Durham City

The 1851 Census

DURHAM CITY
THE 1851 CENSUS

edited by David J. Butler

Durham

1992

Published by
Durham Historical Enterprises
3 Briardene
Margery Lane
Durham
DH1 4QU

© David J. Butler, 1992

ISBN   0 9519088 0 4

British Library Cataloguing-in-Publication Data
A catalogue record for this book is available
from the British Library

All rights reserved.   No part of this
publication may be reproduced,   stored
in a retrieval system or transmitted
in any form or by any means electronic,
mechanical, photocopying, recording or
otherwise, without the prior permission
of the editor.

Crown Copyright material is reproduced
with the permission of the Controller
of Her Majesty's Stationery Office.

CONTENTS

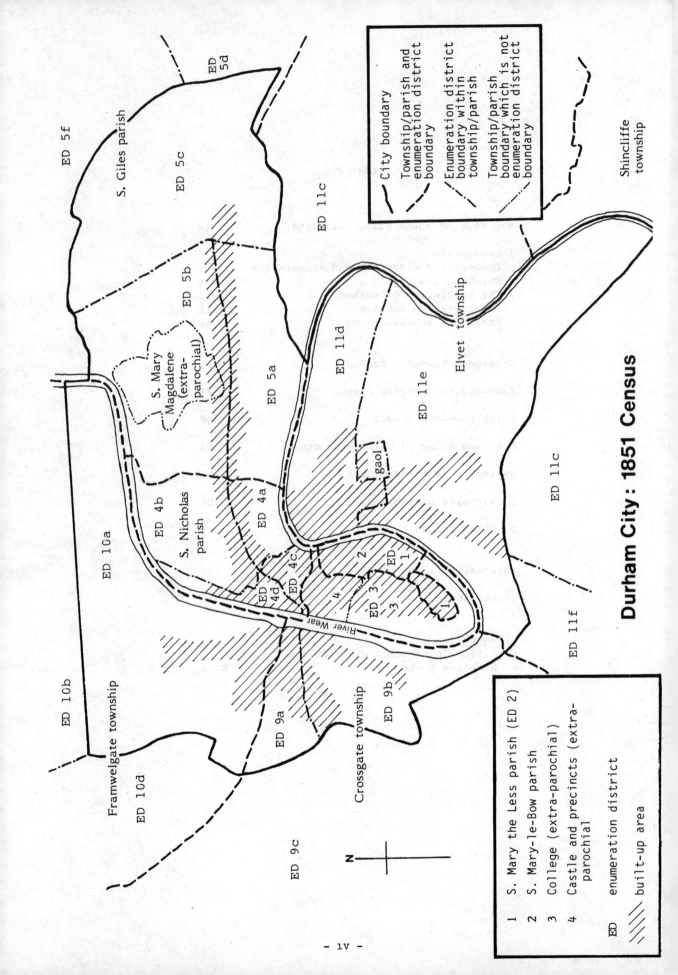

Durham City: 1851 Census

Legend (boundary types):

- City boundary
- Township/parish and enumeration district boundary
- Enumeration district boundary within township/parish
- Township/parish boundary which is not enumeration district boundary

1 S. Mary the Less parish (ED 2)
2 S. Mary-le-Bow parish
3 College (extra-parochial)
4 Castle and precincts (extra-parochial)

ED enumeration district

/// built-up area

ED 5d
ED 5f
ED 5c
ED 11c
S. Giles parish
ED 5b
S. Mary Magdalene (extra-parochial)
ED 5a
ED 11d
ED 11e
Elvet township
Shincliffe township
ED 4b
S. Nicholas parish
ED 4a
gaol
ED 10a
ED 4c
ED 2
ED 1
ED 4d
ED 3
ED 3
ED 1
ED 4
River Wear
ED 11c
ED 10b
Framwelgate township
ED 9a
ED 9b
Crossgate township
ED 11f
ED 10d
ED 9c

N

ENUMERATION DISTRICTS AND ENUMERATORS

For the purposes of the census in 1851 the city was divided into 15 enumeration
districts (see map on page iv),(1) and the responsibility for obtaining
information within the districts was given to 13 individual enumerators.(2)
Since the census was the responsibility of the General Register Office the
existing registration administrative structure was used; thus each enumerator(3)
was appointed by, and responsible to, a registrar who was, in turn, responsible
to a superintendent registrar.   The city was entirely within the Durham Superintendent Registrar's district, but was divided between two Registrar's districts,
those of S. Oswald and S. Nicholas (both of which also extended beyond the city).

The preliminary pages (i-iv) in each enumerator's book give information on the
geographical limits of his district, the total population, the number of houses
and the number of people temporarily present and absent in the district, and that
information is summarised and tabulated below.

S. Oswald district

Enumeration district 9a   Enumerator - Thomas Coxon
Part of Crossgate township 'Framwelgate Bridge End, Milburngate, King Street,
Neville Street, north side of Crossgate, and the whole of Allergate'

Enumeration district 9b   Enumerator - Robert Jackson
Part of Crossgate township 'South Street, Banks Mill House, Prebends Old and New
Gate Houses, Grove House, south side of Crossgate, Union Workhouse and houses
adjoining terminating at Ewbank's House'

Enumeration district 10a   Enumerator - Edward Cornforth
Part of Framwelgate township 'Black House, Crook Hall, Boat House, Gas House,
Sidegate, east and west sides of Framwelgate, Bee's House, Infirmary, and from
Jopling's House (North Road) to Mordew's House (head of North Road)'

Enumeration district 11d   Enumerator - John Salter
Part of Elvet township 'Old Elvet, west side of New Elvet from Elvet Bridge to
the Water Lane including the Lane and houses near the river, east side of New
Elvet to the termination of the street, and Court Lane'

Enumeration district 11e   Enumerator - W[illiam] Peele jn.
Part of Elvet township 'Hallgarth Street, Tollbar head of Hallgarth Street and
one in lane leading to Shincliffe Bridge, Church Lane, west side of New Elvet
from the Water Lane to Elvet churchyard, east side of Church Street to Union
Place, Crawford's House, Anchorage House, and New Row'

Gaol and House of Correction [in Elvet township] - enumerated separately

S. Nicholas district

Enumeration districts 1,2,3   Enumerator - John Newby
North Bailey and South Bailey townships and 'the houses occupied by the
University of Durham including Hatfield Hall ... and extra-parochial houses
adjoining [South Bailey]; the College of Durham (extra-parochial); and houses
built on the site of the old jail (extra-parochial) adjoining North Bailey'

Enumeration district 4a   Enumerator - George R. Thompson
Part of S. Nicholas parish 'the south side of the street of Claypath to Paradise
Lane, including Leazes Place, Leazes House, Paradise Lane, the Foundry and Ebdy's

House'

Enumeration district 4b   Enumerator - Edward Fairclough
Part of S. Nicholas parish 'the north side of Claypath to the Back lane,
including Providence Row'

Enumeration district 4c   Enumerator - Henry Revely
Part of S. Nicholas parish 'Paradise Lane and ... the east side of the Market
Place, the whole of Saddler Street, Fleshergate, Elvet Bridge, the south side of
the Market Place, the south side of Silver Street, Moatside Lane, and Broken
Walls'

Enumeration district 4d   Enumerator - John Morrow
Part of S. Nicholas parish 'the north side of Silver Street, the [west and north
sides of the] Market Place and Claypath Gates, and the whole of the Back Lane
and Freemen's Place'

Enumeration district 5a   Enumerator - Henry Fawcett
Part of S. Giles parish 'the south side of Gilesgate commencing at Tinkler's Lane
to the Tollbar, including the Parsonage House, Scott's Garden House, three
cottages on the opposite side of the path, the Training School and the cottage at
the Waterside, and Ebdy's cottages'

Enumeration district 5b   Enumerator - William Atkinson
Part of S. Giles parish 'the north side of Gilesgate commencing at the Bakehouse
Lane to the Tollbar, including Magdalene Place and two houses beyond but
adjoining the Tollbar, a house at the Glue Garth, a house at the Sands, and a
house at Kepier; also the Railway Station House and the three other houses,
extra-parochial'

Enumeration district 5c   Enumerator - Robert Siddle
Part of S. Giles parish 'from the Tollbar and ... the whole of the houses on both
sides of the turnpike road leading to Sunderland and on both sides of the highway
leading to Sherburn as far as the cross lane from Kepier to Sherburn'

Enumeration District	---------- Population ---------			Occ(4)	--------- Houses --------			Reference numbers
	total	male	female		inhabited	empty	building(5)	
9a	842	399	443	199	121	3	2	1 - 842
9b	1012	488	524	222	138	2	0	843 - 1854
10a	1739	888	851	402	172	3	0	1855 - 3593
11d	1678	780	898	348	235	4	2	3594 - 5271
11e	1746	823	923	377	220	4	0	5272 - 7017
gaol	245	198	47	1	1	-	-	7018 - 7262
1-3	514	181	333	91	85	13	0	7263 - 7776
4a	651	335	316	124	106	4	1	7777 - 8427
4b	859	412	447	190	123	3	0	8428 - 9286
4c	861	429	432	174	115	8	0	9287 - 10147
4d	660	323	337	136	76	1	0	10148 - 10807
5a	809	379	430	183	116	3	0	10808 - 11616
5b	1084	510	574	233	162	5	0	11617 - 12700
5c	488	242	246	109	98	2	0	12701 - 13188
total	13188	6387	6801	2789	1768	55	5	

Notes to table

11d 30 males temporarily in the district 'for the purpose of attending Durham fair'

11e 50 males temporarily in the district due to 'Durham Fair'; 20 males temporarily absent from the district [no
     cause given]

4a   figures given in summary - males 334, females 317; but 8211, a male, was entered and totalled as a female.

45 males and 15 females temporarily in the district due to 'The March Fair for horses and cattle holden in the City of Durham on this day (31st March 1851)'

4b   39 males amd 13 females temporarily in the district due to 'Horse Fair'; 8 males and 5 females temporarily absent from the district [no cause given]

4c   40 males and 10 females temporarily in the district since 'Durham March Fair was held here on the 31st March when many horse dealers and others were here in consequence'

4d   19 males and 3 females temporarily in the district 'on account of Fair being held in Durham on the 31st day of March 1851'

5a   figures given in summary - males 378, females 431; but 11209, a male, was entered and totalled as a female. 6 males and 4 females temporarily absent from the district 'visiting'

5b   40 males and 10 females temporarily in the district since 'the Annual March Fair was held held in Durham on the 31st March which caused many strangers to be in Durham'

5c   6 males temporarily in the district since 'the March Fair for horses and cattle was holden in the city of Durham on this day (31 March 1851)'

COUNTING THE PEOPLE

The 1851 Census was taken in the city of Durham on the night of Sunday 30th March.   In the previous week all householders had received a form (or schedule) on which they were required to provide information on every person present in the house on that night, whether they were permanently resident, lodging or visiting. Nightworkers were to be enumerated at their homes and overnight travellers at the location at which they stopped on 31st March.   The census enumerator was responsible for distributing, collecting and checking the forms, and completing them from information supplied verbally when necessary.

The original schedules which were completed by the head of each household have been destroyed and the only surviving records are the enumeration books, written up by each enumerator from the schedules for his district.   When the enumerator had completed his duties all his records were passed to his supervising registrar who was responsible for checking the information.   The original books are held in the Public Record Office, Kew, London, and microfilm copies are available in the County Record Office, County Hall, Durham.

When the census records were transferred to the Public Record Office they were catalogued by registrar's district and foliated within each district.   The books for the S. Oswald district were catalogued as piece HO 107/2390, and those for the city within that district are covered by folios 110-169, 180-231, 292-398, 411-419.   The volumes for the S. Nicholas district were catalogued as piece HO 107/2391 and those for the city therein are covered by folios 1-190.

Although population totals had been collected every 10 years since 1801 and names and occupations were first recorded in 1841, the 1851 Census is significant since it is the first census which recorded precise ages, birthplaces, marital status and relationships.   The information collected in 1851 remained largely the same for the next five censuses.

THE POPULATION OF DURHAM

The enumerated population of Durham in 1851 was 13188, 6387 males and 6801 females.(6)   Inevitably some usual residents of the city were absent on census night and some visitors were present who usually resided elsewhere, and these two elements could be expected to cancel each other out.   However, a major influx of people was caused by the March horse and cattle fair which was held on Monday 31st March and 320 people (269 males and 51 females) were recorded as temporarily present for that reason.

The population ranged in age from 2 days (Frances Brewster) to 98 years (Ann Stodart), with 33% being under 15 and only 8% being over 60.   Their recorded

birthplaces cover every county in England, eight Welsh, 20 Scottish and 26 Irish counties, the Isle of Man and the Channel Islands. Outside the British Isles birthplaces in each continent except Africa can be found (including Bombay, Quebec and Manila), and three inhabitants are recorded as being born at sea.

The occupations of the inhabitants of the city were equally diverse - over 680 different occupations were enumerated, from an accordion player to a zincworker and including a billiard marker, a female chimney sweep, a ginger-breadmaker and a doll's-eyemaker. As is not surprising in a county and cathedral town a number of well-to-do inhabitants were recorded as independent. The city population also included 226 prisoners in the Gaol in Old Elvet, 96 paupers in the Durham Union Workhouse in Crosssgate, and 22 patients in the County Hospital.

Durham had seen a rapid increase in population in the first half of the nineteenth century, almost doubling in size from about 7000 in 1801 to 13188 in 1851. Thereafter growth was to be more limited and the next fifty years were to see only a modest rise to 14700 in 1901, continuing until the city's peak population (within its 1835 boundaries) of 15400 was reached in 1911.

TRANSCRIPTION DETAILS

The information given in the enumerators' books has been transcribed on the following pages and certain codes and conventions have been employed in order to limit the space required and standardise the information. Each entry (i.e. each person enumerated) has been given a unique number to aid identification and indexing. In order to amplify the information given in the books some additional details have been taken from the 1851 and 1852 Durham Directory, and are given in pointed brackets '< >'.

column 1 REF   Unique identifying number for each entry. This does not appear in the original enumerators' books.

column 2 FOL   Folio reference in group of books, given by the Public Record Office (see page vii above); 'r' for recto, 'v' for verso.

column 3 NO   Number of house in street. Differences of one or two numbers between the census and the Directory have been ignored.
If the street number is not given or supplied as above, a two-letter reference, in square brackets, beginning with 'aa', is used to distinguish separate houses in each street (i.e. those divided by a 'long line'). A single-letter suffix, beginning with 'a', indicates different parts of the same house (i.e. those divided by a 'short line'). Although not enclosed in square brackets this reference does not appear in the enumerators' books.

column 4 STREET   Name of the street/road/house. The spelling in this column is that used in 1992 and has been standardised. An index to the streets etc. in the census is on pages 233-235.

column 5 FORENAME(S)   First forename, with second name and initials if space is sufficient.

column 6 SURNAME   Surname, with 'sn'/'jn' for senior/junior if given.

In columns 5 and 6 abbreviations are expanded. Surname spellings are as in the original but modern spellings have usually been used for forenames.

column 7 REL   Relationship to head of household as a three-letter code (for details see pages ix-x below). If the information has been omitted by the enumerator and the missing entry is obvious it has been supplied.

column 8 C Marital condition; 'm' for married, 'w' for widow(er), 'nk' for not known, blank if unmarried.

It has been necessary to rationalise entries in columns 7 and 8.

column 9 AGE Age in years, but if suffixed with 'm'/'w'/'d' the age is in months/weeks/days.

column 10 OCCUPATION Occupation, trade or profession. Spellings are standardised and 'a', 'the' and '(of) Durham' are omitted. The entry is edited where appropriate and continued in the notes if necessary. Information which is given in the disability column of the census return is transcribed into the right-hand side of the occupation column and enclosed in brackets thus '{blind}'.

column 11 BIRTHPLACE Place of birth in two parts: (a) three-letter county code (for key see pages x-xi below), the code is supplied if it has been omitted by the enumerator but is obvious; (b) parish/township/street (or country). The sequence is standardised, and present-day spellings are used and abbreviated when necessary. If only 'Durham' is given, it is assumed to be the county and not the city. Locations which are in Durham City but which are not stated as such, are indicated by a preceding '[D]'. For this purpose birthplaces given as Crossgate, Framwelgate, S. Margaret, S. Giles/Gilesgate, S. Oswald and Elvet are taken to be within the city. 'Newcastle' and 'Berwick' are regarded as forming part of Northumberland. 'London' is shown as 'Lnd' if no county is given. Those areas of Northumberland which were in Durham until 1844 are regarded as forming part of Northumberland but where the enumerator has entered 'Durham' or 'North Durham' as the birthplace the code '[NDu]' is given after the parish.

The existence of a note at the end of the enumeration district expanding or explaining an entry is shown by an asterisk. The additional information extending into the notes is indicated there by 'xxxxx ...' or '... xxxxx'.

Supplied information, other than in those cases indicated above, is enclosed within square brackets, thus '[xxxxx]'.

Deletions are indicated by 'xxxxx - deleted'.

Doubtful meanings (i.e. where the reading of the entry is clear, but the meaning is in doubt) are indicated by '"xxxxx"', usually following a probable meaning. Uncertain renderings (i.e. where the entry is difficult to read or there is doubt over an interpretation) are indicated by 'xxxx?'.

Registrars' corrections/expansions are included, usually without comment, but checkers' corrections/expansions (usually deletions) are ignored.

CODES AND ABBREVIATIONS

List 1 - Relationship to head of family

app	apprentice	cas	casual [servant]
ass	assistant	cou	cousin
aun	aunt	dau/[d]	daughter/[daughter(?)]
bdr	boarder	dls	daughter-in-law [step-daughter?]
bde	bedesman/bedeswoman		
blw	brother-in-law/brother [in-law(?)]	dlw	daughter-in-law/daughter [in-law(?)]
bro	brother		

flw	father-in-law/father [in-law(?)]	pat	patient
fri	friend	pup/[p]	pupil or scholar/[pupil]
fth	father	rel	relation/relative
gda	grand-daughter/[grand(?)] daughter	sda	step-daughter/[step?] daughter
gfa	grand-father	ser	servant
gmo	grand-mother	sho	shopman/shopwoman
gov	governess	sil	sister-in-law/sister [in-law(?)]
gsn	grand-son/[grand(?)] son		
hea/[h]	head of family/[head]	sis	sister
hou	housekeeper	sls	son-in-law [step-son?]
jny	journeyman	slw	son-in-law/son [in-law(?)]
ldd	lodger's daughter/[lodger's] daughter	smo	step-mother
		son/[s]	son/[son(?)]
ldh	lodger, head	sso	step-son/[step?] son
ldr/[l]	lodger/[lodger]	stu	student
lds	lodger's son/[lodger's] son	swi	son(-in-law)'s wife/[son (in-law)'s] wife
ldw	lodger's wife/[lodger's] wife	unc	uncle
		vis	visitor
mlw	mother-in-law	vsd	[visitor's (?)] daughter
mth	mother	vsh	visitor, head
nce	niece	vss	visitor's son/[visitor's (?)] son
nep	nephew		
nk	not known	vsw	visitor's wife/[visitor's(?)] wife
nse	nurse		
nur	nurse child (probably foster-child)	wif	wife

List 2 - Birthplace counties

England and Wales

Bdf	Bedfordshire	Lin	Lincolnshire
Bkm	Buckinghamshire	Lnd	London
Bre	Brecknockshire	Mdx	Middlesex
Brk	Berkshire	Mgy	Montgomeryshire
Cam	Cambridgeshire	Mon	Monmouthshire
Cgn	Cardiganshire	Nbl	Northumberland
Chs	Cheshire	Nfk	Norfolk
Cmn	Carmarthenshire	Nry	North Riding of Yorkshire
Con	Cornwall	Nth	Northamptonshire
Cul	Cumberland	Ntt	Nottinghamshire
Dby	Derbyshire	Oxf	Oxfordshire
Den	Denbighshire	Pem	Pembrokeshire
Dev	Devonshire	Sal	Shropshire
Dor	Dorset	Sfk	Suffolk
Dur	Durham	Som	Somerset
Eng	England (unspecified)	Sry	Surrey
Ery	East Riding of Yorkshire	Ssx	Sussex
Ess	Essex	Sts	Staffordshire
Fln	Flintshire	War	Warwickshire
Gla	Glamorgan	Wes	Westmorland
Gls	Gloucestershire	Wil	Wiltshire
Ham	Hampshire and Isle of Wight	Wls	Wales (unspecified or unidentified)
Hef	Herefordshire		
Hrt	Hertfordshire	Wor	Worcestershire
Hun	Huntingdonshire	Wry	West Riding of Yorkshire
Ken	Kent	Yks	Yorkshire (unidentified or York)
Lan	Lancashire		
Lei	Leicestershire and Rutland		

Scotland

Abd	Aberdeenshire	Inv	Inverness-shire
Ayr	Ayrshire	Kkd	Kirkcudbrightshire
Ban	Banffshire	Lks	Lanarkshire
Bew	Berwickshire	Nai	Nairnshire
But	Buteshire	Per	Perthshire
Dfs	Dumfriesshire	Rfw	Renfrewshire
Dum	Dumbartonshire	Roc	Ross and Cromarty
Edn	Edinburghshire or Mid Lothian	Sct	Scotland (unspecified or unidentified)
Fif	Fifeshire	ShI	Shetland Isles
For	Forfarshire or Angus	Sti	Stirlingshire
Had	Haddingtonshire or East Lothian		

Ireland

Ant	Antrim	Kik	Kilkenny
Arm	Armagh	Kin	King's County (Offaly)
Cav	Cavan	Ldy	Londonderry
Cla	Clare	Let	Leitrim
Cor	Cork	Lim	Limerick
Don	Donegal	Log	Longford
Dow	Down	Lou	Louth
Dub	Dublin	May	Mayo
Fer	Fermanagh	Mog	Monaghan
Gal	Galway	Ros	Roscommon
Irl	Ireland (unspecified or unidentified)	Sli	Sligo
		Tip	Tipperary
Ker	Kerry	Tyr	Tyrone
Kid	Kildare	Wem	Westmeath

ChI	Channel Islands	IoM	Isle of Man

List 3 – Standard abbreviations

a	acres	gard	garden
app	apprentice(s)	gen	general
asst	assistant	gent	gentleman
bdg	bridge	grad	graduate
brkr	broker	ho	house(s)
BS	British subject	hosp	hospital
cas	castle	insp	inspector
cath	cathedral	jnym	journeyman/journeymen
clk	clerk	kpr	keeper
clry	colliery	labr	labourer(s)
co	company	licd	licensed
coll	college	ln	lane
cott	cottage	merch	merchant
dau	daughter	mfr	manufacturer
dlr	dealer	mkr	maker
dltd	deleted	N	North(ern)
E	East(ern)	nk	not known
emp	employing	nr	near
fcty	factory	off	office(r)
fmly	formerly	par	parish

pen	pensioner		ser	servant
pp	pauper		ser	sergeant
Prim	Primitive		soc	society
prop	proprietor		st	street
prty	property		supt	superintendent
rd	road		surg	surgeon
recg	receiving		toll	tollbar/tollhouse
retd	retired		univ	university
rly	railway		wid	widow
S(S).	Saint(s)		wkr	worker
sch	school		yd	yard

Footnotes

(1) Each enumeration district was to be of a size which allowed an able-bodied and active man to visit every house and enumerate its inhabitants within one day; a maximum size of 200 houses was recommended.

(2) Three small enumeration districts (S. Nicholas 1, 2 and 3) were allocated to one enumerator. The gaol in Old Elvet, since it had more than 200 inmates, was separately enumerated by its governor (as what would, in later censuses, be termed a special enumeration district).

(3) An enumerator was to be aged between 18 and 65, temperate, orderly, respectable and knowledgeable about his district. He was also required to be a person of intelligence and activity (sufficiently fit to undertake the work), able to read and write well, with a knowledge of arithmetic.

(4) Occupiers; the number of occupiers can be taken as the number of households.

(5) i.e. under construction

(6) The published totals give 6385 males and 6803 females, but two men, numbers 8211 and 11209, were entered and totalled as females.

1

Ecclesiastical District of   **City or Borough of** Durham   **Town of** Durham

No. of Schedule	Name of Street, Place, or Road, and Name or No. of House	Name and Surname of each Person who abode in the house, on the Night of the 30th March, 1851	Relation to Head of Family	Condition	Age of Males	Age of Females	Rank, Profession, or Occupation	Where Born		Village of
1	Silver Street	John Bainbrough	Head	Mar.	32		Mustard manufacturer and clerk in the Rate Office	Durham St Giles		
		Eleanor Bainbrough	Wife	Mar.		33	Wife of above	Durham Parish St...		
		Eleanor Morcy	Servant	U.		19	House Servant	Durham Nelson...	—	
2	Silver Street	Mary Wright	Head	Widow		58	Corperess	Venton, Co Ware		
		Anne Wright	Daur.	U.		28		Parish St Nicholas		
		Mary Wright	Daur.	U.		20		Durham	—	
		William G. Wright	Son	U.	17		Cooper	Parish St Nicholas		
		Edward Anderson	Journeyman	U.	33		Cooper	Bedford Northumberland		
3	Silver Street	Owen McIntyre	Head	Mar.	30		Dealer in Hardware	County South Ireland	—	
		Ann McIntyre	Wife	Mar.		24	Do Wife	Bewley South Ireland		
4	Up Silver Street	Hugh Sheridan	Head	Mar.	32		Labourer	Chapelhamshire		
		Bridget Sheridan	Wife	Mar.		23	Do Wife	West Ireland	—	
		James Sheridan	Son	Inf.				Durham	—	
5		Ann Bambrough	Head	Mar.		46	Cook and Confectioner	Afton, Durham		
		Mary Coxon	Serv.	U.		19	House Serv.	Roscommon Ireland	—	

Total of Persons ... 6 | 9

REF	FOL	NO	STREET	FORENAME(S)	SURNAME	REL	C	AGE	OCCUPATION	BIRTHPLACE
1	113v	<135>	Framwelgate Bdg End	Richard W.	Bowey	hea	m	35	grocer <& cheesemonger>	Dur Sunderland Bridge
2	113v			Ann	Bowey	wif	m	40	grocer's wife	Dur Bishop Auckland
3	113v			Jane	Bowey	mth	w	52		Dur Sunderland Bridge
4	113v			Stephen	Bowey	bro		12	scholar	Dur [D] S. Nicholas *
5	113v	133	Framwelgate Bridge	George	Milner	hea	m	29	confectioner *	Nbl Newcastle
6	113v			Sarah	Milner	wif	m	29	confectioner's wife	Dur [D] Crossgate
7	113v			Margaret D.	Milner	dau		6	scholar	Dur [D] S. Nicholas
8	113v			Thomas	Bainbridge	app		20	confectioner's app	Dur [D] Crossgate
9	113v			John	Sheldon	app		18	confectioner's app	Dur Trimdon
10	113v	132	Framwelgate Bridge	John	Colpitts	hea	m	48	innkeeper <'Puncheon'> *	Dur Westerton Gate
11	113v			Mary	Colpitts	wif	m	42	innkeeper's wife	Dur Durham
12	113v			Charlotte	Renney	ser		20	innkeeper's servant	Nbl Morpeth
			one house uninhabited							
13	113v	130	Millburngate	Ann	Cornforth	hea		55	grocer	Dur
14	113v			Ann	Green	ser		17	servant	Dur Gainford *
15	113v	129	Millburngate	Isabella	Hansel	hea	w	49	greengrocer	Dur Brancepeth
16	113v			Elizabeth	Hansel	dau		24	works at paper factory	Dur [D] S. Oswald
17	113v			Margaret	Hansel	dau		14	home work	Dur [D] S. Oswald
18	113v			Joseph	Hansel	son		12	scholar	Dur [D] S. Oswald
19	113v			Anne	Hansel	dau		5	scholar	Dur [D] S. Oswald
20	114r	128	Millburngate	George	Martin	hea	m	37	licensed victualler *	Nbl Crookham
21	114r			Mary	Martin	wif	m	38	licd victualler's wife	Wil Erlestoke
22	114r			Mary J.	Martin	dau		3m		Dur [D] Millburngate
23	114r			May	Martin	ser	w	65	house servant	Sct
24	114r			Sarah	Martin	ser		28	house servant	Nbl Crookham
25	114r			William R.	Jewett	vis		21	farmer	Nbl Gunnerton
26	114r			Thomas	Story	ldr		35	horse breaker	Nbl Gunnerton
27	114r			John	Hepple	ldr	m	36	farm servant	Nbl Gunnerton
28	114r			Henry	Dodds	vis		21	ostler	Dur Brancepeth
29	114r			John	Fallon	vis		23	horse dealer	Nbl Newcastle
30	114r	126 a	Millburngate	John	Richardson	hea	m	37	cartman	Dur Hebburn /"Hebron"
31	114r			Abigail	Richardson	wif	m	35	cartman's wife	Nbl Kenton
32	114r			Row[land?]	Richardson	son		16	coal miner	Dur Hebburn /"Hebron"
33	114r			John	Richardson	son		14	coal miner	Dur Hebburn /"Hebron"
34	114r	126 b	Millburngate	Elizabeth	Milner	hea	w	56	none	Nry Thirsk
35	114r			Joseph	Daurge	ldr		18	solicitor's clerk	Dur Wolsingham
36	114r			Isabella	Young	ser		15	servant	Dur [D] S. Nicholas
37	114r			Israel	Asher	ldr		36	traveller, hawker	Prussia
38	114r			Alexander	Nathan	ldr		25	traveller, hawker	Prussia
39	114r			Morris	Levi	ldr	m	35	traveller, hawker	Russia
40	114v			Phillip	Zickel	ldr		23	commercial traveller	Prussia
41	114v	126 c	Millburngate	William	Reed	hea	m	24	tinner <& brazier>	Dur Stanhope
42	114v			Jane	Reed	wif	m	24	tinner's wife	Dur [D] Crossgate
43	114v			Mary A.	Reed	dau		8m	infant	Dur [D] Crossgate
44	114v	126 d	Millburngate	John	Reed	hea	m	48	brewer	Nbl Haltwhistle
45	114v			Jane	Reed	wif	m	48	brewer's wife	Dur Wolsingham
46	114v			John	Reed	son		15	scholar	Dur [D] S. Nicholas
47	114v			Thomas	Reed	son		13	scholar	Dur [D] S. Nicholas
48	114v			Dawson	Reed	son		2	infant	Dur [D] S. Nicholas
49	114v	126 e	Millburngate	James	Mann	hea	w	67	joiner	Dur [D] Framwelgate
50	114v			Thomas	Mann	son		17	apprentice whitesmith	Dur [D] Framwelgate
51	114v			Hannah	Mann	dau		15	at home	Dur [D] Framwelgate
52	114v			James	Mann	son		12	scholar	Dur [D] Framwelgate
53	114v	126 f	Millburngate	Dominic	Sarsfield	hea	m	64	pensioner, 6 Dragoons	Cor Carrigtohill
54	114v			Jane	Sarsfield	wif	m	43	pensioner's wife	Dur Sedgefield
55	114v			James	Sarsfield	son		14	scholar	Dur [D] Crossgate
56	114v			Louisa	Sarsfield	dau		11	scholar	Dur [D] Crossgate
57	114v			William	Sarsfield	son		8	scholar	Dur [D] Crossgate
58	115r	126 g	Millburngate	Thomas	Wandless	hea	m	35	carpet weaver	Dur Barnard Castle
59	115r			Ann	Wandless	wif	m	30	carpet weaver's wife	Dur Darlington
60	115r			Rachael	Wandless	dau		11	scholar	Dur Darlington
61	115r			Alice	Wandless	dau		10	scholar	Dur Darlington
62	115r			Elizabeth	Wandless	dau		8	scholar	Dur Darlington
63	115r			Thomas	Wandless	son		4	scholar	Dur Darlington
64	115r			Mary	Wandless	dau		2		Dur Darlington
65	115r			John	Wandless	son		1m		Dur Darlington
66	115r			Alice	Nicholson	vis	m	51	washerwoman	Dur Darlington
67	115r	126 h	Millburngate	Charles	Anderson	hea	m	34	carpet weaver	Dur [D] S. Nicholas
68	115r			Mary	Anderson	wif	m	35	carpet weaver's wife	Dur S. John's Chapel
69	115r			Charles	Anderson	son		5	scholar	Dur [D] S. Nicholas
70	115r			Mary	Anderson	dau		3	infant	Dur [D] S. Nicholas
71	115r	126 i	Millburngate	Elizabeth	Baty	hea	w	57	laundress	Dur Seaham Harbour *
72	115r			Mary A.	Baty	dau		22	dressmaker	Dur South Church
73	115r			John	Robson	nur		1	infant	Dur [D] Flass Lane
74	115r	126 j	Millburngate	Matthew	Guire	hea	w	44	shoemaker	Dur
75	115r			Ann	Guire	dau		22	shoebinder	Dur [D] Framwelgate
76	115r			William	Guire	son		20	shoemaker	Dur [D] Framwelgate
77	115r			Mary	Guire	dau		18		Dur [D] Framwelgate
78	115r			Matthew	Guire	son		13	shoemaker	Dur [D] Framwelgate

79	115v	125 a	Millburngate	Ann Grievson	hea w	72	<hatter>	Dur Barnard Castle
80	115v			William Grievson	son	41	hat manufacturer	Dur [D] Millburngate
81	115v			George Temply	gsn	10	scholar	Dur New Durham
82	115v			Ann Temply	gda	12	scholar	Dur Dalton
83	115v	125 b	Millburngate	John Cowens	hea m	50	dealer in marine stores	Dow
84	115v			Mary Cowens	wif m	59	marine stores dlr's wife	Dow Newry
85	115v			George Haley	gsn	11	scholar	Dur
86	115v			Norah Caroll	ser	25	house servant	May
87	115v			William Leigh	ldr m	37	hawker	Mdx Fulham, S. John
88	115v			Jane Leigh	ldr m	41	hawker	Mdx Fulham
89	115v			Joseph Mayall	ldr m	38	hawker	Hrt S. Albans
90	115v			Sophia Mayall	ldr m	37	hawker	Sal Shrewsbury
91	115v			James Richardson	ldr m	24	hawker	Gla Bridgend
92	115v			Mary A. Richardson	ldr m	23	hawker	War Birmingham, Aston
93	115v			Jane Dixon	ldr w	60	hawker	Lan Manchester
94	115v			Ann Dixon	ldr	11	hawker	Lan Manchester
95	115v			John Quin	ldr	53	labourer	Irl Kippy
96	115v			Thomas Hampson	ldr m	35	labourer	Cor Desert /"Deasart"
97	116r	124 a	Millburngate	John Elvin	hea m	52	gardener	Dur [D] Framwelgate
98	116r			Sophia Elvin	wif m	41	gardener's wife	Dur [D] Framwelgate
99	116r			John Elvin	son	11	scholar	Dur [D] Framwelgate
100	116r	124 b	Millburngate	Elizabeth Carter	hea w	42	laundress & servant	Dur Medomsley
101	116r	124 c	Millburngate	Garret Murray	hea m	43	pensioner & labourer	Irl
102	116r			Ellen Murray	wif m	39	pensioner's wife	Irl
103	116r			Mary Murray	dau	3	pensioner's daughter	Sct
104	116r			Ellen Murray	dau	1	pensioner's daughter	Dur [D] Crossgate
105	116r	123 a	Millburngate	Rose O. Gould	hea w	76	proprietor of houses *	Dur Fishburn
106	116r			Mary Gould	dau	46	proprietor of house *	Dur [D] Framwelgate
107	116r			Joseph Gould	gsn	20	printer compositor *	Nbl Newcastle
108	116r	123 b	Millburngate	Matthew Grievson	hea m	32	hatter etc.	Dur
109	116r			Mary Grievson	wif m	31	hatter's wife	Dur Newbottle
110	116r			Sarah Grievson	dau	7	hatter's daughter	Dur
111	116r			Nicholas Palmer	nep	11	scholar	Dur Merrington
112	116r	122 a	Millburngate	Thomas Fallon	hea m	34	stonemason & innkeeper *	Dur [D] Framwelgate
113	116r			Elizabeth Fallon	wif m	30	stonemason's wife	Dur [D] Framwelgate
114	116r			Elizabeth Fallon	dau	10	scholar	Dur [D] Framwelgate
115	116r			Elizabeth Fallon	mth w	70		Dur [D] Framwelgate
116	116r			William Burn	flw w	59	tailor	Dur [D] Framwelgate
117	116v			Isaac Thorp	ldr w	48	tailor	Dur [D] Framwelgate
118	116v			William Thorp	ldr	13	scholar	Dur [D] Framwelgate
119	116v			Joseph Whittaker	ldr	23	tailor	Mdx Westminster
120	116v			Ann Marshall	ser	19	house servant	Dur [D] Framwelgate
121	116v	122 b	Millburngate	Francis Askey	hea m	50	brewer	Nry Ormesby
122	116v			Barbary Askey	wif m	44	brewer's wife	Dur Shotley Bridge
123	116v			Thomas Askey	son	23	maltster	Nbl Newcastle
124	116v			Francis Askey	son	15	shoemaker	Dur Stockton
125	116v			Christiana B. Askey	dau	11	scholar	Dur Hartlepool
126	116v			William Askey	son	9	scholar	Dur Hartlepool
127	116v	8	Millburngate	John Smith	hea m	26	miller <Clock Mill>	Dur Croxdale
128	116v			Alice Smith	wif m	28	miller's wife	Dur [D] Millburngate
129	116v		Millburngate Mill Yd	Thomas Dodsworth	hea w	65	toll collector	British subject
130	116v			Isabella Dodsworth	dau	32	servant	British subject
131	116v			Catherine Dodsworth	gda	6	scholar	British subject
132	116v			John Dodsworth	gsn	1	infant	British subject
133	116v	7	Millburngate	Joseph Rust	hea m	48	university servant	Ess Panfield
134	116v			Mary Rust	wif m	56	cook	Dur Hebburn
135	117r	6 a	Millburngate	Richard Richardson	hea m	47	labourer	Lan Liverpool
136	117r			Susan Richardson	wif m	37	labourer's wife	Dub S. Catherine
137	117r			Martha Richardson	dau	9	scholar	Dur [D] S. Margaret
138	117r			Edward Richardson	son	5	scholar	Dur [D] S. Margaret
139	117r			Henry Richardson	son	5	scholar	Dur [D] S. Margaret
140	117r			Ann Richardson	dau	2	child	Dur [D] S. Margaret
141	117r	6 b	Millburngate	John Jaques	hea m	41	cordwainer	Nry Northallerton
142	117r			Sarah Jaques	wif m	36	cordwainer's wife	Dur
143	117r			Jane Anderson	sda	15		Dur
144	117r			John Jaques	son	5	scholar	Dur
145	117r	6 c	Millburngate	Sarah Scorer	hea w	63	laundress	Dur
146	117r			Robert Scorer	son	29	whitesmith	Dur
147	117r			Christopher Robson	slw m	28	weaver, carpet	Dur
148	117r			Jane Robson	swi m	26	laundress	Dur
149	117r	5 a	Millburngate	Bridget Burke	hea w	30	formerly farm servant	Ros Auchram
150	117r			Edward Burke	son	7	scholar	Ros Auchram
151	117r			Martin McCormic	ldr	28	labourer	Gal Loughrea
152	117r			Thomas Byrnes	ldr m	32	labourer	Kin Muttock
153	117r			Mary Byrnes	ldr m	24	labourer's wife	Let Inchil
154	117r			Martin Byrnes	ldr	1	child	Abd Shipra
155	117r			John Reynolds	ldr	19	labourer	Let Inchill
156	117v	5 b	Millburngate	Michael Nary	hea m	34	hawker	Irl
157	117v			Mary Nary	wif m	32	hawker's wife	Irl
158	117v			Catherine Nary	dau	12	scholar	Irl
159	117v			Patrick Nary	son	10	scholar	Irl

				Name	Rel		Age	Occupation	Birthplace
160	117v	5	b	Millburngate	John Fall	ldr		26	labourer	Irl
161	117v	5	c	Millburngate	James Smith	hea m		73	tobacco-pipemaker	Dur Gateshead
162	117v				Hannah Smith	wif m		71	unable to work	Dur Gateshead
163	117v				Hannah Smith	dau		43	spinster	Wes Kendal
164	117v	5	d	Millburngate	Margaret Baker	hea m		74	hawker	Nbl Berwick
165	117v	5	e	Millburngate	John Linard	hea m		40	labourer	Irl
166	117v				Rose Linard	wif m		40	labourer's wife	Irl
167	117v				Bridget Linard	dau		17	works at paper mill	Lan Manchester
168	117v				Peter Linard	son		12	school	Lan Manchester
169	117v	3	a	Millburngate	William Cairnes	hea w		47	tailor	Dur
170	117v				Elizabeth Cairnes	dau		18	milliner	Dur
171	117v				Anne Cairnes	dau		16	milliner	Dur
172	117v				William Cairnes	son		20	gilder	Dur
173	117v				James Cairnes	son		11	scholar	Dur
174	118r	3	b	Millburngate	William Cowen	hea m		46	groom servant	Dur
175	118r				Cecelies Cowen	wif m		49		Dur Houghton-l-Spring
176	118r				Sarah Cowen	dau		18	maid servant	Dur Sunderland
177	118r				Isabella Cowen	dau		13	school	Dur Witton Gilbert
178	118r				William Cowen	son		8	school	Dur Witton Gilbert
179	118r				Elizabeth Cowen	dau		9	school	Dur Witton Gilbert
180	118r	2	a	Millburngate	Isabella Thwaites	hea w		60	grocer & tea dealer	Dur Plawsworth
181	118r				Hannah Thwaites	dau		32	grocer & tea dealer	Dur [D] Crossgate
182	118r	2	b	Millburngate	Thomas Thwaites	hea m		39	engine builder *	Dur [D] Crossgate
183	118r				Elizabeth Thwaites	wif m		39		Dur [D] S. Nicholas
184	118r				Mary Thwaites	dau		18		Dur [D] Crossgate
185	118r				Isabella Thwaites	dau		16	scholar	Dur [D] Crossgate
186	118r				Rachael Thwaites	dau		14	scholar	Dur [D] Crossgate
187	118r				Thomas Thwaites	son		11	scholar	Dur [D] Crossgate
188	118r				Elizabeth Thwaites	dau		9	scholar	Dur [D] Crossgate
189	118r	1		Millburngate	Samuel Monkhouse	hea m		43	butcher	Dur [D] S. Margaret
190	118r				Margaret Monkhouse	wif m		46	butcher's wife	Dur [D] S. Margaret
191	118r				Mary A. Monkhouse	dau		18	butcher's daughter	Dur [D] S. Margaret
192	118r				Samuel Monkhouse	son		16	butcher	Dur [D] S. Margaret
193	118r				Isabella Monkhouse	dau		14	scholar	Dur [D] S. Margaret
194	118v				Elizabeth Monkhouse	dau		11	scholar	Dur [D] S. Margaret
195	118v				Jacob Monkhouse	son		10	scholar	Dur [D] S. Margaret
196	118v	7		King Street *	Richard Peverall	hea m		41	innkeeper	Dur [D] Framwelgate
197	118v				Isabel Peverall	wif m		40	innkeeper's wife	Dur Wolsingham
198	118v				William Peverall	son		16	ironmonger, apprentice	Dur [D] Framwelgate
199	118v				Isabella Peverall	dau		12	innkeeper's daughter	Dur [D] Framwelgate
200	118v				Mary Peverall	dau		7	innkeeper's daughter	Dur [D] Framwelgate
201	118v				Elizabeth Peverall	dau		4	innkeeper's daughter	Dur [D] Crossgate *
202	118v				Mary Pearson	ser		25	house servant	Dur [D] Elvet *
203	118v				George Walters	vis		21	grocer	East Indies BS
204	118v				George Oliver	vis		27	farmer	Dur Hexham Hill
205	118v				James Thompson	vis		29	farmer	Dur Gould Hill
206	118v				Thomas Heslop	vis		45	cartman	Wes Murton
207	118v	<6>		King Street	William W. Shafto	hea m		46	cabinetmaker <& grocer>	Dur
208	118v				Sarah Shafto	wif m		49		Dur Hartlepool
209	118v				Mary Ann Shafto	dau		22	dressmaker <milliner>	Dur
210	118v				Sarah Shafto	dau		19	milliner <straw-hatmkr>	Dur
211	118v				James Shafto	son		13	scholar	Dur
212	118v				Elizabeth Shafto	dau		12	scholar	Dur
213	118v				Hannah Shafto	dau		10	scholar	Dur
214	119r	[aa]		King Street	George Smith	hea m		41	joiner	Nry Gilling /"Gillon"
215	119r				Jane Smith	wif m		41	joiner's wife	Dur Hamsterley
216	119r				Eleanor Smith	dau		16	joiner's daughter	Dur [D] Gilesgate
217	119r				William Smith	son		14	joiner's son	Dur [D] Gilesgate
218	119r				Frances Smith	dau		12	joiner's daughter	Dur [D] Gilesgate
219	119r				James Smith	son		10	joiner's son	Dur [D] Crossgate *
220	119r				Colin Smith	son		8	joiner's son	Dur [D] Crossgate *
221	119r				Henry Smith	son		6	joiner's son	Dur [D] Crossgate *
222	119r				Jane Smith	dau		4	joiner's daughter	Dur [D] Crossgate *
223	119r				Mary Smith	dau		6m	joiner's daughter	Dur [D] Crossgate *
224	119r	[ab]		King Street	John Swalwell	hea m		34	carpet weaver	Dur Barnard Castle
225	119r				Elizabeth Swalwell	wif m		34		Nry Romaldkirk
226	119r				Ann Swalwell	dau		12	scholar	Nry Romaldkirk
227	119r				John Swalwell	son		5	scholar	Dur [D] S. Nicholas
228	119r				Mary Swalwell	dau		3	at home	Dur [D] S. Nicholas
229	119r				Elizabeth Swalwell	dau		1	at home	Dur [D] S. Nicholas
230	119r	<5>		King Street	Robert Rutherford	hea m		40	tailor *	Dur
231	119r				Margaret Rutherford	wif m		37	tailor's wife	Yks Shofforth
232	119r				Charles Rutherford	son		10	scholar	Wry Shaw Mills
233	119r				Hannah Rutherford	dau		2	infant at home	Wry Leeds
234	119r	<4>a		King Street	John Jackson	hea m		60	joiner	Dur [D] S. Margaret
235	119v				Isabella Jackson	wif m		50	joiner's wife *	Dur [D] S. Oswald
236	119v				Margaret Jackson	dau		23	joiner's daughter	Dur [D] S. Margaret
237	119v				Isabella Jackson	dau		14	joiner's daughter	Dur [D] S. Margaret
238	119v				Jane Jackson	dau		12	joiner's daughter	Dur [D] S. Margaret
239	119v				Mary Jackson	dau		6	joiner's daughter	Dur [D] S. Margaret
240	119v	<4>b		King Street	Robert P. Jackson	hea m		27	joiner	Dur Stockton

No.	Folio	Code	Street	Forename	Surname	Rel	M	Age	Occupation	Birthplace
241	119v	<4>b	King Street	Margaret	Jackson	wif	m	35	joiner's wife	Nbl Newcastle
242	119v			Charles	Jackson	son		1m	joiner's son	Dur
243	119v	<3>	King Street	George	Wright	hea	m	42	cordwainer, master *	Nbl Newcastle
244	119v			Mary	Wright	wif	m	47	cordwainer's wife	Nbl Newcastle
245	119v			Robert C.	Wright	son		12	scholar	Nbl Newcastle
246	119v			Thomas	Wright	son		8	scholar	Dur
247	119v	[ac]	King Street	George	Spedding	hea	w	34	iron merchant agent	Cul [Carlisle?] *
248	119v			Ellen	Clennell	sda		16	agent's step-daughter	Nbl Newcastle All SS.
249	119v			Frances	Clennell	sda		14	agent's step-daughter	Nbl Newcastle All SS.
250	119v			Elizabeth	Clennell	sda		12	scholar	Nbl Newcastle All SS.
251	119v			Sarah	Forster	vis		16	scholar	Nbl Newcastle All SS.
252	119v	[ad]	King Street	Isabella	Clark	hea	w	36	schoolmistress	Dur
253	119v			Sarah	Jopling	nce		9	scholar	Dur
254	120r	[ae]	King Street	William	Charlton	hea	m	38	mason	Dur [D] Framwelgate
255	120r			Abigail	Charlton	wif	m	38	mason's wife	Sct
256	120r			Sarah	Charlton	dau		3	infant	Dur [D] Crossgate
257	120r	[af]	King Street	John	Wilkie	hea	m	47	innkeeper *	Dur
258	120r			Ann	Wilkie	wif	m	57	innkeeper's wife	Dur
259	120r			Catherine	Summins	ser		16	servant	Dur
260	120r	[ag]	King Street	Mark	Jopling	hea	m	45	builder emp 5 men *	Dur
261	120r			Jane	Jopling	wif	m	42	builder's wife	Dur
262	120r			Mark	Jopling	son		17	apprentice chemist	Dur
263	120r			Henry	Jopling	son		15	apprentice currier	Dur
264	120r			Cuthbert	Jopling	son		13	scholar	Dur
265	120r			Ellen	Jopling	dau		10	scholar	Dur
266	120r			George	Jopling	son		5	scholar	Dur
267	120r			John	Jopling	son		1		Dur
268	120r			Ruth	Jopling	sis		57	annuitant	Dur
269	120r			Isabella	Middleton	ser		17	house servant	Nbl Newcastle
270	120r	[ah]	King Street	Elizabeth	Pickering	hea	w	40	proprietor of houses	Dur
271	120r			Mary	Pickering	dau		19		Dur Chester-le-Street
272	120r			Elizabeth A.	Pickering	dau		16		Dur Chester-le-Street
273	120r			William	Pickering	son		14	whitesmith, apprentice	Dur Chester-le-Street
274	120v			George	Pickering	son		12	scholar	Dur Chester-le-Street
275	120v			Richard G.	Pickering	son		10	scholar	Dur Chester-le-Street
276	120v			Elizabeth	Dickson	aun		53		Sct
277	120v			Jane	Sword	sis	w	38	proprietor of houses	Dur Chester-le-Street
278	120v	[ai]	King Street	Thomas	Shevels	hea	m	31	miller *	Dur Brandon
279	120v			Sarah	Shevels	wif	m	31	miller's wife	Dur Raby nr Staindrop
280	120v			Ann	Shevels	dau		5	scholar	Dur
281	120v			Thomas	Shevels	son		3		Dur
282	120v			Robert J.	Shevels	son		6m		Dur
283	120v			Elizabeth	White	vis		33	grocer's daughter	Dur Barnard Castle
284	120v	[aj]	King Street	John	Robson	hea	m	36	miller <North Rd Mill> *	Dur
285	120v			Frances	Robson	wif	m	34	miller's wife	Dur
286	120v			Elizabeth	Robson	dau		12	scholar	Dur
287	120v			Mary	Robson	dau		11	scholar	Dur
288	120v			Fanny H.	Robson	dau		9	scholar	Dur
289	120v			John M.	Robson	son		5	scholar	Dur
290	120v			Alice M.	Robson	dau		1	at home	Dur
291	120v			John	Wood jn	vis		30	farmer	Dur Kimblesworth *
292	120v			Ann	Spedding	ser		24	house servant	Dur Esh
293	120v			Agnes	Bowey	ser		27	house servant	Dur Newbottle
294	121r			Mary	Cockburn	ser		22	house servant	Dur
295	121r	[ak]	King Street	James	Morland	hea	m	27	waggoner	Dur [D] Silver Street
296	121r			Maria	Morland	wif	m	25	dressmaker	Dur [D] New Elvet
297	121r			Mary	Morland	dau		5	scholar	Dur [D] New Elvet
298	121r			Jane	Morland	dau		3m	infant	Dur [D] North Road
299	121r	[al]	King Street	William	Laidler	hea	m	37	engineman	Dur Sunderland
300	121r			Hannah	Laidler	wif	m	44	engineman's wife	Dur Chester-le-Street
301	121r			Ann	Laidler	dau		12	scholar	Dur Sunderland
302	121r			Thomas	Laidler	son		11	scholar	Dur Sunderland
303	121r			Jane	Laidler	dau		5	infant	Dur Sunderland
304	121r	[aa]	Neville Street	William	Richardson	nep		23	assistant architect	Dur Chester-le-Street
305	121r			Elizabeth	Smith	ser		37	housekeeper	Dur
306	121r	[ab]	Neville Street	Ann	Brignal	hea	w	77	annuitant	Dur Merrington
307	121r			Ann	Pattison	dau	w	43	milliner	Dur [D] S. Nicholas
308	121r	[ac]	Neville Street	Mary Ann	Stimpson	dau		23		Lin Lincoln
309	121r			George R.	Stimpson	son		19	solicitor's managing clk	Dur
310	121r			Jane R.	Stimpson	dau		12		Dur
311	121r			John G.	Hargraves	ldr		32	solicitor	Wry Tong
312	121r	<4>	Neville Street	Richard	Frater	hea	m	59	off of Inland Revenue *	Dur N Palatine Grange
313	121r			Mary	Frater	wif	m	50	officer's wife	Yks York
314	121r			William	Frater	son		20	watchmaker, apprentice	Nbl Newcastle
315	121v			Mary	Frater	dau		18	officer's daughter	Nbl North Shields
316	121v			Richard	Frater	son		16	gen clerk in Will Office	Dur Bishopwearmouth
317	121v			Margaret	Frater	dau		13	scholar	Dur Bishopwearmouth
318	121v	[ad]	Neville Street	John	Raitt	hea	m	30	provision dealer *	Dur Houghton-l-Spring
319	121v			Margaret	Raitt	wif	m	30	provision dealer's wife	Dur New Lambton
320	121v			John	Raitt	son		2	provision dealer's son	Dur
321	121v			James	Raitt	son		6m	provision dealer's son	Dur

322	121v	[ad]	Neville Street	Alexander Raitt	nep	9	scholar	Dur Houghton-1-Spring
323	121v			Jane Raitt	sis	15	house servant	Dur East Rainton
324	121v			Catherine Grievson	ser	15	house servant	Dur
325	121v	[ae]	Neville Street	Thomas Wood	hea m	43	painter <& glazier>	Dur Nesbitt
326	121v			Ann Wood	wif m	46	painter's wife	Dur
327	121v			John Wood	son	22	professor of violin	Dur
328	121v			Elizabeth Wood	dau	18	painter's daughter	Dur
329	121v	[af]	Neville Street	William Herring	hea w	75	farmer's man	Dur Sherburn
330	121v			Mary Herring	dau	39		Dur Stranton
331	121v			Isabel Herring	dau	16		Dur
332	121v	[ag]a	Néville Street	James Colpitts	hea m	30	coach proprietor	Dur Bishop Auckland
333	121v			Mary I. Colpitts	wif m	25		Dur Birtley
334	122r			James Colpitts	son	3		Dur
335	122r			John Colpitts	son	1		Dur
336	122r			Elizabeth Colpitts	nce	6	scholar	Dur
337	122r			Anne Colpitts	nce	3		Dur
338	122r	[ag]b	Neville Street	Catherine Wortley	hea w	54	retired innkeeper	Dur Auckland S. Helen
339	122r			John Wortley	son	19	apprentice as chemist	Dur
340	122r			Anne Boag	nce	12	scholar	Dur Auckland S. Helen
341	122r	[ah]	Neville Street	Elizabeth Cochrane	hea	56	laundress	Nry Scarborough
342	122r			Jane Cochrane	dau	26	dressmaker	Dur
343	122r			Mary J. Cochrane	dau	4	scholar	Dur
344	122r			Thomas Cochrane	son	2		Dur
345	122r			Frances Cochrane	dau	9m	infant	Dur
346	122r	<10>	Neville Street	Mary Davison	hea w	57	keeps lodgers	Dur Greatham
347	122r			John Davison	son	27	cabinetmaker	Dur Greatham
348	122r			Jane Davison	dau	17	dressmaker	Dur
349	122r			Mary Davison	dau	10	scholar	Nry Malton
350	122r			Elizabeth Reveby	vis	4	scholar	Nry Malton
351	122r			William Patterson	ldr	19	miller	Nbl Bamburgh
352	122r			George Coxon	ldr	41	plasterer <& sculptor>	Dur Tudhoe
			two houses building one house uninhabited					
353	122v	[ai]	Neville Street	Anthony Hall	hea m	62	tanner	Dur [D] S. Margaret
354	122v			Mary Hall	wif m	60	tanner's wife	Nbl Newcastle
355	122v			Frances Hall	dau	23	dressmaker	Dur Chester-le-Street
356	122v	[aj]	Neville Street	John Howe	hea m	30	joiner	Dur [D] Crossgate
357	122v			Elizabeth Howe	wif m	30	joiner's wife	Dur Shincliffe
358	122v			John Howe	son	4	joiner's son	Yks York, Dandy St
359	122v	[ak]	Neville Street	William Sisson	hea m	51	formerly farmer	Dur Satley
360	122v			Mary L. Sisson	wif m	47		Dur Dalton Piercy
361	122v			John W. Sisson	son	12	scholar	Dur Lanchester
362	122v			C.H. Featherstone..*	ldr	33	clerk	Dur Bishopwearmouth
363	122v	[al]	Neville Street	George Smith	hea m	39	cartwright, master	Dur Houghton-1-Spring
364	122v			Jane Smith	wif m	43	cartwright's wife	Dur [D] S. Nicholas
365	122v	[am]	King Street	John Forster	hea m	41	mason employing 24 men *	Dur Chester-le-Street
366	122v			Mary Forster	wif m	43	mason's wife	Nbl Rothbury
367	122v			Sarah Forster	vis w	61	annuitant	Dur Sedgefield
368	122v			Sarah Maude	ser	15	house servant	Dur Darlington
369	122v	[an]a	King Street	John Biggins	hea m	37	tailor	Dur Durham
370	122v			Phyllis Biggins	wif m	32	tailor's wife	Dur Durham
371	122v			Edward Biggins	son	6	scholar	Dur Durham
372	123r			Mary Biggins	dau	1	infant	Dur Durham
373	123r			Catherine Clyne	ser	13	house servant	Irl
374	123r	[an]b	King Street	Thomas Dickinson	hea m	32	plumber etc.	Dur [D] S. Nicholas
375	123r			Mary Dickinson	wif m	36	plumber's wife	Dur [D] S. Nicholas
376	123r			Charles Dickinson	bro	35	grocer etc.	Dur [D] S. Nicholas
377	123r	[an]c	King Street	John Ebdy	hea	38	roper	Dur [D] North Bailey
378	123r	[an]d	King Street	James Crozier	hea m	66	journeyman currier	Dur [D] S. Margaret
379	123r			Ann Crozier	wif m	64	domestic duties	Dur [D] S. Margaret
380	123r			Charles Crozier	son	17	app as tinner & brazier	Dur [D] S. Nicholas
381	123r	[ao]a	King Street	John Morton	hea w	52	tailor	Dur Sunderland
382	123r			Hannah Morton	dau	20		Mdx Westminster
383	123r	[ao]b	King Street	Solomon Norman	hea m	35	miller	Nry Thimbleby
384	123r			Margaret Norman	wif m	49	dressmaker <milliner>	Nbl Newcastle
385	123r	[ap]a	King Street	James Smith	hea m	37	carpenter	Dur
386	123r			Elizabeth Smith	wif m	37	needlewoman	Dur
387	123r	[ap]b	King Street	Mary Yates	hea w	79	needlewoman	Nry Cleveland
388	123r	<2>	King Street	Mary Lowes	hea w	77	matron; pauper	Dur [D] S. Oswald
389	123r			Elizabeth Guire	dau m	52	bonnetmkr <straw-hatmkr>	Dur [D] S. Margaret
390	123r			John Guire	gsn	22	printer compositor	Dur [D] S. Margaret
391	123v	[aq]	King Street	John Nelson	hea m	79	retired butcher	Nry Melsonby
392	123v			Esther Nelson	wif m	74	butcher's wife	Dur Gainford
393	123v			Mary Nelson	dau	42	sempstress	Dur [D] S. Nicholas
394	123v			George Nelson	son	36	auctioneer's clerk	Dur [D] S. Nicholas
395	123v	[ar]	King Street	Mary Smith	hea w	64	laundress	Dur [D] S. Nicholas
396	123v	<1>a	King Street	Ralph Wilkinson	hea m	23	journeyman grocer	Dur West Rainton
397	123v			Phyllis Wilkinson	wif m	23	grocer's wife	Nbl Newcastle John St
398	123v	<1>b	King Street	John Thompson	hea m	39	grocer	Dur Stockton
399	123v			Mary A. Thompson	wif m	34	grocer's wife	Dur Esh
400	123v			William Thompson	son	8		Dur

401	123v	<5>	King Street	George Jackson	hea	m	30	solicitor's clerk	Dur
402	123v			Margaret Jackson	wif	m	24		Dur
403	123v	[am]	Neville Street	Abraham Stout	hea		21	printer compositor	Dur [D] Crossgate
404	123v			Isabella Stout	sis		28	spinster	Dur [D] Crossgate
405	123v			Emma Stout	nce		4		Dur [D] Crossgate
406	123v			Mary Stout	nce		9		Dur [D] Crossgate
407	123v	<61>a	Crossgate	Robert Plumpton	hea	w	47	nailmaker	Dur Durham
408	123v	<61>b	Crossgate	George Hope	hea	w	60	shoemaker	Dur Durham
409	123v	<61>c	Crossgate	Robert Brown	hea	m	64	bread baker	Sct
410	123v			Mary Brown	wif	m	66	baker's wife	Dur Durham
411	124r			Robert Brown	son		26	bread baker	Dur Durham
412	124r			Isabella Brown	dau		39	baker's daughter	Dur Durham
413	124r			Alice Brown	dau		36	baker's daughter	Dur Durham
414	124r			Mary J. Smith	gda		5	scholar	Nbl Benwell
415	124r	<60>a	Crossgate	T<homas> Hodgson sn	hea	w	46	watchmaker	Dur
416	124r			T<homas> Hodgson jn	son		13	scholar	Dur
417	124r			William Hodgson	son		11	scholar	Dur
418	124r	<60>b	Crossgate	John Marshall	hea	m	49	labourer	Dur
419	124r			Ann Marshall	wif	m	45	labourer's wife	Ery Hull
420	124r			Jane Marshall	dau		25	labourer's daughter	Dur
421	124r			William Marshall	son		20	shoemaker	Dur
422	124r			Elizabeth Marshall	dau		23	labourer's daughter	Dur
423	124r			Henry Marshall	son		9	scholar	Dur
424	124r	<59>a	Crossgate	Michael Flinn	hea	m	59	papermaker	Dub Rathfarnham
425	124r			Ann Flinn	wif	m	59	domestic duties	Dub Rathfarnham
426	124r			Phillip Flinn	son		30	labourer	Dub Rathfarnham
427	124r			Bridget Flinn	dau		28	works at paper mill	Dub Windy Harbour
428	124r			Edward Flinn	son		23	carpet weaver	Dub Dublin, Tallaght
429	124r			Peter Flinn	son		18	carpet weaver	Dub Dublin, Tallaght
430	124r	<59>b	Crossgate	William Wortley	hea	w	56	shoemaker	Dur [D] Framwelgate
431	124v			Mary A. Wortley	dau		25	boot and shoebinder	Dur [D] Silver Street
432	124v			Thomas Wortley	son		16	joiner	Dur [D] Crossgate
433	124v	<58>	Crossgate	William Brown	hea	m	54	cordwainer	Dur [D] S. Margaret
434	124v			Mary Brown	wif	m	50	bonnetmaker	Brk Windsor
435	124v			Margaret Brown	dau		25	bonnetmkr <straw-hatmkr>	Dur [D] S. Margaret
436	124v			William A. Brown	son		14	scholar	Dur [D] S. Margaret
437	124v	<57>a	Crossgate	Esther Charlton	hea		60	parochial aid	Dur Lanchester
438	124v	<57>b	Crossgate	James Gardiner	hea	m	84	annuitant	Dur [D] S. Nicholas
439	124v			Margaret Gardiner	wif	m	75		Dur
440	124v	<57>c	Crossgate	Jane Miller	hea		40		Dur
441	124v	<57>d	Crossgate	William Allan	hea	m	40	carpet weaver	Dur [D] S. Giles
442	124v			Ann Allan	wif	m	39	weaver's wife	Dur [D] Crossgate
443	124v			James Allan	son		10	scholar	Dur [D] Crossgate
444	124v			John Allan	son		8	scholar	Dur [D] Crossgate
445	124v	<57>e	Crossgate	Thomas Cairnes	hea	m	41	cordwainer, master	Dur
446	124v			Ann Cairnes	wif	m	38	cordwainer's wife	Yks York
447	124v			Thomas Cairnes	son		14	bread baker	Dur
448	124v			George Cairnes	son		12	scholar	Dur
449	124v			Elizabeth Cairnes	dau		9	scholar	Dur
450	124v			William Cairnes	son		7	home	Dur
451	125r			John Cairnes	son		5	servant	Dur
452	125r			Jean Cairnes	dau		2	home	Dur
453	125r			William Lasselles	ldr	w	69	cordwainer retired *	Dur
454	125r	<57>f	Crossgate	Thomas Minto	hea	m	20	grocer, journeyman	Dur Kimblesworth
455	125r			Sarah Minto	wif	m	20	grocer's wife	Dur Hartley
456	125r			Elizabeth Minto	dau		8m		Dur Durham
457	125r	<57>g	Crossgate	Peter Carlin	hea	m	45	farm labourer	Irl
458	125r			Catherine Carlin	wif	m	41		Irl
459	125r	<57>h	Crossgate	Agnes Smilie	hea	m	32	carpet weaver's wife	Sct
460	125r			James Smilie	son		14	carpet weaver's son	Sct
461	125r			Mary Smilie	dau		12	carpet weaver's daughter	Dur
462	125r			Elizabeth Smilie	dau		8	carpet weaver's daughter	Dur
463	125r			Sidney Smilie	son		5	carpet weaver's son	Lin
464	125r	<57>i	Crossgate	Mary Hope	hea	w	58		Dur Old Washington
465	125r			William Hope	son	m	31	whitesmith	Dur Chester-le-Street
466	125r			Joseph Hope	son		28	carpet weaver	Dur Chester-le-Street
467	125r	[aa]	Crossgate	Ann Herbert	hea	w	54	private	Dur Lanchester
468	125r			William Charlton	son		34	shoemaker	Dur Lanchester
469	125r			Mary Ann Herbert	dau		20	bootbinder	Dur [D] S. Margaret
470	125r			Ellen Charlton	vis	m	31		Sct
471	125v			William E. Charlton	vis		1	infant	Dur Sunderland
472	125v	<55>	Crossgate	Mary J. Harrison	hea	w	53	let apartments	Dur Shotton
473	125v			Mary A.L. Harrison	dau		25		Dur Castle Eden
474	125v			Stephen C. Scarth	nep		8		Dur Bishopwearmouth
475	125v			Henry C. Dealy	bdr		10	chorister	Sct
476	125v			John W. Maltby	ldr		31	LAC, gen practitioner *	Nbl North Shields
477	125v			Hannah Dixon	ldr	w	81	annuitant	Dur Sunderland
478	125v			Dorothy Dixon	ldr		58	house property	Dur Bishopwearmouth
479	125v	<53>	Crossgate	William H. Engledew	hea		32	teacher *	Dur [D] S. Nicholas
480	125v			Lucretia Engledew	mth	w	66		Mdx London
481	125v			William H. Atkinson	nep		5	scholar	Dur West Auckland

482	125v	<53>	Crossgate	Charles C. Wardell	**bdr**	**12**	scholar	Dur Winlaton
483	125v			John H. Carter	**bdr**	**12**	scholar	Dur West Boldon
484	125v			Jane Barron	**ser**	**18**	house servant	Dur Durham
485	125v	<54>	Crossgate	Robert Vasey	**hea m**	**62**	tailor	Dur [D] S. Nicholas
486	125v			Jane Vasey	**wif m**	**60**	tailor's wife	Dur [D] S. Nicholas
487	125v	[ab]a	Crossgate	Matthew Barron	**hea m**	**37**	carpenter	Dur
488	125v			Ann Barron	**wif m**	**38**	carpenter's wife	Dur
489	125v			Matthew Barron	**son**	**13**	scholar	Dur
490	126r			Margaret Barron	dau	12	scholar	Dur
491	126r			Mary Barron	dau	10	scholar	Dur
492	126r			Isabella Barron	dau	8	scholar	Dur
493	126r			Jane Barron	dau	6	scholar	Dur
494	126r			John Barron	son	2	infant	Dur
495	126r			Ann Barron	dau	6m	infant	Dur
496	126r	[ab]b	Crossgate	John Barron	hea m	47	carpenter	Nbl Stamfordham
497	126r			Mary Barron	wif m	48	carpenter's wife	Nry Snape
498	126r			Ann Barron	dau	23	carpenter's daughter	Dur
499	126r			Sarah Barron	dau	14	scholar	Dur
500	126r			Mary A. Barron	gda	9m	infant	Dur
501	126r	[ac]	Crossgate	Charlotte Shaw	hea	35	annuitant	Dur Brancepeth
502	126r			Margaret Helmerow	ldr	46	dressmaker	
503	126r	<52>	Crossgate	Henry W. Dodd	hea m	43	surgeon, MRCS London	Dur Chester-le-Street
504	126r			Isabella Dodd	wif m	40	surgeon's wife *	East Indies BS
505	126r			Thomas F. Dodd	son	14	scholar	Dur
506	126r			Annie C. Dodd	dau	7	scholar	Dur
507	126r			Mary Collinson	ser	14	servant	Dur
508	126r			Margaret Collinson	vis	8	visitor	Dur
509	126r	<51>a	Crossgate	Mary Turnbull	hea w	65		Dur Lanchester
510	126v	51 a	Crossgate	William Turnbull	son	33	joiner	Dur Durham
511	126v			James Turnbull	son	30	joiner	Dur Durham
512	126v			Elizabeth Turnbull	dau	24	dressmaker	Dur Durham
513	126v	51 b	Crossgate	William Wandless	hea m	27	carpet weaver	Dur Barnard Castle
514	126v			Phyllis Wandless	wif m	26	carpet weaver's wife	Dur Barnard Castle
515	126v			Rachael Wandless	dau	5	scholar	Dur Barnard Castle
516	126v	51 c	Crossgate	William Robinson	hea m	29	joiner	Dur Durham
517	126v			Mary Robinson	wif m	31	joiner's wife	Dur Weardale
518	126v			Mary Robinson	dau	7	scholar	Dur Durham
519	126v			William Robinson	son	6	scholar	Dur Durham
520	126v			Elizabeth Robinson	dau	4	scholar	Dur Durham
521	126v			Margaret Robinson	dau	1	infant	Dur Durham
522	126v	51 d	Crossgate	Jane Maddison	hea w	32	laundress	Dur
523	126v			Ellen Maddison	dau	7	scholar	Dur
524	126v			Elizabeth Maddison	dau	1	infant	Dur
525	126v			William Maddison	son	5	scholar	Dur
526	126v			Edward Maddison	son	3	scholar	Dur
527	126v	[ad]	Crossgate	James Crampton	hea m	49	carpet weaver	Dur Barnard Castle
528	126v			Eleanor Crampton	wif m	65		Dur Barnard Castle
529	126v			James Wandless	gsn	2		Wry Halifax
530	127r	[ae]a	Crossgate	Ralph Craggs	hea	72	Chelsea pensioner *	Dur Sunderland
531	127r	[ae]b	Crossgate	Jane Thompson	hea w	71	parish relief	Dur
532	127r	[ae]c	Crossgate	Mary Brown	hea w	63	money on mortgage *	Dur [D] Crossgate
533	127r	[ae]d	Crossgate	Margaret Bellamy	hea	36	dressmaker	Dur
534	127r	<49>	Crossgate	William E. Dennison	hea	38	maltster & hop merchant	Dur Darlington
535	127r			Jane Ewbank	aun	69		Dur Durham
536	127r			Jessie Hepburn	ser	20	house servant	Dur Easington Lane
537	127r	<48>	Crossgate	James White	hea m	50	house & land proprietor	Dur Aycliffe
538	127r			Sarah White	wif m	49		Ken Hythe
539	127r	[af]	Crossgate	Isabella Spence	hea w	52		Nbl Wallsend
540	127r			John Spence	son w	24	joiner, journeyman	Dur Washington
541	127r			William Spence	son	19	whitesmith's apprentice	Dur Washington
542	127r			Thomas Spence	son	13	scholar	Dur [D] S. Margaret
543	127r			Isabella Spence	gda	4	scholar	Dur [D] S. Margaret
544	127r	[ag]	Crossgate	Edward Rake	hea m	27	carpenter's journeyman	Dur [D] S. Oswald
545	127r			Margaret Rake	wif m	28	carpenter's wife	Dur [D] S. Margaret
546	127r			John Rake	son	5	scholar	Dur [D] S. Margaret
547	127r			William Rake	son	3		Dur [D] S. Margaret
548	127r			Edward Rake	son	1		Dur [D] S. Margaret
549	127r			Margaret Mould	mlw	57	charwoman /"chairwoman"	Dur Chester-le-Street
550	127v	[ah]	Crossgate	John S. Wilson	hea m	48	shoemaker, master *	Lan Royton
551	127v			Jane Wilson	wif m	41	shoemaker's wife	Dur [D] Framwelgate
552	127v			Robert S. Wilson	son	11		Dur Monkwearmouth
553	127v			Elizabeth C. Wilson	dau	9	scholar	Dur Monkwearmouth
554	127v			Mary U. Wilson	dau	8	scholar	Dur [D] Framwelgate
555	127v			Sarah Jane Wilson	dau	6	scholar	Dur [D] Framwelgate
556	127v			William S. Wilson	son	3	scholar	Dur [D] Crossgate
557	127v			John S. Wilson	son	1		Dur [D] Crossgate
558	127v	<47>	Crossgate	Robert Tilly	hea m	42	whitesmith & bellhanger*	Dur [D] Gilesgate
559	127v			Elizabeth Tilly	wif m	44	whitesmith's wife	Dur Witton-le-Wear
560	127v			Jane Tilly	dau	16	whitesmith's daughter	Dur [D] Gilesgate
561	127v			Elizabeth Tilly	dau	13	scholar	Wry Leeds
562	127v			John Tilly	son	11	scholar	Dur [D] Framwelgate

563	127v	<47>	Crossgate	Ann Tilly	dau	7	scholar	Dur [D] Framwelgate
564	127v	[ai]a	Crossgate	Matthew Linsley	hea m	47	blacksmith	Dur Witton Gilbert
565	127v			Elizabeth Linsley	wif m	41	blacksmith's wife	
566	127v			William Linsley	son	18	printer compositor	Dur
567	127v			Sarah Linsley	dau	14	shopgirl	Dur
568	127v	[ai]b	Crossgate	Ann Rutherford	hea w	62		Nbl Newcastle
569	127v	[aj]	Crossgate	James Fargison	hea w	60	labourer	Dur [D] Framwelgate
570	128r	<47>	Crossgate	Mary Thompson	hea	38	grocer etc.	British subject
571	128r			William Peverall	nep	15	painter & glazier	British subject
572	128r	[ak]a	Crossgate	Joseph Perry	hea	50	cordwainer	Sct
573	128r			Mary Perry		46	sis[ter]	Nbl Newcastle
574	128r			John Perry	son	23	cordwainer	Dur
575	128r			Charles Perry	son	16	apprentice [shoemaker?]	Dur
576	128r	[ak]b	Crossgate	Sarah Thompson	hea w	50	pauper	Dur [D] S. Margaret
577	128r			Sarah Thompson	dau	24	pau[per]	Dur [D] S. Oswald
578	128r			George Thompson	son	13	scholar	Dur [D] S. Margaret
579	128r	[ak]c	Crossgate	John Hamilton	hea w	56	retired seaman	Sct
580	128r			John Hamilton	son	15	apprentice roper	Ery Hull
581	128r			Margaret Hamilton	dau	12		Ery Hull
582	128r			Samuel Hamilton	son	10	scholar	Ery Hull
583	128r			William Hamilton	son	7	scholar	Dur Darlington
584	128r			George Hamilton	son	3	infant	Dur
585	128r	[ak]d	Crossgate	Mark Mullen	hea m	36	labourer	Cor
586	128r			Catherine Mullen	wif m	40		Irl Court Hill
587	128r			John Mullen	son	2		Dur [D] Crossgate
588	128r	[ak]e	Crossgate	Thomas Bailes	hea m	20	cordwainer	Dur
589	128r			Jane Bailes	wif m	19		Dur
590	128v	[ak]f	Crossgate	Mary Tilly	hea w	63	laundress	Dby Eckingham
591	128v			Thomas Tilly	son	33	cordwainer, master	Dur [D] S. Giles
592	128v	[ak]g	Crossgate	Elizabeth Bainbridge	hea w	42	pauper	Dur
593	128v			Frederick Bainbridge	son	22	cabinetmaker	Dur
594	128v			James Bainbridge	son	17	pipemaker	Dur
595	128v			Jane Bainbridge	dau	15	scholar	Dur
596	128v			Edwin Bainbridge	son	7	scholar	Dur
597	128v	[ak]h	Crossgate	Batt Mulvel	hea m	53	shoemaker	Irl
598	128v			Margaret Mulvel	wif m	56	housekeeper	Irl
599	128v			Patrick Mulvel	son m	30	labourer	Irl
600	128v			Mary Flarty	dau m	26	laundress	Irl
601	128v			Thomas Mulvell	son	18	labourer	Irl
602	128v			Michael Mulvell	son	16	shoemaker	Irl
603	128v			Maurice Flinn	vis	19	labourer	Irl
604	128v			Patrick Flinn	vis	12	labourer	Irl
605	128v	[al]	Crossgate	William McCloud	hea m	40	labourer	Dur [D] Crossgate
606	128v			Elizabeth McCloud	wif m	50		Sct
607	128v			William McCloud	son	14	whitesmith	Dur [D] Crossgate
608	128v			Andrew Harrison	rel	30	tailor	Dur [D] Elvet
609	128v			Thomas Fenwick	ldr	17	labourer	Dur [D] Crossgate
610	129r	<44>a	Crossgate	William Cummins	hea w	70	carpet weaver	Dur [D] Gilesgate
611	129r			Margaret Cummins	dau	48	housekeeper	Dur [D] Crossgate
612	129r	<44>b	Crossgate	John Campbell	hea m	33	labourer	Irl
613	129r			Margaret Campbell	wif m	32	labourer's wife	Dur [D] Hallgarth St
614	129r			George Campbell	son	13	mason	Dur [D] Hallgarth St
615	129r			John Campbell	son	6	scholar	Dur [D] Crossgate
616	129r	<43>	Crossgate	John Phillips	hea m	35	butcher	Wry Leeds
617	129r			Catherine Phillips	wif m	33	butcher's wife	Nry Masham
618	129r			William Phillips	son	6	butcher's son	Dur Durham
619	129r			John Phillips	son	4	butcher's son	Dur Durham
620	129r			Ann Hope	ser	17	house servant	Dur Witton Gilbert
621	129r	<42>	Crossgate	Ann Humble	hea w	68		Nbl Newcastle
622	129r			Margaret M. Guire	ser	23	house servant	Dur
623	129r	<41>	Crossgate	Mary Kelly	hea w	74	annuitant	Nry Ayton
624	129r			Elizabeth Elcot	sis	78	annuitant {blind}	Nry Ayton
625	129r			Frances Robertshaw	ser	17	house servant	Dur
626	129r		one house unoccupied					
626	129r	<39>	Crossgate, 'Angel'	James Lumsden	hea m	26	innkeeper	Dur
627	129r			Ann Lumsden	wif m	23	innkeeper's wife	Dur
628	129r			Mary H. Lumsden	dau	11m	innkeeper's daughter	Dur
629	129v			Mary Walker	ser	17	house servant	Nbl Bellingham
630	129v			George Robson	vis m	45	farmer	Dur Lanchester
631	129v			John Robson	vis m	43	farmer	Dur Lanchester
632	129v			John Shylock	vis m	60	farmer	Dur Wolsingham
633	129v			William Couthard	vis m	45	farmer	Dur Stanhope
634	129v	<38>a	Crossgate	Jane Hutchinson	hea w	87	recg parish relief *	Dur Lambton
635	129v			Ann Hutchinson	dau	45	laundress	Dur [D] Crossgate
636	129v	<38>b	Crossgate	Ann Prudhoe	hea w	79	past work	British subject
637	129v			Dinah? Prudhoe	dau	46	laundress	British subject
638	129v			Mary Prudhoe	dau	36	laundress	British subject
639	129v	<38>c	Crossgate	Joseph Dickinson	hea	19	cartman	Dur [D] Crossgate
640	129v	<38>d	Crossgate	Thomas Littlefair	hea m	38	tailor	Dur
641	129v			Elizabeth Littlefair	wif m	40	tailor's wife	Nry Reeth
642	129v			Mary A. Littlefair	dau	11	tailor's daughter	Dur

643	129v	<38>d	Crossgate	Elizabeth Littlefair	dau	9	tailor's daughter	Dur Witton-le-Wear
644	129v			Harriet Littlefair	dau	7	tailor's daughter	Dur Witton-le-Wear
645	129v			John C. Littlefair	son	4	tailor's son	Dur Witton-le-Wear
646	129v			Jane Littlefair	dau	1	tailor's daughter	Dur
647	129v	[am]a	Crossgate	Thomas Gott	hea m	32	brickmaker	Dur
648	129v			Jane Gott	wif m	27	brickmaker's wife	Dur
649	130r			Joseph Gott	son	4	scholar	Dur
650	130r			Thomas Gott	son	2	at home	Dur
651	130r	[am]b	Crossgate	Mary Tweedie	hea m	60	laundress	Dfs Dumfries
652	130r			Mary Neasham	vis	40		Dur [D] S. Nicholas
653	130r			Jane Neasham	vis	10		Dur [D] S. Margaret
654	130r	<36>	Crossgate	Stephen Heron	hea m	42	slater <& grocer>	Dur
655	130r			Eleanor Heron	wif m	43	slater's wife	Dur
656	130r			Mary Heron	dau	14	slater's daughter	Dur
657	130r			Stephen Heron	son	12	scholar	Dur
658	130r			Thomas Heron	son	7	scholar	Dur
659	130r			William H. Heron	son	7m	infant	Dur
660	130r	[aa]	Allergate	John Lamb	hea m	60	formerly servant	Nbl
661	130r	[ab]	Allergate	Thomas Jopling	hea m	65	carpenter	Dur
662	130r			Martha Jopling	wif m	67	carpenter's wife	Dur
663	130r			Joseph Jopling	gsn	13	scholar	Cul Keswick
664	130r			William Jopling	gsn	10	scholar	Dur [D] Crossgate
665	130r			Elizabeth Jopling	gda	8	scholar	Dur [D] Crossgate
666	130r	<19>	Allergate	George Talbot	hea m	35	master upholsterer	Dur [D] S. Margaret
667	130r			Ann Talbot	wif m	35	upholsterer's wife	Sfk Newham
668	130r			Mary A. Talbot	dau	12	scholar	Mdx S. Pancras
669	130v			Jane Talbot	dau	9	scholar	Mdx S. Pancras
670	130v			Martha Talbot	dau	6	scholar	Dur [D] S. Margaret
671	130v			Emma Talbot	dau	4	scholar	Dur [D] S. Margaret
672	130v	<18>	Allergate	Jane Robson	hea w	38	annuitant <lodgings>	Dur
673	130v			Thomas Robson	son	11	scholar	Dur
674	130v			Mary Robson	dau	13	scholar	Dur
675	130v			Stephen Parker	vis	18	saddler	Dur Shotley Bridge *
676	130v	<17>	Allergate	John Smith	hea w	41	professor of music *	Sts Lichfield
677	130v			Jane Smith	sis	35	housekeeper	Sts Lichfield
678	130v	<16>	Allergate	Charles Macknally	hea	32	teacher (private) *	Wor Bromsgrove
679	130v			Ann Macknally	mth w	64	housekeeper	Dur Easington
680	130v			Richard T. Winscome	bdr	18	[scholar]	Nbl Warkworth
681	130v			James L. Clarke	bdr	17	[scholar]	War Handsworth
682	130v			Edward Ransford	bdr	15	[scholar]	Edn Edinburgh *
683	130v			Edward G. Fabour	bdr	15	[scholar]	Dur Stockton
684	130v			John J. Brown	bdr	16	[scholar]	Dur Dalton-le-Dale
685	130v			Robert C. Rayson	bdr	15	[scholar]	Dur Stockton
686	130v			John Trotter	bdr	14	[scholar]	Dur Stockton
687	130v			John Arkell	bdr	15	[scholar]	Gls Boddington
688	130v			Henry Arkell	bdr	12	[scholar]	Gls Boddington
689	131r			Arthur Trotter	bdr	12	[scholar]	Dur Stockton
690	131r			Walter J. Collinson	bdr	16	[scholar]	Dur Castle Eden
691	131r			Arthur Carr	bdr	13	[scholar]	Dur South Shields
692	131r			Edwin Carr	bdr	11	[scholar]	Dur South Shields
693	131r	<15>	Allergate	Joseph Law	bdr	13	[scholar]	Dur Sunderland
694	131r			Moyes Preston	bdr	14	[scholar]	Wes Warcop
695	131r			Hamilton Russel	bdr	10	[scholar]	Edn Edinburgh
696	131r			Charles Russel	bdr	9	[scholar]	Edn Edinburgh
697	131r			Eleanor Forster	ser	30	house servant	Nbl Stannington
698	131r			Catherine Dighter	ser	23	house servant	Dur [D] S. Nicholas
699	131r			Isabella Forster	ser	17	house servant	Dur South Hetton
700	131r			Isabella Wilkinson	ser	14	house servant	Dur Chester-le-Street
701	131r	[ac]a	Allergate	Isabella Carlton	hea w	63		Nbl Newcastle
702	131r			Cuthbert M. Carlton	son	19	solicitor's clerk	Dur
703	131r	[ac]b	Allergate	Diana A. Brownrigg	hea	37		Nbl Morpeth
704	131r	[ac]c	Allergate	William Richardson	hea	22	tailor	Dur [D] S. Margaret
705	131r	[ac]d	Allergate	John Ramsbottom	hea m	74	woolcomber	Dur
706	131r			Elizabeth Ramsbottom	wif m	62		Dur
707	131r	[ac]e	Allergate	Thomas Rippon	hea m	21	cabinetmaker	Dur [D] S. Margaret
708	131r			Fanny Rippon	wif m	20		Dur [D] S. Oswald
709	131v			William Rippon	son	2m		Dur [D] S. Margaret
710	131v	<13>	Allergate	Jane Caldcleugh	hea w	45	annuitant	Som Bath
711	131v			Mary A. Caldcleugh	dau	16	at home	Lnd
712	131v			Francis Caldcleugh	son	14	at home	Lnd
713	131v			Thomas N. Caldcleugh	son	4		Dur [D] S. Mary-1-Bow
714	131v			Jane S. Caldcleugh	dau	3		Dur [D] S. Mary-1-Bow
715	131v			Isabella Wass	ser	21	house servant	Dur Darlington
716	131v	[ad]a	Allergate	John Grainger	hea m	30	cordwainer	Nry Manfield
717	131v			Eleanor Grainger	wif m	33	cordwainer's wife	Dur [D] South Street
718	131v			Thomas Grainger	son	6	scholar	Dur [D] South Street
719	131v			Margaret Grainger	dau	4	scholar	Dur [D] Crossgate
720	131v			Elizabeth A. Grainger	dau	2		Dur [D] South Street
721	131v			James Grainger	son	7m		Dur [D] Allergate
722	131v	[ad]b	Allergate	Margaret Bee	hea w	50	laundress; pauper	Dur Sacriston
723	131v			Anne Bee	dau	23	domestic duties at home	Dur Durham

724	131v	[ad]b	Allergate	John Bee	son	16	house carpenter	Dur	Durham
725	131v			James Bee	son	15	mason	Dur	Durham
726	131v	[ad]c	Allergate	William Reed	hea m	63	women's shoemaker	Dur	Bishop Auckland
727	131v			Mary Reed	wif m	57	binder of shoes	Lnd	
728	131v	[ae]	Allergate	James Gillespie	hea m	31	mason	Dur	[D] Crossgate
729	132r			Mary Gillespie	wif m	30	mason's wife	Dur	Shincliffe
730	132r			Mary Gillespie	dau	11	scholar	Dur	[D] Crossgate
731	132r			Bessy Gillespie	dau	9	scholar	Dur	[D] Crossgate
732	132r			Joseph Gillespie	son	7	scholar	Dur	[D] Allergate
733	132r			James Gillespie	son	5	scholar	Dur	[D] Allergate
734	132r			Ann Gillespie	dau	3		Dur	[D] Allergate
735	132r			Francis Gillespie	son	1		Dur	[D] Allergate
736	132r	[af]	Allergate *	Richard Windsor	hea m	62	under verger	Sry	Mitcham
737	132r			Charlotte Windsor	wif m	52	under verger's wife	Ssx	Lindfield
738	132r			Margaret Windsor	dau	27	under verger's daughter	Sry	Carshalton
739	132r			Ellen Windsor	dau	21	under verger's daughter	Sry	Carshalton
740	132r			George S. Windsor	son	13	scholar	Nry	Stokesley
741	132r	[ag]	Allergate *	Elizabeth Eggleston	hea w	55	fmly straw-bonnetmaker	Dur	Shincliffe
742	132r			Elizabeth Eggleston	dau	30	milliner	Nbl	Newcastle
743	132r			Ralph Eggleston	son	27	painter, house	Dur	Gateshead
744	132r	[ah]	Allergate	Edward B. Douthwaite	hea m	52	proprietor of houses	Dur	[D] Allergate
745	132r			Esther Douthwaite	wif m	63	wife	Dur	[D] Gilesgate
746	132r			James Douthwaite	bro	54	annuitant	Dur	[D] Claypath
747	132r			Sarah Scott	vis w	54		Dur	[D] Gilesgate
748	132r			Mary J. McDonald	vis w	49		Dur	[D] Gilesgate
749	132v			Margaret Smith	gda	12	scholar	Dur	[D] Gilesgate
750	132v			Esther McDonald	vis	1		Dur	[D] Allergate
751	132v	<11>a	Allergate	Elizabeth Naggs	hea w	70		Dur	Wolviston
752	132v	<11>b	Allergate	Ralph Parkin	hea m	29	saddler	Dur	Homeside Lane
753	132v			Hannah Parkin	wif m	29	saddler's wife	Dur	Ouston
754	132v	<10>	Allergate	Anthony Douthwaite	hea m	45	pawnbroker	Dur	[D] S. Oswald
755	132v			Jane Douthwaite	wif m	39	pawnbroker's wife	Dur	Lanchester
756	132v			Mary Douthwaite	dau	15	pawnbroker's daughter	Dur	[D] S. Oswald
757	132v			William Douthwaite	son	13	scholar	Dur	[D] S. Oswald
758	132v			Margaret Douthwaite	dau	11	scholar	Dur	[D] S. Oswald
759	132v			Jane Douthwaite	dau	6	scholar	Dur	[D] S. Oswald
760	132v			Anthony Douthwaite	son	4	scholar	Dur	[D] S. Oswald
761	132v			Ann Douthwaite	dau	2		Dur	[D] S. Oswald
762	132v			Mary A. Chapman	nce	18	annuitant	Ess	Leigh [on Sea]
763	132v	[ai]a	Allergate	George Wilson	hea m	43	currier	Dur	[D] Elvet
764	132v			Maria Wilson	wif m	43	currier's wife	Dur	[D] Crossgate
765	132v			Elizabeth Wilson	dau	18	currier's daughter	Sry	Walworth
766	132v			George Wilson	son	12	currier's son	Sry	Walworth
767	132v			Maria Wilson	dau	10	currier's daughter	Sry	Walworth
768	132v			John Wilson	son	9	currier's son	Wes	Kendal
769	133r			William Wilson	son	7	currier's son	Nbl	North Shields
770	133r			Hannah Wilson	dau	6	currier's daughter	Dur	[D] Crossgate
771	133r			Matilda Wilson	dau	3	currier's daughter	Dur	[D] Crossgate
772	133r			Alice Wilson	dau	2	currier's daughter	Dur	[D] Crossgate
773	133r	[ai]b	Allergate	Joseph Littlefair	hea m	62	cabinetmaker	Dur	
774	133r			Ann Littlefair	wif m	58	wife	Dur	
775	133r			Benjamin Littlefair	son	19	miller	Dur	
776	133r			Sophia Littlefair	gda	1m		Dur	
777	133r	[aj]	Allergate	Mary Sumerbell	hea w	66		Dur	Darlington
778	133r			Isabel E. Taylor	dau	27	dressmaker	Dur	Belmont
779	133r			John Southron	ldr	20	printer compositor	Dur	
780	133r	<7>a	Allergate	Elizabeth Wallace	hea	66	laundress	Dur	[D] Crossgate
781	133r			Jane Nattress	nce	26	laundress	Dur	[D] Crossgate
782	133r			John Nattress	nep	1m		Dur	[D] Allergate
783	133r	<7>b	Allergate	Ann Elliot	wif m	23		Dur	[D] Crossgate
784	133r			William Ward Elliot	son	1m		Dur	[D] Crossgate
785	133r	<7>c	Allergate	John Andrews	hea w	46	carpet weaver	Sct	
786	133r			Ann Andrews	dau	12	weaver's daughter	Sct	
787	133r			John Andrews	son	8	scholar	Dur	
788	133r			Mary Andrews	dau	6	scholar	Dur	
789	133v			Jessine Andrews	dau	3	weaver's daughter	Dur	
790	133v			Sarah Johnston	ser w	50	house servant	Cul	Carlisle
791	133v	[ak]	Allergate	Joseph Harrison	hea m	30	tinner & brazier	Dur	[D] S. Margaret
792	133v			Sarah Harrison	wif m	25		Dur	[D] S. Oswald
793	133v	[al]	Allergate	Martha Jopling	hea	29	dressmaker	Dur	[D] Allergate
794	133v			Jane Jopling	dau	7	scholar	Dur	[D] Crossgate
795	133v			Ann Jopling	dau	1		Dur	[D] Allergate
796	133v	<2>a	Allergate	Mary Hopper	hea	23	work at paper mill	Dur	[D] S. Oswald
797	133v			Isabella Hopper	sis	20	work at paper mill	Dur	[D] S. Oswald
798	133v			Rachael Hopper	sis	16		Dur	[D] S. Oswald
799	133v	<2>b	Allergate	John Smith	hea m	41	mason	Dur	[D] S. Margaret
800	133v			Mary Smith	wif m	40	mason's wife	Dur	[D] S. Margaret
801	133v			George Smith	son	13	mason's son	Dur	[D] S. Margaret
802	133v	<2>c	Allergate	Joseph Atkinson	hea m	24	plasterer	Dur	[D] Gilesgate
803	133v			Mary A. Atkinson	wif m	22		Nry	Richmond
804	133v			John Atkinson	son	1		Dur	[D] Allergate

805	133v	[am]	Allergate	Michael McKeenan	hea m	26	tailor	Cul Carlisle
806	133v			Elizabeth McKeenan	wif m	22		Dur South Shields
807	133v			Jane Ann McKeenan	dau	2w		Dur [D] S. Margaret
808	133v	[an]	Allergate	Elizabeth Ward	hea w	55	domestic duties	Nbl Newcastle S. John
809	134r	[ao]	Allergate	William Poulton	hea m	36	tallow chandler	Dur Darlington
810	134r			Rose Ann Poulton	wif m	29	domestic duties at home	Irl
811	134r			John Poulton	son	6	scholar	Dur Durham
812	134r			Robert Poulton	son	5	scholar	Dur Durham
813	134r			William Poulton	son	3		Dur Durham
814	134r			James Poulton	son	1		Dur Durham
815	134r	[ap]a	Allergate	George Robertson	hea m	28	servant footman	Sct
816	134r			Mary A. Robertson	wif m	36	servant's wife	Dur Neasham
817	134r			William Robertson	son	3	servant's son	Dur Darlington
818	134r			Mary A. Robertson	dau	7m	servant's daughter	Dur Durham
819	134r			Sarah Hall	ser	12	house servant	Dur Durham
820	134r	[ap]b	Allergate	John Palmer	hea m	34	printer compositor	Dur Durham
821	134r			Caroline Palmer	wif m	30	compositor's wife	Dur Durham
822	134r			Charlotte C. Palmer	dau	1	compositor's daughter	Dur Durham
823	134r	[ap]c	Allergate	George Todner	hea m	30	engineer ([emp] 2 men)	Dur Washington
824	134r			Jane Todner	wif m	38	wife	Dur South Shields
825	134r			Mary J. Todner	dau	10	scholar	Dur Bishopwearmouth
826	134r			Elizabeth A. Todner	dau	6	scholar	Dur Lanchester
827	134r			Isabella Todner	dau	4	scholar	Dur South Church
828	134r			Sarah Todner	dau	4m		Dur Durham
829	134v	<3>	Allergate	Richard Simpson	hea m	51	retired mason	Dur [D] Framwelgate
830	134v			Jane Simpson	wif m	54		Dur [D] Gilesgate
831	134v	<1>	Allergate	William Herbert	hea m	45	gardener <& florist>	Dur Brancepeth
832	134v			Sarah Herbert	wif m	50	gardener's wife	Dur
833	134v			William J. Herbert	son	18	gardener's son	Dur
834	134v			Robert Herbert	son	15	hairdresser	Dur
835	134v			Joseph Herbert	son	13	scholar	Dur
836	134v			Jane Kilvinton	cou	22		Dur Sunderland
837	134v	<5>	Allergate	Matthew Bee	hea m	70	tinner & brazier	Ery Beverley
838	134v			Jane Bee	wif m	74	laundress	Nbl
839	134v			Margaret Bee	nce	22	servant	Dur [D] S. Oswald
840	134v			Isabella Bee	nce	10		Dur [D] S. Margaret
841	134v			Catherine Richardson	ser	22	servant	Dur [D] S. Margaret
842	134v			Mary A. Crowes	ser	16	servant	Dur [D] S. Giles

Notes - Enumeration District 9a

4	Claypath - deleted	291	/"Kinblehurth"
5	... employing 1 man and 3 boys	312	<& inspector of corn returns>
10	<& brewer>	318	<& bacon factor>
14	/"Gainforth"	362	Featherstonehaugh
20	<'Horns'>	365	<& builder>
71	/"Seam Harbour"	453	... (parish pay)
105-106	... & annuitant	476	<surgeon>
107	... & pressman	479	... classical and mathematical <writing
112	<'Mill'>		master at Grammar School>
182	... employing 8 men and 5 boys	504	... mistress of house
196-206	... 'King William <IV>'	530	"Laybour" ...
201	New North Road - deleted	532	income arises from interest of ...
202	Church Street - deleted	550	... employing 2 men and 1 apprentice
219-223	New North Road - deleted	558	<& parish clerk of S. Margaret>
230	<& dealer in old clothes>	634	... formerly laundress
235	<confectioner & eating house>	675	county given as "Northumberland"
243	... employing 4 men	676	<& lay clerk in Cathedral>
247	... S. Cuthbert	678	classical and commercial ....;
257	<'Traveller's Rest'>		<boarding house>
260	<& joiner & timber merchant>	682	... S. Cuthbert
278	<flour and bacon dealer>	736-740	... Myrtle Cottage
284	<& corn merchant>	741-743	... Red Rose Cottage

REF	FOL	NO	STREET	FORENAME(S) SURNAME	REL	C	AGE	OCCUPATION	BIRTHPLACE
843	138v	[aa]	South Street	Robert Pearson	hea	m	45	cutler	Dur [D] Millburngate
844	138v			Isabella Pearson	wif	m	39	cutler's wife	Dur Whitworth
845	138v			George Pearson	nep		25	cutler	Dur [D] Crossgate
846	138v	[ab]	South Street	Elizabeth Hopton	hea	w	60	proprietor of houses	Dur Staindrop
847	138v			Adelaide Hopton	dau		20	bonnetmaker	Dur Durham
848	138v			Mary Hopton	dau		18	domestic duties	Dur Durham
849	138v			Richard Dodd	ldr		21	currier	Dur Barnard Castle
850	138v			Thomas Dawson	ldr		18	butcher's apprentice	Dur Durham
851	138v	<1>	South Street	John Bland	hea	m	30	surgeon	Dur Chester-le-Street
852	138v			Mary Bland	wif	m	29		Dur [D] S. Margaret
853	138v			William C. Bland	son		3		Dur [D] S. Margaret
854	138v			Jane Ann Walker	ser		23	house servant	Dur
855	138v	<2>	South Street	Ann Dixon	hea	w	55	butcher <& lodgings>	Nry Northallerton
856	138v			George Dixon	son		22	butcher	Dur [D] S. Nicholas
857	138v			Kate Dixon	dau		21		Dur [D] S. Nicholas
858	138v			Charlotte Dixon	dau		19		Dur [D] S. Nicholas
859	138v			Ashton Dixon	son		15		Dur [D] S. Nicholas
860	138v			Sarah Garish	ser		19	house servant	Wry Sheffield
861	139r	[ac]	South Street	Ann Pattison	hea	m	36	house servant	Dur Winlaton
862	139r			Sarah Ann Pattison	dau		9	scholar	Dur Winlaton
863	139r			Robert Wood	ldr		23	journeyman chemist	Sct
864	139r			George Henry Mills	ldr		17	chemist's apprentice	Dur Bishop Auckland
865	139r	<4>	South Street	John Robson	hea	m	33	innkeeper *	Dur
866	139r			Anne Robson	wif	m	29		Dur
867	139r			Elizabeth Robson	dau		10	scholar	Dur
868	139r			Anne Robson	dau		7	scholar	Dur
869	139r			Mary Robson	dau		5		Dur
870	139r			Ellen Robson	dau		3		Dur
871	139r			Barbara Robson	mth	m	57	tailor's wife	Dur
872	139r			Amelia Blythed	ser		20	house servant	Fln S. Asaph? *
873	139r			Margaret Alderson	ser		13	house servant	Dur
874	139r	<4>	South Street	Mary Johnson	hea		52	confectioner	Dur [D] S. Nicholas
875	139v	<5>	South Street	Henry Thompson	hea	w	67	grocer	Dur South Shields
876	139v			Caroline Thompson	dau		35	housekeeper	Dur
877	139v	<6>	South Street	William Robinson	hea	m	54	tailor <& sexton *>	Ess Colchester
878	139v			Mary Robinson	wif	m	60		Dur Sunderland
879	139v			Anne Jane Robinson	dau		27	dressmaker	Dur [D] S. Margaret
880	139v	[ad]a	South Street	Robert Middleton	hea		58	cordwainer	Dur [D] S. Nicholas
881	139v	[ad]b	South Street	Jonathan Johnson	hea	m	74	retd woolcomber; pauper	Dur [D] S. Margaret
882	139v			Alice Johnson	wif	m	73	pauper	Tip Nenagh /"Neanah"
883	140r	[ad]c	South Street	Mary Story	hea	w	45	lodging house keeper	Yks Brunton
884	140r			Thomas Hunter	ldr	w	70	carpet weaver	Dur Durham
885	140r			Richard Maxwell	ldr	m	30	fitter & turner	Dub
886	140r			Elizabeth Maxwell	ldw	m	28	dressmaker	Dub
887	140r			Thomas Wilson	ldr	m	40	labourer	Lnd
888	140r			Joseph Harris	ldr		26	baker	Lan Manchester *
889	140r			Andrew Rutherford	ldr		22	labourer	Ken Maidstone
890	140r			Michael Rutherford	ldr		18	labourer	Nbl Newcastle
891	140r			Samuel March	ldr		23	labourer	Nbl Newcastle
892	140r			John McMahon	ldr		37	labourer	Cor
893	140r			John Armitage	ldr	m	37	labourer	Yks Slourt
894	140r			Peter Brenan	ldr		50	labourer	Fer
895	140r			Thomas Watson	ldr	w	47	tallow chandler	Nbl Newcastle
896	140r			John Wilson	ldr	m	50	labourer	Sts Hamphire
897	140r			William Thompson	ldr		30	linen weaver	Ant Belfast
898	140r	<8>a	South Street	Isabella Thompson	hea	m	29	ragsorter	Sct
899	140r			Robert Thompson	son		10		Sct
900	140r	<8>b	South Street	John Magee	hea	m	75	countryman	Dur Brancepeth
901	140v			Eleanor Magee	wif	m	64		Nry Askrigg
902	140v			Mary Magee	dau		36	<dressmaker>	Nry Richmond
903	140v	<9>	South Street	John Brotherton	hea	m	69	innkeeper & miller *	Yks
904	140v			Isabella Brotherton	wif	m	68		Dur
905	140v			Thomas Thompson	gsn		2		Dur
906	140v	<10>a	South Street	George Hopper	hea	w	79	bookbinder	Dur
907	140v			John Hopper	son		36	bookbinder	Dur
908	140v			Margaret Haley	dau	m	34	housekeeper	Dur
909	140v			Mary Ann Hopper	gda		14	scholar	Dur
910	140v	<10>b	South Street	Margaret Airey Bray	hea		27		Dur [D] Abbey Mill
911	140v			William Bray	son		5		Dur [D] Claypath
912	140v	<10>c	South Street	Isabella Dodds	hea		24	washerwoman	Dur
913	140v			Charles Dodds	son		5		Dur
914	140v			Jane Dodds	dau		5m		Dur
915	140v			Hannah Gill	ldr		45	washerwoman	Dur Brancepeth
916	141r	<10>d	South Street	Elizabeth Pattison	hea	w	56	lodging house keeper	Dur
917	141r			Elizabeth Pattison	dau		18	dressmaker	Dur
918	141r			Jane Pattison	dau		14		Dur
919	141r			Thomas Elliot	ldr	w	65	labourer	Dur Blaydon
920	141r			John Fleming	ldr	m	64	seaman	Rfw Greenock
921	141r			Ann Fleming	ldw	m	54		Ayr

922	141r	<10>d	South Street	Elizabeth Robson	ldr m	30	dressmaker	Lan Preston
923	141r			Peter Mackenzie	ldr	44	labourer	Lks Glasgow
924	141r			Nicholas Ph[a]lan	ldr w	52	music master	Kik
925	141r			John Robson	ldr m	42	labourer	Per Perth
926	141r			Timothy Brien	ldr m	57	labourer {blind}	Cor Kinsale
927	141r			Jane Brien	ldw m	52		Cul Eardmouth
928	141r			Edward Phalan	ldr	50	optician	Kik
929	141r	<11>a	South Street	James Taylor	hea m	47	mason	Dur
930	141r			Mary Taylor	wif m	53		Dur
931	141r			James Taylor	son	21	mason	Dur
932	141r			John Taylor	son	17		Dur
933	141r			Ellen Taylor	dau	15		Dur
934	141v	<11>b	South Street	Joseph Sewell	hea m	77	farm labourer	Dur Witton Gilbert
935	141v			Jane Sewell	wif m	73		Dur [B'p] Middleham
936	141v			Joseph Wilson	gsn	16	carpenter's apprentice	Dur
937	141v			William Hopper	slw m	50	painter & glazier	Dur
938	141v			Elizabeth Hopper	swi m	37		Dur Broom
939	141v			William Hopper	gsn	9	scholar	Dur [D] Crossgate
940	141v			Mary Jane Hopper	gda	7	scholar	Dur [D] Crossgate
941	141v			Edward Hopper	gsn	1		Dur [D] Crossgate
942	141v	<11>c	South Street	Jane Hope	hea m	31	washerwoman	Dur
943	141v			Ann Hope	dau	5		Dur
944	141v	<11>d	South Street	George Douglas	hea m	48	woolspinner	Dur
945	141v			Ellen Douglas	wif m	52		Dur
946	141v			Mary Douglas	dau	10		Dur
947	141v	<11>e	South Street	William Cummings	hea m	34	cordwainer	Dur [D] S. Giles
948	141v			Hannah Cummings	wif m	32		Dur [D] Crossgate
949	141v			William Cummings	son	4		Dur [D] Crossgate
950	141v			Mary Jane Cummings	dau	8m		Dur [D] Crossgate
951	142r	[ae]	South Street	Ann Pace	hea w	66	lodging house keeper	Dur Bishop Auckland
952	142r			Dorothy Ann Pace	gda	13	scholar	Dur [D] South Street
953	142r			Thomas Robson	ldr	30	butcher	Dur [D] Saddler St
954	142r			William Elliott	ldr m	62	hatter	Dur [D] Crossgate
955	142r			John Monkhouse	ldr	49	butcher	Dur [D] Silver Street
956	142r			Joseph Dixon	ldr	36	gardener	Dur Red House
957	142r			Mary Musgrove	ldr m	20		Nry Ingleby
958	142r			Thomas Mitchell	ldr m	25	mason	Fif S. Andrews
959	142r			Sarah Mitchell	ldw m	21		Dur Barnard Castle
960	142r	<12>a	South Street	George Hopper jn	hea m	40	roper	Dur
961	142r			Isabel Hopper	wif m	40		Nbl Tynemouth
962	142r			Robert Hopper	son	17	roper	Dur
963	142r			Ann Jane Hopper	dau	15		Dur
964	142r			George William Hopper	son	12	scholar	Dur
965	142r			Lavinia Marina Hopper	dau	5		Dur
966	142r			James Bannister	ldr m	32	carpet weaver	Wor Kidderminster
967	142r			John Lowes	ldr	21	shoemaker	Nbl Newcastle
968	142r			John Wilson	ldr	20	shoemaker	Nbl Newcastle
969	142r			Henry Beach	ldr	23	carpet weaver	Wor Kidderminster
970	142v	<12>b	South Street	Charlotte Reynolds	hea	60	laundress	Ham Basingstoke
971	142v	<13>	South Street	William Henry Dean	hea m	45	worsted mfr <woolcomber>	Dur Bishop Auckland
972	142v			Ann Dean	wif m	47		Dur Trimdon
973	142v			Samuel Dean	son	21	dyer	Dur
974	142v			Jane Dean	dau	16	clerk's assistant	Dur
975	142v			Emma Dean	dau	7	scholar	Dur
976	142v	<14>a	South Street	William Binns	hea m	69	mason	Dur
977	142v			Jane Binns	wif	66	laundress	Dur
978	142v	<14>b	South Street	Robert Douglas	hea m	24	ropemaker	Dur
979	142v			Emma Douglas	wif m	18		Wry Leeds, S. John
980	142v	<14>c	South Street	William Douglas	hea m	35	ropemaker	Dur
981	142v			Jane Douglas	wif m	40		Dur
982	142v			Agnes Johnson	dls	19	dressmaker	Nbl Newcastle
983	143r	[af]a	South Street	Ann Storey	hea w	78		Dur Witton Gilbert
984	143r			Ellen Storey	dau	36		Dur Aycliffe
985	143r			Ann Storey	gda	15		Dur [D] S. Margaret
986	143r	[af]b	South Street	Mary Scott	hea w	59	pauper	Dur Hartlepool
987	143r			Catherine Scott	dau	34	charwoman	Dur Hartlepool
988	143r			Elizabeth Scott	gda	12	scholar	Dur [D] Crossgate
989	143r			Catherine Ann Scott	gda	9	scholar	Dur [D] Crossgate
990	143r			Robert Francis Scott	gsn	6	scholar	Dur [D] Crossgate
991	143r	[ag]	South Street	Elizabeth Johnson	hea w	43	charwoman; pauper	Dur [D] Framwelgate
992	143r			John Johnson	son	18	currier's apprentice	Dur [D] Crossgate
993	143r			Dorothy Johnson	dau	15	scholar	Dur [D] Crossgate
994	143r			Thomas Johnson	son	11	scholar	Dur [D] Crossgate
995	143r			Mary Johnson	dau	1		Dur [D] Crossgate
996	143r	[ah]	South Street	John Mavers	hea m	30	weaver; pauper	Abd Aberdeen
997	143r			Elizabeth Mavers	wif m	28		Dur [D] Crossgate
998	143r			Edward Mavers	son	1		Dur [D] Crossgate
999	143v	[ai]a	South Street	Henry Fawcett	hea w	39	solicitor's managing clk	Dur [D] S. Margaret
1000	143v	[ai]b	South Street	Peter Grieveson	hea m	66	gardener	Dur
1001	143v			Phoebe Grieveson	wif m	62		Dur [D] Crossgate
1002	143v			John Grieveson	son	27	journeyman cooper	Dur [D] Crossgate

1003 143v	[aj]a	South Street	William Westgarth	hea m	68	woolcomber	Dur Bishop Auckland
1004 143v			Harriet Westgarth	wif m	67		Chs Altrincham
1005 143v			Mary Westgarth	dau	32		Chs Altrincham
1006 143v			John Westgarth	son	25	journeyman nailer	Dur Bishop Auckland
1007 143v			Abraham Westgarth	son	23	smith	Dur Bishop Auckland
1008 143v	[aj]b	South Street	Margaret Cockburn	hea w	42	pauper	Dur Sunderland
1009 143v			William Cockburn	son	18	tinman's apprentice	Dur [D] S. Nicholas
1010 143v			Jane Cockburn	dau	16	works at paper mill	Dur [D] S. Nicholas
1011 143v			John Cockburn	son	10	scholar	Dur [D] Crossgate
1012 143v			Richard Cockburn	son	3		Dur [D] Crossgate
1013 143v			Emma Cockburn	dau	1		Dur [D] Crossgate
1014 144r	[aj]c	South Street	Elizabeth Richardson	hea w	42	pauper	Bkm
1015 144r			Thomas Richardson	son	12	errand boy	Nbl Bradford
1016 144r			Ann Richardson	dau	8	scholar	Dur Darlington
1017 144r			Jane Richardson	dau	10	scholar	Nbl Bradford
1018 144r	[aj]d	South Street	John Pace	hea m	27	ropemaker	Dur [D] Crossgate
1019 144r			Eleanor Pace	wif m	22		Dur [D] Crossgate
1020 144r	[aj]e	South Street	George Alderson	hea w	37	carpet weaver	Dur Barnard Castle
1021 144r			Robert Alderson	son	10	errand boy	Dur Barnard Castle
1022 144r			Mary Alderson	dau	2		Dur Barnard Castle
1023 144r	<17>a	South Street	Elizabeth Suggett	hea	65	dealer in milk	Dur
1024 144r	<17>b	South Street	Jane Davison	hea w	67	pauper	Dur Monk Hesleden
1025 144r			Susan Jackson	vis	39		Dur Whitton
1026 144r	<18>a	South Street	Robert Charlton	hea m	27	shoemaker	Dur Witton Gilbert
1027 144r			Jane Charlton	wif m	21		Nbl Hexham
1028 144r			Robert Charlton	son	4		Dur [D] Crossgate
1029 144v	<18>b	South Street	Joseph Barker	hea m	51	cordwainer	Dur Sedgefield
1030 144v			Mary Barker	wif m	47		Dur [D] Crossgate
1031 144v			William Barker	son	7		Dur [D] Crossgate
1032 144v			Ralph Vasey	ldr	69	tailor	Dur [D] S. Nicholas
1033 144v	<19>	South Street	William Barnes	hea m	49	auctioneer & appraiser	Dur
1034 144v			Mary Barnes	wif m	53		Dur Stockton
1035 144v			Richard Barnes	son	24	bailiff's assistant	Dur Staindrop
1036 144v			John William Barnes	son	20	auctioneer's clerk	Dur Staindrop
1037 144v			Mary Ann Barnes	dau	18		Dur Staindrop
1038 144v			Mary Ann Wrightson	ldr m	47	land agent's wife	Dur
1039 144v			Mary Ann Barnes	ldr w	75		Nbl Berwick
1040 144v			William Wrightson	ldr	8	scholar	Dur Shincliffe
1041 144v			Anna Wrightson	ldr	7	scholar	Dur
1042 144v			Richard Wrightson	ldr	5		Dur
1043 144v			Thomas Wrightson	ldr	3		Dur
1044 145r	<20>	South Street	Thomas Charles Durham	hea	25	mathematical master *	Nth Burton Latimer
1045 145r			Lucy Durham	sis	24	housekeeper	Nth Burton Latimer
1046 145r			Thomas Welbank Fowle	bdr	15	scholar	Nry Northallerton
1047 145r			William Fowle	bdr	14	scholar	Nry Northallerton
1048 145r			Thomas James Schollick	bdr	15	scholar	Lan Pennybridge
1049 145r			George Thomas Allison	bdr	14	scholar	Nry Richmond
1050 145r			Robert Thorp	bdr	12	scholar	Nbl Alnwick
1051 145r			Barbara Lee	ser	30	cook	Dur Penshaw
1052 145r			Mary Anne Scott	ser	21	house maid	Nbl Allendale *
1053 145r			Oran Mann	ser	16	general servant	Dur Tudhoe
1054 145r	<21>	South Street	John Herbert	hea w	69	gardener <florist>	Dur [D] Crossgate
1055 145r			Ellen Herbert	dau	38	needlewoman	Dur Brancepeth
1056 145r			Ellen Herbert jn	gda	11	scholar	Dur [D] Crossgate
1057 145r	<22>	South Street	George Norie	hea w	56	overlooker, carp[et] *	Abd Aberdeen
1058 145r			William Norie	son	19	smith	Dur
1059 145r			Margaret Norie	dau	17	bonnetmaker	Dur
1060 145r			George Norie	son	15	flesher	Dur
1061 145r			Hannah Norie	dau	13	scholar	Dur
1062 145v	[ak]	South Street	William Marshall	hea m	48	coach painter	Nbl Newcastle
1063 145v			Harriet Marshall	wif m	49		Nbl Newcastle
1064 145v			William Marshall	son	19	writing clerk	Cul Carlisle
1065 145v			Thomas Marshall	son	16	writing clerk	Cul Carlisle
1066 145v			Oliver Marshall	son	12	errand boy	Cul Carlisle
1067 145v			Harriet Marshall	dau	7		Dur
1068 145v			Martha Marshall	dau	4		Wry Knaresborough
1069 145v		Banks Mill	William Hutchinson	hea m	43	mason	Dur
1070 145v			Jane Hutchinson	wif m	43		Dur
1071 145v			Thomas Hutchinson	son	18	mason's apprentice	Dur
1072 145v			John Hutchinson	son	9	scholar	Dur
1073 145v			Jane Hutchinson	dau	2		Dur
1074 145v			Robert Revely	slw m	23	mason, journeyman	Dur
1075 145v			Elizabeth Revely	swi m	20		Dur
1076 145v		Prebends' Cottage	David Flintoff	hea m	54	gardener	Nry Northallerton
1077 145v			Beatrice Flintoff	wif m	56		Dur Aycliffe
1078 145v			Mary Anne Flintoff	dau	23		Nry Northallerton
1079 145v			Elizabeth Flintoff	dau	20	lady's maid	Nry Northallerton
1080 145v			David F. Garthwaite	gsn	12	scholar	Dur
1081 146r		Prebends' Gate	Christopher Brown	hea m	60	gentleman's servant	Dur West Boldon
1082 146r			Hannah Brown	wif m	70		Dur [D] Elvet
1083 146r		Grove	Margaret Dance	ser	65	housekeeper	Dur Staindrop

1084	146r	<24>a	South Street	William Hopper	hea m	40	joiner	Dur [D] Elvet
1085	146r			Mary Hopper	wif m	38		Sfk Bury S. Edmunds
1086	146r			Ann Hopper	dau	11		Mdx Pimlico
1087	146r	<24>b	South Street	Margaret Thompson	hea w	55	charwoman	Dur
1088	146r			Edward Thompson	son m	26	cooper	Dur
1089	146r			Isabella Thompson	swi m	23		Dur Chester-le-Street
1090	146r	<24>c	South Street	Ann Laidler	hea	42		Dur Bishop Auckland
1091	146r	<24>d	South Street	John Stoddart jn	hea m	22	journeyman printer	Dur [D] Crossgate
1092	146r			Jane Stoddart	wif m	21	milliner <& strawhatmkr>	Dur [D] Elvet
1093	146r	[al]	South Street	Mary Best	hea	64	washerwoman	Dur [D] Crossgate
1094	146r			Thomas Mitchinson	ldr	56	annuitant	Dur Stockton, Newport
1095	146v	<26>	South Street	Robert Gray	hea m	38	master currier *	Dur
1096	146v			Ann Gray	wif m	35		Dur
1097	146v			Caroline Gray	dau	6	scholar	Dur [D] S. Giles
1098	146v			Elizabeth Gray	dau	5	scholar	Dur [D] S. Giles
1099	146v			Ralph Gray	son	3		Dur [D] S. Giles
1100	146v			George Gray	son	1		Dur [D] S. Giles
1101	146v			Margaret Gill	ser	20	house servant	Dur
1102	146v	<27>a	South Street	Ann Middleton	hea w	85	laundress	Dur [D] Crossgate
1103	146v			Mary Middleton	dau	62	laundress	Dur [D] Crossgate
1104	146v	<27>b	South Street	Ann Blackett	hea w	56	laundress	Dur [D] Crossgate
1105	146v			Mary Ann Blackett	dau	25	dressmaker	Dur [D] S. Nicholas
1106	146v			Margaret Blackett	dau	22	laundress	Dur [D] S. Nicholas
1107	146v			Robert Blackett	son	18	coachmaker's apprentice	Dur [D] S. Nicholas
1108	146v			Elizabeth Blackett	dau	16	scholar	Dur [D] Crossgate
1109	146v	<28>	South Street	John Stoddart	hea w	51	gardener	Dur
1110	146v			Thomas Stoddart	son	28	gardener	Dur
1111	146v			Ann Stoddart	dau	24	laundress	Dur
1112	147r	<29>	South Street	William Worthy	hea w	74	retd gentleman's servant	Nbl Minsteracres
1113	147r			William Worthy	son	44	painter & glazier	Dur Sunderland Bridge
1114	147r			Mary Ann Worthy	dau	36	laundress	Dur [D] S. Giles
1115	147r			Jane Worthy	gda	17	laundress	Dur [D] Crossgate
1116	147r	<30>	South Street	Elizabeth Gray	hea w	65	proprietor of houses	Dur Barnard Castle
1117	147r			Jane Gray	dau	30		Dur
1118	147r			Elizabeth Gray	dau	28		Dur
1119	147r			Caroline Gray	mlw w	93	proprietor of houses	Dur Houghton-l-Spring
			house empty					
1120	147v	[am]	South Street	Henry Stoker	hea m	33	second master *	Dur Durham
1121	147v			Charlotte Stoker	wif m	31		Ken Tunbridge [Wells]
1122	147v			Katherine Stoker	dau	5		Dur Durham
1123	147v			Henry Edward Stoker	son	4		Dur Durham
1124	147v			Frederick W. Stoker	son	2		Dur Durham
1125	147v			Anne Stoker	sis	24	surgeon's daughter	Dur Durham
1126	147v			Elizabeth Ann Pierce	sil	30	gentleman's daughter	Ken Tunbridge [Wells]
1127	147v			Thomas Henry Stokoe	pup	17	scholar	Nbl Hexham
1128	147v			Robert Chapman Richmond	pup	13	scholar	Nbl Haydon Bridge
1129	147v			Joseph Elliot Parsons	pup	17	scholar	Nbl Newcastle
1130	147v			Henry Joy	pup	15	scholar	Dub
1131	147v			Alexander Park	pup	16	scholar	Dur Elwick
1132	147v			George Murray	pup	16	scholar	Sct Dalton
1133	147v			Henry Ritson	pup	15	scholar	Dur Sunderland
1134	147v			Thomas Birkett	pup	15	scholar	Cul Carlisle
1135	147v			Henry John Chaytor	pup	12	scholar	Gal
1136	147v			George T. Raine	pup	12	scholar	Nbl Blyth
1137	147v			Henry Bacon-Grey	pup	13	scholar	Nbl Styford
1138	147v			John William Bacon-Grey	pup	12	scholar	Nbl Styford
1139	148r			William James	pup	13	scholar	Dur Gateshead
1140	148r			Benjamin D. Kennicott	pup	12	scholar	Nbl Woodhorn
1141	148r			Edward Birkett	pup	14	scholar	Nbl Ovingham
1142	148r			William Stow-Stowell	pup	15	scholar	Dur Cockerton
1143	148r			George Saville Streatfield	pup	12	scholar	Ssx Brighton
1144	148r			Henry Fitz. Reynolds	pup	13	scholar	Ery Welton
1145	148r			Walter Reynolds	pup	11	scholar	Ery Welton
1146	148r			Ralph Edward Fenwick	pup	13	scholar	Nbl Ulgham
1147	148r			Margaret Weir	ser	42	house servant	Sct
1148	148r			Elizabeth Titmarsh	ser	23	house servant	Cam Cambridge
1149	148r			Mary Taylor	ser	23	house servant	Dur Durham
1150	148r			Elizabeth Shaw	ser	20	house servant	Dur Easington
1151	148r	[an]	South Street	John Cundill	hea m	38	perpetual curate *	Dur Stockton
1152	148r			Mary Cundill	wif m	37		Cul Crosthwaite
1153	148r			John Ponsonby Cundill	son	7	scholar	Dur
1154	148r			Ann Oley Williams	ser	50	house servant	Dur Shotley Bridge
1155	148r			Mary Wilkinson	ser	20	house servant	Dur Shotley Bridge
1156	148r			Barbara Crow	ser	18	house servant	Nbl Stamfordham
1157	148v	<32>a	South Street	James Elliott	hea m	31	writer	Dur Framwelgate
1158	148v			Jane Elliott	wif m	32		Dur Lumley
1159	148v			Ann Elliott	dau	12	scholar	Dur [D] Crossgate
1160	148v			William Elliott	son	10	scholar	Dur [D] Crossgate
1161	148v			Jane Elliott	dau	8	scholar	Dur [D] Crossgate
1162	148v			Grace Elliott	dau	3		Dur [D] Crossgate
1163	148v			Elizabeth Elliott	dau	1		Dur [D] Crossgate

1164 148v	<32>b	South Street	Grace Elliott	hea w	71	laundress	Dur [D] Crossgate
1165 148v	<32>c	South Street	Charles Sutherst	hea m	41	watchmaker	Dur [D] Framwelgate
1166 148v			Frances Sutherst	wif m	41		Dur Brancepeth
1167 148v	<32>d	South Street	John Sarsfield	hea m	38	gentleman's servant	Dur [D] Elvet
1168 148v			William Sarsfield	son	15	chemist's apprentice	Dur Whitworth
1169 148v			Thomas Sarsfield	son	12	chorister	Dur [D] North Road
1170 148v			Annie Sarsfield	dau	8	scholar	Dur [D] North Bailey
1171 148v			Ralph Sarsfield	son	3		Dur [D] Crossgate
1172 149r	<33>	South Street	John Lidster	hea	67	proprietor of houses *	Dur Ferryhill
1173 149r			Margaret Clarke	sis w	65	landed proprietor	Dur Ferryhill
1174 149r	<34>	South Street	Thomas Richardson	hea m	53	master saddler	Dur Gateshead
1175 149r			Isabella Richardson	wif m	45		Dur Durham
1176 149r			Robert Fewster Liddle	nep	9	chorister	Dur Durham
1177 149r	<35>	South Street	John Jerrems	hea m	31	master chemist & grocer	Lin Gainsborough
1178 149r			Mary Jerrems	wif m	26		Ntt Elkesley
1179 149r			John Giles Jerrems	son	3		Dur
1180 149r			William Henry Jerrems	son	2		Dur
1181 149r			Elizabeth L. Walker	ser	20	house servant	Dur Easington Lane
1182 149r	[ao]a	South Street	Jane Spoore	hea	77	parish relief	Dur Houghton-l-Spring
1183 149r	[ao]b	South Street	Jane Wilson	hea	63	proprietor of houses	Dur Staindrop
1184 149r	[ao]c	South Street	Samuel Cawood	hea m	45	house servant	Wry Tadcaster
1185 149r			Ann Cawood	wif m	45		Sal Shrewsbury
1186 149v	[ao]d	South Street	Ann Linsley	hea	87	spinster; pauper	Dur Bishop Auckland
1187 149v	<37>	South Street	William Peele sn	hea m	60	acting receiver *	Dur
1188 149v			Mary Peele	wif m	60		Dur Witton Gilbert
1189 149v			Eliza Peele	dau	32		Dur
1190 149v			Margaret Peele	dau	26		Dur
1191 149v	<38>	South Street	William Peele jn	hea m	36	proctor's managing clk *	Dur
1192 149v			Mary Peele	wif m	35		Dur South Shields
1193 149v			Isabella Peele	dau	13		Dur
1194 149v			Mary Ann Peele	dau	10		Dur
1195 149v			Elizabeth Peele	dau	7		Dur
1196 149v			Fanny Peele	dau	4		Dur
1197 149v			Robert Turner Peele	son	1		Dur
1198 150r	<39>	South Street	Robert Jackson	hea m	38	solicitor's managing clk	Dur
1199 150r			Susan Jackson	wif m	31		Dur Brancepeth
1200 150r			Henry Jackson	son	10	scholar	Dur
1201 150r			William R. Jackson	son	8	scholar	Dur
1202 150r			Robert Jackson jn	son	6	scholar	Dur
1203 150r			George Jackson	son	4		Dur
1204 150r			John Jackson	son	7m		Dur
1205 150r	<40>a	South Street	Joseph <S.> Rippon	hea m	48	boot and shoemaker	Dur
1206 150r			Elizabeth Rippon	wif m	52		Dur Muggleswick
1207 150r			Mary Jane Rippon	dau	20	dressmaker <& milliner>	Dur
1208 150r	<40>b	South Street	Mary Revely	hea	74	retired house servant	Dur Burdon
1209 150r	<41>	South Street	John Cartwright	hea	46	minor canon *	Wry Halifax
1210 150r			Jane Cairns	ser	38	housekeeper	Dur
1211 150r			Ann Jopling	ser	24	cook	Dur West Rainton
1212 150v	<42>	South Street	Mary Edger	hea	73	proprietor of houses *	Dur Sedgefield
1213 150v			William Finley	ldr	52	private teacher *	Sfk [Long] Melford
1214 150v	<43>	South Street	Sarah Hartley	hea w	33	lodging house keeper	Dur
1215 150v			Surtees Smith	ldr	16	scholar	Dur Cleatlam
1216 150v			Henry Charles Spearman	ldr	15	scholar	Germany BS
1217 150v			Isabella Young	ser	17	house servant	Dur Hetton-le-Hole
1218 150v	<44>	South Street	William Hutchinson	hea w	30	clerk to Water Company	Dur
1219 150v			Thomas Edward Hutchinson	son	6	scholar	Dur
1220 150v			Ellen Thompson	mlw w	54	laundress	Dur Windlestone
1221 150v			Martha Thompson	sil	18	laundress	Dur
1222 150v	[ap]	South Street	James Main	hea m	44	woolsorter	Dur Darlington
1223 150v			Charlotte Main	wif m	33		Wry Harrogate
1224 150v			Sarah Main	dau	17	straw-bonnetmaker	Dur Darlington
1225 150v			James Main	son	6	scholar	Dur
1226 151r	<46>	South Street	Eliza Ponsonby	hea	38	fundholder & annuitant	Cul Keswick
1227 151r			Rachael Greathead	ser	29	house servant	Dur Bishop Auckland
1228 151r	<47>	South Street	John Wheldon	hea m	76	retired farmer	Dur Pelton
1229 151r			Sarah Wheldon	wif m	66		Dur
1230 151r			Sarah Wheldon	dau	32		Dur Chester-le-Street
1231 151r	<48>	South Street	Robert Sutherland	hea m	35	auctioneer <& lodgings*>	Nbl Hexham
1232 151r			Rebecca Sutherland	wif m	56	bookseller & stationer	Dur Greatham
1233 151r			Sarah Nicholson	ser	20	house servant	Dur Easington Lane
1234 151r	<49>	South Street	William Deanham	hea m	42	reporter <& lodgings>	Dur
1235 151r			Sarah Deanham	wif m	43		Dur Union Hall
1236 151r			Sarah Deanham	dau	12	scholar	Dur
1237 151r			Susan Deanham	dau	10	scholar	Dur
1238 151r			Elizabeth Grieveson	sis w	39	milliner	Dur
1239 151r			Mary Scott	ser	19	house servant	Nry Northallerton
1240 151v	[aq]	South Street	Margaret Pinkney	hea w	65		Dur
1241 151v			Peter Pinkney	son	22	carpet weaver	Dur
1242 151v			Hannah Bennett	dau m	20		Dur
1243 151v			George Bennett	slw m	35	journeyman bookbinder	Sal Shrewsbury
1244 151v			George Bennett	gsn	4		War Birmingham

1245	151v	[aq]	South Street	William Bennett	gsn	6m		Dur
1246	151v	<51>	South Street	Thomas Coxon	hea m	45	master tailor *	Dur
1247	151v			Mary Coxon	wif m	45		Dur
1248	151v			Thomas Coxon	son	13	scholar	Dur
1249	151v			George Coxon	son	12	scholar	Dur
1250	151v			William Coxon	son	8	scholar	Dur
1251	151v			John Russell Gray	ldr	50	brewer's traveller	Nbl Newcastle
1252	151v			Maria Madgin	ldr	70	annuitant	Dur
1253	151v			Hannah Mainsforth	ser	17	house servant	Dur
1254	151v	<52>	South Street	Joseph Waite	hea m	68	curate * <& academy>	Nbl Morpeth
1255	151v			Jane Waite	wif m	60		Dur Fatfield House
1256	151v			Jane Eliza Waite	dau	29		Dur S. John's Chapel
1257	151v			Mary Humble	sil	58		Dur North Biddick
1258	152r	<53>	South Street	Eleanor Lowery	hea w	71		Nbl Mitford
1259	152r			John Lowery	son	31	draper's assistant	Nbl Alnwick
1260	152r			Isabella Lowery	dau	27	dressmaker	Nbl Alwinton
1261	152r			John Lowery	gsn	5	scholar	Nbl Morpeth
1262	152r	<54>	South Street	Susanna Ellidge	hea w	57	annuitant	Cam Upwell
1263	152r			Susanna Ellidge	dau	28		Lin Louth
1264	152r			Henry Richardson	gsn	3		Nbl Newcastle
1265	152r	<55>	South Street	Harriet Angas	hea	64	annuitant	Dur Brancepeth
1266	152r			Mary Angas	sis	62	annuitant	Dur Brancepeth
1267	152r			Anne Dickinson	vis	28	annuitant	Cul Alston
1268	152r			Rachael Scrafton	ser	19	house servant	Dur Esh
1269	152r	<56>	South Street	Mary S. Hole	hea	53	teacher	Lnd
1270	152r			Louisa Mitchinson	sis w	51	teacher <boarding sch>	Lnd
1271	152r			John Mitchinson	*	17	scholar, Pembroke Coll *	Dur
1272	152r			Elizabeth Stephenson	pup	17	scholar	Ssx Hastings
1273	152r			John Stephenson	pup	7	scholar	Ssx Hastings
1274	152v			Anne Jackson	pup	13	pupil	Belgium, Antwerp*
1275	152v			Robert Jackson	pup	12	pupil	Belgium, Antwerp*
1276	152v			Frederica Fenwick	pup	11	pupil	Dur Stanhope
1277	152v			Mary Ann Trueman	pup	10	pupil	Dur
1278	152v			Elizabeth Ann Wilson	ser	29	house servant	Dur Lanchester
1279	152v			Isabella Smiles	ser	18	house servant	Dur Seaham Harbour
1280	152v	<57>	South Street	Thomas Clamp	hea m	57	registrar *	Dur Trimdon
1281	152v			Jane Clamp	wif m	47		Dur West Rainton
1282	152v			Thomas Clamp	son	20	attorney's writing clerk	Dur [D] Elvet
1283	152v			John Clamp	son	18	app to cabinetmaker	Dur [D] Elvet
1284	152v			William Clamp	son	17	apprentice to chemist	Dur [D] Elvet
1285	152v			Fanny Hindmarsh	ser	15	domestic servant	Dur Merrington
1286	152v	[ar]	South Street	Henrietta Metcalf	hea	28	lodging house keeper	Dur
1287	152v			Mary Ryle	ldr	52	retd straw-bonnetmaker	Dur
1288	152v			William Turner	ldr	41	bookbinder	Yks
1289	152v			James Cochrane	ldr	39	compositor	Kkd Castle Douglas
1290	152v			Thomas Mills	ldr	21	expectant Excise officer	Dur
1291	152v			Frederick Parker	ldr	20	chemist's apprentice	Dur Darlington
1292	153r	[as]	South Street	Jonah Pattison	hea m	27	horseshoer	Dur [D] Elvet
1293	153r			Margaret Pattison	wif m	27		Dur [D] Crossgate
1294	153r			Margaret Pattison	dau	6	scholar	Dur [D] Crossgate
1295	153r			John Pattison	son	3		Dur [D] Crossgate
1296	153r			Thomas Kelly	ldr	31	carpet weaver	Dur [D] Crossgate
1297	153r			Jane Pattison	dau	1		Dur [D] Crossgate
1298	153r	[at]a	South Street	John Marsden	hea m	27	maltman	Dur [D] Crossgate
1299	153r			Jane Marsden	wif m	24		Dur [D] S. Nicholas
1300	153r	[at]b	South Street	Elizabeth Burnett	hea w	31	lodging ho kpr; pauper	Dur [D] Elvet
1301	153r			John George Burnett	son	5		Dur [D] Crossgate
1302	153r			Mary Burnett	dau	3		Dur Gateshead
1303	153r			Thomas Watson	ldr w	35	spinner, carp[et]	Wry Leeds
1304	153r			Robert Louth	ldr	25	cabinetmaker	Edn Leith
1305	153r			William Brown	ldr	26	bailiff's follower	Nbl Morpeth
1306	153r	[at]c	South Street	Henry Chicken	hea m	23	tobacconist	Dur [D] Elvet
1307	153r			Ann Chicken	wif m	28		Dur [D] Framwelgate
1308	153r			Ann Chicken	dau	2		Dur [D] Crossgate
1309	153v	[at]d	South Street	John Hedley	hea m	30	cloth-capmaker	Lan Liverpool
1310	153v			Ellen Hedley	wif m	28		Lan Liverpool
1311	153v			John Hedley	son	2		Dur Gateshead
1312	153v	[au]a	South Street	John Robson	hea w	74	cordwainer; pauper	Dur
1313	153v	[au]b	South Street	Thomas Wall	hea m	57	journeyman joiner	Dur
1314	153v			Mary Wall	wif m	54		Dur
1315	153v			Alice Wall	nce	10		Dur
1316	153v	[av]	South Street	Mary Dial	hea	50	laundress	Nbl Walker
1317	153v			Joseph Dial	son	14	roper's apprentice	Dur [D] Crossgate
1318	153v	[aw]a	South Street	John Harrison	hea m	49	labourer	Dur
1319	153v			Elizabeth Harrison	wif m	45		Dur
1320	153v			Jane Harrison	dau	19		Dur
1321	153v			Edward Harrison	son	6	scholar	Dur
1322	153v			Margaret Harrison	gda	1		Dur
1323	154r	[aw]b	South Street	William Hall	hea	22	shoemaker	Dur
1324	154r			Margaret Hall	sis	13		Dur
1325	154r			John Hall	bro	8		Dur

				Name		Rel	Cond	Age	Occupation	Birthplace
1326	154r	[ax]	South Street	Thomas	Cockburn	hea	w	36	labourer	Dur [D] Elvet
1327	154r			John	Cockburn	son		13	scholar	Dur [D] Crossgate
1328	154r	<60>	South Street	George	Bone	hea	m	55	fruiterer	Dur
1329	154r			Jane	Harker	dau	w	30	fruiterer	Dur
1330	154r			John	Bone	son		13	scholar	Dur
1331	154r			George	Macdonald	ldr	w	58	tailor	Dur
			house empty							
1332	154v	<1>	Crossgate	John	Collinson	hea	m	45	shoemaker	Dur Whorlton
1333	154v			Jane	Collinson	wif	m	49		Dur
1334	154v			Jane	Collinson	dau		18		Dur
1335	154v			Mary	Collinson	dau		14		Dur
1336	154v			Sarah	Collinson	dau		12	scholar	Dur
1337	154v			Margaret	Collinson	dau		10	scholar	Dur
1338	154v			William	Heslop	ldr	w	38	mason	Dur
1339	154v			Elizabeth	Heslop	ldd		9	scholar	Dur
1340	154v			Mary	Heslop	ldd		2		Dur
1341	154v	<2>a	Crossgate	Eleanor	Cherry	hea	w	66	grocer	Dur Durham
1342	154v			Eleanor	Cherry	dau		45	dressmaker	Dur Durham
1343	154v			Obadiah Miller	Cherry	son		35	journeyman cabinetmaker	Dur Durham
1344	154v			William	Cherry	gsn		20	cabinetmaker's app	Dur Barnard Castle
1345	154v	<2>b	Crossgate	James	Rennison	hea		28	journeyman joiner	Dur
1346	154v			Isabella	Rennison	sis		37	house servant	Dur
1347	154v			John	Rennison	nep		10	scholar	Lnd
1348	155r	[an]a	Crossgate	Jemima	Hunt	hea	w	42	work at paper mill	Dur
1349	155r			Eleanor	Hunt	dau		19	work at paper mill	Dur
1350	155r			Francis	Hunt	son		16	shoemaker's apprentice	Dur
1351	155r			John	Hunt	son		13	joiner's apprentice	Dur
1352	155r			Margaret	Hunt	dau		9	scholar	Dur
1353	155r			Mary	Hunt	dau		5	scholar	Dur
1354	155r	[an]b	Crossgate	John	Blakey	hea	m	23	journeyman cooper	Dur [D] S. Nicholas
1355	155r			Ann	Blakey	wif	m	21		Dur [D] Crossgate
1356	155r	<4>a	Crossgate	Thomas	Hamilton	hea	m	41	husbandman	Nry Thornton-le-Beans
1357	155r			Ann	Hamilton	wif	m	40		Dur Ferryhill
1358	155r			Mary Jane	Hamilton	dau		11	scholar	Dur
1359	155r			Catherine	Hamilton	dau		9	scholar	Dur
1360	155r			Elizabeth	Hamilton	dau		4		Dur
1361	155r			Thomas Pybus	Hamilton	son		2		Dur
1362	155r	<4>b	Crossgate	William	Lumley	hea	m	56	woolcomber	Dur
1363	155r			Ann	Lumley	wif	m	56	laundress	Dur
1364	155r			Matthew	Bee jn	ldr		19	painter's apprentice	Dur
1365	155v	<4>c	Crossgate	John	Hodgson	hea	m	39	tailor *	Dur
1366	155v			Hannah	Hodgson	wif	m	37		Dur
1367	155v			Mary Ann	Hodgson	dau		10	scholar	Dur
1368	155v			Thomas	Hodgson	son		8	scholar	Dur
1369	155v			John	Hodgson	son		5	scholar	Dur
1370	155v			Isabel	Hodgson	dau		1		Dur
1371	155v	<4>d	Crossgate	George	Waddington	hea	m	54	printer's compositor	Dur [D] Crossgate
1372	155v			Elizabeth	Waddington	wif	m	49		Dur Stockton
1373	155v			John Banks	Waddington	son		20	currier's apprentice	Dur [D] Crossgate
1374	155v			Catherine	Waddington	dau		15	scholar	Dur [D] Crossgate
1375	155v			George	Waddington	son		14	mason's apprentice	Dur [D] Crossgate
1376	155v			Margaret	Waddington	dau		8	scholar	Dur [D] Crossgate
1377	155v	<4>e	Crossgate	John	McCulloch	hea	m	49	carpet weaver	Sct
1378	155v			Margaret	McCulloch	wif	m	49		Sct
1379	155v	<4>f	Crossgate	Michael	Divine	hea	m	52	papermaker	Dub
1380	155v			Ann	Divine	wif	m	53		Dub
1381	155v			Catherine	Divine	dau		28	working at paper mill	Dub
1382	155v			Elizabeth	Divine	dau		25	working at paper mill	Dub
1383	155v			Peter	Divine	son		23	journeyman butcher	Dub
1384	155v			Laurence	Divine	son		20	woolsorter	Dub
1385	156r	<4>g	Crossgate	William	Bainbridge	hea	w	78	pauper; jnym joiner	Dur Lanchester
1386	156r	<5>a	Crossgate	Mary	Ward	hea		65	silk dyer; pauper	Dur South Church
1387	156r	<5>b	Crossgate	Thomas	Anderson	hea	m	68	carter	Sct
1388	156r			Elizabeth	Anderson	wif	m	64		Dur South Shields
1389	156r	<5>c	Crossgate	Elizabeth	Mills	hea	w	66	pauper; fmly laundress	Nbl Newcastle
1390	156r	<6>	Crossgate	Jane	Jackson	hea	w	74	proprietor of houses	Dur
1391	156r			Charlotte	Wharton	nce	w	46	retired grocer	Dur
1392	156r			Elizabeth	Smith	ser		16	house servant	Dur Tudhoe
1393	156r	<6>	Crossgate	Richard	Sutcliffe	hea	m	57	master tallow chandler	Wry Leeds
1394	156r			Elizabeth	Sutcliffe	wif	m	48		Dur
1395	156r	<7>	Crossgate	William Law	Robertson	hea	m	35	printer's compositor	Sct
1396	156r			Helen Nelson	Robertson	wif	m	43		Sct
1397	156v	<8>	Crossgate	Mary	Greenwell	hea	w	59	boarding house	Wry Ripon
1398	156v			William	Greenwell	son		20	student in University	Dur Lanchester
1399	156v			Robert	Heaviside	gsn		4	clergyman's son	Dur West Rainton
1400	156v			William	Bulmer	bdr		18	scholar	Dur South Shields
1401	156v			John	Bulmer	bdr		15	scholar	Dur Sunderland
1402	156v			John F.	Powles	bdr		13	scholar	Lan Manchester
1403	156v			William D.	Powles	bdr		11	scholar	Lnd
1404	156v			Charles H.	Badnall	bdr		18	scholar	IoM
1405	156v			John	Mayors	bdr		15	scholar	Dur South Shields

1406	156v	<8>	Crossgate	Joseph Hudson	bdr	16	scholar		Quebec
1407	156v			Mary Wood	ser	22	house servant		Nry Richmond
1408	156v			Margaret Wood	ser	19	house servant		Nry Richmond
1409	156v	<9>	Crossgate	Mary Addison	hea w	61	proprietor of houses		Dur Durham
1410	156v			Mary Addison	dau	28	no occupation		Dur Durham
1411	156v			Charles Addison	son	25	classical teacher		Dur Durham
1412	156v	<10>	Crossgate	Elizabeth Hall	hea w	77	money at interest *		Dur Preston-le-Skerne
1413	156v			Jane Watson	ser	29	house servant		Dur Middle'n-Teesdale
1414	157r	<11>	Crossgate	John Hammond	hea w	76	gentleman		Nry Kilburn
1415	157r			Richard Hammond	son	41	attorney *		Dur
1416	157r			Isabella McDonald	ser	25	housekeeper		Wry Ripon
1417	157r	[aa]	Grape Lane	Rowland Stout	hea w	60	butcher		Dur Durham
1418	157r			John Stout	son	19	shoemaker's apprentice		Dur Durham
1419	157r	[ab]	Grape Lane	William Tweedie	hea m	58	joiner employing 1 man		Sct
1420	157r			William Tweedie	son	19	joiner's apprentice		Dur
1421	157r			Mary Bradley	ser	40	housekeeper		Dur
1422	157r	[ac]	Grape Lane	Thomas Marshall	hea m	37	journeyman cabinetmaker		Dur
1423	157r			Ann Marshall	wif m	40			Dur Piercebridge
1424	157r			Ann Marshall	dau	2			Dur Darlington
1425	157r	[ad]a	Grape Lane	Margaret Pearson	hea w	52	daily labourer		Dur Kelloe
1426	157r			Ruth Pearson	dau	31	dressmaker		Dur Sedgefield
1427	157r	[ad]b	Grape Lane	Isabella Towns	hea w	41	daily labourer		Dur Brandon
1428	157r			Francis James Towns	son	11	scholar		Dur
1429	157r	[ae]	Grape Lane	Thomas Graham	hea w	71	retired millwright		Dur [D] Crossgate
1430	157r	[af]	Grape Lane	Francis Graham	hea m	68	papermaker		Hef Rickermouth
1431	157r			Jane Graham	wif m	67			Dur Staindrop
1432	157r			John Henry Graham	son	17	plasterer's apprentice		Dur Langley
1433	157v	[ao]	Crossgate	Thomas Jacques	hea m	39	cordwainer		Ery Pocklington *
1434	157v			Isabella Jacques	wif m	39			Edn Leith
1435	157v			Thomas Jacques	son	7	scholar		Dur Sunderland
1436	157v			Joseph Jacques	son	4			Dur
1437	157v	[ap]	Crossgate	Robert Lovegreen	hea m	35	shoemaker		Dur Sunderland
1438	157v			Margaret Lovegreen	wif m	33			Dur
1439	157v			Robert R. Lovegreen	son	4			Nbl Newcastle
1440	157v			John Andrew Lovegreen	son	2			Nbl Newcastle
1441	157v			William Lovegreen	son	10m			Dur
1442	157v			John Richardson	ldr	20	cartman		Dur
1443	157v			James Clarke	ldr	37	gardener		Dur
1444	157v	[aq]	Crossgate	William Blair	hea m	35	boot and shoemaker		Dur Tudhoe
1445	157v			Mary Blair	wif m	37			Dur
1446	157v			John Blair	son	13	errand boy		Dur
1447	157v			Joseph Blair	son	11	scholar		Dur
1448	157v			Elizabeth Ann Blair	dau	9	scholar		Dur Merrington
1449	157v			William Blair	son	6	scholar		Dur
1450	157v			Mary Blair	dau	1			Dur
1451	157v			John Hill	ldr	22	journeyman shoemaker		Dur Norton
1452	158r	[ar]a	Crossgate	Hannah Mount	hea w	77	pauper; daily labourer		Dur Witton Gilbert
1453	158r			Anne Butterwith	gda	24	daily labourer		Dur
1454	158r			Michael Butterwith	gsn	1			Dur
1455	158r	[ar]b	Crossgate	Elizabeth Smith	hea w	68	parish relief		Dur
1456	158r			Isabel Smith	dau	40	laundress		Dur
1457	158r			William Smith	gsn	10	scholar		Dur
1458	158r			Mary Smith	gda	13	pauper; scholar		Dur
1459	158r	[ar]c	Crossgate	John French	hea m	21	labourer		Dur
1460	158r			Mary French	wif m	19			Dur
1461	158r	[ar]d	Crossgate	John Lumley	hea m	31	shoemaker		Dur
1462	158r			Mary Ann Lumley	wif m	26			Dur Bishop Auckland
1463	158r			William Lumley	son	1			Dur
1464	158r	<12>	Crossgate	Jane Talbot	hea w	70	licensed victualler *		Dur Wolsingham
1465	158r			Martha Talbot	dau	32	dressmaker		Dur
1466	158r			Jane Talbot	dau	31	dressmaker		Dur
1467	158r			Thomas Punshon	slw m	35	mason * <& builder>		Dur Bishopwearmouth
1468	158r			Elizabeth Punshon	dau m	33	dressmaker <& milliner>		Dur
1469	158v	[as]	Crossgate	Elizabeth Marshall	hea w	67	manglekeeper		Dur
1470	158v			Charles Oswald	slw m	41	boot and shoemaker		Dur Sedgefield
1471	158v			Harriet Oswald	dau m	40			Dur
1472	158v			Henry Oswald	gsn	13	scholar		Dur
1473	158v			Charles C. Oswald	gsn	9	scholar		Dur
1474	158v			Margaret Oswald	gda	4			Dur
1475	158v			Ann Oswald	vis	60			Dur Sedgefield
1476	158v	<14>a	Crossgate	Mary Calvert	hea w	45	shoebinder		Dur
1477	158v			Thomas Thompson	bro	35	shoemaker		Dur
1478	158v	<14>b	Crossgate	Edward Jasper Graham	hea m	23	painter & glazier		Dur Langley
1479	158v			Isabel Graham	wif m	21			Dur
1480	158v			Ann Graham	dau	10m			Dur
1481	158v	<14>c	Crossgate	William Kightley	hea m	26	miller's labourer		Mdx London
1482	158v			Phoebe Kightley	wif m	20			Dur
1483	158v			Ann Kightley	dau	2			ChI Jersey
1484	158v	<14>d	Crossgate	Ann King	hea m	44	papermaker's wife		Dur Witton Gilbert
1485	158v			Mary Ann King	dau	15	scholar		Dur Langley
1486	158v			Elizabeth King	dau	10	scholar		Dur Langley

				Name	Rel		Age	Occupation	Birthplace
1487	158v	<14>d	Crossgate	Isabel King	dau		8	scholar	Dur Langley
1488	159r	<14>e	Crossgate	Elizabeth Turrell	hea	w	64	pauper; daily labourer	Dub Rathfarnham
1489	159r	<15>	Crossgate	George Newton	hea	m	49	cordwainer	Dur
1490	159r			Ann Newton	wif	m	48		Nbl Berwick
1491	159r			Lancelot Newton	son		20	cordwainer's apprentice	Dur
1492	159r			Elizabeth Newton	dau		17		Dur
1493	159r			George Newton	son		12	scholar	Dur
1494	159r			Mary Newton	dau		7	scholar	Dur
1495	159r			Jane Butterwith	vis		4		Dur
1496	159r	<16>	Crossgate	Anne Isabella Hubberthorn	hea	w	48	grocer <& lodgings>	Dur
1497	159r			Jane Hubberthorn	dls		16	house servant	Dur Redworth
1498	159r			Thomas Holston Egglestone	nep		32	journeyman upholsterer	Nbl Newcastle
1499	159r	<17>	Crossgate	Joseph Brownless	hea	m	48	cowkeeper <milk vendor>	Dur Brancepeth
1500	159r			Margaret Brownless	wif	m	59		Dur Thornley Pit Ho
1501	159r			Hannah Scrafton	vis		3	gamekeeper's daughter	Dur Waterhouses
1502	159r			George Brownless	vis	m	58	farmer	Dur Stainton
1503	159r			Henry Brownless	vis		14	farmer's son	Dur Newbiggin
1504	159v	<19>	Crossgate	John Rontree	hea	m	57	cabinetmaker *	Dur
1505	159v			Catherine Rontree	wif	m	60	grocer	Dur
1506	159v			John Rontree	son	w	34	journeyman mason	Dur
1507	159v			Catherine Rontree	gda		10	scholar	Dur
1508	159v			John Rontree	gsn		4	scholar	Dur
1509	159v			Grace Johnson	ldr		38	daily labourer	Dur
1510	159v			John Johnson	ldr		16	forge apprentice	Dur
1511	159v			Ann Johnson	ldr		9	scholar	Dur
1512	159v			Jane Ivison	ldr		36	daily labourer	Dur
1513	159v			Sarah Bickerstaff	ldr		22	servant	Ken
1514	159v			Hannah Ward	ldr		21	dressmaker	Dur
1515	159v			Peter Marran	ldr	m	35	labourer	Irl
1516	159v			Ann Maunan	ldw		27		Irl
1517	159v	<20>	Crossgate	George Cornforth	hea	m	30	land surveyor *	Dur
1518	159v			Jane Cornforth	wif	m	32		Dur
1519	159v			Henry Rontree Cornforth	son		3		Dur
1520	159v			Mary Cornforth	dau		1		Dur
1521	159v			George Cornforth	son		1m		Dur
1522	160r	[at]a	Crossgate	Mary Ward	hea	w	50	washerwoman	Irl
1523	160r			Bridget Ward	dau		15	daily labourer	Dur Wolsingham
1524	160r	[at]b	Crossgate	Thomas Fiddler	hea	m	29	journeyman shoemaker	Dur
1525	160r			Jane Fiddler	wif	m	27		Dur
1526	160r			Margaret Fiddler	dau		5	scholar	Dur
1527	160r			Ellen Fiddler	dau		1		Dur
1528	160r			Thomas Steel	ldr		27	journeyman shoemaker	Nbl Newcastle
1529	160r	[au]a	Crossgate	John Grieveson	hea	m	36	sawyer	Dur
1530	160r			Mary Grieveson	wif	m	42		Dur
1531	160r	[au]b	Crossgate	Ann Fiddler	hea		23	daily labourer	Dur Staindrop
1532	160r	[au]c	Crossgate	George Gardener	hea	m	46	sawmaker	Dur Merrington
1533	160r			Mary Gardener	wif	m	44		Dur
1534	160r			Joseph Gardener	son		22	iron moulder	Dur
1535	160r			George Gardener	son		17	smith's apprentice	Dur
1536	160r			William Gardener	son		12	scholar	Dur
1537	160r			Margaret Gardener	dau		14	scholar	Dur
1538	160r	[au]d	Crossgate	Hannah Dial	hea		40	washerwoman	Nbl Newcastle
1539	160r			Michael Dial	son		12	scholar	Dur West Rainton
1540	160r			Isabella Dial	dau		7	scholar	Dur [D] Crossgate
1541	160r			Mary Dial	dau		2		Dur [D] Crossgate
1542	160v	[av]	Crossgate	Mary Richardson	hea	w	49	laundress	Ken Hastingleigh
1543	160v			Mary Ann Richardson	dau		14	scholar	Dur
1544	160v			John Thomas Richardson	son		6	scholar	Dur
1545	160v	<23>a	Crossgate	George Forster	hea	m	48	cartman & shoemaker	Dur
1546	160v			Jane Forster	wif	m	38		Dur Gibside
1547	160v			Elizabeth Forster	dau		16	at home	Dur
1548	160v			Mary Forster	dau		11	scholar	Dur
1549	160v			Thomas Forster	son		7	scholar	Dur
1550	160v			George Forster	son		4	scholar	Dur
1551	160v	<23>b	Crossgate	Joseph Littlewood	hea	m	29	cutler	Dby Eckington *
1552	160v			Mary Littlewood	wif	m	29		Dur South Shields
1553	160v			John Littlewood	son		6	scholar	Dur
1554	160v			Eliza Jane Littlewood	dau		3	scholar	Dur
1555	160v			Tamar Littlewood	dau		5m		Dur
1556	160v	<23>c	Crossgate	John Thompson	hea	m	83	papermaker	Dur
1557	160v			Isabella Thompson	wif	m	79		Dur
1558	160v	<23>d	Crossgate	William Hutchinson	hea	m	66	coachsmith	Dur
1559	160v			Jane Hutchinson	wif	m	51		Lan Manchester
1560	160v			William Hutchinson	son		20	miller's apprentice	Nry Richmond
1561	160v			Hannah Hutchinson	dau		16	daily labourer	Nry Richmond
1562	160v			Jane Hutchinson	dau		10	scholar	Dur
1563	161r	<23>e	Crossgate	Valentine Roe	hea	m	52	husbandman	Dur Stockton
1564	161r			Mary Roe	wif	m	45		Dur Bishopton
1565	161r			Robert Roe	son		19	app to iron moulder	Dur Bishopton
1566	161r			John Roe	son		11	scholar	Dur
1567	161r			Jane Roe	dau		9	scholar	Dur

1568	161r	<23>e	Crossgate	Valentine Roe	son	6	scholar	Dur
1569	161r			Elizabeth Roe	dau	3		Dur
1570	161r			Thomas Old	blw	30	blacksmith	Dur Bishopton
1571	161r	<23>f	Crossgate	William Nichols	hea m	47	cordwainer	Nbl North Shields
1572	161r			Mary Nichols	wif m	48		Dur Tanfield
1573	161r			Mary Ann Nichols	dau	15	scholar	Nbl North Shields
1574	161r			William John Nichols	son	13	scholar	Nbl North Shields
1575	161r			Isaac Nichols	son	10	scholar	Dur Brandon
1576	161r			Hannah Nichols	dau	8	scholar	Dur Brandon
1577	161r			Isabella Nichols	dau	7	scholar	Dur Brandon
1578	161r	[aw]a	Crossgate	Jane McCormack	hea w	71	teacher	Nbl Haydon Bridge
1579	161r			Matthew Forster	sls	35	journeyman tailor	Dur
1580	161r			Robinson Dowson	gsn	7	scholar	Dur
1581	161v	[aw]b	Crossgate	John Elliott	hea m	51	stonemason	Dur Durham
1582	161v			Sarah Elliott	wif m	47		Dur Durham
1583	161v			John Elliott	son	10	scholar	Dur Durham
1584	161v			Mary Elliott	dau	7	scholar	Dur Durham
1585	161v			Sarah Elliott	dau	3		Dur Durham
1586	161v	[aw]c	Crossgate	William Parker	hea m	72	farm labourer	Dur Lanchester
1587	161v			Elizabeth Parker	wif m	78		Dur Tanfield
1588	161v			William Parker	son	28	journeyman carpenter	Dur
1589	161v	[ax]a	Crossgate	Roger Mole	hea m	30	journeyman plasterer	Nbl Belford
1590	161v			Elizabeth Mole	wif m	26		Dur Durham
1591	161v			Margaret Mole	dau	4	scholar	Dur Durham
1592	161v			John Mole	son	2m		Dur Durham
1593	161v	[ax]b	Crossgate	John Bland	hea m	70	labourer at paper mill	Dur Durham
1594	161v			Ann Bland	wif m	55		Dur Wolsingham
1595	161v	[ax]c	Crossgate'	Margaret Richardson	hea	24	dressmaker	Dur Chester-le-Street
1596	161v			Mary Richardson	sis	19	staymaker	Dur Chester-le-Street
1597	161v	[ax]d	Crossgate	George Dodds	hea m	60	farm labourer	Nry Gilling /"Gillon"
1598	161v			Mary Dodds	wif m	54		Nry Reeth
1599	161v			James Alderson Galloway	gsn	10	scholar	Dur Bishop Auckland
1600	162r	[ax]e	Crossgate	Dorothy Chrishop	hea w	33	laundress; pauper	Dur Houghton-l-Spring
1601	162r			Elizabeth Chrishop	dau	9	scholar	Dur Kelloe
1602	162r			Abraham Chrishop	son	7	scholar	Dur Kelloe
1603	162r	[ax]f	Crossgate	Elizabeth Burton	hea	32	dressmaker; pauper	Dur
1604	162r			Anthony Richardson	ldr	17	app to saddler; pauper	Dur
1605	162r	<26>	Crossgate	William Forster	hea m	63	blacksmith <whitesmith*>	Dur Chester-le-Street
1606	162r			Margaret Forster	wif m	56		Dur Darlington
1607	162r			Elizabeth Laidler	dau m	30		Dur
1608	162r			Margaret Forster	dau	21	at home	Dur
1609	162r			William Laidler	gsn	3		Dur
1610	162r			Margaret Ann Laidler	gda	1		Dur
1611	162r			Thomasin Clark	ser	16	house servant	Nry Wilton
1612	162r	<27>	Crossgate	Christopher Ivison	hea m	76	cowkeeper <milk vendor>	Dur
1613	162r			Elizabeth Ivison	wif m	75		Dur
1614	162r			Robert Ivison	gsn	17	farm labourer	Dur
1615	162r	<28>a	Crossgate	Eleanor Lister	hea	34	washerwoman	Dur
1616	162r			Caroline Lister	dau	9	scholar	Dur
1617	162r			Theophilus Lister	son	7	scholar	Dur
1618	162v	<28>b	Crossgate	James Adamson	hea m	56	journeyman mason	Dur Durham
1619	162v			Margaret Adamson	wif m	63	laundress <& tea dealer>	Dur South Shields
1620	162v			Margaret Adamson	dau	31	laundress	Dur
1621	162v			Ellen Slater	ser	20	laundress	Dur
1622	162v			John Granger	gsn	8	scholar	Dur
1623	162v			William Adamson	rel	78	parish relief {deaf}	Dur
1624	162v	<29>	Crossgate	James Lumsden	hea m	54	iron <& brass> founder *	Dur
1625	162v			Ann Lumsden	wif m	56		Dur
1626	162v			Mary Lumsden	dau	28	at home	Dur
1627	162v			William Lumsden	son	22	apprentice in foundry	Dur
1628	162v			Daniel Lumsden	son	20	apprentice in foundry	Dur
1629	162v			Ann Lumsden	dau	16	scholar	Dur
1630	162v			Mary Ann Richardson	vis	21	annuitant	Dur Bishopton
1631	162v	<30>	Crossgate	Thomas Robson	hea m	43	papermaker & innkeeper *	Dub Dublin
1632	162v			Mary Jane Robson	wif m	38		Dur
1633	162v			Mary Robson	dau	2		Dur
1634	162v			Dorothy Phillips	ser	16	house servant	Dur
1635	162v	[ay]	Crossgate	George Robinson	hea	25	engine builder	Dur Sheriff Hill
1636	162v			Isabella Kenmir	vsw m	42	iron moulder's wife	Nbl Morpeth
1637	162v			John Kenmir	vss	14	iron moulder's app	Nbl Alnwick
1638	163r	<32>a	Crossgate	William Clifton	hea m	39	journeyman mason	Dur
1639	163r			Catherine Clifton	wif m	40		Nbl Earsdon Grange
1640	163r			James Clifton	son	17	mason's apprentice	Dur
1641	163r			Mary Clifton	dau	12	scholar	Dur
1642	163r	<32>b	Crossgate	William Robertshaw	hea m	46	cordwainer	Dur
1643	163r			Isabella Robertshaw	wif m	44		Dur
1644	163r			John Robertshaw	son	11	scholar	Dur
1645	163r			Mary Jane Robertshaw	dau	6	scholar	Dur
1646	163r	<32>c	Crossgate	Caroline Richardson	hea m	26	house servant's wife	Nry Smeaton
1647	163r			Mary Mavin Richardson	dau	1		Nry Smeaton
1648	163r	<32>d	Crossgate	Mary Musgrove	hea m	27	smith's wife	Nry Danby Wiske

1649	163r	<34>a	Crossgate	George Hare	hea	m	55	joiner & farming 17a *	Dur Witton-le-Wear
1650	163r			Ann Hare	wif	m	63		Dur Stanhope
1651	163r			Sarah Hare	dau		20	straw-hatmaker	Dur
1652	163r			Barbara Adamson	sda		36	dressmaker	Dur Stanhope
1653	163r			Mary Ann Adamson	gda		11	scholar	Dur Wolsingham
1654	163r			Ralph Hare	vis	m	46	farmer of 130a	Dur Witton-le-Wear
1655	163r	<34>b	Crossgate	John Boston	hea	m	29	engine smith	Nbl Earsdon
1656	163v			Isabel Boston	wif	m	27		Nbl Longbenton
1657	163v			Jane Hannah Boston	dau		9m		Dur
1658	163v	<34>c	Crossgate	George Ferry	hea	m	48	labourer	Dur
1659	163v			Rebecca Ferry	wif	m	52		Dur
1660	163v			George Ferry	son		20	mason's apprentice	Dur
1661	163v			Eliza Ferry	dau		11	scholar	Dur
1662	163v	[az]	Crossgate	Robert Drysdale	hea	m	38	carpet weaver	Sct
1663	163v			Helen Drysdale	wif	m	34		Sct
1664	163v			Margaret Drysdale	dau		7	scholar	Dur
1665	163v			Thomas Drysdale	son		5	scholar	Dur
1666	163v			Helen Drysdale	dau		1		Dur
1667	163v	[ba]	Crossgate	John Swainston	hea	m	38	labourer	Wry Aldborough
1668	163v			Elizabeth Swainston	wif	m	39		Nry Spennithorne
1669	163v			Hannah Swainston	dau		9	scholar	Dur
1670	163v			Mary Jane Swainston	dau		7	scholar	Dur
1671	163v			Robert Swainston	son		2	scholar	Dur
1672	163v			Thomas Swainston	son		2		Dur
1673	164r	[bb]a	Crossgate	Margaret Wheeler	hea	w	62		Dur Easington
1674	164r			Margaret Wheeler	dau		32	papersorter	Dur Houghton-l-Spring
1675	164r			George Wheeler	son	w	29	labourer	Dur Lintzford *
1676	164r			George Wheeler	gsn		3		Dur
1677	164r			William Wheeler	gsn		7	scholar	Dur
1678	164r	[bb]b	Crossgate	Susanna Pattison	hea	w	50	papersorter	Nbl Slaley
1679	164r			Nicholas Pattison	son		21	wheelwright	Dur
1680	164r			Phoebe Wheeler	ldr		8	scholar	Dur
1681	164r	[bc]	Crossgate	William Proud	hea	m	56	labourer at mill p[aper]	Dur Wolsingham
1682	164r			Mary Proud	wif	m	54	laundress	Dur Tunstall
1683	164r			Elizabeth Proud	dau		16	laundress	Dur
1684	164r			Jane Proud	dau		11	scholar	Dur
1685	164r			John Proud	son		8	scholar	Dur
1686	164r	[bd]	Crossgate	Thomas Renwick	hea	m	47	teacher	Dur Cornforth
1687	164r			Mary Renwick	wif	m	48	working at paper mill	Dur Merrington
1688	164r			Jane Renwick	dau		15	working at paper mill	Dur
1689	164r			Mary Renwick	dau		13	scholar	Dur
1690	164r			Thomas Renwick	son		11	scholar	Dur
1691	164r			Margaret Renwick	dau		8	scholar	Dur
1692	164r			Robert Renwick	son		5	scholar	Dur
1693	164v	[be]	Crossgate	John Dixon	hea	m	32	forgeman	Sct British subject
1694	164v			Agnes Dixon	wif	m	31		Sct British subject
1695	164v			Jessie Dixon	dau		10	scholar	Sct British subject
1696	164v			Alexander Dixon	son		8	scholar	Sct British subject
1697	164v			William Veitch Dixon	son		1		Dur
1698	164v	[bf]	Crossgate	James Craggs	hea	m	41	cartman	Nry Snape
1699	164v			Ann Craggs	wif	m	39		Dur Brafferton
1700	164v			John Craggs	son		11	scholar	Nry Brompton
1701	164v			Robinson Ridley	ldr		20	engineman, p[aper mill]	Dur South Shields
1702	164v			John Fisher	ldr		22	blacksmith	Cul Geenfoot
1703	164v	[bg]	Crossgate	Hannah Seed	hea	m	49	papermaker's wife	Dur Shotley Bridge
1704	164v			James Seed	son		19	iron forgeman	Dur Shotley Bridge
1705	164v			Robert Seed	son		17	papermaker's apprentice	Dur Shotley Bridge
1706	164v			Hannah Seed	dau		15	at home	Dur Shotley Bridge
1707	164v			John Seed	son		11	scholar	Dur Neville's Cross
1708	164v			George Seed	son		9	scholar	Dur Neville's Cross
1709	165r		Union Workhouse	Charles W. Buddle	hea	m	32	master of workhouse	Dur
1710	165r			Ann Buddle	wif	m	32	mistress of workhouse	Nbl Hedley
1711	165r			Thomas Richardson	ser	m	25	asst master of workhouse	Dur Flass
1712	165r			Anne Young	ser		34	nurse to workhouse	Nbl Burton /"Barton"
1713	165r			Elizabeth Wealands			48	pp, fmly house servant	Dur
1714	165r			Sarah Davis			2	pauper	Dur
1715	165r			Joseph Robertson			10	pauper, scholar	Dur
1716	165r			Thomas Goodwin		w	74	pp, fmly lieutenant *	Irl
1717	165r			Thomas Hewett		m	45	pp, fmly farm labourer	Dur Brancepeth
1718	165r			Maria Ward		w	23	pauper, labourer's widow	Irl
1719	165r			William Ward			11m	pauper's son	Dur
1720	165r			John Gascoigne			83	pauper, fmly labourer	Dur Westoe
1721	165r			Ralph Smith	hea	m	39	pauper, fmly pitman	Dur Beamish
1722	165r			Elizabeth Smith	wif	m	30	pauper	Dur Fishburn
1723	165r			Alice Smith	dau		6	pauper, scholar	Dur Cassop Moor
1724	165r			Thomas Smith	son		4	pauper, scholar	Dur Cassop Moor
1725	165r			Robert Smith	son		2	pauper	Dur Cassop Moor
1726	165r			Jane McGough	wif	m	23	pauper, pitman's wife	Dur Gateshead
1727	165r			Jane McGough	dau		3m	pauper	Dur Cassop Moor
1728	165v			Thomas Raffles			9	pauper, scholar	Dur Coxhoe
1729	165v			Robert Harrison			4	pauper, scholar	Dur Coxhoe

Line	Folio	Address	Forename	Surname	Rel	m/w	Age	Occupation	Birthplace
1730	165v	Union Workhouse	Mary Ann	Donaldson	wif m		27	pauper, pitman's wife	Dur Piercebridge
1731	165v		Elizabeth	Donaldson	dau		10m	pauper	Dur Coxhoe
1732	165v		Elizabeth	Hall			20	pp, fmly house servant	Dur Old Hetton
1733	165v		Thomas	Hall	son		2	pauper	Dur Shotton Hill
1734	165v		Margaret	Gamwell	wif m		25	pauper, pitman's wife	Cul Harrington
1735	165v		James	Gamwell	son		6	pauper, scholar	Cul Harrington
1736	165v		Mary Ann	Gamwell	dau		3	pauper	Dur Berry Edge
1737	165v		John	Gamwell	son		6m	pauper	Dur Coxhoe
1738	165v		Sophia	Wild	wif m		27	pauper, sinker's wife	Dur Usworth
1739	165v		Margaret Ann	Wild	dau		6	pauper, scholar	Dur Dalton
1740	165v		Isabella	Wild	dau		4	pauper, scholar	Dur Dalton
1741	165v		Samuel	Wild	son		2	pauper	Dur Seaton
1742	165v		Matthew	Beecroft			62	pp, fmly farm labourer	not known
1743	165v		John	Pallister		w	77	pp, fmly gentleman's ser	Nry Bowes
1744	165v		George	Johnstone			59	pp, fmly farm labourer	Dur Brancepeth
1745	165v		Mary	Hindmarsh		w	81	pauper, pitman's widow	Dur Swalwell
1746	165v		Barbara	Reed			35	pp, tailor's daughter	Dur
1747	166r		Thomasine	Bell			61	pp, fmly housekeeper	Dur
1748	166r		Ann	Walker		w	93	pauper, tailor's widow	Dur
1749	166r		Mary	Jackson	wif m		36	pauper, miller's wife	Dur Sedgefield
1750	166r		Mary Ann	Jackson	dau		1m	pauper's daughter	Dur
1751	166r		Elizabeth	Marsden		w	49	pp, labourer's widow	Dur
1752	166r		William	Wallace		w	61	pauper, fmly baker	Nbl Norham
1753	166r		Joseph	Thwaites		w	71	pauper, fmly joiner	Dur
1754	166r		John	Pattison			67	pauper, fmly coachman	Dur Humbersledge
1755	166r		Mary	Palmer		w	62	pp, shoemaker's widow	Dur
1756	166r		George	Vardy			52	pauper, fmly shoemaker	Dur
1757	166r		William	Smith			49	pauper, fmly labourer	Dur
1758	166r		George	Davison			62	pauper, fmly labourer	Nry Yarm *
1759	166r		Ann	Graham			24	pauper, fmly servant	Dur
1760	166r		John	Graham			1w	pauper	Dur
1761	166r		Peter	Gott		w	66	pauper, fmly heckler	Dur
1762	166r		George	Deanham		w	65	pp, fmly linen weaver	Dur Sunderland
1763	166r		Ann	Sharp		w	91	pauper	not known
1764	166r		Mary	Gibson		w	77	pauper, waiter's widow	Dur Lamesley
1765	166r		Ellen	Conroy	hea w		43	pp, leatherdresser's wid	Wry Leeds
1766	166v		William	Conroy	son		14	pauper, scholar	Wry Leeds
1767	166v		James Merchant	Conroy	son		7	pauper, scholar	born at sea
1768	166v		Thomas	Conroy	son		2	pauper	Nbl Newcastle
1769	166v		John	Hedley	hea m		74	pauper, fmly shoemaker	Nry Kirby Moorside
1770	166v		Catherine	Hedley	wif m		71	pauper	Dur
1771	166v		Sarah	Dodds			24	pauper, fmly servant	Nry Downholme? *
1772	166v		Matthew	Dodds			4	pauper, scholar	Dur Stonebridge
1773	166v		Margaret	Anderson			4	pauper, scholar	not known
1774	166v		Agnes	Laurence			15	pauper, servant	Yks Ladychapel
1775	166v		William	Laurence			4	pauper, scholar	Dur Hartlepool
1776	166v		Jane	Clapperton		w	83	pauper, tailor's widow	Dur
1777	166v		Catherine	Shields		w	81	pp, flaxdresser's widow	Irl
1778	166v		William	Wetherell		w	74	pp, fmly carpet weaver	Dur
1779	166v		Alice	Marks			12	pp, labourer's daughter	Lks Glasgow
1780	166v		Robert	Clasper			54	pauper, fmly pitman	Dur Pittington
1781	166v		Mary Ann	Ogle			18	pauper	Irl
1782	166v		William	Harley			30	pauper, patternmaker	War Birmingham
1783	166v		Francis	Laydon			25	pauper, labourer	Irl
1784	166v		Charles	Towers			50	pauper, labourer	Irl
1785	167r		Elizabeth	Clarkson		w	60	pauper, painter's widow	Nbl Newcastle
1786	167r		John	Price			12	pauper, labourer's son	Irl
1787	167r		Joseph	Herbert			24	pauper, labourer	Lks Glasgow
1788	167r		Elizabeth	Golightly	hea		26	pauper	Dur Stanhope
1789	167r		Matthew	Golightly	son		2	pauper	Dur Houghton-l-Spring
1790	167r		Ann	Golightly	dau		1	pauper	Dur
1791	167r		Margaret	Bell			30	pauper	Lks Glasgow
1792	167r		Thomas	Pickering			26	pauper {deaf/dumb}	Dur
1793	167r		William	Young			11	pauper, scholar	Dur
1794	167r		John	Young			9	pauper, scholar	Dur
1795	167r		Sarah	Young			5	pauper, scholar	Dur
1796	167r		Elizabeth	Young			1	pauper	Dur
1797	167r		George	Gordon			43	pauper, fmly nailmaker	Dur
1798	167r		Isabella	Bradley			71	pauper, servant	Dur
1799	167r		Ann	Walton			86	pauper, fmly laundress	Dur
1800	167r		James	Morgan		m	70	pauper, fmly tailor	Dur
1801	167r		Mary	Green			8	pp, pitman's daughter	Dur
1802	167r		Sarah	Danks		w	69	pauper, labourer's wife	Dur
1803	167r		John	Mowbray			50	pauper, labourer	Yks York
1804	167r		Joseph	Newton			34	pauper, labourer	Nbl Coxlodge
1805	167v	[bh]a Crossgate	Ann	Fairbairn	hea m		46	watchmaker's wife	Dur Chester-le-Street
1806	167v		Thomas	Richardson	son		15	scholar	Dur Chester-le-Street
1807	167v		John	Fairbairn	son		9	scholar	Dur Chester-le-Street
1808	167v		Charles	Fairbairn	son		6	scholar	Dur Chester-le-Street
1809	167v		Anne	Fairbairn	dau		3		Dur
1810	167v	[bh]b Crossgate	John	Thirlwall	hea w		68	farm labourer	Nbl Shotley

1811 167v	[bh]b	Crossgate	Frances Thirlwall	dau	38		Dur	
1812 167v			Susan Woodifield	ser	13	house servant	Dur	
1813 167v	[bi]	Crossgate	Peter Clarke	hea m	31	Prim Methodist minister*	Nbl Wallsend	
1814 167v			Frances Clarke	wif m	32		Wry Whitley	
1815 167v			Peter Watkin Clarke	son	3		Wes Kendal	
1816 167v			James Carver Clarke	son	1		Dur Monkwearmouth	
1817 167v			Mary Ann Fox	vis	12	scholar	Wry Swinefleet	
1818 167v			Jane Hunter	ser	16	house servant	Dur High Moorsley	
1819 168r	[bj]a	Crossgate	Anne Muff	hea w	42	laundress	Dur Chester-le-Street	
1820 168r			Sarah Muff	dau	16		Dur	
1821 168r			Edward Muff	son	7	scholar	Dur	
1822 168r			William Forster	ldr m	56	journeyman saddler	Nbl Rothbury	
1823 168r			Margaret Forster	ldr m	60	jnym saddler's wife	Dur Sunderland	
1824 168r	[bj]b	Crossgate	Thomas Veitch	hea m	44	warehouseman	Dur	
1825 168r			Mary Veitch	wif m	37	dressmaker	Wry Huddersfield	
1826 168r			John Hardinge Veitch	son	13	printer's compositor	Wry Huddersfield	
1827 168r			Ralph Veitch	son	9	scholar	Dur	
1828 168r			Margaret Veitch	dau	4	scholar	Dur	
1829 168r	[bk]a	Crossgate	William Bradford	hea m	30	journeyman tailor	Dur	
1830 168r			Elizabeth Bradford	wif m	27		Dur	
1831 168r			Jane Bradford	dau	8	scholar	Dur	
1832 168r			John Bradford	son	6	scholar	Dur	
1833 168r			William Bradford	son	4	scholar	Dur	
1834 168r			Elizabeth Bradford	dau	2		Dur	
1835 168r			Caroline Bradford	dau	1m		Dur	
1836 168v	[bk]b	Crossgate	John Morton	hea m	25	printer's compositor	Nbl Newcastle	
1837 168v			Rebecca Morton	wif m	25		Dur	
1838 168v	[bl]a	Crossgate	John Usher	hea m	39	cabinetmaker	Dur	
1839 168v			Elizabeth Usher	wif m	37	laundress	Nbl Percy Main	
1840 168v			Jane Elizabeth Usher	dau	16	dressmaker	Dur	
1841 168v	[bl]b	Crossgate	John Robinson	hea m	28	journeyman plasterer	Dur	
1842 168v			Ellen Robinson	wif m	22		Dur Barnard Castle	
1843 168v	[bl]c	Crossgate	John Hansell	hea m	25	journeyman joiner	Dur	
1844 168v			Mary Hansell	wif m	26		Dur Pittington	
1845 168v	[bm]	Crossgate *	Lancelot Robinson	hea m	56	tailor <& artist>	Dur	
1846 168v			Margaret Robinson	wif m	56		Dur	
1847 168v			Francis Robinson	son	22	tailor's apprentice	Dur	
1848 168v			Margaret Robinson	dau	17	dressmaker	Dur	
1849 168v			Frances Robinson	dau	13	scholar	Dur	
1850 169r	[bn]	Crossgate *	Henry Talbot	hea m	28	journeyman joiner	Dur	
1851 169r			Hannah Talbot	wif m	28		Dur Castle Eden	
1852 169r	[bo]	Crossgate *	John Wardell	hea m	65	retired shoemaker	Dur	
1853 169r			Elizabeth Wardell	wif m	62		Dur	
1854 169r	[bp]	Crossgate *	Eleanor Ewbank	hea	63	annuitant	Dur	

Notes - Enumeration District 9b

865	<'Fighting Cocks'>
872	/"Santasa"
877	... of S. Margaret
888	... Salford
903	<'Jolly Waggoner'; & oatmealmaker>
1044	<at Grammar School>
1052	county given as "Cumberland"
1057	<woolcomber>
1095	... employing 11 men and boys
1120	... of Grammar Sch & curate of Shincliffe
1151	... of S. Margaret <principal of Diocesan Training School>
1172	... & annuitant
1187	... to dean and chapter
1191	<& lodgings>
1209	... [of] Durham [Cathedral] <MA>
1212	<lodgings>
1213	... of languages <mathematical teacher & mathematical master at Diocesan Training School>
1231	... & sheriff's officer & inspector of hawkers' licences
1246	<& lodgings>
1254	... of S. John's [Chapel], Weardale
1271	[sister's] son; ... Oxford
1274-1275	... British subject
1280	... <of births, marriages and deaths> & relieving officer <& parish clerk of S. Oswald>
1365	... & letter messenger
1412	houses and ...
1415	<& treasurer to Board of Health & to Borough>
1433	/"Pockerlton"
1464	<'Elm Tree'>
1467	... employing 4 jnym, 4 app and 3 labr
1504	<furniture broker>
1517	<accountant>
1551	/"Heckington"
1605	... & engine builder
1624	... [employing] 7 labourers
1631	<'Bowes' Arms'>
1649	<milk vendor>
1675	/"Linsford", no county given
1716	... in the Army
1758	county given as "Durham"
1771	/"Downham"
1813	<Prim Methodist chapel, Silver St Lane>
1845-1854	<Wardell's or New Buildings>

REF	FOL	NO	STREET	FORENAME(S)	SURNAME	REL	C	AGE	OCCUPATION	BIRTHPLACE
1855	183v	[aa]	New North Road	John	Watson	hea	w	36	councillor, articled clk	Dur Monkwearmouth
1856	183v			Jane	Watson	mth	w	62		Dur Lanchester
1857	183v			Thomas	Watson	son		9	scholar	Dur
1858	183v			Frances	Watson	dau		6	scholar	Dur
1859	183v			Elizabeth	Mains	ser		16	servant	Dur Darlington
1860	183v	[ab]	New North Road	William	Blakey	hea	m	43	clerk, Stamp Office	Nbl Newcastle
1861	183v			Edwarda	Blakey	wif	m	41		Nbl Holy Island [NDu]
1862	183v			Emma /"Emor"	Hall	ser		17	house servant	Dur Medomsley
1863	183v	[ac]	New North Road	Anthony	Wetherall	hea	m	32	professor of music *	Dur
1864	183v			Abigail	Wetherall	wif	m	32		Irl
1865	183v			George	Wetherall	son		4		Dur
1866	183v			Anthony	Wetherall	son		2		Dur
1867	183v			Charles	Wetherall	son		3m		Dur
1868	183v			Mary	Burns	ser		15	servant	Dur
1869	183v	[ad]	New North Road	Mary	Hall	hea	w	40	annuitant	Dur
1870	183v			Ovington	Hall	son		19	miller & corn factor	Dur
1871	183v	[ae]	New North Road	George A.	Scott	hea	m	25	grocer's assistant	Dur Silksworth
1872	183v			Margaret	Scott	wif	m	21		Nry Aldbrough
1873	183v			George F.	Scott	son		4m		Dur
1874	184r	[af]	New North Road	Susan	Walker	hea	w	72	proprietor of houses	Dur Bishop Auckland
1875	184r			Barbara	Peyton	sis	w	78		Dur Bishop Auckland
1876	184r	[ag]	New North Road	Susanna	Booth	hea	w	42	lodgings	Wls
1877	184r			William Henry	Booth	son		15	bookbinder's apprentice	Dur [D] S. Nicholas
1878	184r			Jane	Young	mth	w	68	annuitant <lodgings>	Cul Carlisle
1879	184r			Henry	Revely	[1]		26	grocer's shopman	Dur [D] S. Oswald
1880	184r			Theophas B.	Cowe	[1]		18	scholar	not known
1881	184r	[ah]a	New North Road	John	Redshaw	hea	m	45	master joiner *	Dur Staindrop
1882	184r			Mary	Redshaw	wif	m	39		Dur Sedgefield
1883	184r			Thomas Smith	Redshaw	son		14	apprentice [joiner]	Dur Elwick
1884	184r			John	Redshaw	son		13	scholar	Dur [D] Crossgate
1885	184r			Mary	Readshaw	dau		11	scholar	Dur [D] Crossgate
1886	184r			Emily	Redshaw	dau		5	scholar	Dur [D] Framwelgate
1887	184r	[ah]b	New North Road	Jane	Mitchinson	hea		46	charwoman	not known
1888	184r	[ai]a	New North Road	Peter	Elliott	hea	m	45	joiner	Lan Manchester *
1889	184r			Mary	Elliott	wif	m	50		Dur Brandon
1890	184r			George	Elliott	son		16	shoemaker	Dur [D] Crossgate
1891	184r			Ann	Elliott	dau		12	scholar	Dur [D] Crossgate
1892	184r			Eleanor	Smith	sil	w	49	upholsterer's sewer	Dur Brandon
1893	184v	[ai]b	New North Road	William	Wilson	hea	m	31	woolsorter	Dur [D] Framwelgate
1894	184v			Hannah	Wilson	wif	m	28		Dur [D] Framwelgate
1895	184v			Elizabeth	Wilson	dau		2		Dur [D] Framwelgate
1896	184v			Rebecca	Wilson	dau		2m		Dur [D] Framwelgate
1897	184v	[ai]c	New North Road	Charlotte	Carr	hea	m	25		Dur [D] Framwelgate
1898	184v			Thomas Henry	Carr	son		2		Dur [D] Framwelgate
1899	184v	[ai]d	New North Road	William	Mowbry	hea	m	37	master tailor	Dur [D] S. Margaret
1900	184v			Ann	Mowbry	wif	m	31		Dur [D] S. Margaret
1901	184v			Wharton *	Mowbry	son		5	scholar	Dur [D] S. Margaret
1902	184v			Thomas Walton	Mowbry	son		3	scholar	Dur [D] S. Margaret
1903	184v			James Walton	Mowbry	son		1		Dur [D] S. Margaret
1904	184v	[aj]	New North Road	Thomas	Simpson	hea	m	53	carpet weaver *	Wor
1905	184v			Sarah	Simpson	wif	m	57		Wor
1906	184v			James	Raine	[1]		30	land agent, clerk	Dur West Herrington
1907	184v			John George	Newby	[1]		21	land agent, clerk	Dur Wolviston
1908	184v	[ak]	New North Road	Matthew	Bee	hea	w	47	mason	Dur
1909	184v			John	Bee	son		13	scholar	Dur
1910	184v			Joseph	Bee	son		8	scholar	Dur
1911	184v			Isabella	Bee	dau		5	scholar	Dur
1912	185r	[al]	New North Road	Peter	Gradon	hea	m	44	joiner	Dur Hartlepool
1913	185r			Caroline	Gradon	wif	m	40		Ken Canterbury
1914	185r			Walter	Gradon	son		18	joiner	Sry Epsom
1915	185r			Elizabeth	Gradon	dau		16		Dur Sherburn
1916	185r			Clara Jane	Gradon	dau		13		Dur Sherburn
1917	185r			Peter	Gradon	son		10		Dur Shincliffe
1918	185r			Caroline	Gradon	dau		1		Dur
1919	185r	[am]	New North Road	George	Graham	hea	m	33	blacksmith	Dur [D] Framwelgate
1920	185r			Mary	Graham	wif	m	35		Dur Easington
1921	185r			Mary Ann	Graham	dau		6		Dur [D] Framwelgate
1922	185r			William	Graham	son		4		Dur [D] Framwelgate
1923	185r			Elizabeth	Graham	dau		2		Dur [D] Framwelgate
1924	185r			Jane	Graham	dau		2m		Dur [D] Framwelgate
1925	185r	[an]	New North Road	Major	Dixon	hea	w	36	timber merch emp 4 men *	Nbl Branton
1926	185r			Ann	Dixon	dau		3		Dur [D] Framwelgate
1927	185r			Mary	Foster	ser		22	servant	Dur Jarrow
1928	185r	[ao]	New North Road	John	Snowball	hea		41	cartwright	Dur
1929	185r			Elizabeth	Snowball	mth	w	73	formerly housekeeper	Dur
1930	185r			George	Liddle	app		17	cartwright	Dur
1931	185v	[ap]	New North Road	Samuel	Goodall	hea	m	34	independent minister *	Wry Leeds
1932	185v			Ann	Goodall	wif	m	34		Nbl North Shields
1933	185v			John Charles	Goodall	son		4		Dur [D] Framwelgate

1934	185v	[ap]	New North Road	Hamilton Goodall	son	2		Dur [D] Framwelgate
1935	185v			Catherine Goodall	dau	5m		Dur [D] Framwelgate
1936	185v			Sarah Riddley	ser	23	domestic servant	Dur Middleton
1937	185v	[aq]a	New North Road	John Robinson	hea m	33	carrier	Dur Thornley
1938	185v			Sarah Robinson	wif m	47		Ham Bullington
1939	185v			Jane Robinson	dau	13		Dur [D] Framwelgate
1940	185v	[aq]b	New North Road	Edward Cornforth	hea m	23	bookbinder	Dur [D] Framwelgate
1941	185v			Jane Cornforth	wif m	21		Dur [D] Framwelgate
1942	185v			John Henry Cornforth	son	2		Dur [D] Framwelgate
1943	185v	[aq]c	New North Road	Thomas Wetherall	hea m	26	carpet weaver	Dur [D] Framwelgate
1944	185v			Mary Wetherall	wif m	24		Dur [D] Framwelgate
1945	185v			William Wetherall	son	4	scholar	Dur [D] Framwelgate
1946	185v			Sarah Wetherall	dau	2		Dur [D] Framwelgate
1947	185v			James Wetherall	bro	30	cordwainer	Dur [D] Framwelgate
1948	185v	[ar]	New North Road *	Thomas Pailey	hea m	32	auctioneer <& lodgings>	Nbl Gosforth
1949	185v			Anne Pailey	wif m	26		Dur [D] Framwelgate
1950	185v			John Sullivan	ldr	21	teacher *	Lnd
1951	186r	[as]	New North Road	Thomas White	hea m	47	clerk to miller *	Dur [D] S. Oswald
1952	186r			Mary White	wif m	37		Dur [D] S. Nicholas
1953	186r			Gilbert Wood	vis	57	retired farmer	Dur
1954	186r			Eliza Richardson	ser	21	servant	Dur
1955	186r	[at]	New North Road	Hannah Freemantle	hea w	38	proprietor of houses	Cam Ely
1956	186r			George Freemantle	son	17	organist, articled pupil	Cam Ely
1957	186r			Elizabeth Kempton	nce	17		Cam Ely
1958	186r	[au]	New North Road	Barbara Thompson	hea w	50	spirit merchant	Dur
1959	186r			John Thompson	son	29	spirit merchant	Dur
1960	186r			Eleanor Mowbry	ser	21	servant	Dur Lumley
1961	186r	[av]	New North Road	Sarah Ingham	hea w	83	formerly housekeeper	Wry Batley
1962	186r			Martha Wilson	vis	24		Nbl North Shields
1963	186r			Sarah Carr	ser	33	servant	Dur Chester-le-Street
1964	186r	[aw]	New North Road	Ann Hunter	hea w	66		Dur
1965	186r			Ann Hunter	dau	36		Dur
1966	186r			Margaret Hunter	dau	34		Dur
1967	186r			Thomas Hunter	son	32	county court bailiff	Dur
1968	186r			John Hunter	son	30	draper	Dur
1969	186r	[ax]	New North Road	Thomas Laycock	hea m	47	gardener & publican	Dur Houghton-le-Side
1970	186r			Isabella Laycock	wif m	55		Cul Penrith
1971	186v	[ay]	New North Road	William Stubbs	hea m	42	linen draper<'s asst>	Nry Bulmer
1972	186v			Hannah Stubbs	wif m	34		Nry New Malton
1973	186v			Hannah Stubbs	dau	15	scholar	Yks York
1974	186v			William Stubbs	son	4		Dur
1975	186v			Mary Hodgkins Stubbs	dau	3		Dur
1976	186v			Robert P. Stubbs	son	2		Dur
1977	186v			Henry Stubbs	son	1		Dur
1978	186v			Ann Brewser	ser	20	house servant	Yks York, S. John
1979	186v			Mary Ann Herding	ser	19	house servant	Nry New Malton
1980	186v	[az]	New North Road	John Grievson	hea m	71	whitesmith	Dur [D] S. Oswald
1981	186v			Nerretter Grievson	wif m	69		Ntt Nottingham
1982	186v			Alexander Brewce		42	office[r] of Excise	Sct
1983	186v	[ba]a	New North Road	Richard Christopher	hea m	24	servant	Dur [D] S. Oswald
1984	186v			Margaret Christopher	wif m	30		Dur [D] S. Oswald
1985	186v			Richard Christopher	son	3		Dur
1986	186v	[ba]b	New North Road	William Wealands	hea m	26	coachmaker	Dur [D] Gilesgate
1987	186v			Sophia Wealands	wif m	23	dressmaker	Dur [D] Framwelgate
1988	187r	[bb]	New North Road *	William Bradford	hea w	51	master tailor emp 6 men*	Dur Durham
1989	187r			Caroline Bradford	dau	28	housekeeper	Dur Durham
1990	187r			Thomas Bradford	son	20	tailor	Dur Durham
1991	187r			Charles Bradford	son	17	tailor	Dur Durham
1992	187r			Jane Bradford	dau	15	dressmaker	Dur Durham
1993	187r			Sarah Bradford	dau	14	scholar	Dur Durham
1994	187r			Emma Bradford	dau	9	scholar	Dur Durham
1995	187r			Elizabeth Bradford	dau	7	scholar	Dur Durham
1996	187r	[bc]a	New North Road	Thomas Maughan	hea m	37	sawyer	Dur [D] S. Oswald
1997	187r			Ann Maughan	wif m	33		Dur
1998	187r			Hannah Maughan	dau	3		Dur
1999	187r			John Maughan	fth w	73	farm labourer	Dur
2000	187r	[bc]b	New North Road	George Walker	hea w	81	carpet weaver	Dur Darlington
2001	187r			Catherine Tate	mlw w	69		not known
2002	187r			John Tate	nep	4		Dur Darlington
2003	187r	[bc]c	New North Road	William Wandless	hea m	26	shoemaker	Dur
2004	187r			Ann Wandless	wif m	24		Dur Ferryhill
2005	187r			Thomas Cathron Wandless	son	3		Dur
2006	187r			James Cathron Wandless	son	1		Dur
2007	187v	[bd]	New North Road	Ralph Kirsop	hea m	53	road labourer	Dur Sunderland
2008	187v			Jane Kirsop	wif m	50	laundress	Nry Gatenby
2009	187v			Henry Kirsop	son	17	cabinetmaker, apprentice	Dur
2010	187v			George Kirsop	son	15	cabinetmaker, apprentice	Dur
2011	187v			Robert Hutchinson	slw m	23	stonemason	Nbl Blanchland
2012	187v			Ann Hutchinson	dau m	25		Dur
2013	187v			Alfred Hutchinson	gsn	1		Dur
2014	187v	[be]	New North Road *	Mary Chickin	hea w	56	dairy keeper	Dur [D] Framwelgate

2015	187v	[be]	New North Road *	Mary Chickin	dau	32	dairy keeper	Dur [D] Framwelgate
2016	187v	[bf]	New North Road	John Chickin	hea	29	labouring man <cartman>	Dur
2017	187v	[bg]	New North Road	Isabella Firguson	hea w	37	annuitant	Dur [D] S. Nicholas
2018	187v			Robert N. Firguson	son	5		Cul Wigton
2019	187v		<Wharton's> Tower	Edward Greatorex	hea	27	sacrist of Durham * MA	Dby Newton Solney
2020	187v			Elizabeth Greatorex	mth w	69	annuitant	Nbl Newcastle
2021	187v			Mary Black	ser	25	house servant	Dur
2022	187v			John Long	ser	20	groom	Dby Eckington *
2023	187v	[bh]	New North Road	William Mordew	hea m	39	innkeeper <'Woodman'>	Dur Colliery Dykes
2024	187v			Isabella Mordew	wif m	33		Dur Colliery Dykes
2025	187v			Elizabeth Mordew	dau	12		Dur Coxhoe
2026	187v			Mary Ann Mordew	dau	10		Dur Coxhoe
2027	188r			Jacob Mordew	son	9		Dur Colliery Dykes
2028	188r			Margaret Mordew	dau	7		Dur Colliery Dykes
2029	188r			William Mordew	son	4		Dur Colliery Dykes
2030	188r			Joseph Mordew	son	2		Dur Colliery Dykes
2031	188r			Robert Mordew	son	3m		Dur [D] Framwelgate
2032	188r	[aa]	Bees House	Charles Johnson	hea m	41	tailor	Lan Liverpool
2033	188r			Margaret Johnson	wif m	37		Lan Liverpool
2034	188r			Mary Ellen Johnson	dau	16		Lan Liverpool
2035	188r			Charles Johnson	son	7		Lan Liverpool
2036	188r			Elizabeth Johnson	dau	4		Chs Macclesfield
2037	188r			Walter Johnson	son	2		Chs Macclesfield
2038	188r			Thomas Gelespie	vis	23	tailor	Dur
2039	188r			Thomas Miller	vis m	33	tailor	Sct
2040	188r			Frederick Carter	vis	23	surgeon	Ery Hull
2041	188r	[ab]	Bees House	John Chambers	hea m	43	woolstapler, master *	Wry Wrenthorpe *
2042	188r			Elizabeth Chambers	wif m	49		Dur Brancepeth
2043	188r			George Chambers	son	18	woolsorter	Dur Brancepeth
2044	188r			Micah Chambers	son	13	scholar	Dur Durham
2045	188r			Jabez Chambers	son	8	scholar	Dur Durham
2046	188r			Hannah Braimbrige	ser	19	house servant	Dur Westgate
2047	188v		Durham Co Infirmary	Robert W. Gillespie	hea	35	house surgeon, MRCS, LSA	Dur Merrington
2048	188v			Caroline N. Taylor	*	55	matron	Nbl Newcastle
2049	188v			John S. Adamson	* m	48	porter	Dur Durham
2050	188v			Sarah Duncan	nse m	44	nurse	Dur Durham
2051	188v			Dorothy Ellen Calvert	ser	18	house servant	Dur Winston *
2052	188v			James Hills	pat w	59	coal miner	Dur Chester-le-Street
2053	188v			William Makepeace	pat m	27	coal miner	Dur Houghton-l-Spring
2054	188v			Richard Laing	pat m	35	coal miner	Lan Prescot
2055	188v			Thomas Clark	pat	34	labourer	Dur Durham
2056	188v			Edward Price	pat	18	coal miner	Chs Chester
2057	188v			Edward Smith	pat	24	blacksmith	Dur Bishop Middleham
2058	188v			Samuel Simmons	pat m	51	cowkeeper	Sfk S. Andrew *
2059	188v			James Rowley	pat	40	cook	Mdx London
2060	188v			Thomas Kelly	pat	15		Irl
2061	188v			William Thompson	pat m	25	coal miner	Dur Bishop Auckland
2062	188v			Henry Brown	pat	33	coal miner	Sct
2063	188v			Patrick Carrol	pat w	38	shoemaker	Irl
2064	188v			William Green	pat	30	tailor	Dur Houghton-l-Spring
2065	188v			Thomas Hutchinson	pat	33	nailmaker	Dur Durham
2066	188v			John McDermott	pat	59	tailor	Irl
2067	189r			George Robinson	pat m	32	blacksmith	Dur Haughton-l-Skerne
2068	189r			William Igo	pat	20	coal miner	Irl
2069	189r			John Barrett	pat	10	scholar	Sal
2070	189r			Sarah Rutter	pat m	39	coal miner's wife	Lan Wigan
2071	189r			Mary Johnson	pat m	39	washerwoman	Nbl Newcastle
2072	189r			Jane Young	pat	17	servant	Lan Burnley
2073	189r			Margaret Maughan	pat	17	servant	Dur Westbeck
2074	189r	[aa]a	Sidegate	William Fallon	hea m	35	mason	Dur [D] Framwelgate
2075	189r			Mary Fallon	wif m	32		Dur [D] Framwelgate
2076	189r			John Fallon	son	15	scholar	Dur [D] Framwelgate
2077	189r			Ann Fallon	dau	8	scholar	Dur [D] Framwelgate
2078	189r			Margaret Fallon	dau	6	scholar	Dur [D] Framwelgate
2079	189r			Elizabeth Fallon	dau	3		Dur [D] Framwelgate
2080	189r			William Fallon	son	1		Dur [D] Framwelgate
2081	189r			James Stowell	nep	22	mason	Dur [D] Framwelgate
2082	189r	[aa]b	Sidegate	William Chicken	hea m	27	cartman	Dur
2083	189r			Eleanor Chicken	wif m	26		Dur
2084	189r			Henry Chicken	son	6	scholar	Dur Easington
2085	189r			John Chicken	son	4	scholar	Dur Shildon
2086	189r	[aa]c	Sidegate	William Taylor	hea m	34	cordwainer	Yks Morton Banks
2087	189r			Ellen Taylor	wif m	32	washerwoman	Dur
2088	189v			Robinson Taylor	son	11	scholar	Dur [D] Framwelgate
2089	189v			Ellen Taylor	dau	9	scholar	Dur [D] Framwelgate
2090	189v			Ann Taylor	dau	4	scholar	Dur [D] Framwelgate
2091	189v			Margaret Taylor	dau	2		Dur [D] Framwelgate
2092	189v			Matthew Taylor	son	1m		Dur [D] Framwelgate
2093	189v	[ab]a	Sidegate	John Quilt	hea m	26	shoemaker	Dur [D] Crossgate
2094	189v			Mary Quilt	wif m	24		Dur [D] Elvet
2095	189v			John Quilt	son	5		Dur [D] S. Nicholas

2096 189v	[ab]a	Sidegate	Francis Quilt	son	9m		Dur [D] Framwelgate
2097 189v	[ab]b	Sidegate	Ann Winkop	hea	28	formerly servant	Nry Sheriff Hutton
2098 189v			Thomas Winkop	son	7		Nbl Newcastle
2099 189v			Margaret Suthron	nur	1		Dur
2100 189v			Eleanor Suthron	vis	23	dressmaker	Dur
2101 189v	[ab]c	Sidegate	Richard Morgan	hea w	89	pauper; formerly farmer	Dur Sedgefield
2102 189v	[ab]d	Sidegate	Mary Tugby	hea m	53		Yks Oldl...ly?
2103 189v			Thomas Tugby	son	19	coal miner	Ery Hull
2104 189v			Cornelius Tugby	son	14	coal miner	Dby Derby
2105 189v			Mary Jane Tugby	dau	10	scholar	Dby Derby
2106 189v			William Tugby	son	6	scholar	Dby Derby
2107 189v			William Wooton	ldr w	49	labourer	Dby Melbourne
2108 190r	[ac]	Sidegate	Thomas Stodart	hea w	69	mole catcher	Dur Tanfield
2109 190r			John William		49	hawker	South America
2110 190r	[ad]	Sidegate	John Sheppard	hea m	46	<market> gardener	Dur Castle Eden
2111 190r			Jane Sheppard	wif m	40		Dur Durham
2112 190r			Margaret Sheppard	dau	16		Dur Durham
2113 190r			William Sheppard	son	13	scholar	Dur Durham
2114 190r			Thomas Sheppard	son	5	scholar	Dur Durham
2115 190r	[ae]	Sidegate	James Blenkinsopp	hea w	45	labourer	Dur Durham
2116 190r			Margaret Herison		22	house servant	Dur Durham
2117 190r			Margaret Blenkinsopp	dau	12	scholar	Dur Durham
2118 190r			James Blenkinsopp	son	9	scholar	Dur Durham
2119 190r			John Blenkinsopp	son	7	scholar	Dur Durham
2120 190r			Elizabeth Harrison	dau	3		Dur Durham
2121 190r			Ann Harrison	dau	6m		Dur Durham
2122 190r	[af]	Sidegate	William Maddison	hea	50	basketmaker	Dur [D] Framwelgate
2123 190r			John Davinson	[1] m	66	agricultural labourer	Dur Durham
2124 190r			Isabella Davinson	ldw m	70		Nbl Bywell S. Peter
2125 190r	[ag]	Sidegate	John Spink	hea m	73	gentleman	Yks
2126 190r			Anne Spink	wif m	74		Dur [D] Framwelgate
2127 190r			Thomas Cornforth	gsn m	20	upholsterer	Dur [D] Crossgate
2128 190r			Louisa Cornforth	gda m	21		Dur [D] Framwelgate
2129 190v			Mary Anne Cornforth	*	2		Dur [D] Framwelgate
2130 190v		Pit House	James Furgeson	hea m	62	sawyer	Sct
2131 190v			Jane Furgeson	wif m	52		Sct
2132 190v		Gas House	Joseph Blackett	hea m	36	secretary to City Gas Co	Dur Durham
2133 190v			Sarah Blackett	wif m	31		Lei Leicester *
2134 190v			Thomas Crofts Blackett	son	2		Dur Durham
2135 190v			Sarah Jane Blackett	dau	6m		Dur Durham
2136 190v			Mary Ann Jobey	ser	21	house servant	Dur Durham
2137 190v		Boat House	Joseph Emmerson	hea m	54	smith & nail maker	Dur [D] S. Giles
2138 190v			Isabella Emmerson	wif m	51		Dur Lanchester
2139 190v			Isabella Emmerson	nce	16		Dur [D] S. Giles
2140 190v	[aa]	Crook Hall	James Raine	hea m	60	rector * South Bailey	Nry Ovington
2141 190v			Margaret Raine	wif m	57		Dur Denton
2142 190v			Anne Raine	dau	22		Dur [D] North Bailey
2143 190v			James Raine	son	20		Dur [D] North Bailey
2144 190v			Margaret Raine	dau	19		Dur [D] North Bailey
2145 190v			Mary Robson	ser m	44	house servant	Yks Thornton
2146 190v			Elizabeth Foster	ser	27	house servant	Yks Thornton
2147 191r	[ab]	Crook Hall	George Peverall	hea m	52	farmer 140a emp 3 men *	Dur [D] S. Oswald
2148 191r			Hannah Peverall	wif m	45		Dur [D] S. Oswald
2149 191r			John Peverall	son	11	scholar	Dur [D] S. Oswald
2150 191r			Hannah Peverall	dau	3		Dur [D] S. Oswald
2151 191r			William Thompson	nep	8	scholar	Dur [D] S. Oswald
2152 191r			Mary Ann Allan	ser	15	house servant	Dur [D] S. Oswald
2153 191r	<120>	Framwelgate	Thomas Palmer	hea m	40	mason	Dur Durham
2154 191r			Margaret Palmer	wif m	41		Dur Durham
2155 191r			William Palmer	son	20	mason	Dur Durham
2156 191r			Thomas Palmer	son	16	mason	Dur Durham
2157 191r			Margaret Palmer	dau	13	scholar	Dur Durham
2158 191r			Elizabeth Palmer	dau	11	scholar	Dur Durham
2159 191r			Ann Palmer	dau	8	scholar	Dur Durham
2160 191r			Henry Palmer	son	3		Dur Durham
2161 191r			Elizabeth Palmer	mth w	68		Dur Durham
2162 191r	<121>a	Framwelgate	Anne Charlton	hea	46	laundress	Dur [D] Framwelgate
2163 191r	<121>b	Framwelgate	Ralph Bainbridge	hea m	35	butcher	Dur Lumley Park
2164 191r			Margaret Bainbridge	wif m	38		Yks
2165 191r			Jane E. Bainbridge	dau	10	scholar	Dur Durham
2166 191r			Elizabeth Bainbridge	dau	8	scholar	Dur [D] S. Nicholas
2167 191v			Mary Emma Bainbridge	dau	5	scholar	Dur [D] Framwelgate
2168 191v			Margaret Bainbridge	dau	6m		Dur [D] Framwelgate
2169 191v	<121>c	Framwelgate	Ralph Smith	hea m	36	boot and shoemaker	Dur Ferryhill
2170 191v			Mary Smith	wif m	40		Lin Cumberworth
2171 191v			William Femellow	app	16	apprentice [shoemaker?]	Dur New Stranton
2172 191v	<121>d	Framwelgate	Mary Beavens	hea w	35		Cul Carlisle
2173 191v			Elizabeth Beavens	dau	10	scholar	Dur Beamish
2174 191v			Joseph Beavens	son	5		Dur [D] S. Margaret
2175 191v			John B. Maude	ldr	20	writing clerk	Dur Beamish
2176 191v			William Titmarch		12	scholar	Dur [D] S. Margaret

2177	191v	<121>e	Framwelgate	Thomas Graham	hea	m	44	blacksmith	Dur Durham
2178	191v			Susanna Graham	wif	m	42		Dur Durham
2179	191v			Ann Robinson	dau	m	22		Dur Durham
2180	191v			William Robinson	slw	m	22	cabinetmaker	Dur Durham
2181	191v			William Robinson	gsn		1		Dur Durham
2182	191v	<121>f	Framwelgate	Ann Palmer	hea		29	paperdresser	Dur Durham
2183	191v	<121>g	Framwelgate	Joseph Bond	hea	m	22	labourer	Dur Gainford *
2184	191v			Fanny Bond	wif	m	28		Dur Heworth /"Hauith"
2185	191v			Ann Bond	dau		1		Dur Mo[or]sley
2186	191v	<121>h	Framwelgate	John Kirtley	hea	m	25	tailor	Dur Ferryhill
2187	191v			Jane Kirtley	wif	m	25		Sct
2188	192r			George Coats Kirtley	son		9m		Dur Durham
2189	192r	<119>	Framwelgate	Mary Beckwith	hea	w	50	brewer [&] maltster *	Dur Whitworth
2190	192r			Robert Beckwith	son		17	brewer [&] maltster	Dur Durham
2191	192r			Mary Ann Beckwith	dau		14		Dur Durham
2192	192r			Elizabeth Band	ser		19	house servant	Dur Durham
2193	192r			Dorothy Tindle	mth	w	86		Dur Satley
2194	192r	[aa]	Framwelgate	Cuthbert Elsdon	hea	m	43	labourer	Dur Pittington *
2195	192r			Elizabeth Elsdon	wif	m	36		Dur Houghton-1-Spring
2196	192r			Thomas Elsdon	son		14	butcher's apprentice	Dur Hetton-le-Hole
2197	192r			Isabella Elsdon	dau		12	scholar	Dur Hetton-le-Hole
2198	192r			Jane Elsdon	dau		10	scholar	Dur [D] Crossgate
2199	192r			Henry Elsdon	son		9	scholar	Dur [D] Crossgate
2200	192r			Sarah Elsdon	dau		7	scholar	Dur [D] Crossgate
2201	192r			John Elsdon	dau		1		Dur [D] Crossgate
2202	192r	[ab]	Framwelgate	William Bond	hea	m	57	labourer	Nry Witton
2203	192r			Fanny Bond	wif	m	48		Yks Collerly
2204	192r			John Bond	son	m	28	joiner	Dur Staindrop
2205	192r			Fanny Bond	dau		18	scholar	Nry Skeeby
2206	192r			Sarah Bond	dau		10	scholar	Nry Skeeby
2207	192r			Robert Bond	son		6	scholar	Dur Stockton
2208	192v			Thomas Pallister	vis	m	30	farm labourer	Dur Bradbury
2209	192v	[ac]	Framwelgate	James Hardy	hea	m	72	maltster	Nfk Norwich
2210	192v			John Hardy	gsn		15	basketmaker	Dur [D] Crossgate
			one house uninhabited						
2211	192v	<113>	Framwelgate	George Blagdon	hea		35	currier *	Dur [D] Framwelgate
2212	192v			Thomas Blagdon	fth	m	79	gardener	Dur Bishop Middleham
2213	192v			Elizabeth Blagdon	mth	m	79		Dur Durham
2214	192v	<112>	Framwelgate	Cuthbert Blackett	hea	m	74	worsted & carpet mfr *	Dur Durham
2215	192v			Margaret Blackett	wif	m	75		Dur Darlington
2216	192v			Elizabeth Blackett	dau		45		Dur
2217	192v			Mary Blackett	dau		39	schoolmistress	Dur
2218	192v			Emily A. Palmer	gda		11	pupil	Dur
2219	192v			Henry Jonbey	ldr		26		Ham Romsey /"Romsley"
2220	192v			Margaret Caile	ser		17	servant	Dur Toft Hill
2221	192v	<111>	Framwelgate	John Bramwell	hea	w	56	esquire <solicitor>	Wry Birstal
2222	192v			Ann L. Styring	vis		40	gentlewoman	Wry Sheffield
2223	192v			Jane Styring	ser		24	house servant	Dur High Moorsley
2224	192v	<110>	Framwelgate	Mary Ann Stamp	hea	w	34	householder	Nry Northallerton
2225	192v			Ann Hill	mth	m	68	retired grocer	Nry Northallerton
2226	192v			James J. Hill	*		33	commercial traveller	Nry Northallerton
2227	193r			F.W. Hill	*	m	31	druggist	Nry Northallerton
2228	193r			Thomas Hill	*	m	34	husbandman	Nry Northallerton
2229	193r			Ann Hill	*	m	40		Dur Durham
2230	193r	[ad]	Framwelgate	John Thirlwell	hea	m	35	cartman	Dur Durham
2231	193r			Jane Thirlwell	wif	m	31		Dur Newbottle
2232	193r			Eliza Thirlwell	dau		8	scholar	Dur [D] Framwelgate
2233	193r			John Thirlwell	son		6	scholar	Dur [D] Framwelgate
2234	193r			Thomas Thirlwell	son		2		Dur [D] Framwelgate
2235	193r	<108>a	Framwelgate	Joseph Snowdon	hea	m	47	hatter	Dur
2236	193r			Hannah Snowdon	wif	m	48		Yks
2237	193r			Joseph Snowdon	son		20	hatter	Yks
2238	193r			Gilbert Snowdon	son		18	cartman	Yks
2239	193r			James Snowdon	son		16	smith	Nbl
2240	193r			Richard Snowdon	son		13	scholar	Dur
2241	193r	<108>b	Framwelgate	Josiah Smith	hea	m	39	mason	Dur [D] S. Margaret
2242	193r			Mary Smith	wif	m	40	house servant	Dur [D] S. Margaret
2243	193r			William Smith	son		15		Dur [D] S. Margaret
2244	193r			Ellen Smith	dau		13		Dur [D] S. Margaret
2245	193r			Joseph Smith	son		9		Dur [D] S. Margaret
2246	193r			Henry Smith	son		7		Dur [D] S. Margaret
2247	193v			Jane Smith	dau		5		Dur [D] S. Margaret
2248	193v			Ann Smith	dau		2		Dur [D] S. Margaret
2249	193v			Thomas Smith	son		1m		Dur [D] S. Margaret
2250	193v	<108>c	Framwelgate	Elizabeth Briggs	hea		40	washerwoman	Dur Shincliffe
2251	193v			Mary Ann Briggs	dau		16	washerwoman	Dur Evenwood
2252	193v			Francis Briggs	son		8		Dur Sunderland
2253	193v			Edward Briggs	son		2		Dur [D] Framwelgate
2254	193v			James Briggs	vis		22	shoemaker	Dur [D] S. Giles
2255	193v	[ae]a	Framwelgate	John Lowes	hea	m	55	joiner	Dur [D] Framwelgate
2256	193v			Mary Ann Lowes	wif	m	56		Wor Worcester

2257	193v	[ae]a	Framwelgate	William Lowes	son	21	shoemaker	Dur [D] Framwelgate
2258	193v			Mary Ann Lowes	dau	19		Dur [D] Framwelgate
2259	193v			Matthew Lowes	son	17	mason	Dur [D] Framwelgate
2260	193v			Robert Lowes	son	10		Dur [D] Framwelgate
2261	193v			Elizabeth Boydon	aun w	71		Dur Cowpen /"Couper"
2262	193v			Mark Guire	blw m	50	shoemaker	Chs Macclesfield
2263	193v			William Guire	blw w	35	shoemaker	Dur Durham
2264	193v			Ann Guire	nce	8		Dur [D] Framwelgate
2265	193v			William Guire	nep	6		Dur [D] Framwelgate
2266	193v			Elizabeth Guire	nce	4		Dur [D] Framwelgate
2267	194r	[ae]b	Framwelgate	Thomas Bainbridge	hea m	66	Chelsea pensioner	Dur [D] Framwelgate
2268	194r			"Thomas" Bainbridge	wif m	49		Nai Nairn
2269	194r			John Bainbridge	son	23	mason [&] quarryman	Dur
2270	194r			Caroline Bainbridge	dlw m	24		Dur
2271	194r			Georgina Bainbridge	dau	16		Dur
2272	194r			Martin Lindsley	slw m	26	coal miner	Nbl Wallsend
2273	194r			Ellen Moor	gda	5		Dur
2274	194r			William Smith	vis w	68	annuitant	Dur Easington
2275	194r	[ae]c	Framwelgate	Robert Cummings	hea m	38	cabinetmaker <& carver>	Dur [D] S. Margaret
2276	194r			Jane Cummings	wif m	38		Dur [D] S. Giles
2277	194r			Thomas Cummings	son	17	cabinetmaker	Dur [D] S. Margaret
2278	194r			Julia Cummings	dau	12	scholar	Dur [D] S. Margaret
2279	194r			Margaret Cummings	dau	10	scholar	Dur [D] S. Margaret
2280	194r			John Cummings	son	7		Dur [D] S. Margaret
2281	194r			William Cummings	son	3		Dur [D] S. Margaret
2282	194r			Sarah Cummings	dau	1		Dur [D] S. Margaret
2283	194r	[ae]d	Framwelgate	Israel France	hea m	40	carpet weaver	Wry Heckmondwike
2284	194r			Jane France	wif m	43		Dur Durham
2285	194r			Morgan France	dau	14		Dur Durham
2286	194r			Elizabeth France	dau	9		Dur Durham
2287	194v			Jane France	dau	7		Dur Durham
2288	194v			John France	son	5		Dur Durham
2289	194v			William France	son	3		Dur Durham
2290	194v			Israel France	son	1		Dur Durham
2291	194v			Elizabeth Gainford	mlw w	79	annuitant	Dur Fishburn
2292	194v	<106>	Framwelgate	Ann Swan	hea w	84	sailing master's widow	Dur [D] S. Oswald
2293	194v			Michael Briggs	bro	80	gentleman	Dur [D] S. Oswald
2294	194v			Alice Teasdale	ser	22	house servant	Dur [D] S. Oswald
2295	194v	<105>a	Framwelgate	John Wood	hea m	76	farm labourer	Dur Shotley Bridge
2296	194v			Margaret Wood	wif m	86		Dur [D] S. Oswald
2297	194v			John Wood	son	46	painter (master)	Dur [D] S. Oswald
2298	194v	<105>b	Framwelgate	Mary Neashem	hea w	50	bootbinder; pauper	Nbl Welton
2299	194v			Ellen Neashem	dau	22	bootbinder; pauper	Dur [D] Framwelgate
2300	194v			Frances Neashem	dau	9	scholar	Dur [D] Framwelgate
2301	194v	<105>c	Framwelgate	Susanna Stoker	hea w	75	sweep [employing] 2 boys	Dur Darlington
2302	194v			Henry Stoker	nep	19	sweep	Dur
2303	194v			Alan Steel	app	14	sweep	Wry Bishop Monkton *
2304	194v			John Flin	app	10	sweep	Nbl Carsl...ly?
2305	194v	<105>d	Framwelgate	Matthew Wear	hea m	57	weaver (carpet)	Sct
2306	194v			Elizabeth Wear	wif m	60		Sct
2307	195r	<105>e	Framwelgate	Timothy Blakey	hea m	54	tailor	Dur [D] S. Giles
2308	195r			Elizabeth Blakey	wif m	54		Dur [D] S. Nicholas
2309	195r			Laura Blakey	dau	18	dressmaker	Dur [D] Framwelgate
2310	195r	<105>f	Framwelgate	James Barlow	hea m	36	carpet weaver	Dur Darlington
2311	195r			Dinah Barlow	wif m	31		Dur Durham
2312	195r			Henry Barlow		22	carpet weaver	Dur Darlington
2313	195r			James Barlow	son	10	scholar	Dur Darlington
2314	195r			Edward Barlow	son	8	scholar	Dur Darlington
2315	195r			George Barlow	son	4		Dur Durham
2316	195r			James Barlow	son	2		Dur Durham
2317	195r	<104>a	Framwelgate	Richard McCandrew	hea m	50	labourer, draining	Irl
2318	195r			Bridget McCandrew	wif m	45		Irl
2319	195r			Patrick McCandrew	son	20	labourer, draining	Irl
2320	195r			John McCandrew	son	18	labourer, draining	Irl
2321	195r			Margaret McCandrew	dau	14	scholar	Irl
2322	195r			Mary McCandrew	dau	12	scholar	Irl
2323	195r			James McCandrew	son	10	scholar	Irl
2324	195r			Richard McCandrew	son	8	scholar	Irl
2325	195r			Thomas McCandrew	son	3	scholar	Dur Durham
2326	195r			Michael Mullen	ldr	20	labourer, draining	Irl
2327	195v			John Douley		40	labourer, draining	Irl
2328	195v			Margaret Kelly	nce m	24		Irl
2329	195v	<104>b	Framwelgate	Thomas Caldclaugh	hea w	66	joiner, journeyman	Dur [D] Elvet
2330	195v			John Caldclaugh	son	26	attorney's clerk	Dur [D] Framwelgate
2331	195v			Catherine Caldclaugh	dau	24		Dur [D] Framwelgate
2332	195v			Sarah Caldclaugh	nce	11	scholar	Dur [D] Framwelgate
2333	195v	<104>c	Framwelgate	Thomas Torpy	hea m	70	agricultural labourer	Irl
2334	195v			Mary Torpy	wif m	70		Irl
2335	195v			Mary Torpy	dau	30		Irl
2336	195v	<104>d	Framwelgate	Mary Horan	hea w	53	soldier's widow	Irl
2337	195v			Mary Craig	dau m	18		Irl

				Name	Rel	Age	Occupation	Birthplace
2338	195v	<104>d	Framwelgate	Bridget Horan	dau	13		Irl
2339	195v	<104>e	Framwelgate	William Faigan	hea m	40	labourer to mason	Lnd
2340	195v			Elizabeth Faigan	wif m	28		Dur Tanfield
2341	195v			John Barrowford		5	scholar	Dur [D] S. Margaret
2342	195v			Sarah Shanks	ldr m	35		Irl
2343	195v			John Shanks	lds	8m		Irl
2344	195v			Mary Jane Moggror	ldr	30		Irl
2345	195v	<104>f	Framwelgate	Isabella Caldclaugh	hea	36	laundress	Dur [D] Framwelgate
2346	195v			Frederick Caldclaugh	son	15	grocer's apprentice	Dur [D] Framwelgate
2347	196r			Sarah Caldclaugh	dau	11	scholar	Dur [D] Framwelgate
2348	196r	<103>a	Framwelgate	Elizabeth Miller	hea m	28	washerwoman	Dur
2349	196r			Jane Miller	dau	4		Dur
2350	196r			Ann Miller	dau	2		Dur
2351	196r	<103>b	Framwelgate	John Johnson	hea m	29	labourer	Denmark
2352	196r			Mary Johnson	wif m	27		Sct
2353	196r			John Johnson	son	1		Dur Durham
2354	196r	<103>c	Framwelgate	Gilbert Snowdon	hea m	75	cartman	Dur Durham
2355	196r			Mary Snowdon	wif m	67		Dur Durham
2356	196r			James Smurthwaite	gsn	6	scholar	Dur Durham
2357	196r	<103>d	Framwelgate	Mary Hamalton	hea m	25		Dur Durham
2358	196r			Mary Hamalton	dau	6		Dur Durham
2359	196r			Thomas Hamalton	son	3		Dur Durham
2360	196r			Hannah Hamalton	dau	1		Dur Durham
2361	196r	<103>e	Framwelgate	John Magure	hea m	38	tailor	Irl
2362	196r			Thorid? Magure	son m	21		Sts Alton
2363	196r	<103>f	Framwelgate	Daniel Hind	hea	26	boot and shoemaker	Dur Durham
2364	196r	<103>g	Framwelgate	William Turnbull	hea w	63	countryman	Dur Hunwick
2365	196r			Elizabeth Turnbull	dau	17	dressmaker	Dur [D] Crossgate
2366	196v	<103>h	Framwelgate	Robert Brydon	hea m	29	labourer	Dur [D] S. Margaret
2367	196v			Susanna Brydon	wif m	28		Dur [D] S. Margaret
2368	196v			William Brydon	son	2		Dur [D] S. Margaret
2369	196v			William C. Eckford	flw m	52	blacksmith	Sct
2370	196v			Euphemia Eckford	* m	50		Nbl Morpeth
2371	196v			Mary Eckford	*	14		Sct
2372	196v	<102>a	Framwelgate	John Kellomichel	hea m	50	agricultural labourer	Dur Durham
2373	196v			Margaret Kellomichel	wif m	40		Irl
2374	196v			Mary Ann White	vis w	30		Nbl Newcastle
2375	196v	<102>b	Framwelgate	James Fannon	hea m	50	agricultural labourer	Irl
2376	196v			Ann Fannon	dau	18		Irl
2377	196v			Ellen Fannon	dau	14		Irl
2378	196v			Hannah Fannon	dau	6		Irl
2379	196v			James Fannon	son	1		Dur [D] Framwelgate
2380	196v			Mary Cox	vis m	40		Irl
2381	196v			James Cox	m	30	agricultural labourer	Irl
2382	196v	<102>c	Framwelgate	John Kennir	hea m	51	chimney sweep {deaf}	Wry Sheffield
2383	196v			Ann Kennir	wif m	55		Dur Durham
2384	196v			Thomas Kennir	son	25	chimney sweep	Dur Durham
2385	196v			John Kennir	son	23	tinner & brazier	Dur Durham
2386	197r			Anne Kennir	dau	18		Dur Durham
2387	197r			John Kennir	gsn	2		Dur Durham
2388	197r			Michael Dailey	ser	14	chimney sweep	Nbl Newcastle
2389	197r			James Lions	ser	10	chimney sweep	Dur Stockton
2390	197r	<102>d	Framwelgate	Patrick Loftus	hea m	27		Irl
2391	197r			Susan Loftus	wif m	22		Irl
2392	197r			John Loftus	son	1		Dur [D] S. Oswald
2393	197r	<101>a	Framwelgate	William Clarke	hea m	48	porter <& publican *>	Dur
2394	197r			Frances Clarke	wif m	50		Dur
2395	197r			Henry Clarke	son	13	miller	Dur
2396	197r			Robert Clarke	son	11	scholar	Dur
2397	197r	<101>b	Framwelgate	Edward Scott	hea m	54	maltsman	Nbl Newcastle
2398	197r			Ellen Scott	wif m	54		Nbl Newcastle
2399	197r			Mary Scott	dau	20		Nbl Newcastle
2400	197r			Betsy Scott	dlw	22		Nbl Newcastle
2401	197r			Dorothy Scott	dau	18		Nbl Newcastle
2402	197r			Jane Scott	dau	16		Nbl Newcastle
2403	197r			Elizabeth Scott	dau	4		Nbl Newcastle
2404	197r	<101>c	Framwelgate	George Longstaff	hea	71	coal miner	Dur [D] S. Margaret
2405	197v	[af]a	Framwelgate	Jane Askew	hea w	69	house servant	Dur Chester-le-Street
2406	197v			George Askew	son	35	mason	Dur
2407	197v			John Askew	son	23	joiner	Dur
2408	197v			Alice Howey	gda	13	scholar	Dur
2409	197v			George Scott	gsn	5	scholar	Dur
2410	197v	[af]b	Framwelgate	Mary Todd	hea w	71		Dur Bishop Auckland
2411	197v			Ann Beadnell	nce	35		Dur Darlington
2412	197v			Thomas Beadnell	*	9	scholar	Dur
2413	197v	<99>a	Framwelgate	George Goodfellow	hea m	42	collier	Dur Durham
2414	197v			Christian Goodfellow	wif m	50		Sct
2415	197v	<99>b	Framwelgate	Thomas Sistterson	hea m	78	ship carpenter	Nbl Newburn
2416	197v			Sophia Sistterson	wif m	78		Sct
2417	197v			Isaac Pearson	ldr w	80	tailor	Yks Bowten
2418	197v	<99>c	Framwelgate	Daniel McCartney	hea m	50	dealer in cloth caps	Irl

2419	197v	<99>c	Framwelgate	Mary McCartney	wif m	34		Irl
2420	197v			Margaret McCartney	dau	9		Dur Durham
2421	197v			Susan McCartney	dau	7		Dur Durham
2422	197v			Elizabeth McCartney	dau	5		Dur Durham
2423	197v			Margaret McCartney	dau	8m		Dur Durham
2424	197v			John Hanlin	ldr w	39	dealer in cloth caps	Irl
2425	198r	<99>d	Framwelgate	Thomas O'Riodon	hea m	55	labourer	Irl
2426	198r			Mary O'Riodon	dau	22	washerwoman	Irl
2427	198r			Thomas O'Riodon	son	17	labourer	Irl
2428	198r			John Taylor	ldr	32	labourer	Irl
2429	198r			Dennis Taylor	ldr	35	labourer	Irl
2430	198r			Ann Shepherd	nce	3m		Dur Durham
2431	198r			Margaret Kelly	ldr w	55	labouring woman	Irl
2432	198r	<99>e	Framwelgate	Jane Brice	hea m	45	pauper	Irl
2433	198r			James Brice	son	24	labourer	Sct
2434	198r			George Brice	son	20	blacksmith	Dur [D] Framwelgate
2435	198r			Robert Brice	son	15	iron forgeman	Dur [D] Framwelgate
2436	198r			William Brice	son	11	pipemaker's apprentice	Dur [D] Framwelgate
2437	198r			Alexander Brice	son	9	scholar	Dur [D] Framwelgate
2438	198r			Daniel Brice	son	8	scholar	Dur [D] Framwelgate
2439	198r			John Brice	son	5	scholar	Dur [D] Framwelgate
2440	198r			Richard Brice	son	4	scholar	Dur [D] Framwelgate
2441	198r	<98>	Framwelgate	George Wilkinson	hea m	64	tailor <& publican> *	Dur Wolsingham
2442	198r			Ann Wilkinson	wif m	62		Dur Hunstanworth
2443	198r			Henry Wilkinson	son	31	tailor	Dur [D] Framwelgate
2444	198v	[ag]	Framwelgate	Charles Stott	hea m	48	tallow chandler, jnym	Nbl Alnwick
2445	198v			Isabella Stott	wif m	50		Sct
2446	198v			Ann Stott	dau	24	dressmaker	Nbl Berwick
2447	198v			William Stott	son	16	grocer	Nbl Berwick
2448	198v			Isabella Stott	dau	14	dressmaker	Nbl Berwick
2449	198v			Mary Ann Stott	dau	12	scholar	Nbl Berwick
2450	198v			Martha Stott	dau	10	scholar	Nbl Newcastle
2451	198v			Agnes Stott	dau	7	scholar	Nbl Newcastle
2452	198v			James S. Wilson	slw m	25	cordwainer /"cardwinder"	Mdx Westminster
2453	198v			Margaret Wilson	dau	22		Nbl Berwick
2454	198v			Isabella Wilson	gda	6m		Dur Durham
2455	198v	[ah]a	Framwelgate	Thomas Blagdon	hea m	42	mason, journeyman	Dur [D] S. Margaret
2456	198v			Ann Blagdon	wif m	38		Dur Sedgefield
2457	198v			Elizabeth Blagdon	dau	12	scholar	Dur [D] S. Margaret
2458	198v			Margaret Blagdon	dau	10	scholar	Dur [D] S. Margaret
2459	198v			George Blagdon	son	5		Dur [D] S. Margaret
2460	198v			Mary Jane Blagdon	dau	3		Dur [D] S. Margaret
2461	198v			Thomas Blagdon	son	1		Dur [D] S. Margaret
2462	198v	[ah]b	Framwelgate	Mary Mann	hea m	27		Nbl Wallsend
2463	198v			Mary Mann	dau	9	scholar	Dur Durham
2464	199r			William George Mann	son	1m		Dur [D] Framwelgate
2465	199r	[ai]	Framwelgate	George Thompson	hea m	29	carpet weaver	Dur Barnard Castle
2466	199r			Christiana Thompson	wif m	24		Dur Darlington
2467	199r			Elizabeth Thompson	dau	5		Dur Barnard Castle
2468	199r			William Thompson	son	2		Dur Barnard Castle
2469	199r	[aj]a	Framwelgate	William Ward	hea m	25	woolsorter	Dur [D] Framwelgate
2470	199r			Ann Ward	wif m	24		Dur [D] Framwelgate
2471	199r			Roger Ward	son	3		Dur [D] Framwelgate
2472	199r			Edward Ward	son	2		Dur [D] Framwelgate
2473	199r	[aj]b	Framwelgate	James Carr	hea m	37	currier, journeyman	Dur [D] Framwelgate
2474	199r			Mary Carr	wif m	43		Dur [D] Framwelgate
2475	199r	[ak]a	Framwelgate	Robert Graham	hea m	25	iron moulder	Dur Durham
2476	199r			Hannah Graham	wif m	26		Dur Durham
2477	199r			Robert Graham	son	4		Dur Birtley
2478	199r			George B. Graham	son	2		Dur Durham
2479	199r			William F. Graham	son	1		Dur Durham
2480	199r	[ak]b	Framwelgate	Robert Hodgson	hea m	31	iron and brass founder	Dur Durham
2481	199r			Isabella Hodgson	wif m	35		Dur Durham
2482	199r	[ak]c	Framwelgate	Charles Grant	hea w	65	corporal, artillery *	Sct
2483	199r			Catherine Grant	dau	21	dressmaker	Sct
2484	199v	[ak]d	Framwelgate	Robert Hodgson	hea m	53	shoemaker	Dur Durham
2485	199v			Ann Hodgson	wif m	50		Dur Durham
2486	199v			Ann Hodgson	dau	22		Dur Durham
2487	199v			Rachael Hodgson	dau	14		Dur Durham
2488	199v			Eliza Hodgson	dau	9		Dur Durham
2489	199v	[ak]e	Framwelgate	Ann Dickinson	hea w	46	sempstress; pauper	Dur Durham
2490	199v			Thomas Dickinson	son	11	scholar	Dur Durham
2491	199v	[ak]f	Framwelgate	Elizabeth Elliot	hea m	55	lodging house keeper	Nbl Berwick
2492	199v			Mary Williams	[1] m	23	dressmaker	Sts Birmingham
2493	199v			James Grieves	[1]	40	shoemaker	Bdf
2494	199v			William Haniless?	[1]	40	cutler	New York BS
2495	199v			Henry Abel	[1]	23	basketseller	Deatenhausen
2496	199v			Edward Smith	[1] w	51	basketseller	Hasselboon
2497	199v			Peter Smith	[1]	18	basketseller	Hasselboon
2498	199v			John Sew	[1]	18	basketseller	Hasselboon
2499	199v	[ak]g	Framwelgate	John Dent	hea m	60	weaver	Dur Durham

No.	Folio	Ref	Place	Name	Rel	M	Age	Occupation	Birthplace
2500	199v	[ak]g	Framwelgate	Ann Dent	wif	m	61		Nry Catterick
2501	199v			Elizabeth Dent	dau		28		Dur Barnard Castle
2502	199v			John Dent	son		6		Dur Barnard Castle
2503	199v			Mary Ann Dent	dau		3m		Dur Barnard Castle
2504	200r			Elizabeth Wilson	vis		10		Dur Barnard Castle
2505	200r	[ak]h	Framwelgate	Edward Rynas	hea	m	31	labourer	Log
2506	200r			Julie Rynas	wif	m	28		Log
2507	200r			James Rynas	son		8	scholar	Log
2508	200r			Mary Raynas	dau		9m		Dur Durham
2509	200r	[al]a	Framwelgate	Anthony Kennady	hea	m	48	bagpipe manufacturer	Irl
2510	200r			Mary Kennady	wif	m	47		Irl
2511	200r			Michael Kennady	son		17		Irl
2512	200r			Anthony Kennady	son		12		Irl
2513	200r			Martin Kennady	son		10		Irl
2514	200r			James Kennady	son		8		Irl
2515	200r			Maria Kennady	dau		4		Irl
2516	200r	[al]b	Framwelgate	Hugh Kennady	hea	m	23	agricultural labourer	Irl
2517	200r			Ann Kennady	wif	m	22		Irl
2518	200r			Biddy Kennady	dau		1		Dur Easington Lane
2519	200r	[al]c	Framwelgate	John Holiday	hea	m	58	shoemaker	Dur Sunderland
2520	200r			Catherine Holiday	wif	m	31		Dur Darlington
2521	200r			John Holiday	son		7	scholar	Dur Sunderland
2522	200r			George Holiday	son		4		Dur Sunderland
2523	200r			Thomas Holiday	son		2		Dur Durham
2524	200v	[al]d	Framwelgate	Dennis Haggarty	hea	m	34	agricultural labourer	Irl
2525	200v			Catherine Haggarty	wif	m	30		Irl
2526	200v			Matilda Haggarty	dau		9		Irl
2527	200v			John Haggarty	son		7		Irl
2528	200v			Mary Haggarty	dau		3		Lan Liverpool
2529	200v			Catherine Haggarty	dau		1		Dur Durham
2530	200v			James Corney	vis		30	agricultural labourer	Irl
2531	200v	[al]e	Framwelgate	Mary Rigby	hea		30	charwoman /"chairwoman"	Dur Durham
2532	200v			Eleanor Rigby	dau		6	scholar	Dur Durham
2533	200v	<95>a	Framwelgate	James Shaw	hea	m	50	baker	Wry Selby
2534	200v			Ann Shaw	wif	m	48		Dur Gainford *
2535	200v			James Shaw	son		24	tailor	Dur Durham
2536	200v	<95>b	Framwelgate	Eleanor Walker	hea		21		Dur Sunderland
2537	200v			John George Walker	son		2		Dur Sunderland
2538	200v			William Walker	son		1		Dur Sunderland
2539	200v	<95>c	Framwelgate	Francis Burns	hea	m	41	coal miner	Irl
2540	200v			Mary Burns	wif	m	37		Irl
2541	200v			Catherine Burns	dau		11		Irl
2542	200v			Michael Burns	son		6	scholar	Dur Durham
2543	200v			Mary Ann Burns	dau		1		Irl
2544	201r			Patrick Caire	vis		35	labourer	Irl
2545	201r			James Gibny	vis		21	labourer	Irl
2546	201r			Patrick W. Fillips	vis	m	35	fiddler	Irl
2547	201r			John Stewart	vis		38	labourer	Irl
2548	201r	<95>d	Framwelgate	Elizabeth Wood	hea		59		Dur [D] S. Nicholas
2549	201r			Caroline Lascelles	sis	w	55	nurse	Dur [D] S. Nicholas
2550	201r			Elizabeth Wilkinson	dau	m	22	dressmaker	Dur [D] Framwelgate
2551	201r	<94>a	Framwelgate	Elizabeth Gay	hea	w	72	receiving parish relief	Dur Willington
2552	201r	<94>b	Framwelgate	George Carr	hea	m	44	grocer <& tailor>	Dur Durham
2553	201r			Eleanor Carr	wif	m	46		Dur Durham
2554	201r			William Carr	son		13		Dur Durham
2555	201r			Jane Carr	dau		11		Dur Durham
2556	201r			George Carr	son		7		Dur Durham
2557	201r	<93>a	Framwelgate	John Cowen	hea	m	40	tailor	Dur Durham
2558	201r			Eliza Cowen	wif	m	39		Dur Durham
2559	201r			James Cowen	son		12	scholar	Dur Durham
2560	201r			Mary Ann Cowen	dau		10	scholar	Dur Durham
2561	201r			John Cowen	son		8	scholar	Dur Durham
2562	201r			William Cowen	son		5	scholar	Dur Durham
2563	201v	<93>b	Framwelgate	John Millner	hea	m	44	porter	Nry Bowes
2564	201v			Mary Millner	wif	m	40		Nry Tunstall
2565	201v			Mary Millner	dau		14	scholar	Nry Tunstall
2566	201v			Henry Millner	son		12	scholar	Dur Brancepeth
2567	201v			Thomas Millner	son		3	scholar	Dur [D] Framwelgate
2568	201v			Isabella Millner	dau		3	scholar	Dur [D] Framwelgate
2569	201v	<93>c	Framwelgate	Robert Bradley	hea	m	28	agricultural labourer	Nry Yarm
2570	201v			Jane Bradley	wif	m	30		Castle Busby
2571	201v			Jane Bradley	dau		3		Nry Yarm
2572	201v	<93>d	Framwelgate	Absalom Burton	hea	m	46	miller	Dur Durham
2573	201v			Mary Burton	wif	m	31		Nry Marske
2574	201v			Jane Burton	dau		12		Dur Brandon
2575	201v			William Burton	son		12	scholar	Dur Brandon
2576	201v			Robert Burton	son		6	scholar	Dur Brandon
2577	201v			Joseph Burton	son		4	scholar	Dur Brandon
2578	201v			Thomas Burton	son		11m		Dur Brandon
2579	201v			Absalom Burton	son		3	scholar	Dur Brandon
2580	201v			Joseph Bentley	vis	m	44	millwright	Wry Leeds

2581	201v	<93>d	Framwelgate		not known	vis	28	miller	Wry Leeds
2582	202r	<93>e	Framwelgate	Samuel Gownes		hea m	34	pipemaker emp 2 men	Lan Rainford
2583	202r			Ann Gownes		wif m	34		Wry Sheffield
2584	202r			Isabella Gownes		dau	7	scholar	Dur Stockton
2585	202r			Abigail Gownes		dau	9m		Lan Holden
2586	202r			Thomas Gownes		*	22	pipemaker	Lan
2587	202r			George Gownes		son	5		Lan
2588	202r			Samuel Marland		app	11	pipemaker (apprentice)	Lan Ashton-under-Lyne
2589	202r			Moses Tunstall			20	pipemaker	Lan Rochdale *
2590	202r	[am]	Framwelgate	William Staples		hea m	49	miller	Cam Soham
2591	202r			Elizabeth Staples		wif m	28		Wry Ripon
2592	202r			Gabriel Staples		son	8	scholar	Dur Stockton
2593	202r			Mary Staples		dau	6	scholar	Dur Stockton
2594	202r			Peter Staples		son	3		Dur Stockton
2595	202r	[an]a	Framwelgate	Harriet Bicroft		hea m	21		Dur Shincliffe
2596	202r			Michael Bicroft		[s]	2		Dur [D] S. Margaret
2597	202r			Elizabeth Bicroft		dau	1m		Dur [D] Framwelgate
2598	202r	[an]b	Framwelgate	George Grabham		hea m	33	mason	Dur Sedgefield
2599	202r			Elizabeth Grabham		wif m	31		Nbl Newcastle
2600	202r			Mary J. Grabham		dau	10	scholar	Dur Houghton
2601	202r			Thomason Grabham		dau	5	scholar	Dur Bishop Auckland
2602	202v			George Grabham		son	3		Dur [D] Framwelgate
2603	202v			William Grabham		son	8m		Dur [D] Framwelgate
2604	202v	[ao]a	Framwelgate	Mary Ann Craige		hea m	39		not known
2605	202v			Hannah Craige		dau	10	scholar	Nbl Newcastle
2606	202v			Mary Ann Craige		dau	8	scholar	Nbl Newcastle
2607	202v	[ao]b	Framwelgate	James Ireland		hea m	42	gardener	Cul Penrith
2608	202v			Mary Ireland		wif m	50		Cul Penrith
2609	202v			Margaret Ireland		dau	19		Nbl Sandhoe
2610	202v		Robson's Buildings	Richard W. Chapman		hea m	29	miller	Wes Kirkby Stephen
2611	202v			Esther Chapman		wif m	21		Dur Bishop Middleham
2612	202v			Margaret Chapman		dau	1		Dur Bishop Middleham
2613	202v	[ap]a	Framwelgate	Miles Longmire		hea m	50	blacksmith	Wes Bolton
2614	202v			Sarah Longmire		wif m	29		Dur West Ketton
2615	202v			John Longmire		son	13	labourer	Wes Kirkby Stephen
2616	202v			Elizabeth Longmire		dau	10		Dur Relley
2617	202v			Agnes Longmire		dau	7		Dur Shildon
2618	202v			Joseph Longmire		son	4		Dur Shincliffe
2619	202v			Miles Longmire		son	1		Dur
2620	202v	[ap]b	Framwelgate	Jane Cowley		hea w	36	lodging house keeper	Nbl Newcastle
2621	202v			Elizabeth Welsh		ldr m	22		Wry Wakefield *
2622	203r			Hiram Welsh		lds	4		Wry Leeds
2623	203r	[ap]c	Framwelgate	John Wallace		hea m	58	joiner	Dur
2624	203r			Phoebe Wallace		wif m	61		Nbl Melkirk
2625	203r	[ap]d	Framwelgate	James Barret		hea m	43	agricultural labourer	Irl
2626	203r			Mary Barret		wif m	34		Sal
2627	203r			Margaret Barret		dau	1		Dur [D] Framwelgate
2628	203r			Patrick Kirby		ldr w	45	agricultural labourer	Irl
2629	203r			Patrick Kirby		ldr	8		Irl
2630	203r			Cuthbert Smith		vis	22		Sal
2631	203r	[ap]e	Framwelgate	James Kirby		hea m	35	agricultural labourer	Sli
2632	203r			Mary Kirby		wif m	40		Sli
2633	203r			Peter Kirby		son	13		Sli
2634	203r			Bridget Kirby		dau	9		Sli
2635	203r			Patrick Kirby		son	7		Sli
2636	203r			Michael Kirby		son	3		Dur
2637	203r			Andrew Kirby		son	11m		Dur
2638	203r			James Grey			22	labourer	Irl
2639	203r	[ap]f	Framwelgate	Harvey Fidler		hea m	58	upholsterer	Dur
2640	203r			Mary Fidler		wif m	59		Dur
2641	203r			John Fidler		son	25	carpet weaver	Dur
2642	203v			William Fidler		son	20	shoemaker	Dur Durham
2643	203v			Isabella Fidler		dau	9		Dur Durham
2644	203v	[ap]g	Framwelgate	Robert H. Heslop		hea m	30	nailmaker	Dur Durham
2645	203v			Isabella Heslop		wif m	30		Wry Arkendale
2646	203v			Margaret Heslop		dau	4		Dur
2647	203v			Catherine Heslop		dau	2		Dur
2648	203v			Isabella Heslop		dau	1m		Dur
2649	203v	[ap]h	Framwelgate	Matthew Morley		hea m	67	tripe dresser	Gla Thornton
2650	203v			Elizabeth Morley		wif m	50		Dur Durham
2651	203v			Thomas Morley		son	12	scholar	Yks York
2652	203v			William Morley		son	8	scholar	Dur Durham
2653	203v			Richard Morley		son	5	scholar	Dur Durham
2654	203v	[ap]i	Framwelgate	Robert Pinkerton		hea m	54	rag merchant	Nbl Tynemouth
2655	203v			Mary Pinkerton		wif m	52		Sct
2656	203v	[ap]j	Framwelgate	Matthew Herbert		hea	66	agricultural labourer	Dur Durham
2657	203v	[ap]k	Framwelgate	Sarah Dawsey		hea m	35	laundress	Dur Durham
2658	203v			Mary Dawsey		dau	13	scholar	Dur Durham
2659	203v	[ap]l	Framwelgate	Mary Hodgson		hea	48	washerwoman	Dur Durham
2660	203v			James Dobson			38	agricultural labourer	Dur Lumley
2661	203v	[aq]a	Framwelgate	Ann Solo		hea	25	factory girl, paper	Wry Studley *

2662	204r	[aq]b	Framwelgate	Elizabeth Cummings	hea m	70	innkeeper	Dur Durham
2663	204r			Anthony Stephenson	gsn	11		Dur Durham
2664	204r			Mary Stephenson	dau m	36		Dur Durham
2665	204r			Robert Stephenson	gsn	5		Dur Durham
2666	204r			Margaret Stephenson	gda	2		Dur Durham
2667	204r			Thomas Naught	ser	37	servant	Dur Durham
2668	204r			William Shaw	vis	22	miner	Dur Durham
2669	204r			Elizabeth Stephenson	dau	18		Dur Durham
2670	204r	[aq]c	Framwelgate	Bridget Armstrong	hea w	44	laundress	Dur Lanchester
2671	204r			Isabella Armstrong	dau	19	laundress	Dur [D] Framwelgate
2672	204r			Mary Armstrong	dau	14	scholar	Irl
2673	204r			Thomas Wallace		45	agricultural labourer	Dur Brandon
2674	204r	[aq]d	Framwelgate	John Brown	hea m	43	butcher	Dur [D] Framwelgate
2675	204r			Elizabeth Brown	wif m	35		Dur [D] Framwelgate
2676	204r			Anthony Brown	son	10		Dur [D] Framwelgate
2677	204r			Ann Brown	dau	7		Dur [D] Framwelgate
2678	204r			Mary Brown	dau	9m		Dur [D] Framwelgate
2679	204r	[aq]e	Framwelgate	Thomas Hodgson	hea m	36	nailmaker	Dur [D] S. Oswald
2680	204r			Elizabeth Hodgson	wif m	35		Dur [D] S. Oswald
2681	204r			Thomas Hodgson	son	15	bootcloser (apprentice)	Dur [D] S. Margaret
2682	204v			Robert Hodgson	son	11		Dur [D] S. Margaret
2683	204v			William Hodgson	son	5m		Dur [D] S. Margaret
2684	204v	[aq]f	Framwelgate	Mark Ragan	hea m	60	agricultural labourer	Irl
2685	204v			Bridget Ragan	wif m	58	agricultural labourer	Irl
2686	204v			Michael Ragan	son	24	agricultural labourer	Irl
2687	204v			Patrick Ragan	son	21	agricultural labourer	Irl
2688	204v			Eleanor Ragan	dau	16	agricultural labourer	Irl
2689	204v	[aq]g	Framwelgate	Margaret Wittingham	hea	28	factory girl	Dur
2690	204v			Ellen Wittingham	dau	9		Dur
2691	204v	[ar]a	Framwelgate	William Smith	hea w	30	shoemaker	Dur [D] Crossgate
2692	204v	[ar]b	Framwelgate	Hannah Hind	hea	66	pauper	Dur Lumley
2693	204v	[ar]c	Framwelgate	George Liddle	hea m	57	joiner?	Dur Sheraton
2694	204v			Elizabeth Liddle	wif m	59		Dur Brancepeth
2695	204v			Robert Liddle	son	18	shoemaker	Dur Middle'n-Teesdale
2696	204v	[ar]d	Framwelgate	Francis Littlefaire	hea m	33	hairdresser	Dur Durham
2697	204v			Elizabeth Littlefaire	wif m	25		Dur [D] Framwelgate
2698	204v			William Littlefaire	son	3		Dur [D] Framwelgate
2699	204v			Ann Littlefaire	dau	6		Dur [D] Framwelgate
2700	204v			Sophia Littlefaire	dau	1m		Dur [D] Framwelgate
2701	205r	<80>a	Framwelgate	George Bainbridge	hea m	72	confectioner	Dur Durham
2702	205r			Mary Bainbridge	wif m	53		Dur Durham
2703	205r			Catherine Bainbridge	dau	14	scholar	Dur Durham
2704	205r			Charles Bainbridge	son	12	scholar	Dur Durham
2705	205r			Susanna Bainbridge	dau	10	scholar	Dur Durham
2706	205r			Mary Ann Bainbridge	dau	4		Dur Durham
2707	205r	<80>b	Framwelgate	Margaret Pearson	hea	60	annuitant	Dur [D] Framwelgate
2708	205r			William Barkas	*	22	tailor	Dur [D] Framwelgate
2709	205r	<80>c	Framwelgate	Edward Bentley	hea m	63	tailor	Dur Hutton Henry
2710	205r			Ellen Bentley	wif m	58		Sct
2711	205r	<80>d	Framwelgate	Edward Hargrave	hea m	40	tailor	Dur Durham
2712	205r			Catherine Hargrave	wif m	22	housekeeper	Irl
2713	205r			Henry Hargrave	son	1		Dur Durham
2714	205r	[as]a	Framwelgate	Ann Palmer	hea m	36	worsted spinner	Dur Sunderland
2715	205r			Thomas Briggs		7	scholar	Dur Durham
2716	205r	[as]b	Framwelgate	Laurence Kerbey	hea m	60	labourer	Irl
2717	205r			Mary Kerbey	wif m	60	housekeeper	Irl
2718	205r			Bridget Kerbey	dau	18		Irl
2719	205r	[as]c	Framwelgate	John Stevens	hea m	39	shoemaker	Nbl All Saints *
2720	205r			Mary Stevens	wif m	41		Dur [D] S. Oswald
2721	205v			John Stevens	son	18	mason	Dur [D] Framwelgate
2722	205v			Ann Welands		12		Dur [D] Framwelgate
2723	205v			Catherine Tanby	vis	6		Dur [D] Framwelgate
2724	205v	[as]d	Framwelgate	Patrick Callehan	hea m	40	agricultural labourer	Irl
2725	205v			Helen Callehan	wif m	30		Irl
2726	205v			Mary Callehan	dau	6		Irl
2727	205v			Margaret Callehan	dau	6m		Dur Durham
2728	205v			Ann Kilroy	ser	18	domestic [servant]	Irl
2729	205v			Patrick Riley	vis	22	agricultural labourer	Irl
2730	205v			Laurence Calligan	vis m	59	agricultural labourer	Irl
2731	205v			Richard Carney	vis	20	agricultural labourer	Irl
2732	205v			John Martin	vis	26	agricultural labourer	Irl
2733	205v	[as]e	Framwelgate	Elizabeth Gleson	hea w	32	charwoman /"chairwoman"	Dur [D] Framwelgate
2734	205v			Margaret Gleson	dau	12		Dur [D] Framwelgate
2735	205v			Ann Gleson	dau	10		Dur [D] Framwelgate
2736	205v	[as]f	Framwelgate	William Carr	hea m	65	mason, labourer	Dur Houghton-l-Spring
2737	205v			Margaret Carr	wif m	63		Dur Durham
2738	205v			Margaret Carr	dau	25		Dur [D] Framwelgate
2739	205v			William Carr	son	20		Dur [D] Framwelgate
2740	205v	[as]g	Framwelgate	Hannah Smith	hea	60	pauper	Dur [D] S. Oswald
2741	206r	[as]h	Framwelgate	Mary Gibson	hea w	70		Wes Orton Moor
2742	206r			Isabella Gibson	dau	34		Dur Witton Gilbert

2743	206r	[as]h	Framwelgate	Peter Gibson	gsn		12		Dur Durham
2744	206r			Joseph Gibson	gsn		2		Dur Durham
2745	206r	[at]a	Framwelgate	Patrick Cawlon	hea	m	67	hawker	Irl
2746	206r			Ann Cawlon	wif	m	67		Irl
2747	206r			Edward Danse			30	stationer	Irl
2748	206r	[at]b	Framwelgate	Jane Turnbull	hea	w	65		Dur Butterby
2749	206r			Thomas Turnbull	son		24	mason	Dur Durham
2750	206r			Eleanor Turnbull	dau		18	servant	Dur Durham
2751	206r			Thomas Liddle	gsn		21	tailor	Dur Durham
2752	206r	[at]c	Framwelgate	Joseph Knowles	hea	w	40	carpet weaver	Wor Bewdley
2753	206r			John Knowles	son		12	draw boy	Dur Durham
2754	206r			Catherine C. Knowles	dau		10		Dur Bishop Auckland
2755	206r			Joseph E. Knowles	son		7	scholar	Dur Bishop Auckland
2756	206r			Stephen Knowles	son		4	scholar	Dur Bishop Auckland
2757	206r			James Knowles	son		1		Dur Bishop Auckland
2758	206r			Edwin Knowles	son		36	carpet weaver	Wor Bewdley
2759	206r	[au]a	Framwelgate	Judith Douglass	hea	w	64	annuitant	Dur Durham
2760	206r			Henry Douglass	son		38	master painter	Dur Durham
2761	206v			Henry Douglass	son		24	master painter	Dur Durham
2762	206v	[au]b	Framwelgate	William Savin	hea	w	50	groom	Nth Chacombe
2763	206v			William Smith	slw	m	27	currier	Dur [D] S. Margaret
2764	206v			Anne Smith	dau	m	22		Dur [D] S. Mary-1-Bow
2765	206v			William Smith	gsn		3		Dur [D] S. Margaret
2766	206v			Margaret Smith	gda		4m		Dur [D] S. Margaret
2767	206v	<84>a	Framwelgate	Isaac Thorp	hea	m	69	schoolmaster *	Lan Traworth
2768	206v			Elizabeth Thorp	wif	m	55		Dur [D] Framwelgate
2769	206v	<84>b	Framwelgate	John Watson	hea	m	45	mason	Dur [D] S. Margaret
2770	206v			Margaret Watson	wif	m	46		Cul Preston
2771	206v			Jane Watson	dau		18	dressmaker	Dur Houghton-1-Spring
2772	206v			Janet Watson	dau		14	scholar	Dur Houghton-1-Spring
2773	206v			Maria Watson	dau		10	scholar	Dur [D] S. Margaret
2774	206v			Frances Watson	dau		8	scholar	Dur [D] S. Margaret
2775	206v			Sarah A. Watson	dau		4	scholar	Dur [D] S. Margaret
2776	206v			Jane Farley	nur		2		Dur [D] S. Margaret
2777	206v	<84>c	Framwelgate	William Wilkey	hea		22	tailor	Dur [D] S. Nicholas
2778	206v	<84>d	Framwelgate	William Johnson	hea	m	45	shoemaker	Dur [D] S. Nicholas
2779	206v			Ann Johnson	wif	m	44		Dur [D] S. Oswald
2780	206v			Ellen Johnson	dau		7	scholar	Dur [D] Framwelgate
2781	207r			Mary Ann Johnson	dau		6	scholar	Dur [D] Framwelgate
2782	207r	[av]a	Framwelgate	John Devine	hea	m	35	hawker	Irl
2783	207r			Bridget Devine	wif	m	25		Irl
2784	207r	[av]b	Framwelgate	Thomas Casolin	hea	m	30	coal miner	Irl
2785	207r			Bridget Casolin	wif	m	26		Irl
2786	207r			James Casolin	son		5		Dur [D] Framwelgate
2787	207r			Mary Ann Casolin	dau		1		Dur [D] Framwelgate
2788	207r	[av]c	Framwelgate	Jane Sharp	hea	m	27		Dur [D] Framwelgate
2789	207r			Sarah Sharp	dau		6	scholar	Dur [D] Framwelgate
2790	207r			Esther Sharp	dau		4		Dur [D] Framwelgate
2791	207r			Mary Sharp	dau		10m		Dur [D] Framwelgate
2792	207r	[av]d	Framwelgate	Barnard O'Hare	hea	m	21	dealer in ropes	Irl
2793	207r			Margaret O'Hare	wif		20		Irl
2794	207r	[av]e	Framwelgate	Mary Kerney	hea	m	50	women's capmaker	Irl
2795	207r			Ellen Kerney	dau		12		Irl
2796	207r			Mary Ann Kerney	dau		9	scholar	Dur
2797	207r			Jane Kerney	dau		6	scholar	Dur
2798	207r	[aw]a	Framwelgate	Jane Cornforth	hea	w	64	domestic duties	Dur [D] Framwelgate
2799	207r			George Cornforth	son		26	tailor	Dur [D] Framwelgate
2800	207r			George Cornforth	gsn		14	whitesmith (apprentice)	Dur [D] Framwelgate
2801	207v			Mary Sumbell	dau	m	31		Dur [D] Framwelgate
2802	207v			John Sumbell	gsn		2		Dur [D] Framwelgate
2803	207v			Thomas Sumbell	gsn		9m		Dur [D] Framwelgate
2804	207v	[aw]b	Framwelgate	Robert Gardner	hea	m	50	lamplighter	Dur Birtley
2805	207v			Jane Gardner	wif	m	40		Wes Kendal
2806	207v			Robert Gardner	son		9	scholar	Dur [D] Framwelgate
2807	207v			Jane Gardner	dau		7	scholar	Dur [D] Framwelgate
2808	207v			Margaret Chapman	nce		4	scholar	Dur Sunderland
2809	207v	[aw]c	Framwelgate	Michael Gorman	hea	m	33	labourer	Irl
2810	207v			Bridget Gorman	wif	m	32		Irl
2811	207v			Mary Gorman	dau	m	*		Irl
2812	207v			Michael Gorman	[s]		10		Irl
2813	207v			Ann Gorman	[d]		7		Irl
2814	207v			Mary Mellin	ser		19	servant	Irl
2815	207v	[aw]d	Framwelgate	Dominic Laiven	hea	m	34	labourer	Irl
2816	207v			Catherine Laiven	wif	m	32		Irl
2817	207v			John Laiven	son		7		Irl
2818	207v			Margaret Laiven	dau		5		Irl
2819	207v			Catherine Laiven	dau		5m		Irl
2820	207v			James Welsh	ldr	m	26	labourer	Irl
2821	208r			Thomas Morgan	ldr	m	20	labourer	Irl
2822	208r			Mary Laynora	ldr	m	36	labourer	Irl
2823	208r			John Laynora	lds		7		Irl

Line	Folio	Sched	Address	Name	Rel	Cond	Age	Occupation	Birthplace
2824	208r	<81>	Framwelgate	George Hemmingway	hea	m	32	lay clerk <in Cath *>	Wry Ossett
2825	208r			Elizabeth Hemmingway	wif	m	31		Wry Ossett
2826	208r			Margaret Hemmingway	dau		10	scholar	Wry Ossett
2827	208r			Frederick Hemmingway	son		9	scholar	Wry Ossett
2828	208r			George Hemmingway	son		7	scholar	Wry Dewsbury
2829	208r			Elizabeth Hemmingway	dau		5	scholar	Wry Dewsbury
2830	208r			James W. Hemmingway	son		2		Wry Hunslet *
2831	208r			Anna Hemmingway	dau		3m		Wry Hunslet *
2832	208r			Elizabeth Sidney	mth		70		Wry Leeds
2833	208r	[ax]a	Framwelgate	Thomas Gowland	hea	m	29	currier	Dur Durham
2834	208r			Mary Ann Gowland	wif	m	31		Dur Durham
2835	208r			Richard J. Gowland	son		6		Dur Durham
2836	208r			Elizabeth Gowland	dau		4		Dur Durham
2837	208r			Thomas Gowland	son		2		Dur Durham
2838	208r	[ax]b	Framwelgate	Matthew Hart	hea	m	73	retired weaver	Dur Durham
2839	208r			Mary Hart	wif	m	67		Dur Durham
2840	208v	[ay]a	Framwelgate	Joseph Graves	hea	m	28	gas fitter	Nry Huntington
2841	208v			Elizabeth Graves	wif	m	31		Wry Tadcaster
2842	208v			Mary Graves	dau		4		Hamburg BS
2843	208v	[ay]b	Framwelgate	Bentflower Hill	hea	m	73	fellmonger	Nbl Be[n]well
2844	208v			Eleanor Hill	wif	m	59		Dur [D] Framwelgate
2845	208v			Sarah Hill	dau		27	dressmaker	Dur [D] Framwelgate
2846	208v			Robert Johnson	nep		8	scholar	Dur [D] Framwelgate
2847	208v			Eleanor Hill	dau		25	dressmaker	Dur [D] Framwelgate
2848	208v	<76>	Framwelgate	Thomas Bray	hea		63	<market> gardener 2a	Wry Wakefield
2849	208v			Richard Bray	son		12	joiner	Dur [D] Framwelgate
2850	208v			Joseph Bray	son		12	gardener's apprentice	Dur [D] Framwelgate
			one house uninhabited						
2851	208v	[az]	Framwelgate	John Soggett	hea	m	30	agricultural labourer	Yks
2852	208v			Jane Soggett	wif	m	30		Dur Durham
2853	208v			Charles Soggett	son		1		Dur Durham
2854	208v			John Brown			40	agricultural labourer	Dur Durham
2855	208v	<75>	Framwelgate	Ralph Smith	hea	m	72	flaxdresser	Dur Durham
2856	208v			Mary Smith	wif	m	72	laundress	Dur Penshaw
2857	208v			Sarah Smith	dau		46	laundress	Dur Penshaw
			one house uninhabited						
2858	209r	<79>	Framwelgate	John Smith	hea	m	30	joiner	Dur Durham
2859	209r			Mary Smith	wif	m	27		Sal Wem
2860	209r			Mary A. Smith	dau		2		Lan Manchester
2861	209r			Ralph Smith	son		6m		Dur
2862	209r	<72>a	Framwelgate	Abraham Douglass	hea	m	34	rope & twine mkr, master	Dur Durham
2863	209r			Dorothy Douglass	wif	m	31		Dur Durham
2864	209r			William Douglass	son		14	rope & twine maker (app)	Dur Durham
2865	209r			Mary Douglass	dau		11	scholar	Nbl Newcastle
2866	209r			Helen Douglass	dau		3	scholar	Dur Durham
2867	209r	<72>b	Framwelgate	James Johnson	hea		16	joiner (apprentice)	Dur Durham
2868	209r			Mary Ann Johnson	sis		14	scholar	Dur Durham
2869	209r	<72>c	Framwelgate	Mary Green	hea	w	70	laundress emp 4 women	Dur Bishop Auckland
2870	209r			Ralph Green	son		17	upholsterer's apprentice	Dur Durham
2871	209r			Henry Hodgson	slw	m	20	journeyman mason	D'ir Durham
2872	209r			Ephthlea Hodgson	dau	m	20		Dur Durham
2873	209r			Charles R. Hodgson	gsn		1m		Dur Durham
2874	209r			Jane Longstaff	ser		17	servant	Dur Barnard Castle
2875	209r	<71>a	Framwelgate	Mary Dent	hea	w	39	laundress; pauper	Dur Durham
2876	209r			Isab[el] Dent	dau		4		Dur Durham
2877	209r	<71>b*	Framwelgate	William Wilson	hea	m	27	gardener	Nbl Carslile
2878	209v			Elizabeth Wilson	wif	m	27		Dur Durham
2879	209v			Christopher Wilson	son		5	scholar	Dur Durham
2880	209v			Sarah Wilson	dau		3		Dur Durham
2881	209v			Elizabeth Wilson	dau		10m		Dur Durham
2882	209v	<71>c	Framwelgate	Charles Fallon	hea	m	37	mason	Dur Durham
2883	209v			Jane Fallon	wif	m	38		Dur Durham
2884	209v			Elizabeth Fallon	dau		17		Dur Durham
2885	209v			Hannah Fallon	dau		15		Dur Durham
2886	209v			John Fallon	son		13	scholar	Dur Durham
2887	209v			Thomas Fallon	son		8	scholar	Dur Durham
2888	209v			Mary Jane Fallon	dau		5	scholar	Dur Durham
2889	209v			Emma Fallon	dau		1m		Dur Durham
2890	209v			John R. Fallon	nep		3		Dur Durham
2891	209v	<71>d	Framwelgate	William Waite	hea	m	40	handloom carpet weaver	Wry Sheffield
2892	209v			Dorothy Waite	wif	m	41		Wes Milnthorpe
2893	209v			Elizabeth Waite	dau		12		Wes Kendal
2894	209v			William Waite	son		8	scholar	Dur Durham
2895	209v			Miles Waite	son		5	scholar	Dur Durham
2896	209v			George Waite	son		2		Dur Durham
2897	210r	<71>e	Framwelgate	John Oliver	hea	m	36	mason <& grocer>	Dur [D] Framwelgate
2898	210r			Hannah Oliver	wif	m	35		Dur [D] S. Giles
2899	210r			George Oliver	son		16		Dur [D] Framwelgate
2900	210r			Margaret Oliver	dau		14		Dur [D] Framwelgate
2901	210r			Thomas Oliver	son		10	scholar	Dur [D] Framwelgate
2902	210r			Elizabeth Oliver	dau		9	scholar	Dur [D] Framwelgate

2903	210r	<71>e	Framwelgate	John Oliver	son	7	scholar	Dur [D] Framwelgate
2904	210r			Harriet Oliver	dau	4	scholar	Dur [D] Framwelgate
2905	210r			Eleanor Oliver	dau	2		Dur [D] Framwelgate
2906	210r			Hannah Oliver	dau	3m		Dur [D] Framwelgate
2907	210r	<30>a	Framwelgate	James McJarnen	hea w	73	labourer	Irl
2908	210r			Bridget McJarnen	dau	20		Sct
2909	210r	<30>b	Framwelgate	Robert Balmbrough	hea m	60	bread baker	Yks
2910	210r			William Gowland	slw m	34	shoemaker	Dur [D] S. Oswald
2911	210r			Ann Gowland	dau m	32		Dur [D] S. Oswald
2912	210r			Christopher Gowland	gsn	8	scholar	Dur [D] S. Margaret
2913	210r			Ruth Gowland	gda	6	scholar	Dur [D] S. Margaret
2914	210r			Robert Gowland	gsn	4		Dur [D] S. Margaret
2915	210r			Eleanor Gowland	gda	2		Dur [D] S. Margaret
2916	210r			Mary Ann Proud	ser	14	domestic [servant]	Dur [D] S. Margaret
2917	210r	<30>c	Framwelgate	Susanna Judson	hea	72		Dur [D] S. Margaret
2918	210v	<30>d	Framwelgate	James Ramshaw	hea m	50	agricultural labourer	Sct
2919	210v			Janet Ramshaw	wif m	36		Sct
2920	210v			Janet Ramshaw	dau	9	scholar	Sct
2921	210v			Mary Ramshaw	dau	6	scholar	Sct
2922	210v			Susan Ramshaw	dau	8m		Dur [D] S. Margaret
2923	210v	<30>e	Framwelgate	John O'Coner	hea m	26	agricultural labourer	Irl
2924	210v			Elizabeth O'Coner	wif m	28	nurse	Irl
2925	210v			Catherine O'Coner	dau	9		Irl
2926	210v			James O'Coner	son	6m		Eng
2927	210v	[ba]a	Framwelgate	John Cousin	hea w	76	Chelsea pensioner	Dor Symondsbury
2928	210v	[ba]b	Framwelgate	Mary Binks	hea w	60		Dur Durham
2929	210v			Ann Binks	dau	22	dressmaker	Dur Durham
2930	210v			Henry Binks	son	18	cordwainer	Dur Barnard Castle
2931	210v	[ba]c	Framwelgate	Francis McCabe	hea m	40	labourer	Irl
2932	210v			Catherine McCabe	wif m	43		Irl
2933	210v			Rose Smith	vis	20		Irl
2934	210v	[ba]d	Framwelgate	James Dent	hea m	25	carpet weaver	Dur Barnard Castle
2935	210v			Mary Dent	wif m	21		Dur
2936	210v	[ba]e	Framwelgate	Robert Bell	hea m	26	pipemaker, journeyman	Dur
2937	211r			Jane Bell	wif m	25		Wry Ripon
2938	211r			Robert Bell	son	2		Dur Durham
2939	211r	[ba]f	Framwelgate	Hugh McCan	hea m	40		Irl
2940	211r			Mary McCan	wif m	24		Irl
2941	211r			Ann Mcdonald	mth w	60		Irl
2942	211r			John McCan	son	9		Irl
2943	211r	[ba]g	Framwelgate	George Brown	hea m	41	maltster	Dur Durham
2944	211r			Ann Brown	wif m	41		Dur Durham
2945	211r			Mary Jane Brown	dau	12		Dur [D] Framwelgate
2946	211r			Margaret Brown	dau	4		Dur [D] Framwelgate
2947	211r			Ann Brown	dau	2		Dur [D] Framwelgate
2948	211r	<31>a	Framwelgate	Hannah Doyle	hea m	50	hawker	Irl
2949	211r	<31>b	Framwelgate	Hannah Tate	hea w	72	pauper	Dur Bishopwearmouth
2950	211r	<31>c	Framwelgate	Robert Vasey	hea m	34	tailor	Dur [D] S. Nicholas
2951	211r			Margaret Vasey	wif m	33		Dur [D] S. Margaret
2952	211r			Thomas B. Vasey	son	8	scholar	Dur [D] S. Margaret
2953	211r			Robert Vasey	son	7	scholar	Dur [D] S. Margaret
2954	211r			Horace Vasey	son	5	scholar	Dur [D] S. Margaret
2955	211r			Elizabeth Vasey	dau	8m		Dur [D] S. Margaret
2956	211v	<31>d	Framwelgate	Daniel Cowley	hea m	29	tailor	Cul Whitehaven
2957	211v			Martha Cowley	wif m	28		Sct
2958	211v			William Cowley	son	4		Sct
2959	211v			James Cowley	son	2m		Dur [D] Framwelgate
2960	211v	<31>e	Framwelgate	Elizabeth Smith	hea m	25		Dur
2961	211v			William Smith	son	4		Dur
2962	211v			Joseph Smith	son	2		Dur
2963	211v	<29>a	Framwelgate	George Sewell	hea m	31	tailor	Dur
2964	211v			Jane Sewell	wif m	28		Dur
2965	211v			Susan Sewell	dau	3		Nry Redcar
2966	211v			John Sewell	son	2		Dur Durham
2967	211v	<29>b	Framwelgate	Robert McKenzie	hea m	35	picture gilder	Sct
2968	211v			Mary McKenzie	wif m	36		Sct
2969	211v			Isabella McKenzie	dau	5		Sct
2970	211v			Donald McKenzie	son	3		Dur Durham
2971	211v			Robert McKenzie	son	1		Dur Durham
2972	211v	<29>c	Framwelgate	Daniel Wheatley	hea m	79	woolcomber	Dur Bishop Auckland
2973	211v			Jane Wheatley	wif m	72		Dur
2974	211v	<29>d	Framwelgate	Thomas Penny	hea m	63	joiner, journeyman	Dur West Rainton
2975	211v			Jane Penny	wif m	62		Dur Bishop Auckland
2976	212r			Thomas Penny	son	32	joiner	Dur
2977	212r			William Penny	son	29	joiner	Dur
2978	212r	[bb]a	Framwelgate	Ann Lawrance	hea m	25	stuff weaver	Dur [D] Crossgate
2979	212r			Susan Lawrance	dau	7		Dur Darlington
2980	212r			Matthew Lawrance	son	3		Dur [D] S. Oswald
2981	212r	[bb]b	Framwelgate	Joseph Nattress	hea m	53	quarryman	Cul
2982	212r			Mary Nattress	wif m	53	formerly laundress	Dur [D] Crossgate
2983	212r			Mary Nattress	dau	21	dressmaker	Dur [D] Crossgate

2984	212r	[bb]b	Framwelgate	Isabella Nattress	dau		17		Dur Thornley
2985	212r			Thomas Nattress	son		14	joiner (apprentice)	Dur Thornley
2986	212r	[bb]c	Framwelgate	Sarah Mann	hea		56	fmly straw-bonnetmaker	Dur [D] Framwelgate
2987	212r	[bc]a	Framwelgate	Isabella Gladdley	hea		45	labourer	Dur
2988	212r			Robert Grabham	vis	w	65	labourer	Dur
2989	212r	[bc]b	Framwelgate	Thomas Lambert	hea	m	73	carpet weaver	Wry Stanley
2990	212r			E[lizabeth] Lambert	wif	m	76		Dur Sedgefield
2991	212r	[bc]c	Framwelgate	Thomas Higgs	hea	m	41	house servant	Oxf
2992	212r			Charlotte Higgs	wif	m	40		Dur
2993	212r			George Higgs	son		14		Dur Chester-le-Street
2994	212r			Thomas Higgs	son		11		Dur
2995	212r			James Higgs	son		9		Dur
2996	212v			Charles Higgs	son		5		Dur Durham
2997	212v			Elizabeth Higgs	dau		2		Dur Durham
2998	212v	[bc]d	Framwelgate	John Newby	hea	m	43	labourer	Wry Abbey[dale?]
2999	212v			Mary Newby	wif	m	59		Dur Durham
3000	212v	[bc]e	Framwelgate	Thomas Gorgeson	hea		52	gas fitter	Dur Durham
3001	212v			Robert Beadnell			14	scholar	Dur Durham
3002	212v	<25>	Framwelgate	William Wood	hea	m	65	woolcomber <weaver>	Dur Durham
3003	212v			Elizabeth Wood	wif	m	62		Yks
3004	212v			Samuel Wood	son		22	butcher's man	Dur
3005	212v			Mary Mossam	nce		32	laundress	Dur
3006	212v			William Forster	vis	m	36	traveller, hawker	Dur
3007	212v			Ellen Forster	vis	m	32		Dur
3008	212v	<25>	Framwelgate	Thomas Clarke	hea	m	59	currier *	Dur [D] S. Nicholas
3009	212v			Ann Clarke	wif	m	51		Dur [D] S. Nicholas
3010	212v			Margaret Clarke	dau		17		Dur [D] S. Nicholas
3011	212v			Jane Clarke	dau		14		Dur [D] S. Nicholas
3012	212v			Emmy Clarke	dau		12	scholar	Dur [D] S. Nicholas
3013	212v			Barbara Clarke	dau		8	scholar	Dur [D] S. Nicholas
3014	212v			Alice Clarke	ser		23	house servant	Dur Birtley
3015	213r	<24>	Framwelgate	Robert Barnes	hea	m	58	supervisor *	Lin Louth
3016	213r			Ann Barnes	wif	m	54		Dby Little Hilton
3017	213r			George Barnes	son		20	student	Dur Barnard Castle
3018	213r			Eliza Ann Barnes	dau		18		Dur Barnard Castle
3019	213r			Edwin Barnes	son		13	scholar	Dur Barnard Castle
3020	213r	<23>	Framwelgate	John Embleton	hea	m	68	schoolmaster	Dur Durham
3021	213r			Mary Embleton	wif	m	62	schoolmistress	Dur Durham
3022	213r			Marcella Grievson	sda		19		Dur Durham
3023	213r	<22>	Framwelgate	John G<rant> Telfair	hea		28	accountant	Mdx
3024	213r			James Telfair	fth	w	62	retired tailor	Sct
3025	213r			Margaret Lowes	ser		22	servant	Nbl Newcastle
3026	213r	[bd]	Framwelgate *	Thomas Appleby	hea		50	cartman	Dur [D] Framwelgate
3027	213r			Robert Appleby	nep		23	whitesmith, journeyman	Dur [D] Framwelgate
3028	213r	[be]	Framwelgate	Dorothy Teasdle	hea	w	68		Dur
3029	213r			William Teasdle	son		32	master gunsmith	Dur [D] Framwelgate
3030	213r			Hannah Teasdle	dau		25		Dur [D] Framwelgate
3031	213r	<19>	Framwelgate	Phyllis Williams	hea		39	lady	Dur
3032	213r			Hannah Brown	ser		32	waiting maid	Dur [D] Framwelgate
3033	213r			Ann Conn	ser		20	cook	Dur Lanchester
3034	213v	<18>	Framwelgate	Francis Wharton	hea	m	60	agent * <& bank agent>	Dur Durham
3035	213v			Sarah Wharton	wif	m	54		Dur Gateshead
3036	213v			Sarah H. Wharton	dau		22	daily governess	Dur Durham
3037	213v			Francis Wharton	son		19	assistant in office	Dur Durham
3038	213v			Hannah Wharton	dau		15	scholar	Dur Durham
3039	213v			James F. Wharton	son		14	scholar	Dur Thornley
3040	213v			Mary Cant	vis	w	56	proprietress of houses	Dur Gateshead
3041	213v			Ann Cant	vis		19		Nbl
3042	213v			Ann Gray	ser		21	servant	Dur Whitworth
3043	213v	<17>	Framwelgate	Jane Wheamys	hea	w	60	confectioner	Dur Sunderland
3044	213v			William Wheamys	son	m	34	master cooper	Dur Bishopwearmouth
3045	213v			Julia Wheamys	dlw	m	29		Dur Durham
3046	213v			James Wheamys	gsn		1m		Dur Durham
3047	213v	[bf]a	Framwelgate	William Dykes	hea	m	68	brewer	Nbl North Shields
3048	213v			Elizabeth Dykes	wif	m	64		Nbl North Shields
3049	213v			Thomas Hogg	gsn		6		Nbl Blyth
3050	213v	[bf]b	Framwelgate	Michael Graham	hea	m	55	agricultural labourer	Yks
3051	213v			Mary Graham	wif	m	55		Dur [D] S. Margaret
3052	213v			Jane Graham	dau		31		Dur [D] S. Margaret
3053	213v			John Graham	son		22	miller's waggonman	Dur [D] S. Margaret
3054	214r			Robert Graham	son		14	miller's apprentice	Dur [D] S. Margaret
3055	214r	[bf]c	Framwelgate	Hannah Brown	hea		51	pauper	Dur
3056	214r			Walter Hendry			34	blackingmaker	Wor Kidderminster
3057	214r	[bg]a	Framwelgate	Dorothy Avery	hea		45	laundress	Dur Lanchester
3058	214r			John Avery	son		1		Dur
3059	214r	[bg]b	Framwelgate	George Coxon	hea	m	24	tailor	Dur Houghton-l-Spring
3060	214r			Jane Coxon	wif	m	27		Dur Durham
3061	214r			Thomas Telford	sso		10		Dur [D] S. Margaret
3062	214r			Anne Coxon	dau		1		Dur [D] S. Margaret
3063	214r			Richard Johnson	ldr		18	grocer	Dur [D] S. Giles
3064	214r			Thomas Johnson	ldr		16	tailor's apprentice	Dur [D] S. Giles

3065	214r	[bg]c	Framwelgate	James McDonald	hea	m	58	carpet weaver	Sct
3066	214r			Mary McDonald	wif	m	53		Dur Darlington
3067	214r			James McDonald	son		14	painter's apprentice	Dur Darlington
3068	214r			Thomas McDonald	son		12		Dur Darlington
3069	214r			Christopher Crampton	vis		27	carpet weaver	Sts Stafford
3070	214r	[bg]d	Framwelgate	Elizabeth Carr	hea	w	47	laundress	Dur [D] S. Nicholas
3071	214r	[bg]e	Framwelgate	Robert Morton	hea	m	25	pipemaker, master	Nbl North Shields
3072	214r			Mary Morton	wif	m	40		Dur Sunderland
3073	214r			James Smith	sso		18	pipemaker's apprentice	Dur [D] Framwelgate
3074	214v			Henry Smith	sso		17	grocer's apprentice	Dur Durham
3075	214v			Ann Smith	sda		12	scholar	Dur Durham
3076	214v			George Smith	sso		12	scholar	Dur Durham
3077	214v			Jane Morton	dau		2		Dur Durham
3078	214v	<15>a	Framwelgate	Frances Dixon	hea	w	52	butcher	Dur [D] S. Nicholas
3079	214v	<15>b	Framwelgate	Richard Lowes	hea	m	26	joiner	Dur [D] Framwelgate
3080	214v			Catherine Lowes	wif	m	27		Dur Lanchester
3081	214v			Catherine Lowes	dau		6m		Dur [D] Framwelgate
3082	214v	<14>a	Framwelgate	George Cummings	hea	m	49	cabinetmaker	Dur [D] Framwelgate
3083	214v			Alice Cummings	wif	m	54	laundress	Dur [D] Framwelgate
3084	214v			Jane Cummings	dau		26	dressmaker	Dur [D] Framwelgate
3085	214v			Margaret Cummings	dau		19	scholar	Dur [D] Framwelgate
3086	214v			William Cummings	son		17	grocer (apprentice)	Dur [D] Framwelgate
3087	214v			Joseph Cummings	son		14	scholar	Dur [D] Framwelgate
3088	214v	<14>b	Framwelgate	Wilson Bell	hea	w	53	carpenter <joiner>	Dur
3089	214v			Mary Bell	dau		28		Dur
3090	214v			Francis Bell	son		15	plumber's apprentice	Dur
3091	214v	<14>c	Framwelgate	Isaac Suthers	hea	w	51	woolcomber	Dur
3092	214v			Edward Suthers	son		18	carpet weaver	Dur
3093	215r	<13>a	Framwelgate	William Blagdon	hea	w	50	cordwainer	Dur Durham
3094	215r			Harriet Hall	vis	w	46		Nbl Hexham
3095	215r			Peter Philipps	ldr		26	currier	Dur Stockton
3096	215r			Richard Taylor	ldr		19	currier	Wes Appleby
3097	215r	<13>b	Framwelgate	Thomas Sutters	hea	w	71	worsted manufacturer *	Lan Rawtenstall *
3098	215r			Hannah Sutters	dau		30		Dur Durham
3099	215r			Ephraim Sutters	son		19	tailor	Mdx London
3100	215r	<13>c	Framwelgate	Rebecca Dalton	hea	w	68	shoebinder; pauper	Dur Durham
3101	215r	<13>d	Framwelgate	Elizabeth Burton	hea	w	50	washerwoman	Dur Durham
3102	215r			Deborah Burton	dau		22		Dur
3103	215r			John Burton	son		20	cordwainer	Dur Houghton-l-Spring
3104	215r			Thomas Burton	son		18	mason (apprentice)	Dur
3105	215r			George Burton	son	m	16	mason (apprentice)	Dur
3106	215r	<13>e	Framwelgate	John Maddison	hea	m	61	joiner	Dur
3107	215r			Ann Maddison	wif	m	57		Dur Wolsingham
3108	215r			Catherine Maddison	dau		27	dressmaker	Dur
3109	215r	[bh]a	Framwelgate	Mary Hopper	hea	w	54	washerwoman	Dur Lumley
3110	215r			John Hopper	son		19	mason	Dur Lumley
3111	215r			George Hopper	son		8	scholar	Dur
3112	215v	[bh]b	Framwelgate	William Emmerson	hea	m	34	carpet weaver	Dur Barnard Castle
3113	215v			Elizabeth Emmerson	wif	m	34		Dur
3114	215v			Thomas Emmerson	son		13		Dur
3115	215v			John Emmerson	son		9		Dur
3116	215v			Ann Emmerson	dau		7	scholar	Dur
3117	215v			William Emmerson	son		5		Dur
3118	215v			Hannah Emmerson	dau		3		Dur
3119	215v			Elizabeth Emmerson	dau		1m		Dur
3120	215v	[bh]c	Framwelgate	William Grant	hea	m	31	carpet weaver	on the sea
3121	215v			Jane Grant	wif	m	26		Sct
3122	215v			Mary A. Grant	dau		3		Dur Durham
3123	215v			Elizabeth Grant	dau		2		Dur Durham
3124	215v			Charles Grant	son		3m		Dur Durham
3125	215v	[bi]a	Framwelgate	Margaret Cain	hea	w	69	formerly house servant	Cul Sebergham *
3126	215v			John Dixon	son	w	36	mason	Cul Cockermouth
3127	215v			Elizabeth Dixon	gda		12	scholar	Dur [D] Framwelgate
3128	215v			John Dixon	gsn		10	scholar	Dur [D] Framwelgate
3129	215v			Solomon Dixon	gsn		7	scholar	Dur [D] Framwelgate
3130	215v	[bi]b	Framwelgate	Hugh Moon	hea	m	34	shoemaker	Irl
3131	215v			Ellen Moon	wif	m	24		Irl
3132	216r			John Moon	son		1		Dur Durham
3133	216r			Jane Moon	dau		7m		Dur Durham
3134	216r			Mary Moon	mth	w	60		Irl
3135	216r	[bi]c	Framwelgate	Hugh Duffy	hea	m	34	mason	Nbl Stamfordham
3136	216r			Jane Duffy	wif	m	30		Nbl Newcastle
3137	216r			Ann Duffy	dau		13		Nbl Newcastle
3138	216r			William Duffy	son		8	scholar	Nbl Newcastle
3139	216r			John Duffy	son		5	scholar	Dur Hunwick
3140	216r			Hugh Duffy	son		2		Dur [D] Framwelgate
3141	216r	[bi]d	Framwelgate	George Cockburn	hea	m	40	shoemaker	Dur Waldridge Fell
3142	216r			Ellen Cockburn	wif	m	40		Dur [D] Framwelgate
3143	216r			George Cockburn	son		12	scholar	Dur [D] Framwelgate
3144	216r			Catherine Cockburn	dau		10	scholar	Dur [D] Framwelgate
3145	216r			Isabella Cockburn	dau		8	scholar	Dur [D] Framwelgate

3146	216r	[bi]d	Framwelgate	John Cockburn	son		5	scholar	Dur [D] Framwelgate
3147	216r	[bi]e	Framwelgate	William Smith	hea	m	43	shoemaker, master	Dur [D] Framwelgate
3148	216r			Ellen Smith	wif	m	37		Nbl Newcastle
3149	216r			John Smith	son		17	mason (apprentice)	Dur Durham
3150	216r			Ellen Smith	dau		10		Dur Durham
3151	216r			Margaret Smith	dau		4		Dur Durham
3152	216v			William Smith	son		7m		Dur [D] Framwelgate
3153	216v	<12>a	Framwelgate	Mary Lowes	hea	w	71	annuitant	Dur S. John's Chapel
3154	216v			Emmerson Anderson	gsn		10	scholar	Dur Durham
3155	216v			Margaret Anderson	gda		7	scholar	Dur Durham
3156	216v	<12>b	Framwelgate	Richard Hope	hea	m	43	woolcomber	Dur [D] Framwelgate
3157	216v			Ann Hope	wif	m	30		Dur Aycliffe
3158	216v			Richard Hope	son	w	17	barber (apprentice)	Dur [D] Framwelgate
3159	216v			Robert Hope	son		11	scholar	Dur [D] Framwelgate
3160	216v			William Brown	sso		8	scholar	Dur Aycliffe
3161	216v	<12>c	Framwelgate	William Turnbull	hea	m	41	joiner	Dur [D] S. Margaret
3162	216v			Jane Turnbull	wif	m	47	dressmaker	Dur [D] Framwelgate
3163	216v			William Turnbull	son		16	att[orney']s clerk	Dur [D] Framwelgate
3164	216v			John Turnbull	son		14	currier	Dur [D] Framwelgate
3165	216v			Henry Turnbull	son		7	scholar	Dur [D] Framwelgate
3166	216v			Mary Turnbull	dau		4	scholar	Dur [D] Framwelgate
3167	216v	[bj]	Framwelgate	Michael O'Hanley	hea	m	26	labourer	Irl
3168	216v			Margaret O'Hanley	wif	m	30		Irl
3169	216v			Michael O'Hanley	son		5		Irl
3170	216v			Sarah O'Hanley	dau		3m		Dur Durham
3171	216v			James O'Hanley	bro		20	labourer	Irl
3172	217r			John Sullivan	vis	w	40	labourer	Irl
3173	217r	<11>	Framwelgate	Thomas Oliver	hea	m	64	mason & innkeeper *	Dur [D] Framwelgate
3174	217r			Margaret Oliver	wif	m	64		Dur [D] S. Nicholas
3175	217r			Mary Johnson	gda		15	servant	Dur [D] S. Nicholas
3176	217r			Richard Johnson	gsn		13	scholar	Dur [D] S. Nicholas
3177	217r			William Johnson	nep		21	printer's apprentice	Dur [D] S. Nicholas
3178	217r			Edward Lows	ldr		25	tobacconist	Ken Sandgate
3179	217r	<9>	Framwelgate	Thomas Paxton	hea	m	66	farmer *	Dur Easington
3180	217r			Jane Paxton	wif	m	66		Dur Wolsingham
3181	217r			William Paxton	son		40		Dur [D] Framwelgate
3182	217r			Thomas Paxton	son		37		Dur [D] Framwelgate
3183	217r			Ann Smith	ser		16	house servant	Dur Rainton
3184	217r	<8>a	Framwelgate	Mary Liddle	hea	w	41	grocer	Dur Lanchester
3185	217r			John Liddle	son		16	grocer (apprentice)	Dur
3186	217r			Thomas Liddle	son		14	joiner's apprentice	Dur
3187	217r			Mary Liddle	dau		11	scholar	Dur
3188	217r			William Liddle	son		7	scholar	Dur
3189	217r	<8>b	Framwelgate	Thomas Salter	hea	m	26	mason	Dur Felling Shore
3190	217r			Mary Salter	wif	m	35		Dur [D] S. Giles
3191	217r			Elizabeth Stobbart	sda		9		Dur [D] Framwelgate
3192	217v			Thomas Smith Salter	son		6m		Dur [D] Framwelgate
3193	217v			Thomas Smith	flw	w	65	carpet weaver	Dur Sedgefield
3194	217v	<8>c	Framwelgate	Elizabeth Dixon	hea		57	proprietor of houses	Dur [D] S. Nicholas
3195	217v	[bk]a	Framwelgate	Daniel Robinson	hea	m	41	pensioner	Nbl Alnwick
3196	217v			Sarah Robinson	wif	m	28		Dur Newbottle
3197	217v	[bk]b	Framwelgate	Thomas McEvoy	hea	m	28	labourer	Sct
3198	217v			Mary McEvoy	wif	m	21		Sct
3199	217v	<10>a	Framwelgate	William Thornton	hea	m	31	husbandman	Dur Cornsay
3200	217v			Susan Thornton	wif	m	27		Dur Lumley
3201	217v			Thomas Thornton	son		5	scholar	Dur Lumley
3202	217v			Mary Thornton	dau		3		Dur Brandon
3203	217v	<10>b	Framwelgate	Ann Pearson	hea		44	dyer	Dur [D] Framwelgate
3204	217v	<10>c	Framwelgate	William Wall	hea	m	47	agricultural labourer	Dur
3205	217v			Sarah Wall	wif	m	40		Dur
3206	217v			William Samson			21	baker, journeyman	Dur
3207	217v			John Kelly			21	carpet weaver	Dur
3208	217v			John Smith			21	joiner	Dur
3209	217v	<62>	Framwelgate	Elizabeth Eggelston	hea	w	72	income from mortgages	Nbl Corbridge
3210	217v			Margaret Patterson	ser		19	house servant	Dur Gateshead
3211	217v	<51>	Framwelgate	John Allan	hea	m	34	rope merchant *	Dur [D] S. Mary-1-Bow
3212	218r			Ann Allan	wif	m	25		Dur [D] S. Margaret
3213	218r			Mary Allan	dau		7		Dur [D] S. Margaret
3214	218r			William Allan	son		5		Dur [D] S. Margaret
3215	218r			John E. Allan	son		3		Dur [D] S. Margaret
3216	218r			Samuel Allan	son		2		Dur [D] S. Margaret
3217	218r			Mary Jannest	ser		14	house servant	Nbl Newcastle
3218	218r	[bl]	Framwelgate	Henry Stephens	hea	m	24	cordwainer	Nbl Berwick
3219	218r			Jane Stephens	wif	m	35		Dur Durham
3220	218r			George Wallace	sso		12	cordwainer (apprentice)	Dur Durham
3221	218r			William Wallace	sso		10	scholar	Dur Durham
3222	218r			Thomas Wallace	sso		7	scholar	Dur Durham
3223	218r	<58>	Framwelgate	George Walton	hea	m	78	retired innkeeper	Dur Iveston
3224	218r			Jane Walton	wif	m	75		Dur Witton Gilbert
3225	218r	[bm]	Framwelgate	Henry Redshaw	hea		23	currier	Dur [D] Framwelgate
3226	218r			John Redshaw	bro		9	scholar	Dur [D] Framwelgate

3227	218r	[bm]	Framwelgate	Ann Wilson	vis	w	65		Nry Newham
3228	218r	<63>a	Framwelgate	Robert Morgan	hea	m	54	agricultural labourer	not known
3229	218r			Hannah Morgan	wif	m	36		Lin Normanby
3230	218r			Mary Jane Morgan	dau		14	scholar	Dur [D] Framwelgate
3231	218r			Elizabeth Ann Morgan	dau		7	scholar	Dur [D] Framwelgate
3232	218v			Robert Morgan	son		7	scholar	Dur [D] Framwelgate
3233	218v			Theresa Morgan	dau		4		Dur [D] Framwelgate
3234	218v	<63>b	Framwelgate	William Campbell	hea	m	45	blacksmith	Dur Plawsworth
3235	218v			Ann Campbell	wif	m	50		Nry Melsonby
3236	218v			William Campbell	son		14	grocer (apprentice)	Dur [D] Framwelgate
3237	218v			Thomas Campbell	son		13	scholar	Dur [D] Framwelgate
3238	218v	[bn]	Framwelgate <Head>	Thomas Fenny	hea	m	45	agricultural labourer *	Wry Halton
3239	218v			Mary Fenny	wif	m	45		Dur Durham
3240	218v			Thomas Fenny	son		20	agricultural labourer	Dur Biggen
3241	218v			Isabella Fenny	dau		16		Dur [D] Framwelgate
3242	218v			Hannah Fabley	ser		17	[servant]	Yks
3243	218v	[bo]	Framwelgate	Archibald Stallie	hea		40	labourer	Sct
3244	218v			Mary Johnson			49		Eng
3245	218v	<61>	Framwelgate	Robert Oliver	hea	m	39	mason & innkeeper *	Dur Durham
3246	218v			Mary Oliver	wif	m	35		Dur Whitworth
3247	218v			Jane Oliver	dau		17		Dur Durham
3248	218v			John Oliver	son		15	mason's apprentice	Dur Durham
3249	218v			Margaret Oliver	dau		12		Dur Durham
3250	218v	[bp]	Framwelgate	John Baitson	hea	m	38	bookbinder	Dur Durham
3251	218v			Ann Baitson	wif	m	38		Dur Durham
3252	219r			Margaret B. Batson	dau		12	scholar	Dur [D] Framwelgate
3253	219r			Jane S. Batson	dau		8	scholar	Dur [D] Framwelgate
3254	219r			Thomas G. Batson	son		5	scholar	Dur [D] Framwelgate
3255	219r			Ann S. Batson	dau		2		Dur [D] Framwelgate
3256	219r			Mary E. Batson	dau		2m		Dur [D] Framwelgate
3257	219r	<64>a	Framwelgate	Thomas Oliver	hea	m	31	mason	Dur
3258	219r			Jane Oliver	wif	m	32		Irl
3259	219r	<64>b	Framwelgate	John Hall	hea	w	48	gardener, master	Dur Durham
3260	219r			John Hall	son		22	gardener	Dur Durham
3261	219r			Ann Gowland	ser	w	58	house servant	Nry Marske
3262	219r	<64>c	Framwelgate	James Powney	hea	m	34	quarryman	Dur Merrington
3263	219r			Jane Powney	wif	m	32		Dur Durham
3264	219r			Jane Powney	dau		11		Dur Merrington
3265	219r			John Powney	son		8	scholar	Dur [D] S. Margaret
3266	219r			William James Powney	son		3		Dur [D] S. Margaret
3267	219r			Mary El. Powney	dau		11m		Dur [D] Framwelgate
3268	219r	[bq]	Framwelgate *	Robert Hudson	hea	m	63	cartman	Dur Brancepeth
3269	219r			Jane Hudson	wif	m	62		Dur South Church
3270	219r			John Hudson	son		17	whitesmith, apprentice	Dur Durham
3271	223v*	[br]	Framwelgate	John Swinburn	hea	m	42	tobacconist's clerk	Dur Sunderland
3272	223v			Mary A. Swinburn	wif	m	32		Dur Staindrop
3273	223v			John Swinburn	son		9	scholar	Dur Quarrington Hill
3274	223v			William B. Swinburn	son		7	scholar	Dur Durham
3275	223v			Alice Swinburn	dau		3		Dur Durham
3276	223v			Joseph Swinburn	son		1		Dur Durham
3277	223v			Mary Ann Elgy	ser		16	house servant	Dur Chester-le-Street
3278	223v	[bs]a	Framwelgate	William Turnbull	hea	m	23	mason	Dur Durham
3279	223v			Mary Turnbull	wif	m	21		Dur Durham
3280	223v			Elizabeth Turnbull	dau		2		Dur Durham
3281	223v			William Turnbull	son		3m		Dur Durham
3282	223v	[bs]b	Framwelgate	Ann Clasper	hea	w	42	laundress	Dur Chester-le-Street
3283	223v			John Clasper	son		17	grocer (apprentice)	Dur Lanchester
3284	223v	[bs]c	Framwelgate	Christopher Liddle	hea	w	36	cordwainer	Dur [D] S. Nicholas
3285	223v			Sarah Liddle	dau		8		Dur [D] Framwelgate
3286	223v			William Liddle	son		6		Dur [D] Framwelgate
3287	223v	[bs]d	Framwelgate	Ann Leroy	hea	w	34	pauper	Dur [D] Elvet
3288	223v			Sarah Leroy	dau		14	dressmaker	Dur [D] S. Margaret
3289	223v			Margaret Leroy	dau		12	errand girl	Dur [D] Elvet
3290	223v			Jane Leroy	dau		7	errand girl	Dur [D] S. Margaret
3291	224r			Elizabeth Leroy	dau		5	scholar	Dur [D] S. Margaret
3292	224r			David Leroy	son		1		Dur [D] S. Margaret
3293	224r			Thomas Douglas	ldr		29	retired roper	Dur [D] S. Margaret
3294	224r	[bt]	Framwelgate	George Allan	hea	m	51		Dur
3295	224r			Isabella Allan	wif	m	48		Dur
3296	224r			George Allan	son		26	agricultural labourer	Dur
3297	224r			John Allan	son		23	agricultural labourer	Dur
3298	224r			Joseph Allan	son		18	saddler	Dur
3299	224r			Isabella Allan	dau		12		Dur
3300	224r			Thomas Allan	son	m	11		Dur
3301	224r			Robert Allan	son		7		Dur
3302	224r	[bu]a	Framwelgate	William Wilkinson	hea	m	44	labourer	Dur [D] Framwelgate
3303	224r			Mary Wilkinson	wif	m	44		Dur [D] S. Giles
3304	224r			Thomas Wilkinson	son		21	hairdresser	Dur [D] S. Giles
3305	224r			John Wilkinson	son		16	mason's apprentice	Dur [D] S. Giles
3306	224r			Thomas Wilkinson	bro		48	mason	Dur [D] Framwelgate
3307	224r	[bu]b	Framwelgate	William Liddle	hea	m	32	tailor [&] draper	Dur [D] S. Margaret

3308	224r	[bu]b	Framwelgate	Isabella Liddle	wif m	23		Dur [D] S. Giles
3309	224r			Rosanna Liddle	dau	9	scholar	Dur [D] S. Giles
3310	224r			Charles Liddle	son	7	scholar	Dur [D] S. Margaret
3311	224v			Thomas Liddle	son	7m		Dur [D] S. Margaret
3312	224v	[bu]c	Framwelgate	Caroline Raine	hea m	30	washerwoman	Nry Richmond
3313	224v			Edward Raine	son	2		Dur [D] S. Margaret
3314	224v			Catherine Raine	dau	6m		Dur [D] Framwelgate
3315	224v	[bu]d	Framwelgate	Robert Brown	hea m	32	cordwainer	Dur [D] S. Nicholas
3316	224v			Jane Brown	wif m	31		Dur Durham
3317	224v	[bu]e	Framwelgate	Ann Foster	hea w	61	pauper	Dur Barnard Castle
3318	224v			Timothy Foster	son	20	carpet weaver	Dur [D] S. Nicholas
3319	224v	[bu]f	Framwelgate	William Milburn	hea m	27	coal miner	Nry Danby
3320	224v			Barbara Milburn	wif m	24		Dur [D] S. Nicholas
3321	224v			William Milburn	son	2		Dur [D] Framwelgate
3322	224v	[bv]a	Framwelgate	John Turnbull	hea m	36	cordwainer	Dur [D] S. Margaret
3323	224v			Jane Turnbull	wif m	33		Dur [D] S. Margaret
3324	224v			Joseph Turnbull	son	13	scholar	Dur [D] S. Margaret
3325	224v			Jane Turnbull	dau	11	scholar	Dur [D] S. Margaret
3326	224v			Elias Turnbull	son	9	scholar	Dur [D] S. Margaret
3327	224v			John Turnbull	son	7	scholar	Dur [D] S. Margaret
3328	224v			Ann Turnbull	dau	5	scholar	Dur [D] S. Margaret
3329	224v			Robert Turnbull	son	1		Dur [D] S. Margaret
3330	224v	[bv]b	Framwelgate	William Swinburn	hea m	47	labourer	Nbl Hexham
3331	225r			John Swinburn		23		Nbl Hexham
3332	225r	[bv]c	Framwelgate	Harriet Martin	hea m	32	sempstress	Sts Lichfield
3333	225r	[bv]d	Framwelgate	Benjamin Hill	hea m	40	labourer	Dur Durham
3334	225r			Sarah Hill	wif m	38	formerly servant	Dur Sunderland
3335	225r			Mary A. Newton	sda	21	charwoman /"chairwoman"	Dur Fishburn
3336	225r			Benjamin G. Newton	sso	15	errand boy	Dur Durham
3337	225r			John Newton	sso	12	errand boy	Dur Durham
3338	225r			Isabella Hill	dau	9	scholar	Dur Durham
3339	225r			George Hill	son	6	scholar	Dur Durham
3340	225r	[bw]	Framwelgate	William Walton	hea m	39	tobacconist	Wry Leeds
3341	225r			Martha Walton	wif m	38		Wry Leeds
3342	225r			Elizabeth Walton	dau	13		Wry Leeds
3343	225r			Charles Walton	son	11		Wry Leeds
3344	225r			Mary Walton	dau	7		Dur Durham
3345	225r			Ann Walton	dau	4		Dur Durham
3346	225r			William H. Walton	son	2		Dur Durham
3347	225r	<47>	Framwelgate	Robert Adamson	hea m	28	mason & innkeeper *	Dur Durham
3348	225r			Jane Adamson	wif m	29		Dur Durham
3349	225r			Thomas Adamson	son	5		Dur Durham
3350	225r			Margaret Adamson	dau	2		Dur Durham
3351	225v	[bx]a	Framwelgate	Mary Smith	hea w	71	householder	Nbl Newburn *
3352	225v	[bx]b	Framwelgate	Robert Appleby	hea m	43	joiner	Dur [D] S. Margaret
3353	225v			Jane Appleby	wif m	40		Dur [D] S. Oswald
3354	225v			Henry Appleby	son	17	joiner	Dur [D] S. Margaret
3355	225v			Ann Appleby	dau	15	scholar	Dur [D] S. Margaret
3356	225v			Thomas Appleby	son	10	scholar	Dur [D] S. Margaret
3357	225v			William Appleby	son	6	scholar	Dur [D] S. Margaret
3358	225v			Robert Appleby	son	3		Dur [D] S. Margaret
3359	225v	[bx]c	Framwelgate	Elizabeth Davinson	hea w	74	gingerbread-baker	Dur South Shields
3360	225v			Hannah Davinson	dau	32	laundress	Dur [D] S. Margaret
3361	225v			William Davinson	son	24	ropemaker	Dur [D] S. Margaret
3362	225v	[bx]d	Framwelgate	Thomas Liddle	hea m	35	shoemaker	Dur
3363	225v			Sarah Liddle	wif m	31		Dur
3364	225v			John Liddle	son	11		Dur
3365	225v			Christopher Liddle	son	9		Dur
3366	225v			Robert Liddle	son	4		Dur
3367	225v			Sarah Liddle	dau	2		Dur
3368	225v	[by]	Framwelgate	Robert Forster	hea m	26	mason	Dur
3369	225v			Margaret Forster	wif	23		Dur
3370	225v			Henry Forster	son	2		Dur
3371	226r			George Forster	son	5m		Dur
3372	226r	[bz]a	Framwelgate	Michael Pickring	hea m	46	butcher	Dur Lanchester
3373	226r			Margaret Pickring	wif m	36	dressmaker	Dur [D] Framwelgate
3374	226r	[bz]b	Framwelgate	Thomas Robinson	hea m	83	Chelsea pensioner	Dur [D] Framwelgate
3375	226r	[bz]c	Framwelgate	William Fenwick	hea m	42	agricultural labourer	Dur [D] Framwelgate
3376	226r			Phyllis Fenwick	wif m	42		Dur [D] Framwelgate
3377	226r			George Fenwick	son	12		Dur [D] Framwelgate
3378	226r			Mary A. Fenwick	dau	5		Dur [D] Framwelgate
3379	226r			Elizabeth Sewell	m	47	washerwoman	Dur [D] Framwelgate
3380	226r	[bz]d	Framwelgate	Robert Robson	hea m	36	joiner	Dur [D] Framwelgate
3381	226r			Catherine Robson	wif m	30		Nry Otterington
3382	226r			Thomas Robson	son	14	tailor, apprentice	Dur [D] Framwelgate
3383	226r			Mary Jane Robson	dau	11	scholar	Dur [D] Framwelgate
3384	226r			Mary Ann Robson	dau	7	scholar	Dur [D] Framwelgate
3385	226r			Hannah Robson	dau	3	scholar	Dur [D] Framwelgate
3386	226r			Robert Robson	son	1		Dur [D] Framwelgate
3387	226r	[bz]e	Framwelgate	Thomas Dixon	hea m	26	labourer	Dur [D] Framwelgate
3388	226r			Margaret Dixon	wif m	22		Dur [D] Framwelgate

3389	226r	[bz]e	Framwelgate	Ann Dixon	dau	5		Dur [D] Framwelgate	
3390	226r	[ca]a	Framwelgate	Ann Briggs	hea	29	charwoman /"chairwoman"	Dur Durham	
3391	226v			Phyllis Briggs	dau	3	scholar	Dur Durham	
3392	226v			Matthew Briggs	son	5m		Dur Durham	
3393	226v			Jane Evington	ser	26	servant	Dur Durham	
3394	226v	[ca]b	Framwelgate	John Lewis	hea m	39	husbandman	Nry Guisborough	
3395	226v			Ann Lewis	wif m	40		Ham Isle of Wight	
3396	226v			Ann Lewis	dau	13		Dur Durham	
3397	226v			Mary Lewis	dau	8		Dur Durham	
3398	226v	[ca]c	Framwelgate	Robert Wilson	hea m	28	labourer	Dur Bishop Auckland	
3399	226v			Mary Wilson	wif m	32		Dur Barnard Castle	
3400	226v			Elizabeth Wilson	dau	10	scholar	Dur [D] Framwelgate	
3401	226v			Thomas Wilson	son	6	scholar	Dur [D] Framwelgate	
3402	226v			Hannah Wilson	dau	3		Dur [D] S. Nicholas	
3403	226v	<78>a	Framwelgate	George Gibson	hea m	30	joiner	Dur [D] Framwelgate	
3404	226v			Alice Gibson	wif m	32		Dur [D] Framwelgate	
3405	226v			Margaret Nicholson	sda	12	scholar	Dur	
3406	226v			Frances Gibson	dau	7	scholar	Dur [D] Framwelgate	
3407	226v			Mary A. Gibson	dau	6		Dur Sunderland	
3408	226v			George Gibson	son	9m		Dur [D] Framwelgate	
3409	226v	<78>b	Framwelgate	Robert Laws	hea m	70	labourer	Dur Ryton	
3410	226v			Ann Laws	wif m	67	laundress	Dur Medomsley	
3411	227r	[cb]	Framwelgate	William Winkup	hea w	81	fishmonger	Wry Leeds	
3412	227r			Elizabeth Brown	ser	41	house servant	Nry Cleasby	
3413	227r			William Brown	*	21	labourer	Dur Bishop Auckland	
3414	227r			Fanny Tugby	vis m	26	dressmaker	Lei Whitwick	
3415	227r	[cc]	Framwelgate	John Hind	hea m	45	labourer	Dur Durham	
3416	227r			Margaret Hind	wif m	48		Dur Durham	
3417	227r			Robert Hind	son	19	tailor, apprentice	Dur Durham	
3418	227r			Charlton Hind	son	16	mason, apprentice	Dur Durham	
3419	227r			Mary Hind	dau	13	scholar	Dur Durham	
3420	227r			Emma Hind	dau	7	scholar	Dur Durham	
3421	227r			Thomas Hind	son	4	scholar	Dur Durham	
3422	227r			William Hind	son	1		Dur Durham	
3423	227r	[cd]a	Framwelgate	Anne Bailes	hea m	32		Dur Durham	
3424	227r			Samuel Bailes	son	7		Dur Durham	
3425	227r			Maria Bailes	dau	2		Dur Durham	
3426	227r	[cd]b	Framwelgate	James Cowley	hea m	50	shoemaker	Irl	
3427	227r			Catherine Cowley	wif m	49		Irl	
3428	227r			William Cowley	son	13	shoemaker's apprentice	Irl	
3429	227r			John Cowley	son	9	scholar	Irl	
3430	227r			Patrick Downs	nep	19	shoemaker's apprentice	Irl	
3431	227v			Maurice Connars	nep	18	labourer	Irl	
3432	227v			Catherine Connars	nce	24	worker at paper mill	Irl	
3433	227v	<41>a	Framwelgate	Ann Hall	hea w	49	shopkeeper	Dur Durham	
3434	227v			Ann Hall	dau	22		Dur Durham	
3435	227v			Mary Hall	dau	15		Dur Durham	
3436	227v	<41>b	Framwelgate	William Beugless	hea m	28	police constable	Nbl Elsdon	
3437	227v			Ann Beugless	wif m	30		Nbl Bellingham *	
3438	227v			Edward Beugless	son	3		Dur [D] S. Nicholas	
3439	227v			Jane Beugless	dau	1		Dur [D] S. Oswald	
3440	227v	<41>c	Framwelgate	Edward Hopper	hea m	32	joiner	Dur Durham	
3441	227v			Margaret Hopper	wif m	31		Dur Durham	
3442	227v	<41>d	Framwelgate	Hannah Condon	hea w	73	pauper	Dur Brancepeth	
3443	227v			Hannah Condon	dau	26	pauper	Dur Brandon	
3444	227v	<41>e	Framwelgate	Ann Wascoe	hea w	78	pauper	Dur Whitworth	
3445	227v	<41>f	Framwelgate	Peter Devlin	hea m	39	labourer	Irl	
3446	227v			Margaret Devlin	wif m	35		Sct	
3447	227v			Robert Devlin'	son	9		Sct	
3448	227v			Thomas Devlin	son	4		Irl	
3449	227v			Jonah Byrns	vis w	39	ropemaker	Irl	
3450	227v			Jonah Byrns	vis	13	draw boy	Irl	
3451	228r			Patrick Muldon	vis m	24	plasterer's labourer	Irl	
3452	228r	<41>g	Framwelgate	Patrick Ryness	hea m	40	labourer	Irl	
3453	228r			Ann Ryness	wif m	40		Irl	
3454	228r			Patrick Ryness	son	18	miner	Irl	
3455	228r			Margaret Ryness	dau	14		Irl	
3456	228r			Jonah Ryness	son	12		Irl	
3457	228r			Mary Ryness	dau	7		Irl	
3458	228r	<41>h	Framwelgate	James Emmerson	hea m	35	grocer	Dur [D] S. Margaret	
3459	228r			Ellen Emmerson	wif m	36		Dur [D] S. Margaret	
3460	228r	<40>a	Framwelgate	Joseph Wilson	hea m	26	sawyer	Nry Middleham	
3461	228r			Mary Wilson	wif m	22		Dur Stockton	
3462	228r			Elizabeth Wilson	dau	2		Dur Stockton	
3463	228r			Hannah Wilson	dau	7m		Dur Sunderland	
3464	228r	<40>b	Framwelgate	George Myers	hea m	44	worsted manufacturer	Dur Durham	
3465	228r			Mary Myers	wif m	43		Dur Durham	
3466	228r			John Myers	son	18	worsted manufacturer app	Dur Durham	
3467	228r			Ann Myers	dau	16		Dur Durham	
3468	228r			Mary Myers	dau	14	scholar	Dur Durham	
3469	228r			Margaret Myers	dau	11	scholar	Dur Durham	

3470	228r	<40>b	Framwelgate	George Myers	son		5	scholar	Dur Durham
3471	228v			Elizabeth Myers	dau		7m		Dur Durham
3472	228v	<40>c	Framwelgate	John Wallace	hea m		28	joiner	Dur Durham
3473	228v			Ann Wallace	wif m		29		Dur Newbottle
3474	228v			Ann Wallace	dau		6		Dur Durham
3475	228v			John Wallace	son		1		Dur Durham
3476	228v	<40>d	Framwelgate	Elizabeth Davinson	hea w		66	pauper	Dur Durham
3477	228v			John Tallon	ldr m		35	cutler	Irl
3478	228v			Elizabeth Tallon	ldw		33		Sct
3479	228v	<39>a	Framwelgate	John Taylor	hea m		66	labourer	Yks Norton Banks
3480	228v			Margaret Taylor	wif m		65		Dur [D] Framwelgate
3481	228v			John Taylor	son		29	cordwainer	Dur [D] Framwelgate
3482	228v			James Taylor	son		24	grocer's assistant	Dur [D] Framwelgate
3483	228v			Frances Taylor	dau		22	dressmaker <milliner>	Dur [D] Framwelgate
3484	228v			Robert Nicholson	gsn		11	scholar	Dur [D] Framwelgate
3485	228v			Margaret Taylor	gda		3	scholar	Dur [D] Framwelgate
3486	228v	<39>b	Framwelgate	William Thoubron	hea m		56	labourer	Dur Durham
3487	228v			Elizabeth Thoubron	wif m		55		Dur Durham
3488	228v			James Thoubron	son w		28	tailor	Dur Durham
3489	228v			Thomas Thoubron	son		17	labourer	Dur Durham
3490	228v			Francis Thoubron	son		15	shoemaker's apprentice	Dur Durham
3491	229r			Henry Thobourn	dau		13	miller's apprentice	Dur Durham
3492	229r			Jane Thubron	dau		11	scholar	Dur Durham
3493	229r	<39>c	Framwelgate	William Wallace	hea m		50	labourer	Cul Alston Moor
3494	229r			Dorothy Wallace	wif m		45		Nbl Hartburn *
3495	229r			Elizabeth Wallace	dau		21		Dur [D] S. Nicholas
3496	229r			William Wallace	son		19	shoemaker's apprentice	Dur [D] S. Giles
3497	229r			Catherine Wallace	dau		9		Dur [D] S. Nicholas
3498	229r			Thomas Wallace	son		5	scholar	Dur [D] S. Nicholas
3499	229r			John Wallace	son		4		Dur [D] S. Nicholas
3500	229r			Mary Ann Wallace	dau		3m		Dur [D] Framwelgate
3501	229r	<39>d	Framwelgate	John Gott	hea m		69	labourer	Dur [D] S. Giles
3502	229r			Isabella Gott	wif m		53		Dur [D] S. Giles
3503	229r			John Gott	son m		21	miller	Dur [D] S. Nicholas
3504	229r			Mary A. Gott	dau m		21		Dur Shotley Bridge
3505	229r			Mary J. Gott	dau		10		Dur [D] S. Margaret
3506	229r	[ce]a	Framwelgate	George Ranson	hea m		39	cordwainer	Dur Durham
3507	229r			Elizabeth Ranson	wif m		38		Nbl
3508	229r	[ce]b	Framwelgate	Ellen Oliver	hea m		38	sempstress; pauper	Sct
3509	229r			Catherine Oliver	dau		18		Sct
3510	229r			Betsy Oliver	dau		15	factory girl	Irl
3511	229v			William Oliver	son		11	factory boy	Sct
3512	229v			James Oliver	son		9	scholar	Dur Bishop Auckland
3513	229v			Mary Oliver	dau		6	scholar	Dur Durham
3514	229v			Thomas Oliver	son		3	scholar	Dur Durham
3515	229v	<90>a	Framwelgate	William Wilson	hea w		43	tailor <& publican *>	Dur Durham
3516	229v			John Grey Wilson	son		23	nailer	Dur Durham
3517	229v			William Wilson	son		19	tailor	Dur Durham
3518	229v			Robert Wilson	son		17	cordwainer	Dur Durham
3519	229v			Elizabeth Wilson	dau		14		Dur Durham
3520	229v			Catherine Wilson	dau		12		Dur Durham
3521	229v	<90>b	Framwelgate	William Purvis	hea m		36	carpet weaver	Dur [D] Framwelgate
3522	229v			Hannah Purvis	wif m		31		Dur [D] Framwelgate
3523	229v			Jane Purvis	dau		10		Dur [D] Framwelgate
3524	229v			Eleanor Purvis	dau		7		Dur [D] Framwelgate
3525	229v			Elizabeth Purvis	dau		3		Dur [D] Framwelgate
3526	229v			Hannah Purvis	dau		2m		Dur [D] Framwelgate
3527	229v	[cf]a	Framwelgate	Ann Ross	hea		41	pauper	Dur [D] Framwelgate
3528	229v	[cf]b	Framwelgate	Thomas Laybourn	hea		44	labourer	Dur [D] S. Margaret
3529	229v	[cf]c	Framwelgate	George Brown	hea m		54	miller	Dur [D] S. Margaret
3530	229v			Catherine Brown	wif m		53		Dur Lanchester
3531	230r			George Heslop	slw		25	nailer	Dur [D] S. Margaret
3532	230r	<37>a	Framwelgate	George Ranson	hea m		62	shoemaker	Dur Durham
3533	230r			Mary Ranson	wif m		62		Dur Durham
3534	230r			Dorothy Ranson	gda		12		Dur Durham
3535	230r	<37>b	Framwelgate	John Ainsley	hea m		50	mustard manufacturer	Dur Durham
3536	230r			Hannah Ainsley	wif m		41	milliner <dressmaker>	Dur Durham
3537	230r			William Johnson	sso		11	scholar	Dur Durham
3538	230r	<37>c	Framwelgate	John Longstaff	hea m		42	labourer	Wes Brough
3539	230r			Margaret Longstaff	wif m		39		Nry Catterick
3540	230r			Sarah Longstaff	dau		11	scholar	Dur Durham
3541	230r			Eleanor Longstaff	dau		4		Dur Durham
3542	230r			Jane Brinkly	ldr		27		Nry Catterick
3543	230r			Robert Brinkly	lds		9	scholar	Nry Richmond
3544	230r	<37>d	Framwelgate	John White	hea m		48	fishmonger	Dur [D] S. Nicholas
3545	230r			Mary White	wif m		50		Nbl S. Nicholas *
3546	230r			Barbara White	dau		20	domestic duties	Dur [D] S. Margaret
3547	230r	<37>e	Framwelgate	Ann Tindle	hea		52	washerwoman; pauper	Dur Wingate
3548	230r			Elizabeth Tindle	dau		30	factory girl	Dur Brandon
3549	230r			Robert Tindle	gsn		7		Dur Brandon
3550	230r			Thomas Tindle	gsn		4		Dur Brandon

3551	230v	[cg]a	Framwelgate	Joseph Gibson	hea m	36	carpet weaver	Dur Durham
3552	230v			Hannah Gibson	wif m	35		Dur Durham
3553	230v			George Baker Gibson	son	10	scholar	Dur Durham
3554	230v			Mary Gibson	dau	1		Dur Durham
3555	230v			Ann Gibson	dau	3m		Dur Durham
3556	230v	[cg]b	Framwelgate	James Mitchell	hea m	50	shoemaker	Cul
3557	230v			Alice Mitchell	wif m	45		Dur Durham
3558	230v	[cg]c	Framwelgate	Elizabeth Surtees	hea m	63	charwoman /"chairwoman"	Dur Bishop Auckland
3559	230v			Jane Surtees	dau	22	dressmaker	Dur [D] S. Margaret
3560	230v			Luke Dixon	gsn	5	scholar	Dur Hebburn /"Hebron"
3561	230v			Jane Fishwick	vis	6	scholar	Dur [D] S. Margaret
3562	230v	[ch]a	Framwelgate	John Fewster	hea	57	shoemaker	Dur Durham
3563	230v	[ch]b	Framwelgate	Sarah Gardner	hea	42		Dur Durham
3564	230v			Robert Gardner	son	21	labourer	Dur Durham
3565	230v			Margaret Gardner	dau	17		Dur Durham
3566	230v			Thomas Gardner	son	12		Dur Durham
3567	230v			Edward Gardner	son	9		Dur Durham
3568	230v			Sarah Gardner	dau	4		Dur Durham
3569	230v	[ch]c	Framwelgate	Frances Burnell	hea m	49	dressmaker	Dur Bishopwearmouth
3570	230v	[ch]d	Framwelgate	Joseph Moore	flw m	55	farm labourer	Sts Draycott
3571	231r			Elizabeth Moore	hea m	50		Cul Workington *
3572	231r			Martha Brough	dau	26	dressmaker	Cul Workington *
3573	231r			Elizabeth Brough	dau	15		Cul Workington *
3574	231r			Elizabeth Wilkinson	vis	18		Dur Barnard Castle
3575	231r	[ci]a	Framwelgate	Jane Wortley	hea	58	shopkeeper	Dur [D] Framwelgate
3576	231r	[ci]b	Framwelgate	John Jammerson	hea m	25	carpet weaver	Dur Barnard Castle
3577	231r			Sarah Jammerson	wif m	24		Dur Barnard Castle
3578	231r			Joseph Jammerson	son	8		Dur Durham
3579	231r	[ci]c	Framwelgate	Thomas Hall	hea m	64	woolspinner	Wes Kendal
3580	231r			Jane Hall	wif m	62		Dur Durham
3581	231r			Eubell Hall	dau	18		Dur Durham
3582	231r	[cj]a	Framwelgate	John Vasey	hea m	33	bookbinder	Dur [D] S. Oswald
3583	231r			Elizabeth Vasey	wif m	31		Dur [D] S. Margaret
3584	231r			Harriet Vasey	dau	4		Dur [D] S. Oswald
3585	231r			Eleanor Vasey	dau	3		Dur [D] S. Margaret
3586	231r			Sarah Vasey	dau	1		Dur [D] S. Margaret
3587	231r	[cj]b	Framwelgate	Bridget O'Brien	hea m	30	washerwoman	Irl
3588	231r			Martin O'Brien	son	11		Irl
3589	231r			Patrick O'Brien	son	7	scholar	Irl
3590	231r			Michael O'Brien	son	5	scholar	Dur
3591	231v			Thomas O'Brien	son	4		Dur Durham
3592	231v			Dennis O'Brien	son	2		Dur Durham
3593	231v			John O'Brien	son	8m		Dur Durham

Notes - Enumeration District 10a

1863	... dancing and drawing
1881	... employing 1 man <& builder>
1888	... Salford
1901	/"Worrton"
1904	<& lodgings>
1925	<& slater>
1931	<Independent [Congregational] chapel, 31 Claypath>
1948-1950	<Swiss Cottage>
1950	<master of Blue Coat School, Claypath, & master of Model School to Diocesan Training School>
1951	<accountant & sharebroker>
1988-1995	<Castle Chare>
1988	<& draper>
2014-2015	<Castle Chare>
2019	... [Cathedral] ...
2022	/"Egginton"
2041	... employing 4 men; ... Stanley Lane
2048	matron
2049	porter
2051	county given as "Yorkshire"
2058	[Ilketshall] ...
2129	[great?] grand-daughter
2133	... S. Nicholas
2140	<of S. Mary the Less> <MA>
2147	<& milk vendor>
2183	/"Gainforth"
2189	<& porter merchant>
2194	... Hallgarth
2211	<& leather cutter>
2214	retired ... <lodgings>
2226-2228	son [brother?]
2229	daughter [sister-in-law?]
2303	no county given, /"Bishop Mounton"
2370	[father-in-law's] wife
2371	[father-in-law's] daughter
2393	... 'Artichoke'
2412	[niece's] son
2441	<'Blue Bell'>
2482	... Chelsea [pensioner]
2534	... Bisharpbrig?
2586	son [brother?]
2589	/"Aushdale"
2621	/"Wackifield"
2661	/"Stoudley"
2708	"nav"
2719	[Newcastle?] ...
2767	<market gardener>
2811	"22" and "20" both given
2824	.... & chorister
2830-2831	/"Huntlet"
2877-2881	<number given as "77">
3008	... [employing] 2 men, 3 apprentices
3015	... of Inland Revenue
3026-3027	<2 Castle Chare>
3034	... to Norwich Insurance Society
3097	<& greengrocer>; /"Rodansdale"
3125	/"Sebera"
3173	<'Woolpack'>
3179	<cartman & milk vendor>
3211	<& marine store dealer>
3238	<farmer & milk vendor>
3245	<'Three Horseshoes'>
3268-3270	<Sidegate>
3271	[folios 219v-223r are preliminary pages

	of continuation book]	3494	/"Hearth Burn"
3347	<'Tanners' Arms'>	3515	... 'Buck'
3351	county given as "Durham"	3545	[Newcastle?] ...
3413	[servant's] son	3571-3573	/"Worhinton"
3437	/"Bellington"		

REF	FOL	NO	STREET	FORENAME(S) SURNAME	REL	C	AGE	OCCUPATION	BIRTHPLACE
3594	295v	1	New Elvet	George Howe	hea	w	47	butcher	Dur [D] S. Oswald
3595	295v			John Howe	son		20	butcher	Dur [D] S. Oswald
3596	295v			Mary McAuliffe	ser		50	general servant	Irl
3597	295v	2 a	New Elvet	William V. Johnson	hea	m	46	saddler (master *)	Dur Durham
3598	295v			Jane Johnson	wif	m	48		Dur Durham
3599	295v			Thomas Johnson	nep		17	upholsterer's apprentice	Dur Durham
3600	295v	2*b	New Elvet	William Cornwall	hea	m	44	butcher	Dur [D] S. Oswald
3601	295v			Sarah Cornwall	wif	m	47		Dur [D] S. Oswald
3602	295v			William Cornwall	son		24		Dur [D] S. Oswald
3603	295v			Margaret Cornwall	dau		22		Dur [D] S. Oswald
3604	295v			Mary Cornwall	dau		19		Dur [D] S. Oswald
3605	295v			Ann Cornwall	dau		17		Dur [D] S. Oswald
3606	295v			John Cornwall	son		16		Dur [D] S. Oswald
3607	295v			Sarah Cornwall	dau		14		Dur [D] S. Oswald
3608	295v			Mary M. Cann	ser		17	general servant	Dur Bishop Auckland
3609	295v	4	New Elvet	Thomas Buston	hea	m	63	hairdresser	Dur Darlington
3610	296r			Mary Buston	wif	m	57		Dur [D] S. Oswald
3611	296r	5 & 6 a	New Elvet	Ann Lister	hea	w	80	annuitant	Nbl Newcastle
3612	296r			Elizabeth Lister	dau		42	dressmaker	Dur Chester-le-Street
3613	296r	5 & 6 b	New Elvet	Joseph Lister	hea	m	40	baker (master *)	Dur Chester-le-Street
3614	296r			Mary Lister	wif	m	42		Nry Reeth
3615	296r			James Lister	son		7	scholar	Dur Durham
3616	296r			Joseph Lister	son		6	scholar	Dur Durham
3617	296r			William Sanderson	jny		21	baker's journeyman	Wry Leeds
3618	296r			Ann Belleby	ser		19	general servant	Dur Sherburn
3619	296r			Thomas Richardson	app		12	baker's apprentice	Dur Durham
3620	296r	8	New Elvet	John Ward	hea	m	41	solicitor *	Dur [D] S. Margaret
3621	296r			Rebecca Ward	wif	m	36		Wry Acomb
3622	296r			Elizabeth J. Ward	dau		11	scholar	Dur [D] S. Oswald
3623	296r			Mary Ward	dau		10	scholar	Dur [D] S. Oswald
3624	296r			William C. Ward	son		8	scholar	Dur [D] S. Oswald
3625	296r			John Ward	son		6	scholar	Dur [D] S. Oswald
3626	296v			Fanny Ward	dau		6	scholar	Dur [D] S. Oswald
3627	296v			Henry Ward	son		4	scholar	Dur [D] S. Oswald
3628	296v			Charles Ward	son		3	scholar (at home)	Dur [D] S. Oswald
3629	296v			Rebecca Ward	dau		1		Dur [D] S. Oswald
3630	296v			Esther Turner	ser		29	house servant	Dur Chester-le-Street
3631	296v			Mary Wright	ser		20	house servant	Nry Whitby
3632	296v			Barbara Welsh	ser		20	house servant	Dur Chester-le-Street
3633	296v	9 a	New Elvet	Edward Crickshank	hea		25	servant (footman)	Irl
3634	296v			Ann T. Crickshank	wif		29		Sct
3635	296v			Elizabeth Crickshank	dau		1		Dur Durham
3636	296v	9 b	New Elvet	John Coates	hea	m	62	sawyer	Dur Bishop Auckland
3637	296v			Mabel Coates	wif	m	62		Nbl Hexham
3638	296v			Elizabeth Davidson	ser		56	servant	Nbl Hexham
3639	296v	9 c	New Elvet	William Lister	[h]		25	chemist <& druggist>	Dur Durham
3640	296v	9 d	New Elvet	William H. Forster	hea	m	29	upholsterer	Dur [D] Gilesgate
3641	296v			Jane Forster	wif	m	29		Dur [D] S. Oswald
3642	296v			Henry Forster	son		3		Dur Hartlepool *
3643	296v			George O. Forster	son		1		Nbl Newcastle
3644	296v			John Brammer	vis	m	25	general clerk	Dur [D] S. Oswald
3645	297r	11 e	New Elvet	Sarah Bailey	[h]		62	charwoman	Nbl Ovington *
3646	297r	11 f	New Elvet	Robert Woraker	hea		34	ostler, inn	Mdx S. George
3647	297r			Sarah Woraker	wif		33		Hrt Baldock
3648	297r			Louisa Woraker	dau		9	scholar	Mdx S. George
3649	297r			Robert J. Woraker	son		6	scholar	Mdx S. George
3650	297r			Joseph Woraker	son		3		Mdx S. George
3651	297r			Ann H. Woraker	dau		1		Mdx S. George
3652	297r	11 g	New Elvet	Mary A. Grey	hea		40	seamstress	Mdx not known
3653	297r			Jane Grey	sis		33	seamstress	Mdx not known
3654	297r			Oriah Grey	*		7		Nbl Corbridge
3655	297r	11	New Elvet	John Howe	hea		33	brewer's servant	Dur Ferryhill
3656	297r			Mary Howe	wif		33		Dur Hutton Henry
3657	297r			John Howe	son		9	scholar	Dur Durham
3658	297r			Jonathan Howe	son		6	scholar	Dur Durham
3659	297r			Margaret Howe	dau		2		Dur Durham
3660	297v	11	New Elvet	John Sanders	hea	m	49	porter	Dur Gainford
3661	297v			Ellen Sanders	wif	m	37		Dur Houghton
3662	297v			Jane Sanders	dau		11	scholar	Dur Durham
3663	297v	11	New Elvet	Elizabeth Chapman	hea	w	64	dressmaker	Nry Northallerton
3664	297v			Elizabeth Chapman	dau		35	dressmaker	Nry Northallerton
3665	297v	12	New Elvet	William Oliver	hea	m	53	sheriff's officer	Dur Sherburn
3666	297v			Elizabeth Oliver	wif	m	59		Dby Clowne
3667	297v			John Oliver	son		21	journeyman painter	Dur Durham
3668	297v			Nicholas Oliver	son		15	druggist's apprentice	Dur Durham
3669	297v			John Oliver	bro		48	master butcher *	Dur Sherburn
3670	297v	13 a	New Elvet	Joseph Howe	hea	m	73	tailor	Dur Durham
3671	297v			Isabella Howe	wif	m	74	corsetmaker	Dur Durham

3672	297v	13	b	New Elvet	Edward Brewster	hea	m	22	journeyman upholsterer	Mdx London
3673	297v				Jane Brewster	wif	m	27	<dressmaker & milliner>	Dur Durham
3674	297v				Frances Brewster	dau		2d		Dur Durham
3675	297v	13	a	New Elvet	Mary Tiplady	hea	w	83	kept by daughter	Dur Durham
3676	297v				Ann Tiplady	dau		60	charwoman	Dur Durham
3677	298r	13	b	New Elvet	Mary Smith	hea	w	58	dressmaker	Dur Durham
3678	298r				Jane Smith	dau		25	milliner	Dur Durham
3679	298r				Sarah Smith	dau		18	dressmaker	Dur Durham
3680	298r	14		New Elvet	George Brown	hea	m	49	innkeeper <'Three Tuns'>	Dur [D] Crossgate
3681	298r				Margaret Brown	wif	m	39		Dur Seaton
3682	298r				Edward Miller	blw	m	43	draper	Dur Easington
3683	298r				Jane Miller	*	m	33		Nbl Newcastle
3684	298r				Sarah Pattison	ser		25	servant	Dur Durham
3685	298r				Ann Nixon	ser		25	servant	Nbl Newcastle
3686	298r				Mary Barker	ser		19	servant	Nry Romaldkirk
3687	298r				Jane Harrison	ser		21	servant	Nbl Newcastle
3688	298r				Elizabeth Johnson	ser		21	servant	Dur Durham
3689	298r				John Cochrant	vis		35	gentleman, not known	Irl
3690	298r				George Cross	vis	w	60	gentleman, not known	Dev not known
3691	298r				Richard Langridge	vis		23	gentleman, not known	Gls not known
3692	298r				Charles Barton	vis		21	gentleman, not known	War Birmingham
3693	298r	15	a	New Elvet	Frances Bone	hea	w	75	pauper (laundress)	Dur Durham
3694	298r				James Savage	gsn		7	scholar	Dur Durham
3695	298r	15	b	New Elvet	Mary Maddan	hea	w	65		Irl
3696	298v				Dominic Maddan	son		20	agricultural labourer	Irl
3697	298v				Winnie Maddan	dau		18	carpet factory labourer	Irl
3698	298v	15	c	New Elvet	Robert French	hea	m	51	colliery labourer	Dur Durham
3699	298v				Martha French	wif	m	44		Dur Durham
3700	298v				Sarah French	dau		21	dressmaker	Dur Durham
3701	298v				Robert French	son		19	tailor's apprentice	Dur Houghton-l-Spring
3702	298v				Jane French	dau		17	carpet factory girl	Dur Hetton
3703	298v				Henry French	son		13	tailor's apprentice	Dur Durham
3704	298v				Anne French	dau		10	scholar	Dur Durham
3705	298v				Thomas French	son		7	scholar	Dur Durham
3706	298v				Margaret French	dau		3	scholar	Dur Durham
3707	298v				Edward French	gsn		1		Dur Durham
*										
3708	298v	15		New Elvet	Robert Wake	hea	m	33	maltster	Nbl Morpeth
3709	298v				Sarah Wake	wif	m	26		Dev Plymouth
3710	298v				Elizabeth Wake	dau		4		Dur Sunderland
3711	298v				William Wake	son		9m		Nbl Newcastle
3712	298v	15	a	New Elvet	Joseph Linsley	[h]		50	shoemaker	Dur Durham
3713	298v	15	b	New Elvet	William Bailes	[h]	w	67	pauper (millwright)	Dur Durham
3714	298v	15		New Elvet	Edward Pattison	hea	m	38	drayman	Dur Burdon /"Burdow"
3715	298v				Ann Pattison	wif	m	34		Dur Herrington
3716	299r				Mary Stobert	dls		13		Dur Durham
3717	299r				Thomas Stobert	sls		11	errand boy	Dur Durham
*										
3718	299r	15		New Elvet	William Robinson	hea	m	37	roper	Dur Durham
3719	299r				Dorothy Robinson	wif		38		Dur Durham
3720	299r				Isabella Robinson	dau		8m		Dur Durham
3721	299r	15		New Elvet	John Johnston	hea	m	40	carpet weaver	Sct
3722	299r				Helen Johnston	wif	m	42		Sct
3723	299r				Robert Johnston	son		9	draw boy	Sct
3724	299r				Edward Johnston	son		6	scholar	Sct
3725	299r	15		New Elvet	William Richardson	hea	m	72	tailor	Dur Bishop Auckland
3726	299r				Isabella Richardson	wif	m	70		Nbl Wylam
3727	299r				Sophia Richardspn	dau		49	staymaker	Dur Durham
3728	299r				Sarah Richardson	dau		29	bonnetmaker	Dur Durham
3729	299r				William Richardson	gsn		8	scholar	Dur Durham
3730	299r	15		New Elvet	Isabella Bond	hea	w	46	dressmaker	Dur Durham
3731	299r				Isabella Bond	dau		16	staymaker	Dur Durham
3732	299r				John Bond	son		15	tailor's apprentice	Irl
3733	299r				William Bond	son		12	errand boy	Irl
3734	299v				Alexander Bond	son		8	scholar	Irl
3735	299v	16		New Elvet	William Hinchley	hea	m	30	fruiterer & greengrocer	Mdx West Drayton
3736	299v				Elizabeth Hinchley	wif	m	37		Dur Shincliffe
3737	299v				William Hinchley	son		6	scholar	Mdx Drury Lane
3738	299v				John Hinchley	son		4	scholar	Mdx Gray's Inn Lane
3739	299v				George Hinchley	son		2	scholar	Dur Durham
3740	299v				John S. Hinchley	bro		18	fruiterer's shopman	Mdx Uxbridge
3741	299v	17		New Elvet	George Martin	hea	m	38	tinplate worker	Yks York
3742	299v				Mary Martin	wif	m	36		Nry Newton upon Ouse
3743	299v				William Martin	son		12	scholar	Yks York
3744	299v				George Martin	son		9	scholar	Yks York
3745	299v				Reuben Martin	son		3	scholar	Dur Durham
3746	299v	17	a	New Elvet	John Snowdon	[h]		53	agricultural labourer	Dur Witton-le-Wear
3747	299v	17	b	New Elvet	Christopher Waton	hea	m	55	porter merchant's labr	Dur Ferryhill
3748	299v				Margaret Waton	wif	m	53		Dur Barnard Castle
3749	299v				Ann Waton	dau		19	dressmaker's apprentice	Dur [D] S. Oswald
3750	299v				Charles Waton	gsn		8	scholar	Dur [D] S. Oswald

3751	299v	20	New Elvet	Mary Tiplady	wif	m	44	solicitor's wife	Dur Durham
3752	299v			Ellen Tiplady	dau		20		Dur Durham
3753	300r			John Tiplady	son		19	solicitor's articled clk	Dur Durham
3754	300r			Charles Tiplady	son		15	builder's apprentice	Dur Durham
3755	300r			William Tiplady	son		12	scholar	Dur Durham
3756	300r			Jane Tiplady	dau		9	scholar	Dur Durham
3757	300r			Mary Tiplady	dau		4		Dur Durham
3758	300r			Thomas Caldcleugh	flw	w	79	retired currier	Dur Durham
3759	300r			Ann Coulson	ser		26	house maid	Dur Eastgate
3760	300r			Isabella Coulson	ser		22	cook	Dur Eastgate
3761	300r			Mary Charlten	ser		16	nurse	Nry Bowes
3762	300r	21 a	New Elvet	Ann Pattison	wif	m	27	shoemaker's wife	Dur Wolsingham
3763	300r			Robert Pattison	son		14	coachmaker's apprentice	Dur [D] S. Oswald
3764	300r			John Pattison	son		13	scholar	Dur [D] S. Oswald
3765	300r			Ann Pattison	dau		10	scholar	Dur [D] S. Oswald
3766	300r			Jonathan Pattison	son		5	scholar	Dur [D] S. Oswald
3767	300r			William Pattison	son		5m		Dur [D] S. Oswald
3768	300r	21 b	New Elvet	Mary Carter	wif	m	30	groom's wife	Nry Barton
3769	300r			John Carter	son		6	scholar	Dur [D] S. Oswald
3770	300r	21 a	New Elvet	Dorothy Hodgson	hea	m	44	mason's wife	Dur Durham
3771	300r			John Hodgson	son		18	mason's apprentice	Dur Streatlam
3772	300v			James Hodgson	son		16	carver & gilder's app	Dur Hartlepool
3773	300v	21 b	New Elvet	Joseph Gillespie	hea	m	24	mason	Dur Durham
3774	300v			Elizabeth Gillespie	wif	m	23		Dur Durham
3775	300v	22 a	New Elvet	Mary Southern	hea	w	73	joiner's wid <lodgings>	Dur Durham
3776	300v			Sarah A. Young	gda		10	scholar	Dur Merrington
3777	300v			Ann Dermont	ser		14	servant	Dur Darlington
3778	300v			Henry Dawson	vis		22	druggist	Dur Merrington
3779	300v			Elizabeth Dawson	vis		16	scholar	Dur Merrington
3780	300v	22 b	New Elvet	Mary Marshall	[h]		70	annuitant	Dur Middleton
3781	300v	23	New Elvet	John Sewell	hea		39	cabinetmaker, master *	Dur [D] S. Oswald
3782	300v			William Sewell	fth	m	64	cabinetmaker	Dur [D] S. Giles
3783	300v			Mary Sewell	mth	m	62		Dur Durham
3784	300v			Mary Sewell	sis		26		Dur Durham
3785	300v			Robert Sewell	bro	m	23	cabinetmaker	Dur Durham
3786	300v			Sarah Hunter	*	w	83	annuitant	Dur Ryton
3787	300v	24	New Elvet	Cuthbert J. Hubbick	hea	m	33	veterinary surgeon *	Dur Lanchester
3788	300v			Elizabeth Hubbick	wif	m	34		Dur Chilton
3789	300v			Joseph Hubbick	son		3		Dur [D] S. Oswald
3790	300v			William Hubbick	nep		21	[veterinary surg] asst	Nbl Alnwick
3791	301r			Joseph Burlinson	app		17	horseshoer	Dur Chester-le-Street
3792	301r			Ellen Wilson	ser		18	house servant	Dur Chester-le-Street
3793	301r	25 a	New Elvet	Margaret Hodgson	hea	w	77	ironmonger	Dur Durham
3794	301r			Ralph Hodgson	son	m	45	coachmaker, master *	Dur Durham
3795	301r			Charles Hodgson	son		32	smith & ironmonger *	Dur Durham
3796	301r			Sophia Hodgson	dlw	m	39	Inland Revenue off wife	Dev Ashburton
3797	301r			Thomas Hodgson	gsn		9	scholar	Dur Heworth
3798	301r			Charles Hodgson	gsn		4	scholar	Nfk Norwich
3799	301r			Margaret Hodgson	gda		2		Nfk Norwich
3800	301r			Ralph Bulmer	gsn		15	ironmonger's apprentice	Dur Merrington
3801	301r			Ann Pattison	ser		22	servant	Mdx London, not known
3802	301r	25 b	New Elvet	Simon Herdman	hea	m	22	valet	Yks Brunton
3803	301r			Ann Herdman	wif	m	22		Dur Cockerton
3804	301r			Edward Herdman	son		1		Dur [D] S. Oswald
3805	301r			Hannah Usher	vis		16	visitor	Dur Brandon
3806	301r	25 c	New Elvet	Joseph Snowdon	hea		52	shoemaker	Dur [D] S. Oswald
3807	301r			Jane Snowdon	sis		50	servant	Dur [D] S. Oswald
3808	301r			Dorothy Snowdon	nce		16	dressmaker	Dur [D] S. Oswald
3809	301r	26 a	New Elvet	Henry Nicholson	hea	m	40	iron founder	Dur [D] S. Oswald
3810	301v			Mary Nicholson	wif	m	31		Dur [D] Crossgate
3811	301v			Sarah Nicholson	dau		9	scholar	Dur [D] S. Oswald
3812	301v			Mary Nicholson	dau		7	scholar	Dur [D] S. Oswald
3813	301v			John Nicholson	son		5	scholar	Dur [D] S. Oswald
3814	301v			Henry Nicholson	son		2		Dur [D] S. Oswald
3815	301v	26 b	New Elvet	Joseph Dodds	hea	w	66	whitesmith	Dur Willington
3816	301v			Robert Dodds	bro		64	smith & horseshoer	Dur Willington
3817	301v			Thomas Dodds	son		27	whitesmith	Dur [D] S. Oswald
3818	301v			Robert Dodds	son		25	whitesmith	Dur [D] S. Oswald
3819	301v			Jane Dodds	dau		45	housekeeper	Dur [D] S. Oswald
3820	301v	26	New Elvet	Mary Briggs	hea	w	50	sempstress	Bew Coldstream
3821	301v			Thomas Briggs	son		10	scholar	Nbl Newcastle
3822	301v			James Roggers	vis	w	40	traveller, mason	Sct
3823	301v			John West	vis		17	traveller, not known	Mdx not known
3824	301v			William Ball	vis	w	70	traveller	Wry Leeds
3825	301v			William Miller	vis	m	30	carpet weaver	Bkm Sparam
3826	301v	27	New Elvet	Richard Thwaites	hea	m	34	<boot and> shoemaker	Nry Sedbusk/"Sadbush"
3827	301v			Sarah Thwaites	wif	m	29		Nry Nosterfield
3828	301v			Arthur Thwaites	son		7	scholar	Dur [D] S. Oswald
3829	301v			John Thwaites	son		2		Dur [D] S. Oswald
3830	302r			William Thwaites	nep		14	scholar	Wry Roecliffe
3831	302r			Christopher Iveson	vis	m	37	farmer & butcher	Nry Hawes

3832	302r	27	New Elvet	Christopher Moore	vis	m	46	agricultural labourer	Nry Hardraw
3833	302r			John Moore	vis	m	35	cattle dealer	Nry Hardraw
3834	302r			Arthur Iveson	vis	m	33	farmer, not known	Nry Hawes
3835	302r	28 a	New Elvet	Brian Gilan	hea	m	48	agricultural labourer	Irl
3836	302r			Mary Gilan	wif	m	47	agricultural labourer	Irl
3837	302r			John Gilan	son		21	agricultural labourer	Irl
3838	302r			Sarah Gilan	dau		19	carpet factory girl	Irl
3839	302r			Mary Gilan	dau		16	carpet factory girl	Irl
3840	302r	28 b	New Elvet	William Smith	hea	m	37	carpet weaver	Sct
3841	302r			Helen Smith	wif	m	36		Sct
3842	302r			George Smith	son		8	scholar	Sct
3843	302r			Francis Smith	son		3		Dur [D] S. Oswald
3844	302r	28	New Elvet	George Kirkley	hea		38	mason	Dur [D] S. Oswald
3845	302r	28	New Elvet	Matthew Craggs	hea	m	34	coachman <greengrocer>	Nry North Cowton
3846	302r			Margaret Craggs	wif	m	33		Nbl Warkworth
3847	302r			George Craggs	son		4	scholar	Dur Durham
3848	302v			Ann Craggs	dau		2		Dur Durham
3849	302v	29	New Elvet	John W. Crossling	hea	m	48	grocer & horses for hire	Dur West Auckland
3850	302v			Ann Crossling	ser		36	house servant	Dur Bishop Auckland
3851	302v	29	New Elvet	Thomas Robinson	hea	m	33	ostler, inn	Nry Moorsholm
3852	302v			Catherine Robinson	wif	m	30		Dur Wolsingham
3853	302v			William Robinson	son		16	ostler, inn	Dur Wolsingham
3854	302v			George Robinson	son		8	scholar	Dur Durham
3855	302v			Thomas Robinson	son		6	scholar	Dur Durham
3856	302v			Mary Robinson	dau		3		Dur Durham
3857	302v			Elizabeth Robinson	dau		10m		Dur Durham
3858	302v	29	New Elvet	Ann Dawson	hea	w	66	not known (laundress)	Dur [D] S. Oswald
3859	302v	30	New Elvet	William Morland	hea	m	58	clockmaker	Nry Masham
3860	302v			Mary Morland	wif	m	34		Dur Sunderland
3861	302v			Sarah Morland	dau		14		Dur Sunderland
3862	302v			Thomas Morland	son		12	carpet factory boy	Dur Durham
3863	302v			William Morland	son		9	scholar	Dur Durham
3864	302v			Joseph Morland	son		3		Dur Durham
3865	302v	31	New Elvet	John Bourk	hea	m	35	agricultural labourer	Irl
3866	302v			Margaret Bourk	wif	m	32		Irl
3867	303r			Mary Molone	sil		26	servant	Irl
3868	303r	31	New Elvet	Margaret Hopper	hea	w	80	pauper (innkeeper)	Dur Durham
3869	303r			Elizabeth Paxton	dau	w	46	manglekeeper; pauper	Dur Durham
3870	303r	31	New Elvet	William Maddison	hea	m	69	grocer <& tailor>	Dur [D] S. Oswald
3871	303r			Jane Maddison	wif	m	64		Dur Denton
3872	303r			Jane Maddison	dau		31	straw-bonnetmaker *	Dur [D] S. Oswald
3873	303r			Ann Maddison	dau		29	dressmaker	Dur [D] S. Oswald
3874	303r			Hannah Maddison	dau		27	straw-bonnetmaker	Dur [D] S. Oswald
3875	303r			John Maddison	son		25	officer of Excise	Dur [D] S. Oswald
3876	303r			Susanna Maddison	dau		24	milliner	Dur [D] S. Oswald
3877	303r	32	New Elvet	Robert Long	hea	m	39	agricultural labourer	Nry Boltby
3878	303r			Isabella Long	wif	m	37		Dur Durham
3879	303r			William Long	son		10	scholar	Dur Durham
3880	303r			Margaret Long	dau		8	scholar	Dur Durham
3881	303r			Isabella Long	dau		3		Dur Durham
3882	303r			Anne Long	dau		1		Dur Durham
3883	303r	32	New Elvet	Thomas Grundon	hea	w	50	lemonade manufacturer	Dur Durham
3884	303r			Ellen Liddle	ser	w	62	housekeeper	Dur Durham
3885	303r	32	New Elvet	Margaret Bateson	hea	w	76	pp (fmly schoolmistress)	Dur [D] S. Nicholas
3886	303v	32	New Elvet	William Hopper	hea	m	44	clock and watchmaker	Dur Durham
3887	303v			Jane Hopper	wif	m	42	<straw-hatmaker>	Dur Durham
3888	303v			Francis Hopper	son		21	hairdresser	Dur Durham
3889	303v			Jane Hopper	dau		17	scholar	Dur Durham
3890	303v			Mary Hopper	dau		15	scholar	Dur Durham
3891	303v	33	New Elvet	Joseph Dickinson	hea	m	45	coachmaker	Nbl Newcastle
3892	303v			Elizabeth Dickinson	wif	m	51		Dur [D] S. Oswald
3893	303v			John Salkeld	ldr		23	coachsmith	Wes Kendal
3894	303v			Anthony Story	ldr	m	23	coachsmith	Wes Kendal
3895	303v	34	New Elvet	Thomas Robinson	hea	w	61	confectioner	Dur Durham
3896	303v			Thomas Robinson	son		30	confectioner	Dur Durham
3897	303v	34 a	New Elvet	William Hodgson	hea	m	50	blacksmith	Dur [D] S. Oswald
3898	303v			Mary Hodgson	wif	m	42		Dur Witton-le-Wear
3899	303v	34 b	New Elvet	Mary Bell	[h]		33	charwoman	Dur Durham
3900	303v			William Ainsley	vis		32	blacksmith	Dur Durham
3901	303v	34 c	New Elvet	William James	[h]	w	63	Chelsea pensioner	Irl
3902	303v	34 d	New Elvet	Martha Landragan	hea		32	laundress	Irl
3903	303v			Mary Landragan	dau		5		Dur Durham
3904	303v			Agnes Landragan	dau		1		Dur Durham
3905	304r	34	New Elvet	William Hutchinson	hea	m	42	tilemaker	Dur Norton
3906	304r			Mary Hutchinson	wif	m	39		Dur Durham
3907	304r			William Hutchinson	son		13	scholar	Dur Stockton
3908	304r			John Hutchinson	son		11	scholar	Dur Norton
3909	304r			Mary Hutchinson	dau		8	scholar	Dur Durham
3910	304r			Susanna Hutchinson	dau		5		Dur Durham
3911	304r			Margaret Hutchinson	dau		3		Dur Durham
3912	304r	34	New Elvet	Jonathan Forster	hea	m	34	coal miner	Dur Bishop Auckland

3913	304r	34	New Elvet	Mary Forster	wif	m	39		Dur Marwood
3914	304r			Esther Forster	dau		20	charwoman	Dur Newbiggin
3915	304r			Jonathan Forster	son		2		Dur Bradley Burn
3916	304r			Robert Forster	son		4		Dur Edelsmely
3917	304r			Thomas Forster	[s]		1		Dur Durham
3918	304r	34	New Elvet	William Sedwell	hea	m	35	coachmaker	Ntt Newark
3919	304r			Fanny Sedwell	wif	m	30		Lei Newton
3920	304r			Mary A. Sedwell	dau		9	scholar	Lan Manchester
3921	304r	[aa]a	New Elvet	Robert Wilson	hea	m	36	tailor	Sct
3922	304r			Elizabeth Wilson	wif	m	28		Dev Plymouth
3923	304r			Robert Wilson	son		3		Lan Liverpool
3924	304v			George Wilson	son		10m		Dur South Shields
3925	304v	[aa]b	New Elvet	Isabella Moore	hea		35	laundress	Dur Durham
3926	304v			Phyllis Moore	dau		10	milliner's servant	Dur Durham
3927	304v			John Moore	son		7	scholar	Dur Durham
3928	304v			Sarah Moore	dau		5	scholar	Dur Durham
3929	304v	[ab]a	New Elvet	Mary Brown	hea		57	lodging house keeper	Dur Durham
3930	304v			William Doyle	ldr		35	joiner	Irl
3931	304v			Charles Ferrall	ldr	w	49	cattle drover	Irl
3932	304v			John Bickerdike	ldr		23	groom	Nry Thirsk
3933	304v			Septimus Cooper	ldr	m	24	hawker, not known	Dur not known
3934	304v			Robert Campbell	ldr		25	labourer, not known	Nbl Morpeth
3935	304v			Samuel Ridpith	ldr		32	groom	Nbl Alnwick
3936	304v			Mark Caudle	ldr		21	cartman	Nbl Glanton
3937	304v			James Wood	ldr		39	drover	Wil not known
3938	304v			James Flintoff	ldr		34	groom	Nry Malton
3939	304v	[ab]b	New Elvet	Mary Nicholson	hea	w	93	pp (coachmaker's wife)	Dur Gateshead
3940	304v			Jane Nicholson	dau		45	charwoman	Nbl Newcastle
3941	304v			Henry Pattison	gsn		17	shoemaker's apprentice	Dur Durham
3942	304v	[ab]c	New Elvet	Thomas Herbert	hea	m	22	gardener	Dur Durham
3943	305r			Ann Herbert	wif	m	23		Dur Durham
3944	305r			Thomas Herbert	son		1m		Dur Durham
3945	305r	[ab]d	New Elvet	William Allen	[h]	w	79	tailor	Ess Witham
3946	305r	[ab]e	New Elvet	Ann Maughan	wif	m	44	charwoman	Dur Durham
3947	305r			Joseph W. Maughan	son		11	scholar	Dur [D] S. Oswald
3948	305r	<35>	New Elvet	Thomas Wilkinson	hea	m	42	schoolmaster	Dur Darlington
3949	305r			Elizabeth Wilkinson	wif	m	40		Dur Darlington
3950	305r			Mary H. Wilkinson	dau		11	scholar (at home)	Dur Chester-le-Street
3951	305r			Dorothy J. Wilkinson	dau		10	scholar (at home)	Dur Chester-le-Street
3952	305r			Sarah Wilkinson	dau		2		Dur [D] S. Oswald
3953	305r	<36>	New Elvet	John Winter	hea	m	34	printer compositor *	Dur Durham
3954	305r			Maria Winter	wif	m	30		Dur Pittington
3955	305r			John Winter	son		1		Dur [D] S. Oswald
3956	305r	<37>	New Elvet	Mary Hutchinson	[h]		52	greengrocer	Dur Norton
3957	305r	[ac]a	New Elvet	Michael Vest	hea	m	31	tailor	Dur [D] S. Oswald
3958	305r			Ann Vest	wif	m	38		Dur Sunderland
3959	305r			John Vest	son		6	scholar	Dur [D] S. Oswald
3960	305r			William Vest	son		3	scholar	Dur [D] S. Oswald
3961	305r			Michael Vest	son		1		Dur [D] S. Oswald
3962	305v	[ac]b	New Elvet	John Pattison	hea	m	26	shoemaker (journeyman)	Dur Durham
3963	305v			Eleanor Pattison	wif	m	23		Wry Ripon
3964	305v			Elizabeth Pattison	dau		3		Dur Durham
3965	305v			William Pattison	son		1		Dur Durham
3966	305v	[ac]c	New Elvet	Ann Hall	hea	w	58	pauper (miller's wife)	Dur Coundon
3967	305v			Jane Lockey	vis	m	27	agricultural labr's wife	Dur Barnard Castle
3968	305v			George Mathews	vis	m	20	coachsmith	Dur Barnard Castle
3969	305v			James W. Lockey	vss		6m		Dur Barnard Castle
3970	305v			John Lockey	vis	m	23	agricultural labourer	Nry Boldron
3971	305v	[ac]d	New Elvet	Margaret Young '	hea		54	charwoman	Dur Durham
3972	305v			William Young	son		17	tailor's apprentice	Dur Durham
3973	305v	[ac]e	New Elvet	James Warren	hea	m	70	carpenter	Mdx Spa Fields
3974	305v			Elizabeth Warren	wif	m	69		Dur [D] S. Oswald
3975	305v			James Warren	son		40	carpenter	Dur [D] S. Oswald
3976	305v			Robert Warren	son		30	shoemaker	Dur [D] S. Oswald
3977	305v			Thomas Warren	son		27	coach wheelwright	Dur [D] S. Oswald
3978	305v			Hawdon Warren	son		24	coachsmith	Dur [D] S. Oswald
3979	305v	[ad]a	New Elvet	Simon Gray	hea	m	42	Chelsea pensioner	Nry Osbaldwick
3980	305v			Susan Gray	wif	m	36		Log
3981	305v			Elizabeth Gray	dau		17	dressmaker's apprentice	Irl Ballincole
3982	306r			Henry Gray	son		6	scholar	Tip Clonmel
3983	306r			James Gray	son		5	scholar	Lei Loughborough *
3984	306r	[ad]b	New Elvet	John Smith	hea	m	31	cabinetmaker	Dur Durham
3985	306r			Mary A. Smith	wif	m	29		Nbl Newcastle
3986	306r			Matthew T. Smith	son		4	scholar	Dur Durham
3987	306r			Joseph Smith	son		2		Dur Durham
3988	306r			Anne Smith	dau		1m		Dur Durham
3989	306r	[ad]c	New Elvet	James Vasey	hea	m	28	painter	Dur [D] S. Oswald
3990	306r			Ann Vasey	wif	m	25		Dur Shiney Row
3991	306r			Elizabeth Vasey	dau		6	scholar	Dur [D] S. Oswald
3992	306r			James C. Vasey	son		3	scholar	Dur [D] S. Oswald
3993	306r			Thomas Vasey	son		2		Dur [D] S. Oswald

3994	306r	[ae]a	New Elvet	George Gray	hea	m	47	papermaker	Dur Sunderland Bridge
3995	306r			Ann Gray	wif		47		Dur [D] S. Oswald
3996	306r			Martha Gray	dau		21	paper factory girl	Dur Felling Shore
3997	306r			William Gray	son		15	printer	Dur [D] S. Oswald
3998	306r			George Gray	son		12	scholar	Dur [D] S. Oswald
3999	306r			Sarah Gray	dau		7	scholar	Dur [D] S. Oswald
4000	306v			Thomas Gray	son		5	scholar	Dur [D] S. Oswald
4001	306v			Ann Gray	gda		4	scholar	Dur [D] S. Oswald
4002	306v	[ae]b	New Elvet	Richard Clayton	hea	m	33	agricultural labourer	Nry Catterick
4003	306v			Maria Clayton	wif	m	37		Nry Bilsdale
4004	306v			Margaret Clayton	dau		6	scholar	Dur [D] S. Oswald
4005	306v	[af]a	New Elvet	William Lockey	hea	m	32	agricultural labourer	Nry Boldron
4006	306v			Elizabeth Lockey	wif	m	29		Dur Barnard Castle
4007	306v			Margaret Lockey	dau		7	scholar	Dur Ferryhill
4008	306v			Mary Lockey	dau		5	scholar	Dur Durham
4009	306v			Elizabeth Lockey	dau		3		Dur Durham
4010	306v			William Lockey	son		4m		Dur Durham
4011	306v			John Franklin	vis	w	71	agricultural labourer	Nry Kirkby Ravensw'th
4012	306v	[af]b	New Elvet	Ann Wetherall	hea	w	87	supported by gentleman	Dur Sedgefield
4013	306v			Sarah Wetherall	dau		55	monthly nurse	Dur [D] S. Oswald
4014	306v	<39>	New Elvet	John Shaw	hea	m	35	cabinetmaker, master *	Dur [D] S. Margaret
4015	306v			Mary Shaw	wif	m	31		Dur [D] S. Oswald
4016	306v			Charles Shaw	son		10		Dur [D] S. Oswald
4017	306v			Frances Shaw	dau		7		Dur [D] S. Oswald
4018	306v			William Shaw	son		3		Dur [D] S. Oswald
4019	307r			Mary Shaw	dau		1		Dur [D] S. Oswald
4020	307r			Margaret Golightly	vis		23	dressmaker	Dur Chester-le-Street
4021	307r	[ag]	New Elvet	Thomas S. Lindsley	hea		56	journeyman shoemaker	Dur [D] S. Oswald
4022	307r			Jane Lindsley	sis		49	housekeeper	Dur [D] S. Oswald
4023	307r			Eve Palmer	nce		13	scholar	Dur [D] S. Oswald
4024	307r			Charles Palmer	nep		6	scholar	Dur [D] S. Oswald
4025	307r	<40>a	New Elvet	Charles Graham	hea	w	51	mason	Dur [D] S. Margaret
4026	307r			George Graham	son		26	roper	Dur East Rainton
4027	307r			James Graham	son		23	groom	Dur Houghton-1-Spring
4028	307r			Charles Graham	son		17	coach painter's app	Dur [D] S. Oswald
4029	307r	<40>b	New Elvet	Mary Bell	[h]	w	57	stocking knitter	Nbl Gosforth *
4030	307r	<40>c	New Elvet	William Vasey	hea	m	39	tailor	Dur Durham
4031	307r			Jane Vasey	wif	m	38		Dur Durham
4032	307r			John Vasey	son		6	scholar	Dur Durham
4033	307r			Thomas Vasey	son		5	scholar	Dur Durham
4034	307r			William Vasey	son		2		Dur Durham
4035	307r			Frederick Vasey	son		1m		Dur Durham
4036	307r			Mary Thwaites	sil		24	servant, house maid	Dur Durham
4037	307r	<40>d	New Elvet	Thomas Vasey	hea	m	73	tailor	Dur Durham
4038	307v			Sarah Vasey	wif	m	69		Dur Durham
4039	307v			Thomas Vasey	son		37	painter	Dur Durham
4040	307v	[ah]	New Elvet	George Gill	hea	m	31	cabinetmaker	Dur Brancepeth
4041	307v			Elizabeth Gill	wif	m	25		Dur Shincliffe
4042	307v			Jane Gill	dau		3		Dur Durham
4043	307v			George Gill	son		1		Dur Durham
4044	307v	[ai]a	New Elvet	William Howson	hea	m	26	journeyman whitesmith	Dur Barnard Castle
4045	307v			Elizabeth Howson	wif	m	26		Dur Houghton-1-Spring
4046	307v			William Howson	son		4	scholar	Dur Houghton-1-Spring
4047	307v			George Howson	son		1		Dur Durham
4048	307v	[ai]b	New Elvet	James Allen	hea	m	37	traveller *	Irl
4049	307v			Hannah Allen	wif	m	34		Ery Dunnington
4050	307v			Margaret Allen	dau		9	scholar	Ery Pocklington
4051	307v			Thomas Allen	son		7	scholar	Ery Howden
4052	307v			Mary A. Allen	dau		4		Ery Market Weighton
4053	307v			Hannah Allen	dau		1		Dur Durham
4054	307v			James Magan	vis		34	traveller *	Irl
4055	307v			Terence Magan	vis		28	traveller *	Irl
4056	307v			James Devlin	vis		40	traveller *	Irl
			two houses building						
4057	308r	[aj]	New Elvet	Christopher Thwaites	hea	m	46	printer compositor	Dur Durham
4058	308r			Jane Thwaites	wif	m	44		Dur Durham
4059	308r			John Thwaites	son		19	tailor	Dur Durham
4060	308r			George Thwaites	son		17	writing clerk	Dur Durham
4061	308r			William Thwaites	son		15	printer compositor's app	Dur Durham
4062	308r			Henry Thwaites	son		13	scholar	Dur Durham
4063	308r			Mary J. Thwaites	dau		11	scholar	Dur Durham
4064	308r			Ann S. Thwaites	dau		9	scholar	Dur Durham
4065	308r			Thomas Thwaites	son		5		Dur Durham
4066	308r			Alice Thwaites	dau		3		Dur Durham
4067	308r	[ak]	New Elvet	James Short	hea	m	26	warder in Durham Gaol	Nbl Grindon
4068	308r			Dorothy Short	wif	m	30		Nbl Newcastle
4069	308r			Margaret A. Short	dau		6m		Dur Durham
4070	308r	[al]	New Elvet	Jane Alderson	hea	w	59	housekeeper	Dur Willington
4071	308r			Thomas Alderson	son		32	saddler	Dur [D] S. Nicholas
4072	308r			Elizabeth Alderson	dau		23	dressmaker	Dur [D] S. Margaret
4073	308r			William Alderson	son		21	carpenter	Dur [D] S. Nicholas

4074	308r	[al]	New Elvet	Mary Alderson	dau	10	scholar	Dur [D] S. Nicholas
4075	308r			Richard Alderson	son	8	scholar	Dur [D] S. Nicholas
4076	308v	[am]	New Elvet	Sarah Middleton	hea w	50	formerly sempstress	Dur [D] S. Oswald
4077	308v			Jane Brown	dau m	24	straw-bonnetmaker	Dur [D] S. Oswald
4078	308v			Robert Middleton	son	22	upholsterer	Dur [D] S. Oswald
4079	308v			Thomas Middleton	son	19	tailor's apprentice	Dur [D] S. Oswald
4080	308v			William Middleton	son	17	tailor's apprentice	Dur [D] S. Oswald
4081	308v			John Middleton	nep	4		Dur [D] S. Oswald
4082	308v			Joseph Brown	nep	5m		Dur [D] S. Oswald
4083	308v	[an]	New Elvet *	Thomas Hopper	hea m	59	joiner	Dur Durham
4084	308v			Hannah Hopper	wif m	48		Dur West Auckland
4085	308v			Edmund Hopper	son	19	joiner's apprentice	Dur Durham
4086	308v			Thomas Hopper	son	17	harnessmaker's * app	Dur Durham
4087	308v			James Hopper	son	15	tailor's apprentice	Dur Durham
4088	308v			Charles Hopper	son	12	errand boy	Dur Durham
4089	308v			Henry Hopper	son	8	scholar	Dur Durham
4090	308v			John Hopper	son	4	scholar	Dur Durham
4091	308v	[ao]	New Elvet	Phyllis Moore	hea w	52	charwoman	Dur Stanhope
4092	308v			Thomas Moore	son	19	coachsmith's apprentice	Dur Durham
4093	308v			Joseph Moore	son	13	scholar	Dur Durham
4094	308v	[ap]	New Elvet	Joseph Smith	hea m	33	officer in Durham Gaol	Dur Durham
4095	309r			Mary Smith	wif m	31		Dur Durham
4096	309r	[aq]	New Elvet	John Morgan	hea m	27	traveller *	Irl
4097	309r			Mary Morgan	wif m	29		Irl
4098	309r			Elizabeth Morgan	dau	2		Dur Durham
4099	309r			Rebecca Ribbon	vis	24	sempstress	Irl
4100	309r	[ar]a	New Elvet	Martin Harrison	hea m	21	agricultural labourer	Dur Durham
4101	309r			Ann Harrison	wif m	22		Dur Sunderland
4102	309r	[ar]b	New Elvet	Henry Hopper	hea m	39	saddler	Dur Durham
4103	309r			Jane Hopper	wif m	37		Dur Durham
4104	309r			Margaret Hopper	dau	11	scholar	Nbl Newcastle
4105	309r			Mary Hopper	dau	6	scholar	Dur Durham
4106	309r			Henry Hopper	son	3		Dur Durham
4107	309r	[ar]c	New Elvet	John Laing	hea m	68	shoemaker	Dur Gateshead
4108	309r			Mary Ann Laing	wif m	50		Nry Whitby
4109	309r	[ar]d	New Elvet	John Parkinson	[h] w	69	shoemaker	Nry Stokesley
4110	309r	[ar]e	New Elvet	Margaret Jeffrey	hea w	70	hawker of tapes & thread	Sct
4111	309r			not known	vis nk	40	cattle drover	not known
4112	309v			not known	vis nk	30	cattle drover	not known
4113	309v			not known	vis nk	24	cattle drover	not known
4114	309v			not known	vis nk	17	cattle drover	not known
4115	309v	[as]	New Elvet	Nicholas Palmer	hea m	46	journeyman mason	Dur [D] S. Margaret
4116	309v			Maria Palmer	wif m	46		Dur [D] S. Oswald
4117	309v			Jane Palmer	dau	18	seamstress	Dur [D] S. Oswald
4118	309v			James Palmer	son	16	painter's apprentice	Dur [D] S. Oswald
4119	309v			Nicholas Palmer	son	11	scholar	Dur [D] S. Oswald
4120	309v			Henry Palmer	son	9	scholar	Dur [D] S. Oswald
4121	309v			Robert Palmer	son	2		Dur [D] S. Oswald
4122	309v	[at]	New Elvet	John M. Millbank	hea m	27	joiner	Dur [D] S. Oswald
4123	309v			Mary Millbank	wif m	24		Dur [D] S. Oswald
4124	309v			John Millbank	son	6	scholar	Dur Staindrop
4125	309v			Jane Millbank	dau	4	scholar	Dur Wolsingham
4126	309v			Edward Millbank	son	2		Dur [D] S. Oswald
4127	309v			David Wagner	vis	53	brass moulder	Edn Edinburgh
4128	309v			George Hall	vis	21	joiner	Dur [D] S. Oswald
4129	309v	<42>	New Elvet	Henry Harrison	hea m	34	butcher	Dur Hamsterley
4130	309v			Jane Harrison	wif m	31		Dur [D] S. Nicholas
4131	310r			Henry Harrison	son	5	scholar	Dur [D] S. Oswald
4132	310r			Michael Harrison	son	3	scholar	Dur [D] S. Oswald
4133	310r			Margaret Harrison	dau	5m		Dur [D] S. Oswald
4134	310r			Ann Carr	ser	16	butcher's servant	Dur Hetton
4135	310r	[au]	New Elvet	Ralph Hopper	hea m	47	journeyman painter	Dur Durham
4136	310r			Ellen Hopper	wif m	52		Nbl Newcastle
4137	310r			Thomas Hopper	son	20	painter's apprentice	Dur Durham
4138	310r			Elizabeth Hopper	dau	15	dressmaker's apprentice	Dur Durham
4139	310r			Ellen Hopper	dau	13	scholar	Dur Durham
4140	310r	<42>	New Elvet	Joseph Rickerby	hea m	29	baker, master *	Dur [D] S. Oswald
4141	310r			Mary Rickerby	wif m	25		Dur Westoe
4142	310r			Mary F. Rickerby	dau	2		Dur [D] S. Oswald
4143	310r			Ann E. Rickerby	dau	7m		Dur [D] S. Oswald
4144	310r			Jane Rickerby	sis	21	house servant	Dur [D] S. Oswald
4145	310r			James Leonard	ser	27	baker's journeyman	Dur Gateshead
4146	310r	<43>	New Elvet	George S. Ross	hea m	33	innkeeper *	Nbl Alnwick
4147	310r			Ann Ross	wif m	48		Dur Ferryhill
4148	310r			Mary A. Chilton	nce	15	scholar	Dur Penshaw
4149	310r			Mary [P]reestman	ser	17	general servant	Nry Kirby
4150	310v			Thomas Bell	vis w	71	agricultural labourer	Nry Maltby
4151	310v	[aa]a	Court Lane	Elizabeth Ainsley	hea w	36	charwoman	Mdx not known
4152	310v			Hannah Ainsley	dau	18		Dur Shincliffe
4153	310v			Henry Ainsley	son	8	scholar	Dur [D] S. Oswald
4154	310v			Edward Ainsley	gsn	4m		Dur [D] S. Oswald

4155	310v	[aa]b	Court Lane	James Hanlon	hea m	27	agricultural labourer	Irl
4156	310v			Catherine Hanlon	wif m	25		Irl
4157	310v			Mary Hanlon	dau	7		Irl
4158	310v			Thomas Hanlon	son	2		Eng
4159	310v			Barnabas Hanlon	son	6m		Eng
4160	310v			John Archer	flw m	60	handloom weaver	Irl
4161	310v			Catherine Archer	mlw m	50		Irl
4162	310v			John Archer	blw	16		Irl
4163	310v	[aa]c	Court Lane	Mary Irwin	hea w	62	charwoman　　{deaf}	Dur Monkwearmouth
4164	310v			Mary Hardy	dau	22	dressmaker	Dur [D] S. Nicholas
4165	310v			John Campbell	vis	27	agricultural labourer	Nbl Wooler
4166	310v			James Menzies	vis	16	agricultural labourer	Edn Edinburgh
4167	310v	[aa]d	Court Lane	Mary West	* w	75	pauper (joiner's widow)	Dur Durham
4168	310v			Louisa Allison	hea w	35	pauper (sawyer's widow)	Dur [D] S. Oswald
4169	311r			Matthew Allison	son	16	printer's apprentice	Dur [D] S. Oswald
4170	311r			Louisa Allison	dau	12	scholar	Dur [D] S. Oswald
4171	311r			Mary Allison	dau	9	scholar	Dur [D] S. Oswald
4172	311r			Edward Allison	son	7	scholar	Dur [D] S. Oswald
4173	311r			Elizabeth Allison	dau	5	scholar	Dur [D] S. Oswald
4174	311r			Joseph Allison	son	2		Dur [D] S. Oswald
4175	311r	[ab]a	Court Lane	John Rush	hea m	58	weaver	America BS
4176	311r			Susan Rush	wif m	38		Dow Bryansford
4177	311r			Mary Rush	dau	12	general servant	Dow Bryansford
4178	311r			Peter Rush	son	9	scholar	Irl
4179	311r	[ab]b	Court Lane	Margaret Adamson	wif m	45	chainmaker's wife	Dur Durham
4180	311r			Jane Adamson	dau	14	scholar	Dur Durham
4181	311r			John Adamson	son	12	scholar	Dur Durham
4182	311r			Eleanor Adamson	dau	8	scholar	Dur Durham
4183	311r	[ab]c	Court Lane	Joseph Pattison	hea	40	ostler	Dur Durham
4184	311r	[ab]d	Court Lane	George Lindsey	hea w	71	agricultural labourer	Dur Hett
4185	311r			John Lindsey	son	38	blacksmith	Dur Ferryhill
4186	311r			Mary B. Lindsey	dau	29	dressmaker	Dur [D] S. Oswald
4187	311r			Isabella Lindsey	gda	8	scholar	Dur [D] S. Oswald
4188	311v	[ac]	Court Lane	John Todd	hea m	53	cabinetmaker	Dur [D] S. Oswald
4189	311v			Jane Todd	wif m	51		Dur [D] S. Oswald
4190	311v			Thomas Todd	son	20	plumber's apprentice	Dur [D] S. Oswald
4191	311v			John Todd	son	18	writing clerk	Dur [D] S. Oswald
4192	311v			James Todd	son	15	scholar	Dur [D] S. Oswald
4193	311v			Hannah F. Todd	dau	14	dressmaker's apprentice	Dur [D] S. Oswald
4194	311v			Jane A. Todd	dau	11	scholar	Dur [D] S. Oswald
4195	311v			Joseph Todd	son	8	scholar	Dur [D] S. Oswald
4196	311v	[ad]	Court Lane	Julia Kitchen	hea w	61	laundress	Dur Durham
4197	311v			Jonathan Laverick	vis	19	tailor	Dur Durham
4198	311v			Thompson Ridsdale	vis	22	tinsmith	Dur Ferryhill
4199	311v			Richard T[h]waites	vis m	43	agricultural labourer	Nry Wensleydale
4200	311v			John Thwaites	vis m	39	agricultural labourer	Nry Wensleydale
4201	311v	[ae]	Court Lane	Thomas Platt	hea m	48	groom	Ess Great Baddow
4202	311v			Mary Platt	wif m	45		Dur Stanhope
4203	311v			Sarah Platt	dau	22		Dur Stanhope
4204	311v	[af]	Court Lane	Christopher Robinson	hea m	67	turnkey at Durham Gaol	Dur [D] Gilesgate
4205	311v			Mary Robinson	wif m	64		Dur [D] S. Nicholas
4206	311v	[ag]	Court Lane	Eleanor Morton	hea w	44	pauper (soldier's widow)	Irl
4207	312r			Eleanor Morton	dau	14	scholar	Irl
4208	312r			Robert Morton	son	11	scholar	Sct
4209	312r			Rebecca Morton	dau	7	scholar	Dur [D] Crossgate
4210	312r			Elizabeth Morton	dau	4	scholar	Dur [D] Crossgate
4211	312r	[ah]	Court Lane	Joseph Soulsby	hea m	37	wine merchant	Nbl Benwell
4212	312r			Annie Soulsby	wif m	30	dressmaker	Dur Durham
4213	312r			John C.F. Soulsby	son	7	scholar	Dur Durham
4214	312r			Mary S. Soulsby	dau	6	scholar	Dur Durham
4215	312r			George Charlton	flw w	66	retired clerk	Dur Chester-le-Street
4216	312r	[ai]	Court Lane	Charles Gill	hea m	56	groom	Dur Brancepeth
4217	312r			Elizabeth Gill	wif m	60		Dur Ferryhill
4218	312r			Elizabeth Birbeck	vis	14	scholar	Nry Thirsk
4219	312r	[aj]	Court Lane	John Donnison	hea m	46	prison officer	Dur Merrington
4220	312r			Isabella Donnison	wif m	43	dressmaker	Dur Durham
4221	312r			Ralph Saidler	vis	56	plumber, master *	Dur Durham
4222	312r			James Saidler	vis	23	plumber	Yks York
4223	312r	[ak]	Court Lane	John Mutter	hea m	41	publican <'Court'>	Sct
4224	312r			Jane Ann Mutter	wif m	48		Dur Durham
4225	312r			Ann Thompson	vis	30	dressmaker	Dur Durham
4226	312v			John Thompson	vis m	36	farmer of 60a *	Nry Carlton *
4227	312v	[al]	Court Lane	Jane Robinson	[h] w	60	keeper of County Courts	Dur [D] S. Oswald
4228	312v	[am]	Court Lane	George Ball	hea m	33	schoolmaster	Wry Handsworth Woodho
4229	312v			Jane Ball	wif m	26		Dur New Lambton
4230	312v			Elizabeth Ball	dau	3		Dur Shincliffe
4231	312v			Maria Ball	dau	2		Dur [D] S. Oswald
4232	312v			John Ball	son	4m		Dur [D] S. Oswald
4233	312v			Matilda Clark	ser	15	general servant	Dur Sedgefield
4234	312v			Catherine Holland	ser	18	general servant	Wry Leeds
4235	312v	[an]	Court Lane	Thomas Caygill	hea m	41	storekeeper in Prison	Nry Yarm

4236	312v	[an]	Court Lane	Hannah Caygill	wif m	38	collector of accounts	Dur Bishop Auckland
4237	312v			Mary Sexton	sil	16		Dur Cockerton
4238	312v	[ao]	Court Lane	Edward Dodd	hea m	40	prison officer	Dur Durham
4239	312v			Elizabeth Dodd	wif m	40		Dur Durham
4240	312v			Thomas Dodd	son	18	plumber's apprentice	Dur Durham
4241	312v			Edward Dodd	son	15	upholsterer's apprentice	Dur Durham
4242	312v			Henry Dodd	son	13	chorister	Dur Durham
4243	312v			William Dodd	son	11	scholar	Dur Durham
4244	312v			Elizabeth Dodd	dau	7	scholar	Dur Durham
4245	313r			Wilson Dodd	son	4	scholar	Dur Durham
4246	313r			John Dodd	son	6m		Dur Durham
4247	313r	[ap]	Court Lane	George Ramshaw	hea m	46	clerk at County Gaol	Dur Merrington
4248	313r			Elizabeth Ramshaw	wif m	36		Dur Morley
4249	313r			Thomas Ramshaw	son	17	attorney's general clerk	Dur Westerton
4250	313r			Richard Ramshaw	son	9	scholar	Dur Durham
4251	313r			William Ramshaw	son	6	scholar	Dur Durham
4252	313r			Henry Ramshaw	son	5m		Dur Durham
4253	313r			Elizabeth Studhome	ser	15	house servant	Dur Merrington
4254	313r	[aq]	Court Lane	Robert Booth	hea m	59	deputy governor of Gaol	Dur Monkwearmouth
4255	313r			Margaret Booth	wif m	56	warder in Gaol at Durham	Dur Iveston
4256	313r			Anne Booth	dau	24		Dur Monkwearmouth
4257	313r			James Holburn	nep	12	scholar	Dur Durham
4258	313r	[ar]	Court Lane	John Walker	hea w	59	bookseller	Dur Chester-le-Street
4259	313r			Mary F. Walker	dau	24	dressmaker	Dur [D] S. Oswald
4260	313r			John Walker	son	22	coachmaker	Dur [D] S. Oswald
4261	313r			Eleanor A. Walker	dau	19	milliner	Dur [D] S. Oswald
4262	313r			Mary Ann Cowey	vis	16	milliner	Dur [D] S. Giles
4263	313r	[as]	Court Lane	William Southeron	hea w	44	butcher	Dur [D] S. Oswald
4264	313v			Joseph Sutheron	cou	38	cattle dealer	Dur [D] S. Oswald
4265	313v			William Sutheron	son	15		Dur [D] S. Oswald
4266	313v			Thomas Sutheron	son	13	butcher's apprentice	Dur [D] S. Oswald
4267	313v			Ann Sutheron	dau	7	scholar	Dur [D] S. Oswald
4268	313v			John Sutheron	son	4	scholar	Dur [D] S. Oswald
4269	313v	[at]a	Court Lane	Thomas Turnbull	hea m	55	agricultural labourer	Dur Gainford *
4270	313v			Hannah Turnbull	wif m	55		Dur Moorsley
4271	313v			Elizabeth Turnbull	dau	18	visitor	Dur Hetton
4272	313v			Susanna Turnbull	dau	13	scholar	Dur Thornley
4273	313v			Thomas Turnbull	gsn	5	scholar	Dur Barnard Castle
4274	313v			Elizabeth Turnbull	gda	5m		Dur [D] S. Margaret
4275	313v	[at]b	Court Lane	Henry Wortly	hea m	37	joiner	Dur [D] S. Giles
4276	313v			Elizabeth Wortly	wif m	33		Dur Darlington
4277	313v			Mary A. Wortly	dau	4	scholar	Dur [D] S. Oswald
4278	313v			William Wortly	son	2		Dur [D] S. Oswald
4279	313v	[au]a	Court Lane	Michael Ranaghan	hea m	66	agricultural labourer	Irl
4280	313v			Rose Ranaghan	wif m	56		Irl
4281	313v			Nicholas Ranaghan	son	38	hawker of drapery	Irl
4282	313v	[au]b	Court Lane	Mary Johnson	[h]	56	seamstress; pauper	Dur Durham
4283	314r	[au]c	Court Lane	Mary Pearson	hea w	62	hawker of tapes & thread	Irl
4284	314r	[au]d	Court Lane	Elizabeth French	hea w	57	pauper; solicitor's wife	Irl
4285	314r			Rachael D. French	ser	16	house assistant	Dur [D] S. Oswald
4286	314r	[av]a	Court Lane	Isabella Cairnes	hea w	57	charwoman	Nry Kirby Hill
4287	314r			Barbara Cairnes	dau	26	laundress	Dur [D] S. Oswald
4288	314r			Jane Cairnes	dau	19	carpet weaver warper	Nbl Newcastle
4289	314r			Isaac Cairnes	son	17	whitesmith, apprentice	Nbl Newcastle *
4290	314r			Ann Denham	gda	8	scholar	Nbl Newcastle, S.John
4291	314r			John G. Tenant	gsn	11m		Nbl Tynemouth
4292	314r			Alfred J. Caines	gsn	7m		Dur [D] S. Oswald
4293	314r			Mary Denham	gda	6	scholar	Nbl Newcastle, S.John
4294	314r	[av]b	Court Lane	Joseph Cumming	hea m	34	shoemaker	Dur [D] S. Margaret
4295	314r			Harriet Cumming	wif m	40		Ken Maidstone
4296	314r			Jane M. Cumming	dau	7	scholar	Dur [D] S. Oswald
4297	314r			Margaret E. Cumming	dau	3		Dur [D] S. Oswald
4298	314r			William C. Cumming	son	3m		Dur [D] S. Oswald
4299	314r	[aw]a	Court Lane	William Robson	hea m	31	maltster	Dur Pittington
4300	314r			Margaret Robson	wif m	37		Dur Wapping
4301	314r			Hannah Robson	dau	6	scholar	Dur Moorsley
4302	314v			William Robson	son	3	scholar	Dur Durham
4303	314v			Matthew Robson	son	8	scholar	Dur Durham
4304	314v			Sarah Long	ser	13	servant	Dur Durham
4305	314v	[aw]b	Court Lane	Jane Cox	hea w	52	kept by sons	Irl
4306	314v			Michael Cox	son	15	coal miner	Irl
4307	314v			Bridget Burk	vis m	36	kept by sons	Irl
4308	314v			Ann Burk	vsd	16	agricultural labourer	Irl
4309	314v			Harry Burk	vss	13	coal miner	Irl
4310	314v			Margaret Burk	vsd	11		Irl
4311	314v			Thomas Burk	vss	8		Irl
4312	314v			Edward Burk	vss	2		Irl
4313	314v	[aw]c	Court Lane	John Magash	hea m	32	mason's labourer	Irl
4314	314v			Ann Magash	wif m	30		Sct
4315	314v			Thomas Magash	son	9	scholar	Sct
4316	314v			Ann Magash	dau	3		Dur Durham

No.	Folio	Ref	Street	Name	Rel		Age	Occupation	Birthplace
4317	314v	[aw]c	Court Lane	Isabella * Magash	dau		2		Dur Durham
4318	314v			Janet/"Jenatt" Magash	dau		4m		Dur Durham
4319	314v	[aw]d	Court Lane	John Walsh	hea	m	30	agricultural labourer	Irl
4320	314v			Mary Walsh	wif	m	26		Irl
4321	315r			Thomas Walsh	son		6		Nbl Newcastle
4322	315r			Ann Walsh	dau		1		Nbl Newcastle
4323	315r			Ann O'Doud	vis		60		Irl
4324	315r			"Ommy" O'Doud	vsd		15		Irl
4325	315r	[aw]e	Court Lane	Pat Hanley	hea	m	37	agricultural labourer	Irl
4326	315r			Catherine Hanley	wif	m	35		Irl
4327	315r			Clarrie Hanley	dau		18		Irl
4328	315r			Catherine Hanley	dau		1		Eng
4329	315r			Mary Dinsey	vis		23		Irl
4330	315r			Margaret Dinsey	vis		16		Irl
4331	315r			Francis Dinsey	vis		13	agricultural labourer	Irl
4332	315r			Catherine Dinsey	vis		23		Irl
4333	315r			Ann Gorman	vsw		30	agricultural labourer	Irl
4334	315r			James Gorman	vss		7		Irl
4335	315r			Catherine Gorman	vsd		9		Irl
4336	315r			Ann Gorman	vsd		3		Sct
4337	315r			Owen Gorman	vss		2		Eng
4338	315r			Winifred Deley	vis		27		Irl
4339	315r			Harry Gibbins	vis		30		Irl
4340	315v	[aw]f	Court Lane	Andrew West	[h]		37	auctioneer['s] servant	Dur Durham
4341	315v			John Herd	vis		49	grocer['s] servant	Dur Durham
4342	315v	[aa]	Water Lane	John Daley	hea	m	25	agricultural labourer	Irl
4343	315v			Bridget Daley	wif	m	29		Irl
4344	315v			John Daley	son		2		Dur Durham
4345	315v			Mary Daley	dau		6m		Dur Durham
4346	315v			John Fox	vis		20	dealer in nuts	Irl
4347	315v	[ab]	Water Lane	Sarah Robinson	hea	w	80	lodging house keeper	Dur Bishop Auckland
4348	315v			Ann Robinson	gda		26	dressmaker	Dur Durham
4349	315v			Peter Keenan	vis		60	hawker, not known	Irl
4350	315v			Jonathan Salter	vis		30	draper	Gls Bristol
4351	315v			David Clark	vis	m	58	calico printer	Sct
4352	315v			Elizabeth Clark	vis	m	40	capmaker	Sct
4353	315v			James Johnson	vis	m	25	tailor	Irl
4354	315v			Elizabeth Johnson	vis	m	20		Germany
4355	315v	[ac]	Water Lane	Edward Kelly	hea	m	60	lodging house keeper	Irl
4356	315v			Catherine Kelly	wif	m	40		Irl
4357	315v			Patrick Hanton	ldr	m	35	shoemaker	Irl
4358	315v			Ann Hanton	ldr	m	36	shoemaker's wife	Yks not known
4359	316r			Patrick Gaking *	*	m	40	general labourer	Irl
4360	316r			Bridget Gaking *	ldw	m	35		Irl
4361	316r			John Gaking *	lds		9		Irl
4362	316r			Elizabeth Golightly	vis		26		Dur Stanhope
4363	316r			Matthew Golightly	vis		2		Dur Houghton
4364	316r	[ad]a	Water Lane	Dominic Cane	hea	m	22	bricklayer's labourer	Sli
4365	316r			Margaret Cane	wif	m	21		Ros
4366	316r	[ad]b	Water Lane	James Battle	bro		30	lodging house keeper	Irl
4367	316r			Bridget Battle	sis		28	housekeeper	Irl
4368	316r			Mary Battle	mth	w	60		Irl
4369	316r			Francis McGowen	son	w	50	agricultural labourer	Irl
4370	316r			William McGowen	son		20	coal miner	Irl
4371	316r			Thomas Cane	son		50	coal miner	Irl
4372	316r			Michael Cane	son		9		Irl
4373	316r			James Fynet	son	m	24	coal miner	Irl
4374	316r			Catherine Fynet	swi	m	40		Irl
4375	316r			Thomas Fynet	*		1		Dur [D] S. Oswald
4376	316r			James McDonnogt	*	m	30	agricultural labourer	Dur [D] S. Oswald
4377	316r			Honour McDonnogt,	ldw	m	30	housekeeper	Dur [D] S. Oswald
4378	316v			Patrick Regan	vis	m	18	coal miner	Dur [D] S. Oswald
4379	316v			James Joice	vis	m	20	agricultural labourer	Dur [D] S. Oswald
4380	316v			John Mooran	vis	m	22	agricultural labourer	Dur [D] S. Oswald
4381	316v	[ad]c	Water Lane	William Watson	hea	m	40	iron moulder	Dur Durham
4382	316v			Elizabeth Watson	wif	m	42		Dur Durham
4383	316v			John Watson	son		15	painter's apprentice	Dur Durham
4384	316v			Elizabeth Watson	dau		13	carpet factory girl	Wry Keighley
4385	316v			Ann Watson	dau		9	scholar	Dur Durham
4386	316v			Sarah Watson	dau		7	scholar	Wry Keighley
4387	316v			Jane Watson	dau		1		Dur Durham
4388	316v	[ae]	Water Lane	Elizabeth Wheatley	hea		49	stocking knitter	Dur [D] S. Oswald
4389	316v	[af]a	Water Lane	William Blenkinsopp	hea	m	37	agricultural labourer	Dur Fishburn
4390	316v			Isabella Blenkinsopp	wif	m	40		Dur Sunderland Bridge
4391	316v			William Blenkinsopp	son		17	coachsmith, apprentice	Dur [D] S. Oswald
4392	316v			Richard Blenkinsopp	son		13	carpet factory boy	Dur [D] S. Oswald
4393	316v			Elizabeth Blenkinsopp	dau		10	scholar	Dur [D] S. Oswald
4394	316v			Jane Blenkinsopp	dau		7	scholar	Dur [D] S. Oswald
4395	316v			Ann Blenkinsopp	dau		2		Dur [D] S. Oswald
4396	316v	[af]b	Water Lane	Bridget Kellan	hea	w	60	lodging house keeper	Irl
4397	317r			Martin Kellan	son		20	agricultural labourer	Irl

4398	317r	[af]b	Water Lane	Mary Kellan	dau	18	agricultural labourer	Irl
4399	317r			Michael Kellan	son	16	agricultural labourer	Irl
4400	317r			Michael Kellan	vis w	52	agricultural labourer	Irl
4401	317r			John Kellan	vss	13	agricultural labourer	Irl
4402	317r			Catherine Nelon	*	30	wife	Irl
4403	317r			James Gorman	vis	19	not known	Irl
4404	317r	[af]c	Water Lane	Charles Divine	hea m	69	sawyer	Irl
4405	317r			Frances Divine	wif m	62		Cul Ousby
4406	317r			Henry Divine	son m	30	hawker of blacking	Cul Wigton
4407	317r			William Divine	gsn	10	mason's labourer	Cul Penrith
4408	317r	[af]d	Water Lane	Patrick Dunleary	hea m	32	dealer in handkerchiefs	Irl
4409	317r			Bridget Dunleary	wif m	40		Irl
4410	317r			Edward Reagoin	vis m	50	dealer in cottons	Irl
4411	317r			James Duffy	vis w	50	agricultural labourer	Irl
4412	317r			Thomas Michan	vis	18	coal miner	Irl
4413	317r			Patrick Duffy	vis	20	coal miner	Irl
4414	317r	[ag]a	Water Lane	Hugh Patterson	hea m	44	basketmaker	Dur Gateshead
4415	317r			Mary Patterson	wif m	52		Dur Gateshead
4416	317r	[ag]b	Water Lane	John Rutherford	hea m	58	dyer	Dur Durham
4417	317v			Jane Rutherford	wif m	33		Dur Durham
4418	317v			Elizabeth Rutherford	dau	7	scholar	Dur Durham
4419	317v			Jane Rutherford	dau	1		Dur Durham
4420	317v	[ag]c	Water Lane	Christopher Wall	hea m	46	maltster	Nbl Hartburn
4421	317v			Ann Wall	wif m	44		Dur Hurworth
4422	317v			George Wall	son	12	scholar	Dur Durham
4423	317v			Catherine Wall	dau	10	scholar	Dur Durham
4424	317v			Thomas Wall	son	7	scholar	Nbl Newcastle
4425	317v	[ag]d	Water Lane	Robert Watson	hea m	57	lead miner	Dur Wearhead
4426	317v			Sarah Watson	wif m	52		Dur Wearhead
4427	317v			Joseph Watson	son	23	carpet weaver	Dur Wearhead
4428	317v			Sarah Watson	dau	19	assistant in paper mill	Dur [D] Gilesgate
4429	317v			James Watson	son	12	scholar	Dur [D] Claypath
4430	317v	[ah]	Water Lane	John Macklam	hea w	82	whitesmith (emp 1 man)	Sct
4431	317v			James McQueen	slw m	29	police officer	Nbl Berwick
4432	317v			Elizabeth McQueen	dau m	35		Dur Durham
4433	317v			John J. McQueen	gsn	3	scholar	Dur Durham
4434	317v			Frederick McQueen	gsn	2	scholar	Dur Durham
4435	318r			William McQueen	gsn	2m		Dur Durham
4436	318r	[ai]a	Water Lane	Dennis Gannon	hea m	27	lodging house keeper	Irl
4437	318r			Catherine Gannon	wif m	29	not known	Irl
4438	318r			Annie Foley	vis w	40	not known	Irl
4439	318r			John Berlin	vis	17	not known	Irl
4440	318r			Martin Berlin	vis	12	not known	Irl
4441	318r			John McGill	vis	23	not known	Irl
4442	318r			Charles Richmond	vis	22	not known	Irl
4443	318r	[ai]b	Water Lane	Michael Owens	hea m	40	agricultural labourer	Irl
4444	318r			Bridget Owens	wif m	40	agricultural labourer	Irl
4445	318r			Luke Owens	son	19	agricultural labourer	Irl
4446	318r			Patrick Owens	son	17	agricultural labourer	Irl
4447	318r			Bridget Owens	dau	13		Irl
4448	318r			Michael Owens	son	11		Irl
4449	318r			Margaret Owens	dau	7		Irl
4450	318r			Catherine Owens	dau	5		Irl
4451	318r			James Owens	son	9m		Dur [D] S. Oswald
4452	318r			Ann Owens	dau	9		Irl
4453	318r	[ai]c	Water Lane	Thomas Killion	hea m	30	lodging house keeper	Irl
4454	318v			Ann Killion	wif m	25		Irl
4455	318v			Dennis Clark	vis m	47	agricultural labourer	Irl
4456	318v			Ann Clark	vsw m	36		Irl
4457	318v			Brian Clark	vss	11		Irl
4458	318v			Michael Clark	vss	5		Irl
4459	318v			Stephen * Clark	vss	3m		Dur Durham
4460	318v			John Awl	vis	21	agricultural labourer	Irl
4461	318v			John Cook	vis	17	sailor	Eng not known
4462	318v			Michael Fooley	vis	28	cabinetmaker	Eng not known
4463	318v			John Crow	vis m	30	agricultural labourer	Irl
4464	318v			Margaret Crow	vsw m	36		Irl
4465	318v			William Wilson	vis m	35	cattle drover	Irl
4466	318v			Bridget Wilson	vsw m	35		Irl
4467	310v			John Smith	vis	29	bucklemaker	Lan Manchester
4468	318v	[aj]	Water Lane	Catherine King	hea w	50	lodging house keeper; pp	Irl
4469	318v			Mary A. King	dau	12	scholar	Dur Durham
4470	318v			James King	son	11	coachsmith's apprentice	Dur Durham
4471	318v			Francis King	son	19	tinner's apprentice	Dur Durham
4472	318v			Peter Meghion	vis m	26	hawker of clothes	Irl
4473	318v			Betsy Meghion	vsw m	25	hawker's wife	Irl
4474	319r			Thomas Cranny	[1]	84	watchmaker	War Coventry
4475	319r			Thomas White	[1]	45	agricultural labourer	Ery Hull
4476	319r			Peter Carnell	[1] nk	50	cattle drover	Irl
4477	319r			Joseph Williams	* m	42	groom	Mdx London
4478	319r			Elizabeth Williams	ldw m	41		Mdx London

4479	319r	[aj]	Water Lane	William Millian	[1] nk 50		agricultural labourer	Irl
4480	319r			John Wattas	[1] nk 60		cattle drover	Irl
4481	319r	[av]	New Elvet	Margaret Atkinson	hea w 56		confectioner	Dur Trimdon
4482	319r			Jane Wrangham	sis m 51		farmer's servant	Dur Trimdon
4483	319r	<62>	New Elvet	Charles S. Ilderton	hea m 54		tinner & brazier *	Dur Durham
4484	319r			Mary Ilderton	wif m 54		<staymaker>	Dur Durham
4485	319r			Ann Herbert	mlw w 82		fmly shopkeeper; pauper	Dur Durham
4486	319r			George Pollock	app 19		tinner & brazier's app	Cul Carlisle
4487	319r			Ann Stewart	ser 16		house servant	Lan Liverpool
4488	319r	62 a	New Elvet *	Thomas Hornsby	hea m 56		carpenter	Dur Durham
4489	319r			Margaret Hornsby	wif m 58			Dur Durham
4490	319r			William Hornsby	son 19		currier's apprentice	Dur Durham
4491	319r			John Fawcett	vis 35		brewer	Dur Durham
4492	319v			Jeffery Heslton	vis 30		farmer	Yks not known
4493	319v			Metcalfe * Iverson	vis 25		farmer	Yks not known
4494	319v			Thomas Woodward	vis 28		farmer	Yks not known
4495	319v	62 b	New Elvet *	Thomas Pearson	hea m 55		cartman	Dur Durham
4496	319v			Elizabeth Pearson	wif m 51			Dur Durham
4497	319v			Martha Pearson	dau 19		factory (carpet) girl	Dur Durham
4498	319v			Thomas Pearson	son 14		factory (carpet) boy	Dur Durham
4499	319v	62 c	New Elvet *	Thomas Hutton	hea m 25		joiner	Dur Bishopwearmouth
4500	319v			Elizabeth Hutton	wif m 23			Dur Jarrow
4501	319v	62 d	New Elvet *	William Lindsey	hea m 50		groom	Dur [D] S. Oswald
4502	319v			Ann Lindsey	wif m 52			Dur Gainford
		63	New Elvet	uninhabited				
4503	319v	[aw]	New Elvet	Patrick Gammon	hea m 52		general labourer	Irl
4504	319v			Catherine Gammon	wif m 60			Irl
4505	319v			Pat Smith	vis 20		coal miner	Irl
4506	319v			Robert Brodrick	vis 21		vagrant	not known
4507	319v	<64>a	New Elvet	Thomas Buston <jn>	hea m 30		barber <& news vendor>	Dur [D] S. Oswald
4508	319v			Barbara Buston	wif m 30			Dur Shadforth
4509	319v	<64>b	New Elvet	John Tiplady	hea m 52		joiner	Dur Durham
4510	320r			Elizabeth Tiplady	wif m 44			Nry Newholm
4511	320r			Rebecca Pybus	sda 16		seamstress	Nry Whitby
4512	320r	<64>c	New Elvet	John Maddison	hea m 28		master tailor	Dur [D] S. Oswald
4513	320r			Elizabeth Maddison	wif m 28			Dur [D] S. Oswald
4514	320r			Elizabeth Maddison	dau 6		scholar	Dur [D] S. Oswald
4515	320r			William Maddison	son 4		scholar	Dur [D] S. Oswald
4516	320r	<64>d	New Elvet	Margaret Hopper	hea 24		pauper	Dur Durham
4517	320r			Thomas Hopper	bro 15		scholar	Dur Durham
4518	320r			Henry Hopper	bro 12		scholar	Dur Durham
4519	320r			George Hopper	bro 7		scholar	Dur Durham
4520	320r	<64>e	New Elvet	Matthew Stelling	hea m 24		agricultural labourer	Yks Ashby
4521	320r			Isabella Stelling	wif m 33			Nbl Bedlington
4522	320r			George Stelling	son 3			Dur Shotton
4523	320r			Thomas Stelling	son 1			Dur Durham
4524	320r	<64>f	New Elvet	Arthur McIlion	hea m 28		mason's labourer	May
4525	320r			Sarah McIlion	wif m 24			May
4526	320r			Maria McIlion	dau 6m			Dur Durham
4527	320r			Anthony Gannon	blw 17		mason's labourer	May
4528	320r			Bridget Gannon	mlw w 60		supported by son	May
4529	320v			Mary Reygin	vis w 35		hawker of prints	Sli
4530	320v	<65>	New Elvet	Mary Hutton	hea 48		grocer	Dur [D] S. Oswald
4531	320v			Elizabeth Hutton	mth w 78		retired greengrocer	Dur Brancepeth
4532	320v	<66>	New Elvet	George Fenwick	hea m 48		baker, master *	Dur Durham
4533	320v			Sarah Fenwick	wif m 32			Dur Gateshead
4534	320v			George Fenwick	son 20		butcher's apprentice	Dur Durham
4535	320v			Charles Turnbull	app 20		baker's apprentice	Dur Durham
4536	320v	<68>	New Elvet	George Caldcleugh	hea w 57		porter merchant *	Dur Durham
4537	320v			Ann Caldcleugh	dau 30			Dur Durham
4538	320v			Jane Wilson	sil 63			Nth Peterborough
4539	320v			Ann Ritson	ser 27		house servant	Dur Wolsingham
4540	320v	[ax]	New Elvet	Dinah Charlton	hea w 60		washerwoman	Dur Lanchester
4541	320v			Thomas Charlton	gsn 16		printing pressman app	Dur Lanchester
4542	320v			Jane Charlton	gda 11		scholar	Dur Durham
4543	320v	[ay]	New Elvet	Hannah Bilton	hea m 53		ostler's wife	Dur not known
4544	320v			Ralph Bilton	son 15		printer's apprentice	Dur Durham
4545	320v			Thomas Bilton	son 11		scholar	Dur Durham
4546	320v			John Rutherford	vis m 27		weaver	Nbl Hexham
4547	320v			Mary Rutherford	vis m 23		weaver's wife	Dur Durham
4548	321r			Hannah Rutherford	vsd 5		scholar	Dur Durham
4549	321r			Mary Rutherford	vsd 1			Dur Durham
4550	321r	[az]	New Elvet	Ann Bainbridge	hea w 38		laundress	Dur Durham
4551	321r			Robert Bainbridge	son 15		printer's apprentice	Dur Durham
4552	321r			Mary Ann Bainbridge	dau 12		milliner & errand girl	Dur Durham
4553	321r	[ba]a	New Elvet	George Coleman	hea m 30		hawker of hardware	Irl
4554	321r			Bridget Coleman	wif m 26			Irl
4555	321r			Thomas Coleman	son 9m			Eng
4556	321r			Michael Coleman	bro 28		agricultural labourer	Irl
4557	321r	[ba]b	New Elvet	John Hanby	hea m 35		agricultural labourer	Ros
4558	321r			Catherine Hanby	wif m 35		agricultural labr's wife	Ros

4559 321r	[ba]b	New Elvet	Patrick Moore	vis	24	drainer	Mog
4560 321r			Richard Crudon	vis	25	mason's labourer	Dub
4561 321r			Michael Kerland	vis	17	agricultural labourer	Ros
4562 321r	[ba]c	New Elvet	Thomas Gill	hea	38	agricultural labourer	Ros
4563 321r			Catherine Gill	wif	40	agricultural labr's wife	Ros
4564 321r			Michael Gill	son	15	factory boy	Ros
4565 321r			John Gill	son	13	factory boy	Ros
4566 321r			Patrick Gill	son	10		Ros
4567 321v			Ellen Gill	dau	8		Ros
4568 321v			Maria Gill	dau	1		Dur Durham
4569 321v	[ba]d	New Elvet	Patrick O'Donell	hea m	60	agricultural labourer	Irl
4570 321v			Catherine O'Donell	wif m	45		Irl
4571 321v			Patrick O'Donell	son	15	factory boy	Irl
4572 321v			Michael O'Donell	son	14	factory boy	Irl
4573 321v			Thomas O'Donell	son	10		Irl
4574 321v	[bb]a	New Elvet	John Trahil	hea m	35	agricultural labourer	Lim
4575 321v			Mary Trahil	wif m	40	agricultural labr's wife	Ros
4576 321v	[bb]b	New Elvet	Thomas Haigan	hea m	50	agricultural labourer	Ros
4577 321v			Mary Haigan	wif m	50		Gal
4578 321v			William Haigan	son	16	errand boy	Ros
4579 321v			Catherine Slattery	sil w	28	dressmaker	Gal
4580 321v			Ann Gibbons	vis	19	weaver	Ros
4581 321v			Catherine Connel	sis m	42	agricultural labourer	Ros
4582 321v			Mary Connel	*	15	factory girl	Ros
4583 321v			Martin Connel	*	11	factory boy	Ros
4584 321v			Catherine Connel	*	9	scholar	Ros
4585 321v			Ann Connel	*	5	scholar	Irl
		one house uninhabited					
4586 322r	[bc]	New Elvet	George Young	hea m	34	hairdresser	Cul Carlisle
4587 322r			Elizabeth Young	wif m	35		Dur Shiney Row
4588 322r			George Young	son	3		Nbl Newcastle
4589 322r			Robert Young	son	2m		Dur Durham
4590 322r			Ann Daley	ser	20	house servant	Irl
4591 322r	[bd]	New Elvet	Isabella Wakeman	hea w	66	dressmaker	Dur Sedgefield
4592 322r			Margaret Wakeman	dau	36	dressmaker	Dur [D] S. Oswald
4593 322r			Caroline Wakeman	dau	30	straw-hatmaker	Dur [D] S. Oswald
4594 322r			Isabella C. Stork	nce	12	scholar	Nbl Wooler
4595 322r	<72>	New Elvet	Joseph Brown	hea m	46	brewer & innkeeper *	Dur Shadforth
4596 322r			Maria Brown	wif m	46		Dur [D] S. Oswald
4597 322r			Thomas Brown	son	19	writing clerk	Dur Durham
4598 322r			George Brown	son	17	blacksmith, apprentice	Dur Durham
4599 322r			Jane Brown	dau	14		Dur Durham
4600 322r			Jane Fishwick	vis	45	cook	Nry Kirkleatham
4601 322r			John Forster	vis m	41	horse dealer & farmer *	Cul Nichol Forest
4602 322r			Andrew Forster	vis	22	horse dealer's servant	Cul Nichol Forest
4603 322r	[be]	New Elvet	William Welsh	hea w	40	drayman	Dur Houghton-1-Spring
4604 322r			Mary Welsh	sis	30	housekeeper	Dur Houghton-1-Spring
4605 322v			Matthew Welsh	son	14	printer's apprentice	Dur South Shields
4606 322v			Margaret Welsh	dau	10	scholar	Dur Durham
4607 322v			John Welsh	son	8	scholar	Dur [D] S. Oswald
4608 322v			William Welsh	son	6	scholar	Dur [D] S. Oswald
4609 322v			Ralph Welsh	son	4		Dur [D] S. Oswald
4610 322v	<74>	New Elvet	John Bentham	hea m	70	agent for brewery *	Lin Stamford
4611 322v			Isabella Bentham	wif m	50		Ban Huntley
4612 322v			Hannah Bentham	dau	31	Berlin wool retailer	Nry Yarm
4613 322v			Hannah Turnbull	ser	20	house servant	Dur Darlington
4614 322v	<75>	New Elvet	William Tiplady <sn>	hea w	74	tailor, master *	Dur Kelloe
4615 322v			Henry Tiplady	son	28	painter, master *	Dur [D] S. Oswald
4616 322v			Hannah Tiplady	dau	24		Dur [D] S. Oswald
4617 322v			Frances Tiplady	dau	22		Dur [D] S. Oswald
4618 322v			Margaret Ross	ser	22	house servant	Dur Houghton-1-Spring
4619 322v	[bf]	New Elvet	Sarah Salkeld	[h] w	50	retired innkeeper	Dur Lanchester
4620 322v	<76>	New Elvet	Joseph Rennison	hea m	24	journeyman coachmaker	Dur Durham
4621 322v			Catherine Rennison	wif m	27	milliner	Dur Bishopwearmouth
4622 322v	<77>	New Elvet	John Robson	hea m	56	tailor	Dur [D] S. Giles
4623 322v			Mary E. Robson	dau m	29	milliner	Dur [D] S. Nicholas
4624 323r			Barbara E. Robson	dau m	23	dressmaker	Dur [D] S. Oswald
4625 323r	<78>	New Elvet	William Blackett	hea m	49	turner & grocer *	Dur [D] S. Oswald
4626 323r			Barbara Blackett	wif m	46	wife	Dur Brancepeth
4627 323r			Margaret Blackett	dau	25	schoolmistress *	Dur Brancepeth
4628 323r			Alice Blackett	dau	23	schoolmistress *	Dur Brancepeth
4629 323r			Elizabeth Blackett	dau	18		Dur Brancepeth
4630 323r			Harriet J. Blackett	dau	16		Dur Brancepeth
4631 323r			George P. Blackett	son	13	scholar	Dur Brancepeth
4632 323r			Ann Blackett	dau	6	scholar	Dur Brancepeth
4633 323r			John H. Blackett	son	2		Dur Brancepeth
4634 323r	[bg]a	New Elvet	William Borrowdale	hea m	31	drayman	Wes Appleby
4635 323r			Elizabeth Borrowdale	wif m	31	wife	Nry Masham
4636 323r			Robert W. Borrowdale	son	5		Dur [D] S. Nicholas
4637 323r			William B. Borrowdale	son	3		Dur [D] S. Nicholas
4638 323r			Thomas W. Borrowdale	son	3m		Dur [D] S. Oswald

4639	323r	[bg]b	New Elvet	John Bowey	hea m	28	cabdriver	Dur Durham
4640	323r			Jane Bowey	wif m	27		Dur Durham
4641	323r			Wilson Bowey	son	2		Dur [D] S. Oswald
4642	323r			John Bowey	son	6m		Dur [D] S. Oswald
4643	323v	<79>	New Elvet	Peter Caldcleugh	hea m	56	tailor & draper	Dur Durham
4644	323v			Eliza Caldcleugh	wif m	51		Dur Durham
4645	323v			Jane Caldcleugh	dau m	29		Dur Durham
4646	323v			R.S. Caldcleugh	son	28	tailor & draper's jnym	Dur Durham
4647	323v			Frances M. Caldcleugh	dau	13	school	Dur Durham
4648	323v			Mary Ann Shaw	ser	20	domestic servant	Nbl Newcastle
4649	323v			Robert Nesham	app	19	tailor's apprentice	Dur Durham
4650	323v	<80>a	New Elvet	George Rodham	hea w	71	pensioner (Chelsea)	Dur Staindrop
4651	323v			"Tatune" Price	sis w	57	landed proprietor	Dur Staindrop
4652	323v	<80>b	New Elvet	Mary Addamson	hea w	67	landed proprietor	Dur Cleadon
4653	323v			Jane Addamson	dau	33	dressmkr <straw-hatmkr>	Dur Durham
4654	323v			William Addamson	vis m	70	farmer	Dur Windlestone
4655	323v	<80>	New Elvet	John Cairnes	hea w	60	coachmaker, master *	Dur Barnard Castle
4656	323v			Ann Swallwell	ser	20	home servant	Dur Lambton
			one house uninhabited					
4657	323v	<82>	New Elvet	Paulin Canegham	hea m	36	bootmaker, master *	France
4658	323v			Rose Canegham	wif m	38	<staymaker etc.>	France
4659	323v			Arthur Canegham	son	9	scholar	Ssx Brighton
4660	323v			Alexander Canegham	son	9m		Dur Durham
4661	323v			Ranaghan Shaby	ser	20	servant	Irl
4662	324r			Susanna Forster	ser	17	servant	Dur Durham
			one house uninhabited <'Raby Castle'>					
4663	324r	<84>	New Elvet	George D. Shafto	hea	30	gentleman	Dur [D] S. Oswald
4664	324r			Ann Oswald	ser	21	house servant	Dur Sunderland
4665	324r	<85>	New Elvet	Ralph Robinson	hea m	54	cabinetmaker, master *	Dur Durham
4666	324r			Hannah Robinson	wif m	53		Dur Durham
4667	324r			John J. Robinson	son	26	cabinetmaker	Dur Durham
4668	324r			Mark Robinson	son	23	upholsterer	Dur Durham
4669	324r			William Robinson	son	21	cabinetmaker	Dur Durham
4670	324r			Ralph Robinson	son	19	chemist & druggist	Dur Durham
4671	324r			Anne H. Robinson	dau	16		Dur Durham
4672	324r			Jane Robinson	dau	14		Dur Durham
4673	324r			Francis T. Robinson	son	11	scholar	Dur Durham
4674	324r			Mary Woodifield	ser	16	house servant	Dur Durham
4675	324r	<86>	New Elvet	Sarah Petch	hea	50	innkeeper <'Half Moon'>	Nry Little Broughton
4676	324r			Ann Petch	hea	48	innkeeper <'Half Moon'>	Nry Newby Grange
4677	324r			Alice Walker	sis w	63	annuitant	Dur Long Newton
4678	324r			William Petch	bro	46	farmer, not known *	Nbl not known
4679	324r			Ann Gardiner	ser	19	servant	Dur not known
4680	324v			Margaret Teasdale	ser m	60	house servant	Nry Gilling
4681	324v			John Hudson	m	33	ostler	Dur Ferryhill
4682	324v			Thomas P. Benson	m	43	groom	Nry Kirby Wiske
4683	324v			John Tiplady		55	groom	Yks Shelton
4684	324v			William Jervis		47	groom	Nry Boltby
4685	324v			John Heslop	m	39	builder	Nbl Dissington
4686	324v			John Nicholson	m	57	cattle dealer	Yks not known
4687	324v			Ann Irwins	ser	20	assistant servant	Dur not known
4688	324v	<87>	New Elvet *	Thomas Colpitts	hea m	34	innkeeper <'Wheatsheaf'>	Dur Westerton
4689	324v			Mary Colpitts	wif m	34		Dur Wolsingham
4690	324v			Jane Colpitts	dau	2		Dur Durham
4691	324v			Mary Dunn	ser	20	house servant	Dur Bishop Auckland
4692	324v			Euphemia Robson	ser	26	house servant	Dur Houghton
4693	324v	<88>	New Elvet *	Benjamin Hill <jn>	hea m	39	grocer *	Dur Durham
4694	324v			Sarah Hill	wif m	38		Dur Durham
4695	324v			John Hill	son	17	miller's apprentice	Dur Durham
4696	324v			Frederick Hill	son	15		Dur Durham
4697	324v			Charles Hill	son	12	scholar	Dur Durham
4698	324v			Benjamin Hill	son	10	scholar	Dur Durham
4699	325r			Thomas Hill	son	8	scholar	Dur Durham
4700	325r			Mary J. Hill	dau	6	scholar	Dur Durham
4701	325r			Margaret Hill	dau	3		Dur Durham
4702	325r			Mary H. Robson	vis	46	straw-hatmaker	Nbl Newcastle
4703	325r	[bh]	New Elvet *	Elizabeth Richardson	hea w	41	laundress	Dur Durham
4704	325r			Margaret Richardson	dau	18	straw-hatmaker	Dur Durham
4705	325r			Michael Richardson	son	14	bootbinder's apprentice	Dur Durham
4706	325r	[bi]	New Elvet *	Isabella Smith	hea w	52	nurse	Dur Durham
4707	325r			Thompson Smith	son	31	officer in County Prison	Dur Durham
4708	325r			Frances S. Smith	dau	18	servant (at home)	Dur Durham
4709	325r			Alice Smith	dau	12	scholar	Dur Durham
4710	325r			Eleanor Smith	dau	9	scholar	Dur Durham
4711	325r			Elizabeth Thompson	mth w	76	pauper; Cath charity *	Dur Durham
4712	325r	<91>	New Elvet *	Joseph Worthy	hea m	34	cabinetmaker	Dur [D] S. Giles
4713	325r			Maria J. Worthy	wif m	35	dressmaker <& milliner>	Dur [D] S. Oswald
4714	325r			Henry Worthy	son	3m		Dur [D] S. Oswald
4715	325r			Eleanor Hopper	mlw w	60	supported by son-in-law	Dur not known
4716	325r	<92>	New Elvet *	Robert Grieveson	hea m	24	wood turner & innkeeper*	Dur Stockton
4717	325r			Jane Grieveson	wif m	26	wood turner's wife	Nbl North Shields

4718	325v	<92>	New Elvet *	Jane Ann Grieveson	dau	3		Dur Bishopwearmouth
4719	325v			Grace Grieveson	dau	8m		Dur Gateshead
4720	325v			Jane Grieveson	sis	13		Dur Monkwearmouth
4721	325v			Peter Gib	vis m	61	visitor	Sct
4722	325v	<93>	New Elvet *	Jane Spink	hea w	44	stationer	Dur Durham
4723	325v			Thomas Spink	son	19	chemist, apprentice	Dur Durham
4724	325v			Maria Spink	dau	15		Dur Durham
4725	325v			Jane J. Spink	dau	10	scholar	Dur Durham
4726	325v			Margaret Spink	dau	9	scholar	Dur Durham
4727	325v			Alice S. Spink	dau	7	scholar	Dur Durham
4728	325v			Maria Loughborough	sis	34	annuitant	Dur Durham
4729	325v			Ann Weathell	ser	26	house servant	Dur Stockton
4730	325v	<94>	New Elvet *	George Farrow	hea m	42	veterinary surgeon *	Dur Esh
4731	325v			Jane Farrow	wif m	28		Nbl Lemington
4732	325v			Elizabeth A. Farrow	dau	5m		Dur Durham
4733	325v			George Miller	app	16	app to shoeing smith	Dur Durham
4734	325v			Mary Richardson	ser	15	house servant	Dur Durham
4735	325v	<1>	Old Elvet	William Burn	hea m	26	chemist & druggist	Dur East Rainton
4736	325v			Mary Burn	wif m	25		Dur Gateshead
4737	325v			Mary Burn	dau	5m		Dur [D] S. Oswald
4738	326r			Elizabeth Conner	ser	17	house servant	Wls
4739	326r	<2>	Old Elvet	Joseph Taylor	hea m	43	innkeeper & mason *	Dur [D] S. Oswald
4740	326r			Ann Taylor	wif m	43		Dur Sunderland Bridge
4741	326r			Thomas Taylor	son	17	mason's apprentice	Dur [D] S. Oswald
4742	326r			Joseph Taylor	son	15	mason's apprentice	Dur [D] S. Oswald
4743	326r			Sarah Waite	ser	14	house servant	Dur Washington
4744	326r			Mary Launsdon	ser	21	house servant	Dur Whitworth
4745	326r			William Oliver	nep	6	scholar	Dur Merrington
4746	326r			Joseph Blair	vis	36	woodman	Dur Sunderland Bridge
4747	326r	<3>a	Old Elvet	Margaret Elliott	hea w	51	pauper; laundress	Dur Barnard Castle
4748	326r			James Elliott	son	19	ostler	Dur [D] S. Oswald
4749	326r			Ann Elliott	dau	15	dressmaker	Dur [D] S. Oswald
4750	326r			Sarah Elliott	dau	13	errand girl	Dur [D] S. Oswald
4751	326r			Thomas Fawcett	vis	22	general labourer	Dur [D] S. Oswald
4752	326r	<3>b	Old Elvet	Thomas Hickson	hea m	46	Post Office messenger	Dur Durham
4753	326r			Mary Hickson	wif m	41		Dur Darlington
4754	326r			Emma Hickson	dau	7	scholar	Dur Durham
4755	326r			Mary Hickson	dau	5	scholar	Dur Durham
4756	326r			Frederick Hickson	son	3	scholar	Dur Durham
4757	326v	<3>c	Old Elvet	George Alcock	hea m	29	coachman	Dur Chester-le-Street
4758	326v			Mary Alcock	wif m	29		Edn Edinburgh
4759	326v			George Alcock	son	8	scholar	Nbl North Shields
4760	326v			William Alcock	son	6	scholar	Nbl North Shields
4761	326v			Barbara Alcock	dau	4		Dur Durham
4762	326v			Mary Ann Alcock	dau	2		Dur Durham
4763	326v	<3>d	Old Elvet	William Bowey	hea m	53	groom	Dur Durham
4764	326v			Thomason Bowey	wif m	56		Dur Lanchester
4765	326v			Mary Bowey	dau	22		Dur Durham
4766	326v			George Bowey	son	16	joiner's apprentice	Dur Durham
4767	326v			William Bowey	gsn	1m		Dur Durham
4768	326v	<4>a	Old Elvet	George Shaw	hea	54	MRCSL, LSA * <surgeon>	Dur [D] Framwelgate
4769	327r	<4>b	Old Elvet	Robert Middleton	hea m	49	whitesmith	Dur [D] Framwelgate
4770	327r			Lydia Middleton	wif m	49		Nbl Ovingham
4771	327r			William Middleton	son	15	surgeon's apprentice	Dur [D] S. Oswald
4772	327r			Charles Middleton	son	13	scholar	Dur [D] S. Oswald
4773	327r			Mary Jopling	ser	16	house servant	Dur East Rainton
4774	327r	<5>	Old Elvet	Benjamin Hill	hea w	72	whitesmith *	Dur Hartburn
4775	327r			Hannah Hill	dau	43		Dur Durham
4776	327r			Jane Hill	dau	41		Dur Durham
4777	327r	<6>	Old Elvet	John W. Hays	hea m	62	attorney at law *	Dur Durham
4778	327r			Elizabeth Hays	wif m	59		Nry Whitby
4779	327r			Elizabeth Hays	dau	26		Dur Durham
4780	327r			Eleanor Hays	dau	25		Dur Durham
4781	327r			Anne Hays	dau	23		Dur Durham
4782	327r			Margaret Hays	dau	22		Dur Durham
4783	327r			Isabella Hays	dau	21		Dur Durham
4784	327r			Jane Hays	dau	19		Dur Durham
4785	327r			Abigail Thirkwell	ser	28	house servant	Dur Durham
4786	327r			Sarah Hick	ser	23	house servant	Cam Fen Drayton
4787	327r			Anne M. Taylor	ser	21	house servant	Dur Castle Eden
4788	327v	<7>	Old Elvet	Edwin Tyler	hea	42	general practitioner *	Dur [D] College
4789	327v			Elizabeth Tyler	mth w	76	annuitant	Mdx Marylebone
4790	327v			Susanna Tyler	sis	40	annuitant	Dur [D] College
4791	327v			Anne Wilson	ser	23	servant	Dur Hetton-le-Hole
4792	327v	<8>	Old Elvet	Ann Davison	hea	50	dressmaker	Dur Stockton
4793	327v			Margaret Davison	sis	41	dressmkr <straw-hatmkr>	Dur Durham
4794	327v			Elizabeth Davison	sis	39	bonnetmaker	Dur Durham
4795	327v	<9>	Old Elvet	Hannah Hardinge	hea m	39	annuitant	Ken not known
4796	327v			Henry Hardinge	son	19	soldier, ensign *	Dur Darlington
4797	327v			William Hardinge	son	14	scholar	Dur Darlington
4798	327v			Fanny Hardinge	dau	20		Dur Darlington

4799	327v	<9>	Old Elvet	Hannah Hardinge	dau	16	scholar	Dur Darlington
4800	327v			Emily Hardinge	dau	13	scholar	Dur Darlington
4801	327v			Caroline Hardinge	dau	11	scholar	Dur Darlington
4802	327v			Frances Chaile	nse	50	nurse	Dur Durham
4803	327v			Ann Robson	ser	18	waiting maid	Dur Durham
4804	327v			Ellen Gregg	ser	28	cook	Dur Durham
4805	327v			Phyllis Fordy	ser	25	house maid	Dur Durham
4806	327v	<10>	Old Elvet	William C. King	hea m	50	rector of S. Mary-le-Bow	Sfk Gunton
4807	328r			Sarah King	wif m	46	gentlewoman	Nbl Elswick
4808	328r			Sarah E. King	dau	20	gentlewoman	Nbl Elswick
4809	328r			William King	son	17	undergraduate *	Nbl Backworth
4810	328r			John R. King	son	15	scholar	Nbl Backworth
4811	328r			Anne A. King	dau	14	scholar (at home)	Nbl Backworth
4812	328r			Richard H. King	son	12	scholar	Nbl Backworth
4813	328r			Mary J. King	dau	9	scholar (at home)	Nbl Backworth
4814	328r			Jane King	dau	7	scholar (at home)	Nbl Backworth
4815	328r			Arthur King	son	4		Dur [D] S. Oswald
4816	328r			Isabella H. Lacey	gov	25	teacher	Wil Salisbury
4817	328r			Barbara Proctor	ser	35	[housekeeper]	Nbl Newcastle
4818	328r			Elizabeth Akenhead	nse	48	[nurse]	Nbl Newcastle
4819	328r			Elizabeth Lisle	ser	23	[lady's maid]	Nbl S. John Lee
4820	328r			Susanna Matthew	ser	25	[nursery maid]	Nbl North Shields
4821	328r			Margaret Turnbull	ser	33	[house maid]	Nbl Bellingham
4822	328r			Elizabeth Surtees	ser	21	[house maid]	Nbl Heddon-on-th-Wall
4823	328r			Margaret Cook	ser	28	[laundry maid]	Dur Wolviston
4824	328r			Mary Scott	ser	24	[kitchen maid]	Nbl Bellingham
4825	328r			John Darling	ser	16	[page]	Nbl Wallsend
4826	328r	<11>	Old Elvet	William Brignal	hea m	41	solicitor	Dur [D] S. Nicholas
4827	328v			Sarah F. Brignal	wif m	45		Nbl Newcastle, S. Ann
4828	328v			Sarah S. Oliver	sda	23		Nbl Newcastle
4829	328v			Dorothy A. Oliver	sda	21		Nbl Newcastle
4830	328v			Esther S. Oliver	sda	17		Nbl Newcastle, S.John
4831	328v			Fanny Brignal	dau	10	scholar (at home)	Dur [D] S. Giles
4832	328v			William Brignal	son	7	scholar (at home)	Dur [D] S. Oswald
4833	328v			Emily W. Brignal	dau	5	scholar (at home)	Dur [D] S. Oswald
4834	328v			Ann Liddle	ser	27	cook	Nbl Newcastle
4835	328v			Mary Ranson	ser	23	nurse	Dur Penshaw
4836	328v			Elizabeth Stolling	ser	22	house maid	Nry Leeming
4837	328v	<12>	Old Elvet	Elizabeth A. Arrowsmith	hea w	43	landed proprietor	Dur Sedgefield
4838	328v			Elizabeth A. Arrowsmith	dau	17		Dur [D] S. Giles
4839	328v			Emily M. Arrowsmith	dau	16		Dur Sedgefield
4840	328v			John D. Arrowsmith	son	14	scholar	Dur Sedgefield
4841	328v			William D. Arrowsmith	son	12	scholar	Dur Sedgefield
4842	328v			Sarah Arrowsmith	dau	11	scholar	Dur Sedgefield
4843	328v			Frederick Arrowsmith	son	9	scholar (at home)	Dur Sedgefield
4844	328v			Louisa J. Arrowsmith	dau	6	scholar (at home)	Dur Sedgefield
4845	329r			Jane Charlton	ser	36	house servant	Dur [D] S. Oswald
4846	329r			Isabella Turner	ser	20	house servant	Nbl Alnwick
4847	329r			Mary Ann Nicholson	ser	18	house servant	Dur Hetton-le-Hole
4848	329r	[aa]	Old Elvet	Nicholas Chapman	hea m	47	groom	Dur Thornley
4849	329r			Elizabeth Chapman	wif m	43		Dur Staindrop
4850	329r			Mary Ann Chapman	dau	13	scholar	Dur Witton-le-Wear
4851	329r			Thomas Chapman	son	11	scholar	Dur Durham
4852	329r	<13>	Old Elvet	David H. Stack	hea m	36	barrister at law *	Irl
4853	329r			Margaret Stack	wif m	28		Dur Ford
4854	329r			Morris H. Stack	son	2		Dur [D] S. Oswald
4855	329r			Edwin H. Stack	son	10m		Dur [D] S. Oswald
4856	329r			Margaret Simpson	ser	19	cook	Dur [D] S. Oswald
4857	329r			Elizabeth Emery	ser	17	house maid	Dur [D] S. Oswald
4858	329r	<14>	Old Elvet	Sarah Bowlby	hea w	77	interest of money	Hrt not known
4859	329r			Elizabeth Bowlby	dau	57		Dur [D] S. Mary
4860	329r			Mary Bowlby	gda	28	landed proprietor	Dur [D] S. Oswald
4861	329r			Mary Ord	ser m	49	servant	Dur Eggleston
4862	329r	<15>	Old Elvet	Rosalie Pierre	wif m	32	milliner & dressmaker	France, Paris
4863	329r			Anais Pierre	dau	10		France, Paris
4864	329v			Adela Simon	cou w	35	dressmaker	France, Paris
4865	329v	<16>	Old Elvet	Mary Tindale	hea w	71	lodging house keeper	Dur [D] S. Oswald
4866	329v			Jane Martin	sis w	78	lodging house keeper	Dur [D] S. Oswald
4867	329v			Alice Featonby	sis	81	lodging house keeper	Dur Elwick
4868	329v			Jane Ramsbottom	ser	20	house servant	Dur Chester-le-Street
4869	329v	<17>	Old Elvet	Julia Thompson	hea w	66	house proprietor	Dur Rainton
4870	329v			Jane Wilson	ser	16	servant	Dur Durham
4871	329v	<18>	Old Elvet	Sarah H. Taylor	hea w	48	fundholder	Wry Doncaster
4872	329v			Alice Taylor	dau	27		Nbl Newcastle
4873	329v			Robert Taylor	son	25	law student	Nbl Newcastle
4874	329v			Rosamund Taylor	dau	19		Nbl Newcastle
4875	329v			Lewis Taylor	son	17	scholar	Nbl Newcastle
4876	329v			Mary Cunneen	ser	21	house servant	Lim
4877	329v	<19>a	Old Elvet	David James Stewart	hea m	36	HM inspector of schools*	Sry not known
4878	329v			Louisa Stewart	wif m	33	clergyman's wife	Ssx Brighton
4879	329v			Aubrey Stewart	son	6		Cam Ely

4880	329v	<19>a	Old Elvet	Edward Reeves	ser		25	house servant	Wil Bratton
4881	329v			Hannah Bays	ser	m	58	nurse	Nfk Norwich
4882	329v	<19>b	Old Elvet	Jane Caldcleugh	hea	w	53	board and lodgings (let)	Dur Durham
4883	330r			Thomas Hayes	vis	m	33	ironmonger	Dur Trimdon
4884	330r			Sophia E. Hayes	vis	m	22	ironmonger's wife	Nfk Aylmerton
4885	330r			Sophia Reeves	bdr	m	18		Wil not known
4886	330r			Harry Carter	bdr		27	professor of music	Brk Windsor
4887	330r			Jane Chapman	ser		19	house servant	Yks not known
4888	330r	[ab]	Old Elvet	William Fletcher	hea		51	Roman Catholic priest *	Lan Eccleston
4889	330r			Perpetua Fletcher	sis		49	fundholder	Lan Ormskirk
4890	330r			Winifred Wharton	ser		28	cook	Nry Richmond
4891	330r			Ann Leighton	ser		17	house maid	Nbl Hexham
4892	330r	<20>	Old Elvet	Dorothy Horn	hea	w	61	landed proprietor	Dur Shincliffe
4893	330r			William Horn	son		37	interest of money	Dur Bishopwearmouth
4894	330r			Matthew Murgatroyd	ser	m	70	footman	Dur [D] S. Nicholas
4895	330r			Dorothy Lawes	ser		31	cook	Dur Westoe
4896	330r	<21>	Old Elvet	Priscilla Robson	hea	w	60	annuitant	Gls Moreton-in-Marsh
4897	330r			Alice Forster	ser		20	house servant	Dur Shincliffe
4898	330r	<22>	Old Elvet	Richard Thompson	hea	m	40	solicitor	Dur Durham
4899	330r			Margaret Thompson	wif	m	36		Dur extra-parochial
4900	330r			Mary Thompson	dau		19		Dur Durham
4901	330r			Thomas Thompson	son		4		Dur Durham
4902	330v			Margaret Thompson	dau		2		Dur Durham
4903	330v			Julia Ann Thompson	dau		1		Dur Durham
4904	330v			Isabella Blackett	ser		24	house servant	Dur Durham
4905	330v			Margaret Bulmer	ser		18	house servant	Dur Durham
4906	330v			Ellen Etherington	ser		16	house servant	Dur Lanchester
4907	330v	<23>	Old Elvet	Percival Forster	hea	w	67	land agent *	Nbl Elsdon
4908	330v			Mary S. Forster	dau		29	land agent's daughter	Dur [D] S. Nicholas
4909	330v			Maria Forster	dau		23	land agent's daughter	Dur [D] S. Nicholas
4910	330v			Dorothy J. Forster	dau		19	land agent's daughter	Dur [D] S. Oswald
4911	330v			Jane Bulmer	ser		26	house servant	Dur [D] S. Oswald
4912	330v	<24>	Old Elvet	Robert Waugh	hea	w	54	esquire, proprietor *	Dur Durham
4913	330v			Anne M. Waugh	dau		28		Dur Durham
4914	330v			Mary Gargett	ser		47	house servant	Nry Barton
4915	330v			Ann Saunders	ser		26	house servant	Dur Durham
4916	330v			Robert Turnbull	ser		44	house servant	Dur Lanchester
4917	330v	<25>	Old Elvet	John H. Forster	hea	m	36	mayor (land agent)	Dur Durham
4918	330v			Lucy Forster	wif	m	38	wife	Dur Chester-le-Street
4919	330v			Percival Forster	son		7	scholar	Dur Durham
4920	330v			Richard Forster	son		6	scholar	Dur Durham
4921	331r			Lucy Forster	dau		5	scholar (at home)	Dur Durham
4922	331r			Elizabeth Metcalf	ser		26	servant	Dur Durham
4923	331r			Barbara Robison	ser		22	servant	Dur Auckland S.Andrew
4924	331r			Ann Wardell	ser		17	servant	Dur Houghton-l-Spring
4925	331r	<26>	Old Elvet	Robert D. Smith	hea		32	prop of houses, land etc.	Dur Chester-le-Street
4926	331r			Jane Todd	ser		61	house servant	Dur Chester-le-Street
4927	331r			Elizabeth Todd	ser		18	house servant	Dur Shincliffe
4928	331r	<27>	Old Elvet	Nicholas S. Bouet	[h]	w	60	retired professor *	France, Paris *
4929	331r			Phyllis Best	ser		51	housekeeper	Dur Sunderland Bridge
4930	331r	<28>	Old Elvet	Jane Forster	[h]		55	proprietor of houses	Nbl Newcastle
4931	331r			Eliza Wilson	vis		58	annuitant	Dur Chester-le-Street
4932	331r			Jane Binks	ser		24	general servant	Dur Barnard Castle
4933	331r	<29>	Old Elvet	George Hans Hamilton	hea	m	28	MA, chaplain to Gaol	Irl
4934	331r			Arabella S. Hamilton	wif	m	27	clergyman's wife	Bombay BS
4935	331r			Hans A. Hamilton	son		1		Dur [D] S. Oswald
4936	331r			Henry B. Hamilton	son		5m		Dur [D] S. Oswald
4937	331r			Isabella Skiping	sil		17	clergyman's daughter	Nry Northallerton
4938	331r			Caroline Robson	ser		25	nurse	Ntt East Markham
4939	331r			Ellen Beadline	ser		21	house maid	Ery Hull
4940	331r			Mary Hansby	ser		18	cook	Dur Easington
4941	335v*	<30>a	Old Elvet	Anne Fife	hea	w	74	income from house prty	Nbl Newcastle
4942	335v			Marianna Fife	dau		40	income from house prty	Nbl Newcastle
4943	335v			Elizabeth Fife	dau		38	income from house prty	Nbl Newcastle
4944	335v			Ellen Fife	dau		36	income from house prty	Nbl Newcastle
4945	335v			Frances Bayles Pawson	*	m	36	income from house prty	Nbl Newcastle
4946	335v			Elizabeth Potts	ser		20	servant	Nbl Newcastle
4947	335v	<30>b	Old Elvet	Peter Russel	hea	m	50	tailor <& lodgings>	Dur Brancepeth
4948	335v			Frances Russel	wif	m	50		Ery Hull
4949	335v			Elizabeth Russel	dau		27		Dur Jarrow
4950	335v			John Russel	son		20	medical student *	Dur Bishopwearmouth
4951	335v	<31>a	Old Elvet	Hannah Jopling	hea		50	lodging house keeper	Dur [D] S. Margaret
4952	335v			Mary Hindmarsh	ser		24	servant	Dur Bishopwearmouth
4953	335v	<31>b	Old Elvet	Elizabeth Loin	[h]		60	land proprietor	Lan Manchester
4954	335v	<32>	Old Elvet	George White	hea	m	41	major, army half-pay *	Ken Chatham
4955	335v			Anne White	wif	m	32		Dur Willington
4956	335v			Charles White	son		9	scholar	E Indies, Bengal
4957	335v			Theresa White	dau		7	scholar	E Indies, Bengal
4958	335v			Frederick White	son		5	scholar (at home)	E Indies, Bengal
4959	336r			Alice White	dau		3	scholar (at home)	Dur [D] S. Margaret
4960	336r			Edward White	son		1		Dur [D] S. Oswald

4961	336r	<32>	Old Elvet	Mary Vaux	ser	26	cook	Dur Sedgefield
4962	336r			Jane Reed	ser	19	house maid	Dur Wolsingham
4963	336r			Ellen Charlton	ser	20	head nurse	Nry Bowes
4964	336r			Sarah Charlton	ser	18	nurse	Nry Bowes
4965	336r	<33>a	Old Elvet	Margaret Southeron	hea w	69	lodgings (to let)	Dur Shildon
4966	336r	<33>b	Old Elvet	Elizabeth Sanderson	ldr	58	interest from money *	Nbl not known
4967	336r	[ac]	Old Elvet	Thomas Chapman	hea	39	schoolmaster *	Mdx S. Matthew
4968	336r	<33>	Old Elvet	Mary Daly		20	schoolmistress *	Irl
4969	336r			Anne Kelly		19	schoolmistress *	Irl
4970	336r	<34>a	Old Elvet	Elizabeth Millbank	hea w	67	annuitant & fundholder	Brk Newbury
4971	336r			Christian Brown	ser	67	housekeeper	Edn Dalkeith
4972	336r			Elizabeth Metcalf	ser	19	house maid	Dur Houghton-l-Spring
4973	336v			Mary Kennedy	ser	19	kitchen maid	Dur [D] S. Oswald
4974	336v	<34>b	Old Elvet	Mary Bell	hea	33	charwoman	Dur Durham
4975	336v			William Ainsley	vis	32	blacksmith	Dur Durham
4976	336v	<35>	Old Elvet	Thomas Marsden	hea m	60	proctor <& notary>	Dur Durham
4977	336v			Anne S. Marsden	dau*	11	scholar at home	Dur Shincliffe
4978	336v			Georgiana Marsden	dau*	11	scholar at home	Dur Shincliffe
4979	336v			Dorothy Lake	mlw w	78	interest of money	Dur Heighington
4980	336v			Jane Surtees	ser	25	house maid	Nbl Earsdon
4981	336v			Jane Hall	ser	25	cook	Dur Chester-le-Street
4982	336v	[ad]a	Old Elvet	Elizabeth Watson	hea	82	kept by * charity	Nbl Rothbury
4983	336v	[ad]b	Old Elvet	Gerard Hickson	hea w	69	ostler	Dur Herrington
4984	336v			Margaret Hickson	dau	29	housekeeper	Dur Durham
4985	336v			Charles Fawell	gsn	7	scholar	Dur Durham
4986	336v	<36>a	Old Elvet	Ann Murgatroyd	hea m	50	footman's wife	Dur [D] S. Nicholas
4987	336v			Robert Murgatroyd	son	20	joiner's apprentice	Dur [D] S. Oswald
4988	336v			William Murgatroyd	son	10	scholar	Dur [D] S. Oswald
4989	336v	<36>b	Old Elvet	Ann Rowntree	hea w	57	pp (fmly butcher's wife)	Dur [D] S. Oswald
4990	336v			Mary Rowntree	dau	25	dressmaker	Dur [D] S. Oswald
4991	336v			Ellen Rowntree	dau	15	dressmaker's apprentice	Dur [D] S. Nicholas
4992	337r	<36>c	Old Elvet	Ann Barnes	[h]	51	laundress	Dow Downpatrick
4993	337r	<36>d	Old Elvet	John Dickson	hea m	27	joiner	Dur [D] S. Nicholas
4994	337r			Frances Dickson	wif m	27		Dur [D] S. Giles
4995	337r			Agatha Dickson	dau	4	scholar	Dur [D] S. Giles
4996	337r			Mary F. Dickson	dau	2		Dur [D] S. Nicholas
4997	337r	<37>	Old Elvet	Hannah Grey	hea w	60	innkeeper <'Dun Cow'>	Dur Durham
4998	337r			Mary Grey	dau	32		Dur Durham
4999	337r			William Grey	son	29	tailor	Dur Durham
5000	337r			Hannah Gibson	ser	18	house servant	Dur Durham
5001	337r	<38>a	Old Elvet	Robert Caldcleugh	hea m	47	upholsterer <& lodgings>	Dur [D] S. Nicholas
5002	337r			Mary A. Caldcleugh	wif m	48		Nry Croft
5003	337r			Thomas Caldcleugh	bro w	60	carrier	Dur [D] S. Nicholas
5004	337r			Thomas H. Caldcleugh	nep	14	waiter	Dur [D] S. Oswald
5005	337r			Ellen Carter	sis	36	visitor	Nbl Longwitton
5006	337r			Ellen Carter	nce	12	scholar	Dur Brancepeth
5007	337r			Ellen Carter	nce	6	scholar	Dur Brancepeth
5008	337r	<38>b	Old Elvet	Sarah Hamilton	ldr w	67	annuitant	Irl
5009	337r			Frances B. Hamilton		34	annuitant['s] daughter	Irl
5010	337r	<38>c	Old Elvet	Emma Robinson	ldr	31	fundholder	Mdx London
5011	337v	<39>	Old Elvet	Francis Greenwell	hea m	27	wine merchant	Dur Lanchester
5012	337v			Elizabeth Greenwell	wif m	27		Dur [D] S. Oswald
5013	337v			Hannah Parker	ser	25	house maid	Dur Lanchester
5014	337v			Jane Toward	ser	17	cook	Dur Lanchester
5015	337v	<40>a	Old Elvet	Ann Jackson	hea w	43	lodgings (to let)	Dur Houghton-l-Spring
5016	337v			Mary Jackson	dau	18		Dur Durham
5017	337v			Ann Jackson	dau	16		Dur Durham
5018	337v			George Jackson	son	14	joiner's apprentice	Dur Durham
5019	337v			Sarah Jackson	dau	10	scholar	Dur Durham
5020	337v			Thomas G. Jackson	son	8	scholar	Dur Durham
5021	337v	<40>b	Old Elvet	John Wheeler	hea m	45	proprietor and editor *	Lan Manchester
5022	337v			Jane Wheeler	wif m	49		Ken Aylesford
5023	337v			Margaret F.W. Dyce	*	3		E Indies, Manila
5024	337v			Martha Andrews	nse	25	nurse	Sry Kingston
5025	337v	<41>	Old Elvet	Edward Shafto	hea m	38	wine and spirit merchant	Dur Durham
5026	337v			Eliza Shafto	wif m	40		Nry Richmond
5027	337v			Susanna Loan	ser	25	house servant	Irl
5028	337v	<42>	Old Elvet	Matthew Hepple	hea m	53	LSA gen practitioner *	Dur Bishop Auckland
5029	338r			Elizabeth Hepple	wif m	48		Dur Durham
5030	338r			Isabella C. Hepple	dau	18		Dur Durham
5031	338r			John D. Hepple	son	17	scholar	Dur Durham
5032	338r			Richard Hepple	son	10	scholar	Dur Durham
5033	338r			Matthew Hepple	son	9	scholar (at home)	Dur Durham
5034	338r			Elizabeth Hodgson	ser	21	cook	Dur Houghton-l-Spring
5035	338r			Ann Gleason	ser	19	house maid	Dur Durham
5036	338r	[ae]	Old Elvet	Isabella S. Green	hea	60	interest of money	Dur Durham
5037	338r			Isabella Watson	ser	25	house maid	Dur S. John's Chapel
5038	338r			Elizabeth Wallace	ser	26	cook	Dur Stanhope
5039	338r	<44>	Old Elvet	Margaret Ripley	hea w	51	fundholder	Nbl Morpeth
5040	338r			Margaret Ripley	dau	21		Nbl Morpeth
5041	338r			Horace C. Ripley	son	18	Durham college student	Dur Durham

5042	338r	<45>	Old Elvet	Mary Lonsdale	hea	50	head of boarding school	Dur Arlaw Banks
5043	338r			Catherine Lonsdale	sis	56		Dur Arlaw Banks
5044	338r			Mabel Lonsdale	sis	44	teacher	Dur Arlaw Banks
5045	338r			Mary Tyson	vis	27		Dur Gateshead
5046	338r			Margaret Hartley	pup	16	boarder	Cul Whitehaven
5047	338r			Ellen Hartley	pup	13	boarder	Cul Whitehaven
5048	338v			Susanna Wright	pup	18	boarder	Ery Stamford Bridge
5049	338v			Louisa Russell	pup	18	boarder	India, Bangalore
5050	338v			Elizabeth Hindmarsh	ser	24	house servant	Dur Durham
5051	338v			Jane Peacock	ser	24	house servant	Dur Witton Gilbert
5052	338v	<46>	Old Elvet	William Tiplady <jn>	hea m	31	tailor & draper, master*	Dur Durham
5053	338v			Anne T. Tiplady	wif m	22		Chs Macclesfield
5054	338v			Ann Hutchinson	ser	19	house servant	Dur Durham
5055	338v	<47>	Old Elvet	George Walker <jn>	hea m	43	printer (master *)	Dur [D] S. Nicholas
5056	338v			Frances Walker	wif m	37		Dur [D] S. Oswald
5057	338v			Ann S. Walker	dau	7	scholar (at home)	Dur [D] S. Nicholas
5058	338v			Blackett Lee	nep	16	printer's app compositor	Dur [D] S. Oswald
5059	338v			Mary Ann Walton	ser	19	house servant	Dur Staindrop
5060	338v	<48>	Old Elvet	George Walker	hea w	73	retired printer etc.	Dur Durham
5061	338v			Mary A. Walker	dau	41		Dur Durham
5062	338v			Elizabeth Goodrish	gda	15	scholar (at home)	Dur Durham
5063	338v			Margaret Ridley	ser	24	house servant	Dur Windlestone
5064	338v	<49>	Old Elvet	Eliza Willis	hea*	31	boarding school	Dur Bishopton
5065	338v			Jane Willis	hea*	26	boarding school	Dur Bishopton
5066	338v			Ann Best	aun w	58	matron	Dur Castle Eden
5067	339r			Sarah Willis	sis	18	boarder	Dur Bishopton
5068	339r			Jane Reed	[p]	15	boarder	Dur Knitsley
5069	339r			Ann Turnbull	[p]	14	boarder	Dur Birtley
5070	339r			Margaret Galley	[p]	13	boarder	Lan Manchester
5071	339r			Alice Pallister	[p]	13	boarder	Dur East Rainton
5072	339r			Rachael Bullard	ser	25	house servant	Sfk Southwold
5073	339r	[af]	Old Elvet *	William Pounder	hea m	35	servant in College	Nry Skeeby
5074	339r			Mary A. Pounder	wif m	32	laundress	Nry Richmond
5075	339r			Alice Pounder	mth w	68		Nry Skeeby
5076	339r			Elizabeth Pounder	dau	13		Nry Skeeby
5077	339r			William Pounder	son	11	scholar	Nry Catterick Bridge
5078	339r			Thomas Pounder	son	8	scholar	Nry Catterick Bridge
5079	339r			Alice Pounder	dau	5	scholar	Dur Rushyford
5080	339r			Edward Pounder	son	4	scholar	Dur Sunderland Bridge
5081	339r			Richard Pounder	son	2		Dur Durham
5082	339r	<50>	Old Elvet	William Stoker	hea	31	gen practitioner, MRCS *	Dur Durham
5083	339r			Jane Stoker	sis	27		Dur Durham
5084	339r			Sarah Watson	ser	23	general servant	Dur Houghton-l-Spring
5085	339r			Hannah Watson	ser	15	general servant	Dur Houghton-l-Spring
5086	339r	<51>	Old Elvet	Anthony Wilkinson	hea m	43	JP, esquire, DL	Dur Oswald House
5087	339v			Ann Wilkinson	wif m	40		Nry Thirsk
5088	339v			Ann E. Wilkinson	dau	16		Dur Durham
5089	339v			Mary E. Roberts		25	governess	Fln Mold
5090	339v			Mary Green	ser	46	lady's maid	Dur West Rainton
5091	339v			Margaret Potts	ser	30	house maid	Nbl Heddon-on-th-Wall
5092	339v			Martha Wilson	ser	43	cook	Nbl Whalton
5093	339v	<52>	Old Elvet	Ellen Wilkinson	hea w	88	annuitant	Nfk [Great] Yarmouth
5094	339v			Mary Hall	ser	61	lady's maid	Dur Brancepeth
5095	339v			Jane Robson	ser w	61	house maid	Dur [D] Gilesgate
5096	339v			Ann English	ser	30	cook	Dur Beamish
5097	339v			Henry Easby	ser m	54	house servant	Nry Ayton
5098	339v	<53>	Old Elvet	John Trotter	hea m	55	practising as physician*	Nry Croft
5099	339v			Mary Ann Trotter	wif m	54		Nbl Newcastle
5100	339v			Mary Ann Trotter	dau	23		Dur [D] S. Oswald
5101	339v			Margaret Trotter	dau	22		Dur [D] S. Oswald
5102	339v			Charles D. Trotter	son	19	scholar, University Coll	Dur [D] S. Oswald
5103	339v			Henry Trotter	son	17	scholar (at home)	Dur [D] S. Oswald
5104	339v			George L. Trotter	son	15	scholar (at home)	Dur [D] S. Oswald
5105	339v			Agnes M. Traines	ser	26	servant	Nbl Newcastle
5106	340r			Elizabeth M. Wilkie	ser	17	servant	Dur Hetton-le-Hole
5107	340r			Elizabeth Jane Law	ser	22	servant	Dur Hetton-le-Hole
5108	340r	<54>	Old Elvet	John Ward	hea w	79	solicitor	Dur [D] S. Margaret
5109	340r			Frances L.G. Ward	dau	35		Dur [D] S. Oswald
5110	340r			Ann Elringham	ser	24	maid servant	Nbl Cresswell
5111	340r			Elizabeth Moore	ser	38	cook	Dur Eighton Banks
5112	340r			Ann Windsor	ser	25	house maid	Sry Carshalton
5113	340r			Ellen Haddock	ser	17	kitchen maid	Dur West Rainton
5114	340r	<55>	Old Elvet	William Green	hea m	62	FRCS * surgeon	Nbl not known
5115	340r			Elizabeth Green	wif m	54		Dur Durham
5116	340r			G. Green	son	20		Dur Durham
5117	340r			W.H. Green	son	17	pupil to his father	Dur Durham
5118	340r			S. Carr	vis	30	assistant	Dur Durham
5119	340r			Mary Wilson	ser	26	house maid	Dur Durham
5120	340r			Mary Barker	ser	28	cook	Dur Durham
5121	340r	<56>a	Old Elvet	Fanny Blake	hea	30	boarding school	Bkm Beaconsfield
5122	340r			Charlotte Blake	sis	29	teacher	Bkm Beaconsfield

5123 340r	<56>a	Old Elvet	Isabella Lee	[p]	18	scholar (boarder)	Dur Darlington
5124 340r			Caroline Smith	[p]	16	scholar (boarder)	Dur Sunderland
5125 340v			Elizabeth Anderson	pup	16	scholar, boarder	Nbl Newcastle
5126 340v			Fanny Ward	pup	9	scholar, boarder	Dur Durham
5127 340v			Barbara Bailey	pup	17	scholar, boarder	Dur Chester-le-Street
5128 340v	<56>b	Old Elvet	Martha Castle	hea	55	interest of money	Dur Durham
5129 340v			Hannah Castle	sis	57	interest of money	Dur Durham
5130 340v	[ag]a	Old Elvet	Caroline Storey	wif m	29	waiter's wife	Dur Sunderland
5131 340v			Thomas Storey	son	1m		Dur [D] S. Oswald
5132 340v	[ag]b	Old Elvet	Margaret Wright	[h]	43	dressmaker	Dur [D] S. Oswald
5133 340v	[ag]c	Old Elvet	John Lorimer	hea m	30	dyer	Sct
5134 340v			Maria Lorimer	wif m	31		Sct
5135 340v			George Lorimer	son	4		Sct
5136 340v			Jonas Lorimer	son	2		Dur Durham
5137 340v	[ag]d	Old Elvet	Thomas Benson	hea m	46	ostler	Dur Castle Eden
5138 340v			Elizabeth Benson	wif m	40		Dur Coxhoe
5139 340v	[ag]e	Old Elvet	John Elliott	hea m	22	groom	Dur Barnard Castle
5140 340v			Alice Elliott	wif m	21		Dur Hartlepool
5141 340v			Edward Elliott	son	2		Dur Hartlepool
5142 340v			Jane Elliott	dau	9m		Dur Durham
5143 340v	[ag]f	Old Elvet	Thomas Sidgwick	hea m	37	maltster	Dur Running Waters
5144 341r			Elizabeth Sidgwick	wif m	36		Dur New Lambton
5145 341r			Thomas Sidgwick	son	9	scholar	Dur Durham
5146 341r			Elizabeth Sidgwick	dau	8	scholar	Dur Durham
5147 341r			John Sidgwick	son	6	scholar	Dur Durham
5148 341r			William Sidgwick	son	5	scholar	Dur Durham
5149 341r			Lucy Sidgwick	dau	2	scholar	Dur Durham
5150 341r	[ah]	Old Elvet *.	William Wakeman	hea m	65	mason's labourer	Dur Durham
5151 341r			Mary Wakeman	wif m	60	<dressmaker & milliner>	Dur Durham
5152 341r			Henry Laws	vis	20	coach trimmer * app	Dur Chester-le-Street
5153 341r			George Mack	vis m	39	chaise driver	not known
5154 341r			Joseph Simpson	vis w	30	chaise driver	not known
5155 341r			William Rogerson	vis	31	horse dealer	not known
5156 341r			Frederick Flanders	vis	30	horse dealer	not known
5157 341r	[ai]	Old Elvet	George Smith	hea m	45	cabinetmaker	Dur Durham
5158 341r			Mary Ann Smith	wif m	42		Dur Durham
5159 341r			Mary J. Smith	dau	15	dressmaker's apprentice	Dur Durham
5160 341r			Thomas Smith	son	6	scholar	Dur Durham
5161 341r	[aj]	Old Elvet *	John Wilson	hea m	59	Wesleyan minister *	Wry Skipton
5162 341r			Mary Wilson	wif m	50		Wry Leeds
5163 341v			Jane Wilson	dau	26		Nbl Newcastle
5164 341v			Eliza Wilson	dau	11	scholar (at home)	Ery Bridlington Quay
5165 341v			Lucy E. Wilson	dau	10	scholar (at home)	Lin Brigg
5166 341v			Mary Wardropper	ser	29	servant	Dur Chester-le-Street
5167 341v	[ak]	Old Elvet *	Benjamin Hill	hea m	24	whitesmith & chainmaker	Dur Stockton
5168 341v			Mary Ann Hill	wif m	22		Dur [D] S. Oswald
5169 341v			Benjamin Hill	son	2		Dur [D] S. Oswald
5170 341v			Elizabeth M. Hill	dau	8m		Dur [D] S. Oswald
5171 341v	[al]a	Old Elvet *	George Burnett	[h]	54	mason	Dur [D] S. Oswald
5172 341v	[al]b	Old Elvet *	Joseph Burnett	hea w	60	mason, master emp 1 labr	Dur S. Nicholas
5173 341v			John Burnett	son m	31	mason	Dur [D] Crossgate
5174 341v			Mary Burnett	swi m	21	mason's wife	Irl
5175 341v	[al]c	Old Elvet *	Margaret Punshon	hea	37	house proprietor	Dur Bishopwearmouth
5176 341v			Catherine Pinkney	sis m	29	annuitant	Dur [D] Crossgate
5177 341v			Margaret E. Pinkney	nce	1m		Dur [D] S. Oswald
5178 341v	[am]	Old Elvet	William Storey	hea m	44	chaise driver	Dur Darlington
5179 341v			William Storey	son	15	scholar	Dur Durham
5180 341v			Margaret Storey	dau	17	scholar	Dur Durham
5181 342r			Mary Reed	ser	35	housekeeper	Dur Durham
5182 342r	[an]a	Old Elvet	William Haw	hea m	46	shoemaker	Yks Mellerby
5183 342r			Hannah Haw	wif m	46		Yks Gildens
5184 342r			Maria Haw	dau	3		Wry Knaresborough
5185 342r			Ann Hall	vis	9	scholar	Dur Sherburn
5186 342r	[an]b	Old Elvet	John Robinson	hea m	41	whitesmith	Dur Durham
5187 342r			Jane Robinson	wif m	40		Dur Durham
5188 342r			Jane Robinson	dau	12	scholar	Dur Hartlepool
5189 342r			Georgiana Robinson	dau	10	scholar	Dur Hartlepool
5190 342r			William Robinson	son	7		Dur Hartlepool
5191 342r			Ellen Robinson	dau	4		Dur Stockton
5192 342r	[ao]	Old Elvet	William Wilkie	hea w	33	coachman	Nry Masham
5193 342r			Margaret Wilkie	dau	8	scholar	Nry Guisborough
5194 342r			Thomas Wilkie	son	7	scholar	Nry Guisborough
5195 342r			William Wilkie	son	2		Dur Durham
5196 342r			Margaret Mudd	ser	27	housekeeper	Nry Masham
5197 342r			William Pearson	vis	29	groom	Dur Rushyford
5198 342r	[ap]	Old Elvet	Jane Tempely	hea w	33	pit sinker's widow	Dur [D] Millburngate
5199 342r			John Harding	vis m	44	coachsmith	Dur Darlington
5200 342v			Matthew Smith	vis	25	groom	Dur [D] S. Oswald
5201 342v			John Spenson	vis	44	horse dealer	not known
5202 342v			John Rutledge	vis m	31	horse dealer	not known
5203 342v	[aq]a	Old Elvet *	William Guy	hea m	45	cartman	Dur Durham

5204	342v	[aq]a	Old Elvet *	Mary Guy	wif m	38		Dur Durham
5205	342v			Elizabeth Guy	dau	17		Dur Durham
5206	342v			Jane Guy	dau	12		Dur Durham
5207	342v	[aq]b	Old Elvet *	Ann Ibotson	[h]	80	interest of money	Dur Stanhope
5208	342v	[aq]c	Old Elvet *	Martha Conn	hea w	61	gardener's widow	Dur [D] S. Oswald
5209	342v			Martha Conn	dau	24	dressmaker	Dur [D] S. Oswald
5210	342v			William Conn	son	19	cooper's apprentice	Dur [D] S. Oswald
5211	342v			John Aynsley	vis	32	cooper	Dur Gateshead
5212	342v	[aq]d	Old Elvet *	Jane Brammer	hea w	66	shoemaker's widow	Sct
5213	342v			Mary Brammer	dau	41	dressmaker	Dur [D] S. Oswald
5214	342v			George O. Brammer	son w	33	cabinetmaker	Dur [D] S. Oswald
5215	342v			William Brammer	son	27	cabinetmaker	Dur [D] S. Oswald
5216	342v			Thomas W. Forster	gsn	4	scholar	Dur [D] S. Oswald
5217	342v	<58>	Old Elvet *	Joseph Herbert	hea m	54	grocer & confectioner	Dur [D] S. Nicholas
5218	342v			Sarah Herbert	wif m	56		Dur [D] S. Oswald
5219	343r			John Gelder	vis	38	farmer, not known	Wry Leeds
5220	343r			Robert Richardson	vis m	31	farmer, not known	Wry Leeds
5221	343r	<59>	Old Elvet	John Clifton	hea	84	retired surgeon	Dur [D] S. Nicholas
5222	343r			Jane Sharp	ser w	38	housekeeper	Dur [D] Framwelgate
5223	343r			Ellen Brown	ser	25	house maid	Nbl Netherwitton
5224	343r	<60>	Old Elvet	Elizabeth Garbut *	ser w	64	housekeeper	Wry Airton
5225	343r			Sophia Green	ser	19	bookkeeper	Mdx S. Luke
5226	343r			Margaret Burdon	ser	20	house servant	Dur Lanchester
5227	343r			Sarah Bowden	ser	21	house servant	Dur Houghton-l-Spring
5228	343r			Elizabeth Watson	ser	20	house servant	Dur Lanchester
5229	343r			Mary Laird	ser	18	house servant	Nbl Bywell
5230	343r			John Storey	ser m	37	waiter	Nbl Bywell
5231	343r			John Sanders	ser m	42	boots	Dur Gainford
5232	343r			Joseph Simpson	ser	36	postboy	Nry Catterick
5233	343r			George Mack	ser m	48	postboy	British subject
5234	343r			George Hodgson	vis	33	solicitor	Dur Bishop Auckland
5235	343r	<61>	Old Elvet	John Thwaites	hea m	61	innkeeper <'Waterloo' *>	Dur [D] Framwelgate
5236	343r			Dorothy Thwaites	wif m	58		Nry Askrigg
5237	343v			William Thwaites	son	28		Dur Durham
5238	343v			George M. Thwaites	son	25		Dur Durham
5239	343v			Mary A. Thwaites	dau	20		Nry Askrigg
5240	343v			Jane Thwaites	dau	18		Dur Durham
5241	343v			Mary Thwaites	dau	16		Dur Durham
5242	343v			George Parkinson	ser m	55	postboy	Dur Durham
5243	343v			Robert Hudson	ser	20	postboy	Dur Durham
5244	343v			Maria O'Brien	ser	20	kitchen maid	Irl
5245	343v			Bridget Gilgalon	ser	20	kitchen maid	Irl
5246	343v			Elizabeth Dobson	ser	18	house maid	Dur Durham
5247	343v			Bernard Donern	vis w	60	hawker of linen	Irl
5248	343v			Edward Stichfield	vis w	42	horse dealer	Mdx not known
5249	343v			Mr. Skill	vis m	53	cattle jobber	Lin not known
5250	343v			Mary Ann Spink	vis	16		Dur [D] Framwelgate
5251	343v	<62>	Old Elvet	William Robson	hea m	35	upholsterer *	Dur [D] Elvet
5252	343v			Mary Robson	wif m	39		Nry Ayton
5253	343v			Dorothy Robson	dau	4		Dur [D] Elvet
5254	343v			Mary Robson	dau	3		Dur [D] Elvet
5255	344r			Isabella Robson	dau	1		Dur Durham
5256	344r			Hannah Bulmer	ser	15	under nurse	Dur Durham
5257	344r			Mary Robinson	ser	27	cook	Nry Scotton
5258	344r			Margaret Cuthbert	ser	19	upper nurse	Dur Lumley
5259	344r	[ar]	Old Elvet *	Ridley Thompson	hea m	46	painter, master *	Dur not known
5260	344r			Elizabeth Thompson	wif m	39		Dur Durham
5261	344r			Elizabeth Telford	mlw w	70		Ntt Newark
5262	344r	[as]	Old Elvet	John Hesp	hea m	36	journeyman smith	Nry Ruston
5263	344r			Mary Hesp	wif m	40		Cul Nenthead
5264	344r			Ann Hesp	dau	14		Dur [D] S. Oswald
5265	344r			John Hesp	son	12	scholar	Dur [D] S. Oswald
5266	344r			Mary Hesp	dau	10	scholar	Dur [D] S. Oswald
5267	344r			Margaret Hesp	dau	8	scholar	Dur [D] S. Oswald
5268	344r			James Hesp	son	6	scholar	Dur [D] S. Oswald
5269	344r			Sarah Hesp	dau	5	scholar	Dur [D] S. Oswald
5270	344r			Matthew Hesp	son	3		Dur [D] S. Oswald
5271	344r			Hannah Hesp	dau	7m		Dur [D] S. Oswald

Notes - Enumeration District 11d

3597	... employing 1 man	3659/3660	[entries 3636-3638 repeated and deleted]
3600-3608	<number given as "3">	3669	<publican 'Cock'>
3613	... employing 1 man, 1 apprentice	3683	[brother-in-law's] wife
	<bread and biscuit baker>	3707/3708	[entry 3712 repeated and deleted]
3620	<& deputy prothonotary to court of pleas>	3717/3718	[entry 3712 repeated and deleted]
3642	... S. Hilda	3781	... (employing 2 men) <upholsterer>
3645	/"Obbington"	3786	great-aunt
3654	sister's son	3787	<& blacksmith>

3794	... (emp 6 men and 5 app) <& whitesmith>
3795	... master (employing 3 men & 3 app)
3872	... & letter receiver
3953	<beerhouse keeper>
3983	county given as "Nottinghamshire"
4014	... (employing 4 men)
4029	/"Gosford"
4048	... (dealer in shawls)
4054	... (dealer in shawls and stuffs)
4055	... (dealer in shawls and silk)
4056	... (dealer in linen cloth)
4083-4090	<2 Lister's Buildings>
4086	... and trimmer's ...
4096	... (dealer in shawls)
4140	... (emp 1 man) <bread and biscuit baker>
4146	<'Rose & Crown' & brickmaker>
4167	widow [mother?]
4221	... employing 1 man, 3 apprentices
4226	... (emp 2 labourers); ... in Cleveland
4269	/"Gainforth"
4289	... S. Nicholas
4317	/"Balar"
4359-4361	lodgers at Kelly's
4359	husband [lodger]
4375	[son's] son
4376	head [lodger]
4402	[?'s] wife
4459	/"Sleevin"
4477	husband [lodger]
4483	... employing 1 apprentice
4488-4502	... entrance from Water Lane
4493	/"Medeef"
4532	... (emp 1 app) <bread and biscuit baker>
4536	<& dealer in hats>
4582	[sister's] daughter
4583	[sister's] son
4584-4585	[sister's] daughter
4595	<'Newcastle Arms'>
4601	... of 250a
4610	<manager of Durham Brewery Company>
4614	... (emp 6 men) <& draper & robemaker>
4615	... (employing 1 man)
4625	<worsted and yarn manufacturer>
4627-4628	<Wesleyan day and sabbath school>
4655	... employing 30 men (20 jnym & 10 app) <& lodgings>
4657	... (employing 3 men)
4665	... (emp 5 men and 6 app) <& upholsterer>
4678	<livery stable keeper>
4688-4734	Elvet Bridge
4693	<& cheese and bacon factor>
4711	... (formerly laundress)
4716	<'Ship'>

4730	... & shoeing smith (master employing 3 men & 1 boy)
4739	... master emp 5 men 2 app <'Wheatsheaf'>
4768	... practice as a general practitioner <surgeon to Gaol>
4774	<chainmaker & lodgings>
4777	... & clerk of crown for county
4788	... MRCS and LSA
4796	... 26th Regiment of Foot
4809	... Lincoln College, Oxford
4852	... in practice
4877	... clergyman without cure of souls
4888	... of S. Cuthbert's chapel
4907	<deputy receiver-general of diocese>
4912	... of houses, railways, etc.
4928	... of Durham University <artist>; naturalised Frenchman
4941	[folios 331v-335r are preliminary pages of continuation book]
4945	daughter and visitor
4950	... in [S.] Bartholomew's Hospital
4954	... (county chief constable)
4966	... on railway and houses
4967	... teaches English literature in general, grammar, geography, natural philosophy, algebra and mathematics
4968-4969	<Catholic Free School>
4977-4978	twin daughters
4982	... Miss Spearman's ...
5021	... of newspaper <Durham Chronicle>
5023	adopted child
5028	<surgeon>
5052	... (employing 8 men)
5055	... emp 3 men & 5 boys app <& stationer>
5064-5065	sisters
5073-5081	... Garden Cottage
5082	... and LSA <surgeon>
5098	grad of Edinburgh Univ now ...
5114	... practising as ...
5150-5156	<Chapel Passage>
5152	... and harness maker ...
5161-5166	<Chapel House, Chapel Passage>
5161	<Wesleyan Methodist chapel, 57 Old Elvet>
5167-5170	<Elvet Waterside>
5171-5177	<Chapel Passage>
5203-5220	<Chapel Passage>
5224	head of family not resident <W. Thomas Ward 'Waterloo' & livery stable keeper>
5235	... & livery stable keeper
5251	... & cabinetmaker, master employing 7 men, 7 boys and 3 women <& joiner>
5259-5261	<Elvet Waterside>
5259	... emp 2 men and 1 boy app <& glazier>

REF	FOL	NO	STREET	FORENAME(S)	SURNAME	REL	C	AGE	OCCUPATION	BIRTHPLACE
5272	348v	<60>a	Water Lane	Rachael	Plimmer	hea	w	73	greengrocer; pauper	Dur Barnard Castle
5273	348v			Rachael	Plimmer	gda		18	greengrocer	Dur Durham
5274	348v	<60>b	Water Lane	Benjamin	Binks	hea	m	34	brewer & maltster	Dur
5275	348v			Jane	Binks	wif	m	36		Dur
5276	348v			John	Binks	son		13	scholar	Dur
5277	348v			Elizabeth	Binks	dau		11	scholar	Dur
5278	348v			Joseph	Binks	son		9	scholar	Dur
5279	348v			Benjamin	Binks	son		7	scholar	Dur
5280	348v			Thomas	Binks	son		5	scholar	Dur
5281	348v			Elliott	Binks	son		1		Dur
5282	348v	<60>c	Water Lane	James	Milligan	hea	m	37	hawker	Irl
5283	348v			Jessie	Milligan	wif	m	36	hawker	Nbl Newcastle
5284	348v			Michael	Milligan	son		7	scholar	Dur Durham
5285	348v			John	Johnson	vis		20	scholar	Nbl Newcastle
5286	348v	<60>d	Water Lane	William S.	Addimson	hea	m	23	chainmaker	Dur Durham
5287	348v			Margaret	Addimson	wif	m	23	wife	Dur Durham
5288	348v	<60>e	Water Lane	William	Tytler	hea	m	25	mason	For Brechin
5289	348v			Esther	Tytler	wif	m	22	wife	Dur Durham
5290	349r	<60>	New Elvet	Jane	Forster	hea	w	46	spirit merchant *	Dur Durham
5291	349r			Adelaide	Forster	dau		20	scholar at home	Dur Durham
5292	349r			Samuel Strong	Forster	son		18	scholar at home	Dur Durham
5293	349r			Thomas C.	Forster	son		12	scholar at home	Dur Durham
5294	349r			Ann	Forster	dau		8	scholar at home	Dur Durham
5295	349r			George Graham	Forster	son		5	scholar at home	Dur Durham
5296	349r			Margaret	Pearson	ser		17	general servant	Yks Appleby
5297	349r	<59>	New Elvet	William	Binks	hea	m	31	publican *	Nry Middleton Tyas
5298	349r			Hannah	Binks	wif	m	27	wife	Dur Bishop Middleham
5299	349r			Robert Tobias	Binks	son		1		Dur Durham
5300	349r			Mary	Reed	vis	w	30	schoolmistress	Dur Bishop Middleham
5301	349r			Ann	Winn	vis	m	47	husbandman's wife	Yks Mounfield
5302	349r			Jane	Binks	vis		18	publican's daughter	Nry Middleton Tyas
5303	349r			James	Binks	vis	w	50	publican & farmer	Nry Manfield
5304	349r			Richard	Binks	vis		20	husbandman	Nry Manfield
5305	349r			Joseph	Weatley	vis	w	57	horse dealer	Dur Auckland S.Andrew
5306	349r			Robert	Peacock	vis	m	53	husbandman	Nbl Little Callerton
5307	349r			James	Towers	vis	m	36	blacksmith	Dur Darlington
5308	349r			Isabella	Lulings	ser		18	general servant	Nbl Ponteland
5309	349v	<58>a	New Elvet	Michael	Sewell	hea	m	67	cordwainer	Dur Witton Gilbert
5310	349v			Hannah	Sewell	wif	m	70	wife	Dur Staindrop
5311	349v	<58>b	New Elvet	Ann	Gibson	hea	w	49	washerwoman; pauper	Nbl Corbridge
5312	349v			Mary Ann	Grey	ldr		17	works at paper mill	Dur Durham
5313	349v	<57>	New Elvet	John	Sharp	hea	m	33	publican <'White Swan'>*	Dur Lanchester
5314	349v			Margaret	Sharp	wif	m	36	wife	Dur Whickham
5315	349v			John	Sharp	son		8	scholar	Dur Durham
5316	349v	<56>	New Elvet	John	Rickerby	hea	m	56	bread <& biscuit> baker	Dur Sunderland
5317	349v			Elizabeth	Rickerby	wif	m	54	wife	Dur Chester-le-Street
5318	349v			Thomas	Rickerby	son		16	apprentice baker	Dur Durham
5319	349v			William	Rickerby	son		14	apprentice baker	Dur Durham
5320	349v	[bj]a	New Elvet	Henry	Dawson	hea	m	29	smith	Dur Durham
5321	349v			Maria	Dawson	wif	m	27	wife	on the ocean
5322	349v			Henry	Dawson	son		2		Dur Durham
5323	349v	[bj]b	New Elvet	Thomas	Hall	hea	m	35	blacksmith	Nbl Wooler
5324	349v			Isabella	Hall	wif	m	29	wife	Dur Durham
5325	349v			Elizabeth	Hall	dau		4		Dur Durham
5326	349v			Jane	Hall	dau		3m		Dur Durham
5327	350r	[bk]a	New Elvet	Mary	Walker	hea		35	lodging house keeper	Dur Durham
5328	350r			William	Walker	son		4	scholar	Dur Durham
5329	350r			Sarah	Walker	dau		2	at home	Dur Durham
5330	350r			Daniel	Torran	vis	m	68	traveller, hawker	Irl
5331	350r			Patrick	Fallan	vis	w	30	traveller, hawker	Irl
5332	350r			Michael	Fallon	vis		38	traveller, hawker	Irl
5333	350r			John	Hagaty	vis		20	traveller, hawker	Irl
5334	350r			Patrick	Kenedy	vis		20	traveller, hawker	Irl
5335	350r			Andrew	Gordon	vis		25	mason	Sct
5336	350r	[bk]b	New Elvet	Robert	Innes	hea	m	42	carpet weaver	Sct
5337	350r			Alexander	Innes	son		21	carpet weaver	Sct
5338	350r			William	Innes	son		3	at home	Sct
5339	350r			Margaret	Innes	wif	m	42	wife	Sct
5340	350r			Mary	Innes	dau		16	bonnetmaker	Sct
5341	350r			Margaret	Innes	dau		10	scholar	Dur Durham
5342	350r	<58>	New Elvet	John	Maddison	hea	m	39	journeyman mason	Dur Durham
5343	350r			Jane	Maddison	wif	m	39	wife <straw-hatmaker *>	Dur Durham
5344	350r			Mary Ann	Maddison	dau		10	scholar	Dur Durham
5345	350r			Edward	Maddison	son		6	scholar	Dur Durham
5346	350r			William	Maddison	son		4	scholar	Dur Durham
5347	350v	[bl]	New Elvet	Owen	Malley	hea	m	30	labourer	May
5348	350v			Ann	Malley	wif	m	26		Irl
5349	350v			James	Malley	son		4	scholar	Irl
5350	350v			Betty	McDermot	vis	w	40	traveller	Irl

5351	350v	[bl]	New Elvet	John McDermot	vss		14	traveller (scholar)	Irl
5352	350v			Bridget McDermot	vsd		10	traveller (scholar)	Irl
5353	350v			Martin McDermot	vss		7	traveller (scholar)	Irl
5354	350v			Eliza McDermot	vsd		3	scholar	Irl
5355	350v			Mary Elton	vis w	30	traveller	Eng
5356	350v			John Elton	vis		10	traveller	Eng
5357	350v	[bm]	New Elvet	Patrick Ryan	hea m	25	labourer	May
5358	350v			Catherine Ryan	wif m	20	wife	May
5359	350v			Mary Glary	mth w	50	domestic duty	May
5360	350v			Michael Ryan	son		11m		Dur
5361	350v			Mary Glary	*		13	scholar	May
5362	350v			Catherine Conner	mth w	70	lodger	May
5363	350v			Bridget Glary	*		14	scholar	May
5364	350v			Mary Glary	*		4	scholar	Wry Leeds
5365	350v			John Phillips	vis		21	labourer	May
5366	351r			Margaret Snow	vis m	28	labourer	May
5367	351r			Mary Coulson	dau		2		Dur Durham
5368	351r			John Higgens	vis		21	labourer	Cla
5369	351r	[bn]a	New Elvet	Thomas Dunlay	hea m	25	tailor	May
5370	351r			Mary Dunlay	wif m	24	wife	May
5371	351r			Michael Dunlay	son		1		Dur Durham
5372	351r			Anthony Dunlay	vis w	40	labourer	May
5373	351r			Patrick Dunlay	vis		20	labourer	May
5374	351r			Michael Dunlay	vis		18	labourer	May
5375	351r			Mary Dunlay	vis		16	scholar	May
5376	351r			James Dunlay	vis		2		May
5377	351r			Mary Dunlay	mth w	60	beggar	May
5378	351r			James Pendergad	*		20	labourer	May
5379	351r			Ann Pendergad	*		18	labourer	May
5380	351r	[bn]b	New Elvet	Mary Gannan	wif m	38	beggar	May
5381	351r			Augusta Gannan	son		2		May
5382	351r			Patrick Commons	vis		25	labourer	Gal
5383	351r			Bridget Kelly	vis		13	labourer	Sli
5384	351v	[bn]c	New Elvet	George Riley	hea m	30	labourer	May
5385	351v			Margaret Riley	wif m	21	wife	May
5386	351v			Michael Riley	son		1		Dur Durham
5387	351v			John Walsh	vis m	32	labourer	May
5388	351v			Bridget Walsh	vsw m	30	wife	May
5389	351v			Ann Walsh	vsd		8	scholar	May
5390	351v			Michael Walsh	vss		7	scholar	May
5391	351v			Mary Walsh	vsd		2		Lan Lancaster
5392	351v			Patrick Walsh	vis w	50	labourer	May
5393	351v			Bryan Brynan	vis w	40	labourer	Irl Resanon
5394	351v			James Gannon	vis w	40	labourer	May
5395	351v			Michael Gryn	vis		30	labourer	May
5396	351v			Mary Malone	vis		22	labourer	May
5397	351v			Patrick Gryn	vis		4m		Dur Durham
5398	351v			"Hughfy" Gannan	vis		30	labourer	May
5399	351v	<54>	New Elvet	John Gowland	hea m	55	innkeeper * <& carter>	Dur Barmpton
5400	351v			Ann Gowland	wif m	46	wife	Cul Alston
5401	351v			Mary Gowland	dau		20	scholar	Dur Durham
5402	351v			Thomas Gowland	son		13	scholar	Dur Durham
5403	352r			Ann Gowland	dau		10	scholar	Dur Durham
5404	352r			Margaret Gowland	dau		7	scholar	Dur Durham
5405	352r			John Gowland	son		6	scholar	Dur Durham
5406	352r			John Greenwell	ser		18	farm servant	Dur Merrington
5407	352r			Mary Pasley	ser		26	general servant	Dur Portobello
5408	352r			Alice Forster	ser		20	general servant	Dur Willington
5409	352r			Thomas Ridley	vis m	53	miner	Nbl Allendale
5410	352r			Samuel Richardson	vis m	58	farm servant	Ery Beverley
5411	352r			Thomas Burn	vis m	42	farm servant	Yks Newby
5412	352r			Edward Thompson	vis m	68	farm servant	Dur Stainton
5413	352r			Dennis McCrady	vis		24	farm servant	Irl
5414	352r			John Hunter	vis m	50	farm servant	Dur Norton
5415	352r			Henry Dodds	vis m	35	hay dealer	Nry Middlesbrough
5416	352r			Thomas Lawson	vis m	40	farmer	Dur Egglescliffe
5417	352r			Richard Davison	vis		20	farmer	Dur Crawcrook
5418	352r			Robert Harland	vis		51	cattle dealer	Nry Masham
5419	352r			John Clark	vis m	41	butcher	Dur Darlington
5420	352r			William Thompson	vis		24	butcher	Dur Sadberge
5421	352r			William Oxendale	vis m	46	cattle dealer	Dur Weardale
5422	352r			William Henderson	vis		24	cattle dealer	Dur Sadberge
5423	352r			Thomas Barker	vis m	46	cattle dealer	Bdf East Harley
5424	352v			John Crawhall	vis		25	farmer	Dur Stanhope
5425	352v			Anthony Crawhall	vis		48	cordwainer	Dur Stanhope
5426	352v			Richard Corner	vis		61	farm servant	Nbl Bywell
5427	352v			Samuel Reaves	vis m	46	horse dealer	Bdf Ethenrake
5428	352v			William Palmely	vis		23	labourer	Dur Eggleston
5429	352v			John Thwaites	vis		24	horse dealer	Yks Hans
5430	352v			Richard Thwaites	vis		26	horse dealer	Yks Hans
5431	352v	<53>a	New Elvet	Elizabeth Gowland	hea w	78	dependent	Dur Stainton

5432	352v	<53>a	New Elvet	Ann Archer	ser	15	general servant	Dur Durham
5433	352v	<53>b	New Elvet	Margaret Mayor	hea	38	shopkeeper <grocer>	Lan
5434	352v	[bo]	New Elvet	William Cotton Probert	hea m	37	superintendent of police	Wry Bradford
5435	352v			Elizabeth Probert	wif m	38	wife	Wry Wortley
5436	352v			Ellen Sarah Probert	dau	12	scholar	Wry Sheffield
5437	352v			Louisa Mary Probert	dau	10	scholar	Dur Birtley
5438	352v			Charles Cotton Probert	son	6	scholar	Nbl Walker
5439	352v			Thomas Parkin Probert	son	4	scholar	Dur Coxhoe
5440	352v	<52>	New Elvet	Lincoln Dale	hea m	29	merchant tailor	Dur Pittington
5441	352v			Mary Dale	wif m	25		Dur South Shields
5442	352v			Margaret Dale	dau	1		Dur Durham
5443	353r			Jane Henderson	sil	21	scholar	Dur South Shields
5444	353r			Elizabeth Simm	nce	13	scholar	Dur South Shields
5445	353r	<51>a	New Elvet	Thomas Mowbray	hea m	35	joiner	Dur Iveston
5446	353r			Martha Mowbray	wif m	41	wife	Dur Ushaw
5447	353r	<51>b	New Elvet	James Atkinson	hea m	24	publican *	Dur West Rainton
5448	353r			Eleanor Atkinson	wif m	40	wife	Dur Durham
5449	353r			Eleanor Atkinson	dau	2		Dur Durham
5450	353r			Mary Ann Trotter	nce	10	scholar	Dur Staindrop
5451	353r			Catherine Tragin	ldr w	30	dependent	Irl
5452	353r	<50>a	New Elvet	Patrick Morgan	hea m	30	traveller *	Irl
5453	353r			Mary Ann Morgan	wif m	26	wife	Irl
5454	353r			Ellen Morgan	dau	8m		Dur Durham
5455	353r	<50>b	New Elvet	Thomas Hull	hea m	28	ostler	Dur Merrington
5456	353r			Elizabeth Hull	wif m	26	wife	Dur Coniscliffe
5457	353r			William Hull	son	5	scholar	Dur Durham
5458	353r			Thomas Hull	son	3		Dur Durham
5459	353r			John Hull	son	8m		Dur Durham
5460	353r			Margaret Dawson	mlw	58		Dur Heighington
5461	353r	<50>c	New Elvet	Ralph Mitchell	hea m	49	cooper	Nbl Embleton
5462	353v	<50>d	New Elvet	Sarah Wilkinson	hea w	58	housekeeper	Dur Langley
5463	353v			Elizabeth Wilkinson	dau	23	dressmaker	Dur Durham
5464	353v			Eleanor Wilkinson	dau	22	dressmaker	Dur Durham
5465	353v			Mary Wilkinson	dau	19	dressmaker	Dur Durham
5466	353v	<50>e	New Elvet	Henry Melross	hea m	48	joiner & carpenter	Dur Durham
5467	353v			Jane Melross	wif m	42	wife	Dur Beamish
5468	353v			Henry Melross	son	12	scholar	Dur Durham
5469	353v			Elizabeth Melross	dau	8	scholar	Dur Durham
5470	353v			Catherine Melross	dau	1		Dur Durham
5471	353v			Catherine Melross	mth w	77		Dur Chilton
5472	353v	<50>f	New Elvet	Henry Reavely	hea m	39	coachmaker	Dur South Shields
5473	353v			Mary Reavely	wif m	40	wife	Nbl Bywell
5474	353v			Thomas Reavely	son	7	scholar	Dur Durham
5475	353v			Richard Reavely	son	4	scholar	Dur Durham
5476	353v			Mary Reavely	dau	1		Dur Durham
5477	353v	<50>g	New Elvet	William Cairns	hea m	35	tailor	Dur Durham
5478	353v			Jane Cairns	wif m	42	wife	Nbl Tynemouth
5479	353v			John Cairns	son	2		Dur Durham
5480	353v			Robert Cairns	son	6	scholar	Dur Durham
5481	353v			William Cairns	son	2		Dur Durham
5482	354r	<49>a	New Elvet	John Moorhead	hea m	35	waiter	Dur Throckley Toll
5483	354r			Mary Ann Moorhead	wif m	35	dressmaker	Nry Richmond
5484	354r	<49>b	New Elvet	John Jameson	hea m	32	drayman	Nry Northallerton
5485	354r			Sarah Jameson	wif m	32	wife	Dur Durham
5486	354r			Mary Ann Jameson	dau	9	scholar	Dur Durham
5487	354r			Catherine Jameson	dau	8	scholar	Dur Durham
5488	354r			Sarah Jameson	dau	6	scholar	Dur Durham
5489	354r	<49>c	New Elvet	Jane Noble	wif m	52	grocer & hosier *	Dur Stanhope
5490	354r			Jane Noble	dau	16	scholar	Dur Gateshead
5491	354r			Hannah Moore	vis	16	scholar	Dur Durham
5492	354r	<49>d	New Elvet	Ann Clarke	hea w	67	nurse	Dur Durham
5493	354r	<49>e	New Elvet	John Fowell	hea m	44	cordwainer	Dur Durham
5494	354r			Christiane Fowell	wif m	43	wife	Dur Durham
5495	354r			John Fowell	son	14	scholar	Dur Durham
5496	354r			Martha Fowell	dau	11	scholar	Dur Durham
5497	354r			Margaret Jane Fowell	dau	2		Dur Durham
5498	354r	<47>	New Elvet	Ann Hubbick	hea w	77	domestic duty	Dur Brancepeth
5499	354r			Mary Forster	dau m	54	domestic duty	Dur Esh
5500	354r			Anne Hubbick	gda	15	scholar	Nry Richmond
5501	354v	<48>	New Elvet	Robert Thompson	hea m	59	joiner <& lodgings>	Dur Durham
5502	354v			Sarah Thompson	wif m	57	wife	Ken
5503	354v			Thomas Thompson	son m	24	joiner	Dur Durham
5504	354v			Ann Thompson	swi m	26		War Birmingham *
5505	354v			John Hodgson	vis m	38	coachbuilder	Dur Durham
5506	354v			Henrietta Laing	vis	35	agent to bible depot	Mdx
5507	354v	[aa]	Church Street *	Thomas Etherington	hea w	66	independent	Dur
5508	354v			Thomas Etherington	son m	31	cordwainer	Dur Durham
5509	354v			Mary Etherington	swi m	24	wife	Dur Houghton
5510	354v			John Etherington	gsn	8m		Dur
5511	354v	[ab]a	Church Street *	Elizabeth Harbottle	hea w	67	grocer	Dur
5512	354v			Ann Hopper	dau m	40	domestic duty	Nbl

5513 354v	[ab]a	Church Street *	George Hopper	gsn	9	scholar	Dur
5514 354v			Elizabeth Hopper	gda	8	scholar	Dur
5515 354v	[ab]b	Church Street *	William Irven	hea w	56	gardener	Dur
5516 354v			Mary Ann Irven	dau	24	dressmaker	Dur Bishopwearmouth
5517 354v			Robert Irven	gsn	9	scholar	Dur
5518 354v	[ab]c	Church Street *	John Lowes	hea m	24	mason	Dur
5519 354v		.	Elizabeth Lowes	wif m	22	dressmaker	Dur
5520 355r	[ac]a	Church Street *	John Coates	hea m	33	coach trimmer	Wry Ripon
5521 355r			Lucy Coates	wif m	30	wife	Wry Harrogate
5522 355r	[ac]b	Church Street *	William Robson	hea m	35	butcher	Dur Durham
5523 355r			Sarah Robson	wif m	35	wife	Dur Durham
5524 355r			Thomas Robson	son	10	scholar	Dur Durham
5525 355r			John Robson	son	8	scholar	Dur Durham
5526 355r			Sarah Robson	dau	6	scholar	Dur Durham
5527 355r			Mary Robson	dau	4	scholar	Dur Durham
5528 355r	[ad]a	Church Street *	Mary Shaw	hea w	61	dependent	Dur Gateshead
5529 355r			Isabella Shaw	dau	28	domestic work	Dur Durham
5530 355r			Gibson Shaw	son	20	cabinetmaker	Dur Durham
5531 355r			Emma Shaw	gda	14	scholar	Dur Durham
5532 355r			George Shaw	son m	22	cabinetmaker	Dur Durham
5533 355r			Isabella Shaw	swi m	20	wife	Nbl Bigges Main
5534 355r	[ad]b	Church Street *	Thomas Peele	hea m	37	daguarian artist	Dur Durham
5535 355r			Mary Peele	wif m	24	wife	Dur Durham
5536 355r			Emma Peele	dau	12	scholar	Dur Durham
5537 355r			John Peele	son	1		Dur Durham
5538 355v	[ae]a	Church Street *	William Bellerby	hea m	36	groom	Dur Lanchester
5539 355v			Frances Bellerby	wif m	32	wife	Dur Rainton
5540 355v			Ann Bellerby	dau	9	scholar	Dur Durham
5541 355v			John Bellerby	son	6	scholar	Dur Durham
5542 355v			Elizabeth Bellerby	dau	2		Dur Durham
5543 355v	[ae]b	Church Street *	Richard Renders	hea m	23	servant (at university)	Mdx S. Ann
5544 355v			Elizabeth Renders	wif m	24	wife	Dur Darlington
5545 355v			Isabella Renders	dau	1		Dur Durham
5546 355v	[af]a	Church Street *	John Metcalf	hea m	36	coach painter	Dur Durham
5547 355v			Mary Metcalf	wif m	29	wife	Nbl Newcastle
5548 355v			Helen Metcalf	dau	6	scholar	Dur Durham
5549 355v			Sarah Metcalf	dau	4	scholar	Nbl Newcastle
5550 355v			Thomas Metcalf	son	3	scholar	Dur Durham
5551 355v			John Metcalf	son	1		Dur Durham
5552 355v	[af]b	Church Street *	Elizabeth Loughborough	hea w	51	washerwoman	Dur Low Newton
5553 355v			Mary Loughborough	dau	11	scholar	Dur Durham
5554 355v	[af]c	Church Street *	John Weelands	hea m	49	tailor	Dur Durham
5555 355v			Ann Weelands	wif m	53	wife	Dur Stockton
5556 355v			William Bickston	app	19	[apprentice tailor?]	Mdx Chelsea
5557 356r	[ag]a	Church Street *	Mary O'Connell	hea w	50	servant	Dur Stockton
5558 356r			William O'Connell	son	20	tailor	Dur Durham
5559 356r	[ag]b	Church Street *	Ann Tiplady	hea w	59	dressmaker	Dur Durham
5560 356r			Mary Tiplady	dau	30	dressmaker	Dur Durham
5561 356r			Ellen Tiplady	dau	28	dressmaker	Dur Durham
5562 356r	[ag]c	Church Street *	Jane Blakey	hea w	53	washerwoman	Dur Durham
5563 356r			John Parkinson	ldr w	51	sawyer	Dur Durham
5564 356r	[ag]d	Church Street *	Henry Christy	hea m	42	tailor	Dur Durham
5565 356r			Margaret Christy	wif m	43	wife	Dur Chester-le-Street
5566 356r			Isabel Christy	dau	14	scholar	Dur Durham
5567 356r			Ellen Christy	dau	8	scholar	Dur Durham
5568 356r			Sarah Cecily Christy	dau	3m		Dur Durham
5569 356r			Catherine Christy	dau	11	scholar	Dur Durham
5570 356r	[ah]	Church Street	Elizabeth Burnett	wif m	36	servant's wife	Lan Clitheroe
5571 356r			Elizabeth Burnett	dau	9	scholar	Dur Durham
5572 356r			Thomas Burnett	son	7	scholar	Dur Durham
5573 356r			William John Burnett	son	5	scholar	Dur Durham
5574 356r			Matthew T. Burnett	son	10m		Dur Durham
5575 356r*			Harriet Newby	nce	13	scholar	Dur Byers Green
5576 356v	<34>a	Church Street	Thomas Metcalf	hea m	41	butcher	Dur Haughton-l-Skerne
5577 356v			Maria Metcalf	wif m	37	wife	Sry Chertsey
5578 356v			Thomas Metcalf	son	18	cooper	Dur Norton
5579 356v			Frederick Metcalf	son	15	basketmaker	Dur Norton
5580 356v			Frances E. Metcalf	dau	10	scholar	Dur Durham
5581 356v			John Metcalf	son	8	scholar	Dur Durham
5582 356v			William Metcalf	son	4	scholar	Dur Durham
5583 356v	<34>b	Church Street	John Forster	hea m	72	independent	Dur Shotley Bridge
5584 356v	<34>c	Church Street	Mary Craggs	hea w	46	dependent upon family	Dur Durham
5585 356v			James Craggs	son	24	joiner	Dur Durham
5586 356v			William Craggs	son	20	shoemaker	Dur Durham
5587 356v			Matthew Craggs	son	18	baker	Dur Durham
5588 356v			John Craggs	son	14	cooper	Dur Durham
5589 356v			Mary Jane Craggs	dau	10	scholar	Dur Durham
5590 356v			Margaret Craggs	dau	8	scholar	Dur Durham
5591 356v	<34>d	Church Street	Mary Willis	hea w	57	needlewoman	Dur Durham
5592 356v			Edward Willis	son	30	bookbinder	Dur Durham
5593 356v			Margaret Hopper	dau	44	schoolmistress	Dur Durham

5594	357r	<34>e	Church Street	George Summers	hea	m	29	cordwainer	Dur Durham
5595	357r			Ellen Summers	wif	m	26	wife	Dur Durham
5596	357r			Margaret Summers	dau		5	scholar	Dur Durham
5597	357r			Isabel Summers	dau		4	scholar	Dur Durham
5598	357r			James Summers	son		1		Dur Durham
5599	357r	<33>	Church Street	Daniel McEwen	hea	m	40	lately supt of police	Sct
5600	357r			Catherine McEwen	wif	m	27		Sct
5601	357r			Isabella McEwen	dau		10	scholar at home	Sct
5602	357r			Daniel McEwen	son		3		Dur Durham
5603	357r			Caroline L. McEwen	dau		4m		Dur Durham
5604	357r			Mary McEwen	sis		42	dependent	Sct
5605	357r			Eliza McEwen	nce		13	scholar at home	Sct
5606	357r	<32>	Church Street	Forster Brown	hea	w	56	bookbinder	Nth Peterborough
5607	357r			William Brown	son		20	bookseller's assistant	Dur Durham
5608	357r			Mary Ann Hope	ser		22	house servant	Dur Easington
5609	357r	<31>	Church Street	Sarah Mason	hea	w	77	lodging house keeper	Nry Smeaton
5610	357r			Sarah Telford	dau	m	41	domestic duty	Dur Durham
5611	357r			James Telford	gsn		14	scholar	Dur Durham
5612	357v	<30>	Church Street	Henry James Ellis	hea	m	71	captain & adjutant *	Don Inver
5613	357v			Jane Ellis	wif	m	68	wife	Dur Carlton
5614	357v			Anne Ellis	dau		39	at home	Dur Durham
5615	357v			Jane Ellis	dau		37	at home	Dur Durham
5616	357v			Charlotte F. Ellis	dau		30	at home	Dur Durham
5617	357v			Alexander Ellis	son		21	at home	Dur Durham
5618	357v			Margaret Simpson	ser		41	house maid	Dur Walworth
5619	357v			Anne Dickman	ser		19	cook	Nbl Falloden
5620	357v	<29>	Church Street	William Henderson	hea	m	37	borough JP & alderman *	Dur Merrington
5621	357v			Jane Burlinson	ser		52	general servant	
5622	357v			Mary Thompson	ser		24	general servant	Dur Durham
5623	357v			Robert Cranstoun	ser		19	general servant	Sct
5624	357v	<28>	Church Street	Edward Davison	hea	m	63	perpetual curate *	Dur Brancepeth
5625	357v			Mary P. Davison	wif	m	56	minister's wife	Dur Durham
5626	357v			Edward Davison jn	son		30	scholar	Lnd
5627	357v			Charles Davison	son		23	scholar	Dur Durham
5628	357v			Mary Taylor	ser		36	house servant	Dur West Rainton
5629	357v			Elizabeth Hopper	ser		29	house servant	Dur Durham
5630	357v			Jane Wardell	ser		22	house servant	Dur Houghton-l-Spring
5631	358r	<27>	Church Street	Edward Sneyd	hea	w	56	vicar of S. Oswald <MA>	Irl
5632	358r			Maria Sneyd	mth	w	77	annuitant	Irl
5633	358r			Sarah Maria Sneyd	dau		17	scholar at home	Mdx London
5634	358r			Sarah Sneyd	sis		44	annuitant	Gls Painswick
5635	358r			Sibella Blackler	vis	w	66	annuitant	Dev Devonport
5636	358r			Mary Rutherford	ser		23	servant (general)	Nry East Cowton
5637	358r			Henrietta Steinmetz	ser		23	servant (general)	Germany
5638	358r	<1>a	Hallgarth Street	Ann Fenwick	hea	w	56	grocer	Dur Durham
5639	358r			James Richardson	jny		23	journeyman grocer	Dur Gateshead
5640	358r			Thomas Laidler	ldr		72	Chelsea pensioner	Dur Durham
5641	358r	<1>b	Hallgarth Street	Elizabeth Skelton	hea	w	77	parish relief	Dur Durham
5642	358r	<1>c	Hallgarth Street	Anne Day	hea	w	66	no occupation	Dur Darlington
5643	358r	<1>d	Hallgarth Street	Edward Ramshaw	hea	m	59	master tailor	Dur Durham
5644	358r			Jane Ramshaw	wif	m	59	wife	Dur Stanhope
5645	358r			Jane Ramshaw	dau		34	at home	Dur Durham
5646	358r	<1>e	Hallgarth Street	John Fuller	hea	m	31	coachsmith	Dur Durham
5647	358r			Isabella Fuller	wif	m	32	wife	Dur Durham
5648	358r			Mary Fuller	dau		9	scholar	Dur Durham
5649	358v	<2>a	Hallgarth Street	John Rake	hea	w	68	joiner <& sexton *>	Dur Durham
5650	358v			Mary Rake	dau		42	domestic duty	Mdx London
5651	358v			John Rake	gsn		2		Dur Durham
5652	358v			Margaret Rake	gda		1		Dur Durham
5653	358v	<2>b	Hallgarth Street	Elizabeth Mordy	hea		33	dressmaker	Dur Staindrop
5654	358v			George Mordy	son		11	scholar	Dur Durham
5655	358v			Charles Mordy	son		9	scholar	Dur Durham
5656	358v	<2>c	Hallgarth Street	Thomas Smith	hea	m	56	nailmaker	Dur Durham
5657	358v			Ann Smith	wif	m	51	wife	Dur Durham
5658	358v			William Smith	son		22	joiner	Dur Durham
5659	358v			James Smith	son		24	shoemaker	Dur Durham
5660	358v			Robert Smith	son		22	upholsterer	Dur Durham
5661	358v			Elizabeth Smith	dau		12	servant	Dur Durham
5662	358v			Isabella Smith	dau		14	scholar	Dur Durham
5663	358v			Francis Smith	son		12	scholar	Dur Durham
5664	358v			Eleanor Smith	dau		10	scholar	Dur Durham
5665	358v			Mary Jane Smith	dau		6	scholar	Dur Durham
5666	358v			Elizabeth Stott	mlw	w	82	annuitant	Yks
5667	359r	[aa]	Hallgarth Street	John J. Jackson	hea	m	46	farm labourer	Dur Durham
5668	359r			Mary Jackson	wif	m	39	wife	Dur [South] Shields
5669	359r			Magdalen Jackson	dau		13	scholar	Dur Durham
5670	359r			Robert Jackson	son		11	scholar	Dur Durham
5671	359r			George Jackson	son		9	scholar	Dur Durham
5672	359r			John Jackson	son		6	scholar	Dur Durham
5673	359r			Thomas Pattison	rel		61	farm labourer	Dur Broom
5674	359r	<3>a	Hallgarth Street	William Henry Macklam	hea	m	32	whitesmith & bellhanger	Dur Durham

5675	359r	<3>a Hallgarth Street	Ann Macklam	wif m	32	wife	Dur Durham
5676	359r		Elizabeth Macklam	dau	13	scholar	Dur Durham
5677	359r		Sarah Macklam	dau	10	scholar	Dur Durham
5678	359r		William Henry Macklam	son	8	scholar	Dur Durham
5679	359r		John Macklam	son	3		Dur Durham
5680	359r	<3>b Hallgarth Street	Abraham Marshall	hea m	68	coachmaker	Nbl Newcastle
5681	359r		Ann Marshall	wif m	72	wife	Dur Durham
5682	359r		Mary Marshall	dau	36	domestic duty	Dur Durham
5683	359r		Jane Marshall	dau	27	dressmaker	Dur Durham
5684	359r		William E. Welch	gsn	13	scholar	Dur Durham
5685	359r		Jane Ann Marshall	gda	7m		Dur Durham
5686	359v	<3>c Hallgarth Street	George James Best	hea m	48	painter <& gilder>	Nbl Newcastle
5687	359v		Alice Best	wif m	46	wife	Dur Durham
5688	359v		James Best	son	19	smith	Nbl Newcastle
5689	359v		William Best	son	17	tailor	Dur Durham
5690	359v		Jane Best	dau	14	milliner	Dur Durham
5691	359v		John Best	son	12	scholar	Dur Durham
5692	359v		Henry Best	son	9	scholar	Dur Durham
5693	359v		Alice Best	dau	3		Dur Durham
5694	359v		Dorothy Best	dau	7m		Dur Durham
5695	359v	<4> Hallgarth Street	Robert Jackson <jn>	hea m	43	brewer & innkeeper *	Dur Durham
5696	359v		Phoebe Jackson	wif m	31	wife	Wil Akbourn
5697	359v		Robert Joseph Jackson	son	4	scholar	Dur Durham
5698	359v		Benjamin W. Jackson	son	3		Dur Durham
5699	359v		Sarah Ann Jackson	dau	1		Dur Durham
5700	359v		Mary Owens	ser	16	house servant	Irl
5701	359v	[ab]a Hallgarth Street	William Pattison	hea m	39	brewer	Dur
5702	359v		Elizabeth Pattison	wif m	40	wife	Yks Oldbrough
5703	359v		Margaret Rake	ldr	24	washerwoman	Dur Durham
5704	359v		Thomas Rake	lds	3		Dur Durham
5705	360r	[ab]b Hallgarth Street	Norman Lang	hea m	41	handloom carpet weaver	Abd
5706	360r		Margaret Gordon	wif m	44	servant	Gla
5707	360r		James Milne	vis w	37	handloom carpet weaver	Sct
5708	360r	[ab]c Hallgarth Street	William Johnson	hea m	35	supt of rural police	Dur Burdon
5709	360r		Jane Johnson	wif m	40	wife	Dur Hurworth
5710	360r		Mary Johnson	dau	11	scholar	Dur Hurworth
5711	360r		Thomas Garbutt Johnson	son	7	scholar	Dur Swalwell
5712	360r		William Johnson	son	5	scholar	Dur Houghton-l-Spring
5713	360r		Ann Johnson	dau	3		Dur Houghton-l-Spring
5714	360r		Jane Johnson	dau	9m		Dur Hetton-le-Hole
5715	360r		Elizabeth James	ser	19	house servant	Dur Durham
5716	360r	[ab]d Hallgarth Street	Elizabeth Richardson	hea w	82	needlewoman	Dur Gateshead
5717	360r	<5> Hallgarth Street	Robert Jackson <sn>	hea m	70	farmer emp 1 labourer *	Dur Durham
5718	360r		Ann Jackson	wif m	68	wife	Dur Durham
5719	360r		Mary Jackson	dau	39	farmer's daughter	Dur Durham
5720	360r		Jane Jackson	dau	29	farmer's daughter	Dur Durham
5721	360r		Georgiana Haggiston	ser	17	house servant	Dur Durham
5722	360v	[ac]a Hallgarth Street	Mary Ann Baxter	hea	22	ragsorter at paper mill	Lan Ulverston
5723	360v		Hannah Baxter	sis	21	domestic duty	Cul Skirwith
5724	360v		James Baxter	bro	12	errand boy	Dur Durham
5725	360v		Joseph Baxter	bro	8	scholar	Dur Durham
5726	360v	[ac]b Hallgarth Street	John Sutherst	hea m	43	house carpenter	Dur Durham
5727	360v		Mary Sutherst	wif m	46	wife	Dur Piercebridge *
5728	360v		Agnes Sutherst	dau	13	scholar	Dur Darlington
5729	360v		Samuel Sutherst	son	9	scholar	Dur Norton
5730	360v		John Sutherst	son	6	scholar	Dur
5731	360v		Mary Sutherst	dau	6	scholar	Dur
5732	360v	[ad]a Hallgarth Street	James Mahan	hea m	22	labourer	Ros
5733	360v		Bridget Mahan	wif m	20	wife	Ros
5734	360v		John Mahan	son	6m		Dur Durham
5735	360v		Michael Mahan	vis	18	labourer	Ros
5736	360v		James Mahan	vis	19	labourer	Ros
5737	360v	[ad]b Hallgarth Street	Robert Todd	hea m	31	labourer	Dur Durham
5738	360v		Jemima Todd	wif m	25	wife	Sct
5739	360v		Eliza Ann Todd	dau	3	scholar	Dur Durham
5740	360v		Robert Todd	son	1		Dur Durham
5741	361r	<7>a Hallgarth Street	George Liddle	hea m	43	harnessmaker	Dur Durham
5742	361r		Mary Liddle	wif m	48	laundress	Dur Piercebridge *
5743	361r		Elizabeth Liddle	dau	15	laundress	Dur Durham
5744	361r		Tamar Liddle	dau	14	dressmaker	Dur Durham
5745	361r		Jane Liddle	dau	9	scholar	Dur Durham
5746	361r	<7>b Hallgarth Street	William H. Smith	hea m	23	bootcloser	Dur Sunderland
5747	361r		Elizabeth Smith	wif m	21	wife	Dur South Shields
5748	361r		William Page Smith	son	8m		Dur Durham
5749	361r		Jane Elizabeth Stevenson	vis	20	dressmaker	Dur Gateshead
5750	361r	<7>c Hallgarth Street	James Liddle	hea m	22	master mason	Dur Durham
5751	361r	<7>d Hallgarth Street	George Dodds	hea m	47	labourer	Dur Durham
5752	361r		Jane Dodds	wif m	46	wife	Dur Durham
5753	361r		Thomasine Dodds	dau	14	scholar	Dur Durham
5754	361r		Ann Dodds	dau	10	scholar	Dur Durham
5755	361r		Elizabeth Dodds	dau	6	scholar	Dur Durham

No.	Folio	Schedule	Street	Name	Rel.	Cond.	Age	Occupation	Birthplace
5756	361r	<7>d	Hallgarth Street	George Dodds	son		4		Dur Durham
5757	361r			Robert Dodds	son		2		Dur Durham
5758	361r	<7>e	Hallgarth Street	Mary Spedding	hea	w	35	laundress	Cul Keswick
5759	361r			Elizabeth Palmer	ldr	w	39	washerwoman	Cul Keswick
5760	361r			Jane Palmer	ldd		11	washerwoman	Dur Sunderland
5761	361v	<6>a	Hallgarth Street	John Woodifield	hea	m	49	mason	Brk Windsor
5762	361v			Susan Woodifield	wif	m	43	wife	Dur Durham
5763	361v			Ann Woodifield	dau		11	scholar at home	Dur Durham
5764	361v			William Woodifield	son		8	scholar at home	Dur Durham
5765	361v			Jane Woodifield	dau		6	scholar at home	Dur Durham
5766	361v	<6>b	Hallgarth Street	William Wilkinson	hea	m	40	cordwainer	Dur Barnard Castle
5767	361v			Ann Wilkinson	wif	m	42	wife	Dur Satley
5768	361v			George Wilkinson	son		18	cabinetmaker	Dur Sedgefield
5769	361v			Isabel E. Wilkinson	dau		16	scholar	Dur Durham
5770	361v			Margaret Wilkinson	dau		6	scholar	Dur Durham
5771	361v			John Hopper	ldr		20	cordwainer	Dur Durham
5772	361v	<8>a	Hallgarth Street	William Murray	hea	m	34	labourer	Yks York
5773	361v			Ann Murray	wif	m	32	wife	Dur Durham
5774	361v			Elizabeth Murray	dau		9	scholar	Dur Durham
5775	361v			Henry Murray	son		7	scholar	Dur Durham
5776	361v			Jane Murray	dau		6	scholar	Dur Durham
5777	361v			Fanny Murray	dau		4	scholar	Dur Durham
5778	361v			Matthew Murray	son		2		Dur Durham
5779	361v			Harriet Murray	dau		10m		Dur Durham
5780	361v			Elizabeth Baker	mlw	w	74	confectioner	Dur Durham
5781	362r	<8>b	Hallgarth Street	Christopher Lumley	hea	m	27	cordwainer	Dur Stockton
5782	362r			Elizabeth Lumley	wif	m	21	wife	Dur Durham
5783	362r			Christopher Lumley	son		3		Dur Durham
5784	362r			John Lumley	son		2		Dur Durham
5785	362r	<8>c	Hallgarth Street	Thomas Dodds	hea	m	41	labourer	Dur Durham
5786	362r			Mary Ann Dodds	wif	m	27	wife	Dur Willington
5787	362r			Jane Dodds	dau		4	at home	Dur Durham
5788	362r			Mary Dodds	dau		3	at home	Dur Durham
5789	362r			Thomasine Dodds	dau		6m		Dur Durham
5790	362r			Mary Liddle	ldr		11m		Dur Durham
5791	362r	<8>d	Hallgarth Street	James Dermont	hea	m	46	hawker	Sct
5792	362r			Ann Dermont	wif	m	43	wife	Nry Guisborough
5793	362r			Sarah Dermont	dau		22	servant at home	Nry Yarm
5794	362r			George Palmer	son		20	hawker	Nry Yarm
5795	362r			Mary Dermont	dau		18	scholar at home	Nry Yarm
5796	362r			James Dermont	son		10	scholar at home	Dur Durham
5797	362r			Isaac Dermont	son		8	scholar	Dur Durham
5798	362r			Benjamin Dermont	son		6	scholar	Dur Durham
5799	362r			Rosanna Dermont	dau		4		Dur Durham
5800	362r			Ellen Dermont	dau		10m		Dur Durham
5801	362v	<8>e	Hallgarth Street	John Thompson	hea	m	48	cabinetmaker (master *)	Dur Durham
5802	362v			Faith E. Thompson	wif	m	49	wife	Dur Durham
5803	362v			John Thompson	son		22	cabinetmaker	Dur Durham
5804	362v			Ann Thompson	dau		19	dressmaker	Dur Durham
5805	362v			Thomas Thompson	son		16	cabinetmaker	Dur Durham
5806	362v			Elizabeth Thompson	dau		12	scholar	Dur Durham
5807	362v			Ellen Thompson	dau		9	scholar	Dur Durham
5808	362v	<8>f	Hallgarth Street	George Skelton	hea	m	49	labourer	Dur Chester-le-Street
5809	362v			Ellen Skelton	wif	m	39	wife	Dur Durham
5810	362v			Mary Skelton	dau		19	at home	Dur Durham
5811	362v			Robert Skelton	son		14	at home	Dur Durham
5812	362v			George Skelton	son		2	at home	Dur D'rham
5813	362v			William Skelton	son		2	at home	Dur Durham
5814	362v	[ae]a	Hallgarth Street	John Jewet	hea	m	32	shoemaker (journeyman)	Dur Durham
5815	362v			Isabella Jewet	wif	m	32	wife	Dur Durham
5816	362v			Samuel Jewet	son	m	10	scholar	Dur Durham
5817	362v			Thomas Jewet	son		7	scholar	Dur Durham
5818	362v			John Jewet	son		6	scholar	Dur Durham
5819	362v			Isabella Jewet	dau		9m		Dur Durham
5820	362v			Mary Hives	sil		30	sorter in paper mill	Dur Durham
5821	363r	[ae]b	Hallgarth Street	Robert Parkinson	hea	m	41	labourer	Lan Lancaster
5822	363r			William Ansley	ldr	m	56	labourer	Dur Durham
5823	363r			Mary Franks	ldr	w	52	housekeeper	Dur Durham
5824	363r			William Tatters	sls		8	school	Dur Durham
5825	363r			Ellen Parkinson	dau		6	school	Dur Durham
5826	363r			Jane Parkinson	dau		4	school	Dur Durham
5827	363r			John Franks	gsn		11	school	Dur Durham
5828	363r	<10>	Hallgarth Street	Thomas Jackson	hea	m	33	countryman *	Dur Durham
5829	363r			Elizabeth King Jackson	wif	m	32	wife	Dur Gateshead
5830	363r			Ann Jackson	dau		6	scholar	Dur Durham
5831	363r			Ellen Jackson	dau		3		Dur Durham
5832	363r			George P. Jackson	son		7m		Dur Durham
5833	363r			Eleanor Douley	ser		16	general servant	Nbl Newcastle
5834	363r			John Mitchell	vis		19	cooper	Nbl Alnwick
			one house uninhabited						
5835	363r	[af]	Hallgarth Street	Ann Young	hea	w	49	dependent	Dur Dalton-le-Dale

5836	363r	[af]	Hallgarth Street	William Young	son	15	scholar	Dur Durham
5837	363r			James Young	son	10	scholar	Dur Durham
5838	363v	<13>a	Hallgarth Street	John Winter	hea m	64	mason <& grocer>	Dur Durham
5839	363v			Ann Winter	wif m	70	wife	Dur Darlington
5840	363v	<13>b	Hallgarth Street	Elizabeth Brown	hea w	36	dependent	Dur Durham
5841	363v			Charles Winter Brown	son	9	scholar	Dur Durham
5842	363v			Mary Brown	dau	7	scholar	Dur Durham
5843	363v			Robert Brown	son	5	scholar	Dur Durham
5844	363v	<13>c	Hallgarth Street	David Jackson	hea m	52	labourer	Dur Durham
5845	363v			Mary Jackson	wif m	51	wife	Dur Durham
5846	363v			Ann Jackson	dau	4	at home	Dur Durham
5847	363v			Mary Jackson	dau	2		Dur Durham
5848	363v			Thomas Jackson	son	5m		Dur Durham
5849	363v	<12>a	Hallgarth Street	Jane Fuller	hea	63	washerwoman	Dur Durham
5850	363v			Joseph Dodds	ldr m	41	smith	Dur Durham
5851	363v			Elizabeth Dodds	ldw m	39	wife	Dur Durham
5852	363v			Joseph Dodds	lds	14	coachsmith	Dur Durham
5853	363v			Isabella Dodds	ldd	9	school	Dur Durham
5854	363v			Elizabeth Dodds	ldd	6	school	Dur Durham
5855	363v			Jane Dodds	ldd	4	school	Dur Durham
5856	364r	<12>b	Hallgarth Street	Martin Harrison	hea m	56	countryman	Dur Wolsingham
5857	364r			Isabella Harrison	wif m	42	wife	Dur Durham
5858	364r			Edward Harrison	son	22	countryman	Dur Durham
5859	364r			Jane Harrison	dau	8	countryman's daughter	Dur Durham
5860	364r			Ann Harrison	dau	3		Dur Durham
5861	364r	<12>c	Hallgarth Street	Ralph Gowland	hea m	69	papermaker	Dur Long Newton
5862	364r			Elizabeth Gowland	wif m	69	wife	Dur Chester-le-Street
5863	364r	<17>	Hallgarth Street	Ann Chilton	hea w	50	laundress	Dur
5864	364r			William Chilton	son	22	draper	Dur
5865	364r			Thomas Chilton	son	13	gardener	Dur
5866	364r	[ag]a	Hallgarth Street	George Brown	hea m	48	brickmaker	Dur Durham
5867	364r			Jane Brown	wif m	33	wife	Dur Durham
5868	364r			Phyllis Brown	dau	16	scholar	Dur Durham
5869	364r			Thomas Brown	son	15	scholar	Dur Durham
5870	364r			Elizabeth Brown	dau	5	scholar	Dur Durham
5871	364r			Ann Brown	dau	2		Dur Durham
5872	364r			George Brown	son	6w		Dur Durham
5873	364r	[ag]b	Hallgarth Street	Robert Whitfield	hea m	47	labourer	Dur Durham
5874	364r			Isabella Whitfield	wif m	51	wife	Dur Durham
5875	364v	[ag]c	Hallgarth Street	Thomas Hopper	hea	42	stonemason	Dur Durham
5876	364v			Isabella Ayre	sis w	60	housekeeper; pauper	Dur Durham
5877	364v			Jane Cockburn	nce	8	scholar	Dur Durham
5878	364v	[ag]d	Hallgarth Street	William Calvert	hea m	62	mason	Dur Fishburn
5879	364v			Susanna Calvert	wif m	61	wife	Dur Westgate
5880	364v			William Calvert	son	18	mason's apprentice	Dur Durham
5881	364v	[ag]e	Hallgarth Street	George Hackworth	hea	50	tailor (journeyman)	Dur Durham
5882	364v	[ag]f	Hallgarth Street	Adam Palmer	hea m	23	painter (journeyman)	Dur Durham
5883	364v			Margaret Palmer	wif m	21	wife	Dur Durham
5884	364v	<18>	Hallgarth Street	Stephen Thompson	hea m	63	joiner	Dur Lanchester
5885	364v			Ann Thompson	wif m	63	wife	Dur Durham
5886	364v	<19>	Hallgarth Street	Mary Ann Ellison	hea w	51	worsted dlr <lodgings>	Nbl Berwick
5887	364v			Frances Smith	dau w	26	late innkeeper	Dur Durham
5888	364v			Thomas Joseph Smith	gsn	1		Nbl Newbiggin-by-Sea
5889	364v			Hannah Ellison	dau	22	dressmaker	Dur Durham
5890	364v			Wheatley Ellison	son	19	painter & glazier	Dur Durham
5891	364v			Joseph Ellison	son	15	grocer	Dur Durham
5892	364v			Thomas Cummins Ellison	son	13	scholar at home	Dur Durham
5893	364v			Sarah Jane Ellison	dau	11	scholar at home	Dur Durham
5894	365r		Hallgarth	Anthony Unthank	hea m	48	farmer of 96a emp 2 labr	Dur Thorpe
5895	365r			Harriet Unthank	wif m	50	wife	Dur Long Newton
5896	365r			Robert Petch Unthank	son	14	scholar	Dur Evenwood
5897	365r			William Greenwell	vis	27	farmer	Dur Woodham
5898	365r			Ann Gill	ser	15	servant	Nbl Byker
5899	365r			Robert Erwin	ser	23	servant	Dur Dinsdale
5900	365r			Thomas Teasdale	ser	17	servant	Dur Evenwood
5901	365r	<1>	Hallgarth St *	Ralph Toward	hea m	40	grocer <& hay dealer>	Dur Whickham
5902	365r			Mary Toward	wif m	47	wife	Nbl Haydon Bridge
5903	365r			William Toward	son	9	scholar	Nbl Seaton Terrace
5904	365r			Isabella Ornsby	ser	19	house servant	Dur Picktree
5905	365r			John Geldart	ldr	21	iron moulder	Nry Richmond
5906	365r	<3>a	Hallgarth St *	John Carnes	hea m	39	coachtrimmer	Dur Durham
5907	365r			Mary Carnes	wif m	40	wife	Dur Sedgefield
5908	365r			Ann Carnes	dau	19	at home	Dur Durham
5909	365r			George Carnes	son	17	sailor	Dur Durham
5910	365r			Mary Carnes	dau	11	scholar	Dur Durham
5911	365r			Hannah Carnes	dau	6	scholar	Dur Durham
5912	365r			Emma Carnes	dau	4		Dur Durham
5913	365v	<3>b	Hallgarth St *	Thomas Coates	hea m	40	servant	Dur Sedgefield
5914	365v			Isabella Coates	wif m	27	wife	Dur Pittington *
5915	365v			Jane Coates	dau	4		Wry Sharow
5916	365v			Thomas Coates	son	3		Wry Sharow

5917	365v	<3>b	Hallgarth St *	Isabella Coates	dau	1		Wry Sharow
5918	365v	<2>a	Hallgarth St *	George Robinson	hea m	46	master bread baker	Dur Durham
5919	365v			Mary Robinson	wif m	49	wife	Dur Ferryhill
5920	365v			Catherine Robinson	dau	21	at home	Dur Durham
5921	365v			Mary Robinson	dau	18	at home	Dur Durham
5922	365v			James Robinson	son	16	apprentice [baker?]	Dur Durham
5923	365v			Isabella Robinson	dau	13	scholar	Dur Durham
5924	365v			George Robinson	son	11	scholar	Dur Durham
5925	365v			John Robinson	son	9	scholar	Dur Durham
5926	365v			William Robinson	son	7	scholar	Dur Durham
5927	365v			Alexander Robinson	son	2		Dur Durham
5928	365v	<2>b	Hallgarth St *	Elizabeth Fenwick	hea	61	annuitant	Dur Brancepeth
5929	365v	<4>	Hallgarth St *	Jane Best	hea w	79	lodging house	Nry Smeaton
5930	365v			Jane Corner	dau w	42	sempstress	Dur Durham
5931	365v			Elizabeth Booker	ldr w	46	fundholder *	Mdx London
5932	365v			John Kay Booker	vis	19	commoner, Queen's Coll *	Wor Dudley
5933	366r	<5>a	Hallgarth St *	Catherine Elliott	hea w	40	teacher of school	Dur Penshaw
5934	366r			Jane C. Elliott	dau	12	scholar (at home)	Dur Durham
5935	366r			Catherine C.V. Elliott	dau	10	scholar (at home)	Dur Washington
5936	366r			John Salter	vis	36	teacher, National Sch *	Sry Walton
5937	366r	<5>b	Hallgarth St *	Elizabeth Sowerby	hea w	60	proprietor of houses	Dur Durham
5938	366r	<6>	Hallgarth St *	John Stokoe	hea	74	retired navy surgeon *	Dur Ferryhill
5939	366r			Martha Kell	ser w	45	house servant	Dur Sunderland
5940	366r	[ah]	Hallgarth St *	Jabez Squire	hea m	30	inspector, rural police	Dev Tiverton
5941	366r			Mary Ann Squire	wif m	27	wife	Wes Brough
5942	366r			Edward Squire	son	6	scholar	Dur West Rainton
5943	366r			Ann Squire	dau	3	scholar	Dur Whickham
5944	366r	<8>a	Hallgarth St *	Robert Stewart	hea m	37	coachmaker	Nbl Newcastle
5945	366r			Hannah Stewart	wif m	38	wife	Dur Durham
5946	366r			Thomas Stewart	son	14	plumber	Dur Durham
5947	366r			Mary Stewart	dau	13	scholar	Dur Durham
5948	366r			Hannah Stewart	dau	10	scholar	Dur Durham
5949	366r			Robert Stewart	son	6	scholar	Dur Durham
5950	366r			Charles Stewart	son	3		Dur Durham
5951	366r			Ann Stewart	dau	7m		Dur Durham
5952	366v	<8>b	Hallgarth St *	John Wise	hea m	39	porter merch's cellarman	Yks
5953	366v			Isabella Wise	wif m	32	wife	Yks
5954	366v			Catherine Wise	dau	16	scholar at home	Dur
5955	366v			Ellen Clemment	ser	15	general servant	Dur
5956	366v	[ai]	Hallgarth St *	Charlotte Hope	hea	35	dressmaker	Sct
5957	366v			Elizabeth Hope	sis	39	(invalid)	Ery Driffield
5958	366v			Joseph Fawcett Hope	bro	16	plumber, apprentice	Dur Darlington
5959	366v			John Hope	bro	12	scholar at home	Dur Darlington
5960	366v	[aj]	Hallgarth St *	Anthony Raine	hea m	50	tea dealer	Nry Ovington
5961	366v			Ann Raine	wif m	37	wife	Nry Arkengarthdale
5962	366v			Jane Ann Raine	dau	10	school at home	Dur Bishop Auckland
5963	366v			James Raine	son	8	school at home	Dur Staindrop
5964	366v			Hannah Raine	dau	6	school at home	Dur Staindrop
5965	366v			Amelia Raine	dau	4	school at home	Dur Staindrop
5966	366v			John Raine	son	3m		Dur Durham
5967	366v	[ak]	Hallgarth St *	John Scaif	hea m	31	slater	Nry Cleasby
5968	366v			Elizabeth Scaif	wif m	28	wife	Dur Durham
5969	366v			Frederick Scaif	son	3		Nry Caldwell
5970	366v			Joseph Scaif	son	6m		Dur Durham
5971	367r	<9>	Hallgarth St *	Hannah Hubbick	hea w	53	independent	Dur Kelloe
5972	367r			Jane Welsh	vis m	24	wife	Dur Hart
5973	367r			Mary Gibson	ser	19	house servant	Dur Sedgefield
5974	367r	<10>	Hallgarth St *	John Mattison	hea m	53	retired grocer	Nbl Woodhorn
5975	367r			Mary Mattison	wif m	54	wife	Cul Armathwaite
5976	367r			Ann P. Gibson	nce	19	scholar at home	Nbl North Shields
5977	367r			Margaret Davison	ldr	60	retired teacher	Nbl Morpeth
5978	367r	<11>	Hallgarth St *	James Audas	hea m	32	plumber <lodgings>	Nry Whitby
5979	367r			Ann Audas	wif m	34	wife	Ntt Nottingham
5980	367r			Martha Rippon Audas	dau	5	scholar	Dur Shotley Bridge
5981	367r			Elizabeth H. Audas	dau	2		Dur Durham
5982	367r			Joshua Audas	son	6m		Dur Durham
5983	367r			Andrew Ford	vis m	35	master blacksmith *	Sct
5984	367r	<12>	Hallgarth St *	Thomas Hall	hea m	53	joiner <& lodgings>	Dur Lanchester
5985	367r			Margaret Hall	wif m	54	wife	Nry Middleham
5986	367r			William Walker	vis w	74	late Exciseman	not known
5987	367r			Mary Mowbray	ser	15	servant	Dur Lanchester
5988	367v	<13>a	Hallgarth St *	Mary Cook	hea	24	dressmaker	Dur Durham
5989	367v			William Cook	bro	16	coach painter	Dur Durham
5990	367v			Frances Cook	sis	12	house servant	Dur Durham
5991	367v			Anne Stout	cou	8	no scholar	Dur Durham
5992	367v	<13>b	Hallgarth St *	Thomas Middleton	hea m	50	currier	Dur Durham
5993	367v			Ann Middleton	wif m	54	wife	Dur Durham
5994	367v			Thomas Middleton	son	21	watchmaker	Dur Durham
5995	367v			Jane Middleton	dau	13	scholar	Dur Durham
5996	367v	<13>c	Hallgarth St *	George Alderson	hea m	58	labourer	Dur Hamsterley
5997	367v			Margaret Alderson	wif m	44	wife	Dur Usworth

5998	367v	<13>c	Hallgarth St *	George Alderson	son	27	labourer	Dur Durham
5999	367v	<13>d	Hallgarth St *	Joseph Middleton	hea m	53	porter at University *	Dur Durham
6000	367v			Elizabeth Middleton	wif m	46	wife <laundress>	Dur Durham
6001	367v			Elizabeth Middleton	dau	14	scholar	Lnd Tower of London
6002	367v			Mary Grace Middleton	dau	12	scholar	Canada, Quebec
6003	367v			Catherine A. Middleton	dau	9	scholar	troopship *
6004	367v			Ann Hannah Middleton	dau	6	scholar	Dur Durham
6005	367v	<13>e	Hallgarth St *	Phillip Davis	hea m	56	hawker	Gls
6006	367v			Jane Davis	wif m	57	wife	Dur
6007	367v			Susan Jeferson	vis m	37	labourer's wife	Dur
6008	368r	<21>	Hallgarth Street	John Prest	hea m	36	hay dealer	Cul
6009	368r			Mary Prest	wif m	37	wife	Dur
6010	368r			Anne Prest	dau	9	scholar	Dur
6011	368r			James Prest	son	7	scholar	Dur
6012	368r			Martha Prest	dau	3		Dur
6013	368r			Jane Prest	dau	5d		Dur
6014	368r			Sarah Whitfield	vis	35	dressmaker	Cul Alston Moor
6015	368r	<22>a	Hallgarth Street	Mary Richardson	hea w	66	annuitant	Dur Sherburn
6016	368r	<22>b	Hallgarth Street	William Tindale	hea m	48	sergeant at mace	Dur Brancepeth
6017	368r			Ann Tindale	wif m	50	wife	Dur Durham
6018	368r			John Tindale	son	17	upholsterer	Dur Durham
6019	368r			Joseph Tindale	son	15	painter	Dur Durham
6020	368r			Ann Tindale	dau	14	scholar at home	Dur Durham
6021	368r			William Tindale	son	12	scholar at home	Dur Durham
6022	368r			Michael Tindale	son	7	scholar at home	Dur Durham
6023	368r			William Hall	ldr	36	gentleman	Dur Sunderland
6024	368r	<22>c	Hallgarth Street	John Wilkinson	hea m	23	currier	Dur Hart
6025	368r			Mary Wilkinson	wif m	23	wife	Dur Durham
6026	368r			Thomas Wilkinson	son	1		Dur Durham
6027	368v	<23>	Hallgarth Street	Anne Tristram	hea w	44	fundholder	Sct
6028	368v			Charlotte Tristram	sda	27	fundholder	Nbl Eglingham
6029	368v			Louisa Tristram	sda	22	fundholder	Nbl Eglingham
6030	368v			Jane Tristram	sda	20	fundholder	Nbl Eglingham
6031	368v			Holloway Hastings	nep	10	scholar	Sct
6032	368v			Elizabeth Baines	ser	21	servant (cook)	Gls Bristol
6033	368v			Jane Bell	ser	26	servant (house maid)	Dur Sherburn
6034	368v	<25>	Hallgarth Street	John Maven	hea m	40	iron founder *	Dur
6035	368v			Dorothy Maven	wif m	40	wife	Dur Whickham
6036	368v			George Collon	sso	19	mason	Dur Whickham
6037	368v			Maria Maven	dau	2		Lan Liverpool
6038	368v			Maria Daniel	ldr	65	annuitant	Ham Hambledon
6039	368v	<24>	Hallgarth Street	John Gregson	hea m	38	tailor & draper (master)	Dur Fishburn
6040	368v			Ann Gregson	wif m	33	wife	Dur Brancepeth
6041	368v			Mary Elizabeth Gregson	dau	5	scholar	Dur Fishburn
6042	368v			Anne Gregson	dau	2		Dur Coxhoe
6043	368v			James Gregson	nep	12	errand boy	Dur Fishburn
6044	368v	<27>a	Hallgarth Street	Elizabeth Snowdon	hea w	40	washerwoman; pauper	Dur Rainton
6045	368v			Thomas Snowdon	son	12	scholar	Dur Durham
6046	368v			Jane Snowdon	dau	8	scholar	Dur Durham
6047	369r	<27>b	Hallgarth Street	Matilda Pearson	hea w	47	dressmaker; pauper	Dur Durham
6048	369r			Mary Bamlet	dau m	22	visitor	Dur Durham
6049	369r			Jane Pearson	dau	12	scholar	Dur Durham
6050	369r			Robert Cowans	ldr w	61	butcher	Dur Durham
6051	369r			John Bamlet	gsn	5m		Dur Durham
6052	369r	<27>c	Hallgarth Street	Robert Gent	hea m	38	mason	Dur Wolsingham
6053	369r			Martha Gent	wif m	36	wife	Dur Durham
6054	369r			Margaret Gent	dau	10	scholar	Dur Durham
6055	369r			Susanna Gent	dau	2m		Dur Durham
6056	369r			Isabella Gent	dau	5	scholar	Dur Durham
6057	369r	<27>d	Hallgarth Street	George Keith	hea m	35	countryman	Dur Durham
6058	369r			Margaret Keith	wif m	35	wife	Dur Durham
6059	369r			Frances Keith	dau	13	scholar	Dur Durham
6060	369r			John Keith	son	9	scholar	Dur Durham
6061	369r			George Keith	son	3		Dur Durham
6062	369r	<27>e	Hallgarth Street	Christopher Turnbull	hea m	27	mason	Dur Sunderland Bridge
6063	369r			Elizabeth Turnbull	wif m	27	wife	Dur Durham
6064	369r			Thomas Turnbull	son	1		Dur Durham
6065	369v	[al]	Hallgarth Street	Joseph McGowen	hea m	35	licensed hawker *	Irl
6066	369v			Susanna McGowen	wif m	30	formerly hawker	Dev Devonport
6067	369v			Mary McGowen	dau	5	scholar	Dur Durham
6068	369v			Ellen McGowen	dau	4	scholar	Dur Durham
6069	369v			Bridget McGowen	dau	2		Dur Durham
6070	369v			Elizabeth McGowen	sis	28	servant	Irl
6071	369v	<28>a	Hallgarth Street	Robert Savage	hea m	30	cordwainer	Dur Durham
6072	369v			Margaret Savage	wif m	29	wife	Dur Durham
6073	369v			Robert Savage	son	4	at school	Dur Durham
6074	369v			Frances Savage	dau	3		Dur Durham
6075	369v			William Savage	son	10m		Dur Durham
6076	369v	<28>b	Hallgarth Street	Joseph Snowdon	hea m	52	tailor	Dur Durham
6077	369v			Elizabeth Snowdon	wif m	51	wife	Dur Durham
6078	369v			John Snowdon	son	22	cordwainer	Dur Durham

6079	369v	<28>b	Hallgarth Street	William Snowdon	son	17	house carpenter	Dur Durham
6080	369v			Joseph Snowdon	son	11	at school	Dur Durham
6081	369v			William Williamson	ldr	43	cordwainer	Gla Swansea
6082	369v			Henry Snowdon	son	20	tailor	Dur Durham
6083	370r	<28>c	Hallgarth Street	Simon Sanderson	hea m	66	retired farmer	Nry Kirk Leavington
6084	370r			Dorothy Sanderson	wif m	50	wife	Dur Kelloe
6085	370r			Susanna Sanderson	dau	19	milliner	Dur Kelloe
6086	370r			Sarah Colling	* m	33	visitor	Dur Copley
6087	370r			Joseph Colling	vss	7	visitor	Dur Durham
6088	370r			Rosalie Colling	vsd	6	visitor	Dur Durham
6089	370r			Jane Colling	vsd	7m		Dur Sunderland
6090	370r	<26>	Hallgarth Street	John Day	hea m	39	solicitor's gen clk *	Sct
6091	370r			Mary Day	wif m	34		Dur Durham
6092	370r			Mary Day	dau	4		Dur Durham
6093	370r			Margaret Day	dau	1		Dur Durham
6094	370r			Mary Ann Robson	ser	18	general servant	Nbl Newcastle
6095	370r	[am]	Hallgarth Street	William Fenwick	hea m	67	mason	Dur Durham
6096	370r			Ann Fenwick	wif m	60	wife	Dur Durham
6097	370r			Hannah Fenwick	dau	23	at home	Dur Durham
6098	370r			Thomas Fenwick	son	13	scholar	Dur Durham
6099	370r	[an]	Hallgarth Street *	Robert Wetherell	hea m	26	agent <land surveyor>	Dur Piercebridge *
6100	370r			Mary Ellen Wetherell	wif m	22	wife <milliner>	Dur Durham
6101	370r			Jane Elizabeth Wetherell	dau	1		Dur Durham
6102	370r			Elizabeth Wooler	ser	40	house servant	Nbl Wooler
6103	370v	[ao]	Hallgarth Street	Henry Porter	hea m	55	scripture reader	Ham West Meon
6104	370v			Jane Porter	wif m	50	wife	Ham Preston Candover
6105	370v			Fanny Porter	dau	19	infant school teacher	Ssx Chichester
6106	370v			Lucy Porter	dau	13	infant school assistant	Ssx Chichester
6107	370v			Nathaniel Porter	son	11	scholar	Wry Wentworth
6108	370v			Charles Porter	son	9	scholar	Wry Wentworth
6109	370v			Edward Porter	son	6	at home	Wry Wentworth
6110	370v			George Porter	son	4	at home	Wry Wentworth
6111	370v	[ap]a	Hallgarth Street	John Graham	hea w	80	papermaker; pauper	Edn Mid-Calder
6112	370v	[ap]b	Hallgarth Street	Penelope Johnson	hea w	64	depending on children	Dur Monk Hesleden
6113	370v			Thomas Knowles	ldr	16	cabinetmaker, apprentice	Lan Lancaster
6114	370v	[ap]c	Hallgarth Street	Matthew Johnson	hea m	25	coach-springmaker *	Dur Durham
6115	370v			Ann Johnson	wif m	23	wife	Dur Durham
6116	370v			William Johnson	son	10m		Dur Durham
6117	370v	[ap]d	Hallgarth Street	Frederick Child	hea m	39	servant unemployed	Pem Brawdy /"Brody"
6118	370v			Margaret Child	wif m	30	laundress	Sct Fuge
6119	370v			Harriet Child	dau	10	at school	Inv Fort George
6120	370v			Sophia Child	dau	8	at school	Lks Glasgow
6121	370v			Margaret Child	dau	6	at school	Abd Aberdeen
6122	370v			Sarah E.M. Child	dau	4	at home	Dur Shotley Bridge
6123	370v			Ellen Child	dau	1	at home	Dur Durham
6124	371r	[ap]e	Hallgarth Street	Jane Hutton	hea w	54	charwoman /"chairwoman"	Yks
6125	371r			Henrietta Hutton	dau	13	scholar	Dur Shincliffe
6126	371r			John Hutton	son	10	scholar	Dur Shincliffe
6127	371r	[aq]a	Hallgarth Street	Michael Richardson	hea m	26	master shoemaker	Dur
6128	371r			Ann Richardson	wif m	21	master shoemaker's wife	Dur Heworth
6129	371r			Mary Richardson	dau	10	scholar	Dur
6130	371r	[aq]b	Hallgarth Street	Thomas Briggs Adamson	hea m	42	horse breaker	Dur Durham
6131	371r			Elizabeth Adamson	wif m	26	wife	Nbl Alnwick
6132	371r	[aq]c	Hallgarth Street	Matthew Palmer	hea m	24	mason	Dur Windlestone
6133	371r			Jane Palmer	wif m	22	wife	Dur Durham
6134	371r			Nicholas Palmer	son	1		Dur Durham
6135	371r			Edward Dodd	flw w	75	cordwainer	Dur Durham
6136	371r	[ar]a	Hallgarth Street	John Mensforth	hea m	37	officer of Durham Prison	Dur Durham
6137	371r			Mary Mensforth	wif m	32	wife	Ery Hull
6138	371r			Elizabeth Mensforth	dau	15	servant	Dur Durham
6139	371r			Susanna Mensforth	dau	6	scholar	Dur Durham
6140	371r			George Mensforth	son	4		Dur Durham
6141	371r			John Mensforth	son	2		Dur Durham
6142	371r			Jonathan Robinson	blw	42	gardener	Ery Drypool
6143	371v	[ar]b	Hallgarth Street	Richard Gascoigne	hea m	55	sawyer	Dur Brancepeth
6144	371v			Elizabeth Gascoigne	wif m	56	wife	Dur Houghall
6145	371v			Mary Ann Gascoigne	dau	19	at home	Dur Durham
6146	371v			John Gascoigne	son	17	coachsmith	Dur Durham
6147	371v	[ar]c	Hallgarth Street	Christopher Hickson	hea m	41	butcher	Dur
6148	371v			Julia Hickson	wif m	32	wife	Dur Esh
6149	371v			Mary Martha Hickson	dau	7	scholar	Dur Durham
6150	371v			Margaret Hickson	dau	4	scholar	Dur Durham
6151	371v			John Hickson	son	1		Dur Durham
6152	371v		Hallgarth Tollbar	James Smurthwaite	hea m	43	officer, Durham Prison	Dur Durham
6153	371v			Mary Ann Smurthwaite	wif m	41	toll collector	Dur Durham
6154	371v			Jane Latha Smurthwaite	dau	19	dressmaker	Dur Durham
6155	371v			Agnes Smurthwaite	dau	17	dressmaker	Dur Durham
6156	371v			Mary Ann Smurthwaite	dau	13	scholar	Dur Durham
6157	371v			Charlotte Smurthwaite	dau	4		Dur Durham
6158	371v			James Smurthwaite	son	2		Dur Durham
6159	371v			William Gradon Smurthwaite	son	7m		Dur Durham

6160	371v		Hallgarth Tollbar	Ellen Smurthwaite	dau m	22	straw-bonnetmaker	Dur Durham
6161	371v			James Smurthwaite	gsn	7m		Dur Durham
6162	372r		Hallgarth Peth Gate	William Noble	hea m	49	toll collector	Dur Gateshead
6163	372r	[as]a	Hallgarth Street	William Taylor	hea m	40	slater	Lan Lancaster
6164	372r			Catherine Taylor	wif m	37	wife	Dur Durham
6165	372r			William Taylor	son	17	slater	Dur Durham
6166	372r			Alice Taylor	dau	12	scholar	Dur Durham
6167	372r			Thomas Taylor	son	10	scholar	Dur Durham
6168	372r			Elizabeth Taylor	dau	8	scholar	Dur Durham
6169	372r			Henry Taylor	son	6	scholar	Dur Durham
6170	372r			Jane Taylor	dau	3	at home	Dur Durham
6171	372r			John Taylor	son	1	at home	Dur Durham
6172	372r	[as]b	Hallgarth Street	Jane Penmen	hea		parish relief (servant)	Nbl Ponteland
6173	372r	[as]c	Hallgarth Street	John Banks	hea	50	tailor, journeyman	Dur Durham
6174	372r	[at]	Hallgarth Street	Elizabeth Ayre	hea w	83	parish relief	Dur Haran
6175	372r	[au]	Hallgarth Street	John Fenwick	hea m	61	mason	Dur Sherburn
6176	372r			Dorothy Fenwick	wif m	64	wife	Dur Durham
6177	372r			Richard Fenwick	son	27	mason	Dur Durham
6178	372r			John Fenwick	son	21	butcher	Dur Durham
6179	372r			Jane Fenwick	dau	26	dressmaker	Dur Durham
6180	372r			Ellen Fenwick	dau	19	at home	Dur Durham
6181	376v*	[av]a	Hallgarth Street	Susanna Hopper	hea w	40	washerwoman	Dur Durham
6182	376v	[av]b	Hallgarth Street	Isabella Parker	hea w	65	washerwoman	Ken Tiliam Mickland
6183	376v	[aw]	Hallgarth Street	Thomas Douglas	hea m	48	shoemaker	Nbl Wooler
6184	376v			Mary Douglas	wif m	44	wife	Dur Lumley
6185	376v			John Douglas	son	16	scholar	Nbl Wooler
6186	376v			James Douglas	son	14	scholar	Nbl Wooler
6187	376v			Mary Douglas	dau	11	scholar	Nbl Wooler
6188	376v			Thomas Douglas	son	9	scholar	Nbl Wooler
6189	376v			Isabella Douglas	dau	4	scholar	Nbl Wooler
6190	376v	<38>	Hallgarth Street	George Bell	hea m	62	farmer emp 4 labourers	Dur Medomsley
6191	376v			Margaret Bell	wif m	49	wife	Dur Shotley Bridge
6192	376v			William Bell	son	22	farmer's son	Dur Medomsley
6193	376v			Thomas Bell	son	21	viewer	Dur Medomsley
6194	376v			Joseph Bell	son	16	farmer's son, scholar	Dur Fulforth
6195	376v			Jane Bell	dau	12	farmer's dau, scholar	Dur Fulforth
6196	376v			Mary Bell	dau	10	farmer's dau, scholar	Dur Sherburn
6197	376v			John George Bell	son	7	farmer's son, scholar	Dur Durham
6198	376v			Margaret Anne Bell	dau	4	farmer's daughter	Dur Durham
6199	376v			Mary Smith	ser	16	house servant	Dur Byers Green
6200	377r	<27>a	Hallgarth Street	Ann Gent	hea	68	annuitant	Dur Stockley
6201	377r			Thomas Coates	nep	9	scholar	Dur Durham
6202	377r			George Coates	nep	8	scholar	Dur Durham
6203	377r	<27>b	Hallgarth Street	Ralph Crozier Coates	hea m	30	asst draper & grocer	Dur Sedgefield
6204	377r			Margaret Coates	wif m	31	wife	Dur Whorlton
6205	377r			Susanna Coates	dau	6	scholar	Dur Durham
6206	377r			William Coates	son	4	scholar	Dur Durham
6207	377r			George Coates	son	3		Dur Durham
6208	377r			Ralph Crozier Coates	son	2		Dur Durham
6209	377r	<44>	Hallgarth Street	Edward Peele	hea m	38	chorister in Cathedral *	Dur Durham
6210	377r			Ann Peele	wif m	38	wife	Dur Durham
6211	377r			John Edward Peele	son	17	horse farrier's app	Dur Durham
6212	377r			Robert Peele	son	15	scholar	Dur Durham
6213	377r			Edward Peele jn	son	13	scholar	Dur Durham
6214	377r			Henry Peele	son	10	scholar	Dur Durham
6215	377r			Ann Peele	dau	8	scholar	Dur Durham
6216	377r			Richardson Peele	son	6	scholar	Dur Durham
6217	377r			Maria Peele	dau	4	scholar	Dur Durham
6218	377r			Mary Peele	dau	1		Dur Durham
6219	377r			Hannah Hutchinson	ser	24	house servant	Yks Carlton
6220	377v	<45>	Hallgarth Street	Michael Pearson	hea w	74	landed proprietor	Dur Esh
6221	377v			Ann Booth	ser	20	house servant	Dur Tudhoe
6222	377v	<46>	Hallgarth Street	William Brown	hea m	42	master shoemaker	Holland *
6223	377v			Ann Brown	wif m	45	wife	Nbl Ryde
6224	377v	[ax]a	Hallgarth Street	Hugh Edward Boyd	hea m	58	joiner	Dur Shincliffe
6225	377v			Ann Boyd	wif m	55	wife	Dur Witton Gilbert
6226	377v			Hugh Boyd	son	28	shoemaker	Dur Durham
6227	377v	[ax]b	Hallgarth Street	Jane Sedgwick	hea w	75	laundress	Dur Shadforth
6228	377v	[ay]	Hallgarth Street	Abraham Brown	hea w	88	out of business	Dur Auckland
6229	377v			Elizabeth Brown	dau	59	bonnetmaker	Dur Durham
6230	377v			Elizabeth Canning	gda	33	out of service	Dur Sunderland
6231	377v	[az]a	Hallgarth Street	Ellen Cockburn	hea	50	laundress	Dur Durham
6232	377v			Ann Parkinson	vis	14	scholar	Dur Durham
6233	377v	[az]b	Hallgarth Street	Robert Stevens	hea m	70	hawker; pauper	Sct
6234	377v			Mary Stevens	wif m	73	wife	Nbl
6235	377v	<47>a	Hallgarth Street	John Watson	hea m	27	carpenter	Dur Durham
6236	377v			Margaret Watson	wif m	30	wife	Nry Bedale
6237	377v			Mary Ann Watson	dau	4	scholar	Dur Durham
6238	377v			Isabel Watson	dau	2		Dur Durham
6239	378r	<47>b	Hallgarth Street	Richard Nicholson	hea m	27	master baker	Dur Durham
6240	378r			Jane Nicholson	wif m	25	wife	Dur Durham

6241	378r	<47>c	Hallgarth Street	Catherine Moody	hea		72	retired servant	Dur Durham
6242	378r	<48>	Hallgarth Street	John Patrick	hea m	33	attorney & solicitor	Dur Durham
6243	378r			Anne Patrick	wif m	33	wife	Dur Durham
6244	378r			Anne Patrick	dau	4		Dur Durham
6245	378r			John Patrick	son	3m		Dur Durham
6246	378r			Mary Guhskenan	ser	20	house servant	Mog
6247	378r	<49>a	Hallgarth Street	Thomas Jopling	hea w	72	joiner	Dur Durham
6248	378r			Isabella Jopling	dau	22	domestic duty	Dur Durham
6249	378r			Jane Jopling	vis	10	scholar	Dur Durham
6250	378r	<49>b	Hallgarth Street	William Vest	hea m	55	master tailor	Dur Durham
6251	378r			Maria Vest	wif m	52	wife	Dur Durham
6252	378r			Sarah Vest	dau	22	at home	Dur Durham
6253	378r			William Vest	son	17	at home	Dur Durham
6254	378r			Maria Maddison	nce	8	scholar	Dur Durham
6255	378r	<49>c	Hallgarth Street	John Dickinson	hea m	66	cartman	Dur Weardale
6256	378r			Mary Dickinson	wif m	64	wife	Dur Durham
6257	378v	<49>d	Hallgarth Street	Thomas Jopling	hea m	36	journeyman joiner	Dur Durham
6258	378v			Ann Jopling	wif m	38	wife	Dur Norton
6259	378v			Robert Jopling	son	16	draper	Dur Durham
6260	378v			William Jopling	son	10	scholar	Dur Durham
6261	378v			Margaret Jopling	dau	9	scholar	Dur Durham
6262	378v			Ellen H. Jopling	dau	2		Dur Durham
6263	378v	<49>e	Hallgarth Street	William Jopling	hea m	28	journeyman joiner	Dur Durham
6264	378v			Sarah Jopling	wif m	30	wife	Dur Washbeck
6265	378v	<50>a	Hallgarth Street	Ralph Jopling	hea m	40	joiner & carpenter *	Dur Durham
6266	378v			Mary Jopling	wif m	38	wife	Dur Durham
6267	378v	<50>b	Hallgarth Street	James Jopling	hea m	36	joiner	Dur Durham
6268	378v			Harriet Jopling	wif m	45	wife	Dur Durham
6269	378v			Thomas Brass	sso	19	joiner	Dur Durham
6270	378v			William Brass	sso	17	tailor	Dur Durham
6271	378v			Charles Brass	sso	16	cooper	Dur Durham
6272	378v			Ralph Jopling	son	11	at school	Dur Durham
6273	378v			James Jopling	son	8	at school	Dur Durham
6274	378v			Isabella Jopling	dau	5	at school	Dur Durham
6275	379r	<51>a	Hallgarth Street	Mary Jopling	hea	31	dressmaker <& milliner>	Dur Durham
6276	379r	<51>b	Hallgarth Street	John Hopper	hea m	49	cabinetmaker	Dur Durham
6277	379r			Jane Hopper	wif m	42	wife	Dur Durham
6278	379r			Thomison Hopper	dau	15	scholar	Dur Durham
6279	379r			Edward Hopper	son	12	scholar	Dur Durham
6280	379r			Jane Hopper	dau	9	scholar	Dur Durham
6281	379r			Ann Hopper	dau	7	scholar	Dur Durham
6282	379r			Anna Hopper	dau	5	scholar	Dur Durham
6283	379r			John Hopper	son	2		Dur Durham
6284	379r	<51>c	Hallgarth Street	Charles Maskel Douglass	hea m	38	ropemaker	Dur Durham
6285	379r			Hannah Douglass	wif m	39	wife	Dur Durham
6286	379r			Charles John Douglass	son	2	at home	Dur Durham
6287	379r			Margaret M. Douglass	dau	7m	at home	Dur Durham
6288	379r	[ba]a	Hallgarth Street	Peter Sewell	hea w	60	tailor	Dur Durham
6289	379r			Peter Sewell	son	22	tailor	Dur Durham
6290	379r			Jane Sewell	dau	25	dressmaker	Dur Durham
6291	379r			Sarah Sewell	dau	17	at home	Dur Durham
6292	379r	[ba]b	Hallgarth Street	Joseph Turnbull	hea m	26	mason	Dur Durham
6293	379r			Margaret Turnbull	wif m	25	wife	Dur Durham
6294	379r			Ann Turnbull	dau	6m		Dur Durham
6295	379v	<53>	Hallgarth Street	Robert Young	hea w	51	brewer	Dur Durham
6296	379v			Agnes Rebecca Young	dau	26	at home	Dur Durham
6297	379v			Robert Young	son	20	cooper (apprentice)	Dur Durham
6298	379v			William M. Young	son	16	whitesmith (apprentice)	Dur Durham
6299	379v			Ann Elizabeth Young	dau	13	scholar	Dur Durham
6300	379v			Thomas Young	son	12	scholar	Dur Durham
6301	379v			James Edward Young	son	10	scholar	Dur Durham
6302	379v			Edward Martin Young	son	6	scholar	Dur Durham
6303	379v	<54>	Hallgarth Street	Isabella Howe	hea w	72	linen manufacturer	Dur Durham
6304	379v			Thomas Howe	son	48	linen weaver	Dur Durham
6305	379v			Robert Howe	son	43	linen weaver	Dur Durham
6306	379v			Margaret Gainford	gda	14	scholar	Dur Durham
6307	379v	<55>	Hallgarth Street	Martha Watson	hea	45	spinster	Dur Sherburn House
6308	379v			Isabella Watson	dau	27	dressmaker <& milliner>	Dur Durham
6309	379v			William Craggs	ldr	30	shoemaker	Dur Durham
6310	379v	<56>	Hallgarth Street	Thomas Buddle	hea m	66	retired bread baker	Dur Houghton-1-Spring
6311	379v			Margaret Buddle	wif m	77	wife	Dur Durham
6312	379v			Ann Smales	ser	17	house servant	Dur Gateshead *
			one house uninhabited					
6313	380r	<57>a	Hallgarth Street	Elizabeth Taylor	hea w	75	formerly servant; pauper	Yks Ledbridge
6314	380r	<57>b	Hallgarth Street	Elizabeth Johnson	hea w	82	dependent	Dur Tudhoe
6315	380r	<57>c	Hallgarth Street	Mary Thornton	hea w	33	lodging house	Dur Aycliffe
6316	380r			Ann Allen	dau	12	parish relief	Dur Durham
6317	380r			Jane Allen	dau	10	parish relief	Dur Durham
6318	380r			William Heaviside	bro	25	labourer	Dur Aycliffe
6319	380r			Michael Heaviside	bro	16	labourer	Dur Aycliffe
6320	380r	<57>d	Hallgarth Street	Mary Killion	hea m	40	labourer	Irl

6321 380r	<57>d	Hallgarth Street	Bridget Killion	dau	8	scholar	Irl
6322 380r			John Tigho	ldr m	36	labourer	Irl
6323 380r			James McDonagh	ldr m	20	labourer	Irl
6324 380r			Margaret McDonagh	nce m	18	labourer	Irl
6325 380r			John McManus	ldr m	28	labourer	Irl
6326 380r			Bridget McManus	ldr m	23	labourer	Irl
6327 380r			Ann McManus	ldd	3m	servant (as groom)	Dur Durham
6328 380r	[bb]	Hallgarth Street	James Hodgson	hea m	63	servant (as groom)	Dur Staindrop
6329 380r			Susanna Hodgson	wif m	65	laundress	Dur Whickham
6330 380r			Jane Hodgson	dau	32	laundress	Dur Whickham
6331 380r			Margaret Hodgson	dau	29	laundress	Dur Durham
6332 380v	<58>	Hallgarth Street	Jane Dalyell	hea w	48	daughter of baronet	Lnd
6333 380v			Jane Melvell Dalyell	dau	23	gentlewoman	Sct
6334 380v			Ralph Dalyell	son	16	scholar	Sct
6335 380v			Charlotte Anstruther	sis	46	daughter of baronet	Irl
6336 380v			Margaret Henderson	ser	40	lady's maid	Dur Stockton
6337 380v			Isabel Brodie	ser	38	cook	Sct
6338 380v			Mary Louden	ser	30	house maid	Sct
6339 380v			Dennis Marrin	ser	15	footman	Irl
6340 380v	[bc]	Hallgarth Street	William Cummings	hea m	75	farm labourer	Dur Long Newton
6341 380v			Elizabeth Cummings	wif m	74	wife	Dur Shadforth
6342 380v			Thomas Herring	vis w	71	farm labourer	Dur Shadforth
6343 380v	[bd]a	Hallgarth Street	Robert Calvert	hea m	35	mason	Dur Durham
6344 380v			Sarah Calvert	wif m	31	bootbinder	Ess Harwich
6345 380v	[bd]b	Hallgarth Street	Eliza Oliver	hea m	42	wife of Anthony Oliver *	Ham Fareham
6346 380v			Ellen Oliver	dau	15	scholar	Dur Shadforth
6347 380v			Mary Oliver	dau	12	scholar	Lan Manchester *
6348 380v			Benjamin Oliver	son	10	scholar	Dur Durham
6349 380v			Eliza Oliver	dau	2		Dur Durham
6350 381r	[be]	Hallgarth St *	Isabella Holborn	hea w	73	retired innkeeper	Dur Brancepeth
6351 381r			Mary Holborn	dau	44	at home	Dur Chester-le-Street
6352 381r			Margaret Holborn	dau	30	at home	Dur Durham
6353 381r			James Emerson	nep	17	coachbuilder, apprentice	Dur Sunderland
6354 381r			Isabella Holborn	gda	10	scholar	Dur Durham
6355 381r			Mary Holborn	gda	8	scholar	Dur Durham
6356 381r	<64>	Hallgarth St *	Elizabeth Elliott	hea w	62	innkeeper <'Victoria'>	Dur Durham
6357 381r			Sarah Elliott	dau	33	straw-bonnetmaker {*}	Lnd
6358 381r			William Elliott	son	20	cooper	Lnd
6359 381r			James Layton	ldr	21	butcher	Dur Durham
6360 381r	[bf]	Hallgarth St *	Ann Hannah Jackson	hea w	32	dependant; pauper	Dur Durham
6361 381r			Anne Jackson	dau	10	scholar	Dur Durham
6362 381r			Louisa Jackson	dau	4	scholar	Dur Durham
6363 381r			Mark Jackson	son	2		Dur Durham
6364 381r			Elizabeth Ragan	ser	17	house servant	Irl
6365 381r	[bg]	Hallgarth St *	William Burnett	hea m	28	watchmaker	Sct
6366 381r			Jane Burnett	wif m	29	wife	Dur Durham
6367 381r			Agnes Burnett	dau	2	at home	Dur Durham
6368 381r			Eliza Jane Burnett	dau	11m	at home	Dur Durham
6369 381v	[bh]	Hallgarth St *	William Graham	hea m	46	waiter	Cul Scaleby
6370 381v			Jane Graham	wif m	41	wife	Dfs Dumfries
6371 381v			Henrietta Graham	dau	13	at home (scholar)	Nbl Newcastle
6372 381v			Alexander Graham	son	11	at home (scholar)	Nbl Newcastle
6373 381v			William Graham	son	10	at home (scholar)	Dur Durham
6374 381v			Andrew Graham	son	6	at home (scholar)	Dur Durham
6375 381v			Jane Graham	dau	3		Dur Durham
6376 381v	·[bi]a	Hallgarth St *	Thomas Prince	hea m	40	cartman	Dur Stockton
6377 381v			Mary Prince	wif m	40	wife	Dur Durham
6378 381v			James Prince	son	16	scholar (at home)	Dur Sherburn
6379 381v	[bi]b	Hallgarth St *	Elizabeth Snowdon	hea w	62	dependant on her son	Dur Durham
6380 381v			Michael Snowdon	son	30	maltsman	Dur Durham
6381 381v	[bj]	Hallgarth Street	William Mordy	hea m	61	groom	Dur Haughton-l-Skerne
6382 381v			Isabella Mordy	wif m	61	laundress	Nbl Berwick
6383 381v			Sarah Mordy	dau	33	laundress	Dur Staindrop
6384 381v			Isabella Mordy	gda	3	scholar	Dur Dalton
6385 381v	1	Church Street *	Eleanor Forster	hea	30	grocer & tea dealer	Dur [D] Elvet
6386 381v			Mary Forster	sis	28	grocer & tea dealer	Dur [D] Elvet
6387 382r	<2>	Church Street	Hannah Sewell	hea m	55	domestic duty	Dur Durham
6388 382r			George Jobling	ldr	16	bookbinder	Dur Durham
6389 382r	<3>	Church Street	Ann Wharton	hea w	65	domestic duty	Nbl Newcastle
6390 382r			Ann Smith	ser	17	house servant	Dur Durham
6391 382r	<4>	Church Street	Elizabeth Hines	hea	67	independent <lodgings>	Dur Durham
6392 382r			Ann Hines	sis	55	independent	Dur Durham
6393 382r	<5>	Church Street	Catherine M. Ellis	hea w	40	annuitant	Sct
6394 382r			Robert K.A. Ellis	son	15	scholar	East Indies
6395 382r			Catherine Mactavish	ser	25	house servant	Sct
6396 382r	<6>	Church Street	Robert Hubback	hea m	43	landed proprietor	Dur Cowpen
6397 382r			Frances Hubback	wif m	41	wife	Sry Farnham
6398 382r			Charles Hubback	son	16	scholar (at home)	Ham Shirley
6399 382r			Mark Hubback	son	15	scholar (at home)	Ham Shirley
6400 382r			Eliza Hubback	dau	11	scholar (at home)	Dur Heighington
6401 382r			Walter Hubback	son	9	scholar (at home)	Dur Heighington

6402	382r	<6>	Church Street	Selina Hubback	dau		7	scholar (at home)	Dur Staindrop
6403	382r			Ann Williams	gov		21	governess	Bre Brecon
6404	382r			Ann Cook	ser		23	house servant	Dur Houghton-l-Spring
6405	382r			Ann Taylor	ser		36	house servant	Dur Toft Hill
6406	382r			William Clemishaw	ser		20	house servant	Nry Romanby
6407	382v	<7>	Church Street	Isabella Sewell	hea		55	independent	Dur Durham
6408	382v			Ann Carter	ser		22	house servant	Dur Hartlepool
			one house unoccupied						
6409	382v	[ai]a	Church Street	James Cummings	hea m		21	butcher	Dur Durham
6410	382v			Margaret Cummings	wif m		22	wife	Dur Easington
6411	382v	[ai]b	Church Street	Thomas Lowson	hea m		60	labourer	Dur Durham
6412	382v			Mary Lowson	wif m		52	wife	Dur Durham
6413	382v			Michael Lowson	son		28	labourer	Dur Durham
6414	382v			Thomas Lowson	son		25	labourer	Dur Durham
6415	382v			Joseph Lowson	son		22	engineman	Dur Durham
6416	382v			John Lowson	son		13	scholar	Dur Durham
6417	382v	[aa]	Church Lane	Thomas Chaplin	hea m		38	lady's boot & shoemaker	Wry Ilkley
6418	382v			Elizabeth Chaplin	wif m		34	bootbinder	Wry Harrogate
6419	382v			Charles Chaplin	son		8	scholar	Wry Harrogate
6420	382v			Thomas Chaplin	son		6	scholar	Dur Sunderland
6421	382v			Joshua T. Chaplin	son		4	scholar	Dur Sunderland
6422	382v			Arthur Chaplin	son		3m		Dur Durham
6423	382v	[ab]	Church Lane	James Theakstone	hea m		63	labourer	Nry Constable Burton
6424	382v			Eleanor Theakstone	wif m		62	wife	Lin Sleaford
6425	383r	[ac]	Church Lane	Joseph Dryden	hea m		58	cowkeeper	Dur Carlton
6426	383r			Susanna Dryden	wif m		56	wife	Dur Stanhope
6427	383r			Robert Dryden	son		24	cabinetmaker	Dur Durham
6428	383r			Margaret Dryden	dau		22	at home	Dur Durham
6429	383r			John Dryden	son		19	joiner	Dur Durham
6430	383r			Joseph Dryden	son		17	cabinetmaker	Dur Durham
6431	383r			Thomas Dryden	son		14	scholar	Dur Durham
6432	383r			Joseph McNaughton	nep		14	whitesmith	Dur Durham
6433	383r			James Robinson	vis m		34	tailor	Yks Ullerthorpe
6434	383r			Mary Ann Robinson	vsw m		29	wife	Wry Armley
6435	383r	<10>	Church Street	Robert Ingram Shafto	hea m		41	solicitor	Dur Durham
6436	383r			Sarah Shafto	wif m		41	wife	Dur Hetton
6437	383r			Elizabeth S. Appleby	*		18	at home	Dur Durham
6438	383r			Mary Appleby	*		17	at home	Dur Durham
6439	383r			James Parkin	ser		22	house servant	Dur Lanchester
6440	383r			Dorothy Potts	ser		29	house servant	Nbl Heddon-on-th-Wall
6441	383r			Elizabeth Davison	ser		30	house servant	Dur Houghton-l-Spring
6442	383r			Isabella Elliott	ser		31	house servant	Dur Houghton-l-Spring
6443	383v	<11>	Church Street	Anne Hall	hea w		64	independent	Lnd S. Swithin
6444	383v			Anne C. Hall	dau		29	independent	Dur Bishopwearmouth
6445	383v			Elizabeth Dobison	ser		22	house servant	Dur Aycliffe
6446	383v	<12>	Church Street	Ann Gilhespie	hea w		38	lodging house keeper	Nbl Newcastle
6447	383v			David Thomas	ldr m		27	gentleman	Cmn Abergwilly
6448	383v			Ellen E. Thomas	ldw m		28	wife	Ntt Worksop
6449	383v			William H. Thomas	lds		5	scholar	Cmn Abergwilly
6450	383v			John Dixon Thomas	lds		4	scholar	Dur Durham
6451	383v			Ellen Gossage Thomas	ldd		3		Dur Durham
6452	383v			Margaret A. Thomas	ldd		6m		Dur Witton Gilbert
6453	383v	<13>	Church Street	Eliza Harrison	hea		60	lady (independent)	Dur Hurworth
6454	383v			Martha Thompson	ser		21	house servant	Wry Doncaster
6455	383v	<14>	Church Street	Robert Thompson	hea m		28	joiner <publican *>	Dur Durham
6456	383v			Isabella Thompson	wif m		28	wife	Dur Durham
6457	383v			Ann Thompson	dau		8	scholar	Dur Durham
6458	383v			John Thompson	son		7	scholar	Dur Durham
6459	383v			James Thompson	son		5	scholar	Dur Durham
6460	383v			Isabella Thompson	dau		3m		Dur Durham
6461	383v			Elizabeth Mason	ser		11	house servant	Nbl
6462	384r	<15>	Church Street	John Pearson	hea m		63	tailor	Dur Durham
6463	384r			Sarah Pearson	wif m		60	wife	Dur Durham
6464	384r			Hannah Pearson	dau		26	dressmaker	Dur Durham
6465	384r			Jane Pearson	dau		22	dressmaker	Dur Durham
6466	384r			Elizabeth Pearson	dau		20	dressmaker	Dur Durham
6467	384r			John Thompson	ldr		63	toll agent	Dur Durham
6468	384r	[aj]	Church Street	Anthony Palmer	hea m		53	cordwainer	Dur Durham
6469	384r			Mary Palmer	wif m		43	wife	Dur Birtley
6470	384r			Jane Palmer	dau		23	at home	Dur Durham
6471	384r			George Spoors Palmer	son		15	scholar	Dur Durham
6472	384r			Ann Palmer	dau		11	scholar	Dur Durham
6473	384r			James F. Palmer	son		9	scholar	Dur Durham
6474	384r			Elizabeth Palmer	dau		7	scholar	Dur Elvet Hill
6475	384r			William R. Palmer	son		4	at home	Dur Elvet Hill
6476	384r			Eleanor Palmer	dau		1		Dur Durham
6477	384r			Frances Palmer	gda		7m		Dur Durham
6478	384r	[ak]a	Church Street	Ann Shotton	hea w		54	parish relief	Dur Aycliffe
6479	384r			Robert Shotton	son		21	shoemaker	Dur Durham
6480	384r			John Shotton	son		19	shoemaker	Dur Durham
6481	384v	[ak]b	Church Street	Robert Gray	hea m		27	drayman	Nbl Chatton

6482	384v	[ak]b	Church Street	Jane Gray	wif	m	26	wife	Nbl Lowick
6483	384v			John Gray	son		4	at home	Dur Durham
6484	384v			Mary Gray	dau		1	at home	Dur Durham
6485	384v	[ak]c	Church Street	Eleanor Palmer	hea	w	70	parish relief	Dur Durham
6486	384v			George Palmer	son		35	ostler	Dur Durham
6487	384v			Robert Palmer	son		24	labourer	Dur Durham
6488	384v	[al]a	Church Street	Thomas Thompson	hea	m	36	joiner, master emp 2 app	Dur Durham
6489	384v			Isabella Thompson	wif	m	38	wife	Dur Houghton-1-Spring
6490	384v			Thomas Thompson	son		11	at home	Dur Durham
6491	384v			Isabella Thompson	dau		9	scholar	Dur Durham
6492	384v			Jane Thompson	dau		6	scholar	Dur Durham
6493	384v			Mary Ann Thompson	dau		3		Dur Durham
6494	384v			Emma Thompson	dau		7m		Dur Durham
6495	384v	[al]b	Church Street	Edward Hodgson	hea		23	painter & gilder	Dur Durham
6496	384v	[al]c	Church Street	Isabella Douglass	hea		66	formerly housekeeper	Dur Sedgefield
6497	385r	<18>	Church Street	Thomas Jewet	hea	m	26	solicitor's writing clk*	Dur Durham
6498	385r			Sarah Jewet	wif	m	26	wife	Dur Durham
6499	385r			Isabel Jewet	dau		6	scholar at home	Dur Durham
6500	385r			Thomas Jewet	son		3		Dur Durham
6501	385r			Charles Jewet	son		1		Dur Durham
6502	385r			Robert Lowdon	*	m	30	cartwright, joiner *	Dur Brancepeth
6503	385r			Ellen Lowdon	slw	m	28	dressmaker	Dur Durham
6504	385r	[am]a	Church St *	Jane Greenwood	hea	m	38	wife of gent's valet	Dur Durham
6505	385r			Jane Greenwood	dau		9	scholar	Dur Durham
6506	385r			Mary Greenwood	dau		7	scholar	Dur Durham
6507	385r			Annie Greenwood	dau		3	scholar	Dur Durham
6508	385r			Francis Hopper	ldr	w	69	carpenter	Dur Durham
6509	385r	[am]b	Church St *	Ann Thompson	hea	w	66	bedmaker at Durham Univ	Dur Killerby
6510	385r			Thomas Thompson	son		36	gentleman's servant	Dur Blackwell
6511	385r			Mary Thompson	gda		23	gentleman's servant	Dur Durham
6512	385r	[am]c	Church St *	Margaret Sayer	hea	w	82	annuitant	Nry Ovington
6513	385v	[an]	Church St *	Henry Hogarth	hea	m	41	postman	Wes Kendal
6514	385v			Ann Hogarth	wif	m	25	wife	Dur Gateshead
6515	385v			Mary Hogarth	dau		10	scholar	Dur Durham
6516	385v			Henry Hogarth	son		8	scholar	Dur Durham
6517	385v			John Hogarth	son		6	scholar	Dur Durham
6518	385v			Jane Hogarth	dau		4	scholar	Dur Durham
6519	385v			William Hogarth	son		1		Dur Durham
6520	385v	[ao]	Church St *	Thomas Miller Hopper	hea	m	34	mason	Dur Durham
6521	385v			Ann Hopper	wif	m	31	wife	Dur Durham
6522	385v			Mary Ann Hopper	dau		3	at home	Dur Durham
6523	385v	[ap]	Church St *	William Hodgson	hea	m	26	wardsman at Durham Gaol	Dur Staindrop
6524	385v			Ann Hodgson	wif	m	31	wife	Dur Newbiggin
6525	385v			Ann Hodgson	dau		3		Dur Greatham
6526	385v	<17>	Church St *	William Hodgson	hea	m	29	master painter emp 1 man	Dur Durham
6527	385v			Harriet Hodgson	wif	m	28	wife	Dur Durham
6528	385v			William Joseph Hodgson	son		4		Dur Durham
6529	385v			Jane Hodgson	dau		3		Dur Durham
6530	385v			Margaret Hodgson	dau		2		Dur Durham
6531	385v			John Hodgson	son		7m		Dur Durham
6532	386r	[aq]	Church St *	Robert Robson Almond	hea	m	30	plumber, master no men	Dur Gateshead
6533	386r			Jane Almond	wif	m	31	wife	Nbl Newcastle
6534	386r			Edward Almond	son		7	scholar	Nbl Newcastle
6535	386r			Nicholas W. Almond	son		6	scholar	Dur Durham
6536	386r			Jane Rebecca Almond	dau		4	scholar	Dur Durham
6537	386r			Robert Robson Almond	son		2		Dur Durham
6538	386r	[ar]	Church St *	Joseph Green	hea	m	26	handloom carpet weaver	Lei Market Harborough
6539	386r			Elizabeth Green	wif	m	30	wife	Dur Barnard Castle
6540	386r			Emma Green	dau		2		Dur Darlington
6541	386r			Mary Hannah Green	dau		5m		Dur Durham
6542	386r	<18>	Church St *	Joseph Winter	hea	m	32	mason	Dur Durham
6543	386r			Mary Winter	wif	m	35	wife	Dur Durham
6544	386r			Mary Winter	dau		5	scholar	Dur Durham
6545	386r			Elizabeth Winter	dau		3		Dur Durham
6546	386r			Thomas Winter	son		1		Dur Durham
6547	386r	[as]	Church St *	John Rushforth	hea	m	28	cordwainer	Nry Catterick
6548	386r			Frances Rushforth	wif	m	30	wife	Dur Neasham
6549	386r			Mary Ann Rushforth	dau		4	at home	Dur Stockton
6550	386r			Matthew Rushforth	son		3		Dur Stockton
6551	386r			John Rushforth	son		10m		Dur Durham
6552	386v	[at]	Church St *	Thomas Hopper	hea	m	37	mason	Dur Durham
6553	386v			Sarah Hopper	wif	m	32	wife	Cul Culgaith
6554	386v			Thomas Hopper	son		12	scholar at home	Dur Durham
6555	386v			William Hopper	son		10	scholar	Dur Durham
6556	386v			Ann Hopper	dau		9	scholar	Dur Durham
6557	386v			Mark Hopper	son		7	scholar	Dur Durham
6558	386v			Ralph Hopper	son		6	scholar	Dur Durham
6559	386v			George Hopper	son		3		Dur Durham
6560	386v	<19>a	Church Street	John Jewet	hea	m	64	carpet weaver	Dur Durham
6561	386v			Isabella Jewet	wif	m	64	wife	Dur Durham
6562	386v			Isabella Jewet	dau		36	at home	Dur Durham

6563	386v	<19>a	Church Street	James Jewet	son	28	mason	Dur Durham
6564	386v			Mary Burdon	vis	53	dependent	Dur Durham
6565	386v			Mary Vest	ldr	8		Dur Durham
6566	386v	<19>b	Church Street	William Atkinson	hea m	27	tailor, journeyman	Dur Seaton
6567	386v			Ellen Atkinson	wif m	32	wife	Dur Durham
6568	386v			Ellen Atkinson	dau	2		Dur Durham
6569	386v			Alice Atkinson	mth w	76	dependent	Dur Durham
6570	387r	[au]	Church Street	Thomas Granger	hea m	27	tailor, journeyman	Nry Manfield
6571	387r			Sarah Granger	wif m	26	wife	Dur Chester-le-Street
6572	387r			Thomas Granger	son	1		Dur Durham
6573	387r	<19>	Church Street	William Bell	hea m	22	painter	Dur Durham
6574	387r			Frances Bell	wif m	24	wife	Dur Durham
6575	387r	[av]	Church St *	John Smith	hea m	44	joiner	Dur Durham
6576	387r			Charlotte Smith	wif m	42	wife	Dur Durham
6577	387r			Charlotte Smith	dau	12	scholar	Dur Durham
6578	387r			John Smith	son	9	scholar	Dur Durham
6579	387r			Elizabeth Smith	dau	6	scholar	Dur Durham
6580	387r			Mary Smith	dau	3	at home	Dur Durham
6581	387r	[aw]a	Church St *	Dorothy Walker	hea w	81	parish relief	Dur Durham
6582	387r	[aw]b	Church St *	Robert Jones	hea m	24	tailor	Dur Heworth
6583	387r			Hannah Jones	wif m	24	wife	Ken Sheerness
6584	387r	[ax]a	Church St *	Robert George Charlton	hea m	32	printer compositor	Dur Lanchester
6585	387r			Charlotte Charlton	wif m	30	wife	Dur Durham
6586	387r			Isabella Charlton	dau	4		Dur Durham
6587	387v	[ax]b	Church St *	Cuthbert Robson	hea m	34	labourer	Dur Lanchester
6588	387v			Jane Robson	wif m	33	wife	Dur Pittington *
6589	387v			John Robson	son	7	scholar	Dur Durham
6590	387v			Benjamin Robson	son	5	scholar	Dur Durham
6591	387v			Robert Robson	son	1		Dur Durham
6592	387v	[ay]a	Church St *	William Barrass	hea w	40	shoemaker	Dur Pelton
6593	387v			Elizabeth Barrass	dau	9	scholar	Nbl Newcastle
6594	387v	[ay]b	Church St *	Andrew Burlinson	hea m	56	joiner	Dur Durham
6595	387v			Mary Burlinson	wif m	48	wife	Dur Durham
6596	387v			John Burlinson	son	25	compositor (printer)	Dur Durham
6597	387v			Cuthbert Burlinson	son	21	upholsterer	Dur Durham
6598	387v			Robert Burlinson	son	16	cooper	Dur Durham
6599	387v			Margaret Burlinson	dau	12	scholar	Dur Durham
6600	387v			Mary Jane Burlinson	dau	16	scholar	Dur Durham
6601	387v	[az]a	Church St *	Margaret Hayton	hea w	77	washerwoman	Dur Whickham
6602	387v			Leonard Hayton	gsn	16	apprentice	Dur Darlington
6603	387v			Henry Hayton	gsn	12	scholar	Wry Halifax
6604	387v	[az]b	Church St *	Frances Bulmer	hea	23	dressmaker	Dur Durham
6605	388r	[ba]	Church St *	Margaret Goldsbrough	hea w	43	laundress	Dur Durham
6606	388r			George Goldsbrough	son	15	joiner	Nry Appleton Wiske
6607	388r			Thomas Goldsbrough	son	13	shopboy	Nry Appleton Wiske
6608	388r			Jane Goldsbrough	dau	11	at home	Nry Middlesbrough
6609	388r			Margaret Goldsbrough	dau	2	at home	Dur Durham
6610	388r	[bb]	Church St *	Thomas Alderson	hea m	42	servant	Nry Bowes
6611	388r			Jane Alderson	wif m	34	wife	Nry Barton
6612	388r			Elizabeth Alderson	dau	13	scholar	Nry Barton
6613	388r			George B. Alderson	son	11	scholar	Nry Melsonby
6614	388r			Thomas Alderson	son	5	scholar	Nry Barton
6615	388r			John Alderson	son	2		Dur Hurworth
6616	388r			William Alderson	son	4m		Dur Durham
6617	388r	[bc]a	Church St *	Mary Hopper	hea w	53	dependent	Dur Shincliffe
6618	388r			Henry Hopper	son	22	mason	Dur Durham
6619	388r			John Hopper	son	20	mason	Dur Durham
6620	388r			Mary Byers	dau w	32	dressmaker	Dur Durham
6621	388r			Thomas Byers	*	7	scholar	Dur Durham
6622	388r	[bc]b	Church St *	William Graydon	hea w	50	butcher	Dur Chester-le-Street
6623	388r			Mary Pearson	ser	55	house servant	Dur Kelloe
6624	388v	<20>	Church St *	James Minns	hea m	37	police officer (borough)	Dur Seaham
6625	388v			Frances Minns	wif m	38	wife	Dur Crook
6626	388v			Elizabeth Minns	dau	12	scholar	Dur Sunderland
6627	388v			Thomas Minns	son	7	scholar	Dur Sherburn
6628	388v			Frances Minns	dau	5	scholar	Dur Sherburn
6629	388v			Robert Minns	son	3		Nry Middlesbrough
6630	388v			James Minns	son	7m		Dur Durham
6631	388v	[bd]a	Church St *	James Metcalf	hea m	51	maltster & brewer	Nry Snape
6632	388v			Elizabeth Metcalf	wif m	41	wife	Dur Durham
6633	388v			Christopher I. Metcalf	son	10	scholar	Dur Durham
6634	388v			Morpeath Robyson	ldr	23	coachmaker	Dur Durham
6635	388v	[bd]b	Church St *	William Winter	hea m	41	upholsterer	Dur Durham
6636	388v			Mary Winter	wif m	38	wife	Dur Durham
6637	388v	<21>	Church Street	John Granger	hea m	60	innkeeper *	Dur Sedgefield
6638	388v			Margaret Granger	wif m	50	wife	Nbl Ouseburn
6639	388v			Jane Markham	ser	16	house servant	Dur Durham
6640	388v	<20>	Church Street	Thomas Cooper	hea w	64	formerly house servant	Nry Craike
6641	388v			Catherine Cooper	dau	26	dressmkr <straw-hatmkr>	Wry Knaresborough
6642	388v			Elizabeth Cooper	dau	22	milliner	Dur Sunderland Bridge
6643	389r	<22>a	Church Street	Harriet Muft	hea	32	grocer	Dur Durham

6644	389r	<23>b	Church Street	George Thwaites	hea m	29	slater <grocer>	Dur Durham
6645	389r			Ann Thwaites	wif m	31	wife	Dur Durham
6646	389r			Ann Thwaites	dau	7m		Dur Durham
6647	389r			Thomas Wilson	ldr	22	maltster	Dur Durham
6648	389r	<23>c	Church Street	Thomas Winter	hea w	61	mason	Dur Durham
6649	389r	[be]	Church Street	Ralph Thwaites	hea m	45	joiner	Dur Durham
6650	389r			Hannah Thwaites	wif m	47	wife	Dur West Auckland
6651	389r			Thomas Thwaites	son	24	coach painter	Dur Durham
6652	389r			Ralph Thwaites	son	22	joiner	Dur Durham
6653	389r			Joseph Thwaites	son	19	shoemaker	Dur Durham
6654	389r			Margaret Thwaites	dau	10	scholar	Dur Durham
6655	389r			William Carr	ldr	44	shepherd	Cul Whitehaven
6656	389r	[bf]	Church Street	James Laykin	hea m	50	labourer	Dur Bishop Auckland
6657	389r			Mary Laykin	wif m	47	wife	Dur Langley
6658	389r			John Laykin	nep	10	scholar	Dur Durham
6659	389v	[bg]a	Church Street	Edward Hedley	hea m	73	coal miner	Nbl Hebron
6660	389v			Margaret Hedley	wif m	74	wife	Dur Durham
6661	389v	[bg]b	Church Street	Mary Watson	hea w	78	formerly laundress	Dur
6662	389v			Hannah Anderson	vis	28	laundress	Dur
6663	389v			David Anderson	vss	1m		Dur
6664	389v	[bg]c	Church Street	Henry Marshall	hea	70	writer; pauper	Dur
6665	389v			Ellen Barron	ser	16	house servant	Dur
6666	389v	<24>	Church Street	Margaret Smith	hea w	67	domestic duty	Dur Durham
6667	389v			Martin Smith	son	34	painter	Dur Durham
6668	389v			George Smith	son	25	cabinetmaker	Dur Durham
6669	389v			Michael Smith	son	19	joiner	Dur Durham
6670	389v			James Smith	nep	14	joiner	Dur Durham
6671	389v			Margaret Smith	nce	8	scholar	Dur Durham
6672	389v	[bh]a	Church Street	Robert Ayre	hea m	30	joiner	Dur Sedgefield
6673	389v			Ann Ayre	wif m	22	wife	Dur Hamsterley
6674	389v			Jane Ayre	dau	1m		
6675	389v	[bh]b	Church Street	Sarah Dixon	hea	50	labourer	Dur Marwood
6676	390r	[bi]	Church Street	Joseph Smith	hea m	56	boot and shoemaker	Dur Durham
6677	390r			Jane Smith	wif m	37	wife	Dur Durham
6678	390r			John Vardy	sso	14	coachmaker (apprentice)	Dur Durham
6679	390r			Joseph Smith	son	12	errand boy	Dur Durham
6680	390r			Edward Smith	son	10	scholar	Dur Durham
6681	390r			James Smith	son	8	scholar	Dur Durham
6682	390r			Hannah Smith	dau	5	scholar	Dur Durham
6683	390r			Barbara Smith	dau	3		Dur Durham
6684	390r	[bj]	Church Street	George Henderson	ldr	50	hawker	Dur
6685	390r			James McCain	ldr	45	drover	Irl
6686	390r			Thomas Hutchinson	ldr m	50	drover	Irl
6687	390r			John Richardson	ldr m	34	drover	Irl
6688	390r			Charles Robertson	ldr m	20	bellhanger	Nbl Newcastle
6689	390r			Eliza Robertson	ldw m	20	wife	Dur
6690	390r			Elizabeth Weron	ldr w	31	weaver	Irl
6691	390r			John Dawson	ldr	18	cutler	Irl
6692	390r			Daniel McKinlay	ldr m	23	labourer	Lks Glasgow
6693	390r			Mary McKinlay	ldw m	24	wife	Cul Preston
6694	390r			John Cook	ldr m	45	drover	Irl
6695	390r			William Laing	ldr	25	drover	Irl
6696	390v	[bk]	Church Street	William Patterson	hea m	83	lodging house keeper	Irl
6697	390v			Ann Patterson	wif m	47	wife	Dur
6698	390v			William Patterson	son	14	at home	Dur
6699	390v			James Brown	ldr m	27	labourer	Yks York
6700	390v			Hannah Brown	ldw m	50	needleworker	Yks York
6701	390v			John Harrison	ser	42	cabinetmaker	Nbl Newcastle
6702	390v			Richard Watson	ldr m	40	tinner	Nbl Berwick
6703	390v			Mary Watson	ldw m	50	wife	Nbl Berwick
6704	390v			George Thurlwell	ldr m	50	servant	Dur Darlington
6705	390v			James Skinner	ldr	13	farm labourer	Dur Darlington
6706	390v			Thomas Turner	ldr	10	farm labourer	Irl
6707	390v			James Smith	ldr	26	servant	Dur Darlington
6708	390v			Thomas Dunn	ldr	37	drover	Cul
6709	390v			Henry Thompson	ldr	39	labourer	Dur Darlington
6710	390v			James Richardson	ldr m	54	drover	Dur Darlington
6711	391r	[bl]a	Church Street	Margaret Grace	hea	45	lodging house keeper	Irl
6712	391r			Jane Grace	sis	32	domestic duty	Irl
6713	391r			Sebina Grace	vis w	60		Irl
6714	391r			Barny Blessington	ldr	28	labourer	Irl
6715	391r			Patrick Murray	ldr	22	labourer	Irl
6716	391r			Mary Cronan	ldr	20	labourer	Irl
6717	391r			Bridget Grace	rel*	10	labourer	Irl
6718	391r			Nancy Walsh	vis	22	labourer	Irl
6719	391r			Thomas Owen	vis m	44	labourer	Irl
6720	391r			Mary Green Owen	vsw m	40	labourer	Irl
6721	391r			Dan Owens	vss	16	labourer	Irl
6722	391r			Eliza Owens	vsd	14	labourer	Irl
6723	391r			Patrick Owens	vss	6	labourer	Irl
6724	391r			Margaret Owens	vsd	5		Irl

ID	Folio	Ref	Street	Name	Rel	M	Age	Occupation	Birthplace
6725	391r	[bl]a	Church Street	Thomas Owens	vss		4m		Dur Durham
6726	391r	[bl]b	Church Street	John Battle	hea	m	40	labourer	Irl
6727	391r			Betty Battle	wif	m	36	labourer	Irl
6728	391r			James Battle	son		15	labourer	Irl
6729	391r			Michael Battle	son		13	labourer	Irl
6730	391r			Mary Battle	dau		11	labourer	Irl
6731	391v			Patrick Battle	son		6	labourer	Irl
6732	391v			John Battle	son		5		Irl
6733	391v			Andrew Camel	vis	w	40	mariner	Irl
6734	391v			John Gilmore	vis		24	weaver	Irl
6735	391v			William Wood	vis	m	70	silk weaver	Irl
6736	391v			Margaret Wood	vsw	m	56	wife	Irl
6737	391v			William Clark	vis	m	25	silk weaver	Irl
6738	391v			Elizabeth Clark	vis	m	70	wife	Irl
6739	391v			William Gibson	vis		27	labourer (Protestant)	Eng
6740	391v			Margaret Dowsy	vis		10m	(Catholic)	Irl
6741	391v	[bm]a	Church Street	Christopher Garthwaite	hea	m	32	gardener	Nry Snape
6742	391v			Jane Garthwaite	wif	m	35	wife	Nry Northallerton
6743	391v			Elizabeth Garthwaite	dau		15	scholar	Nry Northallerton
6744	391v			Beatrice Garthwaite	dau		10	scholar	Dur Sherburn Hill
6745	391v			John Garthwaite	son		7	scholar	Dur Durham
6746	391v			Joseph Garthwaite	son		5	scholar	Dur Durham
6747	391v			James Garthwaite	son		1		Dur Durham
6748	391v	[bm]b	Church Street	John Wright	hea	m	55	farm labourer	Dur Auckland S. Helen
6749	391v			Mary Wright	wif	m	55		Dur Westgate
6750	391v			Mary Ann Lumsden	vis		9	scholar	Dur Durham
6751	392r	[bn]a	Church Street	Mary Blanch	hea	w	50	silk weaver	Nry Ravensworth
6752	392r			Thomas Blanch	son		18	farm labourer	Dur Durham
6753	392r	[bn]b	Church Street	Thomas Dodds	hea	m	23	whitesmith	Dur Durham
6754	392r			Sarah Dodds	wif	m	22	wife	Dur Durham
6755	392r			John Dodds	son		1m		Dur Durham
6756	392r	[bn]c	Church Street	William Adamson	hea	m	31	farm labourer	Dur Byers Green
6757	392r			Ann Adamson	wif	m	34	wife	Dur Thinford Mill
6758	392r			George Young	son		11	scholar	Dur Durham
6759	392r			Ann Jemison	vis		65	annuitant	Dur Frosterley
6760	392r			William Parkinson	vis		60	annuitant	Dur Bishopton
6761	392r	[bo]a	Church Street	Robert Young	hea	m	36	railway contractor	Dur Durham
6762	392r			Hannah Young	wif	m	37	wife	Dur Easington
6763	392r			Hannah Young	dau		5	scholar	Dur Durham
6764	392r			Robert Young	son		2		Dur Durham
6765	392r	[bo]b	Church Street	Ann Watson	hea		59	retired from service	Dur Greatham
6766	392r	[bo]c	Church Street	Francis Cummings	hea	m	29	cordwainer	Dur Durham
6767	392r			Jane Cummings	wif	m	30	wife	Dur Darlington
6768	392r			Charlotte Cummings	dau		3	at home	Nry Scarborough
6769	392v	[bp]	Church Street	William Rutherford	hea	m	39	labourer	Dur
6770	392v			Margaret Rutherford	wif	m	38	wife	Dur
6771	392v			Ellen Long	nce		15	scholar	Dur
6772	392v			Ann Armstrong	nce		7	scholar	Dur Durham
6773	392v			Joseph Thornton	vis		42	farm labourer	Dur Lanchester
6774	392v	[bq]	Church Street	John Watson	hea	m	62	carpenter (emp 2 men)	Dur Greatham
6775	392v			Isabella Watson	wif	m	62	wife	Dur Sunderland Bridge
6776	392v			James Watson	son		22	at home	Dur Durham
6777	392v			Isabella Maria Watson	dau		19	at home	Dur Durham
6778	392v	[br]	Church Street	Ann Wilson	hea		50	annuitant	Dur Tudhoe
6779	392v	[bs]	Church Street	Thomas Richardson	hea	m	56	farm labourer	Dur Houghton-l-Spring
6780	392v			Isabella Richardson	wif	m	51	wife	Dur Durham
6781	392v			John Richardson	son		21	joiner	Nbl Newcastle
6782	392v			James Richardson	son		19	shoemaker	Dur Gateshead
6783	392v			Isabella Richardson	dau		15	at home	Dur Durham
6784	392v			Henry Richardson	son		12	scholar	Dur Durham
6785	392v	[bt]	Church Street	George Thompson	hea	m	74	cabinetmaker	Dur Lanchester
6786	392v			Mary Thompson	wif	m	72	wife	Dur Durham
6787	392v			William Thompson	son	m	40	iron moulder	Ham Portsmouth
6788	393r			Isabella Thompson	swi	m	44	moulder's wife	Dur Durham
6789	393r			Robert Thompson	son		35	sa[w]yer	Dur Durham
6790	393r			Thomas Thompson	son		32	sa[w]yer	Dur Durham
6791	393r			Robert Thompson	gsn		17	iron moulder	Dur Durham
6792	393r			Henry Thompson	gsn		14	painter	Dur Darlington
6793	393r			Frederick Thompson	gsn		13	scholar	Dur Darlington
6794	393r			Margaret Thompson	gda		8	scholar	Dur Jarrow
6795	393r	[bu]	Church Street	Edward Dodds	hea	m	43	whitesmith	Dur Durham
6796	393r			Elizabeth Dodds	wif	m	45	wife	Dur Sunderland
6797	393r			Barbara Dodds	dau		17	at home	Dur Houghton-l-Spring
6798	393r			Ann Dodds	dau		12	scholar	Dur Shincliffe
6799	393r			Elizabeth Dodds	dau		7	scholar	Dur Durham
6800	393r			James Dodds	son		4	scholar	Dur Durham
6801	393r			Isabel Dodds	dau		2m	scholar	Dur Durham
6802	393r	[bv]	Church Street	Mary Gibbon	hea	m	36	miller's wife	Wry Sedbergh
6803	393r			Eleanor Gibbon	dau		1		Dur Durham
6804	393r			Jane Ampleby	vis		23	servant	Nry Nosterfield

one house uninhabited

6805	393v	[bw]	Church Street *	Thomas Stephenson	hea w		49	innkeeper	Dur Whorlton
6806	393v			Jane Stephenson	dau		19	at home	Dur Darlington
6807	393v			George Brass Stephenson	son		17	at home	Dur Darlington
6808	393v			Rachael Stephenson	dau		15	at home	Dur Darlington
6809	393v			Mary Ann Stephenson	dau		11	at home	Nry Bowes
6810	393v			Thomas Marchall	vis m		39	labourer	Yks Woodno
6811	393v			Thomas Cramton	vis w		41	horse dealer's servant	Yks Woodno
6812	393v	[bx]	Church Street *	Joseph Hall	hea m		49	farm labourer	Wry Wakefield
6813	393v			Hannah Hall	wif m		45	wife	Dur Great Stainton
6814	393v			John Hall	son		9	scholar	Dur Etherley
6815	393v			Mary Ann Hall	dau		7	scholar	Dur Durham
6816	393v			Sarah Jane Hall	dau		4	scholar	Dur Durham
6817	393v	[by]	Church Street *	George Ridley	hea m		33	farmer of 3a *	Dur Shincliffe
6818	393v			Ann Ridley	wif m		29	wife	Dur Aycliffe
6819	393v			John Hutton Ridley	son		6	scholar	Dur Shincliffe
6820	393v			William Hutton Ridley	son		3	at home	Dur Durham
6821	393v			Alice Hutton Ridley	dau		1		Dur Durham
6822	393v	[bz]a	Church Street *	William Blench	hea		25	farm labourer	Dur Brandon
6823	393v			Robert Blench	son		2m		Dur Brandon
6824	393v			Ann Harling	vis m		39	domestic duty	Dur Benton
6825	394r	[bz]b	Church Street *	John Forster	hea m		47	colliery agent	Nbl Corbridge
6826	394r			Elizabeth Forster	wif m		39	wife	Dur Crowtrees
6827	394r			Robert Forster	son		10	scholar	Dur Durham
6828	394r			Ann Forster	dau		8	scholar	Dur Durham
6829	394r			Mary Forster	dau		6	scholar	Dur Durham
6830	394r			Henry Forster	son		3		Dur Durham
6831	394r			George E. Forster	son		1		Dur Durham
6832	394r	[ca]	Church Street	William Smurthwaite	hea m		54	labourer at colliery	Dur Shotton
6833	394r			Ann Smurthwaite	wif m		53	wife	Dur Felling
6834	394r			Elizabeth Lister	aun w		85	receiving parish relief	Dur Merrington
6835	394r	[cb]a	Church Street *	Mary Ann Heslop	hea		22	dressmaker	Dur Durham
6836	394r			Ellen Wilkey	vis		18	dressmaker	Dur Durham
6837	394r	[cb]b	Church Street *	Mary Ann Bell	hea w		38	lodging house keeper	Irl
6838	394r			Elizabeth Bell	dau		15	scholar	Dur Durham
6839	394r			Ann Bell	dau		11	scholar	Dur Durham
6840	394r			Ellen Bell	dau		7	scholar	Dur Durham
6841	394r			John Bell	son		6	scholar	Dur Durham
6842	394r			Mary Ann Bell	dau		1		Dur Durham
6843	394r			Thomas Bell	son		2m		Dur Durham
6844	394r			Matthew Dowson	ldr		35	coal miner	Cul
6845	394r			James Dowson	ldr		15	coal miner	Dur Durham
6846	394v	[cc]	Church Street	Margaret Dowson	hea w		66	receiving parish relief	Nbl Berwick
6847	394v			Jane Dowson	gda		11	scholar	Dur Durham
6848	394v	[cd]	Church Street *	Richard Moody	hea m		26	shoemaker (journeyman)	Dur Durham
6849	394v			Margaret Jane Moody	wif m		21	wife	Nry Richmond
6850	394v			Isabel Moody	dau		1	at home	Dur Durham
6851	394v	[ce]	Church Street *	Edward Donnalley	hea m		66	weaver of carpets, jnym	Tyr
6852	394v			Mary Donnally	wif m		53	wife	Dur Trimdon
6853	394v	[cf]a	Church Street *	Jeremiah Wood	hea m		40	blacksmith (journeyman)	Wes Barton
6854	394v			Christina Wood	wif m		49	wife	Sct
6855	394v	[cf]b	Church Street *	Mary Collingwood	hea w		50	laundress	Dur Hawthorn
6856	394v			Mary Ann Collingwood	dau		22	laundress	Nbl Humshaugh
6857	394v			Joshua Collingwood	son		9	scholar at home	Dur Sherburn
6858	394v			Ann Harker	ser		17	servant	Dur Durham
6859	394v			Thomas Bulmer	slw m		28	miller	Dur Easington
6860	394v			Elizabeth Bulmer	swi m		24	wife	Nbl Humshaugh
6861	394v	[cg]	Church Street *	Thomas Mavin	hea m		79	sawyer; pauper	Nbl Newcastle
6862	394v			Elizabeth Mavin	wif m		75	wife	Dur Hamsteels
6863	394v			Edward Mavin	son		30	sawyer	Dur Durham
6864	395r	[ch]	Church Street	Robert Milburn	hea m		33	pitman	Dur Hetton
6865	395r			Jane Milburn	wif m		29	wife	Cul Brough Hill
6866	395r			Jonathan Douglas	vis		27	pitman	Cul Low House
6867	395r		Crawford's House *	Mary Smith	hea m		60	independent	Dur Gateshead
6868	395r			Sarah Eleanor Smith	dau		31	at home	Edn Edinburgh
6869	395r			John Whittel Smith	son		28	accountant, Durham Bank	Edn Edinburgh
6870	395r			Robert C. Smith	son		26	banker's clerk	Edn Edinburgh
6871	395r			Charles F. Smith	son		25	carpet manufacturer	Edn Edinburgh
6872	395r			Charlotte Mary Bentley	vis		18	teacher of parish school	Lan Manchester
6873	395r			Jane Hebden	ser		40	cook	Yks York
6874	395r			Mary Bell	ser		20	house maid	Nbl Newcastle
6875	395r	[aa]	Anchorage Row	Thomas Markham	hea m		25	coal miner	Dur Durham
6876	395r			Ann Markham	wif m		20	wife	Dur South Shields
6877	395r	[ab]	Anchorage Row	Henry Bates	hea m		47	colliery cartman	Dur Lanchester
6878	395r			Jane Bates	wif m		49	wife	Dur Lanchester
6879	395r			Jane Bates	dau		18	at home, scholar	Dur Lanchester
6880	395r			Margaret Bates	dau		16	at home, scholar	Dur Lanchester
6881	395r			Henry Bates	son		14	at home, scholar	Dur Lanchester
6882	395r			Martha Bates	dau		11	at home, scholar	Dur Durham
6883	395r			William Forster	vis		1		Dur Durham
6884	395v	[aa]a	Anchorage House	Alexander Kennedy	hea m		45	husbandman <milk vendor>	Nbl
6885	395v			Mary Kennedy	wif m		47	wife	Dur Houghton-1-Spring

6886	395v	[aa]a	Anchorage House	William Kennedy	son	16	smith	Dur Durham
6887	395v			Margaret Kennedy	dau	13	scholar	Dur Durham
6888	395v			Sarah Kennedy	dau	11	scholar	Dur Durham
6889	395v	[aa]b	Anchorage House	William Kennedy	hea m	47	husbandman	Nbl Lowick
6890	395v			Elizabeth Kennedy	wif m	48	wife	Nbl Lucker
6891	395v			Elizabeth Kennedy	dau	10	scholar	Dur Durham
6892	395v			Sarah Kennedy	dau	6	scholar	Dur Durham
6893	395v	[ac]a	Anchorage Row	Edward Atkinson	hea m	50	banksman, coal mine	Dur Durham
6894	395v			Elizabeth Atkinson	wif m	50	wife	Dur Durham
6895	395v			Elizabeth Atkinson	dau	24	at home	Dur Durham
6896	395v			Edward Atkinson	son	18	at home	Dur Durham
6897	395v			Michael Atkinson	son	15	at home	Dur Durham
6898	395v	[ac]b	Anchorage Row	William Young	hea m	29	coal miner	Dur Durham
6899	395v			Hannah Young	wif m	26	wife	Dur Durham
6900	395v			Elizabeth Young	dau	6	scholar at home	Dur Durham
6901	395v			Mary Young	dau	5	scholar	Dur Durham
6902	395v			Ann Young	dau	1		Dur Durham
6903	396r	[ad]	Anchorage Row	Elizabeth Atkinson	hea w	32	washerwoman	Dur Portobello
6904	396r			Mary Atkinson	dau	9	scholar	Dur Durham
6905	396r			Ann Atkinson	dau	7	scholar	Dur Durham
6906	396r			Elizabeth Atkinson	dau	5	scholar	Dur Durham
6907	396r			Eleanor Atkinson	dau	4m		Dur Durham
6908	396r	[ae]a	Anchorage Row	William Harrison	hea m	23	coal miner	Dur Bishopton
6909	396r			Eleanor Harrison	wif m	20	wife	Dur Easington
6910	396r	[ae]b	Anchorage Row	Robert Smurthwaite	hea m	24	coal miner	Dur Durham
6911	396r			Ann Smurthwaite	wif m	23	wife	Dur Durham
6912	396r			William Smurthwaite	son	2w		Dur Durham
6913	396r	[ae]c	Anchorage Row	Benjamin Dowson	hea m	22	coal miner	Lan Preston
6914	396r			Mary Dowson	wif m	26	wife	Dur Durham
6915	396r			Mary Dowson	dau	9m		Dur Durham
6916	396r	[af]a	Anchorage Row	William Walker	hea m	35	coal miner	Dur Durham
6917	396r			Margaret Walker	wif m	32	wife	Dur Durham
6918	396r			Margaret Walker	dau	12	scholar	Dur Durham
6919	396r			John Walker	son	9	scholar	Dur Durham
6920	396r			Charlotte Walker	dau	7	scholar	Dur Durham
6921	396r			William Walker	son	5	scholar	Dur Durham
6922	396r			Isabella Walker	dau	3	at home	Dur Durham
6923	396r			Mary Walker	dau	9m		Dur Durham
6924	396v	[af]b	Anchorage Row	Judah Markham	hea w	50	pauper; washerwoman	Dur Durham
6925	396v			William Markham	son	23	coal miner	Dur Durham
6926	396v			Judah Markham	dau	13	scholar	Dur Durham
6927	396v			Margaret Markham	dau	11	scholar	Dur Durham
6928	396v			Charles Markham	son	7	scholar	Dur Durham
6929	396v			William Taylerson	gsn	3	at home	Dur Durham
6930	396v	[af]c	Anchorage Row	Luke Thew	hea m	48	colliery overman	Dur Middleton
6931	396v			Ann Thew	wif m	44	wife	Dur Durham
6932	396v			Ralph Thew	son	25	coal miner	Dur Durham
6933	396v			Mary Thew	dau	21	dressmaker	Dur Durham
6934	396v			Elizabeth Thew	dau	18	servant	Dur Durham
6935	396v			Margaret Thew	dau	16	milliner	Dur Durham
6936	396v			Hannah Thew	dau	13	scholar	Dur Durham
6937	396v			Ruth Thew	dau	11	scholar	Dur Durham
6938	396v			Luke Thew	son	9	scholar	Dur Durham
6939	396v			Charlotte Thew	dau	6	scholar	Dur Durham
6940	396v	[ab]a	Anchorage House	Robert Dodds	hea m	54	blacksmith	Dur Brancepeth
6941	396v			Martha Dodds	wif m	52	wife	Dur Durham
6942	396v			Robert Dodds	son	23	coal [mine] engineman	Dur Durham
6943	396v			Eleanor Dodds	dau	20	at home	Dur Durham
6944	397r			John Dodds	son	16	apprentice [blacksmith?]	Dur Durham
6945	397r			Richard Dodds	son	14	brakesman	Dur Durham
6946	397r	[ab]b	Anchorage House	John Golightly	hea m	34	coal miner	Dur Seaton
6947	397r			Jane Golightly	wif m	36	wife	Dur Durham
6948	397r			Ann Golightly	dau	12	scholar	Dur Durham
6949	397r			Alice Golightly	dau	10	scholar	Dur Durham
6950	397r			George Golightly	son	9	scholar	Dur Durham
6951	397r			John Golightly	son	7	scholar	Dur Durham
6952	397r			William Golightly	son	5	scholar	Dur Durham
6953	397r			Thomas Golightly	son	1	at home	Dur Durham
6954	397r	[ab]c	Anchorage House	Phoebe Cairns	hea w	62	pauper; charwoman	Dur Westgate
6955	397r	[ag]a	Anchorage Row	William Sexton	hea m	39	cordwainer	Dur Cockerton
6956	397r			Elizabeth Sexton	wif m	31	wife	Dur Durham
6957	397r			Robert Sexton	son	12	scholar	Dur Durham
6958	397r			Ann Sexton	dau	8	scholar	Dur Durham
6959	397r			George Sexton	son	7	scholar	Dur Durham
6960	397r			William Sexton	son	4	at home	Dur Durham
6961	397r			Thomas Sexton	son	2	at home	Dur Durham
6962	397r			Jemima Sexton	dau	10m	at home	Dur Durham
6963	397v	[ag]b	Anchorage Row	Elizabeth Anderson	hea w	52	pauper; charwoman	Dur Fatfield
6964	397v	[ag]c	Anchorage Row	Thomas Donking	hea m	37	cordwainer	Dur Sedgefield
6965	397v			Margaret Donking	wif m	33	wife	Yks Appleby
6966	397v			Jane Donking	dau	12	at home	Dur Durham

6967	397v	[ag]c	Anchorage Row	Thomas Donking	son		10	at home	Dur Durham
6968	397v			Margaret Donking	dau		6	at home	Dur Durham
6969	397v			Elizabeth Donking	dau		3	at home	Dur Durham
6970	397v			Joseph Donking	son		1m	at home	Dur Durham
6971	397v	[ag]d	Anchorage Row	Thomas Grainger	hea m		58	weaver	Dur Sedgefield
6972	397v			Margaret Grainger	wif m		60	wife	Hinghton *
6973	397v			David Taylerson	m		25	miner	
6974	397v	[ah]a	Anchorage Row	Thomas Markham	hea m		84	labourer (parish relief)	Nfk Norwich
6975	397v			Ruth Markham	wif m		67	parish relief	Dur Sunderland Bridge
6976	397v			Hannah Markham	gda		18	servant	Dur Durham
6977	397v			Ruth Markham	gda		3	at home	Dur Durham
6978	397v	[ah]b	Anchorage Row	Eleanor Wright	hea w		36	parish relief	Dur Durham
6979	397v			Eleanor Wright	dau		12	scholar	Dur Durham
6980	397v			William Wright	son		9	scholar	Dur Durham
6981	397v			Sarah Wright	dau		3	scholar	Dur Durham
6982	398r	[ai]a	Anchorage Row	John Forster	hea m		41	coal miner	Dur Bishop Auckland
6983	398r			Eleanor Forster	wif m		48	wife	Dur Darlington
6984	398r			Eleanor Forster	dau		15	at home	Dur Durham
6985	398r			Thomas Forster	son		13	driver in coal mine	Dur Durham
6986	398r			Jonathan Forster	son		11	scholar	Dur Durham
6987	398r			Elizabeth Forster	dau		9	scholar	Dur Durham
6988	398r			Hannah Forster	dau		7	scholar	Dur Durham
6989	398r	[ai]b	Anchorage Row	James Atkinson	hea m		60	coal miner	Dur Durham
6990	398r			Mary Atkinson	wif m		58	wife	Yks Appleby
6991	398r	[aj]a	Anchorage Row	John Dawson	hea m		33	coal miner	Dur Houghton-l-Spring
6992	398r			Jane Dawson	wif m		32	wife	Dur Chester-le-Street
6993	398r			William Dawson	son		10	scholar	Dur Durham
6994	398r			James Dawson	son		8	scholar	Dur Durham
6995	398r			Michael Dawson	son		4	at home	Dur Durham
6996	398r			John Dawson	son		2	at home	Dur Durham
6997	398r	[aj]b	Anchorage Row	Anthony Dowson	hea m		31	coal miner	Dur Durham
6998	398r			Rebecca Dowson	wif m		34	wife	Dur Durham
6999	398r			George Liddell	* w		20	tailor	Dur Durham
7000	398r			Elizabeth Dowson	dau		7	scholar	Dur Durham
7001	398r			Thomas Liddell	vss		6	scholar	Dur Durham
7002	398v			Mary Jane Dowson	dau		5	scholar	Dur Durham
7003	398v			Rebecca Dowson	dau		3m		Dur Durham
7004	398v	[ak]a	Anchorage Row	John Dowson	hea m		25	coal miner	Dur Durham
7005	398v			Ann Dowson	wif m		27	wife	Dur Hylton Ferry
7006	398v			Ann Dowson	dau		3	at home	Dur Durham
7007	398v			William Dowson	son		7m	at home	Dur Durham
7008	398v	[ak]b	Anchorage Row	Richard Taylerson	hea m		27	coal miner	Dur Durham
7009	398v			Ruth Taylerson	wif m		26	wife	Dur Durham
7010	398v			Ruth Taylerson	dau		1		Dur Durham
7011	398v	[ak]c	Anchorage Row	Isabella Dickinson	hea		65	washerwoman	Dur Westgate
7012	398v			John Dickinson	son		29	cabinetmaker & newsagent	Dur Durham
7013	398v	[bp]	New Elvet *	Israel White	hea m		38	carpet weaver	Wor Kidderminster
7014	398v			Mary Ann White	wif m		39	wife	Wor Kidderminster
7015	398v			Eliza White	dau		16	worsted warper	Wor Kidderminster
7016	398v			Jemima White	dau		14	scholar	Wor Kidderminster
7017	398v			Selena White	dau		2		Dur Durham

Notes - Enumeration District 11e

5290	<& brewer, maltster & porter merchant>
5297	... <'Black Horse'> & commercial traveller
5313	<& milk vendor>
5343	... & branch Post Office
5361	[mother's] daughter
5363-5364	[mother's] daughter
5378	[mother's?] son
5379	[mother's?] daughter
5399	<'Hare & Hounds'>
5447	<'Freemasons' Arms'>
5452	... (dealer in shawls)
5489	<& worsted dealer>
5504	county given as "Yorkshire"
5507-5510	<address given as "47 New Elvet">
5511-5519	<address given as "46 New Elvet">
5520-5556	... Ferens' Buildings
5546-5556	<address given as "46 New Elvet">
5557-5569	<address given as "45 New Elvet">
5575	[entries 7013-7017 omitted at this point]
5612	... Northumberland local militia
5620	... woollen carpet manufacturer, drysalter & wooldealer
5624	... of S. Nicholas <MA>
5649	... of S. Oswald
5695	<'Spread Eagle'>
5717	<milk vendor>
5727,5742	county given as "Yorkshire"
5801	... employing 1 man and 2 apprentices
5828	<publican 'Joiners' Arms'>
5901-6007	<New Buildings>
5914	... Hallgarth
5931	clergyman's widow ...
5932	... Oxford
5936	<Church Street>
5938	... with pension
5983	... employing 3 men
5999	... pensioner, late sergeant in Coldstream Guards
6003	Athol ... on passage from Quebec to London
6034	<& lodgings>
6065	... in drapery goods
6086	wife [visitor]
6090	... registrar of births and deaths & asst relieving officer for S. Nicholas district <& parish clerk of S. Nicholas>
6099-6102	<Gladstone's Cottage>
6099	county given as "Yorkshire"
6114	... master employing 1 apprentice

6181	[folios 372v-376r are preliminary pages of continuation book]
6209	... <lay clerk>, overseer & solicitor's managing clerk
6222	... Rotterdam
6265	<& timber merchant>
6312	... Low Fell
6345	... millwright
6347	... Chorlton /"Charlton"
6350-6380	... (Coulson's Buildings)
6357	deaf and dumb
6385-6386	Hallgarth Street & ...
6437-6438	daughters of Sarah Shafto by her former husband, George Appleby, deceased
6455	... 'Coach & Horses'
6497	<& grocer>
6502	lodger, brother-in-law; ... & machinewright

6504-6559	... (Oswald Court)
6575-6636	... (Oswald Place)
6588	... Hallgarth
6621	[daughter's] son
6637	<'Hearts of Gold'>
6717	... lodger
6805-6821	'New Inn' ... <Head>
6817	<market gardener>
6822-6831	... <Head>, Union Place
6835-6845	... <Head>, Union Place
6848-6863	... <Head>, Union Place
6867-6874	<Church Street Head>
6972	... Bisherbridge
6999	brother [in-law?], visitor
7013-7017	[omitted from folio 356r, following 5575]

REF	FOL		FORENAME(S)	SURNAME	POSITION	C	AGE	OCCUPATION	BIRTHPLACE
7018	412v	Gaol	William	Green	governor	m	56	governor of gaol	Dur Durham
7019	412v		Ellen	Green	governor's wife	m	50	governor's wife	Dur Durham
7020	412v		William	Green	[governor's] son		27	colliery viewer	Dur Durham
7021	412v		Frederick	Green	[governor's] son		18	scholar	Dur Durham
7022	412v		Emma	Green	[governor's] daughter		16	scholar at home	Dur Durham
7023	412v		Edward	Green	[governor's] son		14	scholar	Dur Durham
7024	412v		Ann	Green	[governor's] daughter		12	scholar at home	Dur Durham
7025	412v		Rose	Green	[governor's] daughter		9	scholar at home	Dur Durham
7026	412v		Ellen	Emery	governess		25	governess	Nfk [King's] Lynn
7027	412v		Sarah	Dunbar	servant		28	house servant	Nbl Middleton
7028	413r		Frances	Hickson	servant		17	house servant	Dur Durham
7029	413r		George	Hutton	servant		20	house servant	Dur Shincliffe
7030	413r		John	Thompson	door porter	m	41	door porter	Dur Durham
7031	413r		Jane	Thompson	female searcher	m	49	female searcher	Nry Barton
7032	413r		George	Thompson	[door porter's] son		10	scholar	Dur Durham
7033	413r		John	Thompson	[door porter's] son		8	scholar	Dur Durham
7034	413r		Agnes	Johnson	matron		35	matron in gaol	Edn Edinburgh *
7035	413r		Hannah	Spark	schoolmistress		30	schoolmistress in gaol	Wry Wheatley *
7036	413r		Ann	Thurloway	warder		28	warder in gaol	Dur Kip Hill
7037	413v		Ann	Jang	prisoner	w	40	hawker	Ant Belfast
7038	413v		Mary	Logan	prisoner	m	50	domestic affairs	Dur Darlington
7039	413v		Jane	Claig	prisoner		28	prostitute	Cav
7040	413v		Mary	Brown	prisoner	m	32	sempstress	Dur Chester-le-Street
7041	413v		Elizabeth	Rogers	prisoner	m	46	gingerbread-maker	Nry Reeth
7042	413v		Mary Ann	Davison	prisoner	m	45	milliner	Nbl Gosforth
7043	413v		Margaret Jane	Robinson	prisoner		23	prostitute	Dur Stockton
7044	413v		Janet	Messenger	prisoner	m	33	domestic affairs	Roc Fortrose *
7045	413v		Ellen	Holmes	prisoner		19	hawker	Ery Hull
7046	413v		Margaret	Richardson	prisoner	m	45	domestic affairs	Dur Sunderland
7047	413v		Mary	Palmer	prisoner		20	rope spinner	Dur Sunderland
7048	413v		Mary Ann	McGough	prisoner		19	silk weaver	Lan Manchester
7049	413v		Margaret	Watson	prisoner		16	domestic affairs	Dur [Monkwearmouth] *
7050	413v		Rosanna	Dinning	prisoner	w	45	hawker	Edn Edinburgh *
7051	413v		Margaret	Pattison	prisoner		16	knitting	Nry Middlesbrough
7052	413v		Ellen	Cummings	prisoner	m	55	hawker	May
7053	413v		Mary Ann	Cole	prisoner		28	domestic affairs	Nry Worsall
7054	413v		Isabella	Brunning	prisoner	m	38	domestic affairs	Dur Durham
7055	413v		Mary	Mitchell	prisoner	m	45	domestic affairs	Nbl Alnwick
7056	413v		Bridget	McQuire	prisoner		14	ballad singer	Nbl Newcastle
7057	414r		Ellen	McQuire	prisoner		12	ballad singer	Nbl Newcastle
7058	414r		Ellen	O'Brien	prisoner		34	prostitute	Dur [South] Shields
7059	414r		Ann	Moffoot	prisoner		23	prostitute	Dur [South] Shields
7060	414r		Bridget	McQuire	prisoner		16	works in fields	Lan Liverpool
7061	414r		Mary	O'Brien	prisoner	w	48	works in fields	Sli
7062	414r		Mary Ann	Smithson	prisoner	m	23	charwoman /"chairwoman"	Ery Hull *
7063	414r		Elizabeth	Carman	prisoner		40	potter	ChI Jersey
7064	414r		Catherine	Dodds	prisoner	w	40	prostitute	Ant Belfast
7065	414r		Catherine	Salkeld	prisoner		25	prostitute	Dur [South] Shields
7066	414r		Rachael	Taylor	prisoner	m	25	domestic affairs	Yks York
7067	414r		Hannah	Leybourn	prisoner		29	prostitute	Dur Darlington
7068	414r		Mary Ann	Johnson	prisoner	m	31	prostitute	Lan Liverpool
7069	414r		Agnes	Robson	prisoner	w	37	prostitute	Per Perth, S. John
7070	414r		Jane	Atkinson	prisoner		19	prostitute	Dur [South] Shields
7071	414r		Elizabeth	Anderson	prisoner		19	prostitute	Sli
7072	414r		Elizabeth B.	Burn	prisoner	m	39	oakum teaser	Dur Sunderland
7073	414r		Joseph	Colling	prisoner	m	45	auctioneer	Nry Romaldkirk
7074	414r		James	Thomas	prisoner	m	36	general clerk	Gla Swansea
7075	414r		Robert	Shaw	prisoner		34	no trade *	Dur Usworth
7076	414r		Joseph	Scott	prisoner	m	46	potato dealer, master	Dur Greatham
7077	414v		John	Huddlestone	prisoner	m	54	boatbuilder, master	Dur Monkwearmouth
7078	414v		Christopher	Currah	prisoner	m	44	gamekeeper	Dur Durham
7079	414v		William	Ditchburn	prisoner	m	25	grocer, master	Dur Lamesley
7080	414v		Joseph	Green	prisoner	m	46	cartman	Mdx Fulham
7081	414v		John	Littlehailes	prisoner	m	25	bootmaker, master	Edn Edinburgh
7082	414v		Walter	Bates	prisoner	m	25	builder, master	Dur [South] Shields
7083	414v		Henry	Brotherton	prisoner	m	25	grocer, master	Dur Lanchester
7084	414v		Robert	Teasdale	prisoner	m	50	innkeeper, master	Dur Durham
7085	414v		Stephen	Thompson	prisoner	m	50	farmer, master	Nbl Greenhead
7086	414v		William	Lloyd	prisoner		27	surgeon, assistant	Lim
7087	414v		Teasdale	College	prisoner	m	28	master mariner	Dur Sunderland
7088	414v		John	Steele	prisoner	m	55	mason, journeyman	Dur Gateshead
7089	414v		William	Wake	prisoner	m	25	engine driver, rail[way]	Dur Thornley
7090	414v		Daniel	Henry	prisoner	w	65	common labourer	Dur [South] Shields
7091	414v		Thomas	Watson	prisoner	m	24	shipwright	Dur Hylton
7092	414v		George	Cockburn	prisoner		19	coal miner	Nry Crakehall *
7093	414v		Dennis	Cooper	prisoner		24	carpet weaver	Dur Barnard Castle
7094	414v		William	Jameson	prisoner		15	common labourer	Dur Jarrow
7095	414v		Thomas	Henry	prisoner		13	common labourer	Dow Newry, Kilarey
7096	414v		Thomas	Ord	prisoner	m	27	coal miner	Dur Houghton-l-Spring

No.	Folio	Place	Name	Status	Cond	Age	Occupation	Origin
7097	415r	Gaol	John Turnbull	prisoner		15	coal miner	Dur Wrekenton
7098	415r		William Turnbull	prisoner		51	coal miner	Dur Gateshead
7099	415r		James Johnson	prisoner	m	34	common labourer	Nbl Alnwick
7100	415r		Robert Vaughan	prisoner		17	sailor	Lnd Spitalfields
7101	415r		Robert Greatrex	prisoner	w	58	sailor	Dur Sunderland
7102	415r		Robert Garret	prisoner	w	62	blacksmith, journeyman	Dur Sunderland
7103	415r		Thomas Fryer	prisoner	m	28	cabinetmaker	Lan Ashton-under-Lyne
7104	415r		James Wood	prisoner		21	glazier	Dur Westoe
7105	415r		James Jefferson	prisoner		58	common labourer	Dur [South] Shields
7106	415r		John Coates	prisoner	m	29	coaltrimmer	Dur Clilmany, Dilmore
7107	415r		Edward McLaughlin	prisoner		58	common labourer	Nbl Edington
7108	415r		John Clark	prisoner	m	49	gardener	Nry Richmond
7109	415r		Henry Hallgarth	prisoner	m	33	cordialmaker	Dur Rearth, Coleath
7110	415r		John Richardson	prisoner	m	46	plumber	Dur [South] Shields
7111	415r		William Davison	prisoner	m	36	shipwright	Dby Pentrich
7112	415r		John Walters	prisoner	m	33	coal miner	Dur Monkwearmouth
7113	415r		John Evans	prisoner	m	21	boatbuilder	North America BS
7114	415r		William Smith	prisoner		19	sailor	Dur [South] Shields
7115	415r		John Smith	prisoner		18	sailor	Mdx London
7116	415r		John Freeman	prisoner		16	sailor	Dur Sunderland
7117	415v		Frederick B. Handford	prisoner		40	sailor	Dur Sunderland
7118	415v		John Fisher	prisoner		23	sailor	Ess Harwich
7119	415v		William Barron	prisoner		19	coal miner	Dur Ravensworth
7120	415v		William Grant	prisoner		20	sailor	North America *
7121	415v		William Wailes	prisoner	w	40	chainmaker	Nbl Wallsend
7122	415v		Hugh Hutchinson	prisoner		21	sailor	ShI Tolob? /"Tole"
7123	415v		John Bird	prisoner		21	coal miner	Dur Easington Lane
7124	415v		William Robertson	prisoner		19	glassmaker	Dur Sunderland
7125	415v		William Garnet	prisoner		20	painter	Dur Sunderland
7126	415v		James Harding	prisoner		19	common labourer	Lin Spalding
7127	415v		Joseph Maudling	prisoner	m	36	coal miner	Dur Beamish
7128	415v		William Kitchen	prisoner	m	30	shoemaker	Ham Eling
7129	415v		William Christie	prisoner	m	42	shoemaker	Edn Edinburgh
7130	415v		John Kean	prisoner		17	sailor	Kik Rowan
7131	415v		John Toy	prisoner	m	27	common labourer	Dur Durham Gaol
7132	415v		John Antrim	prisoner		19	sailor	Sry Clapham
7133	415v		John Lavin / Hann	prisoner		26	hatter	Ros Kilmore
7134	415v		James Ashcroft	prisoner	m	26	glassmaker	Lan Hatter Heath
7135	415v		Stewart Hewison	prisoner	w	30	sailor	Nbl Bankhead
7136	415v		John Davis	prisoner		18	common labourer	Dow Newry
7137	416r		Robert Thompson	prisoner	m	44	sailor	Dur Sunderland
7138	416r		Abraham Marlow	prisoner	w	27	glassmaker	Sts Horninglow
7139	416r		Peter Kilday	prisoner		33	common labourer	Dev Plymouth
7140	416r		Robert Thirlkeld	prisoner		22	farm servant	Dur Eggleston
7141	416r		Henry Wood	prisoner		16	common labourer	Sry London
7142	416r		Alexander Maddon	prisoner		16	shoemaker	Dub Dublin
7143	416r		William A. Robinson	prisoner		17	sailor	Dur Hetton Hall
7144	416r		Walter M. Robinson	prisoner		15	sailor	Dur Hetton Hall
7145	416r		Joseph Scaife	prisoner		19	bootcloser	Dur Darlington
7146	416r		James Curtis	prisoner		13	tailor	Dur Sunderland
7147	416r		James Howe	prisoner	w	35	potter	Dur West Auckland
7148	416r		William Gibson	prisoner		24	shoemaker	Dur Darlington
7149	416r		Thomas Oates	prisoner	w	42	shipwright	Dur Sunderland
7150	416r		John Smith	prisoner		20	coal miner	Dur Hetton-le-Hole
7151	416r		Thomas Brady	prisoner	m	27	book-keeper	Ros Crossnah
7152	416r		John Delany	prisoner		17	sailor	Lnd S. Nicholas
7153	416r		John Mahon	prisoner		22	common labourer	Mog Tullaneseah
7154	416r		Thomas Pratt	prisoner		27	carpet weaver	Dur Barnard Castle
7155	416r		William Watson	prisoner		18	common labourer	Lan Wigan
7156	416r		William Robison	prisoner		35	brewer's clerk	Dur Stranton
7157	416v		Matthew Martin	prisoner	w	31	common labourer	Arm Fachill
7158	416v		George Mallett	prisoner		23	cabinetmaker	Chs Birkenhead
7159	416v		Thomas Cash	prisoner		20	tinner & brazier	Ntt Nottingham
7160	416v		James Keedy	prisoner		20	common labourer	Nbl Newcastle
7161	416v		Thomas Wibe	prisoner		23	sailor	Norway BS
7162	416v		Philip Martin	prisoner		23	common labourer	Mog Maracloon
7163	416v		Edward Harper	prisoner		24	tailor	Dur Barnard Castle
7164	416v		John Johnson	prisoner	m	36	common labourer	Lin Boston
7165	416v		William Bruce	prisoner	m	20	butcher	Dur Shadforth
7166	416v		Nicholas Cranston	prisoner		18	coal miner	Nbl Newcastle
7167	416v		John Logan	prisoner		47	common labourer	Ldy Gothgarn
7168	416v		Richard Kirk	prisoner		21	brickmaker	Mog Dorally
7169	416v		Thomas McDonald	prisoner		32	common labourer	Sli Farinoy
7170	416v		John D. Watson	prisoner		21	miller	Nry Cotherstone
7171	416v		George Robinson	prisoner		19	common labourer	Nry Easingwold
7172	416v		Thomas Laverick	prisoner		28	miller	Nbl Cramlington
7173	416v		Solomon Spears	prisoner		16	sailor	Ant Belfast
7174	416v		Joseph Taylor	prisoner		21	common labourer	Wil Marlborough
7175	416v		Joseph Smith	prisoner		21	printer	Dur Darlington
7176	416v		James Fleckherty	prisoner	m	42	sailor	Ker
7177	417r		Charles Poskett	prisoner	m	28	common labourer	Wry Fishlake

7178	417r	Gaol	John Riley	prisoner		21	sailor	Mdx London
7179	417r		John Howley	prisoner	m	36	common labourer	May Ballymore
7180	417r		Patrick McKenna	prisoner		26	common labourer	Mog College Hall
7181	417r		Thomas Hann	prisoner		20	coal miner	Dur Sheriff Hill
7182	417r		Thomas Robson	prisoner		20	tobacco manufacturer	Nbl Newcastle
7183	417r		Patrick McGough	prisoner	m	26	coal miner	Mog Lisnekelly
7184	417r		William McPartline	prisoner		27	common labourer	Ros Cormaglee
7185	417r		John Woodhouse	prisoner		40	common labourer	Dub Dublin
7186	417r		Edward Thompson	prisoner		18	miller	Dur Durham
7187	417r		Robert Alderson	prisoner	m	26	glasscutter	Dur Bishopwearmouth
7188	417r		William Atkin	prisoner		16	sailor	Lan Liverpool
7189	417r		John Griffin	prisoner		23	common labourer	Gal Pallinstree
7190	417r		Peter Henry	prisoner		35	common labourer	Ldy Maghera *
7191	417r		Peter Galacher	prisoner		18	common labourer	Dur Gateshead
7192	417r		John Wesley	prisoner		21	sailor	USA
7193	417r		William Jones	prisoner		24	common labourer	Kid Kildare
7194	417r		John McKie	prisoner		26	weaver	Rfw Port Glasgow
7195	417r		Joseph Walton / White	prisoner	m	28	coal miner	Dur Stanhope
7196	417r		Robert James	prisoner		26	woolcomber	Nry Barton
7197	417v		James Graham	prisoner		44	common labourer	Lks Glasgow
7198	417v		William Barclay	prisoner	m	35	innkeeper	Arm Blackwater
7199	417v		James Wilson	prisoner		20	glasscutter	Lan Manchester
7200	417v		George Spencer	prisoner	m	29	potter	Nry Malton
7201	417v		Robert S. Henderson	prisoner		28	millwright	Dur Easington
7202	417v		Thomas Matthews	prisoner	m	27	watchmaker	Nbl Newcastle
7203	417v		Thomas Rogan	prisoner		32	common labourer	Dow
7204	417v		Robert Clark	prisoner		39	common labourer	Dur Gateshead
7205	417v		Craven White	prisoner	w	50	common labourer	Nry Harwood Dale
7206	417v		William Thompson	prisoner	m	30	common labourer	Lan Liverpool
7207	417v		George Farmer	prisoner	m	30	whitesmith	Lan Liverpool
7208	417v		John Thompson	prisoner	m	27	common labourer	Let Belhavel
7209	417v		George Patterson	prisoner	m	26	coal miner	Dur Newbottle
7210	417v		Thomas Kennedy	prisoner	m	23	common labourer	Sli Carrarah
7211	417v		John Wilson	prisoner		19	cotton weaver	Ken Deal
7212	417v		Matthew Mitchell	prisoner	m	42	sailor	But Rothesay *
7213	417v		William Turnbull	prisoner		14	common labourer	Dur Sunderland
7214	417v		James Ginnet	prisoner		20	teaser at cotton factory	Lnd S. Giles
7215	417v		John Harrison	prisoner		22	boilersmith	France BS
7216	417v		George Hill	prisoner		20	common labourer	Ant Belfast
7217	418r		James Mordey	prisoner		23	common labourer	Dur Sunderland
7218	418r		Peter Atkin	prisoner		22	common labourer	Dur Sunderland
7219	418r		John Hooper	prisoner		21	shipwright	Dur Sunderland
7220	418r		William Campbell	prisoner		15	sailor	Dur Sunderland
7221	418r		George Johnson	prisoner	m	24	sailor	Dur [South] Shields
7222	418r		John Lansburg	prisoner	m	29	sailor	Holland, Flushing
7223	418r		Samuel Mitchell	prisoner		25	sailor	ChI Jersey BS
7224	418r		William Vanderside	prisoner	m	40	sailor	Holland *
7225	418r		Bowma de Cloe	prisoner	m	36	sailor	Holland *
7226	418r		William Hardy	prisoner		25	sailor	Dur [South] Shields
7227	418r		John Laws	prisoner		17	shipwright	Dur Sunderland
7228	418r		William Jones	prisoner		20	sailor	Nbl North Shields
7229	418r		John Cain	prisoner		34	common labourer	Sfk Mildenhall
7230	418r		Edward Hewit	prisoner	m	37	sailor	Dur Sunderland
7231	418r		George Pringle	prisoner		19	shipwright	Dur Sunderland
7232	418r		John Oates	prisoner		22	coal miner	Dur Etherley
7233	418r		John Huggett	prisoner		17	sailor	Dur [South] Shields
7234	418r		William Mather	prisoner		20	glassblower	Nbl Newcastle
7235	418r		David Robertson	prisoner		19	sailor	For Dundee
7236	418r		Thomas Brooks	prisoner		18	sailor	Mdx London
7237	418v		Robert Carlton	prisoner	m	65	nailer	Dur Darlington
7238	418v		Joseph Spears	prisoner		30	common labourer	Dow Down
7239	418v		Ralph Watson	prisoner		33	coal miner	Dur Wrekenton
7240	418v		Roger Dinnings	prisoner	m	28	blacksmith	Dur Swalwell
7241	418v		William Grieves	prisoner	m	20	coal miner	Dur Gateshead
7242	418v		James Riley	prisoner	m	24	common labourer	Ken Maidstone
7243	418v		William Stewart	prisoner		17	sailor	Per Perth
7244	418v		Thomas Fenwick	prisoner		44	shoemaker	Dur Fishburn
7245	418v		John Heslop	prisoner	m	24	coal miner	Dur Ouston /"Austin"
7246	418v		James Sparks	prisoner		19	sailor	Ken Sutton
7247	418v		James Horn	prisoner		11	common labourer	Let Drumbolam
7248	418v		Patrick McQuillan	prisoner		20	hawker	Ess
7249	418v		James Williamson	prisoner		19	brushmaker	Sts Newcastle-un-Lyme
7250	418v		Henry Wright	prisoner		18	sailor	Nry Middlesbrough
7251	418v		John Turner	prisoner		20	common labourer	Nbl Newcastle
7252	418v		George Russell	prisoner		18	coal miner	Dur Stanhope
7253	418v		James Dunbar	prisoner	m	31	chainmaker	Nbl Newcastle
7254	418v		James Morton	prisoner	m	24	tinner	Ham Isle of Wight
7255	418v		William Holt	prisoner	m	43	coal miner	Nbl Byker /"Baker"
7256	418v		Cuthbert Wilson	prisoner	m	20	coal miner	Dur [South] Shields
7257	419r		George Rutherford	prisoner		26	joiner	Dur [South] Shields
7258	419r		Patrick Keeron	prisoner		28	common labourer	Lou Louth

7259	419r	Gaol	Robert Barker	prisoner	m	55	common labourer	Dur Sedgefield
7260	419r		George Lowe	prisoner		15	coal miner	Dur Ouston /"Austin"
7261	419r		Fenwick H. Habbard	prisoner	m	37	common labourer	Dur [South] Shields
7262	419r		James Smith	prisoner		40	joiner	Dur Darlington

Notes - Enumeration District   Gaol and House of Correction

7034	... S. Andrew	7092	/"Cracole"
7035	/"Weaterley"	7120	... New York, British subject
7044	county given as "Inverness-shire"	7190	/"Machra"
7049	... S. Peter	7212	county given as "Renfrewshire"
7050	... West Kirk	7224	... Heinewoord
7062	county given as "Durham"	7225	... Zwaite Waol
7075	... has had an annuity but has gone through		

REF	FOL	NO	STREET	FORENAME(S)	SURNAME	REL	C	AGE	OCCUPATION	BIRTHPLACE
			S. Mary the Less parish							
7263	4v	1	South Bailey	Matthew	Woodifield	hea	w	48	landed proprietor	Dur Durham
7264	4v			Anthony	Woodifield	son		22	student of medicine	Dur Durham
7265	4v			Elizabeth	Woodifield	dau		20		Dur Durham
7266	4v			Mary	Arrighi	ser	m	40	housekeeper	Dur Durham
7267	4v			Jane	Forster	ser		30	lady's maid	Dur Durham
7268	4v			Martha	Atkinson	ser		26	house servant	Dur Durham
7269	4v			Hannah	Herring	ser		16	house servant	Dur Durham
7270	4v			Anthony	Arrighi	*		8		Italy
7271	4v	2	South Bailey	Mary	Pearson	ser		40	cook	Yks Deighton
7272	4v			Ann	Wilson	vis		42	housekeeper	Dur
7273	4v	3	South Bailey	John Church	Backhouse	hea	w	39	banker	Dur Darlington
7274	4v			John Henry	Backhouse	son		6	scholar	Dur Blackwell
7275	4v			Eliza	Barclay	sis	w	38		Dur Darlington
7276	4v			Marianne	Lincoln	ser		29	house servant	Nfk Norwich
7277	4v			Ann	Coates	ser		36	house servant	Dur Darlington
7278	4v			Mary	Gregg	ser		30	house servant	Dur Darlington
7279	4v			Sarah	Johnson	ser		18	house servant	Dur Darlington
7280	4v			John	Soung?	ser		38	house servant	Nbl Colwell
7281	4v			George	Best	ser		32	coachman	Dur Coniscliffe
7282	4v	4	South Bailey	Anne Stote	Fox	hea	w	70	landed proprietor	Dur South Shields
7283	5r			George T.	Fox	son		40	curate of St. Oswald	Dur Westoe
7284	5r			Henry Elliott	Fox	gsn		9	scholar at home	East Indies BS
7285	5r			Mary Isabella	Fox	gda		8	scholar at home	East Indies BS
7286	5r			Harriet	Wilkinson	gov		37	governess	War Hartshill
7287	5r			Timothy	Burnett	ser	m	41	butler	Nry Husthwaite
7288	5r			Dorothy	Gargett	ser		31	cook	Nry Brompton
7289	5r			Margaret	Dixon	ser		30	lady's maid	Nbl Quarryhouse
7290	5r			Margaret	Hudson	ser		27	house maid	Nbl Wallsend
7291	5r			Anne	Rowntree	ser		21	house maid	Dur Upper Houses
7292	5r			Elizabeth	Robertshaw	ser		19	kitchen maid	Dur Durham
7293	5r			Jane	Hudson	ser	w	60	nurse	Nbl Walker
7294	5r	5	South Bailey	Isabella	Hope	ser		42	cook	Dur Darlington
7295	5r			Margaret	Hope	ser		24	house maid	Dur Darlington
7296	5r	6	South Bailey	Joseph	Davison	hea	m	40	solicitor *	Dur Sedgefield
7297	5r			Anne Caroline	Davison	wif	m	39	solicitor's wife	Dur Southwick
7298	5r			Frances Anne	Davison	dau		7		Dur Durham
7299	5r			Charlotte	Davison	dau		6		Dur Witton Gilbert
7300	5r			Frederick	Davison	son		5		Dur Durham
7301	5r			Thomas	Davison	son		1		Dur Durham
7302	5r			Dora	Davison	dau		1		Dur Durham
7303	5v			Caroline	Davison	dau		3m		Dur Durham
7304	5v			Elizabeth	Thwaites	ser	m	50	house servant	Dur Fatfield
7305	5v			Mary	Robinson	ser		27	house servant	Dur Durham
7306	5v			Mary Isabella	Gowry	ser		39	house servant	Nbl Whillingham
7307	5v			Isabella	Elder	ser		26	house servant	Nbl Newcastle
7308	5v			Ann	Gainford	ser		19	house servant	Dur Durham
7309	5v	7	South Bailey	Elizabeth	Stuart	hea		50	schoolmistress *	Lnd
7310	5v			Frederica	Anith	*		30	French teacher	Geneva
7311	5v			Dorothy	Ord	pup		16	scholar	Dur Sunderland
7312	5v			Anna	Ordion	pup		13	scholar	Nbl Newcastle
7313	5v			Sarah	Hogg	pup		14	scholar	not known
7314	5v .			Julia	Denten	pup		13	scholar	Dur Sunderland
7315	5v			Hannah	Wright	pup		11	scholar	Nbl Newcastle
7316	5v			Ann	Walker	ser		27	cook	Dur Darlington
7317	5v			Eliza	Lamb	ser		27	house servant	Dur Sunderland
7318	5v			Ann	Bulmer	ser		24	house servant	Dur Durham
7319	5v	8	South Bailey	T.A.	Greenwell	hea	w	65	land holder	Dur
7320	5v			Henry	Greenwell	son		31	solicitor	Dur
7321	5v			Francis	Greenwell	son		25	interest of money	Dur
7322	5v			Charles	Greenwell	son		23	interest of money	Dur
7323	6r			Frances	Lowdon	ser		30	house servant	Dur Brancepeth
7324	6r			Catherine	Brown	ser		40	house servant	Dur
7325	6r			George	Scott	ser		19	house servant	Dur
7326	6r	9	South Bailey	Edward	Shipperdson	hea		70	esquire, magistrate	Dur Pittington
7327	6r			Sarah Ann	Moore	ser		36	house servant	Dur Witton Gilbert
7328	6r			Jane Eliza	Burdon	ser		24	house servant	Dur Houghton-l-Spring
7329	6r			Ann	Barras	ser		19	house servant	Dur Pittington
7330	6r	10	South Bailey	Elizabeth A.	Shields	hea	w	60	annuitant	Ken Greenwich
7331	6r			Elizabeth	Shields	dau		30	teacher	Dur Durham
7332	6r			Jane Eleanor	Shields	dau		25	teacher	Dur Durham
7333	6r			Ann	Grieveson	ser		18	house servant	Dur Durham
7334	6r	11	South Bailey	Edward	Hastings	hea	m	65	artist	Nbl Alnwick
7335	6r			Henrietta	Hastings	wif	m	50	artist's wife	Dur Durham
7336	6r			Jane	Salkeld	sil		56	visitor	Dur Durham
7337	6r			Hannah	Ayre	ser		24	house servant	Dur Barnard Castle
7338	6r	12	South Bailey	William C.	Chaytor	hea		50	solicitor *	Dur Auckland
7339	6r			Ann Jane	Chaytor	sis		53		Lan Smedley

7340	6r	12	South Bailey	Margaret	Welch	ser		39	house servant	Dur Lumley
7341	6r			James	Robson	ser		38	butler	Nbl Wall
7342	6r			Margaret	Simpson	ser		34	house servant	Nry Upleatham
7343	6v			Ellen	Worthy	ser		21	house servant	Dur Durham
7344	6v			Isaac	Coxon	ser		21	house servant	Nbl Wall
			one house uninhabited							
7345	6v	14	South Bailey	Walter	Scruton	hea	m	51	solicitor *	Dur Durham
7346	6v			Marianne	Scruton	wif	m	51	solicitor's wife	Dur Kelloe
7347	6v			Walter	Scruton	son		18	undergraduate of Oxford	Dur Durham
7348	6v			Charles	Scruton	son		14	scholar	Dur Durham
7349	6v			Jane	Kennedy	ser		43	cook	Yks Hadsor
7350	6v			Margaret	Mutter	ser		28	house maid	Nbl Haggerston
7351	6v			George	White	ser		19	footman	Dur Brafferton
7352	6v	16	South Bailey	Henry	Walford	hea		26	MA of Oxford <Rev *>	Ess Hatfield
7353	6v			Jane	Walford	sis		23	gentlewoman	Ess Hatfield
7354	6v			Charles	Walford	bro		18	scholar	Ess Hatfield
7355	6v			Frederick	Walford	bro		13	scholar	Ess Hatfield
7356	6v			Edward B.	Croft	pup		17	scholar	Sry Ripley
7357	6v			Robert Ingham	Salmon	pup		16	scholar	Dur South Shields
7358	6v			Charles C.	Chevallier	pup		16	scholar	Pem Pembroke
7359	6v			James	Hudson	pup		13	scholar	Yks Byssingley
7360	6v			Mary	Littlefair	ser		66	domestic servant	Dur Sunderland Bridge
7361	6v			Joseph	Littlefair	ser		31	domestic servant	Dur Durham
7362	7r			Mary	Hall	ser		23	domestic servant	Dur Washington
7363	7r	17	South Bailey	William Henry	Yarnall	hea		43	<college> cook	Dby Sudbury
7364	7r			Ann	Yarnall	sis		46	housekeeper	Dby Sudbury
7365	7r			Charles Robert	Yarnall	nep		7		Mon Tredegar
7366	7r			Jane	Dawson	ser		18	house servant	Dur Penshaw

S. Mary-le-Bow parish

7367	7v	1	North Bailey	Elizabeth	Alderson	hea		60	milliner <lodgings>	Nry Appleton
7368	7v			Ann	Robinson	sho		22	shopwoman	Dur Durham
7369	7v			Ellen	Burn	ser		18	house servant	Dur Stockton
7370	7v			Clenena	Pelvil	ldr		29	French teacher	France
7371	7v			Joseph	Chapman	ldr	m	35	Wesleyan minister *	Ntt Worksop
7372	7v			Martha	Grey	ser		22	house servant	Dur Lanchester
7373	7v	2	North Bailey	Thomas	Davison	hea	m	31	tailor, draper *	Nbl Hartburn
7374	7v			Mary	Davison	wif	m	34	wife	Dur Staindrop
7375	7v			Mary Sophia	Davison	dau		9	scholar	Dur [D] S. Mary-1-Bow
7376	7v			Sarah Ann	Davison	dau		3	at home	Dur [D] S. Mary-1-Bow
7377	7v			Mary	White	mlw	w	64	mother-in-law	Nry Middleton Tyas
7378	7v			Margaret	Minikin	ser		19	house servant	Dur Wolsingham
7379	7v			Elizabeth	Robson	vis		28	house servant	Dur Chester-le-Street
7380	7v	3	North Bailey	Charlotte E.	Wooler	dau		18	solicitor's daughter	Dur [D] Gilesgate
7381	7v			...b Victoria	Mira	vis		29		Mdx London
7382	7v			Mary	Vardy	ser		39	housekeeper	Dur [D] Elvet
7383	7v			Jane	Haddock	ser		20	house servant	Dur Rainton
7384	7v			Thomas	Baxter	ser		18	butler	Dur Bishop Auckland
7385	7v	4	North Bailey	Edward Cane	Jepson	hea	m	37	surgeon and apothecary *	Lin Gainsborough
7386	7v			Frances Ann	Jepson	wif	m	35	surgeon's wife	Lin Gainsborough
7387	8r			Sarah Flower	Jepson	dau		9	scholar	Dur Durham
7388	8r			Mary	Jepson	dau		7	scholar	Dur Durham
7389	8r			Robert Cane	Jepson	son		6	scholar	Dur Durham
7390	8r			George Hewley	Jepson	son		4	at home	Dur Durham
7391	8r			Edward	Jepson	son		1	at home	Dur Durham
7392	8r			Arthur	Jepson	son		9m	at home	Dur Durham
7393	8r			Mary	Hall	ser		30	house servant	Nbl Wooler
7394	8r			Mary	Cummings	ser		25	house servant	Dur Durham
7395	8r			Hannah	Vasey	ser		22	house servant	Dur Durham
7396	8r	5	North Bailey	Robert N.	Robson	hea	m	35	MRCSL and LSA <surgeon>	Dur Durham
7397	8r			Edward Sheddon	Robson	son		2	at home	Dur Durham
7398	8r			Jane	Thoms	ser		22	house servant	Dur Killerby
7399	8r			Maria	Wilson	ser		21	house servant	Dur Barnard Castle
7400	8r			John	Fawcett	ser		17	servant	Dur Durham
7401	8r	6	North Bailey	Ignatius	Bonomi	hea	m	64	architect	Lnd
7402	8r			Charlotte	Bonomi	wif	m	50	architect's wife	Lnd
7403	8r			Sophia	Feilding	sil		50		Lnd
7404	8r			Sarah	Dent	ser		23	house servant	Nry Romaldkirk
7405	8r			Margaret	Legge	ser		20	house servant	Dur Bishop Middleham
7406	8r	7	North Bailey	Thomas	Davison	hea	m	70	land agent <& surveyor*>	Nbl North Seaton
7407	8v			Dorothy	Davison	wif	m	70	land agent's wife	Dur Sedgefield
7408	8v			John	Wheatley	ser		32	house servant	Dur Langley
7409	8v			William	Robson	ser		26	house servant	Nbl Wreighill
7410	8v			Ann	Thompson	ser		32	house servant	Nbl Hartley
7411	8v			Catherine	Thirlwell	ser		26	house servant	Dur [D] Crossgate
7412	8v			Isabella	Wardell	ser		20	house servant	Dur Houghton-1-Spring
7413	8v		Hatfield Hall	Michael	White	ser	m	32	butler	Dur Brafferton
7414	8v			Susan	White	*	m	33	housekeeper	Nfk Shropham

7415	8v		Hatfield Hall	Elizabeth Forster	ser		20	kitchen maid	Dur Penshaw
7416	8v			Joseph Hall	ser		20	footman	Dur Heighington
7417	8v			Peter Crichton	ser		13	footboy	Dow Bryansford
7418	8v			William Griffiths	bdr		24	gentleman	Sal Kinstock
7419	8v	11	North Bailey	John Moor	hea	m	36	butler	Nbl Kirkharle
7420	8v			Sarah Moor	wif	m	37	wife	Dur Durham
7421	8v			John Moor	son		9	scholar	Dur Durham
7422	8v			Robert Moor	son		7	scholar	Dur Durham
7423	8v			Margaret Moor	dau		4		Dur Durham
7424	8v			Joseph Moor	son		2		Dur Durham
7425	8v	12	Bow Lane	John Burrell	hea	w	56	proctor *	Dur Durham
7426	8v			Robert Anthony Burrell	son		21	articled clerk	Dur Durham
7427	9r			Marianne Burrell	dau		18	at home	Dur Durham
7428	9r			Eliza Burrell	dau		17	at home	Dur Durham
7429	9r			Frances Anne Burrell	dau		13	at home	Dur Durham
7430	9r			Augustus Burrell	dau		11	at home	Dur Durham
7431	9r			Jane Strikley	ser	w	49	house servant	Dur Chester-le-Street
7432	9r			Elizabeth Orton	ser		40	house servant	Nry Easby
7433	9r			Margaret Wheatley	ser		26	house servant	Dur Lanchester
7434	9r			Dorothy Taylor	ser		18	house servant	Dur Lumley
7435	9r	13	Bow Lane	William Henshaw	hea	m	58	organist of Cathedral *	Mdx London
7436	9r			Emily Henshaw	wif	m	53	organist's wife	Mdx London
7437	9r			Mary Anne Rowe	ser		17	house servant	Dur Norton
7438	9r			Elizabeth Dermont	ser		10	house servant	Dur Darlington
7439	9r	14	Bow Lane	George Jackson	hea	w	70	groom	Dur Durham
7440	9r			Hannah Jackson	dau		30		Dur Durham
7441	9r			William Jackson	son		26	solicitor's clerk	Dur Durham
7442	9r	15	Bow Lane	William Kirkley	hea	m	35	writing clerk	Dur Durham
7443	9r			Mary Kirkley	wif	m	37	writing clerk's wife	Dur Lumley Park
7444	9r			Robert William Kirkley	son		8	scholar	Dur Durham
7445	9r			Elizabeth Mary Kirkley	dau		6	scholar	Dur Durham
7446	9r			Matilda Kirkley	dau		1	at home	Dur Durham
7447	9v			Elizabeth Bainbridge	sil		35		Dur Lumley Park
7448	9v	16	North Bailey	Mary Handcock	hea		57	dressmkr <& lodgings *>	Dur Durham
7449	9v			Isabella Handcock	sis		49	dressmkr <& lodgings *>	Dur Durham
7450	9v			Louisa Handcock	nce		13	scholar	Sry Bermondsey
7451	9v	17	North Bailey	Thomas Griffith	hea		55	solicitor *	Dur Durham
7452	9v			Charles Waton	ser		30	house servant	Dur Ferryhill
7453	9v			Mary Raine	ser		43	housekeeper	Dur Witton Gilbert
7454	9v			Catherine Waton	ser		20	house maid	Dur Penshaw
7455	9v	18	North Bailey	Ursula Dodd	hea		27	house servant	Dur Newton Hall
7456	9v			Eleanor Forster	ser		22	house servant	Dur Beamish
7457	9v			John Bryce	ser		23	groom	Dur Wolsingham
7458	9v	19	North Bailey	John Ralph Fenwick	hea	w	90	deputy lieutenant	Nbl Morpeth
7459	9v			John Robson	ser		44	house servant	Nbl Wall
7460	9v			Sarah Heslop	ser		32	house servant	Wes Kirkby Stephen
7461	9v			Jane Crawford	ser		38	house servant	Nbl Newton [on] Moor
7462	9v			Isabella Todd	ser		30	house servant	Nbl Edlingham
7463	9v	20	North Bailey	Henry Stapylton	hea		48	judge of county court *	Lnd
7464	9v			Martyn Stapylton	nep		20	student at university	Dby Barlborough
7465	9v			George Robson	ser		42	house servant	Nbl S. John [Lee]
7466	9v			Mary Rogers	ser		38	house servant	Nbl Hexham
7467	10r			Mary Lister	ser		24	house servant	Dur Ferryhill
7468	10r	21	North Bailey	Mary Griffith	hea		52	gentlewoman	Dur Durham
7469	10r			Frances Griffith	sis		50	gentlewoman	Dur Durham
7470	10r			Eleanor Griffith	sis		44	gentlewoman	Dur Durham
7471	10r			George Griffith	bro		46	solicitor	Dur Durham
7472	10r			Margaret Easby	ser		21	house servant	Dur Durham
7473	10r			Ann Dawson	ser		33	house servant	Dur Stanley
7474	10r			Sarah Wilson	ser		31	house servant	Dur Jarrow
			one house uninhabited						
7475	10r	23	North Bailey	James Brooksbank	hea	m	64	annuitant	Wry Healaugh
7476	10r			Ann Brooksbank	wif	m	57	annuitant	Wry Aberford
7477	10r			Walter Brooksbank	son		20	college student	Dur Durham
7478	10r			Katherine Brooksbank	dau		29		Yks York
7479	10r			Ann Wear	ser		64	servant	Dur Lanchester
7480	10r			Mary Shotton	ser		17	servant	Nbl Ryton
7481	10r	24	North Bailey	Mary Bowlby	hea		59	prop of land and houses	Dur Durham
7482	10r			Anne Young	ser		53	house servant	Dur Shincliffe
7483	10r			Frances Elder	ser		13	house servant	Dur Durham
7484	10r	25	North Bailey	Mary Smith	hea		40	housekeeper	Dur Tudhoe
7485	10r	26	North Bailey	Annie Heppell	ser		32	cook	Nbl Newcastle
7486	10v			Mary Ann Fawcett	ser		22	house maid	Nbl Alnwick
7487	10v	27	North Bailey	Elizabeth Johnson	hea		70	from interest of money	Dur Sunderland
7488	10v			Sarah Minirty	vis	w	80		Dur Sunderland
7489	10v			Isabella Low	vis		55		Cul Great Salkeld
7490	10v			Elizabeth Palmer	ser		28	house servant	Dur Rushyford
7491	10v			Jane Pallister	ser		24	house servant	Dur Windlestone
7492	10v	28	North Bailey	Thomas Tuer	hea	m	43	accountant	Yks York, Parish
7493	10v			Jane Tuer	wif	m	44		Nbl Hexham
7494	10v			John Tuer	son		11	scholar	Dur Durham

No.	Fol.	House	Address	Name	Rel.	Cond.	Age	Occupation	Birthplace
7495	10v	28	North Bailey	Sarah Tuer	dau		8	scholar	Dur Durham
7496	10v			Mary Jane Tuer	dau		7	scholar	Dur Durham
7497	10v			Mary Lowthier	mlw	w	77	late housekeeper	Nbl Ovingham
7498	10v			Elizabeth Calvert	ser		17	house servant	Dur Durham
7499	10v	[aa]a	North Bailey	Mary Clark	wif	m	44	butler's wife	Nbl Bywell
7500	10v	[aa]b	North Bailey	Frances Young	hea	w	76	formerly housekeeper	Dur Wallnook Mill
7501	10v	31 a	Dun Cow Lane	William Dent	hea		46	writing clerk *	Dur Durham
7502	10v			Frances Dent	sis		38	housekeeper	Dur Durham
7503	10v	31 b	Dun Cow Lane	Robert Davidson	hea	m	28	coachman	Nbl Park
7504	10v			Agnes Davidson	wif	m	25	coachman's wife	Sct
7505	10v			Jane Davidson	dau		2		Sct
7506	11r			Isabel Davison	dau		3m		Dur Durham
7507	11r	31 c	Dun Cow Lane	William Taylor	hea	w	54	butler	Nbl Ellingham *
7508	11r			Hannah Cocks	dau	m	26		Dur Durham
7509	11r			William Taylor	son		18	plumber	Dur Durham
7510	11r			Hannah Pinkerton	ser		11	house servant	Nbl Newcastle
7511	11r			William John Taylor	nep		3		Dur Durham
7512	11r	32	Dun Cow Lane	William Evett	hea	m	41	<university> butler	Dev Clayhanger
7513	11r			Ann Evett	wif	m	49	butler's wife	Ham Bullington
7514	11r			Elizabeth Turner	ser		13	house servant	Dur Great Lumley
7515	11r	[aa]	Palace Green	Robert Burrell	hea		49	proctor	Dur Durham
7516	11r			Mary Burrell	sis		58		Dur Durham
7517	11r			Jane Burrell	sis		52		Dur Durham
7518	11r			Elizabeth Burrell	sis		50		Dur Durham
7519	11r			Elizabeth Rutherford	ser		35	house servant	Dur Durham
7520	11r			Anne Hansell	ser		23	cook	Nry Hutton Rudby
7521	11r	34	Dun Cow Lane	John Woodruff <jn>	hea	m	34	coachman <groom>	Dur Brancepeth
7522	11r			Catherine Woodruff	wif	m	30	coachman's wife	Dur West Auckland
7523	11r			Elizabeth Woodruff	dau		10		Dur Witton-le-Wear
7524	11r	35	Dun Cow Lane	Thomas Kaye	hea	m	36	lay clerk *	Wry Almondbury
7525	11r			Priscilla Kaye	wif	m	36	lay clerk's wife	Wry Sheffield
7526	11v			Hannah Bennett Kaye	dau		8	scholar	Ery Norton
7527	11v			Thomas Bennett Kaye	son		6	scholar	Nry Old Malton
7528	11v			Joseph Bennett Kaye	son		2	at home	Dur Durham
7529	11v			Emma Martin	vis		17	house servant	Sts Lichfield
7530	11v			Harriet Suthers	ser		14	house servant	Dur Darlington
7531	11v			Joseph Kaye	nep		17	shopman	Wry Almondbury
7532	11v			Charles B. Kaye	son		1m	at home	Dur Durham
7533	11v	36	Dun Cow Lane	Margaret Newby	hea	w	33	plumber	Dur Durham
7534	11v			George Dixon Newby	son		11	scholar	Dur Durham
7535	11v			Margaret Jane Young	nce		1		Dur Durham
7536	11v			Mary Grisdale	ldr		40	lady	Dur Kirk Merrington
7537	11v			Ann Black	ser		20	house servant	Nbl Alnwick
7538	11v	37	Dun Cow Lane	Mary Newby	hea	w	72	shopkeeper <beerhouse *>	Dur Durham
7539	11v			Mary Elizabeth Hutchinson	gda		11	scholar	Nbl Newcastle
7540	11v			Jane Crooks	ser		15	house servant	Dur South Hetton
7541	11v	38	North Bailey	Catherine Simpson	ser		27	house servant	Dur Kelloe
7542	11v			Jane Bainbridge	ser		27	house servant	Dur Bishop Auckland
7543	11v			Edward Taylor	ser		16	house servant	Lan Manchester
7544	11v	39	North Bailey	George Young Wall	hea	m	46	land agent <& surveyor>	Dur Stainton
7545	11v			Isabella Wall	wif	m	42	land agent's wife	Nbl Newcastle
7546	12r			Hannah Wall	dau		8	scholar	Dur Durham
7547	12r			George Young Wall	son		6	scholar	Dur Durham
7548	12r			Elizabeth Wall	dau		3		Dur Durham
7549	12r			Christopher Wall	fth	m	71	retired farmer	Dur Bishop Auckland
7550	12r			Mary Ann Short	ser		19	house servant	Dur Pittington
7551	12r			Barbara Walker	ser		63	house servant	Lan Manchester
7552	12r			James Wall	son		5		Dur Durham
7553	12r	40	North Bailey	Henry Wetherell	hea	m	36	music & dancing master *	Dur Durham
7554	12r			Mary Ann Wetherell	wif	m	35	music master's wife	Mdx Shoreditch
7555	12r			Jane Pendleton Wetherell	dau		11	scholar	Dur Durham
7556	12r			Mary Wetherell	dau		9	scholar	Dur Durham
7557	12r			Agnes Taylor Wetherell	dau		8	scholar	Dur Durham
7558	12r			Henry Frank Wetherell	son		6	scholar	Dur Durham
7559	12r			Frederick A. Wetherell	son		4		Dur Durham
7560	12r			Emily Wetherell	dau		3		Dur Durham
7561	12r			Frank Wetherell	son		1		Dur Durham
7562	12r			Margaret Stevenson	ser		26	house servant	Dur Easington
7563	12r			Sarah Esther Heaton	ser		22	house servant	Dur Durham
7564	12r			Jane Lightfoot	ser		20	house servant	Dur Durham
			five houses uninhabited						
7565	12v	46	North Bailey	John A. Cory	hea	m	31	architect	Nfk [Great] Yarmouth
7566	12v			Emily Cory	wif	m	29	architect's wife	Mdx Westminster
7567	12v			Robert Cory	son		5		Sry Lambeth
7568	12v			Mary Cory	dau		2		Dur Durham
7569	12v			Emily Cory	dau		9m		Dur Durham
7570	12v			Margaret Chaytor	ser		26	house servant	Dur Jarrow
7571	12v			Elizabeth Todd	ser		21	house servant	Dur Jarrow
7572	12v			Jane Bee	ser		25	house servant	Dur Durham
7573	12v	47	North Bailey	Anthony Brown	hea	w	68	groom	Dur Staindrop
7574	12v	48	North Bailey	John Newby	hea	m	39	tailor & draper *	Dur Durham

7575	12v	48	North Bailey	Charlotte Newby	wif m	40	tailor & draper's wife	Hrt	
7576	12v	49	North Bailey	Thomas C. Maynard	hea m	47	solicitor	Dur Durham	
7577	12v			Jane Frances Maynard	wif m	44	solicitor's wife	Dur Washington	
7578	12v			Jane Fanny Maynard	dau	16	scholar	Dur Durham	
7579	12v			Thomas C. Maynard	son	14	scholar	Dur Durham	
7580	12v			Crofton Maynard	son	13	scholar	Dur Durham	
7581	12v			George Crofton Maynard	son	11	scholar	Dur Durham	
7582	12v			Charles Maynard	son	10	scholar	Dur Durham	
7583	12v			Henry Maynard	son	8	scholar	Dur Durham	
7584	12v			Margaret I. Maynard	dau	1		Dur Durham	
7585	13r			Alice Anderson	vis	47		Dur [South] Shields	
7586	13r			Eleanor Anderson	vis	45		Dur [South] Shields	
7587	13r			Elizabeth Graham	ser	26	house maid	Cul Irthington	
7588	13r			Mary Ann Lee	ser	18	nurse	Dur Houghton-1-Spring	
7589	13r			Ann Smith	ser	21	cook	Dur Houghton-1-Spring	
7590	13r			John Abraham Hunter	vis m	44	butcher	Dur Sunderland	
			two houses uninhabited						
7591	13r	[aa]	Queen Street *	John Lightfoot	bde w	79	[formerly] weaver *	Dur Durham	
7592	13r			John Donnison	bde w	72	[formerly] farm labourer	Dur Kirk Merrington	
7593	13r			Mary Stot	bde w	71	[formerly] servant	Nbl Capheaton	
7594	13r			Jane Snowdon	bde w	79	[formerly] servant	Dur Auckland	
7595	13r			Margaret Vest	bde w	86	[formerly] servant	Dur Lanchester	
7596	13r			Isabella Thackray	bde w	67	[formerly] servant	Dur Sedgefield	
7597	13r			Dinah Thwaites	bde w	79	[formerly] cook	Dur Pelton	
7598	13r	[ab]	Palace Green	John Moor	hea w	54	verger of Cathedral	Nbl Kirkharle	
7599	13r			Jane Catherine Moor	dau	10	scholar	Dur Durham	
7600	13r			Elizabeth Moor	sis	49	housekeeper	Nbl Kirkharle	
7601	13r			Ann Cowel	ser	23	house servant	Nbl Byker	
7602	13r	[ab]	Queen Street	Henry Thomas	hea m	35	house servant	Mdx Bloomsbury	
7603	13r			Mary Thomas	wif m	35	house servant's wife	Nbl Embleton	
7604	13v			William Thomas	son	7	scholar	Nbl Embleton	
7605	13v	[ac]	Queen Street	William Hogg	hea w	47	printer compositor	Lower Canada BS	
7606	13v			Caroline Hogg	sis	48	housekeeper	Dur Chester-le-Street	
7607	13v	[ad]	Queen Street	John Henry Blunt	hea m	27	student in theology	Mdx Chelsea	
7608	13v			Frances Blunt	wif m	27	student's wife	Mdx Chelsea	
7609	13v			Ann Ricketts	ser	21	house servant	Sal Shrewsbury	
7610	13v	[ae]	Queen Street	Timothy Rushworth	hea m	35	carver & gilder *	Wry Lockwood	
7611	13v			Mary Rushworth	wif m	38	carver & gilder's wife	Lan Preston	
7612	13v			Elizabeth Rushworth	dau	12	scholar	Lan Preston	
7613	13v			Alice Rushworth	dau	10	scholar	Dur Durham	
7614	13v			Sarah Rushworth	dau	7	scholar	Dur Durham	
7615	13v			William Rushworth	son	5	scholar	Dur Durham	
7616	13v			Thomas Rushworth	son	7m		Dur Durham	
7617	13v			Catherine Walker	ser	15	house servant	Eng	
7618	13v			James Kent	ser	23	carver & gilder	Lan Manchester	
7619	13v			John P. Scott	ldr	31	artist	Rfw Greenock	
7620	13v	[af]a	Queen Street	John Henry	hea m	35	joiner	Nbl Bamburgh	
7621	13v			Isabella Henry	wif m	36	joiner's wife	Dur Jarrow	
7622	13v			Isabella S. Henry	dau	1		Dur Durham	
7623	13v			Isabella S. Clark	ser	45	servant	Dur South Shields	
7624	14r	[af]b	Queen Street	William Howe	hea m	49	joiner	Dur Durham	
7625	14r			Mary Howe	wif m	48	joiner's wife	Sry Lambeth	
7626	14r			Thomas Howe	son	13	scholar	Dur Durham	
7627	14r			William Howe	son	11	scholar	Dur Durham	
7628	14r			Mary Smurthwate	vis	27	house servant	Dur Sedgefield	
7629	14r	[af]c	Queen Street	Jane Archbold	hea	63	bonnetmaker	Dur Durham	
7630	14r			Margaret Snowdon	nce	47	bonnetmaker	Dur Durham	
7631	14r	[af]d	Queen Street	Mary Ann Graham	wif m	30	butler's wife	War Warwick Barracks	
7632	14r			Margaret Ann Graham	dau	9	scholar	Dur Durham	
7633	14r	[ag]	Queen Street	Judith Hays	hea	72	interest of money	Dur Durham	
7634	14r			Hannah Blackett	ser	27	house servant	Dur Durham	
7635	14r			Margaret Drummond	ser	21	house servant	Dur Lumley	
			two houses uninhabited						

College (extra-parochial)

7636	14v	[aa]	College	Samuel Rowlandson	hea m	45	deputy treasurer *	Dur Gainford	
7637	14v			Hannah Rowlandson	wif m	41	wife	Nry Romaldkirk	
7638	14v			Isabel Mary Rowlandson	dau	14	daughter	Dur Durham	
7639	14v			Christopher Rowlandson	son	11	son	Dur Durham	
7640	14v			Annie Sarah Rowlandson	dau	8	daughter	Dur Durham	
7641	14v			Kate Marion Rowlandson	dau	7	daughter	Dur Durham	
7642	14v			William R. Rowlandson	son	3	son	Dur Durham	
7643	14v			Mary Elizabeth Rowlandson	dau	1	daughter	Dur Durham	
7644	14v			Robert Wiseman	ser	24	groom	Dur Stockton	
7645	14v			Margaret Herdman	ser	29	cook	Nry Northallerton	
7646	14v			Margaret Kendale	ser	21	house maid	Dur Wolsingham	
7647	14v			Sarah Waisman	ser	20	nurse	Dur Durham	
7648	14v			Ann Davison	ser	18	nurse	Dur Auckland	

No.	Fol.	Code	Dwelling	Name	Rel.	Age	Occupation	Birthplace
7649	14v	[ab]	College	Martha Bell	ser	50	house servant	Dur Chester-le-Street
7650	14v	[ac]	College	Jane Lee	ser	60	housekeeper	Nbl Norham
7651	14v	[ad]	College	Henry Douglas	hea m	57	canon of Durham	Wor Worcester
7652	14v			Eleanor Douglas	wif m	49	canon's wife	Gls Newland
7653	14v			Ellen Douglas	dau	21	canon's daughter	Gls Newland
7654	14v			Jane Douglas	dau	16	at home	Dur Whickham
7655	14v			Elizabeth Douglas	dau	13	at home	Dur Whickham
7656	15r			Lucy Douglas	dau	12	at home	Dur Whickham
7657	15r			James Douglas	son	7	at home	Dur Whickham
7658	15r			Emily Maude Douglas	dau	6	at home	Dur Whickham
7659	15r			Adelaide Douglas	dau	5	at home	Dur Durham
7660	15r			Ann Poatten	gov	34	governess	Sry Balham Hill
7661	15r			Joseph Stabler	ser m	33	house servant	Wry Tickhill
7662	15r			Edwin Preece	ser	19	house servant	Gls Mitchel[dean]
7663	15r			Anne Thornton	ser	32	house servant	Dur South Shields
7664	15r			Jane Harker	ser	25	house servant	Dur Durham
7665	15r			Sarah Risk	ser w	46	house servant	Wry Halifax
7666	15r			Hannah Jeckells	ser	20	house servant	Dur Sedgefield
7667	15r			Elizabeth Heslop	ser	20	house servant	Dur Birtley
7668	15r			Emma Melville	vis m	29	wife *	Wem Killary
7669	15r			David W.W. Melville	vss	6m	son of Rev D. Melville	Wor Shelsley
7670	15r			Mary Hunt	ser	23	house servant	Wor Kidderminster
7671	15r	[ae]	College	Ann Clues	ser	30	house servant	Ham Selbourne
7672	15r			Jane Dodd	ser	28	house servant	Dur Ryton
7673	15r	[af]	College	Isabella Bailes	ser w	45	servant	Nbl Newcastle *
7674	15r	[ag]	College	Harriet Jenkins	dau	16	scholar	Dur Durham
7675	15r			Ann Jenkins	dau	10	scholar	Dur Durham
7676	15v			John Jenkins	son	7	scholar	Dur Durham
7677	15v			Arthur Jenkins	son	5	scholar	Dur Durham
7678	15v			Catherine Jenkins	dau	3		Dur Durham
7679	15v			Edith Jenkins	dau	1		Dur Durham
7680	15v			Sarah Penelope Paley	ser	27	governess	Nry Brafferton
7681	15v			Joseph Clark	ser m	47	butler	Nry Strensall
7682	15v			Elizabeth Bewdley	ser w	61	nurse	Ham Newnham
7683	15v			Elizabeth Ann Corp	ser	33	housekeeper	Som Temple Combe
7684	15v			Mary Jane Simpson	ser	22	cook	Dur Hett
7685	15v			Alice Beadley	ser	36	upper house maid	Nry Coatham
7686	15v			Elizabeth Drummond	ser	20	nursery maid	Dur Penshaw
7687	15v			Jane Parkinson	ser	18	under house maid	Dur Bishopton
7688	15v			Ellen Turner	ser	21	kitchen maid	Dur Lumley
7689	15v	[ah]	College	John Edwards	hea w	62	canon of Durham *	Hun Huntingdon
7690	15v			Maria Cook	sil	49	sister	Hun Huntingdon
7691	15v			Anne Walker	ser	32	cook	Nbl Newcastle
7692	15v			Ellen Bentley	ser	32	house maid	Sfk Great Saxham
7693	15v			Hannah Young	ser	18	kitchen maid	Dur
7694	15v			William Denncort?	ser	16	footboy	Nry Yarm *
7695	15v	[ai]	College	Eliza Parker	ser	28	house servant	Ken Wickham
7696	16r			Jane Stout	ser	24	house servant	Dur Durham
7697	16r			Maria Greathead	ser	25	house servant	Dur Durham
7698	16r			William Fenwick	ser	19	house servant	Dur Durham
7699	16r	[aj]	College	Eliza Wilber	ser	50	housekeeper	Dev Exeter
7700	16r			Elizabeth Scott	vis	38		Lei Whitwick
7701	16r			Harriet Grey	ser	37	house maid	Lnd
7702	16r			Elizabeth Harwood	ser	22	kitchen maid	Yks York
7703	16r			Jane Pattison	ser	21	scullery maid	Lnd
7704	16r			Edmund Notley	ser m	51	butler	Sfk Eye
7705	16r			Peter Scott	vis m	56	shipowner	Dur Sunderland
7706	16r			William T. Scott	vis	7	scholar	Dur Sunderland
7707	16r			Thomas Weldon	ser	22	gardener	Dur Conside
7708	16r	[ak]	College	William Hartley	hea m	44	verger & College porter	Mdx London
7709	16r			Phyllis Hartley	wif m	35	verger's wife	Dby Breadsall
7710	16r			Elizabeth Hartley	dau	8	scholar	Dur Durham
7711	16r			Martha Hartley	dau	5	scholar	Dur Durham
7712	16r			Mary Hartley	dau	3	at home	Dur Durham
7713	16r			Catherine Gustand	ser	23	house servant	Dur Newbottle
7714	16r	[al]	College	William Forbes Raymond	hea	64	archdeacon *	Ess [Saffron] Walden
7715	16r			Elizabeth Jones	ser	45	housekeeper	Mgy Machynlleth
7716	16v			Alexander Douglas	ser	27	butler	Sry Putney
7717	16v			Henry Walker	ser	21	house servant	Dur Eggleston
7718	16v			Hutton Elsdon	ser	23	house servant	Nry Richmond
7719	16v			Elizabeth Ascough	ser	25	house servant	Nry Masham /"Mesham"

one house uninhabited

Castle and Precincts (extra-parochial)

No.	Fol.	Dwelling	Name	Rel.	Age	Occupation	Birthplace
7720	17r	Old Grammar School	William Jones	hea m	63	annuitant	Ham South Stoneham
7721	17r		Mary Jones	wif m	57	annuitant's wife	Nbl Stannington
7722	17r		Elizabeth Jones	dau	24	domestic	Nbl Netherwitton
7723	17r		Thomas Jones	son	22	proctor's clerk	Dur Bishopwearmouth

7724	17r		Old Grammar School	Mary Elliot	ser	29	house servant	Nbl Stamfordham
7725	17r		Castle Green	Philip Rudd	*	29	MA, fellow & chaplain *	Wes Musgrave
7726	17r			Charles M. Davies	stu	22	BA, fellow & student	Som Wells
7727	17r			Digby Compton	stu	21	student in arts	Ham Minstead
7728	17r			James Francis Turner	stu	22	student in arts	Nfk [Great] Yarmouth
7729	17r			Christopher Holme	stu	23	student in arts	Wes Orton
7730	17r			James Thompson	stu	20	student in arts	Irl Killeoin
7731	17r			Joseph Rogers Thompson	stu	22	student in arts	Irl Killeoin
7732	17r			George Marshall	ser	34	waiter	Dur Stranton
7733	17r			William Goatley	ser m	58	porter	Brk Newbury
7734	17r			Frances Goatley	* m	68	porter's wife	Sfk S. Margaret?
7735	17r			Emma Sadler	vis	5	grand-daughter of above	Wry Ouseburn *
7736	17r			Frances Bell	ser	55	cook	Nbl Newburn
7737	17r			Hannah Drummond	ser	54	housekeeper	Dur Penshaw
7738	17r			Hannah Johnstone	ser	24	scullery maid	Nbl Newcastle
7739	17r			Mary Waddington	ser	23	kitchen maid	Dur Durham
7740	17v			Frances Waddington	ser	22	house maid	Dur Durham
7741	17v			William Titmarth	ser w	57	waiter	Cam
7742	17v	[ah]	Queen Street	George Moor	hea m	50	attorney	Nbl North Shields
7743	17v			Elizabeth Moor	wif m	47	attorney's wife	Dur Sherburn
7744	17v			Elizabeth Moor	dau	14		Dur Durham
7745	17v			Margaret Moor	dau	6	scholar	Dur Durham
7746	17v			Frederick Moor	son	12	scholar	Dur Durham
7747	17v			Alfred Moor	son	10	scholar	Dur Durham
7748	17v			Elizabeth Hall	ser	31	house servant	Dur West Rainton
7749	17v	[ai]	Queen Street *	Jane Hagen	hea w	55	librarian <& tea dealer>	Dur Hetton
7750	17v			Jane Eliza Hagen	dau	13	scholar	Dur Bishopwearmouth
7751	17v		Library <Queen St>	Charles Reed	hea m	50	librarian *	Dur Durham
7752	17v			Mary Reed	wif m	48	wife	Dur Durham
7753	17v			Frances Reed	dau	9	scholar	Dur Durham
7754	17v		Castle Precincts	Thomas Grey	hea m	28	pig jobber	Dur Durham
7755	17v			Elizabeth Grey	wif m	30	wife	Dur Durham
7756	17v			Thomas Grey	son	7	scholar	Dur Durham
7757	17v			Margaret Grey	dau	5	scholar	Dur Durham
7758	17v			Charles M. Grey	son	3		Dur Durham
7759	17v			Matthew Grey	son	1		Dur Durham
7760	18v*	<51>	Saddler Street	John Brewster	hea m	46	hairdresser <& hatter *>	Lin Friskney
7761	18v*			Mary Brewster	wif m	54	hairdresser's wife *	Lin Boston
7762	18v*			Henrietta A. Brewster	dau	16		Dur [D] S. Nicholas

Houses adjoining South Bailey (extra-parochial)

7763	19r*		Banks Cottage one house uninhabited	Elizabeth Salkeld	hea w	58	dressmaker	Dur Wolviston
7764	19r*		Museum	William Proctor	hea m	53	bird & animal preserver	Dur Lanchester
7765	19r*			Mary Proctor	wif m	44	bird preserver's wife	Nbl Warkworth
7766	19r*			William Proctor	son	16	writing clerk	Dur Durham
7767	19r*			Thomas Proctor	son	14	printer	Dur Durham
7768	19r*			John Proctor	son	11	scholar	Dur Durham
7769	19r*			Joseph Proctor	son	8	scholar	Dur Durham
7770	19r*			Robert Proctor	son	5	scholar	Dur Durham
7771	19r*			Sarah Pearson	ser	14	house servant	Dur Merrington
7772	19r*		Garden Cottage	Thomas Smith	hea m	43	servant	Dur Pittington
7773	19r*			Alice Smith	wif m	43	servant's wife	Nbl Wooler
7774	19r*			Thomas Henry Smith	son	16	apprentice bookbinder	Dur [D] S. Margaret
7775	19r*			Elizabeth Smith	dau	11	scholar	Dur [D] South Bailey
7776	19r*			Margaret P. Smith	dau	9	scholar	Dur [D] South Bailey

Notes - Enumeration Districts 1-3

7270	[servant's son]
7296	<& deputy registrar to bishop, provincial secretary to bishop, clerk of halmote courts & cursitor to court of chancery>
7309	<boarding school>
7310	[employed as?] teacher
7338	<& treasurer of university & registrar to dean and chapter>
7345	<& deputy clerk of peace & registrar to court of chancery>
7352	<assistant classical and mathematical master at Durham School>
7371	<Wesleyan Methodist chapel, 57 Old Elvet>
7373	... & robemaker <& lodgings>
7385	... MRCS and LAC
7406	<& agent to dean and chapter & bishop>
7414	[servant's] wife
7425	<& registrar to archdeacons of Durham, Northumberland and Lindisfarne & deputy registrar to dean and chapter>
7435	<& professor of music>
7448-7449	... & milliner
7451	<& deputy steward of halmote courts & clerk of hanaper>
7463	<for recovery of small debts; & recorder>
7501	<law stationer>
7507	county given as "Durham"
7524	... and musicseller <professor of music>
7538	... & confectioner
7553	<professor of music and dancing, pianoforte tuning & proprietor of Assembly Rooms>
7574	<& lodgings>
7591-7597	<Bishop's almshouses>

7591	<parish clk & sexton of S. Mary the Less>
7610	<& cabinetmaker>
7636	... to dean and chapter
7668	... of Rev. David Melville [principal of Hatfield Hall, tutor in University Coll]
7673	... Gosforth
7689	<& professor of Greek and classical literature at university>
7694	county given as "Durham"
7714	... of Northumb'land <& bishop's chaplain>
7725	in residence; <& pro-proctor of univ & chaplain to University College>

7734	[servant's] wife
7735	/"Osburne"
7749-7750	<48 Saddler Street>
7751	<subscription library and news room, newsagent & lessee of public sale and exhibition rooms>
7760-7776	[entries also made on folio 18r; the transcription takes information from both entries]
7760	... & perfumer & toy dealer
7761	<& register office for servants>

REF	FOL	NO	STREET	FORENAME(S) SURNAME	REL	C	AGE	OCCUPATION	BIRTHPLACE
7777	23v	<64>	Claypath	Ralph Dixon	hea		43	coal owner *	Dur Durham
7778	23v			Ann Hutchinson	ser		22	general servant	Dur Auckland
7779	23v			Alice Hutchinson	ser		13	general servant	Dur Auckland
			two houses uninhabited						
7780	23v	66	Claypath	Thomas Dickens	hea	m	58	mason & builder	Dur Sedgefield
7781	23v			Mary Dickens	wif	m	66		Dur Durham
7782	23v			Sarah Dickens	dau		26		Dur Hill Top
7783	23v			John R. Dickens	son		24	bookbinder & stationer	Dur Durham
7784	23v	<67>	Claypath	William Lightfoot	hea	m	58	butcher	Dur Durham
7785	23v			Jane Lightfoot	wif	m	50		Dur Durham
7786	23v			William Lightfoot	son		33	brewer's labourer	Dur Durham
7787	23v			Robert Lightfoot	son		23	cartman	Dur Durham
7788	23v			Thomas Lightfoot	son		21	cartman	Dur Durham
7789	23v			Joseph Lightfoot	son		19	slater	Dur Durham
7790	23v			George Lightfoot	son		16		Dur Durham
7791	23v			Ann Lightfoot	dau		13		Dur Durham
7792	23v			Henry Lightfoot	son		7		Dur Durham
7793	23v			James Lightfoot	son		5		Dur Durham
7794	23v	1	Leazes Place	William Boyd	hea		33	MRCSL & LAC, * surgeon	Dur [D] S. Nicholas
7795	23v			Clara Boyd	sis		22		Dur [D] S. Nicholas
7796	24r			Elizabeth Grey	ser		19	house servant	Dur [D] S. Oswald
7797	24r	2	Leazes Place	Mary Turner	wif	m	49		Dby Turnditch
7798	24r			Sampson Turner	son		25	draper	Sts Burton-upon-Trent
7799	24r			John Turner	son		19	tailor	Ntt Mansfield
7800	24r			Catherine Turner	dau		16		Lan Oldham
7801	24r			Henry Phillips	vis	w	41	Wesleyan minister	Hef Clodock
7802	24r			Michael Dodds	vis		28	farmer of c90a emp 4 men	Nbl Thorns
7803	24r	3	Leazes Place	Robert Lewis	hea	m	36	Wesleyan minister *	Chs Haughton
7804	24r			Robert M. Lewis	son		4		Dur Shotley Bridge
7805	24r			Elizabeth A. Lewis	dau		3		Nry Whitby
7806	24r			Hannah Witherspoon	ser		18	house servant	Dur Chester-le-Street
7807	24r	4	Leazes Place	Anne H. Gibson	wif	m	32	mistress of day * school	Ken Chatham
7808	24r			Anne Eliza Gibson	dau		13	scholar	Dur Sherburn
7809	24r			Henrietta Hodgson			18	teacher	Dur Sunderland
7810	24r			Isabella Sutton	pup		13	scholar	Nry Middlesbrough
7811	24r			Dorothy A. Moon	pup		11	scholar	Dur Trimdon
7812	24r			Margaret E. Dorvell	pup		10	scholar	Mdx London
7813	24r			Fanny Dorvell	pup		9	scholar	Mdx London
7814	24r			Janet Dorvell	pup		4	scholar	Mdx London
7815	24r			Catherine Ridley	ser		24	house servant	Dur Windlestone
7816	24v	5	Leazes Place	Thomas Tiplady	hea	m	44	tailor & draper	Dur [D] S. Oswald
7817	24v			Elizabeth Tiplady	wif	m	45		Dur Brancepeth
7818	24v			Thomas Tiplady	son		17		Dur [D] S. Giles
7819	24v			Ephraim Tiplady	son		15		Dur [D] S. Giles
7820	24v			Eleanor Tiplady	dau		13	scholar	Dur [D] S. Giles
7821	24v			Elizabeth Tiplady	dau		6	scholar	Dur [D] S. Nicholas
7822	24v			Ellen Newton	ser		20	house servant	Dur [D] S. Giles
7823	24v			William Bryan	ldr		21	railway clerk	Mdx London
7824	24v		Leazes House	John Henderson	hea	m	43	JP, carpet manufacturer*	Dur Durham
7825	24v			Hannah Henderson	wif	m	33		Dur Durham
7826	24v			Emily Henderson	dau		9	scholar	Dur Durham
7827	24v			John G. Henderson	son		4		Dur Durham
7828	24v			Charles W.C. Henderson	son		3		Dur Durham
7829	24v			Annie C. Henderson	dau		1		Dur Durham
7830	24v			Margaret Rowell	vis		49	proprietor of houses	Dur Gateshead
7831	24v			Elizabeth Kirbeck	ser		39	house servant	Dur Newbottle
7832	24v			Ann Coultman	ser		30	house servant	Dur Durham
7833	24v			Elizabeth Hall	ser		27	house servant	Dur Brancepeth
7834	24v			Isabella Hutchinson	ser		16	house servant	Dur Auckland S. Helen
7835	24v	7	Leazes Place	Robert Thwaites	hea	m	63	retd porter merchant, JP	Dur [D] S. Margaret
7836	25r			Ann M. Thwaites	wif	m	49		Gls Lower Swell
7837	25r			William Pucey	vis	m	51	Wesleyan minister	Ntt Newark
7838	25r			Ann Gibson	ser		30	house servant	Dur Houghton-l-Spring
7839	25r	8	Leazes Place	George Usher	hea	w	56	assistant overseer	Dur Shotton
7840	25r			John Harrison Usher	son		23	BA University College	Dur [D] S. Nicholas
7841	25r			Jane Usher	dau		21		Dur [D] S. Nicholas
7842	25r	9	Leazes Place	William Trueman	hea	w	49	chemist & druggist	Nry Whitby
7843	25r			Theresa Agnes Gotha	ser		30	house servant	Dur [D] S. Oswald
7844	25r	10	Leazes Place	Nicholas Oliver	hea	m	36	MRCS Edinburgh, LSA *	Nbl Bamburgh
7845	25r			Jane Maria Oliver	wif	m	30		Dur West Rainton
7846	25r			Charlotte Oliver	sis		29		Nbl Bamburgh
7847	25r			Rebecca Hansell	ser		20	house servant	Dur Langley
7848	25r			Isabella Dawson	ser		22	house servant	Dur West Rainton
7849	25r	11	Leazes Place	Thomas Fawcett	hea	m	60	prop of land & houses	Nbl Ponteland
7850	25r			Margaret Fawcett	wif	m	62		Dur Flass
7851	25r			Margaret Hall	nce		26		Dur Beamish
7852	25r	12	Leazes Place	Jane Brayshay	hea	w	57	proprietor of houses *	Nbl Blyth
7853	25r			James Brayshay	son		32	chemist, druggist *	Dur Durham
7854	25r			Alice Brayshay	dau		30	dressmaker	Dur Durham

7855	25r	12	Leazes Place	Anne Brayshay	dau	28	fancy milliner *	Lan Garstang
7856	25v			Jane Brayshay	dau	23	milliner	Dur Durham
7857	25v			Elizabeth Brayshay	dau	21	milliner	Dur Durham
7858	25v			Hannah Brayshay	dau	17		Dur Durham
7859	25v			John Charles Middleton	vis m	50	annuitant *	Dby Melbourne
7860	25v			Lucy Margaret Middleton	vis m	51		Lan Manchester
7861	25v			Elizabeth Middleton	vis	18	[visitor's] daughter	Dby Melbourne
7862	25v	[aa]	Claypath	Sarah Sanglier	hea w	58	housekeeper	Hef Hereford
7863	25v			Elizabeth Sanglier	dau	21	dressmaker	Hef Hereford
7864	25v	<70>	Claypath	William E. Duncan	hea m	59	newspaper proprietor *	Nbl Newcastle
7865	25v			Sarah Duncan	wif m	53		Dur Durham
7866	25v			Elizabeth Duncan	dau	28		Dur Durham
7867	25v			John Taylor Duncan	son	26	newspaper proprietor *	Dur Durham
7868	25v			William E. Duncan	son	23	newspaper proprietor *	Dur Durham
7869	25v			Sarah Anne Duncan	dau	20		Dur Durham
7870	25v			Henry Duncan	son	18	bookkeeper	Dur Durham
7871	25v			Marianne Duncan	dau	16		Dur Durham
7872	25v			Annie Duncan	dau	13	scholar	Dur Durham
7873	25v			Emma Margaret Duncan	dau	9	scholar	Dur Durham
7874	25v			Elizabeth Taylor	sil	44	annuitant	Dur Durham
7875	25v	<71>	Claypath	Rosamond Egerton	hea m	76	gentlewoman	Wry Burn
7876	26r			John Kirton	ldr m	80	farmer of 80a *	Dur Billy Row
7877	26r	71½	Claypath	Martha Cockill	hea w	54		Wor Kidderminster
7878	26r			Timothy Cockill	son	33	carpet weaver	Wor Kidderminster
7879	26r			Elizabeth Cockill	dau	30	milliner <dressmaker>	Wor Kidderminster
7880	26r			Arabella C. Cockill	dau	20		Dur Durham
7881	26r			Joseph Cockill	son	13	scholar	Dur Durham
7882	26r	72	Claypath	Elizabeth Gowland	hea w	55	temperance hotel keeper	Dur Brancepeth
7883	26r			John George Gowland	son	22	solicitor's writing clk	Dur Durham
7884	26r			Elizabeth Ayre	sis m	21		Dur Durham
7885	26r			James Ayre	nep	4		Dur Durham
7886	26r			Elizabeth Ayre	nce	2		Dur Durham
7887	26r	73	Claypath	Mary Moore	hea w	31	general dealer <toy dlr>	Lan Warrington
7888	26r			Thomas Moore	son	7	scholar	Dur Durham
7889	26r			James Platt	fth m	63	outdoor Chelsea pen *	Lan Warrington
7890	26r			Elizabeth Platt	smo m	63		Lan Warrington
7891	26r	74	Claypath	George Cowl	hea m	59	butcher	Nry Ingleby
7892	26r			Elizabeth Cowl	wif m	67		Nry Yarm
7893	26r			Jane Charlton	ser	15	house servant	Nbl Bedlington [NDu]
7894	26r	75	Claypath	William Murray	hea m	45	quilldresser *	Irl
7895	26r			Isabella Murray	wif m	45		Yks High Benton
7896	26v			William Murray	son	17		Wry Craven, Skipton
7897	26v			Mary Ann Murray	dau	15	scholar	Dur Durham
7898	26v			Martha Murray	dau	9	scholar	Dur Durham
7899	26v			John Murray	son	5	scholar	Dur Durham
7900	26v			Andrew Murray	son	3	scholar	Dur Durham
7901	26v	76*	Claypath	Isabella Taylor	hea w	55	confectioner	Dur [D] S. Nicholas
7902	26v			Bell Drakcup Taylor	dau	22		Dur [D] S. Nicholas
7903	26v	76*	Claypath	William Clark	hea	31	chemist & druggist	Dur Witton Gilbert
7904	26v			Mary Ann Madgin	hou	30	housekeeper	Dur Brandon
7905	26v			Elizabeth Banter	ser	17	house servant	Dur Bishop Middleham
7906	26v	<76>	Claypath	Robert Robson	hea m	44	carpenter & builder *	Dur Chester-le-Street
7907	26v			Susan Robson	wif m	46		Dur Houghton-l-Sprin
7908	26v			Jane M. Robson	dau	20		Dur [D] S. Nicholas
7909	26v			Edward R. Robson	son	16		Dur [D] S. Nicholas
7910	26v			Susan G. Robson	dau	12		Dur [D] S. Nicholas
7911	26v			Henry Robson	son	10		Dur [D] S. Nicholas
7912	26v			Sarah Robson	dau	9		Dur [D] S. Nicholas
7913	26v			George T.E. Ellidge	vis	15		Newfoundland BS
7914	26v			Mary Egglestone	ser	17	[servant]	Dur [D] S. Nicholas
7915	27r	77 a	Claypath	Robert Young	hea m	34	butcher	Dur Staindrop
7916	27r			Jane Young	wif m	34		Dur Darlington
7917	27r			Ann Young	dau	5m		Dur [D] S. Nicholas
7918	27r			William Vaux	app	14	butcher's apprentice	Dur [D] S. Nicholas
7919	27r	77 b	Claypath	Francis Marshall	hea m	38	Post Office messenger	Dur Durham
7920	27r			Jane Marshall	wif m	29		Dur Bishop Auckland
7921	27r			Henry Marshall	son	3		Dur Bishop Auckland
7922	27r			William S. Marshall	son	:		Dur Durham
7923	27r	77 c	Claypath	Elizabeth Meadows	hea w	75	annuitant	Dur Durham
7924	27r			Thomas Robinson	bro	72	painter	Dur Durham
7925	27r			John Robinson	bro	66	draper	Dur Durham
7926	27r	[ab]	Claypath	William Cox	hea m	51	quarryman	Dur Durham
7927	27r			Jane Cox	wif m	62		Dur Durham
7928	27r			John Cox	son	27	printer compositor	Dur [D] S. Nicholas
7929	27r			William Cox	son	25	mason	Dur [D] S. Nicholas
7930	27r			Sarah Cox	dau	20		Dur [D] S. Nicholas
7931	27r			William Cox	gsn	7m		Dur [D] S. Margaret
7932	27r	[ac]	Claypath	Phillip Smith	hea m	30	fruiterer	Irl
7933	27r			Jane Smith	wif m	25		Cul Penrith
7934	27r			Mary Smith	dau	2	scholar	Dur Stockton
7935	27v			Elizabeth Smith	dau	10m		Dur Durham

7936	27v	[ac]	Claypath	Mary Smith	ser	15	house servant	Nry Kirby Moorside *
7937	27v	<78>a	Claypath	Jane Marshall	hea	40	dressmaker	Dur Durham
7938	27v	<78>b	Claypath	George Gleason	hea m	43	tinner & brazier	Dur Bishop Auckland
7939	27v			Martha Gleason	wif m	40		Dur South Shields
7940	27v			Cornelius Gleason	son	17	tinner	Dur Durham
7941	27v			Anthony Gleason	son	14	tinner	Dur Durham
7942	27v			Thomas Gleason	son	12	scholar	Dur Durham
7943	27v			Margaret Gleason	dau	6	scholar	Dur Durham
7944	27v			Ellen Gleason	dau	4	scholar	Dur Durham
			one house uninhabited					
7945	27v	[ad]	Claypath	Mary Hollin	hea m	25	housekeeper (lodgings)	Lan Ashton-under-Lyne
7946	27v			John Mullany	ldr m	35	spectacle-maker	Cul Carlisle
7947	27v			John Cushing	ldr w	34	combmaker	Irl
7948	27v			Hugh McCann	ldr	49	cutler	Irl
7949	27v			Henry Moore	ldr	34	hawker (general)	Irl
7950	27v	[ae]	Claypath	Charles Thwaites	hea m	40	tailor	Dur Durham
7951	27v			Ellen Thwaites	wif m	40		Dur Jarrow
7952	27v			Elizabeth Thwaites	dau	17	dressmaker	Lnd Clerkenwell
7953	27v			Charles Thwaites	son	13	printer's apprentice	Lnd All Souls
7954	28r			Ellen Thwaites	dau	8	scholar	Nry Middlesbrough
7955	28r			William Thwaites	son	6	scholar	Nry Middlesbrough
7956	28r			Emma Thwaites	dau	3	scholar	Nry Middlesbrough
7957	28r			Joseph Thwaites	son	6m		Dur Durham
7958	28r	[af]	Claypath	Michael Bailes	hea m	33	cordwainer	Dur Durham
7959	28r			Mary Ann Bailes	wif m	35		Sfk Hartest
7960	28r			Ann Bailes	dau	2		Dur Durham
7961	28r			Sarah Bailes	dau	1		Dur Durham
7962	28r			Sarah Johnson	mlw w	60	formerly silk weaver	Sfk Glemsford
7963	28r	[ag]	Claypath	Robert Walker	hea m	45	ropemaker	Dur [D] S. Margaret
7964	28r			Mary Walker	wif m	58		Dur [D] S. Giles
7965	28r			Robert Walker	gsn	5		Dur [D] S. Nicholas
7966	28r	<81>	Claypath	Eliza Murphy	hea m	50		Irl
7967	28r			Jane Murphy	dau	26	schoolmistress	Irl
7968	28r			Samuel Murphy	son	9	scholar	Irl
7969	28r			Mary Ann Smith	ser	13	house servant	Dur Stockton
7970	28r	82	Claypath	Thomas Dobson	hea m	58	retired basketmaker	Dur Darlington
7971	28r			Tamar Dobson	wif m	63		Dur South Church
7972	28r			Frances Blakey	gda	14		Dur Durham
7973	28v	[ah]	Claypath	George Franks	hea m	31	coach painter	Dur South Shields
7974	28v			Mary Franks	wif m	32		Dur Durham
7975	28v			William Franks	son	9	scholar	Dur Durham
7976	28v			Elizabeth Franks	dau	8	scholar	Dur Durham
7977	28v			George Franks	son	5	scholar	Dur Durham
7978	28v			John Franks	son	4	scholar	Dur Durham
7979	28v			Robert Franks	son	5m		Dur Durham
7980	28v	[ai]a	Claypath	James Gowland	hea m	27	joiner	Dur Durham
7981	28v			Mary Gowland	wif m	30	dressmaker	Dur Durham
7982	28v			James Gowland	son	2		Dur Durham
7983	28v			Mary Ann Gowland	dau	3		Dur Durham
7984	28v			Hannah Pearson	sil	26	dressmaker	Dur Durham
7985	28v			Elizabeth Pearson	sil	20	dressmaker	Dur Durham
7986	28v			Margaret Swalwell	app	17	dressmaker's apprentice	not known
7987	28v	[ai]b	Claypath	James Swalwell	hea m	48	cordwainer	Dur Barnard Castle
7988	28v			Ann Swalwell	wif m	52		Wry Marsden
7989	28v			William Swalwell	son	22	cordwainer	Ntt Nottingham
7990	28v	82	Claypath	Thomas Maddison	hea m	33	solicitor's general clk	Dur Durham
7991	28v			Jane Maddison	wif m	31	straw-bonnetmaker	Dur Durham
7992	28v			Thomas Maddison	son	1		Dur [D] S. Nicholas
7993	29r			Mary Briggs	ser	18	house servant	Nbl Newcastle
7994	29r	[aj]a	Claypath	George Adam	hea m	28	tinsmith	Edn Edinburgh
7995	29r			Jane Adam	wif m	24		Edn Edinburgh
7996	29r			James Adam	son	4		Edn Edinburgh
7997	29r	[aj]b	Claypath	John Walker	hea m	27	blacksmith	Dur [D] S. Nicholas
7998	29r			Ann Walker	wif m	29		Dur Barnard Castle
7999	29r			Mary Walker	dau	3		Dur [D] S. Nicholas
8000	29r			Isabella Walker	dau	2		Dur [D] S. Nicholas
8001	29r	82*a	Claypath	Mary Johnson	hea w	35	receiving parish relief	Dur Brancepeth
8002	29r			Hannah Johnson	dau	10	scholar	Dur [D] S. Nicholas
8003	29r			Robert Johnson	son	6	scholar	Dur [D] S. Nicholas
8004	29r	82*b	Claypath	William A. Longstaff	hea m	25	general porter	Dur [D] S. Giles
8005	29r			Hannah Longstaff	wif m	22		Dur Barnard Castle
8006	29r			Mary Jane Longstaff	dau	2		Dur [D] S. Nicholas
8007	29r			William Longstaff	son	3		Dur [D] S. Nicholas
8008	29r	83	Claypath	Priscilla Robson	hea w	53	spirit <& wine *> merch	Wry Gomersal
8009	29r			Charles Robson	son	26	spirit merchant	Wry Leeds
8010	29r			Herbert Robson	son	22	spirit merchant	Wry Leeds
8011	29r			George Robson	son	16		Dur [D] S. Nicholas
8012	29r			Elizabeth Lowerison	ser	18	house servant	Dur Lumley
8013	29v			Sarah Lowerison	vis	20		Dur Lumley
8014	29v	<84>	Claypath	William Tindale	hea m	57	plasterer	Dur Brancepeth
8015	29v			Isabella Tindale	wif m	52		Dur Barnard Castle

8016	29v	<84>	Claypath	Robert Tindale	son	21	plasterer	Dur	Durham
8017	29v			George Tindale	son	17	plasterer's apprentice	Dur	Durham
8018	29v			Elizabeth Tindale	dau	19	straw-bonnetmaker's app	Dur	Durham
8019	29v			Jane Tindale	dau	12	scholar	Dur	Durham
8020	29v			Dorothy Tindale	dau	10	scholar	Dur	Durham
8021	29v	[ak]	Claypath	Robert Wright	hea m	29	joiner	Dur	Durham
8022	29v			Sarah Wright	wif m	27		Dur	[D] S. Nicholas
8023	29v			Ann Wright	dau	3		Dur	[D] S. Nicholas
8024	29v	<84>	Claypath	George Moody	hea m	44	joiner & builder *	Dur	Ushaw
8025	29v			Isabella Moody	wif m	40		Dur	Esh
8026	29v			Joseph Moody	son	7	scholar	Dur	[D] S. Nicholas
8027	29v			Mary Ann Moody	dau	2		Dur	[D] S. Nicholas
8028	29v			Jane Wright	ser	16	house servant	Dur	Durham
8029	29v	<84>	Claypath	Robert Prudhoe	hea m	29	grocer & druggist *	Dur	Newbottle
8030	29v			Elizabeth Prudhoe	dau	1		Dur	[D] S. Nicholas
8031	29v			John Prudhoe	bro	32	joiner	Dur	Newbottle
8032	29v			Jane Clark	ser	31	house servant	Dur	Sherburn
8033	29v			Isabella Hawkesley	ser	17	house servant	Dur	Rainton
8034	30r	<85>	Claypath	Thomas Summerbell	hea m	32	Post Office clerk *	Dur	Durham
8035	30r			Margaret Summerbell	wif m	34		Dur	Westoe
8036	30r			John McDonald	ser	19	house servant & ostler	Dur	Durham
8037	30r			Thomas Holborn	sls	6	scholar	Dur	Durham
8038	30r			John Holborn	sls	8	scholar	Dur	Durham
8039	30r	[al]	Claypath	John Alderson	hea m	46	carpet weaver	Dur	Barnard Castle
8040	30r			Mary Alderson	wif m	46		Dur	Barnard Castle
8041	30r			Mary Alderson	dau	17	weftwinder	Dur	[D] S. Nicholas
8042	30r			John Alderson	son	13	woolcarder	Dur	[D] S. Nicholas
8043	30r			Elizabeth Alderson	dau	10	weftwinder	Dur	[D] S. Nicholas
8044	30r			Maria Alderson	dau	7	scholar	Dur	[D] S. Nicholas
8045	30r			George Alderson	son	5	scholar	Dur	[D] S. Nicholas
8046	30r			Elizabeth Bland	nce	28	niece	Dur	[D] S. Nicholas
8047	30r	[am]	Claypath	Neil Boyle	hea m	33	common labourer *	Irl	
8048	30r			Mary Boyle	wif m	23		Irl	
8049	30r			Margaret Boyle	mth	70		Irl	
8050	30r			Mary Brown	ldr	60		Sct	
8051	30r			John Walker	ldh m	30	basketmaker	Cul	Whitehaven
8052	30r			Dorothy Walker	ldw m	33		Wes	Starlen
8053	30v			John Walker	ldh w	80	carpet weaver	Wes	Kendal
8054	30v			Jane Walker	ldd	13		Wes	Kendal
8055	30v			James Walker	lds	7		Wes	Kendal
8056	30v			Samuel Walker	lds	4		Dur	Durham
8057	30v			David Walker	lds	1		Irl	BS
8058	30v			Thomas Cochrane	ldh m	50	common labourer	Irl	
8059	30v			Mary Cochrane	ldw m	47		Wry	Leeds
8060	30v			Catherine Cochrane	ldd	20	capmaker	Wry	Leeds
8061	30v			Mary Cochrane	ldd	17		Wry	Leeds
8062	30v			James Mackintosh	ldr	27	chemist	Edn	Leith
8063	30v			John Reed	ldr	36	not known	Irl	
8064	30v			James Kenmar	ldr	48	carpet weaver	Irl	
8065	30v			James Clark	ldr	45	carpet weaver	Irl	
8066	30v			John Brown	ldh m	24	common labourer	Sct	
8067	30v			Mary Brown	ldw m	30			not known
8068	30v			John Brown	lds	11			not known
8069	30v			Henry Johnson	ldr	30	common labourer	Irl	
8070	30v			William Williamson	ldr	60	drover		not known
8071	30v			Daniel Rafferty	ldr	27	common labourer	Irl	
8072	30v			John Douglas	ldr	19	drover	Sct	
8073	31r			Susan Edmunds	ldr m	36	needlewoman	Lan	Manchester
8074	31r			John Callahan	ldh m	26	shoemaker	Irl	
8075	31r			Ellen Callahan	ldw m	26		Irl	
8076	31r	[an]	Claypath	John Mitchael	hea m	36	fruiterer	Irl	BS
8077	31r			Ann Mitchael	wif m	35		Irl	BS
8078	31r			John Mitchael	son	11	scholar	Dur	[D] S. Nicholas
8079	31r			Ellen Mitchael	dau	9	scholar	Dur	[D] S. Nicholas
8080	31r			Mary J. Mitchael	dau	7	scholar	Dur	[D] S. Nicholas
8081	31r			Christian Mitchael	dau	1		Dur	[D] S. Nicholas
8082	31r	[ao]	Claypath	William James Morgan	hea m	76	general labourer *	Irl	
8083	31r			Ann Morgan	wif m	62		Irl	
8084	31r			Patrick Morgan	son	19	general labourer	Irl	
8085	31r			John Morgan	son	16	fruit seller	Irl	
8086	31r			Susanna Morgan	dau	13	scholar	Irl	
8087	31r			William Fenwick	ldr	45	general labourer	Irl	
8088	31r			James Caufield	ldh w	60	papermaker	Irl	
8089	31r			Edward Caufield	lds	22	tailor	Irl	
8090	31r			Hugh Conlin	ldh m	42	tailor	Irl	
8091	31r			Bridget Conlin	ldw m	24		Irl	
8092	31r			Mary Conlin	ldd	3	scholar	Wes	Kirkby Stephen
8093	31r			James Conlin	lds	1		Cul	Carlisle
8094	31v			Peter McConvel	ldr	66	general hawker	Nry	Wensleydale
8095	31v			Chapman Duidzel	ldr	30	pitman	Nry	Wensleydale
8096	31v			Francis Heseltine	ldr	23	general labourer	Nry	Wensleydale

8097	31v	[ao]	Claypath	Michael Mullen	ldr m	30	general hawker	Irl
8098	31v			James Wallace	ldr m	46	butcher	Sct
8099	31v			Joseph Sill	ldr m	25	whitesmith	Irl
8100	31v			John Armstrong	ldr	18	general hawker	Irl
8101	31v			David Anderson	ldr	18	general hawker	Irl
8102	31v			Joseph Ling	ldr m	26	general hawker	Irl
8103	31v			George Sutherland	ldr	40	carter	Dur Durham
8104	31v	[ap]a	Claypath	James Cave	hea w	72	waiter	Nry Malton
8105	31v	[ap]b	Claypath	Robert Johnson	hea w	71	tailor	Dur [D] S. Nicholas
8106	31v			Michael Johnson	son	13	scholar	Dur [D] S. Nicholas
8107	31v			Elizabeth Johnson	dau	15		Dur [D] S. Nicholas
8108	31v	[ap]c	Claypath	John McLoughlin	hea m	47	blacking manufacturer	Irl BS
8109	31v			Elizabeth McLoughlin	wif m	36		Dur Whickham
8110	31v			Mary McLoughlin	dau	12	scholar	Dur Stockton
8111	31v			Jane McLoughlin	dau	11	scholar	Dur Stockton
8112	32r	[aq]	Claypath	Phillip Renolds	hea m	38	statuary	Italy
8113	32r			Ann Renolds	wif m	30		Sct BS
8114	32r			Douglas Renolds	dau	7	scholar	Nry Scarborough
8115	32r			John Renolds	son	4	scholar	Nbl Newcastle
8116	32r			Louis Renolds	son	1		Dur Durham
8117	32r			Douglas McLaen	ldr w	57	sempster	Sct BS
8118	32r	[ar]	Claypath	John Docherty	hea m	37	tailor	Lks Glasgow
8119	32r			Margaret Docherty	wif m	35		Irl
8120	32r			John Docherty	son	17	tailor	Rfw Greenock
8121	32r			Hugh Docherty	son	15	tailor	Lks Glasgow
8122	32r			William Docherty	son	7	scholar	Rfw Greenock
8123	32r			Thomas Musgrave	ldh m	44	general labourer	Dow Downpatrick
8124	32r			Jane Musgrave	ldw m	28		Cul Whitehaven
8125	32r			Catherine Musgrave	ldd	9	scholar	Cul Whitehaven
8126	32r			Thomas Musgrave	lds	9m		Dur [D] S. Nicholas
8127	32r			William Brodie	ldh m	41	general labourer	Spain, Gibraltar
8128	32r			Jane Brodie	ldw m	32		Sct ...borough
8129	32r	[as]	Claypath	Christopher Meeham	hea m	50	book merchant	Irl
8130	32r			Mary Meeham	wif m	50		Yks
8131	32r			Elizabeth Lister	sil w	56	house servant	Yks
8132	32v			Daniel McCarlan	ldr	30	linen merchant	Irl
8133	32v			Michael McCarlan	ldr	28	linen merchant	Irl
8134	32v			Daniel Fegan	ldr	24	linen merchant	Irl
8135	32v			John Martin	ldr	26	linen merchant	Irl
8136	32v	86	Claypath	William Thompson <sn>	hea m	75	gardener <& carter>	Dur Wolsingham
8137	32v			Elizabeth Thompson	dau	52		Dur [D] S. Nicholas
8138	32v			George Thompson	son	42	tailor	Dur [D] S. Nicholas
8139	32v			Susan Thompson	dau	33		Dur [D] S. Nicholas
8140	32v			Eliza Thompson	nce	13	scholar	Dur [D] S. Nicholas
8141	32v			William Thompson	nep	3		Dur [D] S. Nicholas
8142	32v	88	Claypath	Stephen Nevison	hea m	36	tailor & gen outfitter *	Dur Barnard Castle
8143	32v			Mary Jane Nevison	wif m	33		Wry Leeds
8144	32v			Henry William Nevison	son	6		Dur Darlington
8145	32v			Emma Nevison	dau	4		Dur Darlington
8146	32v			William Todd	flw m	62	tailor	Nry Richmond
8147	32v			Rebecca Todd	mlw m	57		Wry Hunslet
8148	32v			Sarah Edmonson	ser	16	house servant	Nbl Newcastle
8149	32v	<89>a	Claypath	John O'Riordan	hea m	27	hat manufacturer	Irl
8150	32v			Mary O'Riordan	wif m	24		Dur [D] S. Oswald
8151	33r	<89>b	Claypath	Mark Lightfoot	hea m	28	cabinetmaker *	Dur [D] Gilesgate
8152	33r			Elizabeth Lightfoot	wif m	28		Dur Coxhoe
8153	33r			Isabella Dawson	vis	10	scholar	Dur Cornforth
8154	33r	<89>	Claypath	John Wallace	hea m	39	bread baker	Dur Durham
8155	33r			Mary Wallace	wif m	40		Dur Durham
8156	33r			Thomas Wallace	son	10	scholar	Dur Durham
8157	33r			Jane Wallace	dau	8	scholar	Dur Durham
8158	33r			James Wallace	son	6	scholar	Dur Durham
8159	33r			George Wallace	son	4		Dur Durham
8160	33r			Mary Wallace	dau	3		Dur Durham
8161	33r			Isabella Suddick	ser	19	house servant	Dur Lambton
8162	33r	90	Claypath	John Burton	hea m	36	saddler & innkeeper *	Dur Durham
8163	33r			Jane Burton	wif m	28		Dur Bishop Auckland
8164	33r			John Burton	son	6	scholar	Dur Durham
8165	33r			William Burton	son	3		Dur Durham
8166	33r			Mary Surtees	ser	22	house servant	Dur East Rainton
8167	33r	[at]	Claypath	William Haton	hea m	35	general porter & groom	Nry Dalton
8168	33r			Mary Haton	wif m	22		Dur Durham
8169	33r	[au]	Claypath	Joseph Wheatley	hea m	73	servant, University Coll	Nbl Newcastle
8170	33r			Mary Wheatley	wif m	74		Nbl Newcastle
8171	33v			Margaret Westgarth	gda	9	scholar	Dur Durham
8172	33v			Joseph Westgarth	gsn	4	scholar	Dur Durham
8173	33v			Jane Turnbull	ser	18	house servant	Nbl Newcastle
8174	33v	[av]	Claypath	William Paul Jones	hea m	46	carpet weaver	Sal Bridgnorth
8175	33v			Susan Jones	wif m	38		Sal Bridgnorth
8176	33v			William Paul Jones	son	9	scholar	Sal Bridgnorth
8177	33v	[aw]	Claypath	Arthur R. Hunt	hea m	37	supt of waterworks	Irl

8178	33v	[aw]	Claypath	Jane Hunt	wif m	37		Ess Colchester
8179	33v			Rose Hunt	dau	10	scholar	Irl Bonyfobb
8180	33v			Robert Hunt	son	8	scholar	Irl Bonyfobb
8181	33v			Arthur Hunt	son	6	scholar	War Huntingdon
8182	33v			David Hunt	son	4	scholar	War Coventry
8183	33v			Mary Hunt	dau	2		Dur Durham
8184	33v			Bernard Dott Hunt	son	1m		Dur Durham
8185	33v	<91>	Claypath	Benjamin Jackson	hea	25	draper	Dur Annfield Plain
8186	33v			Robert Jackson	bro	24	draper	Dur Annfield Plain
8187	33v			John Jackson	bro	17	draper	Dur Annfield Plain
8188	33v			William Jackson	bro	16	draper	Dur Annfield Plain
8189	33v			Robert Swallow	ass	23	assistant draper	Cul Wigton
8190	33v			William Green	ass	21	assistant draper	Nbl Newcastle
8191	34r			Jane Ridley	ser	20	house servant	Dur Annfield Plain
8192	34r	[ax]	Claypath	Thomas Wheatley	hea	64	grocer	Dur Staindrop
8193	34r	[ay]a	Claypath	Christopher Clark	hea m	57	feltmaker	Dur [D] Gilesgate
8194	34r			Ann Clark	wif m	60	formerly laundress	Wry Littondale
8195	34r			Thomas Clark	son	22	general labourer	Nbl Newcastle
8196	34r			Margaret Clark	dau	14		Dur [D] Framwelgate
8197	34r	[ay]b	Claypath	Mary Snowdon	hea	62	formerly laundress	Dur Hunwick
8198	34r			George Snowdon	son	23	joiner	Dur [D] Claypath
8199	34r	[az]a	Claypath	John McLean	hea m	34	carpet weaver	Sct
8200	34r			Mary McLean	wif m	28		Sct
8201	34r			Donald McLean	son	8	scholar	Sct
8202	34r			James McLean	son	5	scholar	Wry Leeds
8203	34r			Mary McLean	dau	3		Dur Durham
8204	34r			John McLean	son	1		Dur Durham
8205	34r	[az]b	Claypath	Thomas Eggleston	hea m	26	whitesmith	Dur Durham
8206	34r			Jane Eggleston	wif m	25		Dur Durham
8207	34r			Thomas Eggleston	son	1		Dur Durham
8208	34r	[az]c	Claypath	Elizabeth White	hea w	68	waterwoman	Nry Whitby
8209	34r	<91>	Claypath	John Boyd	hea m	62	innkeeper <'Victoria'>	Dur Pinith
8210	34r			Sarah Boyd	wif m	57		Nry Thirsk
8211	34v			Thomas Henry Boyd	son*	28	tallow chandler *	Dur Durham
8212	34v			Robert Currey	ldr	35	cattle dealer	not known
8213	34v	92	Claypath	Jane Wortley	hea w	55	fruiterer	Dur Chilton
8214	34v			Thomas Wortley	son m	24	tinplate wkr <& grocer>	Dur [D] S. Nicholas
8215	34v			Mary Wortley	dlw m	22		Dur [D] S. Margaret
8216	34v			Jane Wortley	dau	20	milliner	Dur [D] S. Nicholas
8217	34v			Ann Wortley	gda	11m		Dur [D] S. Nicholas
8218	34v			Peter Hall	ldr	20	hairdresser	Dur [D] S. Margaret
8219	34v	<92>	Claypath	Robert Rutherford	hea m	70	tailor & lodging ho kpr*	Dur Bishop Auckland
8220	34v			Hannah Rutherford	wif m	68		Yks
8221	34v			Mary Rutherford	dau	28	dressmaker	Dur Durham
8222	34v			Mary Rutherford	gda	8		Nbl Newcastle
8223	34v			John Parks	ldh m	28	upholsterer	Lnd Shoreditch
8224	34v			Ann Parks	ldw m	20		Dur Hartlepool
8225	34v			James Smith	ldr	35	drover	Dur Durham
8226	34v			Ralph Cidero	ldr	26	drover	Sct
8227	34v			Peter Artrick	ldr	21	combmaker	Edn Edinburgh
8228	34v			John Bradley	ldr	55	drover	Irl
8229	34v			Mary Lynch	ldr m	51	confectioner	Irl
8230	34v			Kitty Rare	ldr w	56	general hawker	Irl
8231	35r			Mary Frances	ldh m	32	general hawker	Yks
8232	35r			John Frances	lds	8		Yks
8233	35r			Joseph Frances	lds	12		Yks
8234	35r			Bartholomew Brown	ldr	28	drover	Irl
8235	35r	[ba]	Claypath	Thomas Anderson	hea m	60	general labourer	Ken Challock
8236	35r			Mary Anderson	wif m	55	formerly laundress	Dur [D] Claypath
8237	35r			Sarah Anderson	dau	27	formerly laundress	Dur [D] Claypath
8238	35r			Robert Anderson	son	19	painter	Dur [D] Claypath
8239	35r			Jane Anderson	dau	16	scholar	Dur [D] Claypath
8240	35r	[bb]a	Claypath	Peter Etherington	hea m	37	shoemaker	Lks Glasgow
8241	35r			Mary Etherington	wif m	39	formerly laundress	Sct Addington
8242	35r			James Rabow	sso	16	shoemaker	Ery Hull
8243	35r			Elizabeth Rabow	sda	15	scholar	Wry Rotherham
8244	35r	[bb]b	Claypath	William Todd	hea m	60	general labourer	Dur Shincliffe
8245	35r			Mary Anne Todd	wif m	48	charwoman /"chairwoman"	Dur Portobello
8246	35r			William Todd	son	17	general labourer	Dur [D] Elvet
8247	35r			Thomas Todd	son	13		Dur [D] Gilesgate
8248	35r			John Todd	son	10		Dur [D] Gilesgate
8249	35r	[bb]c	Claypath	Mary Campsey	hea w	48	charwoman /"chairwoman"	Dur [D] Framwelgate
8250	35r	[bb]d	Claypath	Thomas Anderson	hea w	38	nailmaker	Dur Durham
8251	35v			William Anderson	son	16		Dur Durham
8252	35v			Thomas Anderson	son	15		Dur Durham
8253	35v			Mary Anderson	dau	9		Dur Durham
8254	35v	93	Claypath	George Brown	hea m	31	currier & innkeeper *	Dur Durham
8255	35v			Mary Brown	wif m	33		Dur Durham
8256	35v			Jane Elizabeth Brown	dau	4		Dur Durham
8257	35v			Mary S. Brown	dau	6m		Dur Durham
8258	35v			Mary Brown	sis	23		Dur Durham

8259	35v	93	Claypath	Anthony Cair	flw	w	69	cooper	Wry Heaton
8260	35v			Jane Pratt	ser		16	house servant	Dur Rainton
8261	35v			Sarah C. Brown	dau		3		Dur Durham
8262	35v	94 a	Claypath	Mary Hackworth	hea		54	water carrier; pauper	Dur [D] Framwelgate
8263	35v	94 b	Claypath	John Miller	hea	m	66	general labourer	Nry Manfield
8264	35v			Margaret Miller	wif	m	65		Dur Bowes House
8265	35v	[bc]	Claypath	John Londsdale	hea	w	77	annuitant	Dur Bishop Middleham
8266	35v	[bd]a	Claypath	James Mallen jn	hea	m	31	carpet weaver	Dur [D] S. Nicholas
8267	35v			Elizabeth Mallen	wif	m	24		Edn Edinburgh
8268	35v	[bd]b	Claypath	Elizabeth Bowey	hea	w	80		Dur Durham
8269	35v	[be]	Claypath	Ann Howe	hea	w	75	formerly laundress	Dur Stanhope
8270	35v	[bf]	Claypath	Ambrose Fawcett	hea	m	47	coach driver	Dur Aycliffe
8271	36r			Margaret Fawcett	wif	m	28		Dur Staindrop
8272	36r			William Fawcett	son		20	coffee roaster	Dur Durham
8273	36r			Jane Fawcett	dau		18	house servant	Dur Durham
8274	36r			Ambrose Fawcett	son		16	shoemaker	Dur Durham
8275	36r			Joseph Fawcett	son		13	scholar	Dur Durham
8276	36r			John Fawcett	son		1	infant	Dur Durham
8277	36r	[bg]	Claypath	Ann Emery	hea		32	dressmaker	Dur Fatfield
8278	36r			Thomas Emery	son		7	scholar	Dur Durham
8279	36r			William G. Emery	son		5	scholar	Dur Durham
8280	36r			Dorothy Robinson	ser		19	house servant	Dur Easington Lane
			one house unoccupied						
8281	36r	[bh]	Claypath	Henry Sharp	hea	m	53	currier	Dur Durham
8282	36r			Ann Sharp	wif	m	46		Lan Bolton
8283	36r			William Sharp	son		20	cabinetmaker	Dur Durham
8284	36r			John Sharp	son		13	scholar	Dur Durham
8285	36r			Ann Sharp	dau		10	scholar	Dur Durham
8286	36r	[bi]	Claypath	Robert Forster	hea	m	50	groom	Nry Northallerton
8287	36r			Elizabeth Forster	wif	m	49		Wry Ripon
8288	36r			William Forster	son		19	apprentice tailor	Nry Northallerton
8289	36r			Mary Ann Forster	dau		8		Dur [D] New Elvet
8290	36v	<94>	Claypath	Thomas Winter <jn>	hea	m	35	mason <& builder> *	Dur Durham
8291	36v			Eleanor Winter	wif	m	40		Dur Durham
8292	36v			Mary Hutchinson	ser		19	house servant	Nbl Shildon/"Sheldon"
8293	36v	[bj]	Claypath	John Hill Wood	hea	m	22	journeyman miller	Dur Ryhope
8294	36v			Anne Wood	wif	m	20		Dur Sunderland
8295	36v			Louisa Surtees	sil		8		Dur Sunderland
8296	36v	94	Claypath	James T. Hedley	hea	m	32	grocer	Nbl Netherton
8297	36v			Elizabeth Hedley	wif	m	26		Nbl Alnwick
8298	36v			Isabella Hedley	mth	w	67		Nbl Garret Shiels
8299	36v	<96>	Claypath	George Jennings	hea	m	55	innkeeper <'Greyhound'>	Cul Workington
8300	36v			Ellen Jennings	wif	m	60		Dur Gateshead
8301	36v			Ann McMan	ser		17	house servant	Cul Carlisle
8302	36v			Michael Tinney	ldr	m	30	cattle dealer	not known
8303	36v			[blank] Tinney	ldr		28	cattle dealer	not known
8304	36v			not known	ldr	nk	30	cattle dealer	not known
8305	36v			not known	ldr	nk	27	cattle dealer	not known
8306	36v			not known	ldr	nk	32	cattle dealer	not known
8307	36v			not known	ldr	nk	39	cattle dealer	not known
8308	36v			not known	ldr	nk	36	cattle dealer	not known
8309	36v	[bk]	Claypath	Ralph Biggins	hea	m	24	hawker of hardware	Italy, Janeway
8310	37r			Ann Biggins	wif	m	25		Irl
8311	37r			Margaret Biggins	dau		2		Dur [D] S. Nicholas
8312	37r			Henry Biggins	son		8m		Dur [D] S. Nicholas
8313	37r	<97>	Claypath	Ann Peele	hea	w	72	confectioner	Dur Shiney Row
8314	37r			Mary Ann Peele	gda		15		Dur Durham
8315	37r			Thomas Peele	gsn		8	scholar	Dur Durham
8316	37r	[bl]a	Claypath	John W. Metcalf	hea	m	25	teacher of music	Dur Murton
8317	37r			Mary Metcalf	wif	m	23		Dur [D] S. Giles
8318	37r	[bl]b	Claypath	William Harrison	hea	m	30	general labourer	Dur Durham
8319	37r			Jane Harrison	wif	m	26		Dur Durham
8320	37r			Elizabeth Harrison	dau		8		Dur Durham
8321	37r			Samuel Harrison	son		1		Dur Durham
8322	37r	<98>	Claypath	John Thompson	hea	m	42	<boot and> shoemaker *	Dur Durham
8323	37r			Ann Thompson	wif	m	38		Dur Durham
8324	37r			Jane Thompson	dau		15		Dur [D] S. Nicholas
8325	37r			Joseph Thompson	son		12	scholar	Dur [D] S. Nicholas
8326	37r			John Thompson	son		8	scholar	Dur [D] S. Nicholas
8327	37r			Mary Thompson	dau		4	scholar	Dur [D] S. Nicholas
8328	37r			Thomas Thompson	son		1		Dur [D] S. Nicholas
8329	37r	<99>	Claypath	James Fowler	hea	m	38	grocer <& flour dlr> *	Dur Coatham
8330	37v			Eleanor Fowler	wif	m	43		Nry Melsonby *
8331	37v			Matthew Fowler	son		5	scholar	Dur [D] S. Nicholas
8332	37v			Jane Ann Fowler	dau		3		Dur [D] S. Nicholas
8333	37v			James Fowler	son		6m		Dur [D] S. Nicholas
8334	37v			Jane Oliver	sil	w	67		Dur [D] S. Nicholas
8335	37v			Matthew Hind	sho		22	grocer's shopman	Dur Durham
8336	37v			Charles F. White	sho		21	grocer's shopman	Dur Barnard Castle
8337	37v			Thomas Smith	app		19	grocer's apprentice	Dur Croxdale
8338	37v			Phillip Simpson	app		18	grocer's apprentice	Dur Coatham

No.	Folio	Schedule	Address	Name		Rel	Age	Occupation	Birthplace
8339	37v	<99>	Claypath	Washington	Wortley	app	15	grocer's apprentice	Dur Durham
8340	37v			Jane	Selkirk	ser	22	house servant	Nbl Berwick
8341	37v			Ann	Anderson	ser	16	house servant	Dur Durham
8342	37v	100	Claypath	Anne	Burlinson	hea w	72	annuitant	Had
8343	37v			Clement	Burlinson	son	34	portrait * painter	Dur Eggleston
8344	37v			Anne Atchison	Burlinson	dau	23	annuitant	Dur [D] S. Oswald
8345	37v	<101>	Claypath	Thomas	Raine	hea m	31	draper, master emp 2 men	Dur Cockfield
8346	37v			Mary Ann	Raine	wif m	29		Dur Durham
8347	37v			Sarah Frances	Raine	dau	5		Dur [D] S. Nicholas
8348	37v			William	Mawson	sho	20	draper's shopman	Dur Houghton-l-Spring
8349	37v			William	Lappage	sho	20	draper's shopman	Nbl Blyth
8350	38r			Henry R.	Morris	app	17	draper's apprentice	Dur Easington
8351	38r			James	Madgin	app	18	draper's apprentice	Dur Brancepeth
8352	38r			William	Shaw	app	15	draper's apprentice	Dur Cornsay
8353	38r			John	Rayson	app	17	draper's apprentice	Ess Shenfield
8354	38r			George	Hall	app	14	draper's apprentice	Dur Durham
8355	38r			Ellen	Pearson	ser	23	house servant	Dur Lumley
8356	38r			Fanny	Robinson	ser	19	house servant	Dur Durham
8357	38r			Ann	Cook	ser	25	house servant	Nbl North Shields
8358	38r	<102>	Claypath	Nicholson	Iveson	hea m	47	temperance hotel kpr *	Nbl Hexham
8359	38r			Ann	Iveson	wif m	40		Dur Bishop Auckland
8360	38r			James	Iveson	son	19	currier's apprentice	Dur [D] S. Nicholas
8361	38r			Frances	Iveson	dau	17	scholar	Dur [D] S. Margaret
8362	38r			William	Iveson	son	13	scholar	Dur [D] S. Margaret
8363	38r			Elizabeth Anne	Iveson	dau	5	scholar	Dur [D] S. Nicholas
8364	38r			William	Cowell	vis m	50	cattle dealer	Nry Thirsk
8365	38r			James	Hudson	vis	29	boot and shoemaker	Nbl Whittingham
8366	38r			Thomas	Twizle	vis	27	omnibus guard	Nbl Colwell
8367	38r	<103>	Claypath	William	Hall	hea m	48	grocer <& flour dlr> *	Dur Oaks Row
8368	38r			Robert	Hall	son	17	farmer's apprentice	Dur Durham
8369	38r			Joseph	Coulton	app	15	grocer's apprentice	Dur Dalton-le-Dale
8370	38v			Anthony	Smith	app	15	grocer's apprentice	Dur Sunderland Bridge
8371	38v			Mary Ann	Robson	ser	25	house servant	Dur Haram
8372	38v	104	Claypath	Richard	Dixon	hea m	40	brewer's clk & traveller	Cul Whitehaven
8373	38v			Jane	Dixon	wif m	28		Dur Durham
8374	38v			Richard	Dixon	son	12	scholar	Mdx Islington
8375	38v			Ann E.T.	Dixon	dau	6	scholar	Dur Durham
8376	38v			John E.T.	Dixon	son	4		Dur Durham
8377	38v			Robert M.	Dixon	son	2		Dur Durham
8378	38v			Samuel G.	Dixon	son	9m		Dur Durham
8379	38v			Thomas	Thwaites	blw	24	Post Office clerk	Dur Durham
8380	38v	[aa]	Paradise Lane	John	Sime	hea m	60	gardener	Sct
8381	38v			Mary	Sime	wif m	34		Dur Durham
8382	38v			David	Sime	son	18		Dur Durham
8383	38v			John	Sime	son	15	printer's apprentice	Dur Durham
8384	38v			John	Jenkyns	ldr	25	whitesmith	Sct
8385	38v			John	Turner	ldr w	47	land surveyor	Dur Cockfield
8386	38v	[ab]	Paradise Lane	John	Garry	hea	34	whitesmith	Dur Bishop Auckland
8387	38v			Margaret	Garry	sis	16		Dur Bishop Auckland
			one house building						
8388	38v	[ac]	Paradise Lane	Mary	Walker	wif m	45	dressmaker	Dur Durham
8389	38v			Frances I.	Walker	dau	14		Dur Swalwell
8390	39r			Robert S.	Walker	son	10	scholar	Nbl Newcastle
8391	39r			Andrew	James	vis	2		Nbl Newcastle
8392	39r	[ad]	Paradise Lane	Robert	Horn	hea m	52	spirit merchant's porter	Dur [D] Claypath
8393	39r			Margaret	Horn	wif m	41		Dur Elwick
8394	39r			John	Horn	son	23	tailor	Dur [D] Framwelgate
8395	39r			Thomas	Horn	son	6	scholar	Dur [D] S. Nicholas
8396	39r			Anne	Horn	dau	3		Dur [D] S. Nicholas
8397	39r	[ae]	Paradise Lane	George	Bell	hea m	45	butcher	Nry Stainton
8398	39r			Mary	Bell	wif m	45		Dur Auckland S.Andrew
8399	39r	[af]	Paradise Lane	Isabella	Weelands	hea w	47	milliner & dressmaker	Nbl Newcastle
8400	39r			Margaret	Weelands	dau	23	staymaker	Nbl Newcastle
8401	39r			John R.	Weelands	son	21	bookbinder	Dur Seaham Harbour
8402	39r			Richard E.	Weelands	son	17	coach painter's app	Dur Durham
8403	39r			Robert	Weelands	son	10	scholar	Dur Durham
8404	39r	[ag]	Paradise Lane	John W.	Elliott	hea m	46	sheriff's officer *	Dur [D] S. Margaret
8405	39r			Isabella	Elliott	wif m	46		Dur Brancepeth
8406	39r			Anne	Elliott	dau	14	scholar	Dur [D] S. Nicholas
8407	39r			Mary Jane	Elliott	dau	11	scholar	Dur [D] S. Nicholas
8408	39r			Elizabeth Ann	Elliott	dau	6		Dur [D] S. Nicholas
8409	39r		Paradise House	Charles	Ebdy	hea m	54	boatbuilder	Dur Durham
8410	39v			Henrietta	Ebdy	wif m	50		Dur Norton
8411	39v			Henry	Ebdy	son	32	boatbuilder	Dur Durham
8412	39v			Louisa	Ebdy	dau	29		Dur Durham
8413	39v			Charlotte	Ebdy	dau	23		Dur Durham
8414	39v			Eliza	Ebdy	dau	21		Dur Durham
8415	39v			Maria	Ebdy	dau	18		Dur Durham
8416	39v	[aa]	Water Side	John	Chisman	hea m	37	whitesmith & bellhanger*	Dur Durham
8417	39v			Sarah	Chisman	wif m	38		Dur Durham
8418	39v			Lucy	Chisman	dau	9	scholar	Dur Durham

8419	39v	[aa]	Water Side	Anne Chisman	dau		7	scholar	Dur Durham
8420	39v			John Chisman	son		5	scholar	Dur Durham
8421	39v			Fanny Chisman	dau		3	scholar	Dur Durham
8422	39v			Ellen Chisman	dau		1		Dur Durham
8423	39v			Elizabeth Hall	ser		19	house servant	Dur Hetton-le-Hole
8424	39v	[ab]	Water Side	William Kirby	hea	m	54	coachman	Nry Thirsk
8425	39v			Elizabeth Kirby	wif	m	49		Dur Durham
8426	39v			Robert L. Kirby	son		12	scholar	Dur Durham
8427	39v			Anne Kirby	dau		8	scholar	Dur Durham

Notes - Enumeration District 4a

7777	... colliery viewer and manager <Dixon & Thwaites, Kepier Colliery>
7794	... in general practice ...
7803	<Wesleyan Methodist chapel, 57 Old Elvet>
7807	... and boarding ...
7824	<Henderson & Co., Back Lane>
7844	... London, in general practice
7852	<lodgings>
7853	... & teadlr, master emp 10 [men] and boy
7855	... & straw-bonnetmaker, mistress employing 8 women and 1 girl
7859	... agent for British & Foreign Bible Soc
7864	<Durham County Advertiser, & printer>
7867-7868	<Durham County Advertiser, & printer>
7876	<cattle jobber>
7889	... sergeant 16th Light Dragoons
7894	<& bookseller & library>
7901-7902	number given as "66"
7903-7905	number given as "67"
7906	... master emp 14 men and 7 apprentices <& timber merchant>
7936	county given as "Durham"
8001-8007	number given as "28"
8008	... and porter
8024	... master employing [blank] men <& timber merchant>
8029	... master employing 4 men
8034	... & innkeeper <'Newcastle House'>
8047	... & lodging house keeper
8082	... & lodging house keeper
8142	<& ready-made clothes depot>
8151	<& furniture broker>
8162	<'Seven Stars'>
8211	[entered and totalled as "female"]; ... employing 1 journeyman
8219	<dealer in old clothes>
8254	<'Black Swan'>
8290	... master emp [blank] men <& brickmaker>
8322	... master employing 10 men
8329	... master employing 3 men
8330	county given as "Durham"
8343	... and landscape ...
8358	<& eating house & confectioner>
8367	... master employing 3 men
8404	... & auctioneer <& appraiser & gardener>
8416	<& iron and brass founder>

REF	FOL	NO	STREET	FORENAME(S) SURNAME	REL	C	AGE	OCCUPATION	BIRTHPLACE
8428	43v	63	Claypath	Christopher Blyth	hea	m	50	publican *	Nry Melmerby
8429	43v			Ellen Blyth	wif	m	45		Wry Grantley
8430	43v			Elizabeth Anne Blyth	dau		14	scholar	Nry Sutton
8431	43v			James Blyth	son		11	scholar	Nry Sutton
8432	43v	62	Claypath	Martha Atkinson	hea	w	70	hosier	Dur [D] S. Nicholas
8433	43v			Mary Atkinson	dau		39		Dur [D] S. Nicholas
8434	43v			William Atkinson	son	m	47	tailor (master)	Dur [D] S. Nicholas
8435	43v			Jane Atkinson	dlw	m	50		Nbl Ponteland
8436	43v			Sarah Atkinson	gda		22	bonnetmaker	Dur [D] S. Nicholas
8437	43v			Charles Atkinson	gsn		16	tailor (apprentice)	Dur [D] S. Nicholas
8438	43v			Martha Atkinson	gda		7	scholar	Dur [D] S. Nicholas
8439	43v	<61>	Claypath	Richard Gilbertson	hea	m	47	gardener & seedsman *	Dur [D] S. Oswald
8440	43v			Margaret Gilbertson	wif	m	47		Dur [D] S. Oswald
8441	43v			Anne Gilbertson	dau		22		Dur [D] S. Oswald
8442	43v			William Gilbertson	son		20	gardener	Dur [D] S. Nicholas
8443	43v			Matthias Gilbertson	son		14		Dur [D] S. Giles
8444	43v			Margaret Gilbertson	dau		12	scholar	Dur [D] S. Nicholas
8445	43v			Mary Gilbertson	dau		7	scholar	Dur [D] S. Nicholas
8446	44r	60 a	Claypath	Francis Newton	hea	m	39	joiner	Dur Hamsterley
8447	44r			Mary Newton	wif	m	51		Dur Wolsingham
8448	44r			Henry Newton	son		11	scholar	Dur [D] S. Giles
8449	44r	60 b	Claypath	John Allan	hea		50	shoemaker	Dur [D] S. Nicholas
8450	44r	60 c	Claypath	John Newton	hea	m	45	cartman	Dur Hamsterley
8451	44r			Mary Newton	wif	m	53		Dur Bishop Auckland
8452	44r			Rebecca Newton	dau		18		Dur [D] S. Giles
8453	44r	60 d	Claypath	Thomas Young	hea	w	74	coalminer, parish relief	Nbl Newburn
8454	44r	60 e	Claypath	Thomas Crowther	hea	m	41	handloom weaver (carpet)	Sal Farley /"Feirly"
8455	44r			Mary Crowther	wif	m	44		Dur
8456	44r	60 f	Claypath	Robert Summerbell	hea	m	27	handloom weaver (carpet)	Dur [D] S. Giles
8457	44r			Mary Summerbell	wif	m	31		Dur South Shields
8458	44r			Martha Summerbell	dau		5	scholar	Nbl North Shields
8459	44r			Elizabeth Summerbell	dau		1		Dur [D] S. Nicholas
8460	44r	60 g	Claypath	Isabel Maddison	hea	w	74	receiving parish relief	Dur Stanhope
8461	44r			Edward Maddison	son		38	shoemaker	Dur [D] S. Oswald
8462	44r			Eleanor Maddison	gda		18		Dur [D] S. Nicholas
8463	44r	58	Claypath	George Coward	hea	m	46	<wholesale> stationer *	Ery Bridlington
8464	44r			Elizabeth Coward	wif	m	50		Dur Castle Eden
8465	44r			Susanna Coward	dau		20		Dur [D] S. Nicholas
8466	44v			John Coward	son		18	apprentice [stationer?]	Dur [D] S. Margaret
8467	44v			Edward Coward	son		14	scholar	Dur [D] S. Margaret
8468	44v			Henry Coward	son		11	scholar	Dur [D] S. Margaret
8469	44v			Mary Turner	vis		20	dressmaker	Lan Oldham
8470	44v			Jane Thomas	ser		17	house servant	Dur Ferryhill
8471	44v	57 a	Claypath	Thomas Westgarth	hea	m	54	cabinetmaker (master)	Dur Easington
8472	44v			Mary Ann Westgarth	wif		51	<hosier>	Nbl Newcastle All SS.
8473	44v	57 b	Claypath	George Irvine	hea	m	33	grocer	Dur Norton
8474	44v			Frances Irvine	wif	m	34	formerly dressmaker	Dur [D] S. Nicholas
8475	44v	56	Claypath	James F.W. Johnstone	hea	m	52	reader in chemistry *	Sct
8476	44v			Margaret Hamilton	ser		23	house servant	Sct
8477	44v			Catherine J. Alderson	ser		24	house servant	Dur Coatham
8478	44v	55 a	Claypath	Josiah Bell	hea	m	35	pork butcher *	Nry Dalton
8479	44v			Ann Bell	wif	m	23	wife	Wry Bishop Monkton
8480	44v	55 b	Claypath	James Hind	hea		31	shoemaker (master)	Dur Sherburn House
8481	44v	55 c	Claypath	George Knox	hea	m	23	cabinetmaker	Nbl Berwick
8482	44v			Jane Knox	wif	m	20		Nbl Tweedmouth
8483	44v			Jane Gibson Knox	dau		10m		Nbl Tweedmouth
8484	44v	55 d	Claypath	John Herbert	hea	m	30	gardener (master)	Dur
8485	44v			Ann Herbert	wif	m	30	dressmaker	Dur
8486	45r			Sarah Herbert	dau		5	scholar	Dur
8487	45r	55 e	Claypath	Harriet Thomson	hea		20	dressmaker	Dur Ferryhill
8488	45r	53	Claypath	Thomas Brown	hea	m	53	chorister <lay clerk *>	Dur
8489	45r			Margaret Brown	wif	m	53		Dur Brandon
8490	45r			Mary Ann Ridley	ser		27	house servant	Dur Darlington
8491	45r	52	Claypath	Richard G. Rimington	hea	m	30	painter & glazier	Sry Rotherhithe
8492	45r			Ann Rimington	wif	m	32		Dur [D] S. Nicholas
8493	45r			Mary Jane Rimington	dau		7	school	Dur [D] S. Nicholas
8494	45r			John George Rimington	son		4		Dur [D] S. Nicholas
8495	45r			Anne Rimington	dau		2		Dur [D] S. Nicholas
8496	45r			Emma Rimington	dau		9m		Dur [D] S. Nicholas
8497	45r			Jane Rimington	mth	w	60	dressmaker	Dur Kelloe
8498	45r			George Pybus	ldr		30	solicitor's managing clk	Nry Kirkby Fleetham
8499	45r			Catherine Young	ser		14	house servant	Dur Broomside
8500	45r	51	Claypath	Thomas Ebdon	hea		64	vicar of Billingham	Lnd Marylebone
8501	45r			Sarah Thwaites	ser		57	housekeeper	Dur [D] S. Oswald
8502	45r			Sarah Thwaites	ser		21	house servant	Dur [D] S. Oswald
8503	45r	<49>	Claypath	James Jackson	hea		44	annuitant	Dur Brancepeth
8504	45r			Mary Pattison	ser		28	domestic servant	Dur Sunderland
8505	45v	51	Claypath	William Robison	hea	m	36	supt of <borough> police	Nbl Burnfoot
8506	45v			Jane Robison	wif	m	28		Nbl Heatherslaw

8507	45v	51	Claypath	Mary Ann Robison	dau	7	scholar	Dur [D] S. Nicholas
8508	45v			William Robison	son	8m	infant	Dur [D] S. Nicholas
8509	45v	<48>	Claypath	Mary Marshall	hea w	71	proprietor of houses	Cul
8510	45v			Henry Marshall	son	46	alderman & solicitor	Dur
8511	45v			Mary Davidson	ser	22	house servant	Dur
8512	45v	47	Claypath	Elizabeth Elliott	hea	30	milliner	Dur Houghton
8513	45v			Jane Elliott	sis m	40	milliner	Dur Houghton
8514	45v			James Muers	sho	20	shopman	Dur [South] Shields
8515	45v			Elizabeth Shields	ser	19	servant	Dur Merrington
8516	45v	46	Claypath	Lydia E. Painter	hea m	52	scholastic	Lnd Covent Garden
8517	45v			Emma Parker	fri	21	scholastic	Oxf Chalgrove
8518	45v			Mary Irvine	ser	13	servant	Cul Workington
8519	45v			Elijah Craven	ldr m	31	directory publisher	Wry Leeds
8520	45v			Sarah Craven	ldr m	32	wife	Lin Boston
8521	45v			Hannah P. Craven	ldr	4	daughter	Ntt Nottingham
8522	45v			Alonzo Craven	ldr	1	son	Lin Lincoln
8523	45v	45	Claypath	Edward Fairclough	hea m	77	retired builder	Lan Prescot
8524	45v			Ann Fairclough	wif m	73		Dur [D] S. Nicholas
8525	46r			John Fairclough	son	38	joiner	Dur [D] S. Nicholas
8526	46r			Edward Fairclough	son	35	joiner	Dur [D] S. Nicholas
8527	46r			James Henry Fairclough	son	30	upholsterer (master)	Dur [D] S. Nicholas
8528	46r	44	Claypath	James Longstaff	hea m	50	solicitor	Nry Ayton
8529	46r			Sophia Jane Longstaff	wif m	32		Dur [D] S. Nicholas
8530	46r			Ann Sophia Longstaff	dau	10m		Dur [D] S. Nicholas
8531	46r			Mary Jane Lumley	ser	15	house servant	Dur [D] S. Margaret
			one house unoccupied					
8532	46r	42	Claypath	Margaret Watson	hea w	38	publican *	Nry Raskelf
8533	46r			Thomas Watson	son	15	solicitor's clerk	Dur
8534	46r			Hannah Watson	dau	12	scholar	Dur
8535	46r			Francis Watson	son	10	scholar	Dur
8536	46r			Matthew Lamb Thompson	vis	44	butcher	Dur Bishop Auckland
8537	46r	41	Claypath	Robert Chapman	hea m	22	mason	Dur Gateshead
8538	46r			Mary Chapman	wif m	22		Dur [D] S. Nicholas
8539	46r			Jane Dunn	nce	1		Dur [D] S. Giles
8540	46r	41	Claypath	Dorothy Atkinson	hea	35	lodging house keeper	Dur [D] S. Nicholas
8541	46r			Martha McIntosh	nce	8		Gls Bristol
8542	46r			William Fitzjerrald	ldr	25	banker's clerk	Nry Guisborough
8543	46v	40	Claypath	Ann Turner	hea	56	proprietor of houses	Dur Staindrop
8544	46v			Hannah Turner	sis	45	proprietor of houses	Dur Cockfield
8545	46v			Mary Newton	vis w	56	landed proprietor	Dur Whorlton
8546	46v			Margaret Eggleston	ser	20	house servant	Dur [D] S. Nicholas
8547	46v	39	Claypath	Arthur R. Webb	hea w	52	schoolmaster	Ham Southampton
8548	46v			Mary Ann Webb	dau	28		Dur [D] S. Giles
8549	46v			Arthur Webb	son	6		Dur [D] S. Nicholas
8550	46v			Eva Fanny Webb	dau	3		Dur [D] S. Nicholas
8551	46v			Margaret Atchinson	ser	19	servant	Dur New Lambton
			one house uninhabited					
8552	46v	37 a	Claypath	Elizabeth Magistris	hea w	56	dressmaker	Dur [D] S. Margaret
8553	46v	37 b	Claypath	Eleanor Jackson	hea w	70	annuitant	Dur [D] S. Nicholas
8554	46v	<36>	Claypath	William Crowe	hea	62	grocer (master)	Dur [D] S. Nicholas
8555	46v			Catherine Crowe	sis	68		Dur [D] S. Nicholas
8556	46v	35 a	Claypath	Robert Macnamarra	hea w	34	clothes broker	Irl
8557	46v	35 b	Claypath	Jane Webster	hea w	34	cabinetmaker, mistress *	Dur [D] Framwelgate
8558	46v			Mary Webster	dau	10	scholar at home	Dur [D] Framwelgate
8559	46v			Thomas Webster	son	5	scholar at home	Dur [D] S. Nicholas
8560	46v			John Webster	son	10m		Dur [D] S. Nicholas
8561	46v			James Webster	blw	21	cabinetmaker, journeyman	Yks Gowback Hill
8562	47r	35 c	Claypath	John Cain	hea m	25	joiner	Nry Richmond
8563	47r			Elizabeth Cain	wif	24		Dur Stockton
8564	47r			Eleanor Cain	dau	3	scholar	Nry Northallerton
8565	47r	35 d	Claypath	John Kirkley	hea m	30	painter	Dur [D] S. Oswald
8566	47r			Elizabeth Kirkley	wif m	36		Dur [D] S. Giles
8567	47r	35 e	Claypath	Eleanor Dobson	hea w	30	bootbinder	Nry Richmond
8568	47r			Mary Jane Dobson	dau	9	scholar	Dur Haswell
8569	47r			John Roland Dobson	son	2		Dur [D] S. Nicholas
8570	47r	33	Claypath	William Gettins	hea m	40	fruiterer	Irl
8571	47r			Isabella Gettins	wif m	38		Wes Kendal
8572	47r			Isaac Wilson	flw w	75	formerly butcher	Wes Kendal
8573	47r			Catherine Gettins	nce	22	housekeeper	Lan Manchester
8574	47r			Hannah Britton	ser	19	servant	Yks
8575	47r			John Casey	ser	20	servant	Lan Ashton-under-Lyne
8576	47r			Mary Gettins	nce	11	scholar	Lan Manchester
8577	47r			Isabella Gettins	nce	7	scholar	Lan Manchester
8578	47r	[bm]	Claypath	John Swiney	hea m	49	hawker	Ham Portsmouth
8579	47r			Ann Swiney	wif m	34		Nry Stokesley
8580	47r			Robert Brittan	sso	18	woolsorter	Nry Stokesley
8581	47r			Adam Brittan	sso	14	woolsorter	Nry Stokesley
8582	47v			Thomas Moore	ldr	24	horse dealer	Dur Houghton
8583	47v			Richard Young	ldr m	22	horse dealer	Yks Kendale
8584	47v	34	Claypath	Thomas Hopper	hea m	54	upholsterer, master *	Dur
8585	47v			Jane Hopper	wif m	53		Dur Cockerton

8586	47v	34	Claypath	Isabella Hopper	dau	28	milliner etc.	Dur
8587	47v			George Hopper	son	24	off of Inland Revenue *	Dur
8588	47v			Lambton Hopper	son	22	upholsterer *	Dur
8589	47v			Elizabeth Hopper	dau	20	dressmaker	Dur
8590	47v	[aa]a	Providence Row	James Megoran	hea m	26	printer (compositor)	Nbl Newcastle
8591	47v			Ann Megoran	wif m	28		Dur Morton
8592	47v			Hannah Megoran	dau	4		Nbl Newcastle
8593	47v			Sarah Ann Megoran	dau	1m		Dur
8594	47v	[aa]b	Providence Row	Hannah Coverdale	hea m	40	household duties	Dur Darlington
8595	47v			Mary Ann Coverdale	dau	8	scholar	Dur Stockton
8596	47v	[aa]c	Providence Row	Thomas Pickering	hea	19	ironmonger	Cul Garrigill
8597	47v			Jane Smith	ser m	30	servant	Nbl Blyth
8598	47v			George Smith		1	servant's son	Dur
8599	47v	15	Providence Row	James Waistell	hea m	35	prison officer	Dur Darlington
8600	47v			Margaret Waistell	wif m	33		Dur Darlington
8601	47v			Mary Ann Waistell	dau	11	scholar	Dur Darlington
8602	48r			John Waistell	son	6	scholar	Dur [D] S. Nicholas
8603	48r	14	Providence Row	Robert Oswald	hea m	52	watchmaker (master)	Dur [D] S. Nicholas
8604	48r			Mary Oswald	wif m	45		Dur Lanchester
8605	48r			Robert Oswald	son	14		Dur [D] S. Nicholas
8606	48r			Mary Oswald	dau	19		Dur [D] S. Nicholas
8607	48r	13	Providence Row	John Anderson	hea m	37	cabinetmaker (jnym)	Dur [D] S. Nicholas
8608	48r			Mary Anderson	wif m	40		Dur Sunderland
8609	48r			Elizabeth Ann Anderson	dau	11	school	Dur Durham
8610	48r			John Anderson	son	9	school	Dur Durham
8611	48r			Thomas Anderson	son	8	school	Dur Durham
8612	48r	12	Providence Row	Terence Boyle	hea m	40	bookseller	Irl
8613	48r			Mary Boyle	wif m	38		Irl
8614	48r			Alice Boyle	dau	17		Irl
8615	48r			Margaret Boyle	dau	16		Irl
8616	48r			Patrick Boyle	son	14	scholar	Irl
8617	48r			James Boyle	son	11	scholar	Wry Leeds
8618	48r			Mary Anne Boyle	dau	9	scholar	Dur Durham
8619	48r			Terence Boyle	son	7	scholar	Dur Durham
8620	48r			Catherine Boyle	dau	5	scholar	Dur Durham
8621	48r			John Charles Boyle	son	1		Dur Durham
8622	48v	11	Providence Row	Robert Tiplady	hea m	33	currier, master *	Dur [D] S. Oswald
8623	48v			Ann Tiplady	wif m	28		Mdx London
8624	48v			Miriam Tiplady	dau	6		Dur [D] S. Nicholas
8625	48v			Catherine Tiplady	dau	1		Dur [D] S. Nicholas
8626	48v			Elizabeth Taylor	ser	24	house servant	Nbl
8627	48v			Jane Craig	ser	19	house servant	Nbl Newcastle
8628	48v	10	Providence Row	James Oliver	hea m	43	cabinetmaker	Dur
8629	48v			Mary Oliver	wif m	44		Dur
8630	48v	9	Providence Row	John Chapman	hea m	47	mason	Nbl North Shields
8631	48v			Jane Chapman	wif m	47		Nbl North Shields
8632	48v			John Chapman	son	20	solicitor's clerk	Nbl Newcastle
8633	48v			Mary Ann Chapman	dau	17		Dur
8634	48v			George Chapman	son	14		Dur
8635	48v			William Chapman	son	8		Dur
8636	48v			Henry Stobert	*	1m		Dur
8637	48v	8	Providence Row	William Barron	hea m	44	joiner	Nbl Newburn
8638	48v			Ann Barron	wif m	43		Dur Durham
8639	48v			Ann Barron	dau	15		Dur Durham
8640	48v			William Barron	son	13	scholar	Dur Durham
8641	48v			Mary Barron	dau	20	servant	Dur Durham
8642	49r			Susanna Barron	dau	18	service, domestic	Dur Durham
8643	49r			John Barron	son	10	scholar	Dur Durham
8644	49r			Matthew Barron	son	8	scholar	Dur Durham
8645	49r			Thomas Barron	son	5	scholar	Dur Durham
8646	49r			Matilda Louther	gda	4	scholar	Dur Durham
8647	49r	7	Providence Row	Margaret Brownrigg	hea w	33	dressmaker	Dur Sunderland
8648	49r			John Brownrigg	son	12	scholar	Dur [D] S. Nicholas
8649	49r			William Brownrigg	son	3		Dur [D] S. Nicholas
8650	49r			William Wilson	ldr	25	compositor	Dur Stockton
8651	49r			Alfred Porter	ldr	28	compositor	Mdx London
8652	49r			Robert Ayre	ldr	15	joiner	Dur Usworth
8653	49r			William Craggs	ldr m	31	compositor	Dur
8654	49r	6	Providence Row	John Rutherford	hea m	59	hatter	Nbl Hexham
8655	49r			Ann Rutherford	wif m	57		Yks Alston
8656	49r			Edward Rutherford	son	24	shoemaker	Dur
8657	49r	5	Providence Row	Thomas Worthy	hea m	62	shoemaker	Dur [D] S. Nicholas
8658	49r			Margaret Worthy	wif m	61		Dur [D] S. Nicholas
8659	49r			Elizabeth Worthy	dau	30	dressmaker	Dur [D] S. Nicholas
8660	49r			Thomas Worthy	son	26	cooper	Dur [D] S. Nicholas
8661	49r			George Worthy	son	24	basketmaker	Dur [D] S. Nicholas
8662	49v			Francis Worthy	son	22	shoemaker	Dur
8663	49v			William Worthy	son	21	shoemaker	Dur
8664	49v			James Worthy	son	19	shoemaker	Dur
8665	49v			Nicholas Reed	*	15	shoemaker	Dur Sunderland
8666	49v	[ab]a	Providence Row	Ann Mather	hea w	66	laundress	Nry Cleasby

8667	49v	[ab]b	Providence Row	Sarah Porter	hea w	53	laundress	Nbl Haltwhistle
8668	49v			John Porter	son	16	grocer (apprentice)	Nry Lartington
8669	49v			Sarah Porter	dau	14		Nry Lartington
8670	49v			Ann Porter	dau	9	scholar	Nry Lartington
8671	49v	[ac]	Providence Row	Robert Crudass	hea m	60	miller	Nry Danby
8672	49v			Barbara Crudass	wif m	53		Dur [D] S. Giles
8673	49v			Margaret Crudass	dau	26	dressmaker	Dur [D] S. Nicholas
8674	49v	[ad]	Providence Row	Ann Crawford	wif m	45		Dur [D] S. Margaret
8675	49v			William Crawford	son	14	tailor, apprentice	Lan Manchester
8676	49v			Henry Crawford	son	12	scholar	Lan Manchester
8677	49v			Mary Elizabeth Crawford	dau	7	scholar	Lan Manchester
8678	49v			Sarah Crawford	dau	6	scholar	Lan Manchester
8679	49v			Ann Crawford	dau	4	at home	Lan Manchester
8680	49v			Margaret Jane Crawford	dau	1	at home	Lan Manchester
8681	50r	[ae]	Providence Row	Peter Thorpe	hea m	46	quarryman	Dur [D] S. Margaret
8682	50r			Isabel Thorpe	wif m	46		Dur [D] S. Margaret
8683	50r			Isabel Thorpe	dau	22		Dur [D] S. Margaret
8684	50r			Isaac Thorpe	son	15	tailor (apprentice)	Dur [D] S. Margaret
8685	50r			Hannah Thorpe	dau	13	scholar	Dur [D] S. Margaret
8686	50r			Peter Thorpe	son	8	scholar	Dur [D] S. Margaret
8687	50r			Thomas Thorpe	son	3	scholar	Dur [D] S. Margaret
8688	50r		Sands Cottage	William Parker	hea m	31	mason	Dur [D] S. Giles
8689	50r			Eliza Parker	wif m	33		Dur [D] S. Oswald
8690	50r			Thomas Parker	son	11	scholar	Dur [D] S. Margaret
8691	50r			Elizabeth Parker	dau	6	scholar	Dur [D] S. Nicholas
8692	50r			Mary Parker	dau	5	scholar	Dur [D] S. Nicholas
8693	50r	[aa]	Sands	Thomas Parker	hea m	36	joiner	Dur [D] S. Giles
8694	50r			Jane Parker	wif m	39		Dur [D] S. Margaret
8695	50r			William Parker	son	16	joiner	Dur [D] S. Margaret
8696	50r			John Parker	son	14	cabinetmaker	Wry Bramley
8697	50r			Thomas Parker	son	10	scholar	Dur [D] S. Margaret
8698	50r			George Parker	son	8	scholar	Dur [D] S. Margaret
8699	50r	[ab]	Sands	Thomas Palmer	hea m	37	shoemaker	Dur [D] S. Giles
8700	50r			Mary Palmer	wif m	37		Cul Carlisle
8701	50v			Isabella Palmer	dau	14	scholar	Dur [D] S. Nicholas
8702	50v			John Palmer	son	12	scholar	Dur [D] S. Nicholas
8703	50v			Thomas Palmer	son	9	scholar	Dur [D] S. Nicholas
8704	50v			Henry Palmer	son	7	scholar	Dur [D] S. Nicholas
8705	50v			William Palmer	son	5	scholar	Dur [D] S. Nicholas
8706	50v			Mary Jane Palmer	dau	6m		Dur [D] S. Nicholas
8707	50v	[ac]	Sands	George Wilson Cawood	hea m	29	solicitor's managing clk	Dur Sunderland
8708	50v			Frances C. Cawood	wif m	28		Dur Durham
8709	50v			Charles Iveson Cawood	son	1		Dur Durham
8710	50v	[ad]	Sands	Robert French	hea m	63	retired brickmaker	Dur Durham
8711	50v			Margaret French	wif m	63		Dur Durham
8712	50v	[ae]	Sands	John Frazer	hea m	48	farm labourer	Dur Bishopwearmouth
8713	50v			Elizabeth Frazer	wif m	40	laundress	Dur
8714	50v			Margaret Frazer	dau	11	scholar	Dur [D] S. Giles
8715	50v			Ann Frazer	dau	9	scholar	Dur [D] S. Giles
8716	50v			William Frazer	son	5	scholar	Dur [D] S. Giles
8717	50v			John Frazer	son	2		Dur [D] S. Giles
8718	50v	[af]	Providence Row	Simon Binks Tilly	hea m	41	tailor, master emp 1 man	Dur [D] S. Nicholas
8719	50v			Dorothy Tilly	wif m	44		Dur Cockerton
8720	50v			Isabella Tilly	dau	8	scholar	Dur [D] S. Nicholas
8721	51r			Elizabeth Tilly	dau	4	scholar	Dur [D] S. Nicholas
8722	51r	2	Providence Row	Patrick O'Neil	hea m	38	cabinetmaker	Irl
8723	51r			Mary O'Neil	wif m	33		Dur Chester-le-Street
8724	51r			Mary Ann O'Neil	dau	6	scholar	Dur Hetton-le-Hole
8725	51r			Jane Winship	sis m	29	staymaker	Dur Chester-le-Street
8726	51r	[bn]	Claypath	John Champion	hea m	37	teacher, elementary sch	Con Redruth
8727	51r			Ursula Millet Champion	wif m	40		Con Merther
8728	51r			John David Champion	son	1		Dur Durham
8729	51r	33	Claypath	John Brewster Chapman	hea m	43	grocer	Nry Northallerton
8730	51r			Mary Chapman	wif m	36		Dur [D] S. Nicholas
8731	51r			Jane Elizabeth Chapman	dau	12	scholar	Dur [D] S. Nicholas
8732	51r			Mary Chapman	dau	9	scholar	Dur [D] S. Nicholas
8733	51r			George Chapman	son	6	scholar	Dur [D] S. Nicholas
8734	51r			Charles Chapman	son	5		Dur [D] S. Nicholas
8735	51r			Margaret Chapman	dau	3		Dur [D] S. Nicholas
8736	51r			Edwin Francis Chapman	son	1		Dur [D] S. Nicholas
8737	51r			Ann Wright	ser	21	house servant	Dur [D] S. Nicholas
8738	51r			Sarah Hutchinson	ser	17	house servant	Dur [D] S. Nicholas
8739	51v	32	Claypath	John Mohun	hea m	48	blacksmith	Dur Tudhoe
8740	51v			Jane Mohun	wif m	46	<straw-hatmaker>	Dur Norton
8741	51v			Ann Mohun	dau	23		Dur
8742	51v			Henry R. Mohun	son	12	scholar	Dur
8743	51v			Alice Robinson	ldr w	65	lodger	Dur
8744	51v			William M. Evans	ldr	20	student	Cgn Aberystwyth
8745	51v			Eliza Coulthard	ser	17	house servant	Dur Butterknowle
8746	51v	30	Claypath	Mary Raine	hea w	53	maltster	Dur Summerhouse
8747	51v			Elizabeth Raine	dau	26		Dur

8748	51v	30	Claypath	William Cummins	bro w	60	maltman	Dur Heworth
			one house uninhabited					
8749	51v	29 a	Claypath	Richard Palmer	hea m	41	victualler <'Maltman'>	Nth Northampton
8750	51v			Margaret Palmer	wif m	36		Dur Witton Gilbert
8751	51v			Mary Palmer	dau	15		Dur Burdon
8752	51v			Elizabeth Palmer	dau	9	scholar	Dur Durham
8753	51v			William Palmer	son	7	scholar	Dur Durham
8754	51v			Ralph Palmer	son	5	scholar	Dur Durham
8755	51v			Sarah Palmer	dau	4	scholar	Dur Durham
8756	51v			Margaret Palmer	dau	1		Dur Durham
8757	51v			Isaac Miller	ldr m	40	horse dealer	Nbl Hexham
8758	52r			Thomas Donley	ldr	26	horse dealer	Nbl Hexham
8759	52r			John Sowerby	ldr	23	horse dealer	Nbl Hexham
8760	52r	29 b	Claypath	William Whitehead	hea w	69	saddler	Dur [D] S. Oswald
8761	52r	28 a	Claypath	John Bradley	hea m	54	sub verger, Cathedral	Dur
8762	52r			Margaret Bradley	wif m	49		Dur
8763	52r			Eleanor Bradley	dau	20	milliner	Dur
8764	52r			Dorothy Bradley	dau	16	dressmaker	Dur
8765	52r			Frances Bradley	dau	13		Dur
8766	52r			Elizabeth Bradley	dau	9	scholar	Dur
8767	52r			Isabella Bradley	dau	6		Dur
8768	52r			George Dixon	blw	55	labourer	Dur
8769	52r			Ann Barber	dau m	30	visitor	Dur
8770	52r			John Bradley Barber	gsn	3m		Ntt Nottingham
8771	52r	28 b	Claypath	Joseph Hobkirk	hea m	32	fruit merchant	Dur Westoe
8772	52r			Mary Ann Hobkirk	wif m	31		Dur Boldon
8773	52r			James Hobkirk	son	10		Nbl Wallsend
8774	52r			Sarah Hobkirk	dau	6		Dur Durham
8775	52r			Mary Kearns	ser	18	house servant	Irl
8776	52v	<30>	Claypath	Hannah Teasdale	wif m	46		Nry Kirby Hill
8777	52v			Silena Russell	sda	21		Sts Bilston
8778	52v			Robert Russell	sso	14	printer & bookbinder	Lan Burnley
8779	52v			Henry Teasdale	hea m	39	tea dealer <& grocer>	Nbl Newcastle
8780	52v			Mary Ann Teasdale	dau	5		Dur
8781	52v			Hannah Milburn	mlw w	68		Nry Feetham
8782	52v	26	Claypath	Harriet Gill	hea w	36	charwoman /"chairwoman"	Yks Long Counton
8783	52v			John Gill	son	14	shoemaker (apprentice)	Dur Stockton
8784	52v			Hannah Gill	dau	11	scholar	Dur Durham
8785	52v			Henry Gill	son	9	scholar	Dur Durham
8786	52v	27	Claypath	Matthew Wardell	hea m	70	architect	Dur [D] S. Nicholas
8787	52v			Ann Wardell	wif m	82		Dur Fir Tree
8788	52v			Isabella Story	ser	14	house servant	Dur Sherburn Hill
8789	52v	<27>a	Claypath	William Bowey	hea m	32	master joiner *	Dur Durham
8790	52v			Margery Bowey	wif m	32		Dur Fencehouses
8791	52v			Mary Bowey	dau	4		Dur Durham
8792	52v			William Bowey	son	1		Dur Durham
8793	52v			Thomas Bowey	son	2m		Dur Durham
8794	52v			Elizabeth Coxon	vis	26	house servant	Dur Chester-le-Street
8795	52v	<27>b	Claypath	William Preston	hea m	51	porter	Dur
8796	53r			Jane Preston	wif m	48		Dur Sunderland
8797	53r			Elizabeth Preston	nce	14		Dur
8798	53r	<27>c	Claypath	Joseph Longstaff	hea m	25	cartman	Nry Barton
8799	53r			Ellen Longstaff	wif m	30		Dur Darlington
8800	53r			James Longstaff	son	5	scholar	Nry Melsonby
8801	53r			William Longstaff	son	2	scholar	Dur
8802	53r			Edward Longstaff	son	3m		Dur
8803	53r			Joseph Hope	ldr	21	cartman	Dur Witton-le-Wear
8804	53r	<27>d	Claypath	George Salmon	hea m	46	traveller (groceries)	Sfk Ipswich *
8805	53r			Ann Salmon	wif m	46		Wry Ripon
8806	53r			John Smith	vis m	48	cattle driver	Dur Cockerton
8807	53r			John Smith	vis	16	cattle driver	Dur Cockerton
8808	53r	[bo]	Claypath	James Chambers	hea m	45	boot and shoemaker *	Wry Stanley
8809	53r			Ann Chambers	wif m	42		Dur Durham
8810	53r			Ann Chambers	dau	8		Dur Durham
8811	53r			Martha Chambers	dau	7		Dur Durham
8812	53r			Matthew Chambers	son	5		Dur Durham
8813	53r			James Chambers	son	3		Dur Durham
8814	53r			Henry Chambers	son	1		Dur Durham
8815	53r			Sarah Moffet	ser	17	servant	Dur Moorsley
8816	53v	26 a	Claypath	John Raper Kearton	hea	33	hosier & worsted dealer	Dur Sunderland
8817	53v	26 b	Claypath	Mary Hutchinson	hea w	59	lodging house keeper	Dur Lanchester
8818	53v			John Brown	vis	11	visitor	Dur Durham
8819	53v			John Allison	ldr	50	saddler	Dur Chester-le-Street
8820	53v			James Anderson Smart	ldr	38	saddler	Sct
8821	53v	<25>	Claypath	Robert Robson	hea m	29	grocer	Dur Hareholme
8822	53v			Ann Frances Robson	wif m	27		Dur Middle Rainton
8823	53v			John George Robson	son	3		Dur Durham
8824	53v			Thomas Robson	son	1		Dur Durham
8825	53v			Sarah Blackey	ser	14	servant	Dur Durham
8826	53v			Robert Boyes	ser	18	servant	Dur Carlton
8827	53v	<24>	Claypath	Thomas Robson	hea m	79	rope <and twine> maker *	Dur [D] S. Margaret

8828	53v	<24>	Claypath	Hannah Robson	wif m	77		{deaf} Dur Monkwearmouth
8829	53v			Isabella Robson	dau	51		Dur [D] S. Margaret
8830	53v			Hannah Robson	dau	48		Dur [D] S. Giles
8831	53v	[bp]a	Claypath	Frances Hull	hea	74	servant	Dur Chester-le-Street
8832	53v	[bp]b	Claypath	William Laing	hea m	25	carpet weaver	Sct
8833	53v			Margaret Laing	wif m	24		Sct
8834	53v			Isabella Laing	dau	4		Dur [D] S. Oswald
8835	53v			Andrew Laing	son	2		Dur Durham
8836	54r			Catherine Laing	dau	5m		Dur Durham
8837	54r	[bp]c	Claypath	William Watkin	hea m	38	bricklayer's labourer	Dur Durham
8838	54r			Ann Watkin	wif m	32		Nbl Newcastle
8839	54r	[bp]d	Claypath	John Ashworth	hea m	19	mason	Dur Durham
8840	54r			Ann Ashworth	wif m	24	dressmaker	Dur Durham
8841	54r			John Atkinson	sls	5	scholar	Dur Durham
8842	54r			Emily Ashworth	dau	4m		Dur Durham
8843	54r	25	Claypath	George Bland	hea m	27	cordwainer	Dur Durham
8844	54r			Mary Bland	wif m	39		Dur Durham
8845	54r			Sarah Ann Bland	dau	6	scholar	Dur Durham
8846	54r			Eleanor Bland	dau	3		Dur Durham
8847	54r	[bq]	Claypath	Elizabeth Deans	hea w	56	washerwoman	Dur Houghton-1-Spring
8848	54r			Elizabeth Deans	dau	27	seamstress	Dur Houghton-1-Spring
8849	54r			Isabel Deans	dau	16	seamstress	Dur Middle Rainton
8850	54r	[br]	Claypath	Catherine Winnington	hea w	67	parish relief	Irl
8851	54r			Isabella Winnington	dau	30	dressmaker	Irl
8852	54r			Charles Winnington	gsn	1		Dur [D] S. Giles
8853	54r	[bs]a	Claypath	Mary Irvin	hea	50	confectioner	Dur [D] S. Nicholas
8854	54r	[bs]b	Claypath	Harrietta Brooks	hea	54	needleworker	Lnd S. James
8855	54v	25	Claypath	Elizabeth Maguire	hea w	58	confectioner	Dur Durham
8856	54v			William Maguire	son	28	mason's labourer	Dur Durham
8857	54v			Jane Maguire	dau	23	servant	Dur Durham
8858	54v			Teresa Maguire	dau	16	servant	Dur Durham
8859	54v	24	Claypath	William E. Cochrane	hea m	31	grocer & tea dealer	Bew Ayton
8860	54v			Mary Ann Cochrane	wif m	29		Nbl Willington
8861	54v			John Edington Cochrane	son	9	school at home	Nbl Newcastle
8862	54v			William Cochrane	son	4	school at home	Dur Penshaw
8863	54v	<24>	Claypath	Emmerson Heron	hea m	38	plumber & brass founder*	Dur Durham
8864	54v			Mary Heron	wif m	37		Nbl Newbiggin
8865	54v			Ann Heron	dau	13		Dur Durham
8866	54v			Henry Heron	son	11		Dur Durham
8867	54v			Elizabeth Heron	dau	6	scholar	Dur Durham
8868	54v			William Heron	son	4		Dur Durham
8869	54v			Mary Heron	dau	2		Dur Durham
8870	54v			Thomas Brown	ser	21	plumber	Dur Durham
8871	54v			Mary Blacklock	ser	18	house servant	Dur Durham
8872	54v			Elizabeth Brown	mlw w	56	annuitant	Nbl Newbiggin
8873	54v			Alice Brown	vis m	27	tailor's wife	Nbl Harlow Hill
8874	54v			Elizabeth Brown	vis	10m		Nbl Riding /"Ryden"
8875	55r	[bt]a	Claypath	John Melvy	hea w	50	hawker of fruit	Irl
8876	55r			Ann Melvy	dau	15		Chs Stockport
8877	55r	[bt]b	Claypath	Rachael Leith	hea w	37	pauper; formerly hawker	Sct
8878	55r			John Leith	son	5		Dur
8879	55r			Catherine Leith	dau	1		Dur
8880	55r			Michael Battle	ldr m	40	huckster	Irl
8881	55r			Nancy Battle	ldr m	37	huckster's wife	Irl
8882	55r			Catherine Battle	ldr	8	huckster's child	Irl
8883	55r			Ann Battle	ldr	4m	huckster's child	Dur [D] S. Nicholas
8884	55r	<23>a	Claypath	Robert Johnson	hea m	50	labourer (mason's)	Dur
8885	55r			Jane Johnson	wif m	42		Ssx Rye *
8886	55r			John Johnson	son	22	cooper	Dur [D] S. Nicholas
8887	55r			Mary Johnson	dau	16		Dur [D] S. Nicholas
8888	55r			Ellen Johnson	dau	13		Dur [D] S. Nicholas
8889	55r			Ann Johnson	dau	9	scholar	Dur [D] S. Nicholas
8890	55r			Alice Johnson	dau	7	scholar	Dur [D] S. Nicholas
8891	55r			Robert Johnson	son	4	scholar	Dur [D] S. Nicholas
8892	55r			Thomas Johnson	son	2		Dur [D] S. Nicholas
8893	55r	<23>b	Claypath	John Wortley	hea m	31	tinplate wkr emp 1 man *	Dur [D] S. Margaret
8894	55r			Elizabeth Wortley	wif m	29		Dur Gateshead
8895	55v			Mary Ann Wortley	dau	6	scholar	Dur [D] S. Nicholas
8896	55v			Jane Elizabeth Wortley	dau	4		Dur [D] S. Nicholas
8897	55v			Hannah Wortley	dau	2		Dur [D] S. Nicholas
8898	55v	<23>c	Claypath	Ambrose Chapman	hea m	29	carpet weaver, jnym	Dur Barnard Castle
8899	55v			Hannah Chapman	wif m	31		Dur Barnard Castle
8900	55v			Sarah Chapman	dau	5m		Dur [D] S. Nicholas
8901	55v	<23>d	Claypath	Robert Allanby	hea m	37	carpet weaver	Dur Barnard Castle
8902	55v			Sarah Allanby	wif m	39		Dur Barnard Castle
8903	55v			Michael Allanby	son	14	carpet weaver	Dur Barnard Castle
8904	55v			Margaret Allanby	dau	12		Dur Barnard Castle
8905	55v			Thomas Allanby	son	10		Dur Barnard Castle
8906	55v			William Allanby	son	8		Dur [D] S. Nicholas
8907	55v			Robert Allanby	son	6		Dur [D] S. Nicholas
8908	55v			Mary Ann Allanby	dau	4		Dur [D] S. Nicholas

8909	55v	<23>d	Claypath	Jane Ann Allanby	dau		2m		Dur [D] S. Nicholas
8910	55v	<23>e	Claypath	James Gellness	hea m	27	tailor	Irl
8911	55v			Bridget Gellness	wif m	27		Irl
8912	55v			Michael Gellness	son	5		Lan Ashton-under-Lyne
8913	55v			Thomas Gellness	son	1		Dur
8914	55v			Cornelius Malcolm	vis m	31	horse dealer	Nbl Hexham
8915	56r	<23>f	Claypath	Sarah Melvy	hea m	28	fruiterer	Dev Exeter
8916	56r	<21>a	Claypath	William Clark	hea	62	feltmaker	Dur [D] S. Giles
8917	56r	<21>b	Claypath	Patrick Macguigin	hea m	37	cartman	Irl
8918	56r			Phoebe Macguigin	wif m	37		Sct
8919	56r			Frances Macguigin	dau	6m		Dur
8920	56r			Mary Mackinnin	vis w	69	visitor	Sct
8921	56r			Edward Melvy	ldr	18	labourer, mason's	Chs Stockport
8922	56r	<21>c	Claypath	Thomas Largey	hea w	70	pauper; fruiterer	Irl
8923	56r			James Largey	gsn	10		Irl
8924	56r	21	Claypath	Robert Harrison	hea m	48	cordwainer, master	Dur Old Wingate
8925	56r			Eliza Harrison	wif m	43		Ken Dover
8926	56r			George Harrison	son	6	scholar	Dur
8927	56r			Jane Douglass	ser	21	servant	Nbl Newcastle
8928	56r	20	Claypath	James Richardson	hea m	29	tailor <publican *>	Dur
8929	56r			Jane Richardson	wif m	25		Dur
8930	56r			Mary Jane Richardson	dau	4	scholar	Dur
8931	56r			John Richardson	son	6m		Dur
8932	56r	[bu]	Claypath	Patrick Loftes	hea m	55	labourer, railway	Irl
8933	56r			Bridget Loftes	wif m	55		Irl
8934	56r			Susan Loftes	dau	16		Irl
8935	56v			Becky Loftes	dau	16		Irl
8936	56v			William Prestlen	cou	16	labourer, mason's	Irl
8937	56v			John Kennedy	vis	25	beggar, labourer	Irl
8938	56v			Augustine Castle	vis	23	beggar, labourer	Irl
8939	56v	[bv]	Claypath	Bridget Higgins	hea w	60	lodging house keeper	Irl
8940	56v			Mary Higgins	dau	20		Irl
8941	56v			Bridget Higgins	dau	18		Irl
8942	56v			John Higgins	son	16	labourer	Lan Manchester
8943	56v	[bw]a	Claypath	John Rix	hea w	63	shoemaker	Dur Sunderland
8944	56v	[bw]b	Claypath	Margaret Hamilton	hea w	44	formerly laundress	Sct
8945	56v			James Hamilton	son	18	labourer, mason's	Sct
8946	56v			William Hamilton	son	10	scholar	Sct
8947	56v			Mary Hamilton	dau	7	scholar	Dur [D] S. Nicholas
8948	56v			George Macom	ldr	55	labourer, mason's	Sct
8949	56v	[bw]c	Claypath	Matthew Higgins	hea m	23	agricultural labourer	Irl
8950	56v			Honour Higgins	wif m	20		Irl
8951	56v			Michael McDonnell	ldr m	26	agricultural labourer	Irl
8952	56v			Eleanor McDonnell	ldr m	26	agricultural labr's wife	Irl
8953	56v			Ann McDonnell	ldr	4	agricultural labr's dau	Irl
8954	57r	[bx]a	Claypath	Joseph Bourke	hea m	40	lodging house keeper	Irl
8955	57r			Mary Bourke	wif m	40		Irl
8956	57r			Patrick Bourke	son	9	scholar	Irl
8957	57r			Edward Bourke	son	5	scholar	Irl
8958	57r			Bridget Bourke	dau	1		Dur
8959	57r			Bridget Bourke	mth	67		Irl
8960	57r			Honour Bourke	sis	24		Irl
8961	57r			Ellen Bordman	ldr w	52	hawker	Lan Manchester
8962	57r			Samuel Bordman	ldr	9		Lan Manchester
8963	57r			John Power	ldr	24	railway labourer	Irl
8964	57r			Patrick Ronan	ldr	22	railway labourer	Irl
8965	57r	[bx]b	Claypath	John Sim	hea m	33	gardener	Sct
8966	57r			Dorothy Sim	wif m	32		Dur
8967	57r			Dorothy Sim	dau	9	scholar	Dur Lanchester
8968	57r			John Sim	son	6	scholar	Dur Lanchester
8969	57r			James Sim	son	4		Dur Lanchester
8970	57r			David Sim	son	9m		Dur [D] S. Nicholas
8971	57r			Jane Richardson	mlw w	64	annuitant	Dur [D] S. Nicholas
8972	57r			Margaret Richardson	sil	16		Dur [D] S. Nicholas
8973	57v	19 a	Claypath	James Atkinson	hea m	36	<wine &> spirit merchant	Nbl Callaley
8974	57v			Mary Atkinson	wif m	35		Nbl Cambo
8975	57v			Sarah Thewburn	ser	23	house servant	Dur Fishburn
8976	57v			Elizabeth Notley	ldr m	42	annuitant	War Fillongley
8977	57v	19 b	Claypath	Joseph Graham	hea m	65	rope <and twine> maker	Dur [D] S. Nicholas
8978	57v			Joseph Jackson Graham	son m	29	ropemaker	Dur [D] S. Nicholas
8979	57v			Ann Frances Graham	dlw m	34		Wry Boroughbridge
8980	57v			Joseph James Graham	gsn	2		Dur [D] S. Nicholas
8981	57v			Thomas Graham	gsn	9m		Dur [D] S. Nicholas
8982	57v			Mary Ann Bainbridge	ser	19	house servant	Dur [D] S. Nicholas
8983	57v	17	Claypath	Thomas Sheppard	hea m	53	innkeeper *	Ntt Nottingham
8984	57v			Mary Sheppard	wif m	51		Dur
8985	57v			Minos Sheppard	son	20	looking glass maker	Ntt Nottingham
8986	57v			Elizabeth Trotter	nce	12		Dur Staindrop
8987	57v			John Monro	ldr	33	shoemaker	Sct
8988	57v	<16>	Claypath	Christopher Jammison	hea m	51	innkeeper *	Dur Easington
8989	57v			Mary Jammison	wif m	37		Dur Hallgarth

8990	57v	<16>	Claypath	Mary Jane Moody	nce	8	scholar	Dur Hallgarth
8991	57v			Dorothy Ross	ser	16	servant	Dur Lumley
8992	58r	[by]	Claypath	Luke Dickenson	hea m	45	brewer	Dur Pittington
8993	58r			Hannah Dickenson	wif m	43		Dur Hallgarth
8994	58r	15 a	Claypath	John Craig	hea m	34	dealer; laces, hosiery *	Sct
8995	58r			Jane Craig	wif m	30		Dur Darlington
8996	58r			William Craig	son	6		Dur [D] S. Nicholas
8997	58r			E. Tomlinson	sil	20	dressmaker	Dur Darlington
8998	58r	15 b	Claypath	Mary White	hea	26	dressmaker	Nry Sand Hutton
8999	58r			William White	fth m	65	retired farmer	Yks Sutton
9000	58r			Jane White	mth m	65	wife	Wry Calton
9001	58r	15 c	Claypath	Thomas Rennison	hea m	44	porter at rly station	Dur Bishopwearmouth
9002	58r			Ann Rennison	wif m	54		Dur S. John's Chapel
9003	58r			Thomas James Rennison	son	15	at home	Dur [D] S. Nicholas
9004	58r	15 d	Claypath	Richard Jackson	hea m	52	architect	Dur Sunderland
9005	58r			Jane Jackson	wif m	50		Nry Richmond
9006	58r			Mary Jackson	dau	17		Nbl Newcastle
9007	58r	[bz]	Claypath	Jane Elliott	hea m	32	laundress	Nry Redcar
9008	58r			Dorothy Ann Elliott	dau	6		Dur [D] S. Giles
9009	58r	[ca]	Claypath	Rebecca Sanderson	hea w	73	annuitant	Nbl Newcastle
9010	58r	[cb]	Claypath	George Coulson	hea m	36	turner & cabinetmaker	Dur [D] S. Giles
9011	58r			Mary Coulson	wif m	37		Dur Staindrop
9012	58v			Richard S. Coulson	son	12	scholar	Dur Houghton-l-Spring
9013	58v			Joseph Coulson	son	10	scholar	Dur [D] S. Nicholas
9014	58v			Margaret Ann Coulson	dau	2		Dur [D] S. Nicholas
9015	58v			Harry Coulson	son	5m		Dur [D] S. Nicholas
9016	58v	[cc]	Claypath	John Copeland	hea m	35	hawker	Irl
9017	58v			Sarah Copeland	wif m	38	milliner	Irl
9018	58v			Mary Copeland	dau	16	milliner	Nfk Market Dereham
9019	58v	[cd]a	Claypath	Michael Carter	hea m	42	hawker	Irl
9020	58v			Bridget Carter	wif m	30		Irl
9021	58v			John Carter	son	10	scholar	Wry Bradford
9022	58v			Mary Anne Carter	dau	7	scholar	Wry Bradford
9023	58v			Michael Carter	son	3	scholar	Dur
9024	58v			Bridget Carter	dau	1		Dur
9025	58v	[cd]b	Claypath	Daniel McKay	hea m	40	handloom weaver (carpet)	Sct
9026	58v			Christian McKay	wif m	38		Sct
9027	58v			Ann McKay	dau	14	factory worker, carpet	Sct
9028	58v			Christian McKay	dau	12	errand girl	Sct
9029	58v			Daniel McKay	son	9	scholar	Sct
9030	58v			Catherine McKay	dau	6	scholar	Sct
9031	58v			Hugh McKay	son	2		Dur [D] S. Nicholas
9032	59r	[cd]c	Claypath	Charles Tawse	hea m	38	weaver (carpets)	Sct
9033	59r			Jane Tawse	wif m	51		Sct
9034	59r			Charles Tawse	son	11	scholar	Sct
9035	59r	[ce]a	Claypath	Thomas Barnett	hea m	27	shoemaker	Dur Barnard Castle
9036	59r			Isabella Barnett	wif m	25		Wes Kendal
9037	59r	[ce]b	Claypath	James Salmon	hea m	23	joiner	Nry Melsonby
9038	59r			Ann Hall Salmon	wif m	21		Dur Cockerton
9039	59r	[cf]a	Claypath	Isabella Farrow	hea	56	straw-bonnetmaker	Dur
9040	59r			John Farrow	son m	31	painter	Dur
9041	59r			Isabella Farrow	dlw m	33	formerly house maid	Dur Croxdale Village
9042	59r			Jane Wilson Farrow	gda	8	scholar	Dur
9043	59r			Barbary Mary Farrow	gda	4m		Dur
9044	59r	[cf]b	Claypath	William Thompson	hea m	27	printer compositor	Dur Gateshead
9045	59r			Rachael Thompson	wif m	24		Nbl Walker
9046	59r			George Thompson	son	2		Dur Gateshead
9047	59r			William Gill Thompson	son	7m		Dur Gateshead
9048	59r			Margaret Quinton	sil	11		Dur Gateshead Fell
9049	59r	[cf]c	Claypath	James Butler	hea m	40	weaver (carpet)	Wor Kidderminster
9050	59r			Dorcas Butler	wif m	42		Wor Kidderminster
9051	59r			Emma Grubb	nce	11		Wor Kidderminster
9052	59v	14 a	Claypath	George Harden	hea m	34	carpet weaver	Wor Kidderminster
9053	59v			Sarah Harden	wif m	32		Wor Kidderminster
9054	59v			John Harden	son	5	scholar at home	Wor Kidderminster
9055	59v			Thomas Harden	son	3		Wry Leeds
9056	59v	14 b	Claypath	Mary Nisbit	hea w	75	formerly servant	Dur Weardale
9057	59v	14 c	Claypath	Felix Morgan	hea m	21	hawker	Irl
9058	59v			Hannah Morgan	wif m	22		Yks Burlington
9059	59v			Charles Henry Morgan	son	1m		Dur [D] S. Nicholas
9060	59v	<13>a	Claypath	Thomas Caldcleugh	hea m	37	master tailor	Dur [D] S. Margaret
9061	59v			Isabella Caldcleugh	wif m	37		Sct
9062	59v			Isabella Caldcleugh	dau	4		Dur [D] S. Nicholas
9063	59v			Henry Caldcleugh	son	4		Dur [D] S. Nicholas
9064	59v			Thomas Caldcleugh	son	3		Dur [D] S. Nicholas
9065	59v			Elizabeth Caldcleugh	dau	6m		Dur [D] S. Nicholas
9066	59v	<13>b	Claypath	Thomasin Jackson	wif m	57	plumber's wife	Dur Hexham Fell
9067	59v	<13>c	Claypath	Mary Heaviside	hea w	51	laundress	Dur
9068	59v			Thomas Heaviside	son	22	coach trimmer	Dur
9069	59v			Dorothy Heaviside	dau	20	dressmaker	Dur
9070	59v			Ann Heaviside	dau	17	house servant	Nbl Newcastle

9071	59v	<13>c	Claypath	Margaret Heaviside	dau	14	scholar	Dur
9072	60r			Frederick Heaviside	son	14	plumber	Dur
9073	60r	[cg]a	Claypath	Patrick Fegan	hea m	32	general dealer	Irl
9074	60r			Jane Fegan	wif	29	milliner	Dur Iveston
9075	60r	[cg]b	Claypath	Archibald Doinnin	hea m	25	carpet weaver	Sct
9076	60r			Jane Doinnin	wif m	24		Dur [D] S. Nicholas
9077	60r			Elizabeth Doinnin	dau	1		Dur [D] S. Nicholas
9078	60r	<13>a	Claypath	William Liddell	hea m	20	cartman	Dur [D] S. Nicholas
9079	60r			Martha Liddell	wif m	19		Dur [D] S. Nicholas
9080	60r			Robert Liddell	bro	8	scholar	Dur [D] S. Nicholas
9081	60r	<13>b	Claypath	Margaret Simpson	hea w	30	dressmaker	Dur [D] S. Nicholas
9082	60r			Ann Simpson	dau	9	scholar	Dur [D] S. Nicholas
9083	60r			Abraham Simpson	son	7	scholar	Dur [D] S. Nicholas
9084	60r	<13>c	Claypath	William Martin	hea m	25	carpet weaver	Wor Kidderminster
9085	60r			Elizabeth Martin	wif m	24		Wor Kidderminster
9086	60r			William John Martin	son	3m		Dur [D] S. Nicholas
9087	60r			James Graidy	ser	12	draw boy	Irl
9088	60r	[ch]a	Claypath	John Jones	hea m	44	carpet weaver	Sal Bridgnorth
9089	60r			Jane Jones	wif m	43		Sal Bridgnorth
9090	60r			Harriet Jones	dau	11	draws	Sal Bridgnorth
9091	60r			William Jones	son	9	assists [carpet weaver?]	Sal Bridgnorth
9092	60v			Jonathan Cooper	ldr	26	carpet weaver	Wor Kidderminster
9093	60v	[ch]b	Claypath	John Dogherty	hea m	32	carpet weaver	Sct
9094	60v			Jane Dogherty	wif m	35		Sct
9095	60v			Janet Dogherty	dau	9	scholar	Sct
9096	60v			James Dogherty	son	7	scholar	Dur Durham
9097	60v			Robert Dogherty	son	5	scholar	Dur Durham
9098	60v			John Dogherty	son	1		Dur Durham
9099	60v	[ci]	Claypath	William Beecroft	hea m	38	helping hand in dyehouse	Dur Barnard Castle
9100	60v			Mary Ann Beecroft	wif m	44		Lnd Holborn *
9101	60v			Mary Jane Beecroft	dau	8	scholar	Dur [D] S. Nicholas
9102	60v			Ellen Beecroft	dau	5	scholar	Dur [D] S. Nicholas
9103	60v			Alice Lumm	*	13	stranger	Nbl Newcastle, S.John
9104	60v	13	Claypath	George Burdon	hea m	41	town councillor *	Dur [D] S. Oswald
9105	60v			Ann Burdon	wif m	40		Dur Darlington
9106	60v			Mary Frances Burdon	dau	9	scholar	Dur [D] S. Giles
9107	60v			Matthew Burdon	son	7	scholar	Dur [D] S. Nicholas
9108	60v			Thomas Burdon	son	6	scholar	Dur [D] S. Nicholas
9109	60v			Anne Burdon	dau	5		Dur [D] S. Nicholas
9110	60v			Alice Burdon	dau	4		Dur [D] S. Nicholas
9111	60v			Agnes Herbet	ser	24	servant	Sct
9112	61r			Jane Ann Adamson	ser	17	servant	Dur Houghton-1-Spring
9113	61r			Rebecca Cooper	ser	12	servant	Yks Melton
9114	61r	<11>	Claypath	William Milner	hea m	28	confectioner <& baker>	Nbl Newcastle
9115	61r			Ann Milner	wif	31		Dur [D] S. Margaret
9116	61r			Ann Heslop	nce	5	scholar	Dur [D] S. Margaret
9117	61r			John Shaftoe	ser	18	servant	Sct
9118	61r	[cj]	Claypath	William Hering	hea m	38	cabinetmaker	Dur Hunwick
9119	61r			Mary Hering	wif m	40	dressmaker	Dur Billingham
9120	61r			Isabella Hering	dau	12		Dur Sunderland
9121	61r			William Hering	son	8		Dur Durham
9122	61r			Mary Hering	dau	6		Dur
9123	61r			Charles Hering	son	4		Dur
9124	61r			Hardesty Binns	ldr	34	blacking manufacturer	Wry Keighley
9125	61r	<10>a	Claypath	Robert Marriner	hea m	51	boot and shoemaker *	Dur Staindrop
9126	61r			Mary Marriner	wif m	53	<straw-hatmaker>	Dur Barnard Castle
9127	61r			Mary Anne Marriner	dau	23		Nry Aldbrough
9128	61r			Rebecca Marriner	dau	19	milliner	Dur Darlington
9129	61r			Robert Marriner	son	16		Dur Darlington
9130	61r			Matthew Marriner	son	12		Dur Darlington
9131	61v	<10>b	Claypath	John Eggleston	hea m	43	yeoman	Dur
9132	61v			Elizabeth Eggleston	wif	28		Dur Chester-le-Street
9133	61v			Hannah Eggleston	dau	7	scholar	Dur Durham
9134	61v			Mary Ann Eggleston	dau	5	scholar	Dur
9135	61v			John James Eggleston	son	3	scholar	Dur
9136	61v	<10>c	Claypath	Edward T. Kay	hea m	27	printer & bookbinder *	Dur Barnard Castle
9137	61v			Sarah Ann Kay	wif m	29		Dur Barnard Castle
9138	61v			William Thomas Kay	son	5		Dur Barnard Castle
9139	61v			Elizabeth Ann Kay	dau	1		Dur Barnard Castle
9140	61v	[ck]a	Claypath	Robert Robson	hea	41	shoemaker * {deaf}	Dur Lanchester
9141	61v	[ck]b	Claypath	William Smith	hea m	48	grocer's assistant	Dur Quarrington
9142	61v			Margaret Smith	wif m	43		Nry Richmond
9143	61v			Margaret Smith	dau	12		Dur Sunderland Bridge
9144	61v	[ck]c	Claypath	Patrick Ward	hea w	63	labourer	Irl
9145	61v			Ann Ward	dau w	30	washerwoman	Irl
9146	61v			Peter Ward	nep	19	gardener	Irl
9147	61v	[cl]	Claypath	John Dunn	hea m	47	shoemaker	Nry Guisborough
9148	61v			Margaret Dunn	wif m	53		Dur [D] S. Nicholas
9149	61v			John Dunn	son	23	basketmaker	Dur [D] S. Nicholas
9150	61v			Mary Ann Dunn	dau	19		Dur [D] S. Nicholas
9151	62r			Jane Dunn	dau	17		Dur [D] S. Nicholas

9152	62r	[cl]	Claypath	Thomas Dunn	son		14	shoemaker, apprentice	Dur [D] S. Nicholas
9153	62r			Ann Dunn	dau		11	scholar	Dur [D] S. Nicholas
9154	62r	9	Claypath	Ralph Stobart	hea m		45	brewer & publican *	Dur Chester-le-Street
9155	62r			Margaret Stobart	wif m		38		Dur Aycliffe
9156	62r			William Stobart	son		15	currier	Dur Durham
9157	62r			Thomas Stobart	son		11	scholar	Dur Durham
9158	62r			Elizabeth Stobart	dau		9	scholar	Dur Durham
9159	62r			James Stobart	son		5	scholar	Dur Durham
9160	62r			Henry Stobart	son		3m		Dur Durham
9161	62r			Margaret Robinson	ser		18	house servant	Dur Moorsley
9162	62r			Elizabeth Snaith	vis		19	annuitant	Dur Darlington
9163	62r			John Foster	ser		28	house servant	Dur
9164	62r			Elizabeth Snaith	vis		22	annuitant	Dur Houghton
9165	62r			Thomas Gills	vis w		43	horse dealer	Dur
9166	62r			Ralph Snaith	flw w		80	publican	Dur Aycliffe
9167	62r			John Palmer	vis m		50	miller	Dur Staindrop
9168	62r			James Stevenson	vis m		37	horse dealer	Wry Leeds
9169	62v	<8>	Claypath	James Chandler	hea m		43	publican *	Nry Dalton
9170	62v			Mary Chandler	wif m		39		Dur Redworth
9171	62v			Catherine Chandler	dau		13		Dur
9172	62v			Mary Ann Chandler	dau		11		Dur
9173	62v			Jane Chandler	dau		9		Dur
9174	62v			Isabella Graham	ldr		15	servant	Nbl Newcastle
9175	62v			Thomas Wrangham	ldr m		37	butcher	Dur Redworth
9176	62v			William Milston	ldr		25	sergeant 33rd Regiment *	Lei Leicester
9177	62v			Thomas Byrne	ldr m		27	traveller	Irl
9178	62v			James Brignall	ldr		21	groom	Dur Darlington
9179	62v			William Johnson	ldr m		40	butcher	Cul Carlisle
9180	62v			Frederick Potts	ldr		42	horse dealer	Sct
9181	62v			Archibald Scott	ldr		28	cattle dealer	Sct
9182	62v			Johnson Cowen	ldr m		42	butcher	Cul Carlisle
9183	62v	8	Claypath	Sarah Liddle	hea w		70	formerly cook	Nbl Newcastle *
9184	62v	7	Claypath	John Ayre	hea m		50	saddler	Dur
9185	62v			Margaret Ayre	wif m		51		Nbl Newcastle
9186	62v			Thomas Ayre	son		20	saddler	Dur
9187	62v			John Ayre	son		18	currier	Dur
9188	62v			William Ayre	son		11	scholar	Dur
9189	63r			Ann Adamson	ser		16	house servant	Dur Rainton
9190	63r			Margaret Laing	ldr		72	annuitant	Dur Shincliffe
9191	63r	[cm]a	Claypath	William Brown	hea m		30	joiner	Dur Durham
9192	63r			Hannah Brown	wif m		28		Dur
9193	63r			John Brown	son		7		Dur
9194	63r			Ann Brown	dau		5		Dur
9195	63r			William Brown	son		3		Dur
9196	63r			Mary Brown	dau		1		Dur
9197	63r	[cm]b	Claypath	Cortes David Telfair	hea m		31	MRCSL, LAC London *	Lnd Somers Town
9198	63r			Elizabeth Telfair	wif m		31		Dur [D] S. Margaret
9199	63r			Elizabeth Graham	sda		12		Dur [D] S. Margaret
9200	63r			Henry G. Telfair	son		4		Dur Sacriston Clry
9201	63r			Mary Ann J. Telfair	dau		10m		Dur [D] S. Nicholas
9202	63r	<6>	Claypath	William Anderson	hea m		35	innkeeper <'Railway'>	Dur Barnard Castle
9203	63r			Jane Ann Anderson	wif m		32		Dur Darlington
9204	63r			Margaret H. Anderson	dau		6		Dur Heighington
9205	63r			Thomas Brenkley	ldr nk		57	horse dealer	not known
9206	63r			William Brenkley	ldr nk		28	horse dealer	not known
9207	63r			John Iveson	ldr nk		34	horse dealer	not known
9208	63r			William Iveson	ldr nk		28	horse jobber	not known
9209	63v			William Harrison	ldr nk		28	horse dealer	not known
9210	63v			Henry Ranke	ldr nk		19	horse jobber	not known
9211	63v			John Johnson	ldr nk		27	horse dealer	not known
9212	63v			Rebecca Freston	ser		11	house servant	Mdx Bow
9213	63v			Frances Neesham	ser		21	house maid	Dur
9214	63v			Isabella Tod	ser		16	kitchen maid	Dur Pittington
9215	63v			Thomas Reay	ser		55	ostler	Nbl Haltwhistle
9216	63v	<5>	Claypath	Frederick Morgan	hea		26	grocer <& tea dealer *>	Dur Brancepeth
9217	63v			John Baines	*		28	grocer <& tea dealer *>	Lei Burton [Lazars]
9218	63v			William Bait	jny		24	journeyman [grocer]	Dur Houghton-1-Spring
9219	63v			Frederick Foxley	jny		19	journeyman [grocer]	Nth
9220	63v			Mary Dobson	ser		27	housekeeper	Dur Hallgarth
9221	63v	[cn]	Claypath	John Ritson	hea w		64	fmly farm ser {blind}	Dur Hesleden
9222	63v			William Richardson	slw m		30	miller	Nry Thirsk
9223	63v			Jane Richardson	dau m		34		Dur Moorhouse
9224	63v			Margaret Richardson	gda		2		Dur [D] S. Nicholas
9225	63v			Hannah Richardson	gda		8m		Dur [D] S. Nicholas
9226	63v			John Ritson	son		27	butcher	Dur [D] S. Nicholas
9227	63v			Thomas Simpson	ldr		52	groom	Nry Northallerton
9228	64r	<4>a	Claypath	Sarah Vest	hea w		64	lodging house keeper	Dur
9229	64r			Caroline Brown	ldr		9	lodger	Nbl North Shields
9230	64r	<4>b	Claypath	Thomas Kasher	hea m		39	labourer, cartman	Dur [D] S. Nicholas
9231	64r			Mary Kasher	wif m		39		Dur Sherburn
9232	64r			Jane Kasher	dau		12	scholar	Dur [D] S. Nicholas

9233	64r	<4>b	Claypath	Thomas Kasher	son	10	scholar	Dur [D] S. Nicholas
9234	64r			Frances Kasher	dau	8	scholar	Dur [D] S. Nicholas
9235	64r			William Kasher	son	5	scholar	Dur [D] S. Nicholas
9236	64r			Sarah Kasher	dau	2		Dur [D] S. Nicholas
9237	64r			Ruth Kasher	dau	10m		Dur [D] S. Nicholas
9238	64r	5	Claypath	Robert Hornsby	hea m	60	farm labourer	Dur Farewell Hall
9239	64r			Margaret Hornsby	wif m	63		Dur [D] S. Nicholas
9240	64r			Robert Hornsby	slw m	24	dispensing assistant	Dur [D] S. Nicholas
9241	64r			Matilda R. Hornsby	swi m	21		Dur [D] S. Nicholas
9242	64r	<4>	Claypath	John Blagdon	hea m	49	currier & leather cutter	Dur [D] S. Nicholas
9243	64r			Eliza Blagdon	wif m	46		Mdx Brentford
9244	64r			Henrietta Blagdon	dau	19		Dur [D] S. Nicholas
9245	64r			Emily Blagdon	dau	18		Dur [D] S. Nicholas
9246	64r			Eliza Blagdon	dau	16		Dur [D] S. Nicholas
9247	64r			Mary Ann Blagdon	dau	14		Dur [D] S. Nicholas
9248	64v			Clara Blagdon	dau	7		Dur [D] S. Nicholas
9249	64v			John Blagdon	son	5	scholar	Dur [D] S. Nicholas
9250	64v	3	Claypath	William Summerbell	hea m	66	publican <'Wheatsheaf'>	Dur [D] S. Nicholas
9251	64v			Elizabeth Summerbell	wif m	62		Dur Kelloe
9252	64v			Thomas Robson	slw m	35	upholsterer	Dur [D] S. Nicholas
9253	64v			Mary Robson	dau m	35		Dur [D] S. Nicholas
9254	64v			William Robson	gsn	9	scholar	Dur [D] S. Nicholas
9255	64v			Elizabeth Robson	gda	5	scholar	Dur [D] S. Nicholas
9256	64v			Sarah Robson	gda	3	scholar	Dur [D] S. Nicholas
9257	64v			Thomas Robson	gsn	1		Dur [D] S. Nicholas
9258	64v			William Linsley	vis m	29	horse dealer	Dur Barnard Castle
9259	64v			Robinson Linsley	vis	17	earthenware dealer	Dur Barnard Castle
9260	64v			Edward Hepworth	vis	42	clothier	Wry Lindley
9261	64v			Joseph Boroglia	vis	36	traveller	Italy
9262	64v			Henry Walton	vis	23	butcher	Dur Bishop Auckland
9263	64v	<3>a	Claypath	George Summerbell	hea m	32	butcher	Dur [D] S. Nicholas
9264	64v			Hannah Summerbell	wif m	32		Dur [D] S. Nicholas
9265	64v			John Summerbell	son	11	scholar	Dur [D] S. Nicholas
9266	64v			George Summerbell	son	6	scholar	Dur [D] S. Nicholas
9267	64v			Ellen Summerbell	dau	3	scholar	Dur [D] S. Nicholas
9268	65r			William Summerbell	son	8m		Dur [D] S. Nicholas
9269	65r	<3>b	Claypath	Joseph Bland Pearson	hea m	20	hairdresser	Dur [D] S. Nicholas
9270	65r			Elizabeth Pearson	wif m	21		Dur Lumley
9271	65r	[co]a	Claypath	William Summerbell	hea m	26	butcher	Dur [D] S. Nicholas
9272	65r			Mary Summerbell	wif m	28		Dur Darlington
9273	65r	[co]b	Claypath	Patrick Cubit	hea m	35	shoemaker	Irl
9274	65r			Joanna Cubit	wif m	21		Irl
9275	65r			Bridget Cubit	dau	1		Irl
9276	65r			Darby O'Coners	vis	19	agricultural labourer	Irl
9277	65r			Bridget Doherty	vis	20	servant	Irl
9278	65r	[cp]a	Claypath	Thomas Proctor	hea m	60	hawker	Dur Barnard Castle
9279	65r			Ann Proctor	wif m	56		Dur Darlington
9280	65r	[cp]b	Claypath	Maughan Tilly	hea m	27	carpet weaver	Dur [D] S. Nicholas
9281	65r			Ann Tilly	wif m	24		Dur [D] S. Nicholas
9282	65r			Jane Tilly	dau	5		Dur [D] S. Nicholas
9283	65r			Elizabeth Tilly	dau	3		Dur [D] S. Nicholas
9284	65r			Thomas Tilly	son	2		Dur [D] S. Nicholas
9285	65r	[ɔp]c	Claypath	William Cave	hea m	29	shoemaker	Dur [D] S. Nicholas
9286	65r			Ann Cave	wif m	34		Yks York

Notes - Enumeration District 4b

8428	<'Duke of York'>	8885	county given as "Suffolk"
8439	<greengrocer>	8893	<& brazier>
8463	<& paper merchant>	8928	... 'Black Horse'
8475	... and mineralogy in university, MA, FRS	8983	<'Wearmouth Bridge' & 'Nottingham House'>
8478	<& sausage dealer>	8988	<'Bunch of Grapes'>
8488	... & professor of music	8994	... & hardware
8532	<'Masons' Arms'>	9100	... Saffron Hill
8557	... employing 2 men	9103	stranger
8584	... employing son in same occupation	9104	... cabinetmaker <& furniture broker>
8587	expectant ...	9125	<& dealer in old clothes>
8588	... & paperhanger	9136	... journeyman
8622	... employing 5 men and 5 boys	9140	... Chelsea pensioner
8636	young child	9154	<'Bee Hive'>
8665	workman	9169	<'Hope & Anchor'>
8789	<& builder>	9176	... (recruiting)
8804	county given as "Sussex"	9183	... S. Andrew
8808	... master emp 17 men, 1 boy, 2 females	9197	... practising as a general practitioner
8827	{blind}	9216-9217	... & cheesemonger
8863	<& gasfitter>	9217	partner

REF	FOL	NO	STREET	FORENAME(S)	SURNAME	REL	C	AGE	OCCUPATION	BIRTHPLACE
9287	69v	<105>	Claypath	Robert	Tuart	hea	m	56	victualler *	Dur Durham
9288	69v			Ann	Tuart	wif	m	57		Dur Lambton
9289	69v			Mary	Taylor	ser		20	general servant	Dur Lambton
9290	69v			Robert	Heslop	ser		24	horsekeeper	Dur
9291	69v			George	Shield	vis		29	draper	Dur Barnard Castle
9292	69v			John	Plews	vis		30	farmer	Dur Bowon
9293	69v			William	Hurworth	vis		40	farmer	Nry Richmond
9294	69v	106 a	Claypath	Mary A.	Hedley	hea		34	proprietor of houses	Ess Manningtree
9295	69v			Jane E.	Hedley	dau		16		Dur
9296	69v			Elizabeth	Hedley	sis		30	proprietor of houses	Ess Manningtree
9297	69v			Elizabeth M.	Hedley	nce		14	scholar	Dur [D] S. Nicholas
9298	69v			Isabella	Hedley	nce		12	scholar	Dur [D] S. Nicholas
9299	69v			Annie	Hedley	nce		10	scholar	Dur [D] S. Nicholas
9300	69v			Emma	Hedley	nce		5	scholar	Dur [D] S. Nicholas
9301	69v			John	Hedley	bro		41	watchmaker	Dur Sunderland
9302	69v			Magdalen	Hall	ser		17	general servant	Dur Chester-le-Street
9303	69v	106 b	Claypath	James	Harrison	hea	m	49	groom	Yks
9304	69v			Sarah	Harrison	wif	m	48		Nbl
9305	70r	106 c	Claypath	Elizabeth	Craggs	hea		30	charwoman	Dur
9306	70r			Henry	Craggs	son		5	scholar	Dur [D] S. Margaret
9307	70r	106 d	Claypath	Edward	Stout	hea	m	24	carpet weaver	Dur Barnard Castle
9308	70r			Ann	Stout	wif	m	23		Dur Barnard Castle
9309	70r			William	Stout	son		2		Dur Barnard Castle
9310	70r			Elizabeth	Stout	dau		1m		Dur Barnard Castle
9311	70r	106 e	Claypath	Robert	Skelton	hea	m	55	Post [Office] messenger	Dur [D] S. Oswald
9312	70r			Ann	Skelton	wif	m	58		Dur [D] S. Nicholas
9313	70r			Ann	Skelton	dau		18		Dur [D] S. Nicholas
9314	70r			John B.	Pearson	gsn		2		Dur [D] S. Nicholas
9315	70r	106 f	Claypath	William	Elliott	hea	m	32	joiner	Dur
9316	70r			Jane	Elliott	wif	m	33		Cul
9317	70r	106 g	Claypath	William	Clarke	hea	m	24	labourer	Dur Darlington
9318	70r			Margaret	Clarke	wif	m	28	shoebinder	Dur [D] S. Nicholas
9319	70v	106 h	Claypath	Roger	McMahon	hea	m	43	labourer	Irl
9320	70v			Sarah	McMahon	wif	m	43		Irl
9321	70v			Catherine	McMahon	dau		12	scholar	Irl
9322	70v			Roger	McMahon	son		10	scholar	Irl
9323	70v			Sarah	McMahon	dau		2		Irl
9324	70v	106 i	Claypath	Thomas	Neison	hea	m	34	hardware traveller	Gal Loughrea
9325	70v			Ann	Neison	wif	m	22		Irl Crockwell
9326	70v	106 j	Claypath	Martin	Devaney	hea	m	32	general dealer	Irl
9327	70v			Jane	Devaney	wif	m	26		Irl
9328	70v			John	Devaney	son		8		Irl
9329	70v			Michael	Devaney	son		5		Dur
9330	70v			Henry	Devaney	son		2		Dur
9331	70v			Michael	O'Brien	ldr		28	labourer	Sli
9332	70v			John	Davis	blw		24	labourer	May
9333	70v	106 k	Claypath	William	Thompson	hea	m	24	coachman	Yks Brampton
9334	70v			Elizabeth	Thompson	wif	m	23		Yks Allandale
9335	70v			Judith	Thompson	sis		21		Yks Allandale
9336	71r	106 l	Claypath	Catherine	McKany	hea	w	48	charwoman	Irl
9337	71r			Edward	McKany	son		21	labourer	Irl
9338	71r			John	McKany	son		18	cordwainer, apprentice	Irl
9339	71r			Patrick	McKany	son		13	labourer	Irl
9340	71r	106 m	Claypath	Elizabeth	Whiting	hea	w	70		Irl
9341	71r			Thomas	Whiting	son		26	labourer	Dur
9342	71r			Jane	Whiting	dau		24		Dur
9343	71r	107	Claypath	Margaret	Smith	hea	w	64	innkeeper <'Angel'>	Dur Rainton
9344	71r			Margaret	Smith	dau		36		Dur [D] S. Nicholas
9345	71r			William	Smith	son		24	draper	Dur [D] S. Nicholas
9346	71r			John J.	Smith	gsn		6	scholar	Yks
9347	71r			Jonathan	Fairbridge	vis		56	cattle dealer	Dur Hedley
9348	71r			George	Monkester	vis	m	81	cattle dealer	Dur Stainton
9349	71r			John	Henderson	vis		38	farmer	Dur Wolsingham
9350	71r			Johnson	Kirton	vis	m	47	farmer	Dur Shotley Bridge
9351	71r			Joseph	Smith	vis	m	38	groom	Nbl
9352	71r			Elizabeth	Sunn	ser		19	inn servant	Nbl Wallsend
9353	71v	108	Claypath	Robert	Cooke	hea	m	41	draper <& hatter>	Dur [D] S. Oswald
9354	71v			Elizabeth	Cooke	wif	m	34		Dur Monk Hesleden
9355	71v			John L.	Cooke	son		3		Dur [D] S. Nicholas
9356	71v			Charles	Cooke	son		10m		Dur [D] S. Nicholas
9357	71v			Thomas	Cooke	cou		29	draper's shopman	Dur Brancepeth
9358	71v			William	Smith	sho		23	draper's shopman	Dur Ovington
9359	71v			Jonathan	Jeckly	app		22	draper's apprentice	Dur Sedgefield
9360	71v			William	Hardy	app		19	draper's apprentice	Dur Elton
9361	71v			Margaret	Wilkinson	ser		19	general servant	Dur Rainton
9362	71v			Isabel	Hogarth	ser		16	nurse	Wes Kendal *
9363	71v	1 a	Market Place	William	Farmery	hea	m	45	innkeeper <'Griffin'>	Wry Bishop Monkton
9364	71v			Ann	Farmery	wif	m	46		Yks Montin
9365	71v			Hannah	Eales	ser		16	inn servant	Dur

9366	71v	1 a	Market Place	Jane Horn	ser	17	inn servant	Dur
9367	71v			John Bennison	ser m	41	groom	Nry Ayton
9368	71v	1 b	Market Place	John Swinburn	hea m	51	<clock and> watchmaker	Nbl
9369	71v			Ann Swinburn	wif m	51		Dur
9370	71v			John Swinburn	son	31	watchmaker	Dur
9371	72r			George Swinburn	son	29	watchmaker	Dur
9372	72r			Elizabeth Swinburn	dau	24		Dur
9373	72r			Thomas Swinburn	son	19	watchmaker, apprentice	Dur
9374	72r			Mary Swinburn	dau	16		Dur
9375	72r			Jane Swinburn	dau	14		Dur
9376	72r			John Robinson	app	16	watchmaker's apprentice	Dur
9377	72r	[aa]	Market Place	Ann Bulmer	hea w	77	relieved by parish	Dur
9378	72r			Elizabeth Robertson	dau m	35	charwoman /"chairwoman"	Dur
9379	72r			Thomas Bulmer	gsn	15	teacher, assistant	Dur
9380	72r			Nicholas Robertson	gsn	10	scholar	Cul
9381	72r	2	Market Place	John Oliver	hea	52	ironmonger <& nailmaker>	Dur Newbottle
9382	72r			Mary Richardson	nce	20	general servant	Dur
9383	72r			William Hood	nep	11	scholar	Dur
9384	72r			George Forster	sho	26	ironmonger, shopman	Dur [D] S. Giles
9385	72r			Ann Walton	ser	52	housekeeper	Dur Lanchester
9386	72r			George Salkeld	ldr	11	scholar	Dur
9387	72v	3 a	Market Place	Robinson Ferens	hea	33	draper <& hatter>	Dur Rainton
9388	72v			Joseph Ferens	bro	21	draper	Dur Rainton
9389	72v			Robert Dale	sho	24	draper, assistant	Dur Pittington
9390	72v			Joseph Lumley	sho	27	draper, assistant	Dur Gateshead
9391	72v			William H. Bell	app	20	draper, apprentice	Dur Brancepeth
9392	72v			John Hordon	app	19	draper, apprentice	Dur
9393	72v			Bertholomew Danson	app	17	draper, apprentice	Dur Merrington
9394	72v			Lane Cook	app	15	draper, apprentice	Dur Hett
9395	72v			Euphemia Hall	ser	22	general servant	Nbl
9396	72v			Ann Cowans	ser w	30	general servant	Nbl Hexham
9397	72v	3 b	Market Place	William Jackson	hea m	44	innkpr <'Hat & Feather'>	Dur Staindrop
9398	72v			Judith Jackson	wif m	39		Dur Auckland
9399	72v			John Brown	son	19	whitesmith	Dur Auckland
9400	72v			Thomas Brown	son	17		Dur Auckland
9401	72v			Anne E. Brown	dau	15		Dur [D] S. Oswald
9402	72v			Robert Robinson	ser m	50	groom	Dur Dinsdale
9403	72v			Frances Deighton	ser	40	general servant	Nbl
9404	72v			Elizabeth Perry	ser	25	general servant	Dur Penshaw
9405	72v			Isabella Ranson	ser	19	general servant	Dur
9406	73r			Mary Charlton	ser	17	general servant	Dur
9407	73r			William Napier	ser	20	boots	Cul
9408	73r			James Hudson	vis m	48	cattle dealer	Nry Coverdale
9409	73r			Samuel Sagar	vis	32	farmer	Wry Bradford
9410	73r			John Sadler	vis w	53	farmer	Nry Raskelf
9411	73r			Thomas Ross	vis w	47	farmer	Lin
9412	73r			Francis Sagar	vis	59	farmer	Nry Coverdale
9413	73r			Henry Hamnell	vis	42	cattle dealer	Ery Pocklington
9414	73r			Christopher Pybus	vis	50	farmer	Nry Kirkby Fleetham
9415	73r			Henry S. Garforth	vis m	41	butcher	Wry Bradford
9416	73r			Joseph Ackroyd	vis m	30	butcher	Yks
9417	73r			William Scorer	vis m	50	farmer	Dur Brancepeth
9418	73r			Henry Scorer	vis	24	farmer	Nry Westerdale
9419	73r			William Wendran	vis	43	servant	Yks Great Thorpe
9420	73r	4	Market Place	Thomas Millar	hea m	42	innkeeper <'City'>	Nfk
9421	73r			Elizabeth Millar	wif m	33		Dur
9422	73r			John Goodfellow	vis	51	farmer	Cul
9423	73r			Thomas A. Green	vis	27	commercial traveller	Sts
9424	73r			Thomas Hutton	vis	37	commercial traveller	Cul
9425	73v			Ann Raffle	ser	29	cook	Dur
9426	73v			Elizabeth Dixon	ser	28	house maid	Dur Chester
9427	73v			Mary A. Davison	ser	15	waiting maid	Dur Houghton
9428	73v			John Deighton	ser	19	billiard marker	Dur Auckland
9429	73v			Henry Wellington	ser	20	boots	Dur
9430	73v	5	Market Place	John W. Barny	hea	25	banker's clerk *	Nbl
9431	73v			Hannah Barny	sis	27	housekeeper	Nbl Alnwick
9432	73v			John Pickering	ser w	43	bank porter	Cul
9433	73v			Isabella Davison	ser	24	general servant	Nbl
9434	73v	6	Market Place	Francis Stone	hea w	70	hatter employing 1 man	Dur
9435	73v			Hannah Stone	dau	34		Dur
9436	73v			Margaret Pinkney	ser	18	general servant	Dur Darlington
9437	73v	<7>	Market Place	Ann Jackson	hea w	63	hatter employing 1 man	Dur Brancepeth
9438	73v			Hannah Lambert	dau w	38		Dur
9439	73v			John Jackson	gsn	12	scholar	Dur
9440	73v			Ann Dixon	ser	50	general servant	Dur Willington
9441	74r	7 a	Market Place	George Robson	hea m	51	innkpr <'Bowes' Arms'>	Dur
9442	74r			Elizabeth Robson	wif m	51		Dur
9443	74r			Elizabeth Mawson	nce	23	dressmaker	Dur Houghton
9444	74r			Hannah Watson	ser	17	house servant	Dur Hetton
9445	74r	7 b	Market Place	William Thompson	hea m	46	wood turner	Dur
9446	74r			Isabella Thompson	wif m	51		Dur

9447	74r	7 b	Market Place	Samuel Hutchison	bro		40	horsekeeper	Dur
9448	74r			Joseph Hutchison	bro		30	horsekeeper	Dur
9449	74r			Thomas Hutchison	nep		25	nailmaker	Dur
9450	74r	8	Market Place	George Proctor	hea	m	32	printer & stationer *	Dur Hart Moor
9451	74r			Eleanor Proctor	wif	m	32		Dur Carr House
9452	74r			George H. Proctor	son		1		Dur
9453	74r			John G. Proud	blw		15	stationer, apprentice	Dur Cocken
9454	74r			Mary Kirton	vis		12		Dur Belmont
9455	74r			Frances Mossom	ser		21	house servant	Dur Highton
9456	74v	9	Market Place	James Thompson	hea	m	67	ironmonger	Dur
9457	74v			Mary Thompson	wif	m	61		Dur
9458	74v			James Thompson	son		33	ironmonger	Dur [D] S. Nicholas
9459	74v			Sarah Thompson	dau		39		Dur [D] S. Nicholas
9460	74v			Ann Thompson	dau		32		Dur [D] S. Nicholas
9461	74v			Hannah Thompson	dau		28		Dur [D] S. Nicholas
9462	74v			Jane Thompson	dau		24		Dur [D] S. Nicholas
9463	74v			Elizabeth Teasdale	ser		24	house servant	Dur Weardale
9464	74v	10	Market Place	Sarah Gainforth	hea	w	50	hosier	Dur
9465	74v			Elizabeth M. Gainforth	dau		24	private governess	Dur
9466	74v			Margaret Maddison	ser		13	house servant	Dur
9467	74v	1	Fleshergate	Thomas Pyle	hea		26	grocer <cheese * factor>	Nbl
9468	74v			Robert Pyle	bro		24	grocer <cheese * factor>	Nbl
9469	74v			Mary A. Pyle	sis		29	housekeeper	Nbl
9470	74v			George Sewell	ser		30	grocer, assistant	Lnd
9471	74v			Peter Ballan	ser		16	grocer, apprentice	Ssx Hunston
9472	74v			Elizabeth Gray	ser		16	house servant	Dur Kelloe
9473	75r	1 a	Fleshergate	Ann Simpson	hea	w	73	billiard room [keeper]	Nry Newport
9474	75r			Ann Simpson	dau		38		Dur Sunderland
9475	75r			Henry Simpson	son		31	billiard marker	Dur Stockton
9476	75r	1 b	Fleshergate	George Hodgson	hea	m	38	fishmonger	Dur Auckland
9477	75r			Jane Hodgson	wif	m	39		Dur Brandon
9478	75r			Jane Hodgson	dau		11	scholar	Dur Auckland
9479	75r	1 c	Fleshergate	William Smith	hea	m	36	cordwainer	Dur Sunderland
9480	75r			Elizabeth Smith	wif	m	33		Dur Sunderland
9481	75r	1 d	Fleshergate	George R. Brewster	hea	m	26	hairdresser	Mdx London
9482	75r			Jane Brewster	wif	m	30		Dur
9483	75r			John S. Brewster	son		2		Dur S[eaham] Harbour
9484	75r			Margaret H. Brewster	dau		1		Dur Ferryhill
9485	75r	1 e	Fleshergate	Margaret Easby	hea	m	54	laundress	Dur
9486	75r			Robert Easby	son		19	watchmaker, apprentice	Dur [D] S. Nicholas
9487	75r			Sarah Easby	dau		18	dressmaker, apprentice	Dur [D] S. Nicholas
9488	75r			Jane Easby	dau		15		Dur [D] S. Giles
9489	75v	3	Fleshergate	Samuel R. Vann	hea	m	26	grocer <& tea dealer>	Lei Wigston
9490	75v			Emma Vann	wif	m	27		Lei Hinckley
9491	75v			Helen Vann	dau		11m		Dur
9492	75v			William Vann	bro		13	grocer, apprentice	Lei
9493	75v			William Wilkinson	ser		21	grocer, assistant	Dur
9494	75v			Thomas Stimpson	ser		18	grocer, apprentice	Dur
9495	75v			Mary Southeron	ser		19	house servant	Dur Jarrow
9496	75v	4	Fleshergate	George Robson	hea	m	38	chemist & druggist *	Per Perth
9497	75v			Hannah G. Robson	wif	m	41		Dur
9498	75v			Jane Langley	ser		29	house servant	Nbl
9499	75v	5	Fleshergate	Archibald Harper	hea	m	40	draper & tailor *	Sct
9500	75v			Mary A. Harper	wif	m	30		Yks
9501	75v			Alfred Ayton	ser		25	tailor, apprentice	Nry Dalton
9502	75v			Sarah J. Harper	vis		16		Dur
9503	75v			William Maston	ser		13	tailor, apprentice	Yks Dalton
9504	75v			Sarah Summers	ser		21	house servant	Dur
9505	76r	6 a	Fleshergate	Robert Young	hea	m	30	grocer <flour * dealer>	Dur [South] Shields
9506	76r			Fanny Young	dau		3		Dur [D] S. Nicholas
9507	76r			Anne Dixon	sil		30	housekeeper	Dur [D] S. Nicholas
9508	76r			Agnes Russel	ser		18	house servant	Lks Glasgow
9509	76r	6 b	Fleshergate	Mary Bainbridge	hea		35	proprietor of houses	Dur
9510	76r			Eleanor Bainbridge	sis		31		Dur
9511	76r			John Bainbridge	bro		30	painter	Dur
9512	76r	6 c	Fleshergate	James Bayes	hea	m	29	carpet weaver	Wor Kidderminster
9513	76r			Hannah Bayes	wif	m	24		Wes Kendal *
9514	76r	7	Fleshergate	William Marshall	hea	m	35	general merchant *	Dur [D] S. Margaret
9515	76r			Jane Marshall	wif	m	34	<servants' register off>	Dur [D] S. Nicholas
9516	76r			Robert D. Marshall	son		7	scholar	Dur [D] S. Nicholas
9517	76r			Charles Marshall	son		4	scholar	Dur [D] S. Nicholas
9518	76r			Edmund Marshall	son		2	scholar	Dur [D] S. Nicholas
9519	76r			Elizabeth Marshall	mth	w	73		Dur Gateshead
9520	76r			Jane Bulmer	ser		20	shopwoman	Dur [D] S. Margaret
9521	76r			Ann Howe	ser		23	house servant	Dur Birtley
9522	76v	70 a	Fleshergate	Michael Cowans	hea	m	60	butcher	Dur
9523	76v			Ann Cowans	wif	m	60		Dur Stockton
9524	76v			Harriet Cowans	dau		16		Dur
9525	76v			Mary Gascoyne	dau	w	25	annuitant	Dur
9526	76v	70 b	Fleshergate	George Hodgson	hea	m	29	mason	Dur [D] S. Margaret
9527	76v			Jane Hodgson	wif	m	28		Dur [D] S. Oswald

9528	76v	71	Fleshergate	William Thompson	hea	m	35	chemist & druggist *	Dur
9529	76v			Agnes Thompson	wif	m	38		Dur
9530	76v			infant Thompson	dau		11d		Dur
9531	76v			Margaret Gilhespie	nse		50	monthly nurse	Dur Sherburn
9532	76v			Jane Gally	ser		21	house servant	Dur Rainton
9533	76v	72	Fleshergate	Elizabeth Macknight	hea	w	50	grocer <& fishmonger *>	Yks Montons
9534	76v			Jane Macknight	dau		33		Dur
9535	76v			Anne L. Macknight	dau		20		Dur
9536	76v			Joseph Macknight	son		17	chemist, apprentice	Dur
9537	76v			Elizabeth Dixon	ser		20	house servant	Nry Sessay /"Sessan"
9538	77r	72 a	Fleshergate	Thomas Sockett	hea	m	53	gardener	Dur
9539	77r			Mary Sockett	wif	m	50		Dur Shincliffe
9540	77r			Mary Sockett	dau		10	scholar	Dur
9541	77r	72 b	Fleshergate	John Summers	hea	m	38	cordwainer	Dur [D] S. Oswald
9542	77r			Elizabeth Summers	wif	m	41		Dur [D] S. Oswald
9543	77r			Elizabeth Summers	nce		8	scholar	Dur Chester-le-Street
9544	77r	72 c	Fleshergate	Elizabeth Ilderton	hea	w	50	ragsorter	Dur [D] S. Nicholas
9545	77r	74	Fleshergate	William Ainsley	hea	m	40	printer emp 1 man *	Dur
9546	77r			Elizabeth Ainsley	wif	m	35		Dur Sherburn
9547	77r			Elizabeth Ainsley	dau		7	scholar	Dur [D] S. Nicholas
9548	77r			William Ainsley	son		5	scholar	Dur [D] S. Nicholas
9549	77r			Mary Ainsley	dau		3	scholar	Dur [D] S. Nicholas
9550	77r			Ellen Ainsley	dau		1		Dur [D] S. Nicholas
9551	77r			John Ainsley	son		1		Dur [D] S. Nicholas
9552	77r			Mary Fewster	nce		25	proprietor of houses	Dur [D] S. Nicholas
9553	77r			John R. Fewster	nep		22	solicitor['s] clerk	Dur [D] S. Nicholas
9554	77v			Hannah Shotton	ser		20	house servant	Dur
9555	77v			Ann Rowntree	ser		18	house servant	Dur [D] S. Nicholas
9556	77v	75	Fleshergate	Thomas White	hea		29	grocer <& tea dealer>	Yks
9557	77v			Richard White	bro		31	police officer	Dur West Rainton *
9558	77v			Jane White	sis		19	housekeeper	Dur Houghton-Spring *
9559	77v			Roland Lambert	sho		25	grocer, assistant	Dur Newbottle
9560	77v			Samuel Myers	sho		22	grocer, assistant	Dur Sheriff Hill
9561	77v			James Stokoe	sho		18	grocer, assistant	Dur Newbottle
9562	77v			Jane Pattison	ser		15	house servant	Dur Sheriff Hill
			one house uninhabited						
9563	77v	78	Fleshergate	Christopher Nesbitt	hea	m	32	cordwainer emp 18 men *	Nbl
9564	77v			Anne Nesbitt	wif	m	27		Dur [D] S. Giles
9565	77v			Margaret J. Nesbitt	dau		1		Dur [D] S. Nicholas
9566	77v			Mary Welsh	ser		20	house servant	Dur Lumley
9567	77v	<79>	Fleshergate	Jane Hall	hea	w	38	innkpr <'Tailors' Arms'>	Nbl
9568	77v			Mary Brown	ser		19	house servant	Dur
9569	78r	78 a	Fleshergate	Seymour Nelson	hea	m	38	butcher	Dur
9570	78r			Jane Nelson	wif	m	38		Nbl Newcastle
9571	78r			John Nelson	son		15	saddler, apprentice	Dur
9572	78r			William Nelson	son		13	errand boy	Dur
9573	78r			Jane Nelson	dau		4		Dur
9574	78r			Mary A. Nelson	dau		2		Dur
9575	78r			Robert Nelson	bro		40	solicitor's clerk	Dur
9576	78r	78 b	Fleshergate	William Brotten	hea	m	31	cordwainer	Nry Whitby
9577	78r			Ann Brotten	wif	m	39		Had Dunbar
9578	78r			Robert Rolison	nep		8		Dur
9579	78r			Peter Bradley	vis		31	cordwainer	Irl
9580	78r			Thomas Devasey	vis	m	48	cordwainer	Irl
9581	78r	8	Elvet Bridge	Joseph Bridick	hea	m	63	ironmonger <& nailmaker>	Dur Weardale
9582	78r			Maria Bridick	wif	m	62		Yks
9583	78r			John B. Bridick	son		32	MRCS England, LSA *	Dur
9584	78r			Joseph Bridick	son		29	bookseller	Dur
9585	78r			Jane S. Bridick	dau		26		Dur
9586	78v	9	Elvet Bridge	John Readhead	hea		28	draper employing 1 man	Nbl
9587	78v			William Reed	sho		18	draper, assistant	Dur South Shields
9588	78v			Maria Hansel	ser		18	house servant	Dur Langley
9589	78v	10	Elvet Bridge	Jane E. Middleton	hea		41	dressmaker <& milliner>	Dur [D] S. Margaret
9590	78v			Louisa S. Middleton	sis		29	dressmaker <& milliner>	Dur [D] S. Margaret
9591	78v	11	Elvet Bridge	George Dixon	hea	m	38	grocer <& tea dealer>	Sry
9592	78v			Susanna Dixon	wif	m	24		Cam
9593	78v			George Dixon	son		5		War
9594	78v			Robert Dixon	son		4		War
9595	78v			William Dixon	son		1		Dur
9596	78v			Richard Chalk	sho		20	grocer, assistant	Cam
9597	78v			Mary Gray	ser		15	house servant	Dur
9598	78v	12	Elvet Bridge	Thomas Hopper	hea	m	26	fruiterer	Dur
9599	78v			Ann Hopper	wif	m	25		Dur
9600	78v			Isabella Hopper	dau		1		Dur
9601	78v			Thomas R. Hopper	son		3m		Dur
9602	78v			Jane Robinson	mlw	w	50	formerly fruiterer	Dur
9603	79r	12	Elvet Bridge	Thomas Robinson	hea	m	31	gardener	Dur [D] S. Nicholas
9604	79r			Rosanna Robinson	wif	m	35		Ldy Londonderry
9605	79r	13	Elvet Bridge	Eliza Torr	hea	m	30	milliner <hosier *>	Lan
9606	79r			Sarah Charlton			19	milliner, assistant	Lan
9607	79r			Isabella Etherington	ser		22	house servant	Dur

			one house uninhabited						
9608	79r	15	Elvet Bridge	John Cruddas	hea	m	52	watchmaker <& jeweller>	Dur
9609	79r			Jane Cruddas	wif	m	54		Nbl
9610	79r			Henry Cruddas	son		28	watchmaker <& jeweller>	Dur
9611	79r			Ellen Cruddas	dau		18		Dur
9612	79r			William Dalton	app		19	watchmaker, apprentice	Dur Stockton
9613	79r			Mary Forster	ser		17	house servant	Dur
9614	79r	18	Elvet Bridge	Edward Waddingham	hea	m	60	draper & hatter *	Lin
9615	79r			Elizabeth Waddingham	wif	m	60		Hef
9616	79r			William Waddingham	nep	w	24	draper, assistant	Nth
9617	79r			Thomas Sanglier	app		19	draper, apprentice	Dur
9618	79v			Thomas Wetherall	app		15	draper, apprentice	Dur
9619	79v			Jane Taylor	ser		24	house servant	Nbl Newcastle S. John
9620	79v			Jane Pay	ser		13	house servant	Dur
9621	79v	19	Elvet Bridge	Joseph Holmes	hea		49	grocer <& tea dealer>	Yks
9622	79v			William Robinson	ser		17	grocer, apprentice	Yks
9623	79v			George C. Crosby	ser		15	grocer, apprentice	Dur Norton
9624	79v			Isabella Hansel	ser		25	house servant	Dur Langley
9625	79v	20	Elvet Bridge	George Heppel	hea	w	53	cordwainer	Yks
9626	79v			Jane Heppel	dau		20		Dur
9627	79v			Mary Heppel	dau		18		Dur
9628	79v	21	Elvet Bridge	Henry Fenwick	hea	m	54	grocer *	Dur
9629	79v			Jane Fenwick	wif	m	32		Yks
9630	79v			Ann Cowey	ser		18	house servant	Dur
9631	79v	22 a	Elvet Bridge	Mark Hopper	hea	m	58	painter <& glazier *>	Dur
9632	79v			Mary Hopper	wif	m	60		Dur
9633	80r	22 b	Elvet Bridge	Margaret Bateman	hea	w	56	marine store dealer	Dur
9634	80r			John Bateman	son		22	solicitor's clerk	Dur
9635	80r	23	Elvet Bridge	Jane Bland	hea	w	56	confectioner	Dur [D] S. Mary-1-Bow
9636	80r			Ann Bland	dau		30		Dur [D] S. Mary-1-Bow
9637	80r			Jane Bland	dau		28		Dur [D] S. Nicholas
9638	80r			Mary Cateness	ser		23	house servant	Dur
9639	80r	24	Elvet Bridge	Charles Dawson	hea	m	28	painter	Dur
9640	80r			Jane E. Dawson	wif	m	27	dressmaker	Dur
9641	80r	25	Elvet Bridge	William A. Malcolm	hea	m	26	glass and china dealer	Dur
9642	80r			Frances Malcolm	wif	m	25		Dur
9643	80r			Thomas Malcolm	bro		31	ironmonger emp 4 men	Dur
9644	80r			Mary Dowsey	ser		16	house servant	Dur
9645	80r	26	Elvet Bridge	John Downs	hea	m	32	spirit merchant *	Sfk
9646	80r			Amelia Downs	wif	m	39		Ken
9647	80r			John Downs	son		1		Dur
9648	80v			Jemima Downs	sis		24		Sfk
9649	80v			Mary Birk	ser		20	house servant	Dur
9650	80v	29	Saddler Street	George Bailes	hea	m	56	cordwainer	Dur
9651	80v			Mary Bailes	wif	m	50		Dur
9652	80v			George Bailes	son		28	cordwainer	Dur
9653	80v			Thomas Bailes	son		25	hairdresser	Dur
9654	80v			Elizabeth Bailes	dau		12	scholar	Dur
9655	80v			Margaret Bailes	dau		9	scholar	Dur
9656	80v	30	Saddler Street	Michael Bailes	hea	w	82	cordwainer	Dur
9657	80v			Elizabeth Bailes	dau		43		Dur
9658	80v	31	Saddler Street	Hannah Pearson	hea	w	64		Dur
9659	80v			George Pearson	son	w	35	joiner	Dur
9660	80v			William Pearson	son		30	attorney's clerk	Dur
9661	80v	33 a	Saddler Street	Ann Weelands	hea	w	52	cordwainer	Yks
9662	80v			Amelia McDonald	nce		21	dressmaker	Yks
9663	81r	33 b	Saddler Street	Thubron White	hea		21	grocer	Dur
9664	81r			Jane White	sis		23		Dur
9665	81r	34	Saddler Street	Jane Clark	hea		50	cook & confectioner *	Dur
9666	81r			Margaret Holburn	ser		25	[servant]	Dur Houghton
9667	81r			George Hull			13	scholar	Dur
9668	81r	35	Saddler Street	Robert Booth	hea		60	gunmaker	Dur
9669	81r	36	Saddler Street	Robert Dalby	hea	m	35	innkpr <'Royal Tent' *>	Yks
9670	81r			Lavinia Dalby	wif	m	43		Lan
9671	81r			Mary Dalby	dau		8	scholar	Dur
9672	81r			Hannah Dalby	dau		6	scholar	Dur
9673	81r			Sarah Dalby	dau		2		Dur
9674	81r			Ellen Hartley	ser		17	house servant	Lan
9675	81r			Christopher Longstaff	vis		22	farmer's son	Dur Whitburn
9676	81r	37	Saddler Street	Turner Meggeson	hea	m	51	painter <& glazier>	Dur
9677	81r			Mary Meggeson	wif	m	54		Yks
9678	81r			William J. Meggeson	son		24	bank clerk	Dur
9679	81v			Mary Meggeson	dau		21		Dur
9680	81v			Margaret Meggeson	dau		19		Dur
9681	81v			John T. Meggeson	son		16	painter, apprentice	Dur
9682	81v			Jane Meggeson	dau		14	scholar	Dur
9683	81v			Elizabeth Simmons	ser		18	house servant	Dur
9684	81v	38	Saddler Street	Elizabeth Featonby	hea		70	dressmaker <& milliner>	Dur
9685	81v			Isabella Featonby	sis		57	dressmaker <& milliner>	Dur
9686	81v			Ann Tindale	vis		39	dressmaker	Dur Whitworth
9687	81v			Hannah Todd	ser		26	house servant	Dur Chilton

9688	81v	39	Saddler Street	Elizabeth Colling	hea	62	proprietor of houses	Dur
9689	81v			Elizabeth Hardy	ser	16	house servant	Dur Penshaw
9690	81v	40	Saddler Street	George Smith	hea m	35	solicitor	Dur
9691	81v			Mary J. Smith	wif m	26		Dur [D] S. Nicholas
9692	81v			George F. Smith	son	4	scholar	Dur [D] S. Nicholas
9693	81v			Anne L. Smith	dau	1		Dur [D] S. Nicholas
9694	81v			Edmund Smith	son	1		Dur [D] S. Nicholas
9695	82r			Ann Leadbitter	ser	24	house servant	Dur
9696	82r			Elizabeth Johnson	ser	19	house servant	Dur Sunderland
9697	82r	41	Saddler Street	Henry A. Peele	hea m	34	innkeeper *	Dur [D] S. Margaret
9698	82r			Ann Peele	wif m	33		Dur [D] S. Margaret
9699	82r			Henry A. Peele	son	10	scholar	Dur [D] S. Margaret
9700	82r			Catherine Peele	dau	7	scholar	Dur [D] S. Margaret
9701	82r			Mary Peele	dau	5	scholar	Dur [D] S. Oswald
9702	82r			Anne Peele	dau	3		Dur [D] S. Oswald
9703	82r			Mary A. Wardhave	ser	18	house servant	Dur Heworth
9704	82r	42	Saddler Street	William Broadley	hea m	31	perfumer <& hatter *>	Yks
9705	82r			Mary Broadley	wif m	22		Dur
9706	82r			Edith A. Broadley	dau	1		Dur [D] S. Oswald
9707	82r			Ellen Armstrong	ser	18	house servant	Dur Hetton
9708	82r	43	Saddler Street	Anthony Gleason	hea w	77	retired perfumer	Dur [D] S. Nicholas
9709	82r			Mary Turnbull	ser	23	housekeeper	Dur Chester-le-Street
9710	82r			Mary Rawling	ser	54	house servant	Dur Rainton
9711	82v	44	Saddler Street	Dinah Thwaites	hea w	79	housekeeper	Dur
9712	82v			Mary Thwaites	dau	40		Dur [D] S. Nicholas
			two houses uninhabited					
9713	82v	46	Saddler Street	Robert P. Ackroyd	hea m	34	confectioner *	Dur
9714	82v			Sarah Ackroyd	wif m	45		Dur
9715	82v			Sarah B. Ackroyd	dau	15		Dur
9716	82v			Anne B. Ackroyd	dau	13	scholar	Dur
9717	82v			Elizabeth Ackroyd	dau	11	scholar	Dur
9718	82v			George B. Ackroyd	son	9	scholar	Dur
9719	82v			Mary B. Ackroyd	dau	7	scholar	Dur
9720	82v			Jane Jopling	nce	23	confectioner	Dur
9721	82v			Mary Embleton	ser	18	house servant	Dur Gateshead
9722	82v			Henry Jopling	nep	22	tailor	Dur
9723	82v	52	Saddler Street	Mary Shaw	hea w	66		Dur
9724	82v			Margaret Shaw	dau	35	dressmaker	Dur [D] S. Nicholas
9725	82v			John Shaw	gsn	13	solicitor's clerk	Dum Dumbarton *
9726	83r	53 a	Saddler Street	Thomas Hutton	hea	35	bookbinder emp 6 men *	Dur
9727	83r	53 b	Saddler Street	William Moore	hea m	34	whitesmith emp 2 app *	Dur
9728	83r			Margaret Moore	wif m	30		Dur
9729	83r			Phyllis Moore	dau	12	scholar	Dur
9730	83r			Margaret Moore	dau	10	scholar	Dur
9731	83r	54 a	Saddler Street	George E. Boyd	hea m	49	cordwainer	Dur
9732	83r			Elizabeth Boyd	wif m	50		Nbl
9733	83r			Anne Boyd	dau	19		Dur [D] North Bailey
9734	83r			Charles Boyd	son	15	bootcloser	Dur [D] North Bailey
9735	83r			John Boyd	son	13	errand boy	Dur [D] North Bailey
9736	83r	54 b	Saddler Street	Elizabeth Chisman	hea	43	formerly schoolmistress	Dur
9737	83r			Charlotte Chisman	dau	14		Dur Gateshead
9738	83r			Sarah Chisman	sis	33	formerly schoolmistress	Dur
9739	83r	55 a	Saddler Street	John Wilkinson	hea m	44	tailor employing 4 men *	Ess
9740	83r			Eleanor Wilkinson	wif m	37		Dur
9741	83r			Martin Wilkinson	son	19	printer, apprentice	Dur [D] S. Nicholas
9742	83v			John Wilkinson	son	12	scholar	Dur
9743	83v			Eleanor Wilkinson	dau	9	scholar	Dur
9744	83v			Charlotte Wilkinson	dau	7	scholar	Dur
9745	83v	55 b	Saddler Street	William Forster	hea m	39	tailor	Dur
9746	83v			Hannah Forster	wif m	39		Dur
9747	83v			Elizabeth Forster	mth w	79	{blind}	Dur
9748	83v			Susanna Forster	dau	18		Dur
9749	83v			William Forster	son	17	tailor, apprentice	Dur
9750	83v			Robert Forster	son	15		Dur
9751	83v			John Forster	son	11	scholar	Dur
9752	83v			Francis Forster	son	6	scholar	Dur
9753	83v			Edward Forster	son	2		Dur
9754	83v			Ann Forster	dau	15		Dur
9755	83v	57 a	Saddler Street	George Richardson	hea w	59	groom	Dur
9756	83v			Elizabeth Richardson	dau	19	<grocer>	Dur
9757	83v			John Richardson	son	17		Dur
9758	83v			Mary Richardson	dau	14	scholar	Dur
9759	83v			Joseph Hull	vis	24	coachman	Dur Eggleston
9760	83v			William Mossom	vis	21	groom	Dur Sedgefield
9761	84r	57 b	Saddler Street	Mary Waggot	hea	39	dressmaker	Nbl
9762	84r	58	Saddler Street	William Sewell	hea m	37	tailor emp 9 men 5 app *	Dur [D] S. Oswald
9763	84r			Ann Sewell	wif m	35		Dur Langley
9764	84r			John Sewell	son	7	scholar	Yks
9765	84r			William Sewell	son	4	scholar	Yks
9766	84r			Ann Sewell	dau	1m		Dur
9767	84r			Elizabeth Lumley	ser	19	house servant	Dur Stanhope

9768	84r	59	Saddler Street	Ann Nelson	hea w	37	innkeeper *	Dur
9769	84r			Thomas Nelson	son	8	scholar	Dur
9770	84r			Ann Nelson	dau	4	scholar	Dur
9771	84r			Catherine Miller	ser	16	house servant	Dur
9772	84r			Isabella Lumsden	ser	15	house servant	Dur
9773	84r			Thomas Mordue	vis	23	joiner	Dur
9774	84r			James Potts	vis	26	mason	Nbl
9775	84r	60 a	Saddler Street	William Hodgson	hea m	45	confectioner <eating ho>	Yks
9776	84r			Margaret Hodgson	wif m	51		Dur
9777	84r			Mary A. Johnson	nce	12	scholar	Nbl Newcastle
9778	84v	60 b	Saddler Street	Charles Plimmer	hea m	45	cordwainer <sexton *>	Lan
9779	84v			Jane Plimmer	wif m	49		Nbl
9780	84v			Hannah Plimmer	dau	24	dressmaker	Dur
9781	84v			John Plimmer	son	23	cabinetmaker	Dur
9782	84v			Timothy Plimmer	son	21	hairdresser	Dur
9783	84v			Jane Plimmer	dau	14		Dur
9784	84v			Charles Plimmer	son	9	scholar	Dur
9785	84v			Henry Plimmer	son	6	scholar	Dur
9786	84v			William Plimmer	son	2		Dur
9787	84v	60 a	Saddler Street	Joseph McGreger	hea m	27	cabinetmaker	Sct
9788	84v			Margaret McGreger	wif m	28		Dur
9789	84v	60 b	Saddler Street	John Rafferty	hea m	36	porter (grocer's)	Sct
9790	84v			Mary Rafferty	wif m	26		Nbl
9791	84v			Agnes Rafferty	dau	6	scholar	Irl
9792	84v			James Rafferty	son	2		Nbl Newcastle
9793	85r	60 c	Saddler Street	Ralph Thwaites	hea m	51	cordwainer <bellman>	Dur
9794	85r			Elizabeth Thwaites	wif m	49		Dur
9795	85r			John Thwaites	son	28	tailor	Dur
9796	85r	61	Saddler Street	Thomas Hunter	hea m	36	fancy goods dealer *	Dur
9797	85r			Agnes A. Hunter	wif m	37	dressmaker	Dur
9798	85r			Thomas Hunter	son	6	scholar	Dur
9799	85r			Charles Hunter	son	5	scholar	Dur
9800	85r			Edwin Hunter	son	2		Dur
9801	85r			Frederick Hunter	son	8m		Dur
9802	85r			Elizabeth Hall	nce	27	dressmaker	Dur Bishop Auckland
9803	85r			Grace Reavely	ser	17	house servant	Nbl Newcastle
9804	85r	62	Saddler Street	John Gainford	hea m	40	mason <& builder>	Dur
9805	85r			Elizabeth Gainford	wif m	34		Dur [D] S. Oswald
9806	85r			Joseph Gainford	son	13	scholar	Dur [D] S. Oswald
9807	85r			William Gainford	son	10	scholar	Dur [D] S. Oswald
9808	85r	63	Saddler Street	Thomas Bailes	hea m	50	innkpr <'Shakespeare'>	Dur
9809	85r			Mary Bailes	wif m	42		Dur Brandon
9810	85v			Thomas Bailes	son	18	whitesmith, apprentice	Dur
9811	85v			John Bailes	son	14	tailor, apprentice	Dur
9812	85v			Michael Bailes	son	10	scholar	Dur
9813	85v			George Bailes	son	8	scholar	Dur
9814	85v			Mary Bailes	dau	3	scholar	Dur
9815	85v			Mary Crasswell	ser	22	house servant	Dur Hetton
9816	85v			Mary A. Hunter	ser	16	house servant	Dur Haswell
9817	85v	64	Saddler Street	Frances Andrews	hea w	70	bookseller & stationer *	Dur
9818	85v			Frances Andrews	dau	40		Dur
9819	85v			George Andrews	son	37	bookseller, assistant *	Dur
9820	85v			Frances Watson	gda	21		Dur
9821	85v			Jane Watson	gda	20		Dur
9822	85v			Anne Ward	ser	20	house servant	Irl
9823	85v	65 a	Saddler Street	George Lightfoot	hea m	50	agricultural labourer	Nry Scarborough
9824	85v			Elizabeth Lightfoot	wif m	49		Dur
9825	85v			Barbara Lightfoot	dau	14	scholar	Dur
9826	85v			John G. Lightfoot	son	5	scholar	Dur
9827	86r	65 b	Saddler Street	William Gunn	hea w	56	groom	Sct
9828	86r			Harriet Gunn	dau	20	straw-bonnetmaker	Ssx Chichester
9829	86r	65 c	Saddler Street	Ellen Moses	hea w	48		Dur
9830	86r			Elizabeth Moses	dau	19	dressmaker	Dur
9831	86r			Ellen Moses	dau	18	dressmaker	Dur
9832	86r			John Moses	son	12	tailor, apprentice	Dur
9833	86r			Mary A. Moses	dau	10	scholar	Dur
9834	86r			Fanny Moses	dau	8	scholar	Dur
9835	86r	65 d	Saddler Street	William Smith	hea w	39	tailor	Dur
9836	86r			Elizabeth Smith	sis	42	housekeeper	Dur
9837	86r			John Smith	son	7		Dur
			one house uninhabited					
9838	86r	68 a	Saddler Street	James Macknight	hea m	42	fruiterer <& game dlr *>	Dur
9839	86r			Elizabeth Macknight	wif m	42		Dur
9840	86r			James Macknight	son	22	painter	Dur
9841	86r			Mark Macknight	son	21	upholsterer	Dur
9842	86v			John Macknight	son	19	fruiterer	Sfk
9843	86v			William Macknight	son	17	joiner, apprentice	Dur
9844	86v			Joseph Macknight	son	14	tailor, apprentice	Dur
9845	86v			Elizabeth Macknight	dau	12	scholar	Dur
9846	86v			Tom Macknight	son	10	scholar	Dur
9847	86v			Edward Macknight	son	8	scholar	Dur

9848	86v	68 a	Saddler Street	Harry Macknight	son	6	scholar	Dur
9849	86v			Alice Macknight	dau	1		Dur
9850	86v			Catherine French	ser	16	house servant	Dur
9851	86v	68 b	Saddler Street	Christopher Finley	hea m	49	horse breaker *	Dur
9852	86v			Abigail Finley	wif m	43		Dur
9853	86v	69	Saddler Street	William Clarke	hea m	50	innkeeper *	Dur Cole Hill
9854	86v			Jane Clarke	wif m	43		Yks
9855	86v			Anne S. Clarke	dau	21		Dur
9856	86v			Emma J. Clarke	dau	19		Dur Sedgefield
9857	86v			Elizabeth Clarke	dau	17		Dur Sedgefield
9858	86v			John I. Clarke	son	15		Dur Sedgefield
9859	86v			Amelia A. Clarke	dau	12	scholar	Dur Sedgefield
9860	87r			Sarah Clarke	dau	10	scholar	Dur Sedgefield
9861	87r			Frances M. Clarke	dau	7	scholar	Dur Sedgefield
9862	87r			Agnes D. Clarke	dau	2		Dur Stockton
9863	87r			William Reed	vis	15	farmer's servant	Dur Bishop Middleham
9864	87r			George Jackson	vis	64	retired army officer	Dur Stockton
9865	87r	12-14	Market Place	Randal Stevenson	hea	30	draper, assistant *	Dur
9866	87r			George Hudson	ser	27	draper, assistant *	Dur
9867	87r			William Strachan	ser	24	draper, assistant *	Sct
9868	87r			John Lowe	ser	22	draper, assistant *	Dur
9869	87r			Hodgson Henderson	ser	21	draper, assistant *	Dur Stanhope
9870	87r			John Pattison	ser	21	draper, apprentice	Cul
9871	87r			John S. Arthur	ser	19	draper, apprentice	Dur
9872	87r			George Coward	ser	16	draper, apprentice	Dur
9873	87r			Thomas Laycock	ser	20	draper, apprentice	Dur Merrington
9874	87r			John White	ser	31	draper, porter	Yks
9875	87r			Dorothy Carrick	ser	21	house servant	Nbl
9876	87r			Elizabeth Shelton	ser	17	house servant	Dur
9877	87r			Mary White	ser	17	house servant	Dur [D] S. Nicholas
9878	87v	15 a	Market Place	Alan W. Hutchison	hea	51	wine <& spirit> merchant	Dur
9879	87v			Sarah Hutchison	sis	48		Dur
9880	87v			Elizabeth Hutchison	sis	46		Dur
9881	87v			Margaret Sedgwick	ser	32	house servant	Nry Croft
9882	87v			Mary Wright	ser	23	house servant	Dur [D] S. Margaret
9883	87v	15 b	Market Place	Thomas Wright	hea w	49	wine merchant's porter	Dur
9884	87v			Elizabeth Wright	dau	19		Dur [D] S. Nicholas
9885	87v			Harriet Wright	dau	16		Dur [D] S. Nicholas
9886	87v			William Wright	son	12	scholar	Dur [D] S. Nicholas
9887	87v			Jane Wright	dau	7	scholar	Dur [D] S. Nicholas
			one house uninhabited					
9888	87v	16	Market Place	George Emmerson	hea m	32	innkpr <'Rose & Crown'>	Dur
9889	87v			Catherine Emmerson	wif m	32		Nfk Rudham /"Rodham"
9890	87v			Edward Lee	vis m	58	farmer	Nbl
9891	87v			Henry Rutherford	vis m	33	groom	Dur
9892	87v			William Peddie	vis m	27	groom	Sct
9893	87v			Edward Wallace	vis	37	groom	Lks Glasgow
9894	88r			Margaret Borrowdale	ser	20	house servant	Dur
9895	88r			Margaret Bainbridge	ser	20	house servant	Dur Houghton
9896	88r			Thomas Jackson	ser	50	porter	Dur Cockerton
9897	88r			Kate Keerney	ser	23	house servant	Irl
9898	88r			William Bennett	vis m	40	groom	Nbl
9899	88r	1 a	Silver Street	John Caldcleugh	hea	32	ironmonger *	Dur
9900	88r			Elizabeth Caldcleugh	sis	24	housekeeper	Dur
9901	88r			Margaret Liddel	ser	20	house servant	Dur Lumley
9902	88r	1 b	Silver Street	Thomas Storey	hea m	34	innkpr <'Turk's Head'>	Dur
9903	88r			Mary A. Storey	wif m	31		Dur
9904	88r			Elizabeth Snowden	mlw w	74	formerly farmer's wife	Dur
9905	88r			John Storey	son	11	scholar	Dur
9906	88r			Thomas Storey	son	4		Dur
9907	88r			Robert Storey	son	2		Dur
9908	88r			Harriet Dunn	ser	16	house servant	Dur
9909	88r			George Storey	bro m	45	farmer	Dur
9910	88r			Dorothy Storey	sil m	43		Dur
9911	88r			George Storey	nep	13	farmer's son	Dur
9912	88v			Martin Fallon	vis	25		Dur
9913	88v			Thomas Towlan	vis	21		Dur
9914	88v	1 c	Silver Street	George Greenwell	hea m	30	grocer <& tea dealer>	Dur
9915	88v			Barbara H. Greenwell	wif m	29		Dur [D] S. Margaret
9916	88v	1 d	Silver Street	Robert Armstrong	hea m	34	currier	Dur
9917	88v			Agnes Armstrong	wif m	33		Dur Bishop Auckland
9918	88v			Maria Armstrong	dau	2		Dur Bishop Auckland
9919	88v			John F. Armstrong	son	1		Dur Bishop Auckland
9920	88v			John Wade	blw	29	gardener	Dur Wolviston
9921	88v	1 e	Silver Street	John Grey	hea m	38	painter emp 2 men 1 app	Dur
9922	88v			Hannah Grey	wif m	37		Dur Lanchester
9923	88v	1 f	Silver Street	Thomas L. Clarke	hea m	27	currier *	Dur
9924	88v			Mary Clarke	wif m	23		Dur
9925	88v			William Clarke	son	3		Dur
9926	88v			Ann Clarke	dau	6m		Dur
9927	89r	1 g	Silver Street	George Thompson	hea	50	agricultural labourer	Yks

9928	89r	1 g	Silver Street	Mary Hodgson	sil	m	45		Nry Gilling
9929	89r			John Hodgson	nep		8		Dur
9930	89r			William Hodgson	nep		6		Dur
9931	89r	1 h	Silver Street	George Wales	hea	m	71	clogmaker <& lastmaker>	Dur
9932	89r			Margaret Wales	wif	m	66		Dur Houghton
9933	89r	1 i	Silver Street	Robert Greivson	hea	m	38	groom	Dur
9934	89r			Ann Greivson	wif	m	40		Dur
9935	89r			Mary Greivson	dau		16		Dur
9936	89r			Robert Greivson	son		10	scholar	Dur
9937	89r			Thomas Greivson	son		8	scholar	Dur
9938	89r	1 j	Silver Street	Jane Judson	hea	w	52	fishmonger	Dur
9939	89r			Joseph Judson	son		20	mason, apprentice	Dur
9940	89r			Susanna Judson	dau		17		Dur
9941	89r			Phyllis Judson	dau		12	scholar	Dur
9942	89r			Hannah Judson	dau		9	scholar	Dur
9943	89r			John Golightly	vis		19	butcher	Dur
			two houses uninhabited						
9944	89v	5	Silver Street·	Edward Day	hea	m	48	toy and hardwareman	Som Wincanton
9945	89v			Elizabeth Day	wif	m	50		Dur
9946	89v			Joseph Day	nep		17		Lnd
9947	89v	6 a	Silver Street	Charles Brass	hea	m	42	cabinetmaker	Dur
9948	89v			Elizabeth Brass	wif	m	44		Dur
9949	89v			Maschal Brass	son		14	joiner, apprentice	Dur
9950	89v			Jane Brass	dau		12	house servant	Dur
9951	89v			Ann Brass	dau		8	scholar	Dur
9952	89v			Eliza Brass	dau		6	scholar	Dur
9953	89v			Charles Brass	son		4		Dur
9954	89v	6 b	Silver Street	John Chalder	hea	m	27	agricultural labourer	Yks
9955	89v			Frances Chalder	wif	m	19		Dur
9956	89v	6 c	Silver Street	Thomas Clark	hea	w	47	mason	Dur [D] S. Oswald
9957	89v			Matthew Clark	son		21	joiner	Dur [D] S. Oswald
9958	89v			Eleanor Clark	dau		18		Dur [D] S. Oswald
9959	90r	7 a	Silver Street	George Cummings	hea	m	44	innkeeper <'Fleece'>	Dur
9960	90r			Margaret Cummings	wif	m	47		Dur [D] S. Nicholas
9961	90r			Martha Nicholson	ser		21	house servant	Dur Hetton
9962	90r			Frances Hepplewite	ser		21	house servant	Dur Hetton
9963	90r			James Hogg	ser		44	brewer	Dur Chester-le-Street
9964	90r			Robert Patrick	vis		20	carpet weaver	Sct
9965	90r	7 b	Silver Street	William Tilly	hea	m	42	carpet weaver	Dur
9966	90r			Ann Tilly	wif	m	44		Dur Oxclose
9967	90r			Thomas Tilly	son		18	iron moulder, apprentice	Dur [D] S. Nicholas
9968	90r			Henry Kirkham	gsn		3		Dur [D] S. Nicholas
9969	90r	7 c	Silver Street	George Wardell	hea	m	43	cordwainer	Dur Trimdon
9970	90r			Jane Wardell	wif	m	34		Dur [D] S. Giles
9971	90r			Mary Wardell	dau		17		Dur [D] S. Nicholas
9972	90r			Christopher Wardell	son		6	scholar	Dur [D] S. Nicholas
9973	90r			Joseph Wardell	son		4	scholar	Dur [D] S. Nicholas
9974	90r			George Craggs	vis	w	41	cordwainer	Dur [D] S. Margaret
9975	90v	8	Silver Street	George Wilkinson	hea	m	32	grocer employing 2 men *	Nbl
9976	90v			Elizabeth Wilkinson	wif	m	26		Dur
9977	90v			Sarah A.M. Wilkinson	dau		2m		Dur
9978	90v			Anne Weatherill	vis		21		Yks
9979	90v			Mary Rennison	ser		14	house servant	Yks
9980	90v			Sarah Drake	ser		16	house servant	Dur
9981	90v			Edward Todd	ser		17	grocer, apprentice	Yks
9982	90v			John Fatherley	ser		16	grocer, apprentice	Dur
9983	90v	9 a	Silver Street	William Shadforth	hea	m	40	auctioneer *	Dur
9984	90v			Mary A. Shadforth	wif	m	40		Dur [D] S. Nicholas
9985	90v			William R. Shadforth	son		16	builder & joiner, app	Dur [D] S. Nicholas
9986	90v			John M. Shadforth	son		14	architect	Dur [D] S. Nicholas
9987	90v			Margaret Shadforth	dau		8	scholar	Dur [D] S. Nicholas
9988	90v			Thomas Shadforth	son		7	scholar	Dur [D] S. Nicholas
9989	90v	9 b	Silver Street	Thomas Morton	hea	m	64	carpet weaver	Sct
9990	90v			Mary Morton	wif	m	59		Dur
9991	90v			John Morton	son		23	chemist, assistant	Dur
9992	90v			Thomas F. Morton	son		18	carpet weaver	Dur
9993	91r	9 c	Silver Street	James R. Thurlow	hea	m	33	currier *	Dur
9994	91r			Eleanor Thurlow	wif	m	35		Dur
9995	91r			Robert J. Thurlow	son		6	scholar	Dur
9996	91r			Elizabeth Thurlow	dau		4	scholar	Dur
9997	91r			Margaret Thurlow	dau		3		Dur
9998	91r			Eleanor Thurlow	dau		1		Dur
9999	91r			Ann Collinson	ser		18	house servant	Dur
10000	91r	10 a	Silver Street	Matthew Dean	hea	m	40	worsted manufacturer	Dur
10001	91r			Maria Dean	wif	m	34		Dur
10002	91r			Greenwell Smurthwaite	sls		14	scholar	Dur
10003	91r			William Smurthwaite	sls		10	scholar	Dur
10004	91r			Maria Dean	dau		5	scholar	Dur
10005	91r			Matthew Dean	son		2		Dur
10006	91r			Thomas Dean	son		9m		Dur
10007	91r	10 b	Silver Street	Mary Richardson	hea	w	54	charwoman /"chairwoman"	Dur

10008	91r	10 b	Silver Street	Sarah Richardson	dau		18		Dur Newbottle
10009	91v	10 c	Silver Street	William Maude	hea	m	39	dyer	Nbl
10010	91v			Elizabeth Maude	wif	m	40		Dur
10011	91v			John Maude	son		12	scholar	Dur
10012	91v			William Maude	son		10	scholar	Dur
10013	91v			Robert Maude	son		6	scholar	Dur
10014	91v			Martha Maude	dau		4	scholar	Dur
10015	91v			Thomas Maude	son		1		Dur
10016	91v	10 d	Silver Street	Isaac Moses	hea	m	29	cordwainer	Dur Wolsingham
10017	91v			Frances Moses	wif	m	31		Dur [D] S. Margaret
10018	91v			Mary Stephenson	dls		9	scholar	Dur [D] S. Margaret
10019	91v			Mary Moses	dau		4		Dur [D] S. Nicholas
10020	91v			Hannah Moses	dau		1		Dur [D] S. Nicholas
10021	91v	12 a	Silver Street	Charles Biggins	hea	w	41	tinner <& brazier>	Dur [D] S. Nicholas
10022	91v			Eleanor Biggins	dau		19	dressmaker	Dur [D] S. Nicholas
10023	91v			George Biggins	son		17	tinner, apprentice	Dur [D] S. Nicholas
10024	91v			Catherine Biggins	dau		16		Dur [D] S. Nicholas
10025	91v			Charles Biggins	son		13	scholar	Dur [D] S. Nicholas
10026	91v			Robert Biggins	son		11	scholar	Dur [D] S. Nicholas
10027	92r			Elizabeth Biggins	dau		8	scholar	Dur [D] S. Nicholas
10028	92r			Mary A. Biggins	dau		6	scholar	Dur [D] S. Nicholas
10029	92r			Thomas Biggins	son		4		Dur [D] S. Nicholas
10030	92r	12 b	Silver Street	Robert Herbert	hea	m	28	hairdresser	Dur [D] S. Margaret
10031	92r			Ann Herbert	wif	m	29		Dur [D] S. Oswald
10032	92r			Anne Herbert	dau		1		Dur [D] S. Nicholas
10033	92r	12 c	Silver Street	William Dickison	hea		42	plumber	Dur [D] S. Nicholas
10034	92r	13	Silver Street	Francis Henderson	hea	m	42	marine store dealer *	Dur Gateshead
10035	92r			Ann Henderson	wif	m	50		Dur
10036	92r			Frances Henderson	dau		20		Dur [D] S. Margaret
10037	92r			Thomas Henderson	son		18	cordwainer, apprentice	Dur [D] S. Margaret
10038	92r			Isabel Henderson	dau		10	scholar	Dur [D] S. Margaret
10039	92r	14	Silver Street	William Hind	hea	m	60	cordwainer emp 1 man *	Dur Thorpe
10040	92r			Elizabeth Hind	wif	m	57		Yks
10041	92r			Mary A. Hind	dau		20	shoebinder	Dur
10042	92r			Frances Hind	dau		17	shoebinder	Dur
10043	92v	14	Silver Street	William Robinson	hea	m	59	cabinetmaker	Dur
10044	92v			Isabella Robinson	wif	m	56		Nbl Newcastle
10045	92v			John Robinson	son		31	gardener	Dur
10046	92v			Robert Robinson	son		18	painter, apprentice	Dur [D] S. Nicholas
10047	92v			John S. Robson	blw	w	60	cordwainer	Nbl Newcastle
10048	92v			William Robson	blw		58	cordwainer	Nbl Newcastle
10049	92v			Thomas Dryden	vis	w	42	police officer	Dur
10050	92v			Mary Dryden	vis		6	scholar	Dur [D] S. Nicholas
10051	92v	15 a	Silver Street	John Simpson	hea	m	60	groom	Dur Sunderland Bridge
10052	92v			Hannah Simpson	wif	m	55		Dur Ovington
10053	92v			Robert Simpson	son		32	cordwainer	Dur Evenwood
10054	92v			Benjamin Simpson	son		28	tailor	Dur [D] S. Margaret
10055	92v			John Maughan	vis		11	scholar	Dur
10056	92v			Peter Tennet	vis		68	agricultural labourer	Dur
10057	92v	15 b	Silver Street	James Elder	hea	m	31	cabinetmaker	Nbl Newcastle
10058	92v			Mary Elder	wif	m	24	straw-bonnetmaker	Dur
10059	92v			Jane Elder	dau		3		Dur
10060	92v			Isabella Elder	dau		5m		Dur
10061	93r	17	Silver Street	Michael Morris	hea	m	30	tailor & outfitter *	Irl
10062	93r			Margaret Morris	wif	m	28		Nbl Newcastle
10063	93r			Rosanna Morris	dau		4		Nbl Newcastle
10064	93r			Catherine Morris	dau		1		Dur
10065	93r	18	Silver Street	Emmerson Adamson	hea	m	38	innkeeper <'Red Lion'>	Dur
10066	93r			Alice Adamson	wif	m	42		Dur
10067	93r			George Adamson	son		7	scholar	Dur
10068	93r			Thomas Adamson	son		5	scholar	Dur
10069	93r			Hannah Adamson	dau		5	scholar	Dur
10070	93r			Elizabeth Adamson	sis	m	37		Nbl
10071	93r			Sarah Bottom	ser		21	house servant	Gls Bristol
10072	93r			George Anderson	vis	m	37		Dur
10073	93r			Mary A. Anderson	vis	m	38		Dur
10074	93r			Ann E. Anderson	vis		5		Dur
10075	93r			Catherine Anderson	vis		3		Dur
10076	93r			Frances Anderson	vis		2m		Dur
10077	93r			George Anderson	vis		21		Dur
10078	93r			William Forster	vis	w	44		Dur
10079	93r			Johnson Dixon	vis		29		Dur
10080	93v			John Cattron	vis	m	25	blacksmith	Dur
10081	93v			George Robinson	vis		29	porter	Yks
10082	93v	19	Silver Street	Sarah Brewis	hea	w	56	innkeeper *	Nbl
10083	93v			Sarah Brewis	dau		19		Nbl Coxlodge
10084	93v	[aa]	Moatside Lane	Esther Conner	hea		40		Dub Dublin
10085	93v			Joseph Conner	son		12	errand boy	Dur
10086	93v			Elizabeth Hogg	vis		78		{blind} Dur
10087	93v	[ab]	Moatside Lane	Joseph Thackray	hea	m	27	cordwainer	Dur Brancepeth
10088	93v			Mary Thackray	wif	m	25		Dur Bow

10089	93v	[ab]	Moatside Lane	John Merchant	vis	26	cordwainer	Wil
10090	93v			Edward Welsh	vis	24	cordwainer	Cor Cork
10091	93v	[ac]	Moatside Lane	Thomas Boyd	hea m	44	tinner	Dur
10092	93v			Sarah Boyd	wif m	43		Dur
10093	93v			Margaret Boyd	dau	17	scholar	Dur
10094	93v			Thomas Boyd	son	14	currier	Dur
10095	94r	[ad]	Moatside Lane	George Norton	hea m	54	labourer	Lnd
10096	94r			Caroline Norton	wif m	62		Ery Hull
10097	94r			William Norton	son	26	agricultural labourer	Dur
10098	94r			John Norton	son	16		Dur
10099	94r	[ae]	Moatside Lane	George Appleby	hea m	53	cordwainer	Dur [D] S. Margaret
10100	94r			Mary Appleby	wif m	52		Dur Teesdale
10101	94r			John Appleby	son	28	groom	Dur Teesdale
10102	94r			George Appleby	son	26	cordwainer	Dur [D] S. Margaret
10103	94r			Elizabeth Appleby	dau	20	milliner	Dur [D] S. Margaret
10104	94r			Thomas Appleby	son	17	tailor, apprentice	Dur [D] S. Margaret
10105	94r	[af]	Moatside Lane	Joseph Lumley	hea m	55	cordwainer	Dur [D] S. Nicholas
10106	94r			Elizabeth Lumley	wif m	55		Dur [D] S. Nicholas
10107	94r	[ag]	Moatside Lane	Edward Gilmore	hea m	29	bookbinder	Nbl Newcastle *
10108	94r			Elizabeth Gilmore	wif m	28		Sct
10109	94r			Edward Low	sls	7	scholar	Dur
10110	94r			Sarah Low	dls	5	scholar	Dur
10111	94v	[ah]	Moatside Lane	Frederick Wardell	hea m	25	Post [Office] messenger	Dur
10112	94v			Ann Wardell	wif m	24		Dur [D] S. Oswald
10113	94v			John C. Wardell	son	3		Dur [D] S. Oswald
10114	94v			Jane A. Wardell	dau	9m		Dur [D] S. Nicholas
10115	94v	[ai]	Moatside Lane	William Davidson	hea m	26	carpet weaver	Sct
10116	94v			Jane Davidson	wif m	26		Sct
10117	94v			William Davidson	son	3		Dur
10118	94v			Margaret Davidson	dau	2		Dur Gateshead
10119	94v			James Davidson	son	3m		Dur
10120	94v	[aj]	Moatside Lane	William Brown	hea m	39	hairdresser	Nbl Newcastle
10121	94v			Barbara Brown	wif m	41		Nbl Newcastle
10122	94v	[ak]	Moatside Lane	Margaret Smurthwaite	hea	49	rugdresser	Irl
10123	94v			Thomas Smurthwaite	bro w	34	painter	Dur
10124	94v			Edward Smurthwaite	nep	8	scholar	Dur
10125	94v			Ann Smurthwaite	nce	6	scholar	Dur
10126	95r	[aa]	Broken Walls *	George Pearson	hea m	80	cutler <& whitesmith *>	Dur
10127	95r			Mary Pearson	wif m	78		Dur
10128	95r	[ab]	Broken Walls *	George Herring	hea m	36	cooper	Dur Hunwick
10129	95r			Jane Herring	wif m	37		Dur
10130	95r			Mary Herring	dau	11	scholar	Dur
10131	95r			John Herring	son	8	scholar	Dur
10132	95r			George Herring	son	6	scholar	Dur
10133	95r			Jane Herring	dau	3		Dur
10134	95r			Elizabeth Herring	dau	4m		Dur
10135	95r	[ac]	Broken Walls *	John Jennings	hea m	36	fishmonger <& oysterdlr>	not known
10136	95r			Margaret Jennings	wif m	24		Sct
10137	95r	[ad]	Broken Walls	Edward Fidler	hea m	36	upholsterer	Dur
10138	95r			Jessie Fidler	wif m	36		Sct
10139	95r			George Fidler	son	18	stonemason	Dur
10140	95r			Henrietta Fidler	dau	15	scholar	Dur
10141	95r			Edward Fidler	son	13	scholar	Dur Darlington
10142	95v			Ruth Fidler	dau	11	scholar	Dur
10143	95v			Marianna Fidler	dau	9	scholar	Dur Darlington
10144	95v			Henry I. Fidler	son	7	scholar	Dur
10145	95v			Christopher Fidler	son	5	scholar	Dur
10146	95v			Jane Fidler	dau	3	scholar	Dur
10147	95v			Charles Fidler	son	2m		Dur

Notes - Enumeration District 4c

9287	<'King's Arms'>
9362	county given as "Cumberland"
9430	<Backhouse & Co.'s Bank>
9450	<& music and musical instrument seller>
9467-9468	... and bacon ...
9496	<& grocer & lemonade manufacturer>
9499	<& dealer in clothes>
9505	... & cheese and bacon ...
9513	county given as "Cumberland"
9514	<cooper, hamper and basketmaker, dlr in toys (wholesale & retail), riddle and sievemaker, Berlin wool repository & wood turner>
9528	<& grocer>
9533	... & cheese and bacon factor
9545	... 6 boys <& bookseller & stationer>
9557-9558	county given as "Yorkshire"
9563	... 4 women
9583	... London, not practising
9605	... & haberdasher
9614	... <linen & woollen draper> emp 4 men
9628	<& cheese and bacon factor>
9631	... & china dealer
9645	... & porter vaults
9665	<& game dealer & eating house>
9669	... & porter merchant
9697	<'Commerce House'>
9704	... & hairdresser & toy dealer
9713	<& tea and coffee rooms>
9725	/"Dumbotham"
9726	<& paper ruler>
9727	<& bellhanger>
9739	<& draper>
9762	<& draper & robe maker>

9768	<'Buffalo's Head'>
9778	... of S. Nicholas parish
9796	<& Berlin wool repository, saddler & toy dealer>
9817,9819	<& bookbinder & music seller>
9838	... & fishmonger
9851	<livery stable keeper>
9853	<'George & Dragon'>
9865-9869	<to John Shields, draper, grocer & teadlr>
9890	<& tinner, brazier, zincworker, copper- smith & wire blind manufacturer>
9923	<& leathercutter>

9975	<& flour dealer>
9983	... cabinetmaker & upholsterer
9993	<& leathercutter>
10034	<& boot and shoemaker>
10039	... 1 apprentice
10061	<dealer in old clothes>
10082	<'Hole in the Wall'>
10107	... S. Nicholas
10126-10127	<20 Silver Street>
10126	... & bellhanger
10128-10134	<21 Silver Street>
10135-10136	<19 Silver Street>

REF	FOL	NO	STREET	FORENAME(S) SURNAME	REL C AGE	OCCUPATION	BIRTHPLACE
10148	99v	22	Silver Street	John Balmbrough	hea m 29	mustard mfr, grocer *	Dur [D] S. Giles
10149	99v			Eleanor Balmbrough	wif m 33	wife	Dur [D] S. Nicholas
10150	99v			Eleanor Young	ser 19	house servant	Dur Hetton-le-Hole
10151	99v	23	Silver Street	Mary Wright	hea w 53	cooperess	Dur Witton-le-Wear
10152	99v			Anne Wright	dau 23		Dur [D] S. Nicholas
10153	99v			Mary Wright	dau 18		Dur
10154	99v			William G. Wright	son 17	cooper	Dur [D] S. Nicholas
10155	99v			Edward Anderson	jny 33	cooper	Nbl Belford
10156	99v	24 a	Silver Street	Owen McIntyre	hea m 30	dealer in hardware	Lou
10157	99v			Ann McIntyre	wif m 24	hardware dealer's wife	Lou
10158	99v	24 b	Silver Street	Hugh Sheridan	hea m 32	labourer	Let Manorhamilton
10159	99v			Bridget Sheridan	wif m 23	labourer's wife	Sli
10160	99v			James Sheridan	son 2m		Dur
10161	99v	24 c	Silver Street	Ann Bamborough	hea m 46	cook & confectioner	Dur Pelton
10162	99v			Mary Coxon	ser 19	house servant	Ros
10163	100r	24 d	Silver Street	Daniel Bartram	hea m 36	gardener	Wry Leeds, Aberford
10164	100r			Mary Bartram	wif m 34	gardener's wife	Dfs
10165	100r			Thomas Bartram	son 10	at home	Cul Penrith
10166	100r			Agnes Bartram	dau 7	at school	Dur Durham
10167	100r			Nicholas Bartram	son 5	at home	Dur Durham
10168	100r	26	Silver Street	Jane Hall	hea w 49	licensed victualler *	Dur Tan Hills
10169	100r			John Hall	son 24	cabinetmaker	Dur
10170	100r			William Hall	son 22	brewer	Dur
10171	100r			Silas Hall	son 18	miller	Dur
10172	100r			Isabella Hall	dau 15		Dur
10173	100r			Elizabeth Walker	ser 19	house servant	Dur Hetton-le-Hole
10174	100r	27	Silver Street	Joseph Patterson	hea 21	grocer & tea dealer *	Dur Pittington
10175	100r			Anthony Smith	app m 18	apprentice [grocer?]	Dur Pittington
10176	100v	28	Silver Street	John Ord	hea m 40	hatter & clk in Will Off	Dur Tudhoe Mill
10177	100v			Rebecca Anne Ord	wif m 36	hatter's wife	Dur Whitburn
10178	100v			William Henry Ord	son 17	printer & compositor	Dur [D] S. Oswald
10179	100v			Elizabeth Ord	dau 14	at home	Dur [D] S. Giles
10180	100v			Anne Ord	dau 13	scholar	Dur [D] S. Nicholas
10181	100v			John Ord	son 10	scholar	Dur [D] S. Nicholas
10182	100v			Mary Louisa Ord	dau 7	scholar	Dur [D] S. Nicholas
10183	100v			George Ord	son 8m		Dur [D] S. Nicholas
10184	100v			Sarah Eliza Lacy	vis m 22	wife of colliery viewer	Dur Bishop Auckland
10185	100v			Hannah Wilkinson	ser 18	house servant	Dur Chester-le-Street
10186	101r	29 a	Silver Street	Eleanor Ferguson	hea w 70	annuitant	Dur
10187	101r			Elizabeth Ferguson	dau 29		Dur
10188	101r			Eleanor Street	gda 20		Dur
10189	101r			Ashley Street	slw m 43	carpet weaver	Dur
10190	101r			Mary Robinson	ser w 77	house servant	Dur
10191	101r	29 b	Silver Street	William Marley	hea m 36	draper	Dur East Thickley
10192	101r			Margaret Marley	wif m 36	draper's wife	Nbl Rothbury
10193	101r			Joseph Scott Gray	ser 18	draper's assistant	Dur Witton Gilbert
10194	101r			Sarah Jane Lumley	vis 10		Dur Lanchester
10195	101r			Elizabeth Dixon	ser 23	house servant	Dur Denton
10196	101r	30 a	Silver Street	John Longstaff	hea m 34	innkeeper <'Goat'>	Dur Lanchester
10197	101r			Margaret Longstaff	wif m 23	innkeeper's wife	Dur Chester-le-Street
10198	101r			William Longstaff	son 9	scholar	Dur Thorpe
10199	101r			Isabella Longstaff	dau 5	scholar	Dur Chester-le-Street
10200	101r			Thomas Davidson	ldr 39	soldier	Wry Shipley
10201	101r			Stephen Sidnell	ldr 21	soldier	Wil Chippenham
10202	101v	30 b	Silver Street	John Hall	hea m 60	tailor	Dur
10203	101v			Ann Hall	wif m 65	tailor's wife	Dur Staindrop, Barne
10204	101v	30 c	Silver Street	John Mensforth	hea m 59	ostler	Nry Lovesome Hill
10205	101v			Ann Mensforth	wif m 53	midwife	Dur Ferryhill
10206	101v			Mary Mensforth	dau 23	dressmaker	Dur Ferryhill
10207	101v	30 d	Silver Street	Ann Lumley	hea w 81	confectioner	Dur Durham
10208	101v			Ann Davison	dau m 52	confectioner	Dur Durham
10209	101v	31	Silver Street	John Spink <jn>	hea m 44	<wholesale> confectioner	Dur [D] Sidegate
10210	101v			Elizabeth Spink	wif m 37	confectioner's wife	Dur [D] New Elvet
10211	101v			Ann Russell	w 36	dressmaker	Dur [D] New Elvet
10212	101v			Margaret Conn	ser 18	house servant	Dur Old Penshaw
10213	101v	32 a	Silver Street	John Smith	hea m 38	journeyman joiner	Dur [D] S. Oswald
10214	101v			Mary Smith	wif m 38	joiner's wife	Yks York, Walmgate
10215	101v			Hannah Smith	dau 14	scholar	Dur [D] S. Nicholas
10216	101v			George Smith	son 12	scholar	Dur [D] S. Nicholas
10217	101v			John Smith	son 8	scholar	Dur [D] S. Nicholas
10218	102r	32 b	Silver Street	William Robson	hea m 36	hairdresser & toy dealer	Wry Leeds
10219	102r			Elizabeth Robson	wif m 38	hairdresser's wife	Nry Raskelf
10220	102r			Elizabeth Robson	dau 10	scholar	Dur [D] S. Nicholas
10221	102r			William Robson	son 6	scholar	Dur [D] S. Nicholas
10222	102r			Mary Robson	dau 1	home	Dur [D] S. Nicholas
10223	102r	32 c	Silver Street	John Wilson	hea m 59	machinesmith	Dur Darlington
10224	102r			Ann Wilson	wif m 59	wife	Dur Darlington
10225	102r			John Wilson	son m 29	machinesmith	Dur Durham
10226	102r			James Wilson	son 18	machinesmith	Dur Durham

10227	102r	32 c	Silver Street	Ann Wilson	dau		21	milliner	Dur Darlington
10228	102r	33	Silver Street	William Marshall	hea m		46	innkpr <'Albert House'*>	Nbl Longhoughton
10229	102r			Mary Marshall	wif m		37	innkeeper's wife	Dur [D] S. Margaret
10230	102r			Mary Marshall	dau		4	innkeeper's daughter	Dur [D] S. Nicholas
10231	102r			Eleanor Marshall	sis		35	labourer's daughter	Nbl High Buston
10232	102r			Eleanor Marshall	mth w		78	farmer's daughter	Nbl Brandon
10233	102r			Margaret Magee	sil		24	house servant	Dur [D] S. Margaret
10234	102r			Sarah Wilkinson	ser		17	house servant	Dur [D] S. Nicholas
10235	102v	34-35	Silver Street	Thomas O'Neil	hea m		39	<furniture> broker *	Dow Downpatrick
10236	102v			Sarah O'Neil	wif m		26	broker's wife *	Nry Richmond
10237	102v			James O'Neil	son		3	broker's son	Dur Durham
10238	102v			John O'Neil	nep		3	broker's nephew	Dow Newry
10239	102v			James O'Neil	unc m		65	labourer	Dow Downpatrick
10240	102v			Dorothy Liddle	ser		20	house servant	Yks Gales
10241	102v			Mary Ann Liddle	ser		12	house servant	Dur Trimdon
10242	102v	37	Silver Street	Charles Wilson Lowes	hea m		40	tobacco manufacturer *	Ken Cheriton
10243	102v			Jane Ann Lowes	wif m		30	tobacco mfr's wife	Dur South Shields
10244	102v			Charles A. Lowes	son		8	scholar	Dur Durham
10245	102v			Ann Donald	ser		24	house servant	Dur Durham
10246	102v	38	Silver Street	John Morrow	hea m		30	innkpr <'Black Lion' *>	Dur [D] Framwelgate
10247	102v			Mary Ann Morrow	wif m		27	innkeeper's wife	Dur Jarrow
10248	102v			Mary Morrow	dau		1	innkeeper's daughter	Dur [D] Silver Street
10249	102v			Dorothy Angles	ser		27	house servant	Dur Houghton-1-Spring
10250	102v			James Lowry	ldr		56	gardener	Nbl Morpeth
10251	102v			Joseph Lowry	ldr		23	gardener	Nbl Morpeth
10252	102v			John Richardson	flw m		47	miner	Dur Westerton
10253	103r	39	Silver Street	William Caldcleugh	hea w		46	deputy postmaster	Dur Durham
10254	103r			Ann Caldcleugh	dau		14	at home	Dur Durham
10255	103r			Fanny Caldcleugh	dau		12	scholar	Dur Durham
10256	103r			William Caldcleugh	son		12	scholar	Dur Durham
10257	103r			Phyllis Caldcleugh	dau		10	scholar	Dur Durham
10258	103r			Lucy Caldcleugh	dau		8	scholar	Dur Durham
10259	103r			Henry Caldcleugh	son		7	scholar	Dur Durham
10260	103r			Walter Tyler Caldcleugh	son		5	at home	Dur Durham
10261	103r			Horace Caldcleugh	son		3	at home	Dur Durham
10262	103r			Elizabeth Tyler	sil		46	annuitant	Dur Durham
10263	103r			Eliza Best	ser		18	house servant	Dur Easington
10264	103r	40	Silver Street	Gregor McG. Mitchell	hea m		26	hosier <& worsted mfr> *	Sct
10265	103r			Elizabeth Mitchell	wif m		25		Sct
10266	103r			Margaret McG. Mitchell	dau		4		Dur [D] S. Margaret
10267	103r			Elizabeth Mitchell	dau		2		Dur [D] S. Margaret
10268	103r			Duncan Mitchell	son		<1m		Dur [D] S. Nicholas
10269	103r			Margaret Mitchell	sis		24	shopkeeper, hosier	Sct
10270	103r			Marion Liddell	sil		18	housekeeper	Sct
10271	103r			Ivan Graham	ser		17	house servant	Sct
10272	103r			Anne Wright	ser w		55	nurse	Dur [D] S. Oswald
10273	103v	19 a	Market Place	James Monks	hea m		31	chemist, druggist *	Lan Lancaster
10274	103v			Jane Monks	wif m		39	wife	Dur Durham
10275	103v			Mary Ann Hall	ser		20	house servant	Dur Durham
10276	103v	19 b	Market Place	Thomas Scawin	hea m		38	saddler <& harnessmaker>	Dur [D] S. Nicholas
10277	103v			Jane Scawin	wif m		37	saddler's wife	Dur Darlington
10278	103v			Jane Scawin	dau		4	saddler's daughter	Dur [D] S. Margaret
10279	103v			Mary Scawin	dau		1	saddler's daughter	Dur [D] S. Nicholas
10280	103v			Elizabeth Hopper	ser		18	house servant	Dur [D] S. Margaret
10281	103v			Mary Jane Brydon	ser		13	house servant	Nbl Newcastle S. John
10282	103v	20 a	Market Place	Thomas Summers	hea m		49	tanner employing 6 men	Dur Durham
10283	103v			Jane Summers	wif m		44	tanner's wife	Per Scone
10284	103v			Mary Summers	dau		3	tanner's daughter	Dur Durham
10285	103v			Fanny Summers	dau		3	tanner's daughter	Per Scone
10286	103v			Mary Robson	sil		42	annuitant	Dur Durham
10287	103v			Jane Richardson	ser		17	house servant	Dur Hetton-le-Hole
10288	103v			Elizabeth Richardson	ser		15	house servant	Dur Hartlepool
10289	104r	20 b	Market Place	Francis C. Robinson	hea m		45	tailor	Dur [D] Framwelgate
10290	104r			Elizabeth Robinson	wif m		42	wife	Dur [D] S. Margaret
10291	104r			Jane Alice Robinson	dau		16	daughter	Dur [D] S. Nicholas
10292	104r			William Robinson	son		10	scholar	Dur [D] Framwelgate
10293	104r			Joseph Robinson	son		8	scholar	Dur [D] S. Nicholas
10294	104r			Thomas Robinson	son		5	scholar	Dur [D] S. Nicholas
10295	104r			Elizabeth Robinson	dau		3	at home	Dur [D] S. Nicholas
10296	104r	21 a	Market Place	William Rippon	hea w		70	retired tradesman	Dur Durham
10297	104r			Elizabeth Mary Rippon	dau		40		Dur Durham
10298	104r			Jane Walton	sis w		60		Dur Durham
10299	104r			Jane Robinson	ser		20	[servant]	Nfk Walsingham
10300	104r	21 b	Market Place	James Shaw	hea w		46	grocer <& cheesemonger>	Dur Sedgefield
10301	104r			Mary Anne Shaw	dau		17	home	Dur Durham
10302	104r			Emily Jane Shaw	dau		16	home	Dur Durham
10303	104r			Helen E. Shaw	dau		11	scholar	Dur Durham
10304	104r			Mary Jopling	cou		54	housekeeper	Dur Chester-le-Street
10305	104v	22 a	Market Place	John Blenkinsop	hea m		33	carpet weaver	Dur Barnard Castle
10306	104v			Ann Blenkinsop	wif m		33	carpet weaver's wife	Nry Romaldkirk *
10307	104v			John Blenkinsop	son		6	carpet weaver's son	Nry Romaldkirk *

10308	104v	22 a	Market Place	William Hay	ldr	w	35	joiner	Dur Byers Green
10309	104v	22 b	Market Place	William Summers	hea	m	66	coachsmith	Sct
10310	104v			Jane Summers	wif	m	72	coachsmith's wife	Sct
10311	104v			Mary Bone	dau		42	teacher	Sct
10312	104v			William Summers	son		9		Dur [D] S. Nicholas
10313	104v			Melvin Bone	son		9m		Dur [D] S. Nicholas
10314	104v	22 c	Market Place	William Dunn	hea	m	46	innkeeper *	Yks Birkley
10315	104v			Jane Dunn	wif	m	54	innkeeper's wife	Dur [D] S. Nicholas
10316	104v			Jane Dunn	dau		23	dressmaker	Dur [D] S. Nicholas
10317	104v			Elizabeth Dunn	dau		18	innkeeper's daughter	Dur [D] S. Nicholas
10318	104v			James Dunn	son		16	druggist's apprentice	Dur [D] S. Nicholas
10319	104v			Maria Dunn	dau		14	innkeeper's daughter	Dur [D] S. Nicholas
10320	104v			Ellen Dunn	dau		12	innkeeper's daughter	Dur [D] S. Nicholas
10321	105r	22 d	Market Place	William Jackson	hea	m	54	carrier [emp] 4 men	Wry Wadsworth
10322	105r			Isabella Jackson	wif	m	48	carrier's wife	Dur
10323	105r			Mary Jackson	dau		21		Dur
10324	105r			William Jackson	son		19	rolleyman /"rullyman"	Dur
10325	105r			Thomas Jackson	son		15		Dur
10326	105r	22 e	Market Place	Thomas Pickles	hea	m	29	waggon driver	Wry Hebden Bridge
10327	105r			Hannah Pickles	wif	m	27	waggon driver's wife	Wry Wilsden
10328	105r			Elizabeth Pickles	dau		8	scholar	Wry Wilsden
10329	105r			Mary Hannah Pickles	dau		6	scholar	Wry Wilsden
10330	105r			James Harrison Pickles	son		3	scholar	Wry Wilsden
10331	105r			Isabella Agnes Pickles	dau		10m	at home	Dur
10332	105r			Thomas Harrison	flw	w	64	retired foreman *	Wry Keighley
10333	105r	22 f	Market Place	Mary Bridon	hea	w	75		Dur Middle'n-Teesdale
10334	105r			Mary Oliver	dau	w	43	bedmaker at university	Dur Cornforth
10335	105r			Mary Jane Oliver	gda		13	errand girl	Dur [D] Framwelgate
10336	105r			Margaret Summerbell	*		1		Dur [D] S. Nicholas
10337	105v	22 g	Market Place	Andrew Rutherford	hea	m	48	sergt of <boro> police	Bew
10338	105v			Phyllis Rutherford	wif	m	34	sergeant's wife	Dur Hett
10339	105v			Gideon Rutherford	son		6	sergeant's son	Dur Durham
10340	105v			Mary J. Rutherford	dau		4	sergeant's daughter	Dur Durham
10341	105v			William Rutherford	son		3	sergeant's son	Dur Durham
10342	105v	22 h	Market Place	William Dunn	hea	m	62	Brussels carpet weaver	Ayr
10343	105v			Catherine Dunn	wif	m	63	carpet weaver's wife	Sct
10344	105v			Isabella Dunn	dau		23	at home	Dur
10345	105v			Frances Kay	gda		6	scholar	Dur
10346	105v	22 i	Market Place	William Reay	hea	m	28	gardener & seedsman	Dur Houghton-1-Spring
10347	105v			Elizabeth Reay	wif	m	27	milliner	Dur [D] S. Nicholas
10348	105v			Elizabeth Reay	dau		5	daughter	Dur [D] S. Nicholas
10349	105v	22 j	Market Place	John Borrowdale	hea	m	66	omnibus driver	Wes Appleby
10350	105v			Mary Borrowdale	wif	m	55	wife	Wes Brough
10351	106r	22 k	Market Place	Edward Maddison	hea	m	40	basketmaker, master *	Dur Durham
10352	106r			Ann Maddison	wif	m	44	basketmaker's wife	Dur Chester-le-Street
10353	106r			William Maddison	son		15	tailor (apprentice)	Dur [D] S. Nicholas
10354	106r			Elizabeth Maddison	dau		8	scholar	Dur [D] S. Nicholas
10355	106r			Edward Maddison	son		5	scholar	Dur [D] S. Nicholas
10356	106r	23 a	Market Place	Ann Dixon	hea		52	proprietor of house	Dur [D] S. Oswald
10357	106r	23 b	Market Place	Mary Phillips	hea	w	65	butcher	Nry Felixkirk
10358	106r			Elizabeth Phillips	dau		30	milliner *	Wry Leeds
10359	106r			William Petch Phillips	son		22	butcher	Wry Calverley
10360	106r			Mary Phillips	dau		19	milliner *	Wry Calverley
10361	106r			Mary Ann Coulson	ser		20	house servant	Dur Pittington
10362	106r	[ab]	Market Place	George Nettleship	hea	m	27	flour etc. salesman	Nry Yarm
10363	106r			Jane Nettleship	wif	m	30	wife	Nry Yarm
10364	106r			William Nettleship	son		2		Nry Yarm
10365	106r			Thomas Watson Nettleship	son		8m		Nry Yarm
10366	106v	24 a	Market Place	Elizabeth Cummins	hea	w	57	innkeeper <'Goat'>	Dur [D] Back Lane
10367	106v			Thomas Cummins	son		20	joiner	Dur [D] Market Place
10368	106v			John Cummins	son		17	cooper & basketmaker	Dur [D] Market Place
10369	106v			Robert Brown Todd	slw	m	37	waiter	Nry Gilling
10370	106v			Elizabeth Todd	swi	m	27	milliner	Dur [D] Market Place
10371	106v	24 b	Market Place	Thomas Hall	hea	m	35	mason	Dur Durham
10372	106v			Mary Ann Hall	wif	m	30	mason's wife	Dur Durham
10373	106v			Elizabeth Ann Hall	dau			mason's daughter	Dur Durham
10374	106v	24 c	Market Place	Ann Moore	hea	w	68	independent	Lan Hall Carr
10375	106v	25	Market Place	Hornby Hamilton	hea	m	47	innkeeper <'Green Tree'>	Nry Thornton-le-Beans
10376	106v			Ann Hamilton	wif	m	39	innkeeper's wife	Dur Houghton-1-Spring
10377	106v			Hornby Hamilton	son		4	innkeeper's son	Dur Durham
10378	106v			Mary Ann Hamilton	dau		14	innkeeper's daughter	Dur Heworth
10379	106v			Margaret Hamilton	dau		1	innkeeper's daughter	Dur Durham
10380	106v			Mary Hall	ser		17	house servant	Dur Hetton
10381	106v			John Pickersgill	vis	m	52	farmer & toll contractor	Wry Ripon
10382	107r			Thomas Dickinson	vis	m	43	butcher	Nry Topcliffe
10383	107r			Thomas Wright	vis	m	38	labourer	Nbl Lowick
10384	107r			Robert Clark	vis	m	36	horse dealer	Edn Fisherrow
10385	107r			Robert Wright	vis		31	labourer	Nbl Lowick
10386	107r			David Wright	vis		23	labourer	Nbl Lowick
10387	107r			Christopher Cockburn	vis	m	45	labourer	Nbl Etal
10388	107r			John Enderson	vis	m	28	labourer	Sti Redding /"Reddon"

10389	107r	25	Market Place	William Nesbit	vis	22	labourer	Nbl Crookham
10390	107r			James Nesbit	vis	34	labourer	Nbl Crookham
10391	107r			Robert Deighton	vis	27	saddler	Nry Richmond
10392	107r			James Fawcett	vis	14	saddler	Nry Richmond
10393	107r	26	Market Place	William Darling	hea w	68	currier *	Dur [D] S. Nicholas
10394	107r			Henry Darling	son	22	currier's son	Dur [D] S. Nicholas
10395	107r			Elizabeth Jackson	ser	60	house servant	Dur Witton Gilbert
10396	107r	28	Market Place	Matthew Coward Emerson	hea m	44	marine store dealer	Dur [D] S. Nicholas
10397	107r			Ann Emerson	wif m	44	marine store dlr's wife	Yks Brough
10398	107r			Betsy Richardson	dau m	23		Dur Middleton *
10399	107r			Thomas R. Richardson	slw m	23	officer at prison	Dur [D] Framwelgate
10400	107r			Matthew F. Richardson	gsn	3	adult	Dur [D] S. Nicholas
10401	107r			Anne Furness Richardson	gda	1		Dur [D] S. Nicholas
10402	107v	29 a	Market Place	Henry Ashworth	hea m	42	woolcomber	Dur [D] S. Nicholas
10403	107v			Mary Ashworth	wif m	43	woolcomber's wife	Cul Whitehaven
10404	107v			Jane Ashworth	dau	21	woolcomber's daughter	Dur [D] S. Nicholas
10405	107v			Elizabeth Ashworth	dau	17	woolcomber's daughter	Dur [D] S. Nicholas
10406	107v			Christopher Ashworth	son	15	apprentice mason	Dur [D] S. Nicholas
10407	107v			William Ashworth	son	12	scholar	Dur [D] S. Nicholas
10408	107v			Ann Ashworth	dau	10	scholar	Dur [D] S. Nicholas
10409	107v			Robert Ashworth	son	5	scholar	Dur [D] S. Nicholas
10410	107v			Mary Ashworth	dau	2	at home	Dur [D] S. Nicholas
10411	107v			Henry Ashworth	gsn	5m	at home	Dur [D] S. Nicholas
10412	107v	29 b	Market Place	Margaret Dixon	hea w	68		Dur
10413	107v			Robert Dixon	son	44	butcher	Dur
10414	107v			George Dixon	son	31	butcher	Dur
10415	107v			Eliza Dixon	dau	25		Dur
10416	107v			Robert Dixon	son	9	scholar	Dur
10417	107v	29 c	Market Place	William Houston	hea m	44	cordwainer	ChI Guernsey
10418	107v			Mary Houston	wif m	44	cordwainer's wife	Lnd S. Mary-le-Bone
10419	107v			William Houston	son	22	cordwainer's son	Dur [D] Gilesgate
10420	107v			Thomas Houston	son	19	cordwainer's son	Dur [D] Gilesgate
10421	108r			John Houston	son	17	cordwainer's son	Dur [D] Gilesgate
10422	108r			Charles Houston	son	12	cordwainer's son	Dur [D] Gilesgate
10423	108r			Septimus Houston	son	8	cordwainer's son	Dur [D] Gilesgate
10424	108r			Elizabeth Houston	dau	6	cordwainer's daughter	Dur [D] Gilesgate
10425	108r	29 d	Market Place	Richard Lindsley	hea m	28	potter	Dur
10426	108r			Ann Lindsley	wif m	26	potter's daughter	Dur
10427	108r			Hannah Lindsley	dau	7	potter's daughter	Dur
10428	108r			Isabel Lindsley	dau	5	potter's daughter	Dur
10429	108r			Ann Lindsley	dau	2	potter's daughter	Dur Auckland
10430	108r			Robert Lindsley	bro m	22	potter	Dur Barnard Castle
10431	108r			Thomas Lindsley	bro	20	potter	Dur Barnard Castle
10432	108r	29 e	Market Place	Eleanor Kelsey	wif m	29	schoolmistress	Dur
10433	108r			Hannah Kelsey	dau	16	assistant in school	Nbl Newcastle
10434	108r	1	Claypath Gates	Esther Castlehow	hea w	64	confectioner	Dur [D] S. Nicholas
10435	108r			Sophia Bland	sis	57	confectioner	Dur [D] S. Nicholas
10436	108r			Margaret Rutherford	vis m	37	clerk's wife	Dur [D] S. Nicholas
10437	108r			Matthew Stephenson	ldr	29	weigher at colliery	Dur Chester-le-Street
10438	108r			Joseph Rutherford	vis	3		Dur Gateshead
10439	108r			Elizabeth Rutherford		2		Dur [D] S. Nicholas
10440	108v	1	Back Lane	Micah Chambers	hea m	40	foreman boot & shoe shop	Wry Stanley
10441	108v			Mary Chambers	wif m	34		Wry Lofthouse
10442	108v			George Chambers	son	12	scholar	Wry Lofthouse
10443	108v			Martha Chambers	dau	10	scholar	Wry Lofthouse
10444	108v			Sarah Chambers	dau	7	scholar	Dur [D] Crossgate
10445	108v			Luke Chambers	son	4	scholar	Dur [D] Crossgate
10446	108v			Mary Ann Chambers	dau	10m		Dur [D] S. Nicholas
10447	108v			John Palister	ldr	21	merchant grocer	Nry Romaldkirk
10448	108v	[aa]	Back Lane	James Hudson	hea m	53	waiter	Dur Chester-le-Street
10449	108v			Hannah Hudson	wif m	45	waiter's wife	Ery Kirby Underdale
10450	108v			Sophia Hudson	dau	18	waiter's daughter	Nbl Newcastle
10451	108v			James Hudson	son	16	waiter's son	Dur Darlington
10452	108v			John Hudson	son	12	waiter's son	Dur Darlington
10453	108v	[ab]	Back Lane	Patrick Kelly	hea m	40	labourer	Let
10454	108v			Hannah Kelly	wif m	35	labourer's wife	Let
10455	108v			Mary Kelly	dau	12	scholar	Let
10456	108v			John Kelly	son	10	scholar	Let
10457	108v			Ann Kelly	dau	6	scholar	Let
10458	108v			Elizabeth Kelly	dau	9m		Dur [D] S. Nicholas
10459	109r	[ac]	Back Lane	James Westgarth	hea m	30	pipemaker	Chs Altrincham
10460	109r			Isabella Westgarth	wif m	30	pipemaker's wife	Nbl Newcastle
10461	109r			Mary Westgarth	dau	6	school	Dur [D] S. Nicholas
10462	109r			John Westgarth	son	2	at home	Dur [D] S. Nicholas
10463	109r	[ad]	Back Lane	Isabella Brown	hea w	44	bread baker	Dur [D] S. Giles
10464	109r			Ann Brown	dau	20	bread baker	Dur [D] S. Giles
10465	109r			William Brown	son	18	cabinetmaker	Dur [D] S. Giles
10466	109r			Margaret Brown	dau	12	scholar	Dur [D] S. Giles
10467	109r			Thomas Brown	son	10	scholar	Dur [D] S. Giles
10468	109r			Martin Brown	son	6	scholar	Dur [D] S. Nicholas
10469	109r	[ae]a	Back Lane	John Woodness	hea	54	labourer	Dur

ID	Folio	Code	Address	Name	Rel	M	Age	Occupation	Birthplace
10470	109r	[ae]b	Back Lane	John McKewen	hea	m	52	hawker	Arm Armagh
10471	109r			Bridget McKewen	wif	m	51	hawker's wife	Arm Armagh
10472	109r			Peter McKewen	son		18	woolspinner	Dur Durham
10473	109r			Bridget McKewen	dau		14	scholar	Dur Durham
10474	109r			Francis McKewen	son		12	scholar	Dur Durham
10475	109r	[af]a	Back Lane	Joseph Greenwell	hea	m	34	groom	Dur Staindrop
10476	109r			Mary Greenwell	wif	m	31	groom's wife	Nry Richmond
10477	109r			Margaret Greenwell	dau		13	groom's daughter	Dur Staindrop
10478	109v			William Greenwell	son		11	schoolboy	Dur Staindrop
10479	109v			Elizabeth Greenwell	dau		8	school[girl]	Dur Staindrop
10480	109v			Joseph Greenwell	son		6		Dur
10481	109v			James Greenwell	son		1		Dur
10482	109v			Sarah Wilson	nce		15		Dur Barnard Castle
10483	109v			William Vice	ldr		21	grocer	Dur Bishop Middleham
10484	109v	[af]b	Back Lane	Thomas Story	hea	w	74	pensioner	Dur [D] Back Lane BS
10485	109v	[af]c	Back Lane	Joseph Tipping	hea	m	53	shoemaker	Lan Manchester
10486	109v			Ruth Tipping	wif	m	53	shoemaker's wife	Tyr Dungannon
10487	109v			William Miss	ldr		30	doll's eye-maker	Lan Preston
10488	109v	[af]d	Back Lane	Margaret Mather	hea	w	26	dressmaker	Dur [D] Hallgarth St
10489	109v			William Mather	son		6	scholar	Dur [D] Crossgate
10490	109v			James Mather	son		4	at home	Dur [D] Gilesgate
10491	109v	[af]e	Back Lane	Carr Mitchenson	hea	m	21	currier, journeyman	Dur Durham
10492	109v			Ann Mitchenson	wif	m	20	currier's wife	Dur Durham
10493	109v			Henry Mitchenson	son		6m	currier's son	Dur Durham
10494	110r	[ag]	Back Lane	Susanna Lees	hea	w	45	formerly cook	Dur Chester-le-Street
10495	110r			Isabella Lees	dau		12		Dur [D] S. Nicholas
10496	110r			Hannah Lees	dau		11		Dur [D] S. Nicholas
10497	110r			John Lees	son		9		Dur [D] S. Nicholas
10498	110r			William Lees	blw	m	41	Post Office messenger	Dur [D] S. Nicholas
10499	110r			James Cook	ldr	w	42	carpet weaver	Wor Kidderminster
10500	110r			William Baker	ldr	w	33	carpet weaver	Wor Kidderminster
10501	110r			Henry Howes	ldr		31	currier	Nfk Great Yarmouth
10502	110r	[ah]	Back Lane	George Hutchinson	hea	m	36	stonemason	Dur Durham
10503	110r			Susanna Hutchinson	wif	m	40	stonemason's wife	Dur Durham
10504	110r			Mary Ann Hutchinson	dau		13	stonemason's daughter	Dur Durham
10505	110r			Rosanna Baker	mlw	w	84		Dur Durham
10506	110r			John Robinson	vis		30	carpet weaver	Dur Barnard Castle
10507	110r			George Snowdon	vis		21	carpet weaver	Dur Durham
10508	110r	[ai]	Brussels Square *	Ann Lister	hea	w	37	bobbin winder	Dur Barnard Castle
10509	110r			Mary Ann Lister	dau		15	bobbin winder	Dur Barnard Castle
10510	110r			Nicholas Lister	son		13	draw boy to weaver	Dur Barnard Castle
10511	110r			Jane Lister	dau		10	at home	Dur Barnard Castle
10512	110r			Elizabeth Lister	dau		6	school	Dur Durham
10513	110r			Margaret Lister	dau		1	at home	Dur Durham
10514	110v	[aj]	Brussels Square *	John Child	hea	m	35	carpet weaver	Gls Newent
10515	110v			Alice Child	wif	m	35	carpet weaver's wife	Wor Kidderminster
10516	110v			Hannah Child	dau		11	carpet weaver's daughter	Wor Kidderminster
10517	110v	[ak]	Brussels Square *	George Cale	hea	m	37	carpet weaver	Sal Bridgnorth
10518	110v			Hannah Cale	wif	m	35	carpet weaver's wife	Wry Wakefield
10519	110v			Jane Cale	dau		10	carpet weaver's daughter	Sal Bridgnorth
10520	110v			George Cale	son		7	carpet weaver's son	Sal Bridgnorth
10521	110v			Margaret Cale	dau		3	carpet weaver's daughter	Sal Bridgnorth
10522	110v			Henry Beech	ldr		23	carpet weaver	Wor Kidderminster
10523	110v	[al]	Brussels Square *	Hannah Stephenson	hea	w	36	formerly laundress	Dur [D] S. Nicholas
10524	110v			John Stephenson	son		12		Dur [D] S. Nicholas
10525	110v			Hannah Stephenson	dau		10		Dur [D] S. Nicholas
10526	110v			Elizabeth Stephenson	dau		7		Dur [D] S. Nicholas
10527	110v			Joseph Lees	bro		33		Dur [D] S. Nicholas
10528	110v	[am]a	Back Lane	William Byers	hea	m	59	handloom weaver, carpet	Dur Darlington
10529	110v			Elizabeth Byers	wif	m	57	bobbin winder	Dur Bishop Auckland
10530	110v			Ellen Byers	dau		13	at home	Dur Darlington
10531	110v	[am]b	Back Lane	Arthur Cain	hea	m	48	pedlar	Irl
10532	110v			Frances Cain	wif	m	45	pedlar's wife	Nry Richmond
10533	111r	[am]c	Back Lane	Mary Herron	hea		60	pauper	Dur Wolsingham
10534	111r	[am]d	Back Lane	John Troughton	hea	m	44	handloom weaver, carpet	Wes Kendal
10535	111r			Dorothy Troughton	wif	m	44	bobbin winder	Wes Kendal
10536	111r			Edward Troughton	son		20	plumber	Wes Kendal
10537	111r			Agnes Troughton	dau		10	scholar	Dur Durham
10538	111r			Jane Troughton	dau		8	scholar	Dur Durham
10539	111r			Eleanor Troughton	dau		6	at home	Dur Durham
10540	111r			Emma Troughton	dau		2	at home	Dur Durham
10541	111r	[an]a	Green Tree Yard *	Ann White	hea	w	76	greengrocer	Dur Hylton
10542	111r	[an]b	Green Tree Yard *	Robert Brown	hea	w	64	shoemaker	Dur
10543	111r			Robert Brown	son		25	shoemaker	Dur
10544	111r			Thomas Brown	son		20	shoemaker	Dur
10545	111r			Henry Brown	son		13	weaver	Dur
10546	111r	[an]c	Green Tree Yard *	William Minshall	hea	m	37	carpet weaver	Sal Bridgnorth
10547	111r			Hannah Minshall	wif	m	38	carpet weaver's wife	Sal Bridgnorth
10548	111r			Elizabeth Minshall	dau		10m		Dur
			one house unoccupied						
10549	111v	[ao]	Back Lane	Charles McIntyre	hea	m	50	traveller	Arm Jonesborough

10550	111v	[ao]	Back Lane	Mary McIntyre	wif m	40	traveller's wife	Sli
10551	111v			Thomas McIntyre	son	14	app to carpet weaving	Cul Keswick
10552	111v			Catherine McIntyre	dau	9	scholar	Dur Durham
10553	111v			Ann McIntyre	dau	7	scholar	Dur Durham
10554	111v			Charles McIntyre	son	5	scholar	Dur Durham
10555	111v			James McIntyre	son	5	scholar	Dur Durham
10556	111v			Harry McIntyre	son	2	at home	Dur Durham
10557	111v			John Austerfield	vis m	25	clerk	Wry Wakefield
10558	111v			Mary Austerfield	vis m	19	wife	Sli
10559	111v	[ap]	Factory Yd, Back Ln	John Ditchburn	hea m	52	fmly woolcomber & dyer *	Dur [D] S. Nicholas
10560	111v			Elizabeth Ditchburn	wif m	52		Dur Auton Stile *
10561	111v			Thomas Ditchburn	son	26	whitesmith	Dur [D] S. Nicholas
10562	111v			John Ditchburn	son	23	dyer	Dur [D] S. Nicholas
10563	111v			Ann Ditchburn	dau	17		Dur [D] S. Nicholas
10564	111v			Elizabeth Craggs	gda	2		Dur Chester-le-Street
10565	111v	[aq]a	Back Lane	Thomas Atkinson	hea m	25	tailor <& publican *>	Dur [D] S. Giles
10566	111v			Jane Atkinson	wif m	26	tailor's wife	Dur [D] S. Nicholas
10567	111v			Margaret Atkinson	dau	9m	tailor's daughter	Dur [D] S. Nicholas
10568	112r	[aq]b	Back Lane	Richard Sumers	hea m	38	tailor	Dur [D] S. Oswald
10569	112r			Margaret Sumers	wif m	37	tailor's wife	Dur Washington
10570	112r			Thomas Sumers	son	8	tailor's son	Dur Rainton
10571	112r			Robert Sumers	son	2	tailor's son	Dur Sunderland
10572	112r			Richard Sumers	son	4m	tailor's son	Dur [D] S. Nicholas
10573	112r			Anthony Foster	vis	25	labourer	Dur [D] S. Nicholas
10574	112r	[aq]c	Back Lane	John Taylor	hea m	45	woolcomber	Dur Darlington
10575	112r			Ann Taylor	wif m	44	woolcomber's wife	Wry Leeds
10576	112r			James Taylor	son	20	handloom weaver, carpet	Dur Durham
10577	112r			John Taylor	son	18	handloom weaver, carpet	Dur Durham
10578	112r			Hannah Taylor	dau	15	servant at home	Dur Gateshead
10579	112r			Jane Taylor	dau	12	scholar	Dur Durham
10580	112r			Mary Taylor	dau	10	scholar	Dur Durham
10581	112r			Ann Taylor	dau	8	scholar	Dur Durham
10582	112r			Margaret Taylor	dau	5	scholar	Dur Durham
10583	112r			William Taylor	son	2	infant	Dur Durham
10584	112r	[aq]d	Back Lane	William Ward	hea m	58	carpet weaver	Wry Leeds
10585	112r			Mary Ward	wif m	64	pirn winder	Dur
10586	112v	[aq]e	Back Lane	Ann Hutchinson	hea w	40	bootbinder	Cul Carlisle
10587	112v	[aq]f	Back Lane	Margaret Draghorn	hea w	76	widow	Dur Sunderland
10588	112v	[aq]g	Back Lane	Robert Hackworth	hea m	44	cooper	Dur [D] S. Oswald
10589	112v			Margaret Hackworth	wif m	48	cooper's wife	Dur [D] S. Nicholas
10590	112v			Mary Emmerson	sil	54	schoolmaster's daughter	Dur [D] S. Margaret
10591	112v	[ar]	Back Lane	Francis Maris	hea m	32	carpet weaver	Sal Bridgnorth
10592	112v			Mary Maris	wif m	30	carpet weaver's wife	Wry Dewsbury
10593	112v			Mary Ann Maris	dau	10	scholar	Sal Bridgnorth
10594	112v			Theresa Maris	dau	8	scholar	Sal Bridgnorth
10595	112v			Emma Maris	dau	6	scholar	Sal Bridgnorth
10596	112v			Hannah Maris	dau	1		Sal Bridgnorth
10597	112v	[as]	Back Lane	Richard Coltman	hea m	72	woolspinner	Dur [D] Framwelgate
10598	112v			Elizabeth Coltman	wif m	73	woolspinner's wife	Dur [D] S. Giles
10599	112v	[at]	Back Lane	John Lowden	hea	48	whitesmith *	Dur
10600	112v	[au]a	Back Lane	Mary Jamson	wif m	44	wife of William Jamson *	Dur
10601	112v			Mary Jamson	dau	17	scholar	Dur Chilton
10602	112v	[au]b	Back Lane	Robert Baker	hea m	35	cordwainer	Dur [D] S. Giles
10603	112v			Hannah Baker	wif m	33	cordwainer's wife	Dur [D] S. Nicholas
10604	112v			William Baker	son	10	scholar at home	Dur [D] S. Nicholas
10605	113r			Robert Baker	son	7	scholar at home	Dur [D] S. Nicholas
10606	113r			Henry Baker	son	5	scholar at home	Dur [D] S. Nicholas
10607	113r			Elizabeth Jane Baker	dau	3	at home	Dur Seaham Harbour
10608	113r			George Baker	son	1	at home	Dur [D] S. Nicholas
10609	113r	[au]c	Back Lane	William Coltman	hea w	51	woolspinner	Dur Durham
10610	113r			Elizabeth Coltman	dau	29	dressmaker	Dur Durham
10611	113r			Robert Coultman	son	24	ironmonger	Dur Durham
10612	113r			Mary Coultman	dau	18	home	Dur Durham
10613	113r			Thomas Coultman	son	16	butcher	Dur Durham
10614	113r			Camilla Coultman	dau	12	school	Dur Durham
10615	113r			Margaret Coultman	dau	10	school	Dur Durham
10616	113r			William Coultman	son	8	school	Dur Durham
10617	113r	[au]d	Back Lane	John Armour	hea m	40	carpet weaver	Ayr Kilmarnock
10618	113r			Elizabeth Armour	wif m	35	carpet weaver's wife	Ayr Ayr
10619	113r			John Armour	son	15	currier	Ayr Kilmarnock
10620	113r			Robert Armour	son	13	at school	Ayr Kilmarnock
10621	113r			George Armour	son	6	at school	Dur
10622	113r			Jane Armour	dau	3	at home	Dur
10623	113r			Margaret Armour	dau	1	at home	Dur
10624	113r			John Tilly	ldr w	72	at home	Dur
10625	113v	[av]a	Back Lane	Robert Wood	hea m	45	shoemaker	Dur Hart
10626	113v			Margaret Wood	wif m	51	shoemaker's wife	Ess Colchester
10627	113v			Mary Wood	dau	19	dressmaker	Dur
10628	113v			George Wood	son	16	mason	Dur
10629	113v			John Wood	son	13	schoolboy	Dur
10630	113v			Thomas Hill	vis	19	shoemaker	Nbl Hexham

10631	113v	[av]b	Back Lane	Robert Wharton sn	hea m	60	carpet weaver	Dur Darlington
10632	113v			Jane Wharton	wif m	54	carpet weaver's wife	Nbl Seaton Sluice
10633	113v			James Wharton	son w	33	carpet weaver	Nbl Newcastle
10634	113v			Robert Wharton jn	son	30	carpet weaver	Dur Darlington, Carr
10635	113v			Jane Wharton	dau	18	winder	Dur Barnard Castle
10636	113v			Mary Wharton	dau	12	scholar	Dur Barnard Castle
10637	113v			Mary Jane Wharton	gda	6	scholar	Dur
10638	113v			Robert Wharton	gsn	4		Dur
10639	113v			James Melvin Wharton	gsn	1		Dur
10640	113v			Elizabeth Suthers	ldr	19	winder	Dur
10641	113v	[av]c	Back Lane	Thomas Robson	hea m	52	cartman	Dur Lanchester
10642	113v			Elizabeth Robson	wif m	44	cartman's wife	Nry Pickhill
10643	113v			John Robson	son	17	currier	Dur [D] S. Nicholas
10644	114r	[aw]	Back Lane	Isaac Horsfield	hea m	56	agent in carpet fcty *	Dur [D] S. Nicholas
10645	114r			Jane Horsfield	wif m	53	agent's wife	Dur [D] S. Nicholas
10646	114r			Abraham Horsefield	son	27	carpet weaver	Dur Barnard Castle
10647	114r			Charlotte Horsefield	dau	20	at home	Dur [D] S. Nicholas
10648	114r			John Horsefield	son	17	stamper in carpet fcty	Dur [D] S. Nicholas
10649	114r	[ax]	Back Lane	Robert Pearson	hea m	31	plasterer emp 2 men	Dur [D] S. Margaret
10650	114r			Jane Pearson	wif m	30	plasterer's wife	Dur [D] S. Nicholas
10651	114r			Emma Pearson	dau	6	scholar	Dur [D] S. Nicholas
10652	114r			Ann Pearson	dau	3	at home	Dur [D] S. Nicholas
10653	114r	[ay]	Back Lane	William Alexander	hea m	51	carpet weaver	Sct
10654	114r			Isabella Alexander	wif m	58	wife	Dur Brancepeth
10655	114r			Richard Alexander	son	22	carpet weaver	Dur [D] S. Nicholas
10656	114r			Stephen Lumley	ldr	18	tailor	Dur [D] Framwelgate
10657	114r	[az]a	Old Hall, Back Lane	George Clark	hea m	44	painter	Dur Sunderland
10658	114r			Mary Clark	wif m	39	painter's wife	Dur
10659	114r			Margaret Clark	dau	19	painter's daughter	Dur
10660	114r			William Clark	son	14	plumber	Dur
10661	114r			Jane Ann Clark	dau	6	scholar	Dur
10662	114r			James Clark	son	4	scholar	Dur
10663	114r			John Anderson	ldr w	72	carpet weaver	Dur Darlington
10664	114v	[az]b	Old Hall, Back Lane	Francis McArthur	hea m	26	carpet weaver	Sct
10665	114v			Elizabeth McArthur	wif m	25	wife	Dur [D] S. Nicholas
10666	114v			Margaret McArthur	dau	5	at home	Dur [D] S. Nicholas
10667	114v			William McArthur	son	5m	at home	Dur [D] S. Nicholas
10668	114v	[az]c	Old Hall, Back Lane	John Devine	hea m	27	woolsorter	Dub
10669	114v			Margaret Devine	wif m	30	woolsorter's wife	Wem
10670	114v	[az]d	Old Hall, Back Lane	Edward Monks	hea m	30	carpet weaver	Mdx London
10671	114v			Eliza Monks	wif m	30	carpet weaver's wife	Mdx London
10672	114v			Jane Monks	dau	4	carpet weaver's daughter	Lks Glasgow
10673	114v			John Monks	son	1	carpet weaver's son	Dur Durham
10674	114v			Edward Monks	son	1m	carpet weaver's son	Dur Durham
10675	114v	[ba]	Market Place Mill *	William Lee	hea w	39	waregrinder	Wry Leeds
10676	114v			Martha Hannah Lee	dau	15	waregrinder's daughter	Wry Leeds
10677	114v			John William Lee	son	10	waregrinder's son	Wry Leeds
10678	114v			William Appleby	ldr	23	labourer	Dur
10679	114v			Joseph Lee	son	5	waregrinder's son	Wry Leeds
10680	114v	[bb]a	Market Place Mill *	Thomas Gibson	hea m	46	carpet weaver	Sct
10681	114v			Elizabeth Gibson	wif m	36	weaver's wife	Sct
10682	114v			Jane Gibson	dau	16	winder	Sct
10683	114v			Thomas Gibson	son	3		Dur
10684	115r	[bb]b	Market Place Mill *	William Waistell	hea m	39	carpet weaver	Dur Darlington
10685	115r			Mary Waistell	wif m	30	carpet weaver's wife	Dur Stockton
10686	115r			Robert Waistell	son	6	carpet weaver's son	Dur Darlington
10687	115r			William Waistell	son	4	carpet weaver's son	Dur Darlington
10688	115r			Mary Coutley	rel w	70	labourer's widow {blind}	Dur Barmpton
10689	115r	[bb]c	Market Place Mill *	Thomas Smith	hea m	34	corn-miller	Wry Dewsbury
10690	115r			Hannah Smith	wif m	31	corn-miller's wife	Wry Dewsbury
10691	115r			Joseph Smith	son	8	corn-miller's son	Wry Kirkstall
10692	115r			Benjamin Smith	son	7	corn-miller's son	Wry Kirkstall
10693	115r			John Smith	son	3	corn-miller's son	Wry Kirkstall
10694	115r			Sarah Smith	dau	3m	corn-miller's daughter	Dur Durham
10695	115r	[aa]	Freemens Place	William Clarke	hea m	36	carpenter	Dur
10696	115r			Margaret Clarke	wif m	36	carpenter's wife	Dur
10697	115r			Mary Ann Clarke	dau	15	scholar	Dur
10698	115r			John Clarke	son	13	scholar	Dur
10699	115r			Sarah Alice Clarke	dau	7	scholar	Dur
10700	115r			Margaret Jane Clarke	dau	5	scholar	Dur
10701	115r			Eleanor Clarke	dau	2		Dur
10702	115r			Ann Gargett	mlw w	73	formerly laundress	Dur
10703	115v	[ab]	Freemens Place	George Heron	hea m	41	mason	Dur
10704	115v			Ellen Heron	wif m	38	mason's wife	Dur
10705	115v			Ellen Heron	dau	11	scholar	Dur
10706	115v			George Heron	son	9	scholar	Dur
10707	115v			Dorothy Heron	dau	5	scholar	Dur
10708	115v			Emerson Heron	son	2		Dur
10709	115v	[ac]	Freemens Place	William Ayre	hea m	59	cordwainer	Dur [D] Silver Street
10710	115v			Mary Ayre	wif m	59	cordwainer's wife	Dur Wolsingham
10711	115v	[ad]	Freemens Place	Anthony Blakey	hea m	48	cordwainer	Dur [D] S. Giles

10712	115v	[ad]	Freemens Place	Dorothy Blakey	wif m	46	cordwainer's wife	Dur Shadforth
10713	115v			Richard Blakey	son	18	hatter	Dur [D] S. Nicholas
10714	115v			Anthony Blakey	son	15	clerk	Dur [D] S. Nicholas
10715	115v			Ann Blakey	dau	12	cordwainer's daughter	Dur [D] S. Nicholas
10716	115v			Dorothy Blakey	dau	9	daughter	Dur [D] S. Nicholas
10717	115v			William Blakey	son	6	son	Dur [D] S. Nicholas
10718	115v			Margaret Blakey	dau	3	daughter	Dur [D] S. Nicholas
10719	115v	[ae]	Freemens Place	Thomas White	hea m	45	hairdresser	Dur
10720	115v			Jane White	wif m	44	hairdresser's wife	Dur Brancepeth
10721	115v			William White	son	20	joiner	Dur
10722	115v			James White	son	16	currier	Dur
10723	116r			Jane White	dau	10		Dur
10724	116r			Elizabeth White	dau	5		Dur
10725	116r	[af]	Freemens Place	James Trenholm	hea m	25	grocer's assistant	Dur
10726	116r			Ann Trenholm	wif m	24	grocer's asst's wife	Dur
10727	116r			Thomas William Trenholm	son	1		Dur
10728	116r	[ag]	Freemens Place	Charlotte Fawcett	hea w	54	laundress	Yks Bumeholme
10729	116r			Elizabeth Fawcett	dau	24	milliner	Dur
10730	116r			Joseph Fawcett	son	13	scholar	Dur
10731	116r	[ah]	Freemens Place	George Ditchburn	hea m	20	whitesmith	Dur [D] S. Nicholas
10732	116r			Elizabeth Ditchburn	wif m	21	dressmaker	Dur [D] S. Nicholas
10733	116r	[ai]	Freemens Place	Nathaniel Giles	hea m	47	cordwainer	Dur South Shields
10734	116r			Mary Giles	wif m	50	cordwainer's wife	Dur [D] Silver Street
10735	116r	[aj]	Freemens Place	Jonathan Gargett	hea m	28	mason	Dur
10736	116r			Ann Gargett	wif m	26	dressmaker	Dur
10737	116r			Thomas Gargett	son	4m		Dur
10738	116r	[ak]	Freemens Place	Andrew Wall	hea m	22	mason	Dur [D] S. Nicholas
10739	116r			Margaret Wall	wif m	25	mason's wife	Dur [D] S. Margaret
10740	116r	[al]a	Freemens Place	Robert Carr	hea m	67	mason's labr but pen *	Dur
10741	116r			Rachael Carr	wif m	69	domestic duties	Dur
10742	116r			Robert Carr	son	23	stonemason	Dur
10743	116v			Robert Blakey	vsh m	29	commercial clerk	Dur
10744	116v			Elizabeth Blakey	vsw m	28	domestic duties	Dur
10745	116v			Robert Blakey	vss	8	scholar	Dur
10746	116v			Walter Blakey	vss	1		Dur
10747	116v	[al]b	Freemens Place	Henry Hopper	hea m	38	stonemason	Dur [D] S. Oswald
10748	116v			Isabella Hopper	wif m	32	domestic duties	Dur [D] S. Margaret
10749	116v	2	Silver Street Lane	John Waddle	hea m	59	labourer	Nbl Berwick
10750	116v			Isabella Waddle	wif m	70	labourer's wife	Dur
10751	116v			Joanna Lieser	ldr	22	accordion player	Germany
10752	116v			Catherine Horner	ldr	20	image maker	Ant Belfast
10753	116v			Sarah Horner	ldr	14		Tyr
10754	116v			Joseph Horner	ldr	12		Ant
10755	116v			John Rook	ldr	54	drover	Ant Belfast
10756	116v			John Killon	ldr	38	hawker	Gal Tuam
10757	116v			William Paire	ldr m	33	performer	Dur Sunderland
10758	116v			Isabella Paire	ldr m	33	performer's wife	Dur Sunderland
10759	116v			Frances Paire	ldr	13	performer's daughter	Dur Sunderland
10760	116v			Henry Wigdercohen	ldr	43	traveller	Lan Liverpool
10761	116v			Joseph Raye	ldr	40	labourer	Lks Glasgow
10762	117r	[aa]a	Silver Street Lane	Phillip Davison	hea m	34	labourer	Dur
10763	117r			Eliza Davison	wif m	36	labourer's wife	Dur
10764	117r			Ann Davison	dau	13	labourer's daughter	Dur
10765	117r			John Davison	son	10	labourer's son	Dur
10766	117r			Eliza Davison	dau	8	labourer's daughter	Dur
10767	117r			Robert Davison	son	2	labourer's son	Dur
10768	117r			Phillip Davison	son	3m	labourer's son	Dur
10769	117r	[aa]b	Silver Street Lane	Matthew Buddle	hea m	22	tailor	Dur [D] S. Oswald
10770	117r			Margaret Buddle	wif m	28	tailor's wife	Dur Jarrow
10771	117r	[ab]a	Silver Street Lane	James Mallen sn	hea m	56	hatter	Dur [D] S. Nicholas
10772	117r			Mary Mallen	wif m	49	domestic duties	Dur [D] S. Margaret
10773	117r			Isaac Mallen	son	18	cordwainer	Dur [D] S. Nicholas
10774	117r			Ellen Mallen	dau	15	at home	Dur [D] S. Nicholas
10775	117r			John Mallen	son	12	at home	Dur [D] S. Nicholas
10776	117r			John Robinson	vis	38	tailor	Dur [D] S. Nicholas
10777	117r	[ab]b	Silver Street Lane	John Robinson	hea m	68	cabinetmaker	Dur [D] S. Giles
10778	117r			Jane Robinson	wif m	60	cabinetmaker's wife	Dur [D] S. Margaret
10779	117r			Catherine Robinson	dau	24	straw-bonnetmaker	Dur [D] S. Nicholas
10780	117r			Frederick Bulmer	bdr	22	joiner	Dur [D] S. Margaret
10781	117r			Hannah Walker	vis	9		Dur [D] S. Nicholas
10782	117v	[ac]a	Silver Street Lane	Joseph Sandles	hea w	41	carpet weaver	Lan Manchester
10783	117v			Myers Sandles	son	12	carpet weaver's son *	Wes Kendal
10784	117v	[ac]b	Silver Street Lane	William Brandford	hea m	29	carpet weaver	Wor Kidderminster
10785	117v			Elizabeth Brandford	wif m	20	carpet weaver's wife	Dur South Church
10786	117v			Edward Goundry	blw	11	draw boy	Dur Barnard Castle
10787	117v			Mary Goundry	sil	18	factory girl	Dur West Auckland
10788	117v	[ad]a	Silver Street Lane	Isabella Walker	hea m	48	hawker	Edn Edinburgh
10789	117v			Mary Ann Walker	dau	10	hawker's daughter	Wry Ripon
10790	117v			Isabella Walker	dau	8	hawker's daughter	Wry Ripon
10791	117v			James Walker	son	6	hawker's son	Wry Ripon
10792	117v	[ad]b	Silver Street Lane	Isabella Quilt	hea w	64		Nbl Alnwick

10793	117v	[ae]	Silver Street Lane	Joseph Richardson	hea	m	58	labourer	Wes Tullian Bower
10794	117v			Mary Richardson	wif	m	56	labourer's wife	Wes Ormside
10795	117v			Mary Richardson	dau		32	house servant	Wes Garthorn Hall
10796	117v			Joseph Richardson	son		26	labourer	Wes Ormside
10797	117v			George Richardson	gsn		14	factory boy	Wes Sandford, Thorne
10798	117v			Michael Miriman	ldr		37	pedlar	May
10799	117v			Thomas Conner	ldr		20	pedlar	Ros
10800	117v	[af]	Silver Street Lane	Thomas Robinson	hea	m	38	joiner	Dur
10801	117v			Diana Robinson	wif	m	30	joiner's wife	Dur
10802	117v			Mary Robinson	dau		12	joiner's dau, scholar	Dur
10803	117v			Isabella Robinson	dau		16	joiner's daughter	Dur
10804	117v			Emma Robinson	dau		1	joiner's daughter	Dur
10805	117v			Ann Jackson	vis		49	overlooker, paper mill	Dur
10806	117v			Christopher Jackson	ldr		36	miller	Dur
10807	117v			John Denton	ldr		45	carpet weaver	Gls Gloucester

Notes - Enumeration District 4d

10148	... & clerk in Will Office
10168	<'Old Red Lion'>
10174	... employing 1 apprentice
10228	... & spirit and porter vaults
10235	<& cabinetmaker, hardwareman & watchmaker>
10236	<eating house>
10242	<& dealer in cigars>
10246	... & eating house
10264	... managing clerk, carpet trade
10273	... & seed merchant employing 4 men
10306-10307	country given as "Scotland"
10314	... <'Jolly Butcher'> & fancy hearth-rug weaver
10332	... of wool manufactory
10336	great-grand-daughter
10351	... [employing] 1 man
10358,10360	... & straw-bonnetmaker
10393	<& leather cutter>
10398	... in-Teesdale; county given as "Yorkshire"
10508-10527	... Back Lane
10541-10548	... Back Lane
10559	... now foreman
10560	/"Haughton Stye B[ear]P[ark]"
10565	... 'Wool Pack'
10599	<& bellhanger>
10600	... coach driver at Newcastle
10644	<carpet weaver>
10675-10694	... House, Back Lane
10740	... of Chelsea Hospital
10783	scholar

REF	FOL	NO	STREET	FORENAME(S)	SURNAME	REL	C	AGE	OCCUPATION	BIRTHPLACE
10808	122r	221	Gilesgate	William	White	hea	m	51	auctioneer & appraiser *	Dur Durham
10809	122r			Catherine	White	wif	m	51		Dur Durham
10810	122r			Elizabeth	White	dau		20		Dur Durham
10811	122r			Catherine	White	dau		17		Dur Durham
10812	122r			William	White	son		14	scholar	Dur Durham
10813	122r			Margaret	Burt	ser		21	house servant	Dur South Hetton
10814	122r	220	Gilesgate	John Edwin	Marshall	hea	m	41	alderman *	Dur [D] S. Nicholas
10815	122r			Margaret	Marshall	wif	m	40		Dur Houghton-l-Spring
10816	122r			William	Marshall	son		18	articled solicitor's clk	Dur Durham
10817	122r			Harriet	Marshall	dau		17	attorney's daughter	Dur Durham
10818	122r			Mary	Marshall	dau		15	scholar	Dur Durham
10819	122r			Henry	Marshall	son		14	scholar	Dur Durham
10820	122r			Hannah	Bewick	ser		21	house servant	Dur Easington
10821	122r	219 a	Gilesgate	George Farrow	Biggins	hea	m	32	solicitor's managing clk	Dur
10822	122r			Ann	Biggins	wif	m	33		Dur
10823	122r			Charles	Biggins	son		9	scholar	Dur
10824	122r			Ann	Biggins	dau		7	scholar	Dur
10825	122r			Elizabeth	Biggins	mth	w	72	proprietor of houses	Dur
10826	122r			Jane	Nichol	ser		18	house servant	Dur Washington
10827	122r	219 b	Gilesgate	George Prince	Hall	hea	m	27	BA student, university *	Mdx London
10828	122v			Maria Louisa	Hall	wif	m	26		Mdx London
10829	122v			Edith Bagelot	Hall	dau		2m		Dur Durham
10830	122v			Martha	Wilkinson	ser		22	servant	Dur Lambton
10831	122v	218	Gilesgate	James	Anderson	hea	m	32	gardener, master *	Sct
10832	122v			Mary	Anderson	wif	m	37		Dur [D] S. Giles
10833	122v			Mary	Hanson	ser		19	house servant	Dur Kimblesworth
			one house uninhabited							
10834	122v	216	Gilesgate	Maria	Dickson	hea		70	fundholder	Mdx S. Olave
10835	122v			Sarah	Dickson	sis		68	fundholder	Mdx Soho, S. John
10836	122v			Edwin Brodie	Dickson	nep		23	BA University College	Mdx Hanover Square *
10837	122v			Maria C.	Wilson	vis		76	annuitant	Mdx S. Dunstan in E
10838	122v			Margaret	Palling	ser		25	house servant	Lks Lanark
10839	122v			Martha	Metcalf	ser		15	house servant	Dur Barnard Castle
10840	122v	215 a	Gilesgate	Benjamin	Herdman	hea	w	35	butcher	Nry Brompton
10841	122v			John	Herdman	son		12	scholar	Dur [D] S. Giles
10842	122v			Edward	Herdman	son		10	scholar	Dur [D] S. Giles
10843	122v			Ann	Herdman	dau		7	scholar	Dur [D] S. Giles
10844	122v			Margaret	Herdman	dau		4	scholar	Dur [D] S. Giles
10845	122v			Ann	Forsith	ser		19	servant	Nbl Ford
10846	123r	215 b	Gilesgate	George	Forsith	hea	m	52	labourer	Nbl Norham [NDu]
10847	123r			Ann	Forsith	wif	m	44		Nbl Ford
10848	123r			Mary	Forsith	dau		17	dressmaker	Dur [D] S. Giles
10849	123r			Margaret	Forsith	dau		12	scholar	Dur [D] S. Giles
10850	123r	215 c	Gilesgate	John	Buckley	hea	m	46	carpet weaver	Wry Dewsbury
10851	123r			Mary	Buckley	wif	m	49		Dur [D] S. Giles
10852	123r			Elizabeth	Buckley	dau		15		Dur [D] S. Giles
10853	123r			Jane	Buckley	dau		13	scholar	Dur [D] S. Giles
10854	123r			Jonathan	Rain	ldr		29	carpet weaver	Dur Gainford
10855	123r			George	Wise	ldr		20	joiner & builder	Nry Gilling
10856	123r	214	Gilesgate	Charles	Ashton	hea	m	36	professor of music *	Lin Lincoln
10857	123r			Diana V.	Ashton	wif	m	35		Lin Gainsborough
10858	123r			Dian Uvedale	Ashton	dau		10		Lin Lincoln
10859	123r			Charles E.	Ashton	son		8	chorister, Durham Cath	Dur Durham
10860	123r			Katherine F.	Ashton	dau		3		Dur Durham
10861	123r			Madeline L.L.	Ashton	dau		1		Dur Durham
10862	123r			Margaret	Goundry	ser		21	house servant	Dur Coundon /"Cowden"
10863	123r	213	Gilesgate	William	Marshall	hea	m	29	solicitor *	Dur [D] S. Nicholas
10864	123r			Mary Anne	Marshall	wif	m	27		Dur Penshaw
10865	123r			William Henry	Marshall	son		2		Dur [D] S. Giles
10866	123v			Edward	Marshall	son		10m		Dur [D] Gilesgate
10867	123v			Elizabeth	Bailey	vis	w	70		Dur Penshaw
10868	123v			Ellen	Bell	ser		20	[servant]	Dur Penshaw
10869	123v			Jane	Bell	ser		18	[servant]	Dur Penshaw
10870	123v	212	Gilesgate	Mark	Story	hea	m	43	alderman, leather merch	Nry Kildale
10871	123v			Jane	Story	wif	m	42		Dur Durham
10872	123v			Jane Heslop	Story	dau		18		Mdx London
10873	123v			Emma	Story	dau		13	scholar	Dur Durham
10874	123v			Wilson Fawcett	Story	son		9	scholar	Dur Durham
10875	123v			Mark	Story	son		7	scholar	Dur Durham
10876	123v			Jane	Parkinson	ser		24	house servant	Dur Easington Lane
10877	123v			Hannah	Scott	ser		19	house servant	Dur Quarrington
10878	123v	211	Gilesgate	Robert	Hoggett	hea		62	alderman & JP *	Dur Auckland S.Andrew
10879	123v			Ruth	Hoggett	sis		53		Dur [D] S. Nicholas
10880	123v			Isabella	Seymour	ser		20	house servant	Dur Great Lumley
10881	123v	210	Gilesgate	Anna	Bagley	wif	m	34	carpet mfr's wife	Nbl Tynemouth
10882	123v			Anna E.	Bagley	dau		7	scholar at home	Dur
10883	123v			Fanny	Bagley	dau		5	scholar at home	Dur
10884	123v			Alice S.	Bagley	dau		4		Dur
10885	123v			Charles J.	Bagley	son		2		Dur

10886	124r	210	Gilesgate	Jane Blaylock	ser	26	house servant	Dur Middle'n-Teesdale
10887	124r			Ann Cook	ser	29	house servant	Dur
10888	124r	209	Gilesgate	Thomas Hoggett	hea w	60	retired bookseller	Dur Bishop Auckland
10889	124r			Eleanor Thompson	ser	24	house servant	Dur Hurworth
10890	124r	208 a	Gilesgate	Ralph Robinson	hea m	65	gardener	Dur [D] S. Giles
10891	124r			Ann Robinson	wif m	65		Dur [D] S. Nicholas
10892	124r			Mary Ann Mason	gda	2		Dur Bishopwearmouth
10893	124r	208 b	Gilesgate	Jane Ramsbottom	hea w	63	nurse	Wes Long Marton
10894	124r			Jane Summerbell	gda	18	dressmaker	Dur [D] S. Giles
10895	124r	208 c	Gilesgate	Elizabeth Wouldhave	hea w	78	matron	Dur Chester-le-Street
10896	124r	208 d	Gilesgate	Jane Robinson	hea	30	schoolmistress	Dur Durham
10897	124r			Jane Grieveson	nce	8		Dur Sunderland
10898	124r	207 a	Gilesgate	Robert Thompson	hea m	31	shoemaker	Dur Durham
10899	124r			Hannah Thompson	wif m	34		Dur Durham
10900	124r			Elizabeth Bainbridge	vis	21	house servant	Nry Ovington
10901	124r	207 b	Gilesgate	Robert Harrison	hea m	64	Post Office messenger	Dur Durham
10902	124r			Elizabeth Harrison	wif m	63		Dur Durham
10903	124r			Robert Harrison	son	24	labourer	Dur Durham
10904	124r			Robert Richardson	vis	11		Dur Durham
10905	124v	207 c	Gilesgate	John Whillis	hea m	25	police officer, city	Nbl Chatton
10906	124v			Mary Ann Whillis	wif m	23		Nbl Newcastle All SS.
10907	124v			Elizabeth W. Whillis	dau	2		Nbl Newcastle, S. Ann
10908	124v			Mary Ann Whillis	dau	<1m		Dur [D] S. Giles
10909	124v	207 d	Gilesgate	Robert Palmer	hea m	30	painter's journeyman	Dur [D] S. Oswald
10910	124v			Isabella Palmer	wif m	24		Dur [D] S. Giles
10911	124v			John Palmer	son	10m		Dur [D] S. Giles
10912	124v	206	Gilesgate	Jane Martin	hea w	38	dressmaker <lodgings>	Dur Willington
10913	124v			Mary Martin	dau	6		Dur
10914	124v			Ralph Martin	son	13	scholar at home	Dur Hamsterley
10915	124v			James Mellon	ldr	35	bookseller	Lan Liverpool
10916	124v	205 a	Gilesgate	William Williamson <jn>	hea m	27	countryman, innkeeper *	Dur Darlington
10917	124v			Eleanor Williamson	wif m	26		Dur Durham
10918	124v	205 b	Gilesgate	Matthew Anderson	hea m	26	railway labourer	Dur Houghton-l-Spring
10919	124v			Jane Anderson	wif m	25		Dur [D] S. Oswald
10920	124v			Robert Anderson	son	3m		Dur [D] S. Giles
10921	124v	204	Gilesgate	Thomas Hall	hea m	52	shoemaker emp 1 man	Stamford Merfoot
10922	124v			Eleanor Hall	wif m	50		Dur [D] S. Giles
10923	124v			John Hall	son	28	shoemaker	Dur [D] S. Giles
10924	124v			Thomas Hall	son	26	shoemaker	Dur Sunderland
10925	125r			William Hall	son	21	grocer	Dur [D] S. Giles
10926	125r			Mary Hall	dau	24	dressmaker	Dur Sunderland
10927	125r			Henry Hall	son	18	miller	Dur [D] S. Giles
10928	125r			Elizabeth Newton	cou	22	dressmaker	Yks Preston Waller
10929	125r	203	Gilesgate	Peter Bradley	hea m	58	farm labr <mole catcher>	Dur Durham
10930	125r			Margaret Bradley	wif m	58		Dur Greatham
10931	125r			Peter Burnip Bradley	gsn	6	scholar	Dur [D] S. Giles
10932	125r	202 a	Gilesgate	Nathaniel Herdman	hea m	30	butcher	Nry Brompton
10933	125r			Mary Herdman	wif m	30		Dur Whorlton
10934	125r			Ann Gibbon	sil	17	servant	Dur Whorlton
10935	125r	202 b	Gilesgate	Edward Houston	hea m	23	boot and shoemaker	Dur [D] S. Giles
10936	125r			Elizabeth Houston	wif m	22		Dur [D] Milburngate
10937	125r	201 a	Gilesgate	George Robinson	hea m	29	grocer	Dur Hetton
10938	125r			Sarah Robinson	wif m	26		Dur Westoe
10939	125r	201 b	Gilesgate	William Sharp	hea	18	printer compositor	Dur [D] Framwelgate
10940	125r			Mary Sharp	sis	19	dressmaker	Dur [D] Framwelgate
10941	125r			Catherine Sharp	sis	14		Dur [D] Framwelgate
10942	125r			Anthony Sharp	bro	8		Dur [D] Framwelgate
10943	125r	200	Gilesgate	Ann Erskine	hea m	39	wife [of] R. Erskine *	Nbl Norham [NDu]
10944	125r			Margaret L. Erskine	dau	16		East Indies
10945	125v			Esther Hall Erskine	dau	14	scholar	East Indies
10946	125v			Mary Ann Erskine	dau	10	scholar	East Indies
10947	125v			Robert Sturt Erskine	son	8	scholar	East Indies
10948	125v			Sophia Anne Erskine	dau	5	scholar	East Indies
10949	125v			Margaret Rule	mth w	70	visitor	Nbl Norham [NDu]
10950	125v	199	Gilesgate	Matthew Brown	hea m	49	chorister <lay clerk *>	Dur [D] S. Oswald
10951	125v			Barbara Brown	wif m	52		Nbl Simonburn
10952	125v			Elizabeth Brown	dau	27		Dur [D] S. Nicholas
10953	125v			Margaret Brown	dau	25		Dur [D] S. Nicholas
10954	125v			Granville L.G. Ward	ldr	27	solicitor	Dur [D] S. Oswald
10955	125v	198	Gilesgate	William Hutchinson	hea	50	boot & shoemaker retired	Dur Sedgefield
10956	125v			Hannah Sugden	ser	29	housekeeper	Dur Houghton Gate
10957	125v	197	Gilesgate	Ann Hall	hea w	50	<lodgings>	Dur Brandon
10958	125v			Thomas Crossman	ldr	27	curate of S. Giles	Gls Olveston
			one house uninhabited					
10959	125v	195	Gilesgate	Ann Barron	hea	47	proprietor of houses *	Dur Bishop Auckland
10960	125v			Sarah Rowlandson	ldr w	74	proprietor of houses	Dur Barnard Castle *
10961	125v			Ann Story	ser	16	[servant]	Dur Chester-le-Street
10962	125v	194	Gilesgate	Elizabeth Ovington	hea w	69	proprietor of houses	Nfk
10963	125v			Elizabeth James	ser	42	[servant]	Dur [D] S. Giles
10964	126r	193 a	Gilesgate	George Medcalf	hea	74	Chelsea pensioner	Dur Bishopwearmouth
10965	126r			Jane Medcalf	dau	32		Dur [D] S. Giles

10966	126r	193 b	Gilesgate	John Wouldhave	hea	40	nailer	Dur [D] S. Nicholas
10967	126r	193 c	Gilesgate	William Kirk	hea m	50	waggoner	Wry Wetherby
10968	126r			Margaret Kirk	wif m	42		Dur [D] S. Nicholas
10969	126r			William Kirk	son	10	scholar	Nry Leeming Lane
10970	126r			Ann Kirk	dau	8	scholar	Dur Merrington
10971	126r			Thomas Kirk	son	5	scholar	Dur [D] S. Nicholas
10972	126r			Elizabeth Kirk	dau	3		Dur [D] S. Nicholas
10973	126r	193 d	Gilesgate	William Briggs	hea m	29	woodmar	Dur Shincliffe
10974	126r			Mary Ann Briggs	wif m	27		Dur [D] S. Giles
10975	126r			Eleanor Briggs	dau	7		Dur [D] S. Giles
10976	126r			Edward Briggs	son	4		Dur Bishop Auckland
10977	126r			William Briggs	son	2		Dur [D] S. Giles
10978	126r	193 e	Gilesgate	Robert Hall	hea m	39	blacksmith	Dur Medistead
10979	126r			Katherine Hall	wif m	41		Nbl Wooler
10980	126r			Margaret Hall	dau	14	scholar	Nbl Wooler
10981	126r			Jane Hall	dau	8	scholar	Nbl Newcastle
10982	126r	192 a	Gilesgate	Isabella Longstaff	hea w	61	bread baker	Dur Lanchester
10983	126r			Elizabeth Ann Longstaff	dau	19	dressmaker	Dur [D] S. Giles
10984	126v	192 b	Gilesgate	Thomas Reed	hea m	36	rail platelayer	Dur Rainton
10985	126v			Mary Ann Reed	wif m	29		Dur [D] S. Giles
10986	126v			Anthony Reed	son	10	scholar	Dur Pittington *
10987	126v			Catherine Reed	dau	9	scholar	Dur Pittington *
10988	126v			Elizabeth Reed	dau	2		Dur [D] S. Giles
10989	126v			Mary Jane Reed	dau	10m		Dur [D] S. Giles
10990	126v	192 c	Gilesgate	George Atkinson	hea w	67	Chelsea pen, shoemaker	Dur
10991	126v			Elizabeth Atkinson	dau	27	dressmaker	Dur
10992	126v			Eliza Ann Atkinson	gda	3		Dur
10993	126v			William C. Atkinson	gsn	1		Dur
10994	126v	192 d	Gilesgate	Joseph Burnell	hea m	38	railway porter	Dur Bishop Auckland
10995	126v			Jane Burnell	wif m	31		Dur Stranton
10996	126v			Thomas S. Burnell	son	16	whitesmith, apprentice	Dur [D] Framwelgate
10997	126v			Emma Burnell	dau	13		Dur [D] Framwelgate
10998	126v	192 e	Gilesgate	William Thompson	hea m	46	gardener	Dur [D] S. Nicholas
10999	126v	192 f	Gilesgate	Corbitt Stewart	hea m	34	mason	Dur [D] S. Oswald
11000	126v			Margaret Stewart	wif m	26		Dur [D] S. Oswald
11001	126v			Elizabeth Ann Stewart	dau	4	scholar at home	Dur [D] S. Giles
11002	126v			John Stewart	son	2		Dur [D] S. Giles
11003	126v			Jane Stewart	dau	6m		Dur [D] S. Giles
11004	127r			Joseph Stewart	bro m	31	mason	Dur Stanhope
11005	127r			Alice Stewart	sil m	32		Nry Whitby
11006	127r	191	Gilesgate	Michael Cowans <jn>	hea m	29	butcher	Dur [D] S. Nicholas
11007	127r			Mary Cowans	wif m	26		Nbl Wall House
11008	127r	190	Gilesgate	David Jack	hea m	30	basketmaker	Lks Glasgow
11009	127r			Elizabeth Jack	wif m	31	dressmaker	Sti Stirling
11010	127r			Janet Jack	dau	10	scholar	Lks Glasgow
11011	127r			Margaret Jack	dau	7	scholar	Dur Durham
11012	127r			Elizabeth Jack	dau	5	scholar	Dur Durham
11013	127r			David Jack	son	3	scholar	Dur Gateshead
11014	127r			Robert Andrew Jack	son	1		Dur Durham
11015	127r	189	Gilesgate	John Clarke	hea w	69	cabinetmaker, master	Dur Durham
11016	127r			Sarah Clarke	dau	33	teacher, infant school	Dur Durham
11017	127r			Mary Ann Lynn	ldr	30	dressmaker	Dur Durham
11018	127r	188 a	Gilesgate	Michael Hills	hea m	72	miner	Nbl [Newcastle?] *
11019	127r			Ann Hills	wif m	65		Dur Sunderland
11020	127r			Michael Hills	son	33	grocer	Dur Penshaw
11021	127r	188 b	Gilesgate	James Shafto	hea m	76	joiner	Dur [D] S. Giles
11022	127r			Hannah Shafto	wif m	73		Dur [D] S. Margaret
11023	127r			Mary Shafto	dau	26		Dur [D] S. Nicholas
11024	127v	187 a	Gilesgate	Thomas Heaviside	hea m	36	master tailor	Dur Stockton
11025	127v			Elizabeth Heaviside	wif m	34		Dur Bishop Middleham
11026	127v			William Heaviside	son	11	scholar at home	Dur Durham
11027	127v			Elizabeth Heaviside	dau	6	scholar at home	Dur Durham
11028	127v	187 b	Gilesgate	Isabella Wilson	hea	70	shopkeeper	Dur Billingham
11029	127v			Hannah Wood	vis	31		Dur Boldon
11030	127v			James William Wood	vss	5m		Dur Boldon
11031	127v	186 a	Gilesgate	Henry Gray	hea	31	labourer	Dur [D] S. Nicholas
11032	127v			Sarah Clift	ser	33	[servant]	Lan Blackburn
11033	127v	186 b	Gilesgate	Anthony Burnett	hea w	49	cartman	Dur Wolsingham
11034	127v			Jane Burnett	dau	13		Dur [D] S. Giles
11035	127v			George Burnett	son	6		Dur [D] S. Giles
11036	127v	186 c	Gilesgate	John Smith	hea m	36	cooper	Dur [D] S. Oswald
11037	127v			Mary Ann Smith	wif m	34		Dur [D] S. Nicholas
11038	127v			Elizabeth Smith	dau	7	scholar	Dur [D] S. Margaret
11039	127v			Esther Smith	dau	4		Dur [D] S. Margaret
11040	127v			Louisa Smith	dau	1		Dur [D] S. Giles
11041	127v	[aa]	Leazes Cottages	James Thompson	hea m	31	carpet weaver	Dur Barnard Castle
11042	127v			Elizabeth Thompson	wif m	30		Sct
11043	127v			Elizabeth Mary Thompson	dau	10	scholar at home	Dur Barnard Castle
11044	128r			John Thompson	son	7	scholar at home	Dur Barnard Castle
11045	128r			George Thompson	son	5		Dur Barnard Castle
11046	128r			James Thompson	son	3		Dur Barnard Castle

11047	128r	[aa]	Leazes Cottages	Mary Jane Thompson	dau	7m		Dur [D] S. Giles
11048	128r	[ab]	Leazes Cottages	Anne Molesworth	hea	26	straw-bonnetmaker	Dur Bishopwearmouth
11049	128r	[ac]	Leazes Cottages	Thomas Crampton	hea m	30	carpet weaver	Dur Barnard Castle
11050	128r			Jane Crampton	wif m	29		Dur Barnard Castle
11051	128r			Margaret Crampton	dau	2		Dur [D] S. Margaret
11052	128r			Ellen Crampton	dau	7w		Dur [D] S. Giles
11053	128r	[ad]	Leazes Cottages	Henry G. Cunningham	hea m	35	earthenware dealer	Dur S. John's Chapel
11054	128r			Ann Cunningham	dau	14		Yks York
11055	128r			Hannah Cunningham	dau	12		Dur Stockton
11056	128r			Henry Cunningham	son	10		Dur [D] S. Giles
11057	128r			John Cunningham	son	8		Dur [D] S. Giles
11058	128r			Mary Cunningham	dau	5		Dur [D] S. Nicholas
11059	128r	185 a	Gilesgate	James Gray	hea m	47	hairdresser *	Sct
11060	128r			Ann Gray	wif m	42		Dur Washington
11061	128r			Hannah Gray	dau	1		Dur Durham
11062	128r	185 b	Gilesgate	Thomas Forster	hea m	27	hairdresser	Dur
11063	128r			Mary Forster	wif m	25		Dur Brandon
11064	128v			Isabel Forster	dau	4		Dur
11065	128v			Thomas Forster	son	1		Dur
11066	128v			Robert Burn	gfa m	83	labourer	Dur West Auckland
11067	128v			Isabella Burn	gmo m	81		Dur Lanchester
11068	128v	184 a	Gilesgate	Robert Atkinson	hea m	49	tailor	Dur [D] S. Giles
11069	128v			Jane Atkinson	wif m	46		Dur [D] S. Nicholas
11070	128v			John Atkinson	son	19	tailor	Dur [D] S. Giles
11071	128v			Isabella Atkinson	dau	16	dressmaker	Dur [D] S. Giles
11072	128v			Elizabeth Atkinson	dau	14	scholar at home	Dur [D] S. Giles
11073	128v			Henry Atkinson	son	9	scholar at home	Dur [D] S. Giles
11074	128v			Robert Atkinson	son	6	scholar at home	Dur [D] S. Giles
11075	128v			Susanna Atkinson	dau	3	scholar at home	Dur [D] S. Giles
11076	128v	184 b	Gilesgate	John Steele	hea m	38	cordwainer	Dur [D] S. Giles
11077	128v			Jane Steele	wif m	36		Dur [D] S. Giles
11078	128v			Jane Elizabeth Steele	dau	12	scholar	Dur [D] S. Giles
11079	128v			Robert Steele	son	8	scholar	Dur [D] S. Giles
11080	128v	184 c	Gilesgate	Thomas Carlton	hea m	41	carpet weaver	Dur Darlington
11081	128v			Ann Carlton	wif	47		Dur [D] S. Giles
11082	128v			Isabella Carlton	dau	19	doubler	Dur [D] S. Giles
11083	128v			Jane Carlton	dau	16	spinner	Dur [D] S. Giles
11084	128v			Anne Carlton	dau	14	dressmaker	Dur Darlington
11085	129r			William Carlton	son	12	apprentice hairdresser	Dur [D] S. Nicholas
11086	129r			Elizabeth Burn	sda	22	ragcutter	Dur Brandon
11087	129r			John Burn	sso	<1m		Dur [D] S. Giles
11088	129r	184 d	Gilesgate	Ralph Snowdon	hea m	45	cordwainer	Dur [D] S. Giles
11089	129r			Ann Snowdon	wif m	49		Dur [D] S. Giles
11090	129r			John William Snowdon	son	16	tanner, apprentice	Dur [D] S. Giles
11091	129r			Thomas Snowdon	son	15	printer, apprentice	Dur [D] S. Giles
11092	129r			Margaret Snowdon	dau	13	scholar at home	Dur [D] S. Giles
11093	129r			Charles W. Snowdon	son	10	scholar at home	Dur [D] S. Giles
11094	129r			Sarah J. Snowdon	dau	5	scholar at home	Dur [D] S. Giles
11095	129r	183 a	Gilesgate	Thomas Sewell	hea m	41	labourer	Dur
11096	129r			Margaret Sewell	wif m	47		Dur
11097	129r			Mary Ann Bennet	dau	24		Dur
11098	129r			Thomas Hardy	son	21	joiner	Dur
11099	129r			Margaret Sewell	dau	15		Dur
11100	129r			Joseph Sewell	son	13		Dur
11101	129r			Bennet Sewell	son	10		Dur
11102	129r			James Sewell	son	10		Dur
11103	129r			John Bennet	gsn	2		Dur
11104	129v	183 b	Gilesgate	Peter Owens	hea m	29	labourer	Irl
11105	129v			Alice Owens	wif m	30		Irl
11106	129v			Elizabeth Owens	dau	1		Dur [D] S. Giles
11107	129v			James Goggins	blw	40	labourer {deaf & dumb}	Irl
11108	129v			Mary Owens	sis	18		Irl
11109	129v			Henry Savage	ldr	40	labourer	Irl
11110	129v			Thomas Tiernan	ldr	31	labourer	Irl
11111	129v			Patrick Byrne	ldr	50	bookseller	Irl
11112	129v	183 c	Gilesgate	Joseph Bell Dixon	hea m	53	tailor	Cul Westwood
11113	129v			Mary Ann Dixon	wif m	35		Nbl Berwick
11114	129v			John Dixon	son	14	tailor	Nbl Berwick
11115	129v	183 d	Gilesgate	Jacob Anderson	hea m	60	carpet weaver	Dur [D] S. Nicholas
11116	129v			Mary Anderson	wif m	61		Dur [D] Framwelgate
11117	129v			Thomas Anderson	son	26	nailer	Dur Darlington
11118	129v			John Anderson	son	24	carpet weaver	Dur Darlington
11119	129v			George Anderson	son	20	woolsorter	Dur Darlington
11120	129v	183 e	Gilesgate	Jane Jackson	hea m	44	capmaker	Nry Romaldkirk
11121	129v			Mary Howson	dau	16	capmaker	Dur Barnard Castle
11122	129v	182	Gilesgate	James Smith	hea m	50	labourer	Wor Bevere /"Beverly"
11123	129v			Ann Smith	wif m	40		Dur
11124	130r			William Coplin	vis	18	labourer	Dur
11125	130r	181	Gilesgate	John Robinson	hea m	26	seedsman & florist	Dur Darlington
11126	130r			Ann Robinson	wif m	23		Dur Darlington
11127	130r			Robert Scott		22	gardener <& florist>	Nbl

ID	Folio		Address	Name	Rel		Age	Occupation	Birthplace
11128	130r		Pelaw Leazes	Jane Worth Procter	hea	w	36	charwoman	Yks
11129	130r			Joseph Worth Procter	son		15	hawker	Gls
11130	130r			Richard Procter	son		14	scholar at home	Wry Sheffield
11131	130r			Ann Worth Procter	dau		11	scholar at home	Wry Sheffield
11132	130r			Jane Worth Procter	dau		5	scholar at home	Lan Manchester
11133	130r			John Worth Procter	son		2		Dur
11134	130r			Richard Gordon	slw m		21	hawker	Wry Bradford
11135	130r			Elizabeth Gordon	dau m		21		Wry Sheffield
11136	130r			John Gordon	gsn		2		Lan Liverpool
11137	130r			Joseph Gordon	gsn		1m		Dur
11138	130r	180	Gilesgate	George Burlinson	hea m		75	millwright	Dur Auckland S. Helen
11139	130r			Mary Burlinson	wif m		73		Dur Sedgefield
11140	130r			Jane Burlinson	dau		38	dressmaker	Dur Sedgefield
11141	130r			Fanny Burlinson	dau		34	bonnetmaker <dressmaker>	Dur Bishop Auckland
11142	130r			George Carr	gsn		8	scholar at home	Dur [D] S. Nicholas
11143	130r			Thomas Birkinshow	ldr		27	shoemaker	Yks York, S. Peter
11144	130v	179 a	Gilesgate	John Johnson	hea w		55	shoemaker, journeyman	Dur
11145	130v	179 b	Gilesgate	William Peatters	hea		52	labourer	Dur [D] S. Giles
11146	130v	179 c	Gilesgate	Mary Newton	hea		70	pauper; [deleted] widow	Nbl Hartley
11147	130v	178 a	Gilesgate	Richard McGregor	hea m		36	picture-framemaker	Sct
11148	130v			Margaret McGregor	wif		40		Sct
11149	130v			John McGregor	son		14	scholar at home	Sct
11150	130v	178 b	Gilesgate	Joseph Stoker	hea		23	pitman	Dur Hetton-le-Hole
11151	130v			Margaret Stoker	wif		22		Dur [D] S. Giles
11152	130v	177	Gilesgate	William Fleming	hea m		28	cabinetmaker, journeyman	Dur Field Houses
11153	130v			Ann Fleming	wif m		35		Dur [D] Old Elvet
11154	130v			Henry Fleming	son		5		Dur [D] S. Giles
11155	130v			John George Fleming	son		3		Dur Lanchester
11156	130v			Alice Fleming	dau		1		Dur Witton Gilbert
11157	130v		Woolloommoolloo Cott	Thomas Wardropper	hea m		29	mason	Dur Chester-le-Street
11158	130v			Jane Wardropper	wif m		29		Dur [D] S. Giles
11159	130v			William Wardropper	son		4		Dur [D] S. Giles
11160	130v			Robert Wardropper	son		1m		Dur [D] S. Giles
11161	130v		Mount Slowly	Jane Milbourne	hea w		59	landed proprietor	Yks York
11162	130v			John Milbourne	son		33	chandlery business	Yks York
11163	130v			Edward Hills	gsn		6		
11164	131r		not known		ser nk		21	servant	not known
11165	131r	176	Gilesgate	Roger Rule	hea m		35	master slater emp 2 men*	Nbl Norham [NDu]
11166	131r			Elizabeth Rule	wif m		36		Dur [D] S. Giles
11167	131r			Thomas Rule	son		9	scholar at home	Dur [D] S. Giles
11168	131r			Margaret Ann Rule	dau		6	scholar at home	Dur [D] S. Giles
11169	131r			Elizabeth R. Rule	dau		3		Dur [D] S. Giles
11170	131r			Robert Renney Rule	son		1		Dur [D] S. Giles
11171	131r			Mary Ramshaw	ser		17	house servant	Dur Gateshead
11172	131r	175	Gilesgate	Ann Rutherford	hea w		79	proprietor of houses *	Dur [D] S. Giles
11173	131r			Mary Rutherford	nce		15		Dur Witton Gilbert
11174	131r	174	Gilesgate	Angelo Arrighi	hea m		43	servant	Italy
11175	131r			Hugh Condon	vis m		29	miller	Dur
11176	131r			Elizabeth Condon	vis m		26		Dur Chester-le-Street
11177	131r			William Condon	vss		2m		Dur
11178	131r			Magdalen Gilbertson	vis w		77		Dur Trimdon
11179	131r	173	Gilesgate	George Harle	hea w		80	retired drawing master *	Dur [D] S. Oswald
11180	131r			Sarah Bailes	ser		16	[servant]	Dur [D] S. Giles
11181	131r	172 a	Gilesgate	John Wills	hea m		38	printer pressman	Dur [D] S. Oswald
11182	131r			Hannah Wills	wif m		29		Dur Denton
11183	131r			Alice Wills	dau		5	scholar	Dur [D] S. Giles
11184	131v			Emily Ann Wills	dau		9m		Dur [D] S. Giles
11185	131v	172 b	Gilesgate	Thomas Wills	hea w		67	shoemaker	Dur Trimdon
11186	131v			Thomas Wills	son		34	joiner & cabinetmaker	Dur [D] S. Oswald
11187	131v			Alice Wills	dau		28		Dur [D] S. Oswald
11188	131v			Christopher Wills	son		26	plumber	Dur [D] S. Oswald
11189	131v	172 c	Gilesgate	John Shepherd	hea w		41	journeyman slater	Wry Chapel-le-Dale
11190	131v			Alice Jane Shepherd	dau		10	scholar at home	Dur Stockton
11191	131v			John Wills Shepherd	son		8	scholar at home	Dur [D] S. Giles
11192	131v			Susanna Wills	sil		36	housekeeper	Dur [D] S. Oswald
11193	131v		Parsonage House	Francis Thompson	hea m		37	MA, perpetual curate *	Nry Melsonby
11194	131v			Margaret Thompson	wif m		35		Dur [D] S. Nicholas
11195	131v			Elizabeth Smithson	ser		22	house servant	Dur Easington Lane
11196	131v	171	Gilesgate	Benjamin Ord	hea m		41	innkpr <'Turk's Head'>	Dur [D] Crossgate
11197	131v			Jane Ord	wif m		43		Dur [D] Framwelgate
11198	131v			Margaret Ord	dau		20		Dur [D] Framwelgate
11199	131v			Dorothy Ord	dau		18		Dur [D] Framwelgate
11200	131v			Benjamin Ord	son		16		Dur [D] Framwelgate
11201	131v			Mary Ann Ord	dau		13		Dur Bishopwearmouth
11202	131v			Isabel Ord	dau		11		Dur Heworth
11203	131v			John Ord	son		9	scholar	Dur [D] Crossgate
11204	132r			William Ord	son		6	scholar at home	Dur [D] Crossgate
11205	132r			Thomasin Ord	dau		4		Dur [D] Crossgate
11206	132r	[aa]a	house in yard	Henry Robertson	hea m		41	slater	Wes Orton
11207	132r			Jane Robertson	wif m		32		Dur Windy Nook
11208	132r			Elizabeth Robertson	dau		6		Dur Sacriston

			Name	Rel	Cond	Age	Occupation	Birthplace
11209	132r	[aa]a house in yard	John Robertson	son*		2		Wes Ravenstonedale
11210	132r		Mary A. Robson	sil		14	scholar	Nbl Newburn
11211	132r	[aa]b house in yard	Robert Elliott	hea		72	outbrother Sherburn Hosp	Dur [D] S. Giles
11212	132r	[aa]c house in yard	James Cummings	hea	m	23	tinplate worker	Dur Durham
11213	132r		Esther J.W. Cummings	wif	m	24		Wry Leeds
11214	132r		Robert W.W. Cummings	son		7m		Dur Durham
11215	132r	170 Gilesgate	William Wills	hea	m	31	journeyman tailor	Dur [D] S. Giles
11216	132r		Harriet Wills	wif	m	29		Dur [D] Elvet
11217	132r		Thomas Wills	son		6	scholar	Dur [D] Silver Street
11218	132r		John Wills	son		3		Dur [D] S. Giles
11219	132r		Ann Walton	vis	w	69	proprietor of houses	Nbl Elsdon
11220	132r		Robert Thompson	vis		23	journeyman tailor	Dur [D] S. Margaret
11221	132r		Frances Brogden	ser		13	[servant]	Dur Jarrow
11222	132r	169 a Gilesgate	John Mallon	hea	w	40	labourer	Irl
11223	132r		James Mallon	son		11		Dur Sunderland
11224	132v		Catherine Higgins	ser		30	house servant	Irl
11225	132v		Joseph Anderson	vis	m	28	flaxdresser	Irl
11226	132v		Margaret Anderson	vsw	m	23		Irl
11227	132v		Jean Anderson	vsd		16		Irl
11228	132v	169 b Gilesgate	Joseph Wood	hea	m	21	mason	Dur Durham
11229	132v		Agnes J. Wood	wif	m	19		Dur Durham
11230	132v	169 c Gilesgate	William Petrie	hea	m	49	carpet weaver	Sct
11231	132v		Ann Petrie	wif	m	40		Sct
11232	132v	169 d Gilesgate	William Trevor Scott	hea	m	20	bookbinder	Dur Durham
11233	132v		Anne Scott	wif	m	23		Dur Stanhope
11234	132v		Mary Scott	dau		2		Dur Durham
11235	132v	169 e Gilesgate.	Henry Brogden	hea	m	38	shoemaker	Nbl North Shields
11236	132v		Jane Brogden	wif	m	41		Nbl Slaley Ford
11237	132v		John Brogden	son		11	ropemaker, apprentice	Dur Jarrow
11238	132v		Michael Stoker	vis	m	40	miner	Cul
11239	132v		Agnes Stoker	vsw	m	41		Dur Darlington
11240	132v		Ann Stoker	vsd		6		Dur Shotton
11241	132v	169 f Gilesgate	Elizabeth Holmes	hea	w	79	dressmaker	Wry Roundhay
11242	132v		William Holmes	son		44	draper	Dur Durham
11243	169 g Gilesgate		John Medcalf	hea	m	30	grocer's assistant	Dur Durham
11244	133r		Ann L. Medcalf	wif	m	26		Dur Chester-le-Street
11245	133r		George William Medcalf	son		5	scholar at home	Dur Durham
11246	133r		John Medcalf	son		4		Dur Stockton
11247	133r		David Medcalf	son		6m		Dur Durham
11248	133r	168 Gilesgate	George Mitchinson	hea	w	55	groom	Dur Durham
11249	133r		Jane Mitchinson	dau		32		Dur Durham
11250	133r		William Mitchinson	son		12	scholar	Dur Durham
11251	133r		William H. Liddell			5	scholar	Dur Durham
		one house uninhabited						
11252	133r	166 Gilesgate	Hannah Atkinson	hea	w	51		Dur Stanhope
11253	133r		Richard Atkinson	son		11	scholar	Dur [D] S. Giles
11254	133r		Mary Jane Atkinson	dau		7		Dur [D] S. Giles
11255	133r		John Nicholson Atkinson	sso	w	28	cabinetmaker	Dur [D] S. Giles
11256	133r		Thomas Atkinson	sso		19	tailor	Dur [D] S. Giles
11257	133r		John Scorer Atkinson	gsn		5		Dur [D] S. Giles
11258	133r	165 Gilesgate	Richard W. Garth	hea		48	proprietor of houses	Dur Blackwell
11259	133r		Ann Bell	ser		26	housekeeper	Dur Coxgreen
11260	133r		Ann Bell			7		Dur [D] S. Giles
11261	133r		William Bell			6		Dur [D] S. Giles
11262	133v		Jane Bell			4		Dur [D] S. Giles
11263	133v		George Bell			1		Dur [D] S. Giles
11264	133v	164 a Gilesgate	John Bulmer	hea	m	62	master shoemkr emp 3 men	Dur [D] S. Oswald
11265	133v		Elizabeth Bulmer	wif	m	61		Nbl [Newcastle?] *
11266	133v		William Bulmer	son		27	printer compositor	Dur [D] S. Oswald
11267	133v		John Bulmer	son		24	shoemaker	Dur [D] S. Oswald
11268	133v		Anne Bulmer	dau		22		Dur [D] S. Giles
11269	133v		Jane Bulmer	dau		18		Dur [D] S. Giles
11270	133v		Thomas Bulmer	son		17		Dur [D] S. Giles
11271	133v	164 b Gilesgate	Robert Crofton	hea	m	63	tailor	Dur Pittington *
11272	133v		Alice Crofton	wif	m	57	dressmaker	Dur Eppleton
11273	133v		Elizabeth Brown	*	m	73		Dur Pittington *
11274	133v	164 c Gilesgate	Elizabeth Craggs	hea		71		Dur Stockton
11275	133v	163 a Gilesgate	Edward Ferry	hea	m	59	miner	Dur Witton Gilbert
11276	133v		Dinah Ferry	wif	m	54		Dur Winlaton
11277	133v	163 b Gilesgate	Ann Wilson	hea	w	60	pauper	Dur Coatham
11278	133v		Ann Stodart	ldr	w	98		Dur [D] S. Giles
11279	133v	163 c Gilesgate	Catherine Parker	hea	w	60	straw-bonnetmaker	Sry Lambeth
11280	133v	163 d Gilesgate	Thomas Robson	hea	m	54	roper	Dur [D] Claypath
11281	133v		Elizabeth Robson	wif	m	50		Nry Swainby
11282	134r		Margaret Robson	dau		10	scholar	Dur [D] Gilesgate
11283	134r		Alice Moor	ldr		8m		Dur [D] Gilesgate
11284	134r		William B. Greenwell	ldr	m	60	butcher	Dur Crook
11285	134r	163 e Gilesgate	Elizabeth Robinson	hea	m	56		Nbl Newcastle
11286	134r		Jonathan Robinson	son		16	coal miner	Nbl Newcastle
11287	134r	162 Gilesgate *	John Smith	hea	m	63	labourer	Dur Ferryhill
11288	134r		Katherine Smith	wif	m	46		Sct

11289	134r	162	Gilesgate *	Henry Smith	son	9	scholar	Dur [D] Crossgate
11290	134r			George Smith	son	7	scholar	Dur [D] S. Giles
11291	134r			Margaret Smith	dau	5	scholar	Dur [D] S. Giles
11292	134r			Edward Smith	son	3		Dur [D] S. Giles
11293	134r			Robert Herbert		23	cordwainer	Dur [D] Claypath
11294	134r	161	Gilesgate *	Thomas Ballan	hea m	32	woodman	Yks Hanter
11295	134r			Laura Ballan	wif m	26	dressmaker	Ntt Nottingham
11296	134r			Sarah Ballan	mth w	77	formerly housekeeper	Nry Middleham
11297	134r	158	Gilesgate *	James Delayney	hea m	36	lodging house kpr, labr	Irl
11298	134r			Bridget Delayney	dau	13		Wry Halifax
11299	134r			John Golden	ldr	30	labourer	Irl
11300	134r			Patrick Drum	ldr m	40	labourer	Irl
11301	134r			Ann Drum	ldr m	30		Irl
11302	134v			Mary Drum	ldr	8		Irl
11303	134v			Patrick Brown	ldr	20	labourer	Irl
11304	134v			James Murphy	ldr m	29	labourer	Irl
11305	134v			Mary Murphy	ldr m	30		Irl
11306	134v			Patrick Murphy	ldr	5		Irl
11307	134v	157	Gilesgate	Stewart Stewart	hea m	67	basketmaker, formerly *	Nbl Birtley
11308	134v			Mary Stewart	wif m	50		Dur Gateshead
11309	134v			Hugh Stewart	son	13		Yks
11310	134v			William Stewart	son	10		Nry Whitby
11311	134v			Septimus Stewart	son	8		Yks
11312	134v	156	Gilesgate	Thomas Pinkerton	hea m	56	capmaker	Wor Worcester
11313	134v			Ann Pinkerton	wif m	54		Dur South Shields
11314	134v			William Pinkerton	son	18	coal miner	Dur Houghton-l-Spring
11315	134v			George Pinkerton	son	12	coal miner	Dur Durham
11316	134v	155 a	Gilesgate	Robert Laws	hea m	38	coal miner	Dur South Shields
11317	134v			Elizabeth Laws	wif m	35		Nbl West Moor
11318	134v			Isabella Laws	dau	10		Nbl Kenton
11319	134v			Mary Laws	dau	7		Dur Cassop
11320	134v			Elizabeth Laws	dau	5		Nbl Kenton
11321	134v			Jane Laws	dau	1		Dur Cassop
11322	135r	155 b	Gilesgate	Eleanor Sweeting	hea w	63	laundress	Dur Castle Eden
11323	135r			John Sweeting	son	23	labourer	Dur Easington
11324	135r	155 c	Gilesgate	Anthony Punshon	hea m	35	tanner	Dur Chester-le-Street
11325	135r			Ann Punshon	wif m	35		Dur Chester-le-Street
11326	135r			Catherine Punshon	dau	12	scholar	Dur Chester-le-Street
11327	135r			Henry Punshon	son	10	scholar	Dur Chester-le-Street
11328	135r			John Punshon	son	8	scholar	Dur Chester-le-Street
11329	135r			Anthony Punshon	son	6	scholar	Dur Chester-le-Street
11330	135r			Elizabeth Punshon	dau	3	scholar	Dur Durham
11331	135r	154	Gilesgate	William Forster	hea m	42	butcher <baker>	Dur [D] S. Giles
11332	135r			Jane Forster	wif m	50		Dur Hunwick
11333	135r			Barnabas Forster	son	14		Dur [D] S. Giles
11334	135r			Elizabeth Forster	dau	11	scholar	Dur [D] S. Giles
11335	135r			Rebecca Forster	dau	9	scholar	Dur [D] S. Giles
11336	135r			Mary Ann Forster	dau	7	scholar	Dur [D] S. Giles
11337	135r	153	Gilesgate	Thomas Robson	hea m	46	joiner	Dur [D] S. Giles
11338	135r			Ann Robson	wif m	46		Dur [D] S. Nicholas
11339	135r			Carr Robson	son	18	currier, apprentice	Dur [D] S. Oswald
11340	135r			John Robson	son	11	scholar	Dur [D] S. Giles
11341	135r			Eleanor Robson	dau	8	scholar	Dur [D] S. Giles
11342	135v			Mary Robson	dau	5	scholar	Dur [D] S. Giles
11343	135v			Arthur O'Bryon	ldr	21	tanner	Cul Workington
11344	135v	152	Gilesgate	Hannah Ovington	hea	20	landed proprietor	Dur [D] Gilesgate
11345	135v			Elizabeth Hope	ser	20	[servant]	Dur Moorsley
11346	135v	150 a	Gilesgate	James Mather	hea m	24	coal miner	Dur [D] S. Giles
11347	135v			Mary Mather	wif m	25		Dur [D] S. Giles
11348	135v			Jane Mather	dau	5		Dur [D] S. Giles
11349	135v			Mary Mather	dau	1		Dur [D] S. Giles
11350	135v			Joseph Smith	vis	22	coal miner	Dur [D] S. Giles
11351	135v	150 b	Gilesgate	Michael Briggs	hea w	48	coal miner	Dur Shincliffe
11352	135v			Elizabeth Briggs	dau	16		Dur [D] S. Giles
11353	135v			John Briggs	son	18	coal miner	Dur [D] S. Giles
11354	135v			Isabella Briggs	dau	14	scholar	Dur [D] S. Giles
11355	135v			Thomas Briggs	son	11	scholar	Dur [D] S. Giles
11356	135v			Dorothy Briggs	dau	9	scholar	Dur [D] S. Giles
11357	135v	150 c	Gilesgate	James Woodward	hea m	49	pavior	Nry Arkengarthdale
11358	135v			Mary Woodward	wif m	38		Nry Ovington
11359	135v			John Woodward	son	16	shoemaker	Dur
11360	135v			Ann Woodward	dau	12	scholar	Dur
11361	135v			John Woodward	nep	25	miner	Dur Barnard Castle
11362	136r			Jane Hutchinson	vis	23		Nry Arkengarthdale
11363	136r			Joseph Blacklock	vis	18	carpet weaver	Dur
11364	136r	150 d	Gilesgate	John Smith	hea m	28	nailer	Dur [D] S. Giles
11365	136r			Mary Ann Smith	wif m	29		Dur [D] S. Nicholas
11366	136r	149	Gilesgate	George Scarth	hea m	54	marine store dealer	Dur Easington
11367	136r			Jane Scarth	wif m	35		Dur Coundon
11368	136r			Mary Scarth	dau	6		Dur [D] S. Giles
11369	136r			George Scarth	son	3		Dur [D] S. Giles

11370	136r	149	Gilesgate	Ellen Harbit	ser	17	maid servant	Dur Houghton
11371	136r	148	Gilesgate	Jonathan Duncan	hea m	56	master tailor & draper	Dur Penshaw
11372	136r			Ann Duncan	wif m	51		Sal Oswestry
11373	136r			Henry Thomas Duncan	son	21	solicitor's managing clk	Lnd S. Pancras
11374	136r			James Duncan	son	11	scholar	Dur Hetton-le-Hole
11375	136r	147 a	Gilesgate	John Hedley	hea m	62	nailer	Sts Withereb Mill
11376	136r			Elizabeth Hedley	wif m	64		Dur [D] S. Giles
11377	136r			John Hedley	son	20	tailor	Dur [D] S. Giles
11378	136r	147 b	Gilesgate	Ralph Emmerson	hea m	35	coal miner	Dur Brancepeth
11379	136r			Mary Emmerson	wif m	36		France BS
11380	136r			John Emmerson	son	15	coal miner	Dur [D] S. Giles
11381	136r			Ralph Emmerson	son	13	coal miner	Dur [D] S. Giles
11382	136v			William Emmerson	son	10		Dur [D] S. Giles
11383	136v			George Emmerson	son	8		Dur [D] S. Giles
11384	136v			Robert Emmerson	son	6		Dur [D] S. Giles
11385	136v			Hedley Emmerson	son	3		Dur [D] S. Giles
11386	136v			Elizabeth Emmerson	dau	4m		Dur [D] S. Giles
11387	136v	146 a	Gilesgate	John Elliott	hea m	42	mason, master	Dur [D] S. Giles
11388	136v			Ann Elliott	wif m	36		Dur [D] S. Giles
11389	136v			Mary Ann Elliott	dau	15		Dur [D] S. Giles
11390	136v			John Elliott	son	13	mason, apprentice	Dur [D] S. Giles
11391	136v			Robert Elliott	son	12		Dur [D] S. Giles
11392	136v			Joseph Elliott	son	10		Dur [D] S. Giles
11393	136v			Isabella Elliott	dau	8		Dur [D] S. Giles
11394	136v			Dixon Elliott	son	6		Dur [D] S. Giles
11395	136v			Margaret M. Elliott	dau	3		Dur [D] S. Giles
11396	136v			William Elliott	son	1		Dur [D] S. Giles
11397	136v	146 b	Gilesgate	James Mather	hea m	64	cordwainer	Dur [D] Elvet
11398	136v			Jane Mather	wif m	62		Dur [D] S. Giles
11399	136v			Joseph Mather	son	23	cooper	Dur [D] S. Giles
11400	136v			Mary Mather	dau	20		Dur [D] S. Giles
11401	137r	145 a	Gilesgate	William Stewart	hea m	24	coal miner	Dur Easington
11402	137r			Ann Stewart	wif m	23	dressmaker	Dur [D] S. Giles
11403	137r			John Stewart	son	2		Dur [D] S. Giles
11404	137r	145 b	Gilesgate	Joseph Atkinson	hea m	52	labourer	Dur [D] S. Giles
11405	137r			Mary Atkinson	wif m	49		Nbl Berwick
11406	137r			James Atkinson	son	23	coal miner	Dur [D] S. Giles
11407	137r			Joseph Atkinson	son	20	coal miner	Dur [D] S. Giles
11408	137r			Alice Atkinson	dau	11	scholar	Dur [D] S. Giles
11409	137r			John Atkinson	son	9	scholar	Dur [D] S. Giles
11410	137r	144 a	Gilesgate	James Newton	hea m	33	skinner	Dur Hamsterley
11411	137r			Ann Newton	wif m	33		Dur [D] Crossgate
11412	137r			Eleanor Newton	dau	11	scholar	Dur [D] Framwelgate
11413	137r			Mary Newton	dau	9	scholar	Dur [D] S. Giles
11414	137r			James Newton	son	7	scholar	Dur [D] S. Giles
11415	137r			Elizabeth Newton	dau	5	scholar	Dur [D] S. Giles
11416	137r			Phoebe Newton	dau	3		Dur [D] S. Giles
11417	137r			Jane Newton	dau	1		Dur [D] S. Giles
11418	137r	144 b	Gilesgate	William Swan	hea m	24	coal miner	Nbl Wallsend
11419	137r			Margaret Swan	wif	26		Dur [D] S. Giles
11420	137v	143 a	Gilesgate	Robert Ramshaw	hea m	42	brass founder	Dur Gateshead
11421	137v			Ann Ramshaw	wif m	37		Dur Gateshead
11422	137v			Robert Ramshaw	son	15	apprentice brass founder	Dur Gateshead
11423	137v			John Ramshaw	son	13	scholar	Dur Gateshead
11424	137v			Joseph Ramshaw	son	2	scholar	Dur Gateshead
11425	137v			Catherine Ramshaw	dau	6	scholar	Dur Gateshead
11426	137v			Anne Ramshaw	dau	4	scholar	Dur Gateshead
11427	137v	143 b	Gilesgate	Thomas Bridon	hea m	44	labourer	Dur Esh
11428	137v			Catherine Bridon	wif	40		Dur Wrekenton
11429	137v	142	Gilesgate	John Boyd <jn>	hea m	31	ironmonger	Dur Durham
11430	137v			Margaret Boyd	wif m	28		Dur Durham
11431	137v			Thomas Boyd	son	6	scholar	Dur Durham
11432	137v			Mary Boyd	dau	1		Dur Durham
11433	137v			Louisa Wilson	ser	17	house servant	Dur Barnard Castle
11434	137v	141 a	Gilesgate	Robert Kipling	hea m	52	farm servant	Nry Melsonby
11435	137v			Alice Kipling	wif m	48		Dur Wolsingham
11436	137v			Hannah Kipling	dau	16		Dur
11437	137v			William Etherington	gsn	12		Dur Bishop Auckland
11438	137v	141 b	Gilesgate	William Oliver	hea m	24	butcher	Dur Durham
11439	137v			Dorothy Oliver	wif m	21		Dur Durham
11440	138r			Christiana Oliver	dau	2		Dur Durham
11441	138r			Sarah Fanny Oliver	dau	2w		Dur Durham
11442	138r	140 a	Gilesgate	Faith Forster	hea w	30	laundress	Nry Layton Moor
11443	138r			Elizabeth I. Forster	dau	9	scholar at home	Dur [D] S. Giles
11444	138r			Mary Ann Forster	dau	6	scholar	Dur [D] S. Giles
11445	138r			Jane Forster	dau	3		Dur [D] S. Giles
11446	138r			Faith Forster	dau	6m		Dur [D] S. Giles
11447	138r			Jane Wilton	ser	19	[servant]	Dur [D] S. Nicholas
11448	138r	140 b	Gilesgate	Robert Allison	hea m	28	nail manufacturer	Dur [D] S. Nicholas
11449	138r			Ann Allison	wif m	35		Dur [D] S. Margaret
11450	138r			Robert Allison	son	3		Dur [D] S. Giles

11451	138r	140 b	Gilesgate	William Allison	son		9m		Dur [D] S. Giles
11452	138r	139	Gilesgate	Thomas Hall	hea		27	coal miner	Dur [D] S. Giles
11453	138r			Elizabeth Hall	wif		27		Dur Bishop Auckland
11454	138r			Isabella Hall	dau		1		Dur [D] S. Giles
11455	138r	138 a	Gilesgate	William Hall	hea	m	61	coal miner	Dur Witton Gilbert
11456	138r			Ann Hall	wif	m	65		Dur Chester-le-Street
11457	138r			William Hall	son		29	coal miner	Dur [D] S. Giles
11458	138r			James Hall	son		22	joiner	Dur [D] S. Giles
11459	138r			Ann Hall	dau		20	dressmaker	Dur [D] S. Giles
11460	138v	137 b	Gilesgate	Isabella Allison	hea		23		Dur [D] S. Nicholas
11461	138v			Elizabeth Allison	sis		8		Dur [D] S. Giles
11462	138v	136	Gilesgate	William Winter	hea	m	56	surveyor *	Dur Durham
11463	138v			Charlotte Winter	wif	m	54		Dur Durham
11464	138v			Jane Kell	ser	w	25	house servant	Dur Durham
11465	138v	135 a	Gilesgate	Francis Harper	hea	m	64	cartman	Dur Lanchester
11466	138v			Priscilla Harper	wif	m	67	household work	Dur Lanchester
11467	138v			John Harper	son		25	cartwright, journeyman	Dur Hallgarth
11468	138v			Elizabeth Craggs	nce*		15	kin	Dur Satley
11469	138v	135 b	Gilesgate	Thomas Smith	hea	w	63	cartman	Dur Brancepeth
11470	138v			Mary Smith	dau		21		Dur [D] S. Giles
11471	138v			Mary Smith	mth	w	87		Dur Esh
11472	138v	134	Gilesgate	George Estell	hea	m	28	shipowner	Nbl Newcastle All SS.
11473	138v			Ann Estell	wif	m	32		Dur Bedburn
11474	138v			Ann Estell	dau		1		Dur Westoe
11475	138v			not known	dau		2d		Dur [D] S. Giles
11476	138v			Margaret Hackworth	vis	m	48	nurse	Dur [D] S. Nicholas
11477	138v			Margaret Punshon	ser		14	house servant	Dur Chester-le-Street
11478	138v			John Dodds sn	vis	m	72	cutler, firm Dodds & Co	Nbl Shotley
11479	139r			Ann Dodds	vsw	m	66		Nbl Morpeth
11480	139r			John Dodds jn	vss	m	30	journeyman engineer	Nbl Newcastle *
11481	139r			Edward Dodds	vss		26	cutler	Dur Houghton-1-Spring
11482	139r	133	Gilesgate	William Child	hea	m	58	house and land prop *	Dur Durham
11483	139r			Margaret Child	wif	m	54		Dur Durham
11484	139r			Mark Child	son		20	articled clk to attorney	Dur Durham
11485	139r			Mary Ann Archbold	ser		20	house servant	Dur Philadelphia
11486	139r	132	Gilesgate	Thomas Carr Child	hea	m	28	master tanner emp 4 men	Nbl Newcastle
11487	139r			Anna Child	wif	m	29		Dur Durham
11488	139r			Thomas Carr Child	son		5	scholar	Dur Durham
11489	139r			Charlotte E. Child	dau		3		Dur Durham
11490	139r			Fanny Child	dau		9m		Dur Durham
11491	139r			Elizabeth Thornton	ser		20	house servant	Dur Pittington
11492	139r			Jane Tilly	ser		11	house servant	Dur Durham
11493	139r	131	Gilesgate	Thomas T. Atkinson	hea	m	50	coal miner	Dur [D] Crossgate
11494	139r			Mary Atkinson	wif	m	33		Dur [D] Framwelgate
11495	139r			Hannah F. Atkinson	dau		26	dressmaker	Dur West Rainton
11496	139r			Thomas Atkinson	son		19	currier	Dur West Rainton
11497	139r			John Atkinson	son		17	printer compositor	Dur [D] Crossgate
11498	139r			Ellen D. Atkinson	dau		3		Dur [D] Crossgate
11499	139v			Ann Blakiston Atkinson	dau		1		Dur [D] Crossgate
11500	139v	130	Gilesgate	Richard Steele	hea	m	47	shoemaker, master	Dur Durham
11501	139v			Phoebe Steel	wif	m	44		Dur Durham
11502	139v			Ann Chilton	dau	m	22	dressmaker	Dur Durham
11503	139v			Katherine Muir	vis		20	visitor	Sct
11504	139v			John Harker	app		19	shoemaker's apprentice	Dur Durham
11505	139v			Thomas Chilton	gsn		3	scholar	Dur Durham
11506	139v	[ab]	Head of Gilesgate	Michael Mackchlen	hea	m	40	labourer	Dur [D] S. Giles
11507	139v			Margaret Mackchlen	wif	m	44		Dur Chester-le-Street
11508	139v			Thomas Mackchlen	son		12		Dur [D] S. Giles
11509	139v			William Mackchlen	son		10		Dur [D] S. Giles
11510	139v			Margaret Mackchlen	dau		2		Dur [D] S. Giles
11511	139v	131	Gilesgate	Edward Weddle	hea	m	43	sawyer	Dur Herrington
11512	139v			Susanna Weddle	wif	m	40		Dur Durham
11513	139v			Ellen Weddle	dau		14		Dur Durham
11514	139v			John Weddle	son		12	scholar	Dur Durham
11515	139v			Jane Weddle	dau		11	scholar	Dur Durham
11516	139v			Ann Weddle	dau		7	scholar	Dur Durham
11517	139v			Elizabeth Weddle	dau		5	scholar	Dur Durham
11518	139v			Robert Weddle	son		3		Dur Durham
11519	140r			Susanna Weddle	dau		3m		Dur Durham
11520	140r	130	Gilesgate	Robert Punshon	hea	m	37	tanner	Dur Chester-le-Street
11521	140r			Mary Punshon	wif	m	35		Dur Chester-le-Street
11522	140r			Anthony Punshon	son		10		Dur Chester-le-Street
11523	140r			Dorothy Punshon	dau		8		Dur Chester-le-Street
11524	140r			Jane Punshon	dau		6		Dur Chester-le-Street
11525	140r			Robert Punshon	son		4		Dur [D] S. Giles
11526	140r			George Punshon	son		2		Dur [D] S. Giles
11527	140r			Catherine Punshon	dau		11m		Dur [D] S. Giles
11528	140r	129	Gilesgate	Mary Mather	hea	w	33		Dur [D] S. Giles
11529	140r			Jane Mather	dau		13		Dur [D] S. Giles
11530	140r			George Mather	son		9		Dur [D] S. Giles
11531	140r			Elizabeth Mather	dau		7		Dur [D] S. Giles

11532	140r	129	Gilesgate	Mary Ann Mather	dau		5		Dur [D] S. Giles
11533	140r	128	Gilesgate	Eleanor James	hea w	78	milk vendor	Dur Chester-le-Street
11534	140r			Ann James	dau	46	milk vendor	Dur [D] S. Giles
11535	140r	127	Gilesgate	John Burdiss	hea m	31	railway porter	Dur West Rainton
11536	140r			Barbara Burdiss	wif m	28		Dur Houghton-1-Spring
11537	140r			John Burdiss	son	3		Dur [D] S. Giles
11538	140r			Ann Burdiss	dau	1		Dur [D] S. Giles
11539	140v	126	Gilesgate	Harrison Allison	hea m	35	coal miner	Dur Stanhope
11540	140v			Margaret Allison	wif m	32		Nry Arkengarthdale
11541	140v	125	Gilesgate	Pybus Hamilton	hea m	38	labourer	Nry Otterington
11542	140v			Jane Hamilton	wif m	32		Dur Old Durham
11543	140v	124	Gilesgate	Peter Morgan	hea m	50	traveller, hawker	Irl
11544	140v			Sarah Morgan	wif m	44		Nry Appleton-le-Moor
11545	140v			John Morgan	son	23	tailor	Nry Pickering
11546	140v			Felix Morgan	son	19	tailor	Nry Pickering
11547	140v			Sarah Ann Morgan	dau	18		Yks York
11548	140v			Mary Ann Morgan	dau	16		Yks York
11549	140v	123	Gilesgate	Elizabeth Slack	hea w	66		Nry Harwood
11550	140v			Ralph Slack	son	41	coal miner	Nry Arkengarthdale
11551	140v			Barnaby Slack	son	38	coal miner	Nry Arkengarthdale
11552	140v			Matthew Slack	son	23	coal miner	Nry Arkengarthdale
11553	140v			Mary Middleton	ser	12	house servant	Dur Hartlepool
11554	140v	122	Gilesgate	John Burnell	hea m	23	tallow chandler	Dur [D] S. Giles
11555	140v			Elizabeth Burnell	wif m	23		Dur [D] S. Margaret
11556	140v			Elizabeth Burnell	dau	1		Dur Witton Gilbert
11557	140v	121 a	Gilesgate	Elizabeth Morrell	hea	26	dressmaker	Dur
11558	140v	121 b	Gilesgate	Ann Harland	hea w	77		Dur Thornley
11559	141r	120	Gilesgate	Ralph Smith	hea m	32	skinner	Dur [D] S. Giles
11560	141r			Jane Smith	wif m	29		Dur Shadforth
11561	141r			Margaret Smith	dau	5	scholar	Dur [D] S. Giles
11562	141r			Marie Smith	dau	4	scholar	Dur [D] S. Giles
11563	141r			Phyllis Smith	dau	3	scholar	Dur [D] S. Giles
11564	141r			Mary Smith	dau	1		Dur [D] S. Giles
11565	141r			Mary Smith	ser	14	[servant]	Dur [D] S. Giles
11566	141r	119		John Turnbull	hea m	37	cordwainer	Dur
11567	141r			Elizabeth Turnbull	wif m	43	shoebinder	Dur
11568	141r			Edward Turnbull	son	12	scholar	Dur
11569	141r			John Turnbull	son	10	scholar	Dur
11570	141r			Elizabeth Turnbull	dau	8	scholar	Dur
11571	141r			Jane Turnbull	dau	4	scholar	Dur
11572	141r	118	Gilesgate	John Pearson	hea m	42	corver	Lan Manchester
11573	141r			Ann Pearson	wif m	36		Dur [D] S. Giles
11574	141r			Mary Pearson	dau	16		Dur [D] S. Giles
11575	141r			John Pearson	son	13		Dur Sherburn
11576	141r			Ann Pearson	dau	11		Dur [D] S. Giles
11577	141r			Elizabeth Pearson	dau	1		Dur [D] S. Giles
11578	141r			William Elerington	nep	27		Dur [D] S. Giles
11579	141v	117	Gilesgate	Annetta Drummond	hea w	41		Dur Brancepeth
11580	141v			John A. Oswald	ldr m	66	shoemaker	Dur [D] S. Nicholas
11581	141v	116	Gilesgate	Joseph Hall	hea m	52	coal miner	Dur Pittington
11582	141v			Hannah Hall	wif m	50		Dur Gateshead
11583	141v			Elizabeth Hurst	sil m	50		Dur Gateshead
11584	141v			William Hall	son	20	coal miner	Dur [D] S. Giles
11585	141v			Thomas Hall	son	18	coal miner	Dur [D] S. Giles
11586	141v			James Hall	son	16	coal miner	Dur [D] S. Giles
11587	141v			Mary Ann Stapylton	gda	2		Dur [D] S. Giles
11588	141v	115	Gilesgate	Jane Moody	hea w	67		Dur Eggleston
11589	141v	114	Gilesgate	Henry Robson	hea m	27	woodman	Dur [D] S. Giles
11590	141v			Elizabeth Robson	wif m	27		Dur Stockton
11591	141v			Robert Robson	son	5	scholar	Dur Primrose Side
11592	141v			Jane Robson	dau	3	scholar	Dur [D] S. Giles
11593	141v		Turnpike Gate *	Thomas Bulmer	hea w	65	tailor	Dur Durham
11594	141v			Elizabeth Bulmer	dau	26		Dur Durham
11595	141v			Ann Bulmer	dau	23		Dur Durham
11596	141v		The Cottage	Rachel Jemima Skene	hea w	55	annuitant	Nbl Tynemouth
11597	141v			Margaret A. Walmsley	sis	57	annuitant	Nbl Tynemouth
11598	141v			Margaret Cowey	ser	20	house servant	Dur Middle Rainton
11599	142r			Mary Ramshaw	ser	32	cook	Dur [D] S. Oswald
11600	142r		Training School *	John Gabriel Cromwell		27	MA, vice-principal *	Chs Macclesfield
11601	142r			Joseph Moses Burn		26	student	Lan Lancaster
11602	142r			William Allen Snaith		18	student	Dur Gateshead Fell
11603	142r			George Scott		19	student	Dur Greatham
11604	142r			Charles Forster		23	student	Dur Durham
11605	142r			William Jackson		27	student	Nbl Alnmouth
11606	142r			Abraham Wilson		25	student	Dur Jarrow
11607	142r			Richard Underwood		17	student	Wor Abberley
11608	142r			John Fish		17	student	Nbl Hartburn
11609	142r			Adam Potts		17	student	Nbl Ponteland
11610	142r			Andrew Allan		22	student	Nbl Ford
11611	142r			William Stokoe		19	student	Nbl Allendale
11612	142r			Thomas Whinney		19	student	Dur Lanchester

11613 142r	Training School	Thomas Shaw		18	student	Cul Alston
11614 142r		James Reed		22	student	Nbl Berwick
11615 142r		Mary Crow	ser	50	cook	Dur Houghton-1-Spring
11616 142r		Mary Hogg	ser	24	house maid	Nbl Newcastle

Notes - Enumeration District 5a

10808	... bailiff of county court
10814	... practising attorney & clerk of county court in Circuit no. 2
10827	... proprietor of houses
10831	... employing 4 men <nursery & seedsman>
10836	... S. George
10856	<chorister/lay clerk>
10863	<clerk to Board of Health and borough JPs>
10878	... retired currier & leather dealer
10916	<'Nag's Head'>
10943	... engineer
10950	... & professor of music
10959	<lodgings>
10960	... West Park
10986-10987	... Hallgarth
11018	... All Saints
11059	<& hair restorer>
11165	... and 2 apprentices, grocer & draper
11172	<lodgings>
11179	... proprietor of houses
11193	... of S. Giles
11209	[entered and totalled as "female"]
11265	... All Saints
11271	... Hallgarth
11273	sister, visitor; ... Hallgarth
11287-11306	Church Lane ...
11307	... in Artillery
11462	<to Board of Health and inspector of nuisances>
11468	... visitor
11480	... S. Nicholas
11482	... and fundholder
11593-11595	... Head of Gilesgate
11600-11616	<Leazes Lane>
11600	... of Training Sch, chaplain of workhouse

REF	FOL	NO	STREET	FORENAME(S)	SURNAME	REL	C	AGE	OCCUPATION	BIRTHPLACE
11617	146v	1	Gilesgate	John	Hancock	hea	w	75	nursery and seedsman	Nry Thirsk
11618	146v			John	Hancock	son		21	nursery and seedsman	Dur
11619	146v			James	Sime	ser		20	gardener	Dur
11620	146v			Ann	Burnip	ser		21	house servant	Dur
11621	146v	2	Gilesgate	Thomas	Brown	hea		71	prop of land and houses	Dur Thornley
11622	146v			Isabella	Atkinson	ser		20	house servant	Dur West Rainton
11623	146v	3	Gilesgate	Robert	Stafford	hea	m	43	solicitor	Dur Bishopwearmouth
11624	146v			Susanna	Stafford	wif	m	38		Dur
11625	146v			Robert H.	Stafford	son		16	scholar	Dur
11626	146v			John Carrick	Stafford	son		14	scholar	Dur
11627	146v			William Sisson	Stafford	son		12	scholar	Dur
11628	146v			Sarah Susanna	Stafford	dau		11	scholar	Dur
11629	146v			George Shaw	Stafford	son		9	scholar	Dur
11630	146v			Charles Edward	Stafford	son		6	scholar	Dur
11631	146v			Eleanor Mary	Stafford	dau		4		Dur
11632	146v			Sarah	Greenwood	ser		33	house servant	Wes Kendal
11633	146v	4 a	Gilesgate	John	Carr	hea	m	46	tailor	Dur
11634	146v			Elizabeth	Carr	wif	m	43		Dur Hamsterley
11635	146v			William	Carr	son		17	solicitor's clerk	Dur
11636	146v			Elizabeth	Carr	dau		14	scholar	Dur
11637	147r			Eleanor	Carr	dau		12	scholar	Dur
11638	147r			John	Carr	son		8	scholar	Dur
11639	147r			Henry	Carr	son		4		Dur
11640	147r			James	Carr	son		1		Dur
11641	147r	4 b	Gilesgate	Thomas	Eggleston	hea	m	54	whitesmith emp a boy	Nry Richmond
11642	147r			Jane	Eggleston	wif	m	49		Dur Gateshead
11643	147r			James	Eggleston	son		15	whitesmith (apprentice)	Dur
11644	147r			John	Eggleston	son		12	scholar	Dur
11645	147r			Jane	Eggleston	dau		10	scholar	Dur
11646	147r			Susanna	Eggleston	dau		7	scholar	Dur
11647	147r	4 c	Gilesgate	John	Stephenson	hea	m	37	nailmaker	Dur Sunderland
11648	147r			Margaret	Stephenson	wif		37		Dur
11649	147r			John	Stephenson	son		13	scholar	Dur
11650	147r			Margaret	Stephenson	dau		11	scholar	Dur
11651	147r			William	Stephenson	son		8	scholar	Dur
11652	147r			James	Stephenson	son		6		Dur
11653	147r			Andrew	Stephenson	son		3		Dur
11654	147r			Robert	Stephenson	son		7m		Dur
11655	147v	4 d	Gilesgate	Thomas	Parker	hea	m	25	brickmaker	Ery Hemingbrough
11656	147v			Elizabeth	Parker	wif	m	20		Ery Barlby
11657	147v			Jane Ann	Parker	dau		1m		Dur
11658	147v	[ac]a	Gilesgate	Ann	Lonsdale	hea		67	washerwoman	Dur
11659	147v			Peter	Grieveson	ldr		28	cooper	Dur
11660	147v	[ac]b	Gilesgate	Thomas	Jackson	hea	m	51	carpet weaver	Dur
11661	147v			Isabella	Jackson	wif		51		Nry Kirk Leavington
11662	147v			Isabella	Jackson	dau		12		Dur Barnard Castle
11663	147v	[ac]c	Gilesgate	Isabella	Hewlett	hea	m	50	wife of Henry Hewlett *	Sal Stottesden
11664	147v			David	Hewlett	son		10	scholar	Wor Bewdley
11665	147v	[ad]a	Gilesgate	Amelia	Burnell	wif	m	33	tallow chandler's wife	Sts
11666	147v			Amelia	Burnell	dau		3		Nbl Newcastle
11667	147v			Sarah Ann	Burnell	dau		1		Nbl Newcastle
11668	147v	[ad]b	Gilesgate	James	Metcalfe	hea	m	34	carpet weaver	Dur Barnard Castle
11669	147v			Sarah	Metcalfe	wif		34		Dur Barnard Castle
11670	147v			Hannah	Metcalfe	dau		15	scholar	Dur Barnard Castle
11671	147v			William	Metcalfe	son		11	scholar	Dur Barnard Castle
11672	147v			Mary	Metcalfe	dau		9	scholar	Dur Barnard Castle
11673	147v			Catherine	Metcalfe	dau		7	scholar	Dur
11674	147v			Sarah	Metcalfe	dau		5	scholar	Dur
11675	148r			James	Metcalfe	son		3	scholar	Dur
11676	148r			Henry	Metcalfe	son		9m		Dur
11677	148r	[ad]c	Gilesgate	John	Young	hea	m	40	butcher	Dur Staindrop
11678	148r			Jane	Young	wif	m	38		Dur Windlestone
11679	148r			John	Young	son		15	scholar	Dur New Shildon
11680	148r			Robert	Young	son		12	scholar	Dur Windlestone
11681	148r			Eleanor	Young	dau		8	scholar	Dur South Church
11682	148r			George	Young	son		3	scholar	Dur
11683	148r	<4>	Gilesgate	William	Grieveson	hea	m	63	cooper	Lnd Wapping
11684	148r			Elizabeth	Grieveson	wif	m	64		Dur Newbottle
11685	148r			Mary	Grieveson	dau		26		Dur
11686	148r	5 a	Gilesgate	John	Lidster	hea	m	36	mason, journeyman	Dur Ferryhill
11687	148r			Esther	Lidster	wif		33		Dur
11688	148r			Isabella	Lidster	dau		13	scholar	Dur
11689	148r			John	Lidster	son		10	scholar	Dur
11690	148r			William	Lidster	son		7	scholar	Dur
11691	148r			Margaret	Lidster	dau		4	scholar	Dur
11692	148r	5 b	Gilesgate	David	Winter	hea	w	38	labourer at coal mine	Dur
11693	148r			Ann	Winter	dau		12	scholar	Dur Gateshead
11694	148r			Jane	Winter	dau		7	scholar	Dur Quarrington
11695	148v	5 c	Gilesgate	Martin	Winter	hea	m	35	cabinetmaker	Dur

11696	148v	5 c	Gilesgate	Sarah Winter	wif m	31		Dur
11697	148v			William Winter	son	7	scholar	Dur
11698	148v			Martin Winter	son	4	scholar	Dur
11699	148v			Isabella Winter	dau	2	scholar	Dur
11700	148v			Elizabeth Winter	dau	7m		Dur
11701	148v	6	Gilesgate	William Raine	hea m	50	pawnbroker	Lnd
11702	148v			Hannah Eliza Raine	wif m	59		Yks
11703	148v			Elizabeth Scorer	ser	24	house servant	Dur
11704	148v	9	Gilesgate	Elizabeth Nelson	hea w	67	gentlewoman, annuitant	Dur Brancepeth
11705	148v			Jane Nelson	dau	43	gentlewoman, annuitant	Dur Aycliffe
11706	148v			Samuel Nelson	son	38	tenant farmer *	Dur Aycliffe
11707	148v			Jane King	ser	17	house servant	Dur
11708	148v	10	Gilesgate	Thomas L. Watkin	hea	36	physician MRCSL *	Dur Penshaw
11709	148v			Mary Harle	ser	51	housekeeper	Dur Chester-le-Street
11710	148v			Ellen Taylor	ser	29	house servant	Dur Chester-le-Street
11711	148v			Mary Jane Dodds	vis	19	house servant	Dur
11712	148v	11 a	Gilesgate	Ralph Salkeld	hea m	30	solicitor's general clk	Mdx London
11713	148v			Ann Salkeld	wif m	28		Dur Lanchester
11714	148v			Elizabeth Salkeld	dau	7	scholar	Dur
11715	149r			Ralph Salkeld	son	5	scholar	Dur
11716	149r			George Salkeld	son	3		Dur
11717	149r			Lydia Salkeld	dau	5m		Dur
11718	149r	11 b	Gilesgate	Robert M. Cummings	hea m	31	journeyman saddler	Dur
11719	149r			Mary Cummings	wif m	30		Dur
11720	149r			Ann Cummings	dau	7	scholar	Dur
11721	149r			William M. Cummings	son	2		Dur
11722	149r	11 c	Gilesgate	William Chambers	hea m	60	cap manufacturer	Irl
11723	149r			Mary Chambers	wif m	55		Dur
11724	149r	[ae]	Gilesgate	Henry Browning	hea m	30	carpet weaver	Wil Wilton
11725	149r			Ann Browning	wif m	42		Wes Kendal
11726	149r	[aa]	Bakehouse Lane	James White	hea m	38	university servant	Irl
11727	149r			Mary White	wif m	36		Nry Ovington
11728	149r			John White	son	14	attorney's clerk	Dur
11729	149r			Mary Jane White	dau	10	scholar	Dur
11730	149r			James G. White	son	8	scholar	Dur
11731	149r			Daniel White	son	6	scholar	Dur
11732	149r			Hannah White	dau	4	scholar	Dur
11733	149r			Mary Burn	ser	16	house servant	Dur
11734	149v	[ab]	Bakehouse Lane	William Walls	hea m	31	university servant	Yks
11735	149v			Isabella Walls	wif m	36		Nbl
11736	149v			Annabella Walls	dau	7	scholar	Dur
11737	149v			John Walls	son	2		Dur
11738	149v			Ann Wilson	vis w	74		Nbl
11739	149v			Ann Macrow	nce	17	dressmaker	Nbl
11740	149v			Isabella Dunn	ser	17	house servant	Dur
11741	149v	[ac]	Bakehouse Lane	Jacob Pattison	hea m	27	mason's labourer	Dur
11742	149v			Margaret Pattison	wif m	27		Dur Shincliffe
11743	149v			Mary Pattison	dau	1		Dur
11744	149v			H. Battonsby	ldr	16	grocer (apprentice)	Dur Shincliffe
11745	149v	[ad]	Bakehouse Lane	George Fletcher	hea m	42	journeyman mason	Dur Sedgefield
11746	149v			Jane Fletcher	wif m	45		Dur Bishopwearmouth
11747	149v			Mary Jane Fletcher	dau	20	sempstress	Dur Elwick
11748	149v			Thomas Fletcher	son	17	mason (apprentice)	Dur Hartlepool
11749	149v			Ann Elizabeth Fletcher	dau	13	scholar	Dur Gateshead
11750	149v	12	Gilesgate	William Davison	hea m	66	retired bootmaker	Dur Houghton
11751	149v			Eliza Davison	wif m	43		Cul Penrith
11752	149v			Mary Bell	ser	25	house servant	Dur Shiney Row
11753	150r	13	Gilesgate	Mary Seymour	hea	79	fundholder	Dur Summerhouse
11754	150r			Margaret Hodgson	sis w	78	annuitant	Dur Summerhouse
11755	150r			Thomas Seymour	bro	68	retired farmer	Dur Burtree House
11756	150r			Jane Mowbray	ser	20	house servant	Dur Chester-le-Street
11757	150r	14	Gilesgate	John Burdon	hea m	33	chemist & druggist	Dur
11758	150r			Mary Anne Burdon	wif m	32		Dur Jarrow
11759	150r			Mary Burdon	dau	6	scholar	Dur
11760	150r			Jane Burdon	dau	5		Dur
11761	150r			Fanny Burdon	dau	3		Dur
11762	150r			Ellen Burdon	dau	11m		Dur
11763	150r			Jane Pounder	ser	19	house servant	Dur Hallgarth
11764	150r			Jane Henderson	ser	15	house servant	Dur Preston
11765	150r	15 a	Gilesgate	Henry William Allison	hea m	28	nailmaker	Dur
11766	150r			Ann Allison	wif m	28		Abd Aberdeen
11767	150r			William Allison	son	3		Dur
11768	150r			Mary Dobbie	sil	8	scholar	Dur Bishopwearmouth
11769	150r	15 b	Gilesgate	Ann Allan	hea w	74	needlewoman	Dur Ferryhill
11770	150r	15 c	Gilesgate	Isabella Blakey	hea w	70	shopkeeper <mangle>	Dur Bishopwearmouth
11771	150r			John Johnson	vis	26	mason (journeyman)	Dur
11772	150r			Dorothy Blyth	vis	30	dealer in saddlery	Nbl Hexham
11773	150v	15 d	Gilesgate	Samuel Richardson	hea m	32	cabinetmaker	Dur
11774	150v			Sarah Richardson	wif m	33		Dur
11775	150v			Robert Richardson	son	5	scholar	Dur
11776	150v			John Richardson	son	3	scholar	Dur

No.	Folio	Sched.		Address	Name	Rel.	Cond.	Age	Occupation	Birthplace
11777	150v	15	d	Gilesgate	Elizabeth Richardson	dau		1		Dur
11778	150v	16		Gilesgate	Ann Smith	hea w		83	proprietor of houses	Nry Melsonby
11779	150v				Ann Smith	dau w		44	seamstress	Dur
11780	150v				George Mason	vis m		38	smith	Dur Winlaton
11781	150v	17		Gilesgate	Joseph Robson	hea m		25	slater (agent *)	Lan Liverpool
11782	150v				Caroline Robson	wif m		27		Sts Bilston
11783	150v				Anthony Robson	son		2		Dur Darlington
11784	150v				John Tower Robson	son		6m		Dur
11785	150v				Mary Goth	nce		11		Wes Orton
11786	150v	18		Gilesgate	George Goundry	hea m		52	schoolmaster *	Dur Bildershaw
11787	150v				Jane Goundry	dau		21	dressmaker	Dur
11788	150v				Elizabeth Goundry	dau		20	dressmaker	Dur
11789	150v				George Goundry	son		18	assistant schoolmaster	Dur
11790	150v				William Goundry	son		16	assistant schoolmaster	Dur
11791	150v				Sarah Goundry	dau		11	scholar	Dur
				one house uninhabited						
11792	151r	20	a	Gilesgate	William Coulson	hea m		60	land & house proprietor	Nbl Reedsmouth
11793	151r				Jane Coulson	wif m		50		Dur [D] Gilesgate
11794	151r				Robert C. Coulson	son		29	clerk to auditor *	Dur [D] Gilesgate
11795	151r				Ann Hannah Coulson	dau		24		Nbl Lonsdale Cottage
11796	151r	20	b	Gilesgate	John Goodfellow	hea w		37	shoemaker	Dur
11797	151r				Mary Gargett	sil		61	staymaker	Dur
11798	151r				George Burnip	ldr		20	tallow chandler	Dur
11799	151r	21		Gilesgate	George Armstrong	hea m		36	joiner <furniture brkr>	Sct
11800	151r				Jane Armstrong	wif m		39		Sct
11801	151r	22		Gilesgate	Barbara Calvert	hea w		41	proprietor of houses	Wry Pateley Bridge
11802	151r				Thomas Calvert	son		16	solicitor's general clk	Dur
11803	151r				James Calvert	son		12	scholar	Dur
11804	151r				Ellen Calvert	dau		10	scholar	Dur
11805	151r				Edward Calvert	son		8	scholar	Dur
11806	151r				Mary Hodgson	mth w		79		Dur Bishop Auckland
11807	151r	23	a	Gilesgate	Nathan Beebey	hea m		23	railway labourer	Cul
11808	151r				Jane Beebey	wif m		20		Dur
11809	151r				Catherine Jane Beebey	dau		1		Dur
11810	151r				Elizabeth Beebey	dau		4m		Dur
11811	151v	23	b	Gilesgate	Richard Christopher	hea m		54	innkeeper <'Woodman'>	Yks Stockem
11812	151v				Catherine Christopher	wif m		52		Dur Sedgefield
11813	151v				Margaret Christopher	dau		18		Dur
11814	151v				Frances Christopher	dau		14		Dur
11815	151v				Elizabeth Christopher	dau		11		Dur
11816	151v				Joseph Worthey	vis m		63	countryman	Dur Hartburn
11817	151v	24		Gilesgate	Robert Forster	hea		23	dyer	Nry Scarborough
11818	151v				Alfred Freith	blw m		21	dyer	War Birmingham
11819	151v				Mary Ann Freith	sis m		20		Nbl North Shields
11820	151v				Thomas W. Sturdy	nep		14		Nbl North Shields
11821	151v	24½		Gilesgate	Alexander Souter	hea m		35	hat mfr employing 1 man	Lan Bolton
11822	151v				Jane Souter	wif m		28	hat trimmer	War Atherstone
11823	151v	25		Gilesgate	Robert Maddison	hea m		37	grocer	Dur
11824	151v				Ann Maddison	wif m		38		Dur
11825	151v				William S. Maddison	son		9	scholar	Dur
11826	151v				Robert John Maddison	son		3		Dur
11827	151v				Elizabeth Jane Young	ser		27	house servant	Dur Rainton
11828	151v	26	a	Gilesgate	Elizabeth Saunders	hea m		67	shopkeeper	Nry Stainton
11829	151v				John Saunders	son		36	labourer	Dur Billingham
11830	151v				Elizabeth Saunders	dau		29	dressmaker	Dur
11831	152r	26	b	Gilesgate	Matthew Stephenson	hea m		70	millwright	Dur
11832	152r				Alice Stephenson	wif m		69		Dur
11833	152r				Agnes Stephenson	gda		14	needlewoman	Dur
11834	152r	26	c	Gilesgate	Mary Brown	hea w		45	needlewoman	Dur Chester-le-Street
11835	152r				Thomas Brown	son		20	cartman	Dur
11836	152r				William Brown	son		18	joiner (apprentice)	Dur
11837	152r				Matthew Brown	son		15	scholar	Dur
11838	152r				John Brown	son		13	scholar	Dur
11839	152r				Robert Brown	son		10	scholar	Dur
11840	152r	26	d	Gilesgate	Lawrence Blakey	hea m		28	journeyman mason	Dur
11841	152r				Bridget Blakey	wif m		29		Dub Dublin
11842	152r				William Blakey	son		4		Dur
11843	152r				John Blakey	son		1		Dur
11844	152r	26	e	Gilesgate	Ann Frances Moses	hea m		34	shoemaker's wife	Dur Washington
11845	152r				Elizabeth Moses	dau		14		Dur Thornley
11846	152r				John Moses	son		12		Dur
11847	152r				Mary Moses	dau		8		Dur
11848	152r				Lancelot Moses	son		6		Dur
11849	152r				Robert Moses	son		2		Dur
11850	152r				Jane Moses	dau		15		Dur Auckland S. Helen
11851	152v	26	f	Gilesgate	William Anderson	hea m		31	carpet weaver	Dur
11852	152v				Agnes Anderson	wif m		27		Wes Kendal
11853	152v				Joseph Anderson	son		5	scholar	Wes Kendal
11854	152v				Mary Anderson	dau		2	scholar	Wes Kendal
11855	152v	26	g	Gilesgate	William Talbot	hea m		40	coachmaker, journeyman	Dur
11856	152v				Mary Talbot	wif m		41		Nry Yarm

11857	152v	26 g	Gilesgate	John Talbot	son		12		Dur
11858	152v			Elizabeth Talbot	dau		8		Dur
11859	152v			Anthony Talbot	son		5		Dur
11860	152v			William Talbot	son		2		Dur
11861	152v			Thomas Talbot	bro		36	shoemaker	Dur
11862	152v	27 a	Gilesgate	John Tinmouth Blakey	hea m		40	mason employing 3 men	Dur
11863	152v			Isabella Blakey	wif m		36		Dur
11864	152v	27 b	Gilesgate	John Eales	hea m		33	cordwainer	Dur Auckland S. Helen
11865	152v			Margaret Eales	wif m		23		Dur
11866	152v	28	Gilesgate	Charles Wetherell	hea m		42	solicitor's * clerk	Dur
11867	152v			Jane Wetherell	wif m		40		Dur
11868	152v			Jane Wetherell	dau		5		Dur
11869	153r	29	Gilesgate	William Atkinson	hea m		25	<borough> rate collector	Dur [D] Gilesgate
11870	153r			Mary Atkinson	wif m		24		Dur Barnard Castle
11871	153r			Deborah Atkinson	dau		3		Dur [D] Gilesgate
11872	153r			William D. Atkinson	son		1		Dur [D] Gilesgate
11873	153r	30	Gilesgate	John White	hea m		70	grocer & tea dealer	Nry Hunderthwaite *
11874	153r			Elizabeth White	wif m		63		Dur Barnard Castle
11875	153r			Eleanor White	dau		22		Dur Barnard Castle
11876	153r	31	Gilesgate	Thomas Greenwell	hea m		70	retired miller *	Dur Chilton
11877	153r			Ann Greenwell	wif m		70		Dur Bishop Auckland
11878	153r			Elizabeth Ann Spencer	vis		14	scholar	Dur
11879	153r	32	Gilesgate	Matthew Eales	hea m		56	innkeeper & cordwainer *	Dur Thornley
11880	153r			Jane Eales	wif m		62		Dur Witton Castle
11881	153r			Matthew Eales	son		22	journeyman cordwainer	Dur Cockerton
11882	153r			Ann Pearson	ser		25	house servant	Dur
11883	153r			John Flintift	ldr		26	journeyman cordwainer	Nry Northallerton
11884	153r			John Ovington	ldr w		29	journeyman cordwainer	Chs Nantwich
11885	153r			Thomas Spence	ldr		21	puddler	Nry Whitby
11886	153r			William Shale	ldr		21	puddler	Sts Bilston
11887	153r			Elizabeth Ridley	ldr		21	spinster	Nbl Haydon? Bridge *
11888	153r			Richard Cowsick	ldr		19	puddler	Ant Belfast
11889	153v	33 a	Gilesgate	Margaret Myers	hea w		60	shopkeeper	Dur
11890	153v			William Myers	son		30	tailor	Dur
11891	153v			Mary Myers	gda		11	scholar	Dur
11892	153v			Mary Brown	gda		7	scholar	Dur
11893	153v			John Spinks	ser		19	cartman	Dur
11894	153v			Patrick Callaghan	vis		28	labourer	Irl
11895	153v	33 b	Gilesgate	Mary Snowdon	hea w		70	needle[wo]man	Dur
11896	153v	33 c	Gilesgate	John Pepper	hea m		29	labourer	Irl
11897	153v			Mary Pepper	wif m		25		Irl
11898	153v			Thomas Pepper	son		1m		Dur
11899	153v	33 d	Gilesgate	James Callaghan	hea m		44	shoemaker	Irl
11900	153v			Anne Callaghan	wif m		36		Irl
11901	153v			Bridget Callaghan	dau		6		Irl
11902	153v			Edward McKinney	vis w		56	labourer	Irl
11903	153v	33 e	Gilesgate	Eleanor Sheridan	hea w		50		Irl
11904	153v			John Sheridan	son		19	coal miner	Irl
11905	153v			Patrick Sheridan	son		14	labourer	Irl
11906	153v			Margaret Rodden	dau m		22		Irl
11907	153v			Thomas Rodden	slw m		24	labourer	Irl
11908	154r	34 a	Gilesgate	John Wells	hea m		51	botanist	Dur Ferryhill
11909	154r			Ann Wells	wif m		54	<baker>	Dur
11910	154r			Thomas Wells	son		17	slater (apprentice)	Dur
11911	154r			Richard Wells	son		16	cordwainer (apprentice)	Dur
11912	154r	34 b	Gilesgate	John Burlinson	hea m		43	<clock and> watchmaker	Dur Sedgefield
11913	154r			Elizabeth Burlinson	wif m		43		Dur Easington
11914	154r	34 c	Gilesgate	Susanna Tilly	hea w		68		Dur
11915	154r			Elizabeth Tilly	dau		27	dressmaker	Dur Felling Shore
11916	154r	[af]	Gilesgate	Mary Gardener	hea		43	laundress	Dur Frosterley
11917	154r			Elizabeth Gardener	dau		20	laundress	Lnd
11918	154r			William Gardener	son		5	scholar	Dur
11919	154r		Ellis Leazes House	John Williamson	hea m		48	farmer of 63a of land	Yks
11920	154r			Mary Williamson	wif m		59		Dur Stanhope
11921	154r			Mary Williamson	dau		17		Dur Darlington
11922	154r			Robert Eggleston	slw m		34	farm labourer	Yks Broadbury
11923	154r			Hannah Eggleston	dau m		27		Dur Darlington
11924	154r			Elizabeth Eggleston	gda		12		Dur Sherburn
11925	154r			John Eggleston	gsn		2		Dur
11926	154v	35	Gilesgate	George Mavin	hea m		48	builder <& joiner>	Dur
11927	154v			Ann Mavin	wif m		40		Nry Guisborough
11928	154v			Ann Mavin	dau		10		Dur
11929	154v			Isabel Mavin	dau		7		Dur
11930	154v			Margaret Mavin	dau		5		Dur
11931	154v			Mary Mavin	dau		10m		Dur
11932	154v	36 a	Gilesgate	Nathan Beeby	hea m		57	railway labourer	Cul
11933	154v			Elizabeth Beeby	wif m		58		Cul
11934	154v	36 b	Gilesgate	Peter Gibson	hea m		37	journeyman mason	Dur Witton Gilbert
11935	154v			Elizabeth Gibson	wif m		32		Dur
11936	154v			Mary Jane Gibson	dau		9	scholar	Dur
11937	154v			Isabella Gibson	dau		7	scholar	Dur

11938	154v	36 b	Gilesgate	Fanny Gibson	dau	2	scholar	Dur
11939	154v			Margaret Gibson	dau	2m		Dur
11940	154v	36 c	Gilesgate	John Smith	hea m	40	nailmaker	Dur
11941	154v			Hannah Smith	wif m	36		Dur Bishop Auckland
11942	154v			Frederick Smith	son	13	scholar	Dur
11943	154v			Mary Ann Smith	dau	10	scholar	Dur
11944	154v			Elizabeth Smith	dau	8	scholar	Dur
11945	154v			Jane Smith	dau	1		Dur
11946	155r	36 d	Gilesgate	Timothy Blakey	hea m	33	journeyman mason	Dur
11947	155r			Elizabeth Blakey	wif m	32		Dur Barnard Castle
11948	155r			William T. Blakey	son	9	scholar	Dur
11949	155r			Isabella Blakey	dau	4		Dur
11950	155r			John Blakey	son	2		Dur
11951	155r			Agnes Blakey	dau	3m		Dur
11952	155r			Grace Howson	sil	21	house servant	Dur
11953	155r	36 e	Gilesgate	Eleanor Newton	hea w	76		Dur Witton Gilbert
11954	155r			William Newton	son	36	cooper	Dur Hamsterley
11955	155r	37 a	Gilesgate	Stephen Banks	hea m	62	tailor	Dur
11956	155r	37 b	Gilesgate	Ann Palmer	hea	53	washerwoman	Dur Sunderland
11957	155r			Isabella Brown	sis m	45	washerwoman	Dur
11958	155r	38 a	Gilesgate	Thomas Cook	hea m	41	cartman <oatmeal-maker>	Dur
11959	155r			Margaret Cook	wif m	36		Dur
11960	155r			Jane Cook	dau	10	scholar	Dur
11961	155r			Mary Ann Cook	dau	6	scholar	Dur
11962	155r			James Cook	son	3	scholar	Dur
11963	155r			Susan Birbeck	vis	56		Dur
11964	155r			Elizabeth Cook	vis	31		Dur
11965	155r			Mary Sheradon	vis	18		Dur
11966	155v	38 b	Gilesgate	Patrick Grogans	hea m	48	labourer	Irl
11967	155v			Catherine Grogans	wif m	30		Irl
11968	155v			Mary Grogans	dau	8		Irl
11969	155v			Peter Grogans	son	6		Dur
11970	155v			Elizabeth Grogans	dau	4		Dur
11971	155v			Thomas Grogans	son	2		Dur
11972	155v			Mary Duffy	mlw w	50		Irl
11973	155v			Edward Brady	vis	54		Irl
11974	155v			Patrick McWhade	ldr w	62		Irl
11975	155v			Patrick McWhade	ldr	8		Irl
11976	155v			Thomas Codey	ldr	35		Irl
11977	155v	38 c	Gilesgate	Mary Hughs	hea w	40		Irl
11978	155v			Neal Hughs	son	13		Irl
11979	155v			Patrick Hughs	son	12		Irl
11980	155v			Ann Hughs	dau	10		Irl
11981	155v	39	Gilesgate	Ann Renney	hea w	60	innkeeper <'Bull & Dog'>	Nry Hackness
11982	155v			Robert Renney	son	34	mason	Dur
11983	155v			Ann E. Boyd	gda	2		Dur
11984	155v			Martha Fenwick	ser	19	house servant	Dur Sherburn Hill
11985	155v			Esther Harrison	sis m	47	farmer's wife	Dur
11986	156r	40	Gilesgate	Evan Reece	hea w	38	confectioner	Cmn Carmarthen
11987	156r	41 a	Gilesgate	William Boyd	hea w	32	coffee roaster	Dur Brancepeth
11988	156r	41 b	Gilesgate	Mary Park	hea w	49	washerwoman	Nry Northallerton
11989	156r			John Park	son w	27	shoemaker	Nry Northallerton
11990	156r			James Park	son	19	carpet weaver	Dur Darlington
11991	156r			Hannah Park	dau	18	servant	Dur Darlington
11992	156r			George Park	son	12	scholar	Dur
11993	156r	41 c	Gilesgate	Michael Graham	hea m	27	railway porter	Dur
11994	156r			Mary Graham	wif m	27		Dur Hetton
11995	156r			Mary Ann Graham	dau	2		Dur
11996	156r	42	Gilesgate	John Sheldon	hea	40	tallow merchant *	Dur Jarrow
11997	156r			Arabella Sheldon	sis	32		Dur Jarrow
11998	156r			Sarah Ann Sheldon	sis	24		Dur Jarrow
11999	156r			Eleanor Kellett	ser	19	house servant	Dur Houghton-l-Spring
12000	156r	[aa]	Railway Lane	Robert Paul Robinson	hea m	44	railway porter	Dur Burnopfield
12001	156r			Ann Robinson	wif m	34		Nbl Brunton
12002	156r			Thomas Paul Robinson	son	8	scholar	Dur Castle Eden
12003	156r			Robert B. Robinson	son	6	scholar	Dur
12004	156r			William A. Robinson	son	4	scholar	Dur
12005	156r			Mary Robinson	dau	2		Dur
12006	156v			George Robinson	son	3m		Dur
12007	156v	[ab]	Railway Lane	Thomas Brown	hea m	53	coal miner *	Dur Coxhoe
12008	156v			Sarah Brown	wif m	62		Dur Hill Top
12009	156v			James Wade	ldr	6		Dur
12010	156v			George Pickering	ldr	44	whitesmith	Dur Sunderland
12011	156v			Peter Conolly	ldr w	50	gardener	Irl
12012	156v			Owen Clark	ldr	25	shoemaker	Irl
12013	156v			David Rogers	ldr w	40	traveller	Irl
12014	156v			James Nelless	ldr	35	joiner	Nbl Newcastle
12015	156v			Peter McCall	ldr	40	cattle jobber	Irl
12016	156v			William Goulden	ldr	21	traveller	Lan Wigan
12017	156v			Michael McHall	ldr m	26	traveller	Lan Preston
12018	156v			James Timonay	ldr m	24	traveller	Lan Bolton

12019	156v	[ab]	Railway Lane	Hannah Timonay	ldr m	20	traveller	Lan Preston
12020	156v			Patrick Kann	ldr m	40	traveller	Irl
12021	156v			James Cook	ldr	25	cattle jobber	Irl
12022	156v			David Rice	ldr m	34	cattle dealer	Irl
12023	156v			Abraham Myers	ldr	30	general trader	Poland
12024	156v			Thomas Kilgollon	ldr	30	labourer	Irl
12025	157r	[ac]a	Railway Lane	William Snowdon	hea m	42	cowkeeper	Dur
12026	157r			Elizabeth Snowdon	wif m	40		Nry Cowton
12027	157r	[ac]b	Railway Lane	William Elliott	hea	48	journeyman mason	Dur
12028	157r	[ad]	Railway Lane	George Gowland	hea m	36	butter dealer	Wry Burton Leonard
12029	157r			Elizabeth Gowland	wif m	35		Nry Masham, Leighton
12030	157r			George Gowland	son	11		Nry Burrill
12031	157r			Ann Gowland	dau	10		Nry Burrill
12032	157r			Peter Gowland	son	9		Nry Burrill
12033	157r			Elizabeth Gowland	dau	7		Nry Burrill
12034	157r			Cecilia Gowland	dau	6		Nry Burrill
12035	157r	[ae]	Railway Lane	John Thompson	hea m	56	joiner	Dur
12036	157r			Mary Thompson	wif m	56		Dur
12037	157r			Sarah Thompson	dau	30	dressmaker	Dur
12038	157r			Ann Thompson	dau	19		Dur
12039	157r			Susanna Thompson	dau	17		Dur
12040	157r			Andrew Thompson	son	15	chainmaker (apprentice)	Dur
12041	157r			George Thompson	son	15	foundry boy	Dur
12042	157r			Elizabeth Thompson	gda	9	scholar	Dur
12043	157r			Mary Ann Thompson	gda	8	scholar	Dur
12044	157r			John Thompson	gsn	1		Dur
12045	157v	[af]	Railway Lane	George Swales	hea m	41	dealer in earthenware	Wry Sedbergh
12046	157v			Margaret Swales	wif m	38		Wry Sedbergh
12047	157v			Christian Swales	dau	11		Dur
12048	157v			John Swales	son	9	scholar	Dur
12049	157v			Dinah Swales	dau	7	scholar	Dur
12050	157v			Jane Swales	dau	5	scholar	Dur
12051	157v			Elizabeth Swales	dau	1		Dur
12052	157v	45	Gilesgate	John Moore	hea m	64	mason <publican *>	Dur Lanchester
12053	157v			Isabella Moore	wif m	63		Dur Lamesley
12054	157v			Susan Moore	dau	40		Dur Ebchester
12055	157v			John Moore	son	27	joiner	Dur
12056	157v			John Moore	gsn	5		Dur
12057	157v	46 a	Gilesgate	John Steel	hea m	74	gardener	Dur [D] Gilesgate
12058	157v			Mary Steel	wif m	65		Dur [D] Gilesgate
12059	157v	46 b	Gilesgate	George Myers	hea m	39	cinder burner	Dur [D] Gilesgate
12060	157v			Jane Myers	wif m	36		Dur [D] Gilesgate
12061	157v			John Myers	son	17	gardener	Dur [D] Gilesgate
12062	157v			Robert Myers	son	13	scholar	Dur [D] Gilesgate
12063	157v			Mary Myers	dau	10	scholar	Dur [D] Gilesgate
12064	157v			Jane Myers	dau	7	scholar	Dur [D] Gilesgate
12065	158r			Thomas Myers	son	5	scholar	Dur [D] Gilesgate
12066	158r	47	Gilesgate	William Atkinson	hea m	55	cordwainer <publican *>	Dur [D] Gilesgate
12067	158r			Ann Atkinson	wif m	53		Dur [D] Gilesgate
12068	158r			William Atkinson	son	25	cordwainer	Dur [D] Gilesgate
12069	158r			Ann Atkinson	dau	23		Dur [D] Gilesgate
12070	158r			Stephen Atkinson	son	20	tailor (apprentice)	Dur [D] Gilesgate
12071	158r			Isabel Atkinson	dau	14	scholar	Dur [D] Gilesgate
12072	158r			Elizabeth Atkinson	dau	11	scholar	Dur [D] Gilesgate
12073	158r			Thomas Atkinson	son	8	scholar	Dur [D] Gilesgate
12074	158r	48	Gilesgate	Henry Ward	hea m	29	labourer	Nry Pickering
12075	158r			Ann Ward	wif m	26		Dur [D] Gilesgate
12076	158r			Mary Ann Ward	dau	7	scholar	Dur [D] Gilesgate
12077	158r			Jane Ward	dau	4	scholar	Dur [D] Gilesgate
12078	158r	49	Gilesgate	Walter Bermingham	hea m	30	labourer	Irl
12079	158r			Catherine Bermingham	wif m	30		Irl
12080	158r			Mary Bermingham	dau	4		Irl
12081	158r			Catherine Bermingham	dau	1		Dur
12082	158r			Lacky Grymes	flw w	70	labourer	Irl
12083	158r			Bridget Waters	*	14		Irl
12084	158r			Michael Mahon	ldr m	26	labourer	Irl
12085	158v			Mary Mahon	ldr m	27		Irl
12086	158v			Mary Anne Mahon	ldr	10m		Chs Chester
12087	158v	49 a	Gilesgate	William Harrey	hea m	30	coach-springmaker	Mdx
12088	158v			Margaret Harrey	wif m	28		Per Perth
12089	158v			Christian Harrey	dau	3		Lks Glasgow
12090	158v			William Harrey	son	2m		Dur
12091	158v	49 b	Gilesgate	Neil Hood	hea m	36	labourer	Sct
12092	158v			Margaret Hood	wif m	40		Nbl Newcastle
12093	158v	50	Gilesgate	Magdalen Patton	hea w	53	lodging house keeper	Dur Trimdon
12094	158v			Thomas Richardson	gsn	13		Dur
12095	158v			James Lloyd	ldr	63	bookseller	Sry Southwark
12096	158v			Edward Smith	ldr m	28	boilermaker	Sct
12097	158v			Augusta Smith	ldr m	27		Sct
12098	158v			John Rilley	ldr m	37	labourer	Irl
12099	158v			William Paxton	ldr m	40	moulder	Nbl Alnwick

12100	158v	50	Gilesgate	Isabella Paxton	ldr m	40		Sct	
12101	158v			Jane Paxton	ldr	5		Nbl Newcastle	
12102	158v			James Larkin	ldr m	34	labourer	Irl	
12103	158v			Sarah Larkin	ldr m	34		Nfk Norwich	
12104	158v			Edward Lynn	ldr m	50	hawker	Irl	
12105	159r			Alexander McDonald	ldr	40	labourer	Sct	
12106	159r			James Byrne	ldr m	60	labourer	Irl	
12107	159r			Alexander Ferris	ldr	24	labourer	Irl	
12108	159r			John Carter	ldr	38	labourer	Nry Richmond	
12109	159r	51	Gilesgate	John Coltman	hea m	41	gardener	Dur Sedgefield	
12110	159r			Jane Coltman	wif m	38		Dur	
12111	159r			Mary Coltman	dau	22		Dur	
12112	159r			Isabella Coltman	dau	20		Dur	
12113	159r			Eleanor Coltman	dau	17		Dur	
12114	159r			Jane Coltman	dau	15	scholar	Dur	
12115	159r			Elizabeth Coltman	dau	10	scholar	Dur	
12116	159r			John Coltman	son	9	scholar	Dur	
12117	159r			Margaret Coltman	dau	6	scholar	Dur	
12118	159r			Ann Coltman	dau	4	scholar	Dur	
12119	159r			Sarah Coltman	dau	2		Dur	
12120	159r	52 a	Gilesgate	Elizabeth Clark	hea w	64	washerwoman	Dur	
12121	159r			Mary Clark	dau	25	washerwoman	Lan	
12122	159r	52 b	Gilesgate	John Palmer	hea w	73	brickmaker	Ssx Lyminster	
12123	159r	52 c	Gilesgate	William Palmer	hea	33	tailor, journeyman	Dur	
12124	159r			Sarah Clarke	ser	32	housekeeper	Lan Liverpool	
12125	159v			John Palmer	son*	14	slater (apprentice)	Dur Durham	
12126	159v			Isabella Palmer	dau*	12	scholar	Dur Durham	
12127	159v			William Palmer	son*	9	scholar	Dur Durham	
12128	159v			George Palmer	son*	4	scholar	Dur Durham	
12129	159v			Elizabeth Palmer	dau*	9m		Dur Durham	
12130	159v	52 d	Gilesgate	Thomas Brown	hea m	69	labourer	War	
12131	159v			Isabella Brown	wif m	67		Nbl Newcastle	
12132	159v			John Brown	son	28	labourer	Dur	
12133	159v			Isabella Lilley	gda	3	scholar	Dur Sunderland	
12134	159v	52 e	Gilesgate	James Wilkey	hea w	47	labourer	Dur Stanhope	
12135	159v			Ann Wilkey	dau	13		Dur	
12136	159v	52 f	Gilesgate	Thomas Cummings	hea m	57	mason's labourer	Dur	
12137	159v			Jane Cummings	wif m	46		Dur Stanhope	
12138	159v			Thomas Cummings	son	15	pitman	Dur	
12139	159v			Ellen Cummings	dau	17		Dur	
12140	159v			Jane Cummings	dau	13		Dur	
12141	159v			John Cummings	son	11	scholar	Dur	
12142	159v			Mary Elizabeth Cummings	dau	6	scholar	Dur	
12143	159v	52	Gilesgate	Arthur Wilkinson	hea m	69	tinplate worker	Dur	
12144	159v			Elizabeth Wilkinson	wif m	72		Dur Blackwell	
12145	160r	[ag]	Gilesgate	Sarah Smith	hea	25	labouring woman	Dur Sunderland	
12146	160r			Dorothy Smith	sis	23	labouring woman	Dur	
12147	160r			Eleanor Smith	sis	20	labouring woman	Dur	
12148	160r			Jane Smith	nce	4	scholar	Dur	
12149	160r			Richard Smith	nep	1		Dur	
12150	160r			Edward Smith	son	1		Dur	
12151	160r	53	Gilesgate	Emanuel Kellett	hea m	47	slater & innkeeper *	Dur	
12152	160r			Mary Ann Kellett	wif m	50		Dur	
12153	160r			William Thomas Kellett	son	17	currier (apprentice)	Dur	
12154	160r			Mary Ann Kellett	dau	16	scholar	Dur	
12155	160r			Elizabeth Kellett	dau	12	scholar	Dur	
12156	160r	54	Gilesgate	Joseph Dawson	hea m	36	grocer	Nry Stokesley	
12157	160r			Hannah Dawson	wif m	40		Dur	
12158	160r			Robert Dawson	son	7		Dur	
12159	160r			Jane Wilson	ldr	21		Dur	
12160	160r			John Wilson	ldr	19		Dur	
12161	160r	55	Gilesgate	George Taylor	hea m	37	high bailiff *	Dur	
12162	160r			Katherine L. Taylor	wif m	34		Nry Reeth /"Keeth"	
12163	160r			Elizabeth Mary Taylor	dau	15	scholar	Dur Houghton-l-Spring	
12164	160r			Katherine A. Taylor	dau	13	scholar	Dur Houghton-l-Spring	
12165	160v			Isabella Jane Taylor	dau	11	scholar	Dur Houghton-l-Spring	
12166	160v			Margaret Bowes Taylor	dau	9	scholar	Dur	
12167	160v			Georgiana L. Taylor	dau	7	scholar	Dur	
12168	160v			Thomas George Taylor	son	5	scholar	Dur	
12169	160v			Henrietta Taylor	dau	3		Dur	
12170	160v			George Bowes Taylor	son	1		Dur	
12171	160v	56	Gilesgate	John Bungey	hea m	57	half pay in army *	Dur	
12172	160v			Sarah Grace Bungey	wif m	60		Dur	
12173	160v			Elizabeth Markham	ser	19	house servant	Dur	
12174	160v	57	Gilesgate	William Scott	hea m	34	gentleman's ser <groom>	Nry Marske	
12175	160v			Hannah Scott	wif m	34		Wry Nesfield	
12176	160v			John Edward Scott	son	1		Dur	
12177	160v			David Henderson	nep	6		Dur	
12178	160v			Mary Palmer	ser	18	house servant	Dur	
12179	160v	58	Gilesgate	Elizabeth Forster	hea w	72	laundress	Nry Gammersgill	
12180	160v			Elizabeth Gibson	dau w	32	laundress	Dur	

12181	160v	58	Gilesgate	Margaret Gibson	gda	9	scholar	Dur	
12182	160v			Henry John Arighi	gsn	1		Dur	
12183	160v	59	Gilesgate	Jane Mort	hea m	32	wife of Robert Mort *	Nbl	Boldon
12184	160v			Mary Ann Mort	dau	13	scholar	Nbl	Boldon
12185	161r			Margaret Jane Mort	dau	9	scholar	Dur	
12186	161r			Thomas Mort	son	8	scholar	Dur	
12187	161r	60	Gilesgate	Charles Theakston	hea m	28	journeyman draper	Dur	
12188	161r			Mary Ann Theakston	wif m	25		Dur	
12189	161r			Frederick C. Theakston	son	3		Dur	
12190	161r			James Ambrose Theakston	son	2		Dur	
12191	161r			Margaret Baker	ser	15	house servant	Dur	
12192	161r	61	Gilesgate	William Smith	hea m	34	engine driver	Nbl	Haydon Bridge
12193	161r			Jane Smith	wif m	32		Dur	Shotton
12194	161r			James William Smith	son	8	scholar	Dur	Fatfield
12195	161r	62 a	Gilesgate	William Tilly	hea m	51	schoolmaster * <shoemkr>	Dur	
12196	161r			Eleanor Tilly	wif m	46		Dur	
12197	161r			Eleanor Tilly	dau	15		Dur	
12198	161r			Catherine Tilly	dau	14		Dur	
12199	161r			Frances Tilly	dau	12		Dur	
12200	161r			Elizabeth Tilly	dau	9		Dur	
12201	161r			Margaret Tilly	dau	6		Dur	
12202	161r	62 b	Gilesgate	John Tilly	hea w	55	journeyman tailor	Dur	
12203	161v	63	Gilesgate	William Lightfoot	hea w	51	joiner <& grocer>	Dur	
12204	161v			Jane Lightfoot	dau	22		Dur	
12205	161v			John Lightfoot	son	21	joiner	Dur	
12206	161v			Mary Lightfoot	dau	18		Dur	
12207	161v			Ann Lightfoot	dau	16		Dur	
12208	161v			William Lightfoot	son	15	joiner (apprentice)	Dur	
12209	161v			Thomas Lightfoot	son	12		Dur	
12210	161v			Margaret Fletcher	sil	55		Dur	Sedgefield
12211	161v	64	Gilesgate	James Lambert	hea m	39	lay clerk or teacher *	Wry	Leeds
12212	161v			Harriet Lambert	wif m	38		Wry	Huddersfield
12213	161v			Mary Lambert	dau	17		Wry	Leeds
12214	161v			Ann Lambert	dau	14	scholar	Wry	Huddersfield
12215	161v			John Lambert	son	8	scholar	Yks	York
12216	161v			Harriet Lambert	dau	6	scholar	Dur	
12217	161v			James Hiley Lambert	scn	4	scholar	Dur	
12218	161v			Elizabeth F. Lambert	dau	1		Dur	
12219	161v	65	Gilesgate	William Bates	hea m	31	chorister <lay clerk>	Wry	Netherthong
12220	161v			Catherine Bates	wif m	26		Cul	Carlisle
12221	161v			Jane Ann Bates	dau	3		Dur	
12222	161v			John Bates	son	1		Dur	
12223	162r	66	Gilesgate	John Heaton	hea m	59	tailor	Dur	
12224	162r			Hannah Heaton	wif m	57		Dur	Bishopwearmouth
12225	162r			Ann Heaton	dau	36	dressmaker	Sct	
12226	162r			Anthony Heaton	son	32	schoolmaster	Dur	
12227	162r			John Heaton	son	30	solicitor's clerk	Dur	
12228	162r			Robert Heaton	son	17	joiner (apprentice)	Dur	
12229	162r			Mary Heaton	dau	15	scholar	Dur	
12230	162r			Margaret Heaton	dau	13	scholar	Dur	
12231	162r	67	Gilesgate	Jonathan Calvert	hea m	66	mason	Dur	Stockton
12232	162r			Isabella Calvert	wif m	67		Nbl	Berwick
12233	162r			Jane Calvert	dau	29		Dur	
12234	162r			William Henry Calvert	gsn	3		Dby	Belper
12235	162r			Sophia Smith	ldr	55	independent	Lnd	
12236	162r	68	Gilesgate	John Smith	hea m	59	miller & cartman	Dur	Tudhoe
12237	162r			Elizabeth Smith	wif m	54		Dur	Sunnybrow
12238	162r			Frances Smith	dau	21		Dur	Croxdale
12239	162r			Mary Smith	dau	14	scholar	Dur	Croxdale
12240	162r			Ann Smith	sis	55	nurse	Dur	Tudhoe
12241	162r	69	Gilesgate	John Hardinge Veitch	hea m	47	editor of newspaper *	Dur	Swalwell
12242	162r			Isabella Veitch	wif m	48		Dur	Chester-le-Street
12243	162v			Dorothy Jane Veitch	dau	19		Dur	
12244	162v			Ann Margaret Veitch	dau	17		Dur	
12245	162v			John Hardinge Veitch	son	9	scholar	Dur	
12246	162v			Thomas Kelsey Veitch	son	5	scholar	Dur	
12247	162v	70	Gilesgate	William Rollin	hea w	43	butcher	Dur	Barnard Castle
12248	162v			Isabella Mary Rollin	dau	11	scholar	Dur	
12249	162v			John George Rollin	son	10	scholar	Dur	
12250	162v			Jane Calvert Rollin	dau	7	scholar	Dur	
12251	162v			James Calvert Rollin	son	5	scholar	Dur	
12252	162v			Sarah Lee	ser	20	house servant	Nbl	Hartley
12253	162v	71	Gilesgate	John West	hea m	42	coach painter	Dur	
12254	162v			Mary West	wif m	48		Dur	
12255	162v			Ann West	dau	18		Dur	
12256	162v			Elizabeth West	dau	16	<milliner>	Dur	
12257	162v			Joseph West	son	14		Dur	
12258	162v			John West	son	11		Dur	
12259	162v			George West	son	9		Dur	
12260	162v			Francis West	son	6		Dur	
12261	162v			Dominic McEutgart	ldr	30	cutler	Irl	

12262	162v	71	Gilesgate	George Bennett	ldr w	57	painter	Ntt Southwell
12263	163r			John Bennett	ldr	22	painter	Dur
12264	163r	72	Gilesgate	Mary Kipling	hea w	70	laundress	Nbl North Shields
12265	163r			Sarah Kipling	dau	45	laundress	Nbl Chipchase
12266	163r			James Kipling	gsn	7	scholar	Sal Woodcote
12267	163r			Mary Dawson	ser	17	house servant	Nbl Hebron
12268	163r	73	Gilesgate	Robert Harrison	hea m	42	off of Inland Revenue *	Wry Snaith
12269	163r			Margaret Harrison	wif m	37		Wry Leeds
12270	163r			Emily Ann Harrison	dau	13	scholar	Nry Thirsk
12271	163r			Anne Elizabeth Harrison	dau	11	scholar	Wry Leeds
12272	163r			Mary Ann Harrison	dau	9	scholar	Nbl Newcastle
12273	163r			Alfred Harrison	son	6	scholar	Nbl Newcastle
12274	163r			Edwin Harrison	son	4		Dur
12275	163r			Albert Harrison	son	1		Dur
12276	163r	74 a	Gilesgate	Matthew Bone	hea m	54	coal miner	Dur Chester-le-Street
12277	163r			Jane Bone	wif m	58		Dur Brancepeth
12278	163r			John Blackbird Bone	son	20	joiner (apprentice)	Dur
12279	163r			Jane Elizabeth Bone	dau	17	milliner <& strawhatmkr>	Dur
12280	163r			Jane Blackbird	mlw w	84		Dur
12281	163r	74 b	Gilesgate	John Dobson	hea	71	relieving officer *	Dur Haswell
12282	163v	<73>	Gilesgate	Robert Skelton	hea m	31	printer compositor	Dur
12283	163v			Elizabeth Skelton	wif m	28	<dressmaker>	Dur
12284	163v	74	Gilesgate	Elizabeth Coulson	hea	68	laundress	Nbl Newcastle
12285	163v	75	Gilesgate	Mary Willis	hea w	65	proprietor of houses	Nry Catterick
12286	163v			Eleanor Willis	dau	22	dressmaker	Nry Gilling
12287	163v			Elizabeth Willis	dau	19	straw-bonnetmaker	Dur
12288	163v	76	Gilesgate	William Forster	hea w	63	joiner employing 8 men *	Dur Digginhouse
12289	163v			Ann Forster	dau	35		Dur
12290	163v			Mary Forster	dau	31		Dur
12291	163v			Isabella Gradon	dau m	33		Dur
12292	163v			John George Gradon	slw m	31	joiner <& builder>	Nbl Stamford[ham]
12293	163v			John George Gradon	gsn	4		Dur
12294	163v			Anne Gradon	gda	2		Dur
12295	163v			William Gradon	gsn	3m		Dur
12296	163v			Mary Jane Campbell	ser	16	house servant	Dur Bishop Middleham
12297	163v	77	Gilesgate	George Raine	hea	70	retired maltster	Dur Stanhope
12298	163v			Mary Raine	sis	79	retired innkeeper	Dur Stanhope
12299	163v			Margaret Newton	ser	33	[servant]	Dur
12300	163v	78 a	Gilesgate	Jane Jackson	hea	25	dressmaker	Dur Norton
12301	163v			John Pattinson	vis	3		Dur Southwick
12302	164r	78 b	Gilesgate	Elizabeth Clarke	hea w	70	laundress	Dur
12303	164r			Margaret Appleby	vis	30		Dur Rainton
12304	164r	78 c	Gilesgate	Mary Wilson	hea	43	retired innkeeper	Dur Wolsingham
12305	164r	78 d	Gilesgate	Tamar Richardson	hea w	73	retired plumber etc.	Dur Wolsingham
12306	164r	79	Gilesgate	John J. Douglass	hea m	32	proprietor of houses	Dur
12307	164r			Margaret Douglass	wif m	30		Nbl Rothbury
12308	164r			Phoebe Douglass	dau	10	scholar	Dur
12309	164r			Mary Douglass	dau	9	scholar	Dur
12310	164r			James Douglass	son	7	scholar	Dur
12311	164r			William Douglass	son	9m		Dur
12312	164r	80	Gilesgate	Joseph Peacock	hea m	59	brewer (emp 1 man) *	Nry Yarm
12313	164r			Jane Peacock	dau	29		Dur Tudhoe
12314	164r			William Peacock	son	28	grocer	Dur Tudhoe
12315	164r			Mary Peacock	dau	24		Dur Tudhoe
12316	164r	81	Gilesgate	Thomas Earle	hea m	27	innkeeper *	Dur
12317	164r			Jane Earle	wif m	20		Dur
12318	164r			Ann Burrell Earle	dau	2m		Dur
12319	164r			Dinah Pratt	ser	14	house servant	Dur Rainton
12320	164r	82 a	Gilesgate	John Bailes	hea m	42	tanner <shopkeeper>	Dur
12321	164r			Margaret Bailes	wif m	42		Cul Alston
12322	164v			Margaret Bailes	dau	10	scholar	Dur
12323	164v			John Bailes	son	8	scholar	Dur
12324	164v			George Bailes	son	6	scholar	Dur
12325	164v			Mary Bailes	dau	2	scholar	Dur
12326	164v			Elizabeth Bailes	dau	2	scholar	Dur
12327	164v	82 b	Gilesgate	William Bailes	hea m	22	tanner	Dur
12328	164v			Jane Bailes	wif m	22		Dur
12329	164v			John Bailes	son	6m		Dur
12330	164v	82 c	Gilesgate	Robert Myers	hea m	25	cartman	Dur
12331	164v			Mary Ann Myers	wif m	19		Dur Shincliffe
12332	164v	83	Gilesgate	Jane Usher	hea	25	innkeeper <'Britannia'>	Dur
12333	164v			Thomas C. Usher	bro	30	mason	Dur
12334	164v			Ann Welsh	sis w	27		Dur
12335	164v			Michael Welsh	nep	2		Sax S. Leonards
12336	164v			Elizabeth Palmer	ser	17	house servant	Dur
12337	164v			William Hutchinson	vis m	60	farmer	Dur Elwick
12338	164v			Thomas G. Potts	vis m	39	farmer	Dur Castle Eden
12339	164v			John Aird	vis	16	cattle dealer	Dur Houghton
12340	164v			John Dixon	vis	32	cattle dealer	Yks
12341	164v			John Hodgson	vis m	28	farmer	Wes
12342	165r	84 a	Gilesgate	William Baker	hea m	40	mason	Dur

No.	Folio	Sched.	Address	Name		Rel.	Cond.	Age	Occupation	Birthplace
12343	165r	84 a	Gilesgate	Hannah	Baker	wif	m	38		Dur
12344	165r			Mary Ann	Baker	dau		16		Dur
12345	165r			Thomas	Baker	son		14		Dur
12346	165r			Margaret	Baker	dau		11		Dur
12347	165r			Jane	Baker	dau		8		Dur
12348	165r			Isabella	Baker	dau		5		Dur
12349	165r			William	Baker	son		2		Dur
12350	165r			William	Batey	ldr		50	mason's labourer	Dur
12351	165r	84 b	Gilesgate	Owen	Mooran	hea	m	50	labourer	Irl
12352	165r			Mary	Mooran	wif	m	40		Irl
12353	165r			John	Mooran	son		19		Irl
12354	165r			Bridget	Mooran	dau		12		Irl
12355	165r			Andrew	Mooran	son		10		Irl
12356	165r			Patrick	Mooran	son		8		Irl
12357	165r			Mary	Mooran	dau		5		Irl
12358	165r			Owen	Mooran	son		3		Irl
12359	165r	85 a	Gilesgate	Ann	Pallister	hea	w	44	washerwoman	Dur Willington
12360	165r			James	Pallister	son		18	coal miner	Dur Wolsingham
12361	165r			Julian	Pallister	dau		15	carpet factory girl	Dur Wolsingham
12362	165v			Henry	Pallister	son		8	scholar	Dur
12363	165v			Edward	Pallister	son		4	scholar	Dur
12364	165v			Ralph	Pallister	son		1		Dur
12365	165v			Thomas	Smith	ldr		40	labourer	Dur
12366	165v	85 b	Gilesgate	Mary	Thornton	hea	w	64	recg parochial relief	Dur Chester-le-Street
12367	165v	85 c	Gilesgate	Thomas	Thompson	hea	m	31	farm labourer	Dur Sherburn House
12368	165v			Alice	Thompson	wif	m	31		Dur Sunderland
12369	165v			Joseph	Thompson	son		9		Dur
12370	165v			Mary Ann	Thompson	dau		6		Dur
12371	165v			Alice	Thompson	dau		4		Dur
12372	165v			Thomas	Thompson	son		2		Dur
12373	165v	86	Gilesgate	Rowland B.	Wilson	hea	w	79	fruiterer	Dur
12374	165v	87 a	Gilesgate	Ann	Heslop	hea	w	60		Dur
12375	165v			Robert	Heslop	son		25	boot and shoemaker	Dur
12376	165v			Charles Henry	Heslop	son		23	upholsterer	Dur
12377	165v			Isabella	Heslop	dau		20	servant	Dur
12378	165v			William	Troughton	*		2		Dur
12379	165v	87 b	Gilesgate	William	Race	hea		23	tailor	Dur Middle Rainton
12380	165v			Richard	Calvert	blw	m	22	brickmaker	Yks
12381	165v			Mary Ann	Calvert	sis	m	22		Dur Middle Rainton
12382	166r	87 c	Gilesgate	Henry	Burn	hea	m	39	tanner	Dur Lanchester
12383	166r			Selini	Burn	wif	m	31		Nth
12384	166r			Ann	Burn	dau		6	scholar	Nth
12385	166r			Jane	Burn	dau		4	scholar	Nth
12386	166r	87 d	Gilesgate	Peter	McManners	hea	m	31	hawker	Irl
12387	166r			Margaret	McManners	wif	m	31		Irl
12388	166r			Patrick	McManners	son		4		Lan Manchester
12389	166r			Thomas	McManners	son		2		Lan Manchester
12390	166r			Mary	Malone	ser		20	house servant	Irl
12391	166r	87 e	Gilesgate	John Robinson	Emmerson	hea	w	70	proprietor of houses	Dur
12392	166r			Robert	Reed	slw	m	32	colliery waggonrider	Dur Sherburn
12393	166r			Sarah	Reed	dau	m	30		Dur
12394	166r			John Robinson	Reed	gsn		10	scholar	Dur
12395	166r			Jane Ann	Reed	gda		3		Dur
12396	166r	88	Gilesgate	James Jackson	Ferens	hea	m	35	grocer	Nbl Newcastle
12397	166r			Martha	Ferens	wif	m	37		Dur
12398	166r			John	Ferens	son		5		Dur
12399	166r			Robert	Ferens	son		4		Dur
12400	166r			Eleanor	Best	ser		20	house servant	Dur Bishopwearmouth
12401	166v	89	Gilesgate	Thomas	Brown	hea	w	57	farmer (of 40a)	Dur
12402	166v			Sarah	Brown	dau		33		Dur
12403	166v			Margaret	Brown	dau		29		Dur
12404	166v			Smith	Brown	son		27	farm labourer	Dur
12405	166v			Robert	Laws	vis		36	farmer	Nbl Horsley
12406	166v			Jane	Mawson	ser		19	house servant	Dur
12407	166v	90	Gilesgate	James	Ogleby	hea	m	52	husbandman	Dur
12408	166v			Ann	Ogleby	wif	m	46		Dur
12409	166v			William	Ogleby	son		23	butcher	Dur
12410	166v			Ann	Ogleby	dau		16		Dur
12411	166v			Thomas	Coulthard	vis		23	butcher	Dur Sunderland
12412	166v			Richard	Backhouse	ldr		42	husbandman	Dur
12413	166v	91	Gilesgate	Robert	Siddle	hea	m	54	agricultural labourer	Dur
12414	166v			Isabella	Siddle	wif	m	50		Dur
12415	166v			Jane	Siddle	dau		21	schoolmistress	Dur
12416	166v			Esther	Siddle	dau		19		Dur
12417	166v			Thomas	Siddle	son		17	shoemaker (apprentice)	Dur
12418	166v			William	Siddle	son		16	scholar	Dur
12419	166v	[ah]	Gilesgate	Thomas	Mowbray	hea	m	42	dealer in china, glass *	Dur Witton Gilbert
12420	166v			Ann	Mowbray	wif	m	42		Dur Barnard Castle
12421	167r			Eleanor	Wheldon	ldr	m	59	property owner	Dur Middle'n-Teesdale
12422	167r	[ai]	Gilesgate *	John	Stodart	hea	m	44	saddler & harnessmaker	Dur
12423	167r			Elizabeth	Stodart	wif	m	40		Dur

12424	167r	[ai]	Gilesgate *	Ellen Stodart	dau		9	scholar	Dur
12425	167r			John Stodart	son		6	scholar	Dur
12426	167r			Henry Deighton	ldr		16	coal miner	Dur Houghton-l-Spring
12427	167r	[aa]	Magdalen Place	Ralph Adam	hea m		42	cordwainer	Dur
12428	167r			Alice Adam	wif m		49		Dur
12429	167r	[ab]	Magdalen Place	John Bell	hea m		56	stonemason	Dur
12430	167r			Honour Bell	wif m		58		Dur
12431	167r			Ralph Bell	son		22	stonemason	Dur
12432	167r			Davison Bell	son		14	stonemason (apprentice)	Dur
12433	167r			Elizabeth Davison	dau		36		Dur
12434	167r	[ac]	Magdalen Place	Michael Churchill	hea m		43	draper	Irl
12435	167r			Mary Churchill	wif m		43		Irl
12436	167r			Susanna Boland	nce		12	scholar	Lan Manchester
12437	167r			Catherine McKinna	ser		23	house servant	Irl
12438	167r	[ad]	Magdalen Place	George White	hea w		53	travelling draper	Irl
12439	167r			Elizabeth White	dau		20	dressmaker	Nry Guisborough
12440	167r			Anne White	dau		17	scholar	Dur Sunderland
12441	167v			Elizabeth Tumelty	sis w		55	formerly innkeeper	Irl
12442	167v	[ae]	Magdalen Place	Thomas Falknham	hea m		60	cowkeeper	Dur
12443	167v			Elizabeth Falknham	wif m		60		Dur
12444	167v	[af]	Magdalen Place	Peter John Wilson	hea m		37	teacher	Nbl Gosforth
12445	167v			Elizabeth Wilson	wif m		37		Nbl Benton
12446	167v			Mary Ann Wilson	dau		12		Nbl Newcastle
12447	167v	[ag]	Magdalen Place	George Thornton	hea m		34	mason	Dur
12448	167v			Ann Thornton	wif m		31		Dur
12449	167v			Barbara Thornton	dau		10	scholar	Dur
12450	167v			Mary Thornton	dau		8	scholar	Dur
12451	167v			Henry Thornton	son		5	scholar	Dur
12452	167v			George Thornton	son		7m		Dur
12453	167v	[ah]	Magdalen Place	John Palling	hea m		44	worsted dealer	Irl
12454	167v			Lydia Palling	wif m		47		Nry Richmond
12455	167v			John Palling	son		19	app [worsted dealer's?]	Sct
12456	167v			Jane Palling	dau		15	teacher	Sct
12457	167v			Mary Palling	dau		13	scholar	Sct
12458	167v			David Palling	son		7	scholar	Dur
			one house uninhabited						
12459	168r	[ai]	Magdalen Place	Margaret Wallace	hea w		69	house proprietor	Dur Newbottle
12460	168r			Martha Wallace	dau		30		Dur
12461	168r			Elizabeth Nesbitt	gda		1		Dur
12462	168r	[aj]	Magdalen Place	Thomas Hyde	hea m		26	butler	Dur Norton, Whitehall
12463	168r			Margaret Hyde	wif m		28		Yks
12464	168r			Mary Hyde	dau		2		Dur
12465	168r			Elizabeth Hyde	dau		9m		Dur
12466	168r	[ak]	Magdalen Place	William Henry Wilson	hea m		34	shoemaker	Dur Wolviston
12467	168r			Margaret Wilson	wif m		45		Dur
12468	168r			Joseph Hall	sls		16	tallow chandler (app)	Dur Stanley Cottage
12469	168r			Margaret Hall	dls		14	factory girl	Dur Stanley Cottage
12470	168r			Anne Hall	dls		11		Dur Ship House
12471	168r			Alexander A. Wilson	son		7	scholar	Dur
12472	168r	[al]	Magdalen Place	Matthew Bodger	hea m		51	off of Inland Revenue	Cam Littleport
12473	168r			Isabella Bodger	wif m		49		Dur Gateshead
12474	168r			John Bodger	son		5	scholar	Nbl Newcastle
12475	168r	[am]	Magdalen Place	Robert Burns	hea m		64	labourer	Nbl Long Horsley
12476	168r			Ann Burns	wif m		61		Dur Monkwearmouth
12477	168r			William Burns	son		26	engineman	Nbl
12478	168r			Edward Burns	son		22	portrait painter	Nbl
12479	168v			Margaret Burns	dau		20		Nbl
12480	168v	[an]	Magdalen Place	George Cresswell	hea m		30	engine driver	Dur Houghton-l-Spring
12481	168v			Ann Cresswell	wif m		31		Dur South Shields
12482	168v			Caroline Cresswell	dau		5	scholar	Dur Gateshead
12483	168v			Sarah Cresswell	dau		3	scholar	Dur
12484	168v			Jane Ann Cresswell	dau		1		Dur
12485	168v			Jane Ann Miller	nce		18		Lnd
12486	168v	[ao]	Magdalen Place	Thomas Miller	hea m		72	gardener	Wes Stainmore
12487	168v			Hannah Miller	wif m		68	laundress	Ery Hull
12488	168v			Elizabeth Miller	dau		24	laundress	Dur
12489	168v			Sarah Miller	dau		22	laundress	Dur
12490	168v	[ap]	Magdalen Place	Matthew Lautherdale	hea m		67	pensioner (artillery)	Dur
12491	168v			Elizabeth Lautherdale	wif m		67		Dur Wolsingham
12492	168v			Elizabeth Raw	dau m		47		Dur Hamsterley
12493	168v			Sarah Raw	dau		20	dressmaker	Dur Brandon
12494	168v	[aq]	Magdalen Place	Robert Davison	hea m		34	nailmaker	Dur
12495	168v			Mary Davison	wif m		32		Dur
12496	168v			Richard Davison	son		12	scholar	Dur
12497	168v			Mary Davison	dau		9	scholar	Dur
12498	168v			Robert Davison	son		6	scholar	Dur
12499	169r			Jackson Davison	son		4	scholar	Dur
12500	169r			George Davison	son		4m		Dur
12501	169r	[ar]	Magdalen Place	Jane Mawson	hea w		60	milk vendor	Dur
12502	169r			John Mawson	son		29	painter	Dur
12503	169r			Mary Mawson	dau		26	dressmaker	Dur

12504	169r	[ar]	Magdalen Place	Anthony Mawson	son	19	shoemaker	Dur
12505	169r			Michael Mawson	son	19	joiner & cartwright	Dur
12506	169r	[as]	Magdalen Place	William Milburn	hea m	40	labourer	Wry Leeds
12507	169r			Elizabeth Milburn	wif m	36		Nbl
12508	169r			William P. Milburn	son	17	coal miner	Dur Lyons Town
12509	169r			Henry Shield Milburn	son	13	scholar	Dur Easington Lane
12510	169r			Ann Eliza Milburn	dau	11	scholar	Dur
12511	169r			Elizabeth M. Milburn	dau	7	scholar	Dur
12512	169r			Sarah Jane Milburn	dau	2		Dur
12513	169r	[at]	Magdalen Place	John Smithson	hea m	25	railway servant	Dur Whorlton
12514	169r			Mary Smithson	wif m	25		Yks
12515	169r			Margaret Harrison	mlw w	62		Yks
12516	169r	[au]	Magdalen Place	Margaret Short	hea w	72		Dur Houghton-1-Spring
12517	169r			Hannah Short	dau	24		Dur Houghton-1-Spring
12518	169r			John Short	gsn	12	scholar	Dur Houghton-1-Spring
12519	169r	[av]	Magdalen Place	Richard Davison	hea m	31	painter	Dur
12520	169v			Isabella Davison	wif m	33		Nbl Wylam
12521	169v			William Davison	son	5		Nbl Seaton Burn
12522	169v			Robert Davison	son	3		Dur
12523	169v			Mary Ann Davison	dau	7m		Dur
12524	169v	[aw]	Magdalen Place	William Wells	hea m	47	mason employing 2 men	Dur Ferryhill
12525	169v			Jane Wells	wif m	47		Dur
12526	169v			George Wells	son	25	mason	Dur
12527	169v			Jane Wells	dau	24		Dur
12528	169v			Mary Ann Wells	dau	20	<straw-hatmaker>	Dur
12529	169v			Joseph Wells	son	17	shoemaker	Dur
12530	169v			Edward Wells	son	12		Dur
12531	169v	[aj]	Gilesgate *	George Worthy	hea m	42	<boot and> shoemaker	Dur
12532	169v			Margaret Worthy	wif m	47		Dur Lanchester
12533	169v			Susanna Worthy	dau	7	scholar	Dur
12534	169v			Henry Atkinson	ldr	18	shoemaker, apprentice	Dur Kelloe
12535	169v	[ak]	Gilesgate	Dorothy Irven	hea w	52	clergyman's widow	Dur Great Lumley
12536	169v			Edward Irven	son	14	(apprentice)	Dur Chester-le-Street
12537	169v			Elizabeth Mary Watson	vis w	70	proprietor of houses	Dur Great Lumley
12538	170r	<94>	Gilesgate	Mary Stafford	hea	44	annuitant	Dur Bishopwearmouth
12539	170r			Ann Atkinson	sis m	50	annuitant	Dur Bishopwearmouth
12540	170r			Sophia Ann Carrick	nce	17	landed prop & scholar	Nbl
12541	170r			Amelia Letitia Lambert	ldr	27	governess	Lnd
12542	170r			Elizabeth Collinson	ser	21	cook servant	Dur Staindrop
12543	170r			Alice Smith	ser	17	house servant	Dur Stockton
12544	170r	<95>a	Gilesgate	Robert Winder	hea m	56	Post Office messenger	Dur Sunderland
12545	170r			Jane Winder	wif m	58		Dur
12546	170r			Jane Winder	dau	26	<straw-hatmaker>	Dur
12547	170r			Jane Patterson	gda	7		Dur Sunderland
12548	170r	<95>b	Gilesgate	Jane Atkinson	hea w	67	needlewoman	Nbl Hexham
12549	170r	<96>a	Gilesgate	Archibald Lamb	hea m	56	coal miner <publican *>	Dur Winlaton
12550	170r			Mary Lamb	wif m	53		Dur Houghton-1-Spring
12551	170r	<96>b	Gilesgate	John Parkinson	hea m	42	blacksmith	Dur Etherley
12552	170r			Eleanor Parkinson	wif m	33		Dur Bishop Auckland
12553	170r			Mary Anna Parkinson	dau	2		Dur Sunderland
12554	170r	<97>c	Gilesgate	James Chambers	hea m	23	police officer <borough>	Sct
12555	170r			Agnes Chambers	wif m	24		Sct
12556	170r			Elizabeth Chambers	dau	2		Sct
12557	170r			Jane Chambers	dau	4m		Dur
12558	170v	[al]a	Gilesgate	Deborah Herbert	hea w	59	shopkeeper	Nbl Blanchland *
12559	170v	[al]b	Gilesgate	Thomas Valks	hea m	50	mason	Dur Sedgefield
12560	170v			Elizabeth Valks	wif m	55		Dur Evenwood
12561	170v	[am]	Gilesgate	Elizabeth Forster	hea w	36	shopkeeper	Dur Wapping
12562	170v			Mary Forster	dau	9	scholar	Dur Shotton
12563	170v			Margaret Forster	dau	7	scholar	Dur Shotton
12564	170v			Ellen Forster	dau	5	scholar	Dur Carrville
12565	170v	98	Gilesgate	James Blenkinsop	hea m	34	cartwright	Dur
12566	170v			Ann Blenkinsop	wif m	37		Dur
12567	170v			John Blenkinsop	son	11	scholar	Dur
12568	170v	100	Gilesgate	Alexander Q. Ward	hea m	31	surveyor of taxes	Sct
12569	170v			Mary Ward	wif m	29		Lan Blackburn
12570	170v			Henry Brooks Ward	son	5		Wry Leeds
12571	170v			Walter William Ward	son	3		Wry Leeds
12572	170v			Alexander Q. Ward	son	1		Dur
12573	170v			Daniel Ward	son	2m		Dur
12574	170v			Alice Brooks	mlw w	59		Lan Blackburn
12575	170v			Mary Jane Dodds	ser	15	house servant	Dur
12576	170v	101 a	Gilesgate	William Tate	hea m	38	waggonman	Dur Lumley Thicks
12577	170v			Alice Tate	wif m	35		Dur
12578	171r			Elizabeth Tate	dau	1		Dur
12579	171r	101 b	Gilesgate	Thomas Hanson	hea m	49	farm labourer	Dur Willington
12580	171r			Mary Hanson	wif m	47		Dur Castle Eden
12581	171r			Jane Hanson	dau	22	farm servant	Dur Jarrow
12582	171r			George Hanson	son	20	pitman	Dur Red Briar
12583	171r			Mary Hanson	dau	19	house servant	Dur Red Briar
12584	171r			Thomas Hanson	son	16	pitman	Dur

12585	171r	101 b	Gilesgate	Elizabeth Hanson	dau		13	scholar	Dur
12586	171r			Margaret Hanson	dau		9	scholar	Dur
12587	171r			William Hanson	son		6	scholar	Dur
12588	171r			John Hanson	son		4	scholar	Dur
12589	171r			William Doby	ldr		25	pitman	Dur
12590	171r	101 c	Gilesgate	James Benton	hea	m	50	pedlar	Lan Manchester
12591	171r			Margaret Benton	wif	m	40		Nbl Berwick
12592	171r			Margaret Benton	dau		8		Dur
12593	171r			Catherine Benton	dau		5		Dur
12594	171r	102 a	Gilesgate	Francis Walker	hea	m	37	barber	Dur
12595	171r			Isabel Walker	wif	m	36		Dur
12596	171r	102 b	Gilesgate	Patrick Lee	hea	m	53	brickmaker	Irl
12597	171r			Catherine Lee	wif	m	32		Irl
12598	171v			Margaret Lee	dau		11		Irl
12599	171v			William Lee	son		8	scholar	Irl
12600	171v			Judah Waters	vis		23	house servant	Irl
12601	171v	102 c	Gilesgate	Ellen Fenwick	hea		43	needlewoman	Dur Sherburn
12602	171v			George Fenwick	son		3		Dur
12603	171v			James Fenwick	son		1		Dur
12604	171v			Eliza Baster	sis	m	20	wife of Edward Baster	Dur Sherburn
12605	171v	102 d	Gilesgate	Ann Nesbitt	hea	w	73	farmer's servant	Dur
12606	171v			Sarah Nesbitt	dau		43		Dur
12607	171v			John George Nesbitt	gsn		1		Dur
12608	171v	103	Gilesgate	Thomas Barras	hea	m	37	sinker & innkeeper *	Dur Oxclose
12609	171v			Euretta Barras	wif	m	34		Dur
12610	171v			Mary Ann Barras	dau		11		Dur
12611	171v			Catherine Barras	dau		9		Dur
12612	171v			Elizabeth Barras	dau		7		Dur
12613	171v			Edward Barras	son		2		Dur Houghton-l-Spring
12614	171v			John Barras	son		2m		Dur
			one house uninhabited						
12615	171v	<105>	Gilesgate	Joanna Brown	hea	w	53	property owner	Dur
12616	171v			Jane Louisa Brown	dau		24	milliner <dressmaker>	Dur
12617	172r	106	Gilesgate	James Cummins	hea	m	22	chemist, druggist *	Dur
12618	172r			Mary Ann Cummins	wif	m	24		Dur
12619	172r	107	Gilesgate	John Wallace	hea	m	36	cartwright emp 1 man	Dur
12620	172r			Ann Wallace	wif	m	42		Dur
12621	172r			Elizabeth Ryle Wallace	dau		9	scholar	Dur
12622	172r			Mary Ann Wallace	dau		6	scholar	Dur
12623	172r			Margaret Wallace	dau		2		Dur
12624	172r			Thomas Atkinson	ldr		16	cartwright (apprentice)	Dur Quarrington
12625	172r	108	Gilesgate	George Goundry	hea	w	70	retired tallow chandler	Dur
12626	172r			Mary Goundry	dau		42	house servant	Dur
12627	172r			Mary Ann Thompson	gda		8		Dur
12628	172r	109	Gilesgate	Thomas Skelton	hea	m	42	colliery agent	Dur
12629	172r			Mary Skelton	wif	m	39		Wes Kendal
12630	172r			John Skelton	son		19	engineman	Dur
12631	172r			William Skelton	son		13	scholar	Dur
12632	172r			Mary Ann Skelton	dau		6	scholar	Dur
12633	172r			Jane Skelton	dau		4		Dur
12634	172r			Thomas Skelton	son		1		Dur
12635	172r	110	Gilesgate	George Stockdale	hea	m	38	innkeeper <'Sun'>	Nry Scotton
12636	172r			Elizabeth Stockdale	wif	m	36		Dur
12637	172v			Ann Smith	dls		16		Dur
12638	172v			Fanny Stockdale	dau		4		Dur
12639	172v			Jane Stockdale	dau		1		Dur
12640	172v	111	Gilesgate	George Proudlock	hea	m	49	coal miner <fruiterer>	Dur Chester-le-Street
12641	172v			Isabella Proudlock	wif	m	41		Nbl Newcastle
12642	172v			Peter Proudlock	son		22	coal miner	Dur Chester-le-Street
12643	172v			Jane Proudlock	dau		18	<dressmaker & milliner>	Dur Sherburn Hill
12644	172v			Isabella Proudlock	dau		16		Dur Sherburn Hill
12645	172v			Thomas Proudlock	son		13	coal miner	Dur Broomside
12646	172v			Mary Ann Proudlock	dau		9	scholar	Dur
12647	172v	[an]	Gilesgate	William Lumley	hea	m	41	colliery overman	Dur
12648	172v			Mary Lumley	wif	m	43		Dur
12649	172v			Joseph Swales Lumley	son		1		Dur
12650	172v			John Swales Ruttedge	nep		5		Dur Gateshead
12651	172v	[aa]	Gilesgate Moor	Robert Moon	hea	m	45	farm hind	Dur
12652	172v			Barbara Moon	wif	m	47		Dur
			two houses uninhabited						
12653	172v	[ab]	Gilesgate Moor	Thomas Williamson	hea	m	23	innkeeper	Dur Darlington
12654	172v			Margaret Williamson	wif	m	27		Dur Moorsley
12655	172v			Sarah Ann Hindmarch	dls		3		Dur Trimdon
12656	173r			John Burnett	vis		20	butcher	Yks
12657	173r		Glue Garth	James Hutchinson	hea	m	70	cartman	Nry Melsonby
12658	173r			Jane Hutchinson	wif	m	75		Dur Usworth
12659	173r			Richard Hutchinson	son		35	cartman	Dur Rainton
12660	173r			William Hutchinson	son		32	cartman	Dur Rainton
12661	173r		Kepier <Mill>	Thomas Gibson	hea	m	46	miller <gardener *>	Dur Evenwood
12662	173r			Matilda Gibson	wif	m	49		Dur
12663	173r			William Gibson	son		17	miller	Dur

12664	173r		Kepier <Mill>	Margaret Gibson	dau	14		Dur
12665	173r			Thomas Gibson	son	10	scholar	Dur
12666	173r			Robert Gibson	son	8	scholar	Dur
12667	173r			Richard Mothersell	ldr	52	garden servant	Dur Sedgefield
12668	173r			Martha Blenkinsop	ldr	17	house servant	Dur Newbottle
12669	173r	[af]a	Sands	Jonathan Wilson	hea m	60	gardener	Cul
12670	173r			Sarah Wilson	wif m	50		Cul
12671	173r			Mary Wilson	dau	30		Cul
12672	173r			Jonathan Wilson	son	20	currier (apprentice)	Cul
12673	173r			Robert Wilson	son	11	scholar	Cul
12674	173r	[af]b	Sands	Christopher Plews	hea m	39	husbandman	Yks
12675	173r			Elizabeth Plews	wif m	41		Dur Ebern Park
12676	173v			Ann Plews	dau	13	scholar	Dur Sherburn
12677	173v			James Plews	son	12	scholar	Dur
12678	173v	[af]c	Sands	John Worthy	hea m	32	shoemaker	Dur
12679	173v			Mary Worthy	wif m	38		Dur Flass
12680	173v			Thomas Worthy	son	6	scholar	Dur

S. Mary Magdalene chapelry (extra-parochial)

12681	174r	43	Gilesgate	George Fowler	hea m	28	grocer	Nry Coatham
12682	174r			Diana Fowler	wif m	29		Nry Stokesley
12683	174r			Jane Venus	sis m	36	joiner's wife	Nry Stokesley
12684	174r			John Venus	nep	1	joiner's son	Dur Norton
12685	174r			Richard Fowler	son	3		Dur
12686	174r			George Fowler	son	1		Dur
12687	174r			Catherine Gautter	ser	23	house servant	Irl
12688	174r			Magnus Green	ldr m	21	railway porter	ShI
12689	174r			Frances Green	ldr m	23		Nbl Berwick
12690	174r			Margaret Green	ldr	3		Nbl Newcastle
12691	174r	44	Gilesgate	Ellen Hedley	hea w	72	dealer in woollen goods	Dur
12692	174r			Charles Clarke Stodart	gsn	14	saddler (apprentice)	Dur
12693	174r		Railway Station	Thomas John Bungay	hea m	32	railway stationmaster	Dur
12694	174r			Mildred Bungay	wif m	51		Lnd
12695	174r			Elizabeth Turner	ser	26	house servant	Dur Lumley
12696	174r		Brickyard	Joseph Spavin	hea w	52	brickmaker	Dur Coxhoe
12697	174r			Mary Ann Spavin	dau	13	scholar	Dur Coxhoe
12698	174r			Maria Spavin	dau	7	scholar	Dur Coxhoe
12699	174r			Robert Spavin	son	9	scholar	Dur Coxhoe
12700	174r			Joseph Spavin	son	15	brickmaker	Dur Coxhoe

Notes - Enumeration District 5b

11663	... of Yorkshire, lecturer on astronomy
11706	... & landed proprietor
11708	... & graduate of Edinburgh University
11781	<to J. & A. Preston, slate merchants>
11786	<& collector of borough rates>
11794	... of landed proprietor
11866	... managing ... <sharebroker>
11873	county given as "Durham"
11876	... landed proprietor, house proprietor & interest of money
11879	<'Fox & Partridge'>
11887	/"Eden Bridge"
11996	... & candle manufacturer
12007	... & lodging house keeper
12052	... 'Grand Junction'
12066	... 'Railway Tavern'
12083	[father-in-law's?] grand-child
12125-12129	illegitimate ...
12151	<'Joiners' Arms'>
12161	... of county court, Circuit no. 2 <professor of music & pianoforte tuner>
12171	<captain>
12183	... railway contractor
12195	... & parish clerk
12211	... of music <& pianoforte tuner>
12241	<Durham County Advertiser>
12268	... Excise Department
12281	<registrar of births, deaths and marriages for St. Nicholas district>
12288	<& builder>
12312	<brickmaker & porter merchant>
12316	<'Cordwainers' Arms'>
12378	illegitimate [grand?] child
12419	... and earthenware
12422-12426	<New Buildings>
12531-12534	<New Buildings>
12549	... 'Four Alls'
12558	county given as "Durham"
12608	<'Smiths' Arms'>
12617	... & grocer
12661	... & publican 'White Bear'

REF	FOL	NO	STREET	FORENAME(S)	SURNAME	REL	C	AGE	OCCUPATION	BIRTHPLACE
12701	178v	[aa]	Sunderland Road	Andrew	Bell	hea	m	29	grocer, master emp 1 app	Wes Brough
12702	178v			Mary	Bell	wif	m	23		Wes Winton
12703	178v			Robert	Bell	son		2		Dur [D] S. Oswald
12704	178v			Elizabeth	Hutchinson	vis		29		Wes Winton
12705	178v			Sarah	Fallowfield	ser		21	general servant	Wes Great Strickland
12706	178v			James	Bell	bro		15	grocer (apprentice)	Wes Brough
12707	178v	[ab]	Sunderland Road	Charles	Turnbull	hea	m	38	platelayer, insp on rly	Dur Chilton
12708	178v			Jane	Turnbull	wif	m	40		Dur Easington
12709	178v			George	Turnbull	son		13	scholar	Dur Boldon
12710	178v	[ac]	Sunderland Road	Ralph	Forster	hea	m	29	publican *	Dur Washington
12711	178v			Mary	Forster	wif	m	28		Dur [D] Framwelgate
12712	178v			Ann	Goundry	vis	m	20+		not known
12713	178v	[ad]a	Sunderland Road	Phillip	Philipps	hea	m	53	umbrella-maker	High Germany BS
12714	178v			Elizabeth	Philipps	wif	m	42		Sct
12715	178v	[ad]b	Sunderland Road *	Thomas	Clark	hea	m	42	gatekeeper on railway	Dur Durham
12716	178v			Margaret	Clark	wif	m	41		Dur Durham
12717	178v			John George	Clark	son		12	roper's assistant	Dur
12718	178v			Charlotte	Clark	dau		10	scholar	Dur
12719	178v	[ad]c	Sunderland Road *	Thomas	Heslop	hea	m	29	grocer	Dur Durham
12720	178v			Martha	Heslop	wif	m	28		Dur Gateshead
12721	179r	[ae]	Sunderland Road	James	Watchman	hea	m	56	coal miner	Dur Lanchester
12722	179r			Ann	Watchman	wif	m	53		Cul Workington
12723	179r			Isabella	Watchman	dau		19	dressmaker	Dur Hetton-le-Hole
12724	179r			Mary Jane	Watchman	dau		11	scholar	Dur Eppleton
12725	179r			John James	Watchman	gsn		11	scholar	Dur Eppleton
12726	179r	[af]	Sunderland Road	John William	James	hea	m	44	painter, coal miner	Dur [D] S. Giles
12727	179r			Mary	James	wif	m	42		Ery Grimston
12728	179r			Ellen	James	dau		16	dressmaker	Wry Hunslet
12729	179r			Clementine	James	dau		13		Wry Leeds
12730	179r			Elizabeth	James	dau		10	scholar	Dur West Rainton
12731	179r			Mary	James	dau		7		Dur West Rainton
12732	179r			Robert	James	son		4		Dur [D] S. Giles
12733	179r	[ag]	Sunderland Road	John	Cummings	hea	m	63	tailor	Dur [D] S. Giles
12734	179r			Jane	Cummings	wif	m	65		Dur [D] Framwelgate
12735	179r	[ah]	Sunderland Road	James	Taylor	hea	w	61	agricultural labourer *	Dur Durham
12736	179r			Henry	Taylor	son		32	currier (journeyman)	Dur Durham
12737	179r			Ann	Taylor	sil	w	60		Dur Durham
12738	179r			Ann	Roseberry	vis		9	scholar	Dur Bishopwearmouth
12739	179r	[ai]	Sunderland Road	Hannah	Grey	hea	w	57	annuitant	Dur Houghton-1-Spring
12740	179r	[aj]	Sunderland Road	Elizabeth	Simmons	hea	m	50	confectioner	Dur Hett
12741	179v			Thomas	Simmons	son		17	coal miner	Dur [D] S. Nicholas
12742	179v			Lydia	Simmons	dau		11	scholar	Dur [D] S. Giles
12743	179v	[ak]	Sunderland Road	Anthony	Hamilton	hea	m	76	tollbar keeper	Nry Northallerton
12744	179v			Mary	Hamilton	wif	m	73		Nry Helmsley
			one house uninhabited							
12745	179v	[al]	Sunderland Road	John	Dixon	hea	m	35	platelayer	Dur Wolsingham
12746	179v			Isabella	Dixon	wif	m	32		Dur Shotley Bridge
12747	179v			William	Dixon	son		7	scholar	Dur Chester-le-Street
12748	179v			John	Dixon	son		6	scholar	Dur Houghton-1-Spring
12749	179v			Mary Jane	Dixon	dau		4	scholar	Dur [D] S. Giles
12750	179v			Isabella	Dixon	dau		2		Dur [D] S. Giles
12751	179v			Elizabeth	Dixon	dau		9m		Dur [D] S. Giles
12752	179v	[am]	Sunderland Road	William	Hills	hea	m	73	coal miner	Cul Alston Moor
12753	179v			Mary	Hills	wif	m	70		Nbl Swalwell
12754	179v			Ann	Hills	dau	m	25		Dur Rainton
12755	179v			Sarah	Hills	dau		23		Dur Rainton
12756	179v			Isabella	Hills	dau		19		Dur Pittington
12757	179v			Sarah	Hills	gda		7		Dur South Hetton
12758	179v	[an]a	Sunderland Road	Ann	Dawson	hea	w	62	coal miner's widow	Nbl Newcastle
12759	179v			William	Dawson	son		36	coal miner	Dur Houghton-1-Spring
12760	180r			George	Dawson	son		17	coal miner	Dur Hetton-le-Hole
12761	180r	[an]b	Sunderland Road	William	Watchman	hea	m	27	coal miner	Dur
12762	180r			Elizabeth	Watchman	wif	m	24		Dur Lanchester
12763	180r			Robert	Watchman	son		1		Dur Cassop
12764	180r	[ao]	Sunderland Road	John	Lightfoot	hea	m	59	butcher	Nry Scarborough
12765	180r			Mary	Lightfoot	wif	m	57		Dur [D] S. Giles
12766	180r			Elizabeth	Lightfoot	dau		20		Dur [D] S. Giles
12767	180r			Mary	Lightfoot	dau		14	scholar	Dur [D] S. Giles
12768	180r			Thomas	Lightfoot	son		12	scholar	Dur [D] S. Giles
12769	180r	[ap]	Sunderland Road	Margaret	Pattinson	hea	w	30	innkeeper	Dur [D] Framwelgate
12770	180r			Ann	Pattinson	dau		10	scholar	Dur Coxhoe
12771	180r			Elizabeth	Pattinson	dau		7	scholar	Dur Coxhoe
12772	180r			George	Pattinson	son		5	scholar	Dur
12773	180r			George	Dodds	ldr		27	joiner	Nbl Corbridge
12774	180r			John	Potts	ldr		40	retired clockmaker	Nry Yarm
12775	180r			Thomas	Blackburn	ldr		32	butcher	Dur Elwick
12776	180r			Ann	Stone	vis	w	41	boarding house keeper	Dur [D] Framwelgate
12777	180r	[aq]	Sunderland Road	Charles	Ebdy	hea	m	39	roper (master *)	Dur Durham
12778	180r			Jane	Ebdy	wif	m	40		Dur Houghton-1-Spring

12779	180r	[aq]	Sunderland Road	Barron Wright Ebdy	son	13	scholar	Dur [D] S. Giles
12780	180v			Thomas Charles Ebdy	son	11	scholar	Dur [D] S. Giles
12781	180v			Joseph Gibson Ebdy	son	7	scholar	Dur [D] S. Giles
12782	180v			Christopher Fishwick	ldr	24	roper (journeyman)	Wry Leeds
12783	180v			Mary Adelaide Wandless	ser	19	general servant	Nry Coatham
12784	180v	[ar]	Sunderland Road	John Barnes	hea w	62	Excise officer *	Ntt Bingham
12785	180v	[as]a	Sunderland Road	Joseph Bannister	hea m	35	engine driver at clry	Mgy
12786	180v			Mary Bannister	wif m	37		Dur Sunderland
12787	180v			Joseph Bannister	son	6	scholar	Dur [D] S. Giles
12788	180v	[as]b	Sunderland Road	Ann Crosby	hea w	70	pauper; coal miner's wid	Dur Fatfield
12789	180v			Mary Ann Bowron	gda	15	scholar	Dur Pittington
12790	180v	[as]c	Sunderland Road	Sarah Morris	hea w	77	pauper; shoemaker's wid	Yks Little Brauton
12791	180v	[at]	Sunderland Road	Hannah Barron	hea w	79	glovemaker	Dur Wolsingham
12792	180v			Hannah Barron	dau	44	glovemaker	Dur Houghton-1-Spring
12793	180v			Thomas John Archbold	gsn	24	solicitor	Dur [D] S. Giles
12794	180v	[au]	Sunderland Road	Morrison Harle	hea m	38	blacksmith (journeyman)	Nbl Tynemouth
12795	180v			Elizabeth Harle	wif m	31		Nbl Longbenton
12796	180v			Margaret Harle	dau	4	scholar	Nbl Earsdon
12797	180v			George Harle	son	2		Dur [D] S. Giles
12798	180v			Maria Harle	dau	5m		Dur [D] S. Giles
			one house uninhabited					
12799	181r	[av]	Sunderland Road	John Ebdy	hea m	67	retired roper	Nry Yarm
12800	181r			Ann Ebdy	wif m	68		Dur Hetton-le-Hole
12801	181r			Thomas Ebdy	son m	36	roper (journeyman)	Dur [D] S. Nicholas
12802	181r			John Ebdy	son	24	roper (master emp 1 man)	Dur [D] S. Nicholas
12803	181r	[aw]	Sunderland Road	Edmund Ebdy	hea m	30	roper (master emp 1 boy)	Dur [D] S. Nicholas
12804	181r			Anne Ebdy	wif m	30		Dur Shincliffe
12805	181r			Edmund John B. Ebdy	son	1		Dur [D] S. Giles
12806	181r	[ax]	Sunderland Road	Joseph Thompson	hea m	56	agricultural labourer	Dur Redmarshall
12807	181r			Mary Thompson	wif m	52		Dur [D] S. Oswald
12808	181r			John Thompson	son	25	gardener (journeyman)	Dur Sherburn House
12809	181r	[ay]	Sunderland Road	John Suggett	hea m	27	coal miner	Dur Gateshead
12810	181r			Elizabeth Suggett	wif m	31		Dur Gateshead
12811	181r			William Suggett	son	11	coal miner	Dur Kelloe
12812	181r			Mary Ann Suggett	dau	7	scholar	Dur Witton Gilbert
12813	181r			John Suggett	son	5	scholar	Dur Kelloe
12814	181r			Hannah Suggett	dau	1		Dur Castle Eden
12815	181r			William Suggett	bro	17	coal miner	Dur Chester-le-Street
12816	181r			Thomas Suggett	bro	13	coal miner	Dur Shildon
12817	181r			Jane Suggett	sis	11	scholar	Dur Lamesley
12818	181r	[az]	Sunderland Road	Robert Mavin	hea m	42	sawyer	Dur [D] S. Oswald
12819	181v			Isabella Mavin	wif m	38		Dur Thornley
12820	181v			James Mavin	son	8	scholar	Dur Houghton-1-Spring
12821	181v			Jane Mavin	dau	5	scholar	Dur Thornley
12822	181v	[ba]	Sunderland Road	John Earle	hea m	57	blacksmith (journeyman)	Dur Wolsingham
12823	181v			Barbara Earle	wif m	63		Dur Pelton
12824	181v			William Earle	son	22	plumber (journeyman)	Dur [D] S. Oswald
12825	181v			Eleanor Earle	dau	13	scholar	Dur [D] S. Margaret
12826	181v			Elizabeth Earle	dau	10	scholar	Dur [D] S. Margaret
12827	181v	[bb]	Sunderland Road	Thomas Mark	hea w	61	rag gatherer	Cul Castle Sowerby
12828	181v			Mary Richardson	nce w	35		Dur Bishop Auckland
12829	181v			Jane Richardson	*	9	scholar	Dur [D] S. Oswald
12830	181v	[bc]	Sunderland Road	Andrew Herring	hea m	29	tailor	Dur Sunderland
12831	181v			Hannah Herring	wif m	24		Dur Sunderland
12832	181v			George Herring	son	4	scholar	Dur Sunderland
12833	181v			Margaret Herring	dau	3	scholar	Dur Sunderland
12834	181v			Isabella Herring	dau	1		Dur [D] S. Giles
12835	181v	[bd]a	Sunderland Road	William Usher	hea m	40	mason (master emp 2 men)	Dur Witton Gilbert
12836	181v			Matilda Usher	wif m	45		Dur Middle'n-Teesdale
12837	181v	[bd]b	Sunderland Road	Hannah Bilton	hea w	66	confectioner	Dur Witton Gilbert
12838	181v			Ann Ogleby	vis w	49	agricultural labr's wid	Dur Brandon
12839	182r	[be]	Sunderland Road	William Charman	hea m	45	shoemaker	Gls
12840	182r			Ann Charman	wif m	41		Dur Durham
12841	182r	[bf]	Sunderland Road	George Watson	hea m	47	coal miner, publican	Dur Chester-le-Street
12842	182r			Ann Watson	wif m	45		Dur Washington
12843	182r			John Watson	son	20	coal miner	Dur Penshaw
12844	182r			George Watson	son	18	coal miner	Dur Penshaw
12845	182r			Mary Watson	dau	15		Dur [D] S. Giles
12846	182r			Hugh Watson	son	12	coal miner	Dur [D] S. Giles
12847	182r			Sarah Watson	dau	9		Dur Shincliffe
12848	182r			Ann Watson	dau	7		Dur Shincliffe
12849	182r			Jane Watson	dau	5		Dur Shincliffe
12850	182r	[bg]	Sunderland Road	William Bozman	hea m	53	coal miner	Dur Great Stainton
12851	182r			Mary Bozman	wif m	43	laundress	Dur Darlington
12852	182r			Ann Armer	dau	13		Dur [D] S. Giles
12853	182r	[bh]	Sunderland Road	James Gilroy	hea m	46	coal miner	Dur Washington
12854	182r			Jane Gilroy	wif m	42		Dur Washington
12855	182r	[bi]	Sunderland Road	Joseph Stephenson	hea m	39	coal miner	Dur Houghton-1-Spring
12856	182r			Ann Stephenson	wif m	43		Nbl Longbenton
12857	182r			Hannah Stephenson	dau	21	dressmaker	Dur Elwick
12858	182r	[bj]	Sunderland Road	John Burn	hea m	42	coal miner	Dur Penshaw

12859	182v	[bj]	Sunderland Road	Mary Burn	wif	m	25		Dur Washington
12860	182v			Elizabeth J. Burn	dau		2		Dur [D] S. Giles
12861	182v	[bk]	Sunderland Road	Dinah Wardle Waters	wif	m	31	coal miner's wife	Dur Stockton
12862	182v			Ann Waters	dau		10		Dur Shincliffe
12863	182v			Dinah Waters	dau		8		Dur Cassop
12864	182v			Mary Waters	dau		6		Dur Wrekenton
12865	182v			William Waters	son		4		Dur Whitworth
12866	182v			Margaret Waters	dau		1		Dur Whitworth
12867	182v	[bl]	Sunderland Road	Jane Watson	wif	m	32	coal miner's wife	Nbl Byker Hill
12868	182v			Matthew Watson	son		6	scholar	Dur [D] Framwelgate
12869	182v			Elizabeth Watson	dau		4	scholar	Dur Bishop Auckland
12870	182v			William Watson	son		2		Dur Crook
12871	182v	[bm]	Sunderland Road	George B. Hall	hea	m	39	coal miner	Nbl Tynemouth
12872	182v			Jane Hall	wif	m	30		Dur Gateshead
12873	182v			John Hall	son		14	coal miner	Dur Coxhoe
12874	182v			Joseph Hall	son		9	scholar	Dur Wynyard
12875	182v			George Hall	son		6	scholar	Nbl Cramlington
12876	182v			Robert Hall	son		4		Dur Wynyard
12877	182v			Elizabeth Hall	dau		2		Dur Pelton Fell
12878	182v	[bn]	Sunderland Road	William Hall	hea	m	36	coal miner	Nbl North Shields
12879	183r			Isabella Hall	wif	m	35		Dur Lamesley
12880	183r			Simpson P. Hall	son		13	coal miner	Dur Easington
12881	183r			Sarah Hall	dau		12		Dur Easington
12882	183r			John Hall	son		10	coal miner	Dur Kelloe
12883	183r			George Hall	son		8	scholar	Dur Kelloe
12884	183r			William Hall	son		6	scholar	Dur Pittington
12885	183r			Mary Ann Hall	dau		3	scholar	Dur Kelloe
12886	183r			Dorothy Hall	dau		1		Dur [D] S. Giles
12887	183r	[aa]	Sherburn Road	Leonard Cundill	hea	m	39	agricultural labourer	Nry Boltby
12888	183r			Maria Cundill	wif	m	38		Nry Yarm
12889	183r	[ab]	Sherburn Road	Elizabeth Maugham	hea	w	64	prop of house and land	Dur [D] S. Nicholas
12890	183r			John Maugham	son	m	24	coal miner	Nbl Longbenton
12891	183r			Margery Maugham	dlw		23		Dur Houghton-1-Spring
12892	183r	[ac]	Sherburn Road	Robert Barnett	hea	m	23	coal miner	Nry West Rounton
12893	183r			Ann Barnett	wif	m	26		Nry Hudswell, Scarcot
12894	183r			Mary Ann Barnett	dau		2		Dur Coundon
12895	183r			Ruth Barnett	dau		11m		Dur [D] S. Oswald
12896	183r	[ad]	Sherburn Road	Thomas Peart	hea	m	29	coal miner	Dur Stanhope
12897	183r			Sarah Peart	wif	m	25		Dur Houghton-1-Spring
12898	183r	[ae]	Sherburn Road	Hannah Oswald	hea	m	49	bootmaker's wife	Dur Durham
12899	183v			Robert Oswald	son		34	bootmaker (master *)	Dur Houghton-1-Spring
12900	183v			John Oswald	son		33	butcher	Dur Houghton-1-Spring
12901	183v			James Oswald	son		32	butcher	Dur Houghton-1-Spring
12902	183v	[af]	Sherburn Road	William Wilson	hea	m	49	platelayer on railway	Ntt Ayer
12903	183v			Alice Wilson	wif	m	51		Dur Darlington
12904	183v	[ag]	Sherburn Road	William Hunter	hea	m	36	tailor	Dur Chester-le-Street
12905	183v			Ann Hunter	wif	m	36		Dur Usworth
12906	183v			Mary J. Hunter	dau		12		Dur Easington
12907	183v			Sarah A. Hunter	dau		3		Dur Leadgate
12908	183v			William B. Hunter	son		9m		Dur Chester-le-Street
12909	183v	[ah]	Sherburn Road	James Reynolds	hea	m	50	coal miner, prop of ho *	Dur [D] Framwelgate
12910	183v			Margaret Reynolds	wif	m	50		Dur [D] Framwelgate
12911	183v			Mary Ann Reynolds	dau		18	dressmaker	Dur Lumley
12912	183v			Margaret Reynolds	dau		14	scholar	Dur [D] S. Giles
12913	183v			Jane Reynolds	dau		12	scholar	Dur [D] S. Giles
12914	183v			William Embleton	vis		16	carrier's son and asst	Dur Fatfield
12915	183v	[ai]	Sherburn Road	Thomas Stark	hea	m	44	engineman on railway	Dur Winlaton
12916	183v			Isabella Stark	wif	m	41		Dur Winlaton
12917	183v			William Stark	son		17	fireman on railway	Dur Winlaton
12918	183v			Thomas Stark	son		15	cleaner on railway	Dur Derwenthaugh
12919	184r			Richard Stark	son		12	scholar	Dur Blaydon
12920	184r			Isabella Stark	dau		10	scholar	Dur Gateshead
12921	184r			John S. Stark	son		5		Dur Blaydon
12922	184r			Joshua Stark	son		5		Dur Blaydon
12923	184r	[aj]	Sherburn Road	Thomas Fisher	hea	m	40	boilersmith	Gls Gloucester
12924	184r			Margaret Fisher	wif	m	30	milliner	Sct
12925	184r			Elizabeth Fisher	dau		10		Dur Gateshead
12926	184r			Isabella Fisher	dau		8	scholar	Dur Gateshead
12927	184r			John Fisher	son		6	scholar	Dur Houghton-1-Spring
12928	184r			Catherine Fisher	dau		2		Dur [D] S. Giles
12929	184r	[ak]a	Sherburn Road	Anthony Reynolds	hea	m	84	proprietor of houses	Dur [D] S. Oswald
12930	184r			Jane Reynolds	wif	m	80		Nry Pickering
12931	184r	[ak]b	Sherburn Road	Mary Johnson	wif	m	48	innkeeper's wife *	Dur Esh
12932	184r			Elizabeth Johnson	dau		20		Dur [D] S. Margaret
12933	184r			Caroline Johnson	dau		12	scholar	Dur [D] S. Giles
12934	184r			Hannah Johnson	dau		11	scholar	Dur [D] S. Giles
12935	184r	[al]	Sherburn Road	Thomas Watson	hea	m	52	agricultural labourer	Dur [D] S. Oswald
12936	184r			Rose Watson	wif	m	53		Dur Bishop Middleham
12937	184r			Thomas Watson	son		24	agricultural labourer	Dur Bishop Middleham
12938	184r			Elizabeth Watson	dau		22		Dur Bishop Middleham
12939	184v			Margaret Watson	dau		16		Dur Bishop Middleham

12940	184v	[al]	Sherburn Road	Ann Watson	dau	14		Dur Bishop Middleham
12941	184v			Mary Ann Watson	gda	3		Dur [D] Framwelgate
12942	184v	[am]	Sherburn Road	James Gilroy	hea m	36	shoemaker (master *)	Irl
12943	184v			Catherine Gilroy	wif m	35		Irl
12944	184v			Thomas Gilroy	son	13	shoemaker (apprentice)	Irl
12945	184v			Mary Gilroy	dau	11	scholar	Irl
12946	184v			John Gilroy	son	7		Dur [D] S. Nicholas
12947	184v			James Gilroy	son	5		Dur [D] S. Giles
12948	184v			Alice McDonnahey	vis	40	agricultural labourer	Irl
12949	184v			Bridget McDonnahey	vis	17	agricultural labourer	Irl
12950	184v			Catherine McCormack	vis m	30	agricultural labr's wife	Irl
12951	184v			Mary McCormack	vis	7		Irl
12952	184v			Patrick McCormack	vis	5		Irl
12953	184v			John McCormack	vis	2		Irl
12954	184v	[an]	Sherburn Road	Lawrence Stakem	ldr m	44	pedlar	Irl
12955	184v			Catherine Stakem	ldw m	36	agricultural labourer	Irl
12956	184v			Patrick Dougharty	ldr m	39	agricultural labourer	Irl
12957	184v			Mary McKeenan	ldr	18	agricultural labourer	Irl
12958	184v	[ao]	Sherburn Road	Eleanor Gilroy	hea w	67		Irl
12959	185r			Mary Gilroy	dau	30	milliner	Irl
12960	185r			Eleanor Gilroy	dau	20	milliner	Irl
12961	185r	[ap]	Sherburn Road	John Emmerson	hea w	62	coal miner	Dur
12962	185r			Sarah J. Emerson	dau	18	bonnetmaker	Dur Hetton
12963	185r	[aq]	Sherburn Road	William Cowell	hea m	27	joiner (journeyman)	Dur Penshaw
12964	185r			Phyllis Cowell	wif m	26		Dur Durham
12965	185r			Ralph Cowell	son	6	scholar	Dur [D] S. Giles
12966	185r			Ann Cowell	dau	4	scholar	Dur Thornley
12967	185r			Thomas Cowell	son	2		Dur [D] S. Oswald
12968	185r			Elizabeth Cowell	dau	1m		Dur [D] S. Giles
12969	185r	[ar]	Sherburn Road	William Armstrong	hea m	38	joiner & enginewright	Dur Jarrow
12970	185r			Ann Armstrong	wif m	33		Dur [D] S. Nicholas
12971	185r			Thomas Armstrong	son	11	scholar	Dur [D] S. Giles
12972	185r			Mary Ann Armstrong	dau	9	scholar	Dur [D] S. Giles
12973	185r			Barbara Armstrong	dau	6	scholar	Dur [D] S. Giles
12974	185r	[as]	Sherburn Road	Jane Bowron	hea w	41	<publican *>	Dur Rainton
12975	185r			William Bowron	son	19	brewer's labourer	Dur Rainton
12976	185r			Jane Bowron	dau	12		Dur Durham
12977	185r			Thomas Bowron	son	9	scholar	Dur Durham
12978	185r			John Bowron	son	7	scholar	Dur Durham
12979	185v			Henry Bowron	son	5	scholar	Dur Durham
12980	185v			Ann Bowron	dau	3		Dur Durham
12981	185v			Hannah Bowron	dau	1		Dur Durham
12982	185v	[at]	Sherburn Road	James Blackburn	hea m	54	engineman at colliery	Dur Chester-le-Street
12983	185v			Elizabeth Blackburn	wif m	34		Dur Hetton-le-Hole
12984	185v			George Michael Blackburn	son	12	scholar	Dur Hetton-le-Hole
12985	185v			James Blackburn	son	8	scholar	Dur Kelloe
12986	185v	[au]	Sherburn Road	Francis Bowman	hea m	27	blacksmith (journeyman)	Dur Wolsingham
12987	185v			Jane Bowman	wif m	22		Dur [D] S. Margaret
12988	185v			Robert H. Bowman	son	2		Dur [D] S. Margaret
12989	185v			Jane Ann Bowman	dau	6m		Dur [D] S. Giles
12990	185v			John Richardson	ldr	30	agricultural labourer	Dur Esh
12991	185v	[av]	Sherburn Road	George Whitelock	hea m	28	brickmaker	Yks York
12992	185v			Mary Ann Whitelock	wif m	22		Dur Hetton
12993	185v			James Robinson	blw	20	tilemaker	Dur Hetton
12994	185v			Elizabeth Golightly	nce	9		Dur Hetton
12995	185v			John Patterson	ldr	52	coal miner	Dur Wingate
12996	185v	[aw]	Sherburn Road	William Elsbury	hea m	49	coal miner	Dur [D] S. Giles
12997	185v			Margaret Elsbury	wif m	45		Dur [D] S. Oswald
12998	185v			William Elsbury	son	20	coal miner	Dur Pittington
12999	186r			James Elsbury	son	15	coal miner	Dur Pittington
13000	186r			Jane Elsbury	dau	12	bonnetmaker's apprentice	Dur [D] S. Margaret
13001	186r			Matthew Elsbury	son	10	scholar	Dur [D] S. Giles
13002	186r			Robert Elsbury	son	7	scholar	Dur [D] Framwelgate
13003	186r	[ax]	Sherburn Road	Richard Ford	hea m	36	coal miner	Lan Ancoats /"Uncote"
13004	186r			Mary Ford	wif m	28		Dur Durham
13005	186r			Robert Ford	son	7	scholar	Dur Durham
13006	186r			James Ford	son	5	scholar	Dur Durham
13007	186r			Jane Ford	dau	3		Dur Durham
13008	186r			Henry Ford	son	1		Dur Durham
13009	186r			Nicholas Ford	vis w	63	coal miner	Lan Clayton
13010	186r	[ay]	Sherburn Road	John Butterfield	hea m	30	cordwainer	Dur Bishop Auckland
13011	186r			Richard Butterfield	son	2		Dur Durham
13012	186r			Ann Butterfield	mth m	50	clogger's wife	Dur Redmarshall
13013	186r	[az]	Sherburn Road	William Fenney	hea m	36	agricultural labourer	Nry Yarm
13014	186r			Hannah Fenney	wif m	34		Nry Skelton
13015	186r			William Fenney	son	13	coal miner	Yks Greatham
13016	186r			Mary Ann Fenney	dau	11	scholar	Dur Durham
13017	186r			John Fenney	son	8	scholar	Dur Sherburn
13018	186r			Elizabeth Jane Fenney	dau	5		Dur Washington
13019	186v			Rosanna Fenny	dau	1		Dur Durham
13020	186v	[ba]	Sherburn Road	John Kidd	hea m	58	farmer of 96a *	Dur Stanhope

13021	186v	[ba]	Sherburn Road	Elizabeth Kidd	wif m	50		Dur Wolsingham
13022	186v			Thomas Kidd	son	11	scholar	Dur Durham
13023	186v	[bb]	Sherburn Road	John Parkinson	hea m	34	hay dealer	Dur Bishopton
13024	186v			Elizabeth Parkinson	wif m	33		Dur Stockton
13025	186v			Ellen Parkinson	dau	9		Dur Durham
13026	186v			John George Parkinson	son	7		Dur Durham
13027	186v			Edmund N. Parkinson	son	5		Dur Durham
13028	186v			Elizabeth C. Parkinson	dau	3		Dur Durham
13029	186v			Robert H. Parkinson	son	1		Dur Durham
13030	186v	[bc]	Sherburn Road	William Brown	hea m	62	horsekeeper at colliery	Dur West Auckland
13031	186v			Mary Brown	wif m	46		Nbl Haltwhistle
13032	186v			William Brown	son	19	solicitor's general clk	Nbl Newcastle
13033	186v			Elizabeth Brown	dau	17		Dur [D] S. Nicholas
13034	186v			Isaac Brown	son	14	blacksmith	Dur [D] S. Nicholas
13035	186v			Thomas H. Brown	son	9	scholar	Dur [D] S. Nicholas
13036	186v			Margaret A. Brown	dau	2		Dur [D] S. Giles
13037	186v	[bd]	Sherburn Road	George Alderson	hea m	43	coal miner	Nry Romaldkirk
13038	186v			Margaret Alderson	wif m	28		Nbl Morpeth
13039	187r			William Alderson	son	14	coal miner	Dur Hebburn
13040	187r			Elizabeth Alderson	dau	13		Dur New Durham
13041	187r			Charles Alderson	son	11	coal miner	Dur [D] S. Nicholas
13042	187r			John Alderson	son	8	scholar	Dur [D] S. Nicholas
13043	187r			Jane Alderson	dau	5	scholar	Dur [D] S. Nicholas
13044	187r			Mary Ann Alderson	dau	2		Dur [D] S. Nicholas
13045	187r			Sarah Alderson	dau	11m		Dur [D] S. Nicholas
13046	187r			Thomas Magee	ldr w	64	overlooker at colliery	Dur [D] S. Oswald
13047	187r			Thomas Richardson	ldr w	58	coal miner	Dur Houghton-l-Spring
13048	187r	[be]	Sherburn Road	Jane Blackburn	hea	54	grocer	Dur Chester-le-Street
13049	187r	[bf]	Sherburn Road	Peter Mitchell	hea m	44	coal miner	ChI Guernsey
13050	187r			Rosanna Mitchell	wif m	38		Sct
13051	187r			Ann Mitchell	dau	14		Sct
13052	187r			Thomas Mitchell	son	8		Cul
13053	187r			Mary Mitchell	dau	7		Dur Chester-le-Street
13054	187r			Margaret Mitchell	dau	5		Dur Easington
13055	187r			Jane Mitchell	dau	2		Dur Pittington
13056	187r	[bg]	Sherburn Road	Thomas Park	hea m	24	coal miner	Dur Darlington
13057	187r			Elizabeth Park	wif m	20		Dur Rainton
13058	187r			Jane Park	dau	1		Dur Durham
13059	187v	[bh]	Sherburn Road	John Bateman	hea m	41	agricultural labourer	Nry Bedale
13060	187v			Jane Bateman	wif m	41		Dur Durham
13061	187v			Michael Bateman	son	12	roper (apprentice)	Wry Denton
13062	187v			William Bateman	son	4	scholar	Dur Shincliffe
13063	187v	[bi]	Sherburn Road	John Adamson	hea m	40	painter & glazier	Dur Durham
13064	187v			Ann Adamson	wif m	39		Dur South Biddick
13065	187v			John Adamson	son	20	fireman at colliery	Dur Shiney Row
13066	187v			Barbara Adamson	dau	12		Dur East Rainton
13067	187v			Elizabeth Adamson	dau	9	scholar	Dur West Rainton
13068	187v			Ann Adamson	dau	7	scholar	Dur West Rainton
13069	187v			Isabella Adamson	dau	4	scholar	Dur West Rainton
13070	187v	[bj]	Sherburn Road	Thomas Robinson	hea	32	butcher (master *)	Dur High Coniscliffe
13071	187v			Elizabeth Robinson	sis	29	dressmaker	Dur High Coniscliffe
13072	187v			William Robinson	bro	24	butcher	Dur Hetton-le-Hole
13073	187v	[bk]	Sherburn Road	William Walker	hea m	74	grocer	Nbl Bywell
13074	187v			Barbara Walker	wif m	64		Dur Lamesley
13075	187v			William Walker	son w	41	guard on railway	Nbl Ovingham
13076	187v	[bl]a	Sherburn Road	Alexander Maughan	hea m	47	shoemaker (master *)	Dur Sherburn
13077	187v			Dinah Maughan	wif m	45		Nbl Benwell
13078	187v			Matthew Maughan	son	18	shoemaker (apprentice)	Nbl Willington
13079	188r			Anthony Maughan	son	14	shoemaker (apprentice)	Dur Houghton-l-Spring
13080	188r	[bl]b	Sherburn Road	Ann Hopper	hea	58	needlewoman	Dur Lamesley
13081	188r	[bl]c	Sherburn Road	Mary Wilkinson	hea	73	annuitant	Nbl Newcastle
13082	188r	[bm]	Sherburn Road	Joseph Elliott	hea m	61	mason (master emp 1 man)	Dur Sherburn
13083	188r			Elizabeth Elliott	wif m	62		Nbl North Shields
13084	188r			John Elliott	son	32	mason	Dur Durham
13085	188r			William Elliott	son	35	mason	Dur Durham
13086	188r	[bn]	Sherburn Road	John Donnahey	hea m	49	innkpr <'Queen's Head'>	Irl
13087	188r			Mary Donnahey	wif m	41		Nry Brompton
13088	188r			Mary Ann Donnahey	dau	19	milliner	Dur [D] S. Giles
13089	188r			James Donnahey	son	18	joiner (apprentice)	Dur [D] S. Giles
13090	188r			Elizabeth Donnahey	dau	16	pupil teacher	Dur [D] S. Giles
13091	188r			Jane Donnahey	dau	14	scholar	Dur [D] S. Giles
13092	188r			Henry Donnahey	son	12	scholar	Dur [D] S. Giles
13093	188r			William Donnahey	son	6	scholar	Dur [D] S. Giles
13094	188r			Thomas Edmund Donnahey	son	4	scholar	Dur [D] S. Giles
13095	188r			Elizabeth Donnahey	mth w	79	agricultural labr's wid	Irl
13096	188r			John Thornton	ldr	27	agricultural labourer	Dur Easington
13097	188r			James Hamilton	ldr m	30	horse dealer	Nry Appleton
13098	188r			William Hamilton	ldr	26	horse dealer	Nbl Tynemouth
13099	188v	[bo]	Sherburn Road	Elizabeth Blenkinsop	hea w	70	grocer	Dur Houghton-l-Spring
13100	188v			Thomas Blenkinsop	son	40	butcher	Dur Penshaw
13101	188v			Isabella Blenkinsop	dau	30		Dur Houghton-l-Spring

13102	188v	[aa]	Milburn Street	John Watson	hea	m	40	miller's labourer	Nbl
13103	188v			Mary Watson	wif	m	35		Dur [D] S. Giles
13104	188v			John Watson	son		9	scholar	Dur Pittington
13105	188v			Elizabeth Watson	dau		7	scholar	Dur Pittington
13106	188v			Robert Watson	son		4	scholar	Dur Pittington
13107	188v	[ab]	Milburn Street	Samuel Agnew	hea	m	64	agricultural labourer	Sct
13108	188v			Hannah Agnew	wif	m	44		Sct
13109	188v	[ac]	Milburn Street	William Bell	hea	m	28	porter at rly station	Nbl East Lilburn
13110	188v			Mary Bell	wif	m	27		Nbl Whittingham
13111	188v			John A. Bell	son		2		Dur [D] S. Giles
13112	188v	[ad]	Milburn Street	Robert Dixon	hea	m	29	mason	Dur Trimdon
13113	188v			Ann Dixon	wif	m	27		Dur Hebburn
13114	188v			Elizabeth Ann Dixon	dau		6m		Dur [D] S. Giles
13115	188v			Mary L. Todd	sis		8	scholar	Dur Hebburn
13116	188v			Robert Thompson	ldr	w	83	pauper (former trade nk)	Dur Evenwood
13117	188v	[ae]	Milburn Street	Thomas Hall	hea	m	35	screenman at colliery	Dur Stockburn
13118	188v			Elizabeth Hall	wif	m	32		Dur Penshaw
13119	189r			Charles Hall	son		9	scholar	Dur Pittington
13120	189r			William Hall	son		7	scholar	Dur Trimdon
13121	189r			Isabella Hall	dau		2		Dur Wolsingham
13122	189r			John J. Hall	son		1m		Dur [D] S. Giles
13123	189r			Margaret Hall	vis		29	needlewoman	Dur Houghton-1-Spring
13124	189r	[af]	Milburn Street	Joseph Scarth	hea	m	36	coal miner	Dur Escomb /"Eskam"
13125	189r			Isabella Scarth	wif	m	38		Dur Penshaw
13126	189r			James Scarth	son		18	coal miner	Dur Lumley
13127	189r			Joseph Scarth	son		13	coal miner	Dur [D] S. Giles
13128	189r			George Scarth	son		10	coal miner	Dur [D] S. Giles
13129	189r			Thomas Scarth	son		8	scholar	Dur [D] S. Giles
13130	189r			Mary Ann Scarth	dau		6	scholar	Dur [D] S. Giles
13131	189r			Isabella Scarth	dau		4	scholar	Dur [D] S. Giles
13132	189r			Elizabeth Scarth	dau		2		Dur [D] S. Giles
13133	189r	[ag]	Milburn Street	Thomas Scorer	hea	m	48	tea dealer (master)	Dur
13134	189r			Mary Scorer	wif	m	49		Nry Gatenby
13135	189r			Hannah Scorer	dau		21		Dur [D] S. Margaret
13136	189r			Thomas Scorer	son		20	screenman at colliery	Dur [D] S. Margaret
13137	189r			Mary Jane Scorer	dau		18		Nry Cleveland
13138	189r			Martin Scorer	son		13	scholar	Nry Middlesbrough
13139	189v			Ann Scorer	dau		11	scholar	Dur [D] S. Margaret
13140	189v			Isabella Scorer	dau		8	scholar	Dur [D] S. Giles
13141	189v			Sarah A. Scorer	dau		3		Dur [D] S. Giles
13142	189v	[ah]	Milburn Street	George Young	hea	m	56	coal miner	Dur Sedgefield
13143	189v			Margaret Young	wif	m	49		Dur Washington
13144	189v			Elizabeth Young	dau		18	dressmaker (apprentice)	Dur Pittington
13145	189v			Robert Young	son		15	coal miner	Dur Pittington
13146	189v			Jane Young	dau		13	scholar	Dur [D] S. Giles
13147	189v			George Young	son		10	scholar	Dur [D] S. Giles
13148	189v			Isabella Young	dau		7	scholar	Dur [D] S. Giles
13149	189v	[ai]	Milburn Street	Joseph Coulterd	hea	m	42	coal miner	Dur Wolsingham
13150	189v			Eleanor Coulterd	wif	m	38		Dur Lanchester
13151	189v			Jane Coulterd	dau		15	scholar	Dur Hamsterley
13152	189v			Joseph Coulterd	son		14	coal miner	Dur Hamsterley
13153	189v			Dorothy Coulterd	dau		10	scholar	Dur Hamsterley
13154	189v			John Coulterd	son		9	scholar	Dur Hamsterley
13155	189v			William Coulterd	son		7	scholar	Dur [D] S. Giles
13156	189v			Eleanor Coulterd	dau		3		Dur [D] S. Giles
13157	189v			John White	vis		1m		Dur Lanchester
13158	189v	[aj]	Milburn Street	John Slack	hea	m	25	coal miner	Nry Arkengarthdale
13159	190r			Elizabeth Slack	wif	m	24		Dur Washington
13160	190r			Margaret Slack	dau		2		Dur [D] S. Giles
13161	190r	[ak]a	Milburn Street	Charles Swan	hea		22	coal miner	Nbl Wallsend
13162	190r	[ak]b	Milburn Street	Charles Scarth	hea	m	34	coal miner	Dur [D] S. Giles
13163	190r			Isabella Scarth	wif	m	34		Dur [D] S. Giles
13164	190r	[al]	Milburn Street	William Cummings	hea		41	attorney at law	Dur Stockton
13165	190r			Mary Mavin	hou		38	[housekeeper]	Dur [D] S. Oswald
13166	190r			William Mavin	*		16	scholar	Dur Middle Rainton
13167	190r			Thomas Mavin	*		12	scholar	Dur Bishopwearmouth
13168	190r			Isabella Mavin	*		10	scholar	Dur [D] S. Oswald
13169	190r	[am]	Milburn Street	John Elliott	hea	m	37	coal miner	Dur Lumley
13170	190r			Elizabeth Elliott	wif	m	38		Dur Sunderland
13171	190r			Joseph Elliott	son		12	coal miner	Dur Thornley
13172	190r			John Elliott	son		10	scholar	Dur South Hetton
13173	190r			Mary A. Elliott	dau		8	scholar	Dur South Hetton
13174	190r			Margaret Elliott	dau		5	scholar	Dur Coxhoe
13175	190r			William Elliott	son		3	scholar	Dur Coxhoe
13176	190r			Thomas Elliott	son		1		Dur Coxhoe
13177	190r	[an]a	Milburn Street	William Robinson	hea		26	shoemaker (journeyman)	Dur Hetton
13178	190r	[an]b	Milburn Street	David Scarth	hea	m	29	shoemaker (master *)	Dur Evenwood
13179	190v			Elizabeth Scarth	wif	m	34		Dur [D] S. Giles
13180	190v			Joseph Scarth	son		1m		Dur [D] S. Giles
13181	190v	[bo]	Sunderland Road	John Lightfoot	hea		23	agricultural labourer *	Dur [D] S. Giles
13182	190v	[ac]	Gilesgate Moor	John Bland	hea	m	51	shoemaker	Sct

13183	190v	[ac]	Gilesgate Moor	Elizabeth Bland	wif m	46		Dur Durham
13184	190v	[bp]	Sherburn Road	William Roberts	hea m	44	brickmaker (journeyman)	Lei Coleorton
13185	190v			Jane Roberts	wif m	43		Lei Coleorton
13186	190v			Thomas Roberts	nep	14	brickmaker (apprentice)	Lei Coleorton
13187	190v			Reuben Abbott	ldr	35	brickmaker's labourer	Lan Manchester *
13188	190v			William Gage	ldr	24	carpenter (journeyman)	Gls Bristol

Notes - Enumeration District 5c

12710	... <'Londonderry Arms'> waggonway-wright	12942	... employing 1 boy
12715-12720	Gilesgate Moor ...	12974	... 'Railway Coach'
12735	... contractor on railway	13020	... (employing 4 men)
12777	... employing 2 men and 2 boys	13070	... employing 1 boy
	<& curled hair>	13076	... employing 2 boys
12784	... (on superannuation list)	13166-13167	housekeeper's son
12829	niece's daughter	13168	housekeeper's daughter
12899	... emp 8 men, 2 apprentices & 1 woman	13178	... employing 2 men
12909	... and land	13181	... (formerly butcher)
12931	<'Railway Tavern'>	13187	county given as "Yorkshire"

PERSONAL NAME INDEX

Composite entries have been created in this index by linking surnames with minor variations; the variations are indicated by bracketed letters, e.g. 'AD(D)AMSON', in this case entries will be found in the main text for 'Adamson' and 'Addamson'.

Second forenames and initials are ignored.

Surname	Forename	Numbers
ABBOTT	Reuben	13187
ABEL	Henry	**2495**
ACKROYD	Anne	9716
	Elizabeth	9717
	George	9718
	Joseph	9416
	Mary	9719
	Robert	9713
	Sarah	9714 9715
ADAM	Alice	12428
	George	7994
	James	7996
	Jane	7995
	Ralph	12427
AD(D)AMSON	Alice	10066
	Ann	6757 9189 13064 13068
	Barbara	1652 13066
	Eleanor	4182
	Elizabeth	6131 10070 13067
	Emmerson	10065
	George	10067
	Hannah	10069
	Isabella	13069
	James	1618
	Jane	3348 4180 4653 9112
	John	2049 4181 13063 13065
	Margaret	1619 1620 3350 4179
	Mary	1653 4652
	Robert	3347
	Thomas	3349 6130 10068
	William	1623 4654 6756
ADDIMSON	Margaret	5287
	William	5286
ADDISON	Charles	1411
	Mary	1409 1410
AGNEW	Hannah	13108
	Samuel	13107
A(I)NSLEY	Edward	4154
	Elizabeth	4151 9546 9547
	Ellen	9550
	Hannah	3536 4152
	Henry	4153
	John	3535 9551
	Mary	9549
	William	3900 4975 5822 9545 9548
AIRD	John	12339
AKENHEAD	Elizabeth	4818
ALCOCK	Barbara	4761
	George	4757 4759
	Mary	4758 4762
	William	4760
ALDERSON	Catherine	8477
	Charles	13041
	Elizabeth	4072 6612 7367 8043 13040
	George	1020 5996 5998 6613 8045 13037
	Jane	4070 6611 13043
	John	6615 8039 8042 13042
	Margaret	873 5997 13038
	Maria	8044
	Mary	1022 4074 8040 8041 13044
	Richard	4075
	Robert	1021 7187
	Sarah	13045
	Thomas	4071 6610 6614
	William	4073 6616 13039
ALEXANDER	Isabella	10654
	Richard	10655
	William	10653
ALLAN	Andrew	11610
	Ann	442 3212 11769
	George	3294 3296
Allan	Isabella	3295 3299
	James	443
	John	444 3211 3215 3297 8449
	Joseph	3298
	Mary	2152 3213
	Robert	3301
	Samuel	3216
	Thomas	3300
	William	441 3214
ALLANBY	Jane	8909
	Margaret	8904
	Mary	8908
	Michael	8903
	Robert	8901 8907
	Sarah	8902
	Thomas	8905
	William	8906
ALLEN	Ann	6316
	Hannah	4049 4053
	James	4048
	Jane	6317
	Margaret	4050
	Mary	4052
	Thomas	4051
	William	3945
ALLISON	Ann	11449 11766
	Edward	4172
	Elizabeth	4173 11461
	George	1049
	Harrison	11539
	Henry	11765
	Isabella	11460
	John	8819
	Joseph	4174
	Louisa	4168 4170
	Margaret	11540
	Mary	4171
	Matthew	4169
	Robert	11448 11450
	William	11451 11767
ALMOND	Edward	6534
	Jane	6533 6536
	Nicholas	6535
	Robert	6532 6537
AMPLEBY	Jane	6804
ANDERSON	Agnes	11852
	Alice	7585
	Ann	8341 10074
	Catherine	10075
	Charles	67 69
	David	6663 8101
	Edward	10155
	Eleanor	7586
	Elizabeth	1388 5125 6963 7071 8609
	Emmerson	3154
	Frances	10076
	George	10072 10077 11119
	Hannah	6662
	Jacob	11115
	James	10831
	Jane	143 8239 9203 10919
	Jean	11227
	John	8607 8610 10663 11118
	Joseph	11225 11853
	Margaret	1773 3155 9204 11226
	Mary	68 70 8236 8253 8608 10073 10832 11116 11854
	Matthew	10918
	Robert	8238 10920
	Sarah	8237
	Thomas	1387 8235 8250 8252 8611 11117

Surname	Forename	Numbers
BAILES	Ann(e)	3423 7960
	Elizabeth	9654 9657 12326
	George	9650 9652 9813 12324
	Isabella	7673
	Jane	589 12328
	John	9811 12320 12323 12329
	Margaret	9655 12321 12322
	Maria	3425
	Mary	7959 9651 9809 9814 12325
	Michael	7958 9656 9812
	Samuel	3424
	Sarah	7961 11180
	Thomas	588 9653 9808 9810
	William	3713 12327
BAILEY	Barbara	5127
	Elizabeth	10867
	Sarah	3645
BAINBRIDGE	Ann	4550
	Caroline	2270
	Catherine	2703
	Charles	2704
	Edwin	596
	Eleanor	9510
	Elizabeth	592 2166 7447 10900
	Frederick	593
	George	2701
	Georgina	2271
	James	594
	Jane	595 2165 7542
	John	2269 9511
	Margaret	2164 2168 9895
	Mary	2167 2702 2706 4552 8982 9509
	Ralph	2163
	Robert	4551
	Susanna	2705
	Thomas	8 2267 2268
	William	1385
BAINES	Elizabeth	6032
	John	9217
BAIT	William	9218
BAITSON	Ann	3251
	John	3250
BAKER	Elizabeth	5780 10607
	George	10608
	Hannah	10603 12343
	Henry	10606
	Isabella	12348
	Jane	12347
	Margaret	164 12191 12346
	Mary	12344
	Robert	10602 10605
	Rosanna	10505
	Thomas	12345
	William	10500 10604 12342 12349
BALL	Elizabeth	4230
	George	4228
	Jane	4229
	John	4232
	Maria	4231
	William	3824
BALLAN	Laura	11295
	Peter	9471
	Sarah	11296
	Thomas	11294
BALMBROUGH	Eleanor	10149
	John	10148
	Robert	2909
BAMBOROUGH	Ann	10161
BAMLET	John	6051
	Mary	6048
BAND	Elizabeth	2192
BANKS	John	6173
	Stephen	11955
BANNISTER	James	966
	Joseph	12785 12787
	Mary	12786
BANTER	Elizabeth	7905
BARBER	Ann	8769
	John	8770
BARCLAY	Eliza	7275
Barclay	William	7198
BARKAS	William	2708
BARKER	Joseph	1029
	Mary	1030 3686 5120
	Robert	7259
	Thomas	5423
	William	1031
BARLOW	Dinah	2311
	Edward	2314
	George	2315
	Henry	2312
	James	2310 2313 2316
BARNES	Ann	3016 4992
	Edwin	3019
	Eliza	3018
	George	3017
	John	1036 12784
	Mary	1034 1037 1039
	Richard	1035
	Robert	3015
	William	1033
BARNETT	Ann	12893
	Isabella	9036
	Mary	12894
	Robert	12892
	Ruth	12895
	Thomas	9035
BARNY	Hannah	9431
	John	9430
BARRAS(S)	Ann	7329
	Catherine	12611
	Edward	12613
	Elizabeth	6593 12612
	Euretta	12609
	John	12614
	Mary	12610
	Thomas	12608
	William	6592
BARRET(T)	James	2625
	John	2069
	Margaret	2627
	Mary	2626
BARRON	Ann	488 495 498 8638 86 10959
	Ellen	6665
	Hannah	12791 12792
	Isabella	492
	Jane	484 493
	John	494 496 8643
	Margaret	490
	Mary	491 497 500 8641
	Matthew	487 489 8644
	Sarah	499
	Susanna	8642
	Thomas	8645
	William	7119 8637 8640
BARROWFORD	John	2341
BARTON	Charles	3692
BARTRAM	Agnes	10166
	Daniel	10163
	Mary	10164
	Nicholas	10167
	Thomas	10165
BASTER	Eliza	12604
BATEMAN	Jane	13060
	John	9634 13059
	Margaret	9633
	Michael	13061
	William	13062
BATES	Catherine	12220
	Henry	6877 6881
	Jane	6878 6879 12221
	John	12222
	Margaret	6880
	Martha	6882
	Walter	7082
	William	12219
BAT(E)SON	Ann	3255
	Jane	3253
	Margaret	3252 3885
	Mary	3256

Surname	Name	Numbers
Broadley	Mary	9705
	William	9704
BRODIE	Isabel	6337
	Jane	8128
	William	8127
BRODRICK	Robert	4506
BROGDEN	Frances	11221
	Henry	11235
	Jane	11236
	John	11237
BROOKS	Alice	12574
	Harrietta	8854
	Thomas	7236
BROOKSBANK	Ann	7476
	James	7475
	Katherine	7478
	Walter	7477
BROTHERTON	Henry	7083
	Isabella	904
	John	903
BROTTEN	Ann	9577
	William	9576
BROUGH	Elizabeth	3573
	Martha	3572
BROWN	Abraham	6228
	Alice	413 8873
	Ann(e)	2677 2944 2947 5871 6223 9194 9401 10464
	Anthony	2676 7573
	Barbara	10121 10951
	Bartholomew	8234
	Caroline	9229
	Catherine	3530 7324
	Charles	5841
	Christian	4971
	Christopher	1081
	Elizabeth	2675 3412 5840 5870 6229 8872 8874 10952 11273 13033
	Ellen	5223
	Forster	5606
	George	2943 3529 3680 4598 5866 5872 8254
	Hannah	1082 3032 3055 6700 9192
	Henry	2062 10545
	Isaac	13034
	Isabella	412 10463 11957 12131
	James	6699
	Jane	3316 4077 4599 5867 8256 12616
	Joanna	12615
	John	684 2674 2854 8066 8068 8818 9193 9399 11838 12132
	Joseph	4082 4595
	Margaret	435 2946 3681 8489 10466 10953 12403 13036
	Maria	4596
	Martin	10468
	Mary	410 434 532 2678 2945 3929 5842 7040 8050 8067 8255 8257 8258 9196 9568 11834 11892 13031
	Matthew	10950 11837
	Patrick	11303
	Phyllis	5868
	Robert	409 411 3315 5843 10542 10543 11839
	Sarah	8261 12008 12402
	Smith	12404
	Thomas	4597 5869 8488 8870 9400 10467 10544 11621 11835 12007 12130 12401 13035
	William	433 436 1305 3160 3413 5607 6222 9191 9195 10120 10465 11836 13030 13032
BROWNING	Ann	11725
	Henry	11724
BROWNLESS	George	1502
	Henry	1503
	Joseph	1499
	Margaret	1500
BROWNRIGG	Diana	703
Brownrigg	John	8648
	Margaret	8647
	William	8649
BRUCE	William	7165
BRUNNING	Isabella	7054
BRY(N)AN	Bryan	5393
	William	7823
BRYCE	John	7457
BRYDON	Mary	10281
	Robert	2366
	Susanna	2367
	William	2368
BUCKLEY	Elizabeth	10852
	Jane	10853
	John	10850
	Mary	10851
BUDDLE	Ann	1710
	Charles	1709
	Margaret	6311 10770
	Matthew	10769
	Thomas	6310
BULLARD	Rachael	5072
BULMER	Ann(e)	7318 9377 11268 11595
	Elizabeth	6860 11265 11594
	Frances	6604
	Frederick	10780
	Hannah	5256
	Jane	4911 9520 11269
	John	1401 11264 11267
	Margaret	4905
	Ralph	3800
	Thomas	6859 9379 11270 11593
	William	1400 11266
BUNGAY	Mildred	12694
	Thomas	12693
BUNGEY	John	12171
	Sarah	12172
BURDISS	Ann	11538
	Barbara	11536
	John	11535 11537
BURDON	Alice	9110
	Ann(e)	9105 9109
	Ellen	11762
	Fanny	11761
	George	9104
	Jane	7328 11760
	John	11757
	Margaret	5226
	Mary	6564 9106 11758 11759
	Matthew	9107
	Thomas	9108
BURK(E)	Ann	4308
	Bridget	149 4307
	Edward	150 4312
	Harry	4309
	Margaret	4310
	Thomas	4311
BURLINSON	Andrew	6594
	Anne	8342 8344
	Clement	8343
	Cuthbert	6597
	Elizabeth	11913
	Fanny	11141
	George	11138
	Jane	5621 11140
	John	6596 11912
	Joseph	3791
	Margaret	6599
	Mary	6595 6600 11139
	Robert	6598
BURNELL	Amelia	11665 11666
	Elizabeth	11555 11556
	Emma	10997
	Frances	3569
	Jane	10995
	John	11554
	Joseph	10994
	Sarah	11667
	Thomas	10996
BURNETT	Agnes	6367
	Anthony	11033

Surname	Forename	Numbers
CHERRY	Eleanor	1341 1342
	Obadiah	1343
	William	1344
CHEVALLIER	Charles	7358
CHICKEN	Ann	1307 1308
	Eleanor	2083
	Henry	1306 2084
	John	2085
	William	2082
CHICKIN	John	2016
	Mary	2014 2015
CHILD	Alice	10515
	Anna	11487
	Charlotte	11489
	Ellen	6123
	Fanny	11490
	Frederick	6117
	Hannah	10516
	Harriet	6119
	John	10514
	Margaret	6118 6121 11483
	Mark	11484
	Sarah	6122
	Sophia	6120
	Thomas	11486 11488
	William	11482
CHILTON	Ann	5863 11502
	Mary	4148
	Thomas	5865 11505
	William	5864
CHISMAN	Anne	8419
	Charlotte	9737
	Elizabeth	9736
	Ellen	8422
	Fanny	8421
	John	8416 8420
	Lucy	8418
	Sarah	8417 9738
CHRISHOP	Abraham	1602
	Dorothy	1600
	Elizabeth	1601
CHRISTIE	William	7129
CHRISTOPHER	Catherine	11812
	Elizabeth	11815
	Frances	11814
	Margaret	1984 11813
	Richard	1983 1985 11811
CHRISTY	Catherine	5569
	Ellen	5567
	Henry	5564
	Isabel	5566
	Margaret	5565
	Sarah	5568
CHURCHILL	Mary	12435
	Michael	12434
CIDERO	Ralph	8226
CLAIG	Jane	7039
CLAMP	Jane	1281
	John	1283
	Thomas	1280 1282
	William	1284
CLAPPERTON	Jane	1776
CLARK(E)	Agnes	9862
	Alice	3014
	Amelia	9859
	Ann(e)	3009 4456 5492 8194 9855 9926
	Barbara	3013
	Brian	4457
	Charlotte	12718
	Christopher	8193
	David	4351
	Dennis	4455
	Eleanor	9958 10701
	Elizabeth	4352 6738 9857 12120 12302
	Emma/Emmy	3012 9856
	Frances	1814 2394 9861
	George	10657
	Henry	2395
	Isabella	252 7623
	James	681 1443 1816 8065 10662
Clark(e)	Jane	3011 8032 9665 9854 10661
	John	5419 7108 9858 10698 11015 12717
	Joseph	7681
	Margaret	1173 3010 8196 9318 10659 10696 10700 12716
	Mary	7499 9924 10658 10697 12121
	Matilda	4233
	Matthew	9957
	Michael	4458
	Owen	12012
	Peter	1813 1815
	Robert	2396 7204 10384
	Sarah	9860 10699 11016 12124
	Stephen	4459
	Thomas(in)	1611 2055 3008 8195 9923 9956 12715
	William	2393 6737 7903 8916 9317 9853 9925 10660 10695
CLARKSON	Elizabeth	1785
CLASPER	Ann	3282
	John	3283
	Robert	1780
CLAYTON	Margaret	4004
	Maria	4003
	Richard	4002
CLEMISHAW	William	6406
CLEMMENT	Ellen	5955
CLENNELL	Elizabeth	250
	Ellen	248
	Frances	249
CLIFT	Sarah	11032
CLIFTON	Catherine	1639
	James	1640
	John	5221
	Mary	1641
	William	1638
CLUES	Ann	7671
CLYNE	Catherine	373
COATES	Ann	7277
	George	6202 6207
	Isabella	5914 5917
	Jane	5915
	John	3636 5520 7106
	Lucy	5521
	Mabel	3637
	Margaret	6204
	Ralph	6203 6208
	Susanna	6205
	Thomas	5913 5916 6201
	William	6206
COCHRANE	Catherine	8060
	Elizabeth	341
	Frances	345
	James	1289
	Jane	342
	John	8861
	Mary	343 8059 8061 8860
	Thomas	344 8058
	William	8859 8862
COCHRANT	John	3689
COCKBURN	Catherine	3144
	Christopher	10387
	Ellen	3142 6231
	Emma	1013
	George	3141 3143 7092
	Isabella	3145
	Jane	1010 5877
	John	1011 1327 3146
	Margaret	1008
	Mary	294
	Richard	1012
	Thomas	1326
	William	1009
COCKILL	Arabella	7880
	Elizabeth	7879
	Joseph	7881
	Martha	7877
	Timothy	7878
COCKS	Hannah	7508
CODEY	Thomas	11976

Surname	Name	Numbers
COLE	Mary	7053
COLEMAN	Bridget	4554
	George	4553
	Michael	4556
	Thomas	4555
COLLEGE	Teasdale	7087
COLLING	Elizabeth	9688
	Jane	6089
	Joseph	6087 7073
	Rosalie	6088
	Sarah	6086
COLLINGWOOD	Joshua	6857
	Mary	6855 6856
COLLINSON	Ann	9999
	Elizabeth	12542
	Jane	1333 1334
	John	1332
	Margaret	508 1337
	Mary	507 1335
	Sarah	1336
	Walter	690
COLLON	George	6036
COLPITTS	Anne	337
	Elizabeth	336
	James	332 334
	Jane	4690
	John	10 335
	Mary	11 333 4689
	Thomas	4688
CO(U)LTMAN	Ann	7832 12118
	Camilla	10614
	Eleanor	12113
	Elizabeth	10598 10610 12115
	Isabella	12112
	Jane	12110 12114
	John	12109 12116
	Margaret	10615 12117
	Mary	10612 12111
	Richard	10597
	Robert	10611
	Sarah	12119
	Thomas	10613
	William	10609 10616
COMMONS	Patrick	5382
COMPTON	Digby	7727
CONDON	Elizabeth	11176
	Hannah	3442 3443
	Hugh	11175
	William	11177
CONLIN	Bridget	8091
	Hugh	8090
	James	8093
	Mary	8092
CONN	Ann	3033
	Margaret	10212
	Martha	5208 5209
	William	5210
CONNARS	Catherine	3432
	Maurice	3431
CONNEL	Ann	4585
	Catherine	4581 4584
	Martin	4583
	Mary	4582
CONNER	Catherine	5362
	Elizabeth	4738
	Esther	10084
	Joseph	10085
	Thomas	10799
CONOLLY	Peter	12011
CONROY	Ellen	1765
	James	1767
	Thomas	1768
	William	1766
COOK(E)	Ann	6404 8357 10887
	Charles	9356
	Elizabeth	9354 11964
	Frances	5990
	James	10499 11962 12021
	Jane	11960
	John	4461 6694 9355
	Lane	9394
Cook(e)	Margaret	4823 11959
	Maria	7690
	Mary	5988 11961
	Robert	9353
	Thomas	9357 11958
	William	5989
COOPER	Catherine	6641
	Dennis	7093
	Elizabeth	6642
	Jonathan	9092
	Rebecca	9113
	Septimus	3933
	Thomas	6640
COPELAND	John	9016
	Mary	9018
	Sarah	9017
COPLIN	William	11124
CORNER	Jane	5930
	Richard	5426
CORNEY	James	2530
CORNFORTH	Ann	13
	Edward	1940
	George	1517 1521 2799 2800
	Henry	1519
	Jane	1518 1941 2798
	John	1942
	Louisa	2128
	Mary	1520 2129
	Thomas	2127
CORNWALL	Ann	3605
	John	3606
	Margaret	3603
	Mary	3604
	Sarah	3601 3607
	William	3600 3602
CORP	Elizabeth	7683
CORY	Emily	7566 7569
	John	7565
	Mary	7568
	Robert	7567
COULSON	Ann	3759 11795
	Elizabeth	12284
	George	9010
	Harry	9015
	Isabella	3760
	Jane	11793
	Joseph	9013
	Margaret	9014
	Mary	5367 9011 10361
	Richard	9012
	Robert	11794
	William	11792
COULTERD	Dorothy	13153
	Eleanor	13150 13156
	Jane	13151
	John	13154
	Joseph	13149 13152
	William	13155
COU(L)THARD	Eliza	8745
	Thomas	12411
	William	633
COULTON	Joseph	8369
COUSIN	John	2927
COUTLEY	Mary	10688
COVERDALE	Hannah	8594
	Mary	8595
COWANS	Ann	9396 9523
	Harriet	9524
	Mary	11007
	Michael	9522 11006
	Robert	6050
COWARD	Edward	8467
	Elizabeth	8464
	George	8463 9872
	Henry	8468
	John	8466
	Susanna	8465
COWE	Theophas	1880
COWELL	Ann	12966
	Elizabeth	12968
	Phyllis	12964

Cowell	Ralph	12965			
	Thomas	12967			
	William	8364	12963		
COWEN(S)	Cecelies	175			
	Eliza(beth)	179	2558		
	Isabella	177			
	James	2559			
	John	83	2557	2561	
	Johnson	9182			
	Mary	84	2560		
	Sarah	176			
	William	174	178	2562	
COWEY	Ann	9630			
	Margaret	11598			
	Mary	4262			
COW(E)L	Ann	7601			
	Elizabeth	7892			
	George	7891			
COWLEY	Catherine	3427			
	Daniel	2956			
	James	2959	3426		
	Jane	2620			
	John	3429			
	Martha	2957			
	William	2958	3428		
COWSICK	Richard	11888			
COX	James	2381			
	Jane	4305	7927		
	John	7928			
	Mary	2380			
	Michael	4306			
	Sarah	7930			
	William	7926	7929	7931	
COXON	Anne	3062			
	Elizabeth	8794			
	George	352	1249	3059	
	Isaac	7344			
	Jane	3060			
	Mary	1247	10162		
	Thomas	1246	1248		
	William	1250			
CRAGGS	Ann	1699	3848		
	Elizabeth	9305	10564	11274	11468
	George	3847	9974		
	Henry	9306			
	James	1698	5585		
	John	1700	5588		
	Margaret	3846	5590		
	Mary	5584	5589		
	Matthew	3845	5587		
	Ralph	530			
	William	5586	6309	8653	
CRAIG(E)	Hannah	2605			
	Jane	8627	8995		
	John	8994			
	Mary	2337	2604	2606	
	William	8996			
CRAM(P)TON	Christopher	3069			
	Eleanor	528			
	Ellen	11052			
	James	527			
	Jane	11050			
	Margaret	11051			
	Thomas	6811	11049		
CRANNY	Thomas	4474			
CRANSTO(U)N	Nicholas	7166			
	Robert	5623			
CRASSWELL	Mary	9815			
CRAVEN	Alonzo	8522			
	Elijah	8519			
	Hannah	8521			
	Sarah	8520			
CRAWFORD	Ann	8674	8679		
	Henry	8676			
	Jane	7461			
	Margaret	8680			
	Mary	8677			
	Sarah	8678			
	William	8675			
CRAWHALL	Anthony	5425			
	John	5424			
CRESSWELL	Ann	12481			
	Caroline	12482			
	George	12480			
	Jane	12484			
	Sarah	12483			
CRICHTON	Peter	7417			
CRICKSHANK	Ann	3634			
	Edward	3633			
	Elizabeth	3635			
CROFT	Edward	7356			
CROFTON	Alice	11272			
	Robert	11271			
CROMWELL	John	11600			
CRONAN	Mary	6716			
CROOKS	Jane	7540			
CROSBY	Ann	12788			
	George	9623			
CROSS	George	3690			
CROSSLING	Ann	3850			
	John	3849			
CROSSMAN	Thomas	10958			
CROW(E)	Barbara	1156			
	Catherine	8555			
	John	4463			
	Margaret	4464			
	Mary	11615			
	William	8554			
CROWES	Mary	842			
CROWTHER	Mary	8455			
	Thomas	8454			
CROZIER	Ann	379			
	Charles	380			
	James	378			
CRUDASS	Barbara	8672			
	Margaret	8673			
	Robert	8671			
CRUDDAS	Ellen	9611			
	Henry	9610			
	Jane	9609			
	John	9608			
CRUDON	Richard	4560			
CUBIT	Bridget	9275			
	Joanna	9274			
	Patrick	9273			
CUMMING	Harriet	4295			
	Jane	4296			
	Joseph	4294			
	Margaret	4297			
	William	4298			
CUMMIN(G)S	Alice	3083			
	Ann	11720			
	Charlotte	6768			
	Elizabeth	2662	6341	10366	
	Ellen	7052	12139		
	Esther	11213			
	Francis	6766			
	George	3082	9959		
	Hannah	948			
	James	6409	11212	12617	
	Jane	2276	3084	6767	12137 12140 12734
	John	2280	10368	12141	12733
	Joseph	3087			
	Julia	2278			
	Margaret	611	2279	3085	6410 9960
	Mary	950	7394	11719	12142 12618
	Robert	2275	11214	11718	
	Sarah	2282			
	Thomas	2277	10367	12136	12138
	William	610	947	949	2281 3086 6340 8748 11721 13164
CUNDILL	John	1151	1153		
	Leonard	12887			
	Maria	12888			
	Mary	1152			
CUNNEEN	Mary	4876			
CUNNINGHAM	Ann	11054			
	Hannah	11055			
	Henry	11053	11056		
	John	11057			
	Mary	11058			

Surname	Name	Numbers
DIAL	Hannah	1538
	Isabella	1540
	Joseph	1317
	Mary	1316 1541
	Michael	1539
DICKENS	John	7783
	Mary	7781
	Sarah	7782
	Thomas	7780
DICKENSON	Hannah	8993
	Luke	8992
DICKI(N)SON	Ann(e)	1267 2489
	Charles	376
	Elizabeth	3892
	Isabella	7011
	John	6255 7012
	Joseph	639 3891
	Mary	375 6256
	Thomas	374 2490 10382
	William	10033
DICKMAN	Anne	5619
DICKSON	Agatha	4995
	Edwin	10836
	Elizabeth	276
	Frances	4994
	John	4993
	Maria	10834
	Mary	4996
	Sarah	10835
DIGHTER	Catherine	698
DINNING(S)	Roger	7240
	Rosanna	7050
DINSEY	Catherine	4332
	Francis	4331
	Margaret	4330
	Mary	4329
DITCHBURN	Ann	10563
	Elizabeth	10560 10732
	George	10731
	John	10559 10562
	Thomas	10561
	William	7079
DIVINE	Ann	1380
	Catherine	1381
	Charles	4404
	Elizabeth	1382
	Frances	4405
	Henry	4406
	Laurence	1384
	Michael	1379
	Peter	1383
	William	4407
DIXON	Agnes	1694
	Alexander	1696
	Ann(e)	94 855 1926 3389 8375 9440 9507 10356 13113
	Ashton	859
	Charlotte	858
	Dorothy	478
	Eliza(beth)	3127 3194 9426 9537 10195 10415 12751 13114
	Frances	3078
	George	856 8768 9591 9593 10414
	Hannah	477
	Isabella	12746 12750
	Jane	93 8373
	Jessie	1695
	John(son)	1693 3126 3128 8376 10079 11114 12340 12745 12748
	Joseph	956 11112
	Kate	857
	Luke	3560
	Major	1925
	Margaret	3388 7289 10412
	Mary	11113 12749
	Ralph	7777
	Richard	8372 8374
	Robert	8377 9594 10413 10416 13112
	Samuel	8378
	Sarah	6675
	Solomon	3129
Dixon	Susanna	9592
	Thomas	3387
	William	1697 9595 12747
DOBBIE	Mary	11768
DOB(I)SON	Eleanor	8567
	Elizabeth	5246 6445
	James	2660
	John	8569 12281
	Mary	8568 9220
	Tamar	7971
	Thomas	7970
DOBY	William	12589
DOCHERTY	Hugh	8121
	John	8118 8120
	Margaret	8119
	William	8122
DODD(S)	Ann(ie)	506 5754 6798 11479
	Barbara	6797
	Catherine	7064
	Charles	913
	Edward	4238 4241 6135 6795 11481
	Eleanor	6943
	Elizabeth	4239 4244 5755 5851 5854 6796 6799
	George	1597 5751 5756 12773
	Henry	28 503 4242 5415
	Isabel(la)	504 912 5853 6801
	James	6800
	Jane	914 3819 5752 5787 5855 7672
	John	4246 6755 6944 11478 11480
	Joseph	3815 5850 5852
	Martha	6941
	Mary	1598 5786 5788 11711 12575
	Matthew	1772
	Michael	7802
	Richard	849 6945
	Robert	3816 3818 5757 6940 6942
	Sarah	1771 6754
	Thomas(ine)	505 3817 4240 5753 5785 5789 6753
	Ursula	7455
	William	4243
	Wilson	4245
DODSWORTH	Catherine	131
	Isabella	130
	John	132
	Thomas	129
DO(G)HERTY	Bridget	9277
	James	9096
	Jane	9094
	Janet	9095
	John	9093 9098
	Robert	9097
DOINNIN	Archibald	9075
	Elizabeth	9077
	Jane	9076
DONALD	Ann	10245
DONALDSON	Elizabeth	1731
	Mary	1730
DONERN	Bernard	5247
DONKING	Elizabeth	6969
	Jane	6966
	Joseph	6970
	Margaret	6965 6968
	Thomas	6964 6967
DONLEY	Thomas	8758
DONNAHEY	Elizabeth	13090 13095
	Henry	13092
	James	13089
	Jane	13091
	John	13086
	Mary	13087 13088
	Thomas	13094
	William	13093
DONNALL(E)Y	Edward	6851
	Mary	6852
DONNISON	Isabella	4220
	John	4219 7592
DORVELL	Fanny	7813
	Janet	7814

Dorvell	Margaret	7812			
DOUGHARTY	Patrick	12956			
DOUGLAS(S)	Abraham	2862			
	Adelaide	7659			
	Alexander	7716			
	Charles	6284	6286		
	Dorothy	2863			
	Eleanor	7652			
	Elizabeth	7655			
	Ellen	945	7653		
	Emily	7658			
	Emma	979			
	George	944			
	Hannah	6285			
	Helen	2866			
	Henry	2760	2761	7651	
	Isabella	6189	6496		
	James	6186	7657	12310	
	Jane	981	7654	8927	
	John	6185	8072	12306	
	Jonathan	6866			
	Judith	2759			
	Lucy	7656			
	Margaret	6287	12307		
	Mary	946	2865	6184	6187 12309
	Phoebe	12308			
	Robert	978			
	Thomas	3293	6183	6188	
	William	980	2864	12311	
DOULEY	Eleanor	5833			
	John	2327			
DOUTHWAITE	Ann	761			
	Anthony	754	760		
	Edward	744			
	Esther	745			
	James	746			
	Jane	755	759		
	Margaret	758			
	Mary	756			
	William	757			
DOWNS	Amelia	9646			
	Jemima	9648			
	John	9645	9647		
	Patrick	3430			
DOWS(E)Y	Margaret	6740			
	Mary	9644			
DOWSON	Ann	7005	7006		
	Anthony	6997			
	Benjamin	6913			
	Elizabeth	7000			
	James	6845			
	Jane	6847			
	John	7004			
	Margaret	6846			
	Mary	6914	6915	7002	
	Matthew	6844			
	Rebecca	6998	7003		
	Robinson	1580			
	William	7007			
DOYLE	Hannah	2948			
	William	3930			
DRAGHORN	Margaret	10587			
DRAKE	Sarah	9980			
DRUM	Ann	11301			
	Mary	11302			
	Patrick	11300			
DRUMMOND	Annetta	11579			
	Elizabeth	7686			
	Hannah	7737			
	Margaret	7635			
DRYDEN	John	6429			
	Joseph	6425	6430		
	Margaret	6428			
	Mary	10050			
	Robert	6427			
	Susanna	6426			
	Thomas	6431	10049		
DRYSDALE	Helen	1663	1666		
	Margaret	1664			
	Robert	1662			
	Thomas	1665			

DUFFY	Ann	3137			
	Hugh	3135	3140		
	James	4411			
	Jane	3136			
	John	3139			
	Mary	11972			
	Patrick	4413			
	William	3138			
DUIDZEL	Chapman	8095			
DUNBAR	James	7253			
	Sarah	7027			
DUNCAN	Ann(ie)	7872	11372		
	Elizabeth	7866			
	Emma	7873			
	Henry	7870	11373		
	James	11374			
	John	7867			
	Jonathan	11371			
	Marianne	7871			
	Sarah	2050	7865	7869	
	William	7864	7868		
DUNLAY	Anthony	5372			
	James	5376			
	Mary	5370	5375	5377	
	Michael	5371	5374		
	Patrick	5373			
	Thomas	5369			
DUNLEARY	Bridget	4409			
	Patrick	4408			
DUNN	Ann	9153			
	Catherine	10343			
	Elizabeth	10317			
	Ellen	10320			
	Harriet	9908			
	Isabella	10344	11740		
	James	10318			
	Jane	8539	9151	10315 10316	
	John	9147	9149		
	Margaret	9148			
	Maria	10319			
	Mary	4691	9150		
	Thomas	6708	9152		
	William	10314	10342		
DURHAM	Lucy	1045			
	Thomas	1044			
DYCE	Margaret	5023			
DYKES	Elizabeth	3048			
	William	3047			
EALES	Hannah	9365			
	Jane	11880			
	John	11864			
	Margaret	11865			
	Matthew	11879	11881		
EARLE	Ann	12318			
	Barbara	12823			
	Eleanor	12825			
	Elizabeth	12826			
	Jane	12317			
	John	12822			
	Thomas	12316			
	William	12824			
EASBY	Henry	5097			
	Jane	9488			
	Margaret	7472	9485		
	Robert	9486			
	Sarah	9487			
EBDON	Thomas	8500			
EBDY	Ann(e)	12800	12804		
	Barron	12779			
	Charles	8409	12777		
	Charlotte	8413			
	Edmund	12803	12805		
	Eliza	8414			
	Henrietta	8410			
	Henry	8411			
	Jane	12778			
	John	377	12799	12802	
	Joseph	12781			
	Louisa	8412			
	Maria	8415			
	Thomas	12780	12801		

Surname	Given name	Numbers
Fallon	Jane	2883
	John	29 2076 2886 2890
	Margaret	2078
	Martin	9912
	Mary	2075 2888
	Michael	5332
	Thomas	112 2887
	William	2074 2080
FALLOWFIELD	Sarah	12705
FANNON	Ann	2376
	Ellen	2377
	Hannah	2378
	James	2375 2379
FARGISON	James	569
FARLEY	Jane	2776
FARMER	George	7207
FARMERY	Ann	9364
	William	9363
FARROW	Barbary	9043
	Elizabeth	4732
	George	4730
	Isabella	9039 9041
	Jane	4731 9042
	John	9040
FATHERLEY	John	9982
FAWCETT	Ambrose	8270 8274
	Charlotte	10728
	Elizabeth	10729
	Henry	999
	James	10392
	Jane	8273
	John	4491 7400 8276
	Joseph	8275 10730
	Margaret	7850 8271
	Mary	7486
	Thomas	4751 7849
	William	8272
FAWELL	Charles	4985
FEATHERSTONEHAUGH	C.H.	362
FEATONBY	Alice	4867
	Elizabeth	9684
	Isabella	9685
FEGAN	Daniel	8134
	Jane	9074
	Patrick	9073
FEILDING	Sophia	7403
FEMELLOW	William	2171
FENN(E)Y	Elizabeth	13018
	Hannah	13014
	Isabella	3241
	John	13017
	Mary	3239 13016
	Rosanna	13019
	Thomas	3238 3240
	William	13013 13015
FENWICK	Ann	5638 6096
	Dorothy	6176
	Elizabeth	5928
	Ellen	6180 12601
	Frederica	1276
	George	3377 4532 4534 12602
	Hannah	6097
	Henry	9628
	James	12603
	Jane	6179 9629
	John	6175 6178 7458
	Martha	11984
	Mary	3378
	Phyllis	3376
	Ralph	1146
	Richard	6177
	Sarah	4533
	Thomas	609 6098 7244
	William	3375 6095 7698 8087
FERENS	James	12396
	John	12398
	Joseph	9388
	Martha	12397
	Robert	12399
	Robinson	9387
FERGUSON	Eleanor	10186
Ferguson	Elizabeth	10187
FERRALL	Charles	3931
FERRIS	Alexander	12107
FERRY	Dinah	11276
	Edward	11275
	Eliza	1661
	George	1658 1660
	Rebecca	1659
FEWSTER	John	3562 9553
	Mary	9552
FID(D)LER	Ann	1531
	Charles	10147
	Christopher	10145
	Edward	10137 10141
	Ellen	1527
	George	10139
	Harvey	2639
	Henrietta	10140
	Henry	10144
	Isabella	2643
	Jane	1525 10146
	Jessie	10138
	John	2641
	Margaret	1526
	Marianna	10143
	Mary	2640
	Ruth	10142
	Thomas	1524
	William	2642
FIFE	Anne	4941
	Elizabeth	4943
	Ellen	4944
	Marianna	4942
FILLIPS	Patrick	2546
FINLEY	Abigail	9852
	Christopher	9851
	William	1213
FIRGUSON	Isabella	2017
	Robert	2018
FISH	John	11608
FISHER	Catherine	12928
	Elizabeth	12925
	Isabella	12926
	John	1702 7118 12927
	Margaret	12924
	Thomas	12923
FISHWICK	Christopher	12782
	Jane	3561 4600
FITZJERRALD	William	8542
FLANDERS	Frederick	5156
FLARTY	Mary	600
FLECKHERTY	James	7176
FLEMING	Alice	11156
	Ann	921 11153
	Henry	11154
	John	920 11155
	William	11152
FLETCHER	Ann	11749
	George	11745
	Jane	11746
	Margaret	12210
	Mary	11747
	Perpetua	4889
	Thomas	11748
	William	4888
FLIN(N)	Ann	425
	Bridget	427
	Edward	428
	John	2304
	Maurice	603
	Michael	424
	Patrick	604
	Peter	429
	Phillip	426
FLINTIFT	John	11883
FLINTOFF	Beatrice	1077
	David	1076
	Elizabeth	1079
	James	3938
	Mary	1078
FO(O)LEY	Annie	4438

Fo(o)ley	Michael	4462			
FORD	Andrew	5983			
	Henry	13008			
	James	13006			
	Jane	13007			
	Mary	13004			
	Nicholas	13009			
	Richard	13003			
	Robert	13005			
FORDY	Phyllis	4805			
FORSITH	Ann	10845	10847		
	George	10846			
	Margaret	10849			
	Mary	10848			
FO(R)STER	Adelaide	5291			
	Alice	4897	5408		
	Andrew	4602			
	Ann	3317	5294	6828	9754 12289
	Anthony	10573			
	Barnabas	11333			
	Charles	11604			
	Dorothy	4910			
	Edward	9753			
	Eleanor	697	6385	6983	6984 7456
	Elizabeth	1547	2146	6826	6987 7415
		8287	9747	11334	11443 12179
		12561			
	Ellen	3007	12564		
	Esther	3914			
	Faith	11442	11446		
	Francis	9752			
	George	1545	1550	3371	3643 5295
		6831	9384		
	Hannah	6988	9746		
	Henry	3370	3642	6830	
	Isabel(la)	699	11064		
	Jane	1546	3641	4930	5290 7267
		11332	11445		
	John	365	4601	4917	5583 6825
		6982	9163	9751	
	Jonathan	3912	3915	6986	
	Lucy	4918	4921		
	Margaret	1606	1608	1823	3369 12563
	Maria	4909			
	Mary	366	1548	1927	3913 4908
		5499	6386	6829	8289 9613
		11063	11336	11444	12290 12562
		12711			
	Matthew	1579			
	Percival	4907	4919		
	Ralph	12710			
	Rebecca	11335			
	Richard	4920			
	Robert	3368	3916	6827	8286 9750
		11817			
	Samuel	5292			
	Sarah	251	367		
	Susanna	4662	9748		
	Thomas	1549	3917	5216	5293 6985
		11062	11065		
	Timothy	3318			
	William	1605	1822	3006	3640 6883
		8288	9745	9749	10078 11331
		12288			
)WELL	Christiane	5494			
	John	5493	5495		
	Margaret	5497			
	Martha	5496			
)WLE	Thomas	1046			
	William	1047			
)WLER	Diana	12682			
	Eleanor	8330			
	George	12681	12686		
	James	8329	8333		
	Jane	8332			
	Matthew	8331			
	Richard	12685			
)X	Anne Stote	7282			
	George	7283			
	Henry	7284			
	John	4346			

Fox	Mary	1817	7285
FOXLEY	Frederick	9219	
FRANCE(S)	Elizabeth	2286	
	Israel	2283	2290
	Jane	2284	2287
	John	2288	8232
	Joseph	8233	
	Mary	8231	
	Morgan	2285	
	William	2289	
FRANKLIN	John	4011	
FRANKS	Elizabeth	7976	
	George	7973	7977
	John	5827	7978
	Mary	5823	7974
	Robert	7979	
	William	7975	
FRATER	Margaret	317	
	Mary	313	315
	Richard	312	316
	William	314	
FRAZER	Ann	8715	
	Elizabeth	8713	
	John	8712	8717
	Margaret	8714	
	William	8716	
FREEMAN	John	7116	
FREEMANTLE	George	1956	
	Hannah	1955	
FREITH	Alfred	11818	
	Mary	11819	
FRENCH	Anne	3704	
	Catherine	9850	
	Edward	3707	
	Elizabeth	4284	
	Henry	3703	
	Jane	3702	
	John	1459	
	Margaret	3706	8711
	Martha	3699	
	Mary	1460	
	Rachael	4285	
	Robert	3698	3701 8710
	Sarah	3700	
	Thomas	3705	
FRESTON	Rebecca	9212	
FRYER	Thomas	7103	
FULLER	Isabella	5647	
	Jane	5849	
	John	5646	
	Mary	5648	
FURGESON	James	2130	
	Jane	2131	
FYNET	Catherine	4374	
	James	4373	
	Thomas	4375	
GAGE	William	13188	
GAINFORD	Ann	7308	
	Elizabeth	2291	9805
	John	9804	
	Joseph	9806	
	Margaret	6306	
	William	9807	
GAINFORTH	Elizabeth	9465	
	Sarah	9464	
GAKING	Bridget	4360	
	John	4361	
	Patrick	4359	
GALACHER	Peter	7191	
GALL(E)Y	Jane	9532	
	Margaret	5070	
GALLOWAY	James	1599	
GAMMON	Catherine	4504	
	Patrick	4503	
GAMWELL	James	1735	
	John	1737	
	Margaret	1734	
	Mary	1736	
GANNAN	Augusta	5381	
	Hughfy	5398	
	Mary	5380	

GANNON	Anthony	4527				
	Bridget	4528				
	Catherine	4437				
	Dennis	4436				
	James	5394				
GARBUT	Elizabeth	5224				
GARDENER	Elizabeth	11917				
	George	1532	1535			
	Joseph	1534				
	Margaret	1537				
	Mary	1533	11916			
	William	1536	11918			
GARD(I)NER	Ann	4679				
	Edward	3567				
	James	438				
	Jane	2805	2807			
	Margaret	439	3565			
	Robert	2804	2806	3564		
	Sarah	3563	3568			
	Thomas	3566				
GARFORTH	Henry	9415				
GARGETT	Ann	10702	10736			
	Dorothy	7288				
	Jonathan	10735				
	Mary	4914	11797			
	Thomas	10737				
GARISH	Sarah	860				
GARNET	William	7125				
GARRET	Robert	7102				
GARRY	John	8386				
	Margaret	8387				
GARTH	Richard	11258				
GARTHWAITE	Beatrice	6744				
	Christopher	6741				
	David	1080				
	Elizabeth	6743				
	James	6747				
	Jane	6742				
	John	6745				
	Joseph	6746				
GASCOIGNE	Elizabeth	6144				
	John	1720	6146			
	Mary	6145				
	Richard	6143				
GASCOYNE	Mary	9525				
GAUTTER	Catherine	12687				
GAY	Elizabeth	2551				
GELDART	John	5905				
GELDER	John	5219				
GELESPIE	Thomas	2038				
GELLNESS	Bridget	8911				
	James	8910				
	Michael	8912				
	Thomas	8913				
GENT	Ann	6200				
	Isabella	6056				
	Margaret	6054				
	Martha	6053				
	Robert	6052				
	Susanna	6055				
GETTINS	Catherine	8573				
	Isabella	8571	8577			
	Mary	8576				
	William	8570				
GIB	Peter	4721				
GIBBINS	Harry	4339				
GIBBON(S)	Ann	4580	10934			
	Eleanor	6803				
	Mary	6802				
GIBNY	James	2545				
GIBSON	Alice	3404				
	Ann(e)	3555	5311	5976	7807	7808
		7838				
	Elizabeth	10681	11935	12180		
	Fanny/Frances	3406	11938			
	George	3403	3408	3553		
	Hannah	3552	5000			
	Isabella	2742	11937			
	Jane	10682				
	Joseph	2744	3551			
	Margaret	12181	12664	11939		

Gibson	Mary	1764	2741	3407	3554	597
		11936				
	Matilda	12662				
	Peter	2743	11934			
	Robert	12666				
	Thomas	10680	10683	12661	12665	
	William	6739	7148	12663		
GILAN	Brian	3835				
	John	3837				
	Mary	3836	3839			
	Sarah	3838				
GILBERTSON	Anne	8441				
	Magdalen	11178				
	Margaret	8440	8444			
	Mary	8445				
	Matthias	8443				
	Richard	8439				
	William	8442				
GILES	Mary	10734				
	Nathaniel	10733				
GILGALON	Bridget	5245				
GILHESPIE	Ann	6446				
	Margaret	9531				
GILL(S)	Ann	5898				
	Catherine	4563				
	Charles	4216				
	Elizabeth	4041	4217			
	Ellen	4567				
	George	4040	4043			
	Hannah	915	8784			
	Harriet	8782				
	Henry	8785				
	Jane	4042				
	John	4565	8783			
	Margaret	1101				
	Maria	4568				
	Michael	4564				
	Patrick	4566				
	Thomas	4562	9165			
GILLESPIE	Ann	734				
	Bessy	731				
	Elizabeth	3774				
	Francis	735				
	James	728	733			
	Joseph	732	3773			
	Mary	729	730			
	Robert	2047				
GILMORE	Edward	10107				
	Elizabeth	10108				
	John	6734				
GILROY	Catherine	12943				
	Eleanor	12958	12960			
	James	12853	12942	12947		
	Jane	12854				
	John	12946				
	Mary	12945	12959			
	Thomas	12944				
GINNET	James	7214				
GLADDLEY	Isabella	2987				
GLARY	Bridget	5363				
	Mary	5359	5361	5364		
GLE(A)SON	Ann	2735	5035			
	Anthony	7941	9708			
	Cornelius	7940				
	Elizabeth	2733				
	Ellen	7944				
	George	7938				
	Margaret	2734	7943			
	Martha	7939				
	Thomas	7942				
GOATLEY	Frances	7734				
	William	7733				
GOGGINS	James	11107				
GOLDEN	John	11299				
GOLDSBROUGH	George	6606				
	Jane	6608				
	Margaret	6605	6609			
	Thomas	6607				
GOLIGHTLY	Alice	6949				
	Ann	1790	6948			
	Elizabeth	1788	4362	12994		

Hall	Katherine	10979				
	Magdalen	9302				
	Margaret	1324	5985	7851	10980	12469
		13123				
	Maria	10828				
	Mary	354	1869	3435	5094	6815
		7362	7393	10275	10372	10380
		10926	12885			
	Ovington	1870				
	Peter	8218				
	Robert	8368	10978	12876		
	Sarah	819	6816	12881		
	Silas	10171				
	Simpson	12880				
	Thomas	1733	3579	5323	5984	10371
		10921	10924	11452	11585	13117
	William	1323	6023	8367	10170	10925
		11455	11457	11584	12878	12884
		13120				
HALLGARTH	Henry	7109				
HAMALTON	Hannah	2360				
	Mary	2357	2358			
	Thomas	2359				
HAMILTON	Ann	1357	10376			
	Anthony	12743				
	Arabella	4934				
	Catherine	1359				
	Elizabeth	1360				
	Frances	5009				
	George	584	4933			
	Hans	4935				
	Henry	4936				
	Hornby	10375	10377			
	James	8945	13097			
	Jane	11542				
	John	579	580			
	Margaret	581	8476	8944	10379	
	Mary	1358	8947	10378	12744	
	Pybus	11541				
	Samuel	582				
	Sarah	5008				
	Thomas	1356	1361			
	William	583	8946	13098		
HAMMOND	John	1414				
	Richard	1415				
HAMNELL	Henry	9413				
HAMPSON	Thomas	96				
HANBY	Catherine	4558				
	John	4557				
HAN(D)COCK	Isabella	7449				
	John	11617	11618			
	Louisa	7450				
	Mary	7448				
HANDFORD	Frederick	7117				
HANILESS	William	2494				
HANLEY	Catherine	4326	4328			
	Clarrie	4327				
	Pat	4325				
HANLIN	John	2424				
HANLON	Barnabas	4159				
	Catherine	4156				
	James	4155				
	Mary	4157				
	Thomas	4158				
HANN	John	7133				
	Thomas	7181				
HANSBY	Mary	4940				
HANSEL(L)	Anne	19	7520			
	Elizabeth	16				
	Isabella	15	9624			
	John	1843				
	Joseph	18				
	Margaret	17				
	Maria	9588				
	Mary	1844				
	Rebecca	7847				
HANSON	Elizabeth	12585				
	George	12582				
	Jane	12581				
	John	12588				
	Margaret	12586				
Hanson	Mary	10833	12580	12583		
	Thomas	12579	12584			
	William	12587				
HANTON	Ann	4358				
	Patrick	4357				
HARBIT	Ellen	11370				
HARBOTTLE	Elizabeth	5511				
HARDEN	George	9052				
	John	9054				
	Sarah	9053				
	Thomas	9055				
HARDING(E)	Caroline	4801				
	Emily	4800				
	Fanny	4798				
	Hannah	4795	4799			
	Henry	4796				
	James	7126				
	John	5199				
	William	4797				
HARDY	Elizabeth	9689				
	James	2209				
	John	2210				
	Mary	4164				
	Thomas	11098				
	William	7226	9360			
HARE	Ann	1650				
	George	1649				
	Ralph	1654				
	Sarah	1651				
HARGRAVE(S)	Catherine	2712				
	Edward	2711				
	Henry	2713				
	John	311				
HARKER	Ann	6858				
	Jane	1329	7664			
	John	11504				
HARLAND	Ann	11558				
	Robert	5418				
HARLE	Elizabeth	12795				
	George	11179	12797			
	Margaret	12796				
	Maria	12798				
	Mary	11709				
	Morrison	12794				
HARLEY	William	1782				
HARLING	Ann	6824				
HARPER	Archibald	9499				
	Edward	7163				
	Francis	11465				
	John	11467				
	Mary	9500				
	Priscilla	11466				
	Sarah	9502				
HARREY	Christian	12089				
	Margaret	12088				
	William	12087	12090			
HARRIS	Joseph	888				
HARRISON	Albert	12275				
	Alfred	12273				
	Andrew	608				
	Ann(e)	2121	4101	5860	12271	
	Edward	1321	5858			
	Edwin	12274				
	Eleanor	6909				
	Eliza(beth)	1319	2120	6453	8320	8925
		10902				
	Emily	12270				
	George	8926				
	Henry	4129	4131			
	Isabella	5857				
	James	9303				
	Jane	1320	3687	4130	5859	8319
	John	1318	6701	7215		
	Joseph	791				
	Margaret	1322	4133	12269	12515	
	Martin	4100	5856			
	Mary	472	473	12272		
	Michael	4132				
	Robert	1729	8924	10901	10903	12268
	Samuel	8321				

Surname	Given name	Numbers
Harrison	Sarah	792 9304
	Thomas	10332
	William	6908 8318 9209
HART	Mary	2839
	Matthew	2838
HARTLEY	Elizabeth	7710
	Ellen	5047 9674
	Margaret	5046
	Martha	7711
	Mary	7712
	Phyllis	7709
	Sarah	1214
	William	7708
HARWOOD	Elizabeth	7702
HASTINGS	Edward	7334
	Henrietta	7335
	Holloway	6031
HAW	Hannah	5183
	Maria	5184
	William	5182
HAWKESLEY	Isabella	8033
HAY	William	10308
HAY(E)S	Anne	4781
	Eleanor	4780
	Elizabeth	4778 4779
	Isabella	4783
	Jane	4784
	John	4777
	Judith	7633
	Margaret	4782
	Sophia	4884
	Thomas	4883
HA(Y)TON	Henry	6603
	Leonard	6602
	Margaret	6601
	Mary	8168
	William	8167
HEATON	Ann	12225
	Anthony	12226
	Hannah	12224
	John	12223 12227
	Margaret	12230
	Mary	12229
	Robert	12228
	Sarah	7563
HEAVISIDE	Ann	9070
	Dorothy	9069
	Elizabeth	11025 11027
	Frederick	9072
	Margaret	9071
	Mary	9067
	Michael	6319
	Robert	1399
	Thomas	9068 11024
	William	6318 11026
HEBDEN	Jane	6873
HEDLEY	Annie	9299
	Catherine	1770
	Edward	6659
	Elizabeth	8297 9296 9297 11376
	Ellen	1310 12691
	Emma	9300
	Isabella	8298 9298
	James	8296
	Jane	9295
	John	1309 1311 1769 9301 11375 11377
	Margaret	6660
	Mary	9294
HELMEROW	Margaret	502
HEMMINGWAY	Anna	2831
	Elizabeth	2825 2829
	Frederick	2827
	George	2824 2828
	James	2830
	Margaret	2826
HENDERSON	Ann(ie)	7829 10035
	Charles	7828
	David	12177
	Emily	7826
	Frances	10036
Henderson	Francis	10034
	George	6684
	Hannah	7825
	Hodgson	9869
	Isabel	10038
	Jane	5443 11764
	John	7824 7827 9349
	Margaret	6336
	Robert	7201
	Thomas	10037
	William	5422 5620
HENDRY	Walter	3056
HENRY	Daniel	7090
	Isabella	7621 7622
	John	7620
	Peter	7190
	Thomas	7095
HENSHAW	Emily	7436
	William	7435
HEPBURN	Jessie	536
HEPPEL(L)	Annie	7485
	George	9625
	Jane	9626
	Mary	9627
HEPPLE	Elizabeth	5029
	Isabella	5030
	John	27 5031
	Matthew	5028 5033
	Richard	5032
HEPPLEWITE	Frances	9962
HEPWORTH	Edward	9260
HERBE(R)T	Agnes	9111
	Ann(e)	467 3943 4485 8485 1003
		10032
	Deborah	12558
	Ellen	1055 1056
	John	1054 8484
	Joseph	835 1787 5217
	Mary	469
	Matthew	2656
	Robert	834 10030 11293
	Sarah	832 5218 8486
	Thomas	3942 3944
	William	831 833
HERD	John	4341
HERDING	Mary	1979
HERDMAN	Ann	3803 10843
	Benjamin	10840
	Edward	3804 10842
	John	10841
	Margaret	7645 10844
	Mary	10933
	Nathaniel	10932
	Simon	3802
HERISON	Margaret	2116
HER(R)ON	Ann	8865
	Dorothy	10707
	Eleanor	655
	Elizabeth	8867
	Ellen	10704 10705
	Em(m)erson	8863 10708
	George	10703 10706
	Henry	8866
	Mary	656 8864 8869 10533
	Stephen	654 657
	Thomas	658
	William	659 8868
HER(R)ING	Andrew	12830
	Charles	9123
	Elizabeth	10134
	George	10128 10132 12832
	Hannah	7269 12831
	Isabel(la)	331 9120 12834
	Jane	10129 10133
	John	10131
	Margaret	12833
	Mary	330 9119 9122 10130
	Thomas	6342
	William	329 9118 9121
HESELTINE	Francis	8096
HESLOP	Ann	9116 12374

Surname	Given name	Numbers
Holme(s)	Elizabeth	11241
	Ellen	7045
	Joseph	9621
	William	11242
HOLT	William	7255
HOOD	Margaret	12092
	Neil	12091
	William	9383
HOOPER	John	7219
HOPE	Ann	620 943 3157
	Charlotte	5956
	Elizabeth	5957 11345
	George	408
	Isabella	7294
	Jane	942
	John	5959
	Joseph	466 5958 8803
	Margaret	7295
	Mary	464 5608
	Richard	3156 3158
	Robert	3159
	William	465
HOPPER	Ann(a)	963 1086 5512 6281 6282 6521 6556 9599 13080
	Charles	4088
	Edmund	4085
	Edward	941 3440 6279
	Eleanor	4715
	Elizabeth	938 4138 5514 5629 8589 10280
	Ellen	4136 4139
	Francis	3888 6508
	George	906 960 964 3111 4519 5513 6559 8587
	Hannah	4084
	Henry	4089 4102 4106 4518 6618 10747
	Isabel(la)	797 961 8586 9600 10748
	James	4087
	Jane	3887 3889 4103 6277 6280 8585
	John	907 3110 4090 5771 6276 6283 6619
	Lambton	8588
	Lavinia	965
	Margaret	3441 3868 4104 4516 5593
	Mark	6557 9631
	Mary	796 909 940 1085 3109 3890 4105 6522 6617 9632
	Rachael	798
	Ralph	4135 6558
	Robert	962
	Sarah	6553
	Susanna	6181
	Thomas	4083 4086 4137 4517 5875 6520 6552 6554 8584 9598 9601
	Thomison	6278
	William	937 939 1084 3886 6555
HOPTON	Adelaide	847
	Elizabeth	846
	Mary	848
HORAN	Bridget	2338
	Mary	2336
HORDON	John	9392
HORN	Anne	8396
	Dorothy	4892
	James	7247
	Jane	9366
	John	8394
	Margaret	8393
	Robert	8392
	Thomas	8395
	William	4893
HORNER	Catherine	10752
	Joseph	10754
	Sarah	10753
HORNSBY	Margaret	4489 9239
	Matilda	9241
	Robert	9238 9240
	Thomas	4488
Hornsby	William	4490
HORS(E)FIELD	Abraham	10646
	Charlotte	10647
	Isaac	10644
	Jane	10645
	John	10648
HOUSTON	Charles	10422
	Edward	10935
	Elizabeth	10424 10936
	John	10421
	Mary	10418
	Septimus	10423
	Thomas	10420
	William	10417 10419
HOWE(S)	Ann	8269 9521
	Elizabeth	357
	George	3594
	Henry	10501
	Isabella	3671 6303
	James	7147
	John	356 358 3595 3655 365'
	Jonathan	3658
	Joseph	3670
	Margaret	3659
	Mary	3656 7625
	Robert	6305
	Thomas	6304 7626
	William	7624 7627
HOWEY	Alice	2408
HOWLEY	John	7179
HOWSON	Elizabeth	4045
	George	4047
	Grace	11952
	Mary	11121
	William	4044 4046
HUBBACK	Charles	6398
	Eliza	6400
	Frances	6397
	Mark	6399
	Robert	6396
	Selina	6402
	Walter	6401
HUBBERTHORN	Anne	1496
	Jane	1497
HUBBICK	Ann(e)	5498 5500
	Cuthbert	3787
	Elizabeth	3788
	Hannah	5971
	Joseph	3789
	William	3790
HUDDLESTONE	John	7077
HUDSON	George	9866
	Hannah	10449
	James	7359 8365 9408 10448 1045?
	Jane	3269 7293
	John	3270 4681 10452
	Joseph	1406
	Margaret	7290
	Robert	3268 5243
	Sophia	10450
HUGGETT	John	7233
HUGHS	Ann	11980
	Mary	11977
	Neal	11978
	Patrick	11979
HULL	Elizabeth	5456
	Frances	8831
	George	9667
	John	5459
	Joseph	9759
	Thomas	5455 5458
	William	5457
HUMBLE	Ann	621
	Mary	1257
HUNT	Arthur	8177 8181
	Bernard	8184
	David	8182
	Eleanor	1349
	Francis	1350
	Jane	8178
	Jemima	1348

Surname	Forename	Numbers
Lambert	Harriet	12212 12216
	James	12211 12217
	John	12215
	Mary	12213
	Roland	9559
	Thomas	2989
LANDRAGAN	Agnes	3904
	Martha	3902
	Mary	3903
LANGLEY	Jane	9498
LANGRIDGE	Richard	3691
LANSBURG	John	7222
LAPPAGE	William	8349
LARGEY	James	8923
	Thomas	8922
LARKIN	James	12102
	Sarah	12103
LASCELLES	Caroline	2549
LASSELLES	William	453
LAUNSDON	Mary	4744
LAURENCE	Agnes	1774
	William	1775
LAUTHERDALE	Elizabeth	12491
	Matthew	12490
LAVERICK	Jonathan	4197
	Thomas	7172
LAVIN or Hann	John	7133
LAWES	Dorothy	4895
LAWRANCE	Ann	2978
	Matthew	2980
	Susan	2979
LAW(S)	Ann	3410
	Elizabeth	5107 11317 11320
	Henry	5152
	Isabella	11318
	Jane	11321
	John	7227
	Joseph	693
	Mary	11319
	Robert	3409 11316 12405
LAWSON	Thomas	5416
LAYBOURN	Thomas	3528
LAYCOCK	Isabella	1970
	Thomas	1969 9873
LAYDON	Francis	1783
LAYKIN	James	6656
	John	6658
	Mary	6657
LAYNORA	John	2823
	Mary	2822
LAYTON	James	6359
LEADBITTER	Ann	9695
LEE(S)	Barbara	1051
	Blackett	5058
	Catherine	12597
	Edward	9890
	Hannah	10496
	Isabella	5123 10495
	Jane	7650
	John	10497 10677
	Joseph	10527 10679
	Margaret	12598
	Martha	10676
	Mary	7588
	Patrick	12596
	Sarah	12252
	Susanna	10494
	William	10498 10675 12599
LEGGE	Margaret	7405
LEIGH	Jane	88
	William	87
LEIGHTON	Ann	4891
LEITH	Catherine	8879
	John	8878
	Rachael	8877
LEONARD	James	4145
LEROY	Ann	3287
	David	3292
	Elizabeth	3291
	Jane	3290
	Margaret	3289
Leroy	Sarah	3288
LEVI	Morris	39
LEWIS	Ann	3395 3396
	Elizabeth	7805
	John	3394
	Mary	3397
	Robert	7803 7804
LEYBOURN	Hannah	7067
LIDDEL(L)	George	6999
	Margaret	9901
	Marion	10270
	Martha	9079
	Robert	9080
	Thomas	7001
	William	9078 11251
LIDDLE	Ann	4834
	Charles	3310
	Christopher	3284 3365
	Dorothy	10240
	Elizabeth	2694 5743
	Ellen	3884
	George	1930 2693 5741
	Isabella	3308
	James	5750
	Jane	5745
	John	3185 3364
	Mary	3184 3187 5742 5790 10241
	Robert	1176 2695 3366
	Rosanna	3309
	Sarah	3285 3363 3367 9183
	Tamar	5744
	Thomas	2751 3186 3311 3362
	William	3188 3286 3307
LIESER	Joanna	10751
LIGHTFOOT	Ann	7791 12207
	Barbara	9825
	Elizabeth	8152 9824 12766
	George	7790 9823
	Henry	7792
	James	7793
	Jane	7564 7785 12204
	John	7591 9826 12205 12764 13181
	Joseph	7789
	Mark	8151
	Mary	12206 12765 12767
	Robert	7787
	Thomas	7788 12209 12768
	William	7784 7786 12203 12208
LILLEY	Isabella	12133
LINARD	Bridget	167
	John	165
	Peter	168
	Rose	166
LINCOLN	Marianne	7276
LINDSEY	Ann	4502
	George	4184
	Isabella	4187
	John	4185
	Mary	4186
	William	4501
LIN(D)SLEY	Ann	1186 10426 10429
	Elizabeth	565
	Hannah	10427
	Isabel	10428
	Jane	4022
	Joseph	3712
	Martin	2272
	Matthew	564
	Richard	10425
	Robert	10430
	Robinson	9259
	Sarah	567
	Thomas	4021 10431
	William	566 9258
LING	Joseph	8102
LIONS	James	2389
LISLE	Elizabeth	4819
LI(D)STER	Ann	3611 10508
	Caroline	1616
	Eleanor	1615
	Elizabeth	3612 6834 8131 10512

Surname	Forename	References
Maddison	Ellen	523
	Hannah	3874
	Isabel	8460
	Jane	522 3871 3872 5343 7991
	John	3106 3875 4512 5342
	Margaret	9466
	Maria	6254
	Mary	5344
	Robert	11823 11826
	Susanna	3876
	Thomas	7990 7992
	William	525 2122 3870 4515 5346 10353 11825
MADDON	Alexander	7142
MADGIN	James	8351
	Maria	1252
	Mary	7904
MAGAN	James	4054
	Terence	4055
MAGASH	Ann	4314 4316
	Isabella	4317
	Janet	4318
	John	4313
	Thomas	4315
MAGEE	Eleanor	901
	John	900
	Margaret	10233
	Mary	902
	Thomas	13046
MAGISTRIS	Elizabeth	8552
MAGU(I)RE	Elizabeth	8855
	Jane	8857
	John	2361
	Teresa	8858
	Thorid?	2362
	William	8856
MAHAN	Bridget	5733
	James	5732 5736
	John	5734
	Michael	5735
MAHON	John	7153
	Mary	12085 12086
	Michael	12084
MAIN(S)	Charlotte	1223
	Elizabeth	1859
	James	1222 1225
	Sarah	1224
MAINSFORTH	Hannah	1253
MAKEPEACE	William	2053
MALCOLM	Cornelius	8914
	Frances	9642
	Thomas	9643
	William	9641
MALLEN	Elizabeth	8267
	Ellen	10774
	Isaac	10773
	James	8266 10771
	John	10775
	Mary	10772
MALLETT	George	7158
MALLEY	Ann	5348
	James	5349
	Owen	5347
MALLON	James	11223
	John	11222
MALONE	Mary	5396 12390
MALTBY	John	476
MANN	Hannah	51
	James	49 52
	Mary	2462 2463
	Oran	1053
	Sarah	2986
	Thomas	50
	William	2464
MARCH	Samuel	891
MARCHALL	Thomas	6810
MARIS	Emma	10595
	Francis	10591
	Hannah	10596
	Mary	10592 10593
	Theresa	10594
MARKHAM	Ann	6876
	Charles	6928
	Elizabeth	12173
	Hannah	6976
	Jane	6639
	Judah	6924 6926
	Margaret	6927
	Ruth	6975 6977
	Thomas	6875 6974
	William	6925
MARK(S)	Alice	1779
	Thomas	12827
MARLAND	Samuel	2588
MARLEY	Margaret	10192
	William	10191
MARLOW	Abraham	7138
MARRAN	Peter	1515
MARRIN	Dennis	6339
MARRINER	Mary	9126 9127
	Matthew	9130
	Rebecca	9128
	Robert	9125 9129
MARSDEN	Anne	4977
	Elizabeth	1751
	Georgiana	4978
	Jane	1299
	John	1298
	Thomas	4976
MARSHALL	Abraham	5680
	Ann	120 419 1423 1424 5681
	Charles	9517
	Edmund	9518
	Edward	10866
	Eleanor	10231 10232
	Elizabeth	422 1469 9519
	Francis	7919
	George	7732
	Harriet	1063 1067 10817
	Henry	423 6664 7921 8510 10819
	Jane	420 5683 5685 7920 7937 9515
	John	418 10814
	Margaret	10815
	Martha	1068
	Mary	3780 5682 8509 10229 10230 10818 10864
	Oliver	1066
	Robert	9516
	Thomas	1065 1422
	William	421 1062 1064 7922 9514 10228 10816 10863 10865
MARTIN	Elizabeth	9085
	Emma	7529
	George	20 3741 3744
	Harriet	3332
	Jane	4866 10912
	John	2732 8135
	Matthew	7157
	Ma(r)y	21 22 23 3742 10913
	Philip	7162
	Ralph	10914
	Reuben	3745
	Sarah	24 368
	William	3743 9084 9086
MASON	Elizabeth	6461
	George	11780
	Mary	10892
	Sarah	5609
MASTON	William	9503
MATHER	Ann	8666
	Elizabeth	11531
	George	11530
	James	10490 11346 11397
	Jane	11348 11398 11529
	Joseph	11399
	Margaret	10488
	Mary	11347 11349 11400 11528 11532
	William	7234 10489
MATTHEW	Susanna	4820
MAT(T)HEWS	George	3968
	Thomas	7202

MATTISON	John	5974	
	Mary	5975	
MAUDE	Elizabeth	10010	
	John	2175	10011
	Martha	10014	
	Robert	10013	
	Thomas	10015	
	William	10009	10012
MAUDLING	Joseph	7127	
MAUGHAM	Elizabeth	12889	
	John	12890	
	Margery	12891	
MAUGHAN	Alexander	13076	
	Ann	1997	3946
	Anthony	13079	
	Dinah	13077	
	Hannah	1998	
	John	1999	10055
	Joseph	3947	
	Margaret	2073	
	Matthew	13078	
	Thomas	1996	
MAUNAN	Ann	1516	
MAVEN	Dorothy	6035	
	John	6034	
	Maria	6037	
MAVERS	Edward	998	
	Elizabeth	997	
	John	996	
MAVIN	Ann	11927	11928
	Edward	6863	
	Elizabeth	6862	
	George	11926	
	Isabel(la)	11929	12819 13168
	James	12820	
	Jane	12821	
	Margaret	11930	
	Mary	11931	13165
	Robert	12818	
	Thomas	6861	13167
	William	13166	
MAWSON	Anthony	12504	
	Elizabeth	9443	
	Jane	12406	12501
	John	12502	
	Mary	12503	
	Michael	12505	
	William	8348	
MAXWELL	Elizabeth	886	
	Richard	885	
MAYALL	Joseph	89	
	Sophia	90	
MAYNARD	Charles	7582	
	Crofton	7580	
	George	7581	
	Henry	7583	
	Jane	7577	7578
	Margaret	7584	
	Thomas	7576	7579
MAYOR(S)	John	1405	
	Margaret	5433	
McARTHUR	Elizabeth	10665	
	Francis	10664	
	Margaret	10666	
	William	10667	
McAULIFFE	Mary	3596	
McCABE	Catherine	2932	
	Francis	2931	
McCAIN	James	6685	
McCALL	Peter	12015	
McCAN(N)	Hugh	2939	7948
	John	2942	
	Mary	2940	
McCANDREW	Bridget	2318	
	James	2323	
	John	2320	
	Margaret	2321	
	Mary	2322	
	Patrick	2319	
	Richard	2317	2324
	Thomas	2325	

McCARLAN	Daniel	8132	
	Michael	8133	
McCARTNEY	Daniel	2418	
	Elizabeth	2422	
	Margaret	2420	2423
	Mary	2419	
	Susan	2421	
McCLOUD	Elizabeth	606	
	William	605	607
McCONVEL	Peter	8094	
McCORMACK	Catherine	12950	
	Jane	1578	
	John	12953	
	Mary	12951	
	Patrick	12952	
McCORMIC	Martin	151	
McCRADY	Dennis	5413	
McCULLOCH	John	1377	
	Margaret	1378	
McDERMOT(T)	Betty	5350	
	Bridget	5352	
	Eliza	5354	
	John	2066	5351
	Martin	5353	
McDONAGH	James	6323	
	Margaret	6324	
M(a)cDONALD	Alexander	12105	
	Amelia	9662	
	Ann	2941	
	Esther	750	
	George	1331	
	Isabella	1416	
	James	3065	3067
	John	8036	
	Mary	748	3066
	Thomas	3068	7169
McDONNAHEY	Alice	12948	
	Bridget	12949	
McDONNELL	Ann	8953	
	Eleanor	8952	
	Michael	8951	
McDONNOGT	Honour	4377	
	James	4376	
McEUTGART	Dominic	12261	
McEVOY	Mary	3198	
	Thomas	3197	
Mc(K)EWEN	Bridget	10471	10473
	Caroline	5603	
	Catherine	5600	
	Daniel	5599	5602
	Eliza	5605	
	Francis	10474	
	Isabella	5601	
	John	10470	
	Mary	5604	
	Peter	10472	
McGILL	John	4441	
McGOUGH	Jane	1726	1727
	Mary	7048	
	Patrick	7183	
McGOWEN	Bridget	6069	
	Elizabeth	6070	
	Ellen	6068	
	Francis	4369	
	Joseph	6065	
	Mary	6067	
	Susanna	6066	
	William	4370	
McGREGER	Joseph	9787	
	Margaret	9788	
McGREGOR	John	11149	
	Margaret	11148	
	Richard	11147	
MacGUIGIN	Frances	8919	
	Patrick	8917	
	Phoebe	8918	
McHALL	Michael	12017	
McILION	Arthur	4524	
	Maria	4526	
	Sarah	4525	
McINTOSH	Martha	8541	

McINTYRE	Ann	10157	10553	
	Catherine	10552		
	Charles	10549	10554	
	Harry	10556		
	James	10555		
	Mary	10550		
	Owen	10156		
	Thomas	10551		
McJARNEN	Bridget	2908		
	James	2907		
McKANY	Catherine	9336		
	Edward	9337		
	John	9338		
	Patrick	9339		
McKAY	Ann	9027		
	Catherine	9030		
	Christian	9026	9028	
	Daniel	9025	9029	
	Hugh	9031		
MacKCHLEN	Margaret	11507	11510	
	Michael	11506		
	Thomas	11508		
	William	11509		
McKEENAN	Elizabeth	806		
	Jane	807		
	Mary	12957		
	Michael	805		
McKENNA	Patrick	7180		
M(a)cKENZIE	Donald	2970		
	Isabella	2969		
	Mary	2968		
	Peter	923		
	Robert	2967	2971	
McKIE	John	7194		
McKINLAY	Daniel	6692		
	Mary	6693		
McKINNA	Catherine	12437		
McKINNEY	Edward	11902		
MacKINNIN	Mary	8920		
MacKINTOSH	James	8062		
MacKLAM	Ann	5675		
	Elizabeth	5676		
	John	4430	5679	
	Sarah	5677		
	William	5674	5678	
MacKNALLY	Ann	679		
	Charles	678		
MacKNIGHT	Alice	9849		
	Anne	9535		
	Edward	9847		
	Elizabeth	9533	9839	9845
	Harry	9848		
	James	9838	9840	
	Jane	9534		
	John	9842		
	Joseph	9536	9844	
	Mark	9841		
	Tom	9846		
	William	9843		
McLAEN	Douglas	8117		
McLAUGHLIN	Edward	7107		
McLEAN	Donald	8201		
	James	8202		
	John	8199	8204	
	Mary	8200	8203	
McLOUGHLIN	Elizabeth	8109		
	Jane	8111		
	John	8108		
	Mary	8110		
McMAHON	Catherine	9321		
	John	892		
	Roger	9319	9322	
	Sarah	9320	9323	
McMAN	Ann	8301		
McMANNERS	Margaret	12387		
	Patrick	12388		
	Peter	12386		
	Thomas	12389		
McMANUS	Ann	6327		
	Bridget	6326		
	John	6325		

MacNAMARRA	Robert	8556		
McNAUGHTON	Joseph	6432		
MacOM	George	8948		
McPARTLINE	William	7184		
McQUEEN	Elizabeth	4432		
	Frederick	4434		
	James	4431		
	John	4433		
	William	4435		
McQUILLAN	Patrick	7248		
McQUIRE	Bridget	7056	7060	
	Ellen	7057		
MacROW	Ann	11739		
MacTAVISH	Catherine	6395		
McWHADE	Patrick	11974	11975	
MEADOWS	Elizabeth	7923		
MEDCALF	Ann	11244		
	David	11247		
	George	10964	11245	
	Jane	10965		
	John	11243	11246	
MEEHAM	Christopher	8129		
	Mary	8130		
MEGGESON	Jane	9682		
	John	9681		
	Margaret	9680		
	Mary	9677	9679	
	Turner	9676		
	William	9678		
MEGHION	Betsy	4473		
	Peter	4472		
MEGORAN	Ann	8591		
	Hannah	8592		
	James	8590		
	Sarah	8593		
MELLIN	Mary	2814		
MELLON	James	10915		
MELROSS	Catherine	5470	5471	
	Elizabeth	5469		
	Henry	5466	5468	
	Jane	5467		
MELVILLE	David	7669		
	Emma	7668		
MELVY	Ann	8876		
	Edward	8921		
	John	8875		
	Sarah	8915		
MENSFORTH	Ann	10205		
	Elizabeth	6138		
	George	6140		
	John	6136	6141	10204
	Mary	6137	10206	
	Susanna	6139		
MENZIES	James	4166		
MERCHANT	John	10089		
MESSENGER	Janet	7044		
METCALF(E)	Catherine	11673		
	Christopher	6633		
	Elizabeth	4922	4972	6632
	Frances	5580		
	Frederick	5579		
	Hannah	11670		
	Helen	5548		
	Henrietta	1286		
	Henry	11676		
	James	6631	11668	11675
	John	5546	5551 5581 8316	
	Maria	5577		
	Martha	10839		
	Mary	5547	8317 11672	
	Sarah	5549	11669 11674	
	Thomas	5550	5576 5578	
	William	5582	11671	
MICHAN	Thomas	4412		
MIDDLETON	Ann	1102	5993 6004	
	Catherine	6003		
	Charles	4772		
	Elizabeth	6000	6001 7861	
	Isabella	269		
	Jane	5995	9589	
	John	4081	7859	

Surname	Given name	References
Re(y)nolds	Douglas	8114
	Henry	1144
	James	12909
	Jane	12913 12930
	John	155 8115
	Louis	8116
	Margaret	12910 12912
	Mary	12911
	Phillip	8112
	Walter	1145
RIBBON	Rebecca	4099
RICE	David	12022
RICHARDSON	Abigail	31
	Ann(e)	140 1016 6128 10401
	Anthony	1604
	Betsy	10398
	Caroline	1646
	Catherine	841
	Edward	138
	Eliza(beth)	1014 1954 4703 5716 9756 10288 11777
	George	9755 10797
	Hannah	9225
	Henry	139 1264 6784
	Isabella	1175 3726 6780 6783
	James	91 5639 6710 6782 8928
	Jane	1017 8929 8971 9223 10287 12829
	John	30 33 1442 1544 6687 6781 7110 8931 9757 10252 11776 12990
	Joseph	10793 10796
	Margaret	1595 4704 7046 8972 9224
	Martha	137
	Mary	92 1542 1543 1596 1630 1647 4734 6015 6129 8930 9382 9758 10007 10794 10795 12828
	Matthew	10400
	Michael	4705 6127
	Richard	135
	Robert	5220 10904 11775
	Rowland	32
	Samuel	5410 11773
	Sarah	3728 10008 11774
	Sophia	3727
	Susan	136
	Tamar	12305
	Thomas	1015 1174 1711 1806 3619 6779 10399 12094 13047
	William	304 704 3725 3729 9222
RICHMOND	Charles	4442
	Robert	1128
RICKERBY	Ann	4143
	Elizabeth	5317
	Jane	4144
	John	5316
	Joseph	4140
	Mary	4141 4142
	Thomas	5318
	William	5319
RICKETTS	Ann	7609
RID(D)LEY	Alice	6821
	Ann	6818
	Catherine	7815
	Elizabeth	11887
	George	6817
	Jane	8191
	John	6819
	Margaret	5063
	Mary	8490
	Robinson	1701
	Sarah	1936
	Thomas	5409
	William	6820
RIDPITH	Samuel	3935
RIDSDALE	Thompson	4198
RIGBY	Eleanor	2532
	Mary	2531
RIL(L)EY	George	5384
	James	7242
Ril(l)ey	John	7178 12098
	Margaret	5385
	Michael	5386
	Patrick	2729
RIMINGTON	Ann(e)	8492 8495
	Emma	8496
	Jane	8497
	John	8494
	Mary	8493
	Richard	8491
RIPLEY	Horace	5041
	Margaret	5039 5040
RIPPON	Elizabeth	1206 10297
	Fanny	708
	Joseph	1205
	Mary	1207
	Thomas	707
	William	709 10296
RISK	Sarah	7665
RITSON	Ann	4539
	Henry	1133
	John	9221 9226
RIX	John	8943
ROBERTS	Jane	13185
	Mary	5089
	Thomas	13186
	William	13184
ROBERTSHAW	Elizabeth	7292
	Frances	625
	Isabella	1643
	John	1644
	Mary	1645
	William	1642
ROBERTSON	Charles	6688
	David	7235
	Eliza(beth)	6689 9378 11208
	George	815
	Helen	1396
	Henry	11206
	Jane	11207
	John	11209
	Joseph	1715
	Mary	816 818
	Nicholas	9380
	William	817 1395 7124
ROBINSON	Alexander	5927
	Alice	8743
	Ann(e)	879 2179 4348 4671 7368 10891 11126 12001
	Catherine	3852 5920 10779
	Christopher	4204
	Daniel	3195
	Diana	10801
	Dorothy	3719 8280
	Elizabeth	520 3857 10290 10295 11285 13071
	Ellen	1842 5191
	Emma	5010 10804
	Fanny/Frances	1849 8356
	Francis	1847 4673 10289
	George	1635 2067 3854 5918 5924 7171 10081 10937 12006
	Georgiana	5189
	Hannah	4666
	Isabella	3720 5923 10044 10803
	James	5922 6433 12993
	Jane	1939 4227 4672 5187 5188 9602 10291 10299 10778 10896
	John	1841 1937 4667 5186 5925 7925 9376 10045 10506 10776 10777 11125
	Jonathan	6142 11286
	Joseph	10293
	Lancelot	1845
	Margaret	521 1846 1848 7043 9161
	Mark	4668
	Mary	517 518 878 3856 4205 5257 5919 5921 6434 7305 10190 10802 12005
	Ralph	4665 4670 10890
	Robert	9402 10046 12000 12003

Robinson	Rosanna	9604
	Sarah	1938 3196 4347 10938
	Thomas	3374 3851 3855 3895 3896 7924 9603 10294 10800 12002 13070
	Walter	7144
	William	516 519 877 2180 2181 3718 3853 4669 5190 5926 7143 9622 10043 10292 12004 13072 13177
ROB(I)SON	Agnes	7069
	Alice	290
	Ann(e)	866 868 4803 8822 11338
	Anthony	11783
	Barbara	871 4624 4923
	Benjamin	6590
	Caroline	4938 11782
	Carr	11339
	Catherine	3381
	Charles	8009
	Christopher	147
	Cuthbert	6587
	Dorothy	5253
	Edward	7397 7909
	Eleanor	11341
	Elizabeth	286 867 922 7379 9255 9442 10219 10220 10642 11281 11590
	Ellen	870
	Euphemia	4692
	Fanny/Frances	285 288
	George	630 7465 8011 9441 9496
	Hannah	3385 4301 8828 8830 9497
	Henry	7911 11589
	Herbert	8010
	Isabella	5255 8829
	James	7341
	Jane	148 672 5095 6588 7908 8506 11592
	John	73 284 289 631 865 925 1312 4622 5525 6589 7459 8823 10047 10643 11340 11784
	Joseph	11781
	Margaret	4300 11282
	Mary	287 674 869 1632 1633 2145 3383 3384 4623 4702 5252 5254 5527 6094 8371 8507 9253 10222 10286 11210 11342
	Matthew	4303
	Priscilla	4896 8008
	Robert	3380 3386 6591 7396 7906 8821 9140 11591
	Sarah	5523 5526 7912 9256
	Susan	7907 7910
	Thomas	673 953 1631 3382 5524 7182 8824 8827 9252 9257 10641 11280 11337
	William	4299 4302 5251 5522 7156 7409 8505 8508 9254 10048 10218 10221
ROBYSON	Morpeath	6634
RODDEN	Margaret	11906
	Thomas	11907
RODHAM	George	4650
ROE	Elizabeth	1569
	Jane	1567
	John	1566
	Mary	1564
	Robert	1565
	Valentine	1563 1568
ROGAN	Thomas	7203
ROG(G)ERS	David	12013
	Elizabeth	7041
	James	3822
	Mary	7466
ROGERSON	William	5155
ROLISON	Robert	9578
ROLLIN	Isabella	12248
	James	12251
Rollin	Jane	12250
	John	12249
	William	12247
RONAN	Patrick	8964
ROOK	John	10755
ROSEBERRY	Ann	12738
ROSS	Ann	3527 4147
	Dorothy	8991
	George	4146
	Margaret	4618
	Thomas	9411
ROWE	Mary	7437
ROWELL	Margaret	7830
ROWLANDSON	Annie	7640
	Christopher	7639
	Hannah	7637
	Isabel	7638
	Kate	7641
	Mary	7643
	Samuel	7636
	Sarah	10960
	William	7642
ROWLEY	James	2059
RO(W)NTREE	Ann(e)	4989 7291 9555
	Catherine	1505 1507
	Ellen	4991
	John	1504 1506 1508
	Mary	4990
RUDD	Philip	7725
RULE	Elizabeth	11166 11169
	Margaret	10949 11168
	Robert	11170
	Roger	11165
	Thomas	11167
RUSH	John	4175
	Mary	4177
	Peter	4178
	Susan	4176
RUSHFORTH	Frances	6548
	John	6547 6551
	Mary	6549
	Matthew	6550
	Alice	7613
	Elizabeth	7612
	Mary	7611
	Sarah	7614
	Thomas	7616
	Timothy	7610
	William	7615
RUSSEL(L)	Agnes	9508
	Ann	10211
	Charles	696
	Elizabeth	4949
	Frances	4948
	George	7252
	Hamilton	695
	John	4950
	Louisa	5049
	Peter	4947
	Robert	8778
	Silena	8777
RUST	Joseph	133
	Mary	134
RUTHERFORD	Andrew	889 10337
	Ann	568 8655 11172
	Charles	232
	Edward	8656
	Elizabeth	4418 7519 10439
	George	7257
	Gideon	10339
	Hannah	233 4548 8220
	Henry	9891
	Jane	4417 4419
	John	4416 4546 8654
	Joseph	10438
	Margaret	231 6770 10436
	Mary	4547 4549 5636 8221 8222 10340 11173
	Michael	890
	Phyllis	10338
	Robert	230 8219

Thom(p)son	Francis	11193
	Frederick	6793
	George	578 2465 6785 7032 8138 9046 9927 11045 12041
	Hannah	9461 10899
	Harriet	8487
	Henry	875 6709 6792
	infant	9530
	Isabella	898 1089 1557 6456 6460 6489 6491 6788 9446
	James	205 6459 7730 9456 9458 11041 11046
	Jane	531 6492 7031 8324 9462
	John	398 1556 1959 4226 5801 5803 6458 6467 7030 7033 7208 8322 8326 11044 12035 12044 12808
	Joseph	7731 8325 12369 12806
	Judith	9335
	Julia	4869 4903
	Margaret	1087 4899 4902 6794 11194
	Martha	1221 6454
	Mary	399 570 4900 5622 6493 6511 6786 8327 9457 11047 12036 12043 12370 12627 12807
	Matthew	8536
	Rachael	9045
	Richard	4898
	Ridley	5259
	Robert	899 5501 6455 6789 6791 7137 10898 11220 13116
	Sarah	576 577 5502 9459 12037
	Stephen	5884 7085
	Susan(na)	8139 12039
	Thomas	905 1477 4901 5503 5805 6488 6490 6510 6790 8328 12367 12372
	William	400 897 2061 2151 2468 5420 6787 7206 8136 8141 9044 9047 9333 9445 9528 10998
THOMS	Jane	7398
THORNTON	Ann(e)	7663 12448
	Barbara	12449
	Elizabeth	11491
	George	12447 12452
	Henry	12451
	John	13096
	Joseph	6773
	Mary	3202 6315 12366 12450
	Susan	3200
	Thomas	3201
	William	3199
THORP(E)	Elizabeth	2768
	Hannah	8685
	Isaac	117 2767 8684
	Isabel	8682 8683
	Peter	8681 8686
	Robert	1050
	Thomas	8687
	William	118
TH(O)UBRON	Elizabeth	3487
	Francis	3490
	James	3488
	Jane	3492
	Thomas	3489
	William	3486
THURLOW	Eleanor	9994 9998
	Elizabeth	9996
	James	9993
	Margaret	9997
	Robert	9995
THURLOWAY	Ann	7036
THURLWELL	George	6704
THWAITES	Alice	4066
	Ann	4064 6645 6646 7836
	Arthur	3828
	Charles	7950 7953
	Christopher	4057
	Dinah	7597 9711
	Dorothy	5236
Thwaites	Elizabeth	183 188 7304 7952 9794
	Ellen	7951 7954
	Emma	7956
	George	4060 5238 6644
	Hannah	181 6650
	Henry	4062
	Isabella	180 185
	Jane	4058 5240
	John	3829 4059 4200 5235 5429 9795
	Joseph	1753 6653 7957
	Margaret	6654
	Mary	184 4036 4063 5241 5239 9712
	Rachael	186
	Ralph	6649 6652 9793
	Richard	3826 4199 5430
	Robert	7835
	Sarah	3827 8501 8502
	Thomas	182 187 4065 6651 8379
	William	3830 4061 5237 7955
TIERNAN	Thomas	11110
TIGHO	John	6322
TILLY	Ann	563 9281 9966
	Catherine	12198
	Dorothy	8719
	Eleanor	12196 12197
	Elizabeth	559 561 8721 9283 11915 12200
	Frances	12199
	Isabella	8720
	Jane	560 9282 11492
	John	562 10624 12202
	Margaret	12201
	Mary	590
	Maughan	9280
	Robert	558
	Simon	8718
	Susanna	11914
	Thomas	591 9284 9967
	William	9965 12195
TIMONAY	Hannah	12019
	James	12018
TIND(A)LE	Ann	3547 6017 6020 9686
	Dorothy	2193 8020
	Elizabeth	3548 8018
	George	8017
	Isabella	8015
	Jane	8019
	John	6018
	Joseph	6019
	Mary	4865
	Michael	6022
	Robert	3549 8016
	Thomas	3550
	William	6016 6021 8014
TINNEY	Michael	8302
	[blank]	8303
TIPLADY	Ann(e)	3676 5053 5559 8623
	Catherine	8625
	Charles	3754
	Eleanor	7820
	Elizabeth	4510 7817 7821
	Ellen	3752 5561
	Ephraim	7819
	Frances	4617
	Hannah	4616
	Henry	4615
	Jane	3756
	John	3753 4509 4683
	Mary	3675 3751 3757 5560
	Miriam	8624
	Robert	8622
	Thomas	7816 7818
	William	3755 4614 5052
TIPPING	Joseph	10485
	Ruth	10486
TITMARCH	William	2176
TITMARSH	Elizabeth	1148
TITMARTH	William	7741
TOD(D)	Edward	9981

Surname	Given name	Numbers
Tod(d)	Eliza(beth)	4927 5739 7571 10370
	Hannah	4193 9687
	Isabella	7462 9214
	James	4192
	Jane	4189 4194 4926
	Jemima	5738
	John	4188 4191 8248
	Joseph	4195
	Mary	2410 8245 13115
	Rebecca	8147
	Robert	5737 5740 10369
	Thomas	4190 8247
	William	8146 8244 8246
TODNER	Elizabeth	826
	George	823
	Isabella	827
	Jane	824
	Mary	825
	Sarah	828
TOMLINSON	E.	8997
TORPY	Mary	2334 2335
	Thomas	2333
TORR	Eliza	9605
TORRAN	Daniel	5330
TOWARD	Jane	5014
	Mary	5902
	Ralph	5901
	William	5903
TOWERS	Charles	1784
	James	5307
TOWLAN	Thomas	9913
TOWNS	Francis	1428
	Isabella	1427
TOY	John	7131
TRAGIN	Catherine	5451
TRAHIL	John	4574
	Mary	4575
TRAINES	Agnes	5105
TRENHOLM	Ann	10726
	James	10725
	Thomas	10727
TRISTRAM	Anne	6027
	Charlotte	6028
	Jane	6030
	Louisa	6029
TROTTER	Arthur	689
	Charles	5102
	Elizabeth	8986
	George	5104
	Henry	5103
	John	686 5098
	Margaret	5101
	Mary	5099 5100 5450
TROUGHTON	Agnes	10537
	Dorothy	10535
	Edward	10536
	Eleanor	10539
	Emma	10540
	Jane	10538
	John	10534
	William	12378
TRUEMAN	Mary	1277
	William	7842
TUART	Ann	9288
	Robert	9287
TUER	Jane	7493
	John	7494
	Mary	7496
	Sarah	7495
	Thomas	7492
TUGBY	Cornelius	2104
	Fanny	3414
	Mary	2102 2105
	Thomas	2103
	William	2106
TUMELTY	Elizabeth	12441
TUNSTALL	Moses	2589
TURNBULL	Ann	3328 5069 6294
	Charles	4535 12707
	Christopher	6062
	Edward	11568
Turnbull	Eleanor	2750
	Elias	3326
	Elizabeth	512 2365 3280 4271 4274 6063 11567 11570
	George	12709
	Hannah	4270 4613
	Henry	3165
	James	511
	Jane	2748 3162 3323 3325 8173 11571 12708
	John	3164 3322 3327 7097 11566 11569
	Joseph	3324 6292
	Margaret	4821 6293
	Mary	509 3166 3279 9709
	Robert	3329 4916
	Susanna	4272
	Thomas	2749 4269 4273 6064
	William	510 2364 3161 3163 3278 3281 7098 7213
TURNER	Ann	8543
	Catherine	7800
	Elizabeth	7514 12695
	Ellen	7688
	Esther	3630
	Hannah	8544
	Isabella	4846
	James	7728
	John	7251 7799 8385
	Mary	7797 8469
	Sampson	7798
	Thomas	6706
	William	1288
TURRELL	Elizabeth	1488
TWEEDIE	Mary	651
	William	1419 1420
TWIZLE	Thomas	8366
TY(T)LER	Edwin	4788
	Elizabeth	4789 10262
	Esther	5289
	Susanna	4790
	William	5288
TYSON	Mary	5045
UNDERWOOD	Richard	11607
UNTHANK	Anthony	5894
	Harriet	5895
	Robert	5896
USHER	Elizabeth	1839
	George	7839
	Hannah	3805
	Jane	1840 7841 12332
	John	1838 7840
	Matilda	12836
	Thomas	12333
	William	12835
VALKS	Elizabeth	12560
	Thomas	12559
VANDERSIDE	William	7224
VANN	Emma	9490
	Helen	9491
	Samuel	9489
	William	9492
VARDY	George	1756
	John	6678
	Mary	7382
VASEY	Ann	3990
	Eleanor	3585
	Elizabeth	2955 3583 3991
	Frederick	4035
	Hannah	7395
	Harriet	3584
	Horace	2954
	James	3989 3992
	Jane	486 4031
	John	3582 4032
	Margaret	2951
	Ralph	1032
	Robert	485 2950 2953
	Sarah	3586 4038
	Thomas	2952 3993 4033 4037 4039
	William	4030 4034

Fleshergate	Saddler St	1- 7, 70-79	9467- 9580	4c	167-169
Framwelgate		8- 31, ba-bk	2907- 3208	10a	51- 56
(inc. Sidegate and		37- 78 } bl-cj	3209- 3593	10a	56- 62
Castle Chare)		90 }			
		71- 84, ap-az	2613- 2906	10a	46- 51
		93-121, aa-ao	2153- 2609	10a	38- 46
Framwelgate Bridge (End)	132-135		1- 12	9a	1
Freemans Place		aa-al	10695-10748	4d	189
Gaol and House of Correction			7018- 7262	-	123-127
Garden Cottage			7772- 7776	3	136
Gas House			2132- 2136	10a	38
Gilesgate		1- 42, ac-af	11617-11999	5b	206-212
(inc. Bakehouse Lane,		43- 44	12681-12692	5b	223
Ellis Leazes Ho, Leazes		45- 91, ag-ai	12052-12426	5b	213-219
Cott, Pelaw Leazes,		94-111, aj-an	12531-12650	5b	221-223
Woolloommoolloo Cott,		114-221, aa-ab	10808-11592	5a	192-204
Mount Slowly and					
Parsonage House)					
Gilesgate Moor		aa-ab	12651-12656	5b	223
		ac	13182-13183	5c	232
Glue Garth			12657-12660	5b	223
Grape Lane		aa-af	1417- 1432	9b	25
Green Tree Yard	Back Lane	an	10541-10548	4d	186
Grove			1083	9b	19
Hallgarth			5894- 5900	11e	103
Hallgarth Street		1- 19, aa-ag	5638- 5893	11e	99-103
(inc. Coulson's		21- 28, al-ar	6008- 6151	11e	105-107
Buildings)		27- 64, as-bj	6163- 6384	11e	107-111
Hallgarth St. New Buildings		1- 13, ah-ak	5901- 6007	11e	103-105
Hallgarth Tollbar/Gate			6152- 6162	11e	107
Hatfield Hall			7413- 7418	1	130
Kepier			12661-12668	5b	223
King Street		1- 5, am-ar	365- 402	9a	7
(inc. (New) North Road)		3- 7, aa-al	196- 303	9a	4- 6
Leazes Cottages		aa-ad	11041-11058	5a	195-196
Leazes House			7824- 7834	4a	138
Leazes Place		1- 5	7794- 7823	4a	138
		7- 12	7835- 7861	4a	139
Library			7751- 7753	3	136
Magdalen Place		aa-aw	12427-12530	5b	219-221
Market Place		1- 10, aa	9363- 9466	4c	166-167
	12/14- 16		9865- 9898	4c	174-175
	19- 29, ab		10273-10433	4d	182-184
Market Place Mill House	Back Lane	ba-bb	10675-10694	4d	188-189
Milburn Street		aa-an	13102-13180	5c	231-232
Millburngate		1- 8	127- 195	9a	3- 4
	122-130		13- 126	9a	1- 3
Moatside Lane		aa-ak	10084-10125	4c	178
Mount Slowly			11161-11164	5a	197
Neville Street		4, 10, aa-al	304- 364	9a	6- 7
		am	403- 406	9a	7
New Elvet		1- 43, aa-au	3594- 4150	11d	64- 73
(inc. Elvet Bridge and		48- 60, bj-bo	5272- 5506	11e	93- 96
Water Lane)		62- 94, av-bi	4481- 4734	11d	78- 82
		bp	7013- 7017	11e	121
North Bailey		1- 49, aa	7367- 7590	1	129-133
(inc. Hatfield Hall, Bow					
Lane and Dun Cow Lane)					